DATE DUE

DEC	1 1987		

DEMCO 38-297

The Psychobiology
of Consciousness

The Psychobiology of Consciousness

Edited by

Julian M. Davidson

Stanford University
Stanford, California

and

Richard J. Davidson

State University of New York at Purchase
Purchase, New York

PLENUM PRESS · NEW YORK AND LONDON

Library of Congress Cataloging in Publication Data

Main entry under title:

The Psychobiology of consciousness.

Includes index.
1. Consciousness—Physiological aspects.
I. Davidson, Julian M. II. Davidson, Richard J. [DNLM: 1. Consciousness. WL 705 H918]
BF311.H78   153   79-316
ISBN 0-306-40138-X

BF
311
.P785

First Printing — March 1980
Second Printing — May 1982

© 1980 Plenum Press, New York
A Division of Plenum Publishing Corporation
233 Spring Street, New York, N.Y. 10013

Printed in the United States of America

Contributors

SEYMOUR M. ANTELMAN • Department of Psychiatry, University of Pittsburgh, School of Medicine, and Western Psychiatric Institute and Clinic, Pittsburgh, Pennsylvania

MONTE S. BUCHSBAUM • Biological Psychiatry Branch, Division of Clinical and Behavioral Research, National Institute of Mental Health, Bethesda, Maryland

ANTHONY R. CAGGIULA • Departments of Psychology and Pharmacology, University of Pittsburgh, Pittsburgh, Pennsylvania

JULIAN M. DAVIDSON • Department of Physiology, Stanford University, Stanford, California

RICHARD J. DAVIDSON • Department of Psychology, State University of New York, Purchase, New York

STEPHEN FRANKLIN • Department of Mathematics, School of Physical Sciences, University of California at Irvine, Irvine, California

ELLIOT S. GERSHON • Biological Psychiatry Branch, Division of Clinical and Behavioral Research, National Institute of Mental Health, Bethesda, Maryland

GORDON GLOBUS • Department of Psychiatry, University of California at Irvine, Medical Center, Orange, California

CARROLL E. IZARD • Department of Psychology, University of Delaware, Newark, Delaware

E. ROY JOHN • Department of Psychiatry, New York University Medical Center, New York, New York

ARNOLD J. MANDELL • Department of Psychiatry, University of California, San Diego, La Jolla, California

KENNETH S. POPE • Director of Psychological Services, Gateways Hospital and Mental Health Center, 1891 Effie Street, Los Angeles, California

WILLIAM T. POWERS • 1138 Whitfield Road, Northbrook, Illinois

KARL H. PRIBRAM • Department of Psychology, Stanford University, Stanford, California

ARYEH ROUTTENBERG • Department of Psychology and Biological Science, Northwestern University, Evanston, Illinois

MARJORIE SCHUMAN • Department of Psychiatry, University of California at Los Angeles, Los Angeles, California

JEROME L. SINGER • Department of Psychology, Yale University, New Haven, Connecticut

CHARLES T. TART • Department of Psychology, University of California, Davis, California

Foreword

Consciousness and the Brain Self-Regulation Paradox

The relationship of consciousness to biology has intrigued mankind thoroughout recorded history. However, little progress has been made not only in understanding these issues but also in raising fundamental questions central to the problem. As Davidson and Davidson note in their introduction, William James suggested, almost a century ago in his *Principles of Psychology,* that the brain was the organ of mind and behavior. James went so far as to suggest that the remainder of the *Principles* was but a "footnote" to this central thesis.

This volume brings together diverse biobehavioral scientists who are addressing the various aspects of the mind/brain/body/behavior issue. Although some of the authors have previously published together in other volumes, by and large the particular combination of authors and topics selected by the editors makes this volume unique and timely. Unlike the *Consciousness and Self-Regulation* series (Schwartz & Shapiro, 1976, 1978), also published by Plenum, this volume is devoted entirely to a psychobiological approach to consciousness. Although readers will differ in their interest in specific chapters, the well-rounded investigator who is concerned with the psychobiology of consciousness will want to become intimately acquainted with all the views presented in this volume.

As noted by the individual contributors, the topic of this volume stimulates fundamental questions which, on the surface, may appear trivial, yet, on further reflection, turn out to have deep significance. Rather than list here the various fundamental questions raised by the contributors, let me pose one more question which I believe is central to this volume. I have recently referred to this question as the brain self-regulation paradox (Schwartz, 1977, 1978). Simply stated, if the brain is ultimately responsible for the regulation of itself, and therefore one's thoughts, feelings, and actions, why is it that the brain has no direct experience of the fact that it is actually responsible for all this? And what implications does this state of affairs have for our understanding of our own consciousness and that of others?

It is common knowledge that, for all practical purposes, people have no direct conscious experience of the brain processes that underlie their thoughts, feelings, and actions. Most of our consciousness; curiously, is *displaced* from the organ (the brain) which is hypothesized to construct the experience of consciousness. When we move our hands, for example, we consciously experience a pattern of sensations localized *away* from our brain in three-dimensional space. We do not experience the fact that the movement of the muscles in our hands is actually controlled by patterns of brain processes, nor do we directly experience the fact that the conscious registration of the movement in the periphery is actually constructed out of patterns of subcortical and cortical processes located within the skull.

Although this aspect of brain function has obvious adaptive significance for human behavior, it has some paradoxical "side effects" which emerge when the brain tries to understand itself. I have proposed that this lack of direct experience of brain processes may contribute to numerous erroneous conclusions that the general public and scientists alike derive about their own behavior and its regulation (see Schwartz, 1978). For example, consider the research on EEG biofeedback. Prior to the early 1960s, few people talked about, let alone even thought about, learning to control their brains. It was not until the research on biofeedback and the operant conditioning of EEG activity appeared that people began to consider seriously the possibility that learned voluntary control of body responses implied learned brain control (since people had no direct experience that learned voluntary control *was* learned brain control). The average person assumed, for example, that he learned to control his "hands" rather than his "brain" (whose effects were observed overtly as learning to control his hands).

The height of absurdity related to the brain self-regulation paradox occurred when one clever biofeedback researcher (Barbara Brown) connected a child's EEG to an electronic relay circuit so that the child could now "learn to control an electric train with his brain." This demonstration attracted international attention. The question is why all this public and scientific interest? Part of the reason is actually quite simple and may be related to the brain self-regulation paradox. Most people assume that a normal child plays with trains by controlling his "hands." The average person never stops to think that what a child actually does is use his brain to play with the train, employing a biological effector organ (the muscle) as the means of closing the relay. Having no direct experience of either the child's brain or one's own brain, the normal person comes to the erroneous conclusion that people control their hands, not their brains. Placed in more technical terms, Power's concept (see Chapter 10) of behavior as the control of perception (rather than the control of behavior *per se*) is an elaboration of this general point.

One might think that the above illustration is "trivial" because most psychobiologists should know better than that. Unfortunately, this is not yet the case. The same mistake is made by most psychobiologists, since their own cognitive processing is constrained by the identical false perception. Consider also the current research on mechanisms of learned EEG control with biofeedback. Many researchers are systematically assessing what subjects are doing, thinking, or feeling when they control their EEG. In more technical terms, researchers are looking for cognitive, affective, or somatic processes involved in the learned EEG control.

Consider a hypothetical researcher who is investigating mechanisms of learned occipital alpha blocking. When he systematically assesses the subjects' verbal reports, and also measures indices of overt behavior such as eye movements, let us speculate that the researcher discovers that his subjects report generating visual images and/or moving their eyes to turn the feedback on (which may occur when occipital alpha is blocked). Most researchers would be tempted to conclude from such data that the subjects had "controlled their EEG by thinking certain thoughts or generating certain behaviors." Having reached that conclusion, most researchers would make the implicit or explicit presumption that they have "explained" learned EEG control as being "caused" by the voluntary control of specific thoughts and actions.

However, this kind of conclusion is probably not only erroneous but also begs the question. If we assume for the moment that people block their occipital alpha when, for example, they generate visual images (Davidson & Schwartz, 1977), then the question of "how did they generate the images?" is left open. Having once asked that question, the psychobiologist should hypothesize that in all likelihood people generate such images by regulating their brains. What is one physiological indication that they have regulated their brains to generate visual image? Changes in occipital alpha. And who is the "they" that regulated the brain? Maybe the brain itself; hence the concept of brain self-regulation.

If we take seriously the notion that EEG tracings, verbal reports of visual images, and eye movements are *each indirect indications of patterns of brain processes*, we should not be tempted to "explain" learned EEG control by resorting to simple mental or behavioral descriptions. In fact, although the subject may *consciously* experience that when he moves his eyes, for example, his EEG changes, the *reverse* may actually be the case. The EEG may *precede* the movement, even though the subject's *experience* of the process may be quite different.

Since psychobiologists are as constrained by their brains as are their subjects, they may be tempted to accept the subject's explanations at face value (because these explanations also agree with the investigator's personal experience). But if the subject and experimenter are constrained by similar properties of the central nervous system, and therefore come to the same erroneous conclusion, scientific progress is going to be affected accordingly. One of the reasons that researchers in the EEG biofeedback field have not been studying the *timing* of processes in learned EEG control may be that their implicit conceptual model of how people ultimately control their behavior is essentially identical to the erroneous conceptual model of the public that was shocked initially by EEG demonstrations that a child could learn to control a train with his brain (Schwartz, 1977, 1978).

As noted by Globus in this volume (see Chapter 15), there are various implications of theories about the neural creation of conscious experience that should have impact on the kind of research we conduct and the nature of the conclusions that we draw. I use the concept of the brain self-regulation paradox to highlight how our inability to experience directly our own brains may interfere with our ability to perceive correctly, and therefore study, how the nervous system regulates itself. It is hoped that the reader interested in the psychobiology of consciousness will come away from the present volume not only with details about specific techniques, theories, and findings but also with a set of new questions about consciousness that can have broad implications for further research and perspective about human nature in general.

GARY E. SCHWARTZ

Yale University
New Haven, Connecticut

REFERENCES

DAVIDSON, R. J., & SCHWARTZ, G. E. Brain mechanisms subserving self-generated imagery: Electrophysiological specificity and patterning. *Psychophysiology,* 1977, *14,* 598–602.

SCHWARTZ, G. E. Psychosomatic disorders and biofeedback: A psychobiological model of disregulation. In J. D. Maser & M. E. P. Seligman (Eds.), *Psychopathology: Experimental models.* San Francisco: W. H. Freeman, 1977.

SCHWARTZ, G. E. Psychobiological foundations of psychotherapy and behavior change. In S. L. Garfield & A. E. Bergin (Eds.), *Handbook of psychotherapy and behavior change* (2nd edition). New York: Wiley, 1978.

SCHWARTZ, G. E., & SHAPIRO, D. (Eds.). *Consciousness and self-regulation: Advances in research.* Volume I. New York: Plenum, 1976.

SCHWARTZ, G. E., & SHAPIRO, D. (Eds.). *Consciousness and self-regulation: Advances in research.* Volume II. New York: Plenum, 1978.

Contents

CHAPTER 6
Multipotentiality: A Statistical Theory of Brain Function—Evidence and Implications 129

E. ROY JOHN

CHAPTER 7
Genetic Factors in EEG, Sleep, and Evoked Potentials 147

MONTE S. BUCHSBAUM AND ELLIOT S. GERSHON

CHAPTER 8
The Waking Stream of Consciousness 169

KENNETH S. POPE AND JEROME L. SINGER

CHAPTER 9

The Emergence of Emotions and the Development of Consciousness in Infancy 193

CARROLL E. IZARD

CHAPTER 10

A Systems Approach to Consciousness 217

WILLIAM T. POWERS

CHAPTER 13

The Psychophysiological Model of Meditation and Altered
States of Consciousness: A Critical Review 333

MARJORIE SCHUMAN

CHAPTER 14

Toward a Psychobiology of Transcendence: God in the Brain 379

ARNOLD J. MANDELL

CHAPTER 15

Prospects for the Scientific Observer of Perceptual Consciousness

GORDON GLOBUS AND STEPHEN FRANKLIN

1
Introduction: The Scientific Study of Human Consciousness in Psychobiological Perspective

Richard J. Davidson and Julian M. Davidson

Only within the past decade has the subject of consciousness been re-established as a legitimate area of central concern in the behavioral sciences, following its virtual disappearance from the literature during the strongly behaviorist era of the 1950s and early 60s. A number of factors can be identified which helped to usher in the new Zeitgeist out of which the present volume has emerged. These include new developments in the area of species-specific learning which have called certain behavioral principles into serious question; the growth of the developmental-maturational perspective; perceptual research which substantiated constructivist concepts; and contemporary work in the general area of self-regulation which indicated that changes in certain physiological parameters can have significant behavioral consequences. A more detailed discussion of each of these factors can be found in the chapter by R. J. Davidson. However, it should be noted here that what was of major significance in all of these advances was a refocusing of scientific attention on processes within the organism which significantly modulate both its perception of and response to the environment.

It became apparent to many investigators that the behavioral expressions of an organism were not simply a function of the external reinforcement contingencies but were very much dependent upon its internal state. Thus the same stimulus could result in very different responses as a function of changes in particular internal parameters. The critical importance of the organism's internal workings began to be observed in many different research contexts. For example, it has been repeatedly demonstrated that schizophrenics often respond to complex stimuli in a manner which is different from that of nonschizophrenic

Richard J. Davidson • Department of Psychology, State University of New York, Purchase, New York 10577. Julian M. Davidson • Department of Physiology, Stanford University, Stanford, California 94305.

individuals. The response can be "normalized" partially by changing the central nervous system "software" of these individuals through pharmacological manipulation. This type of research has provided important clues concerning differences between normal and schizophrenic brains. In addition, such work has served to highlight the necessity of considering the internal workings of the organism in any attempt to understand complex behavior.

Current research related to the psychobiology of consciousness is grappling mostly with classical problems which were posed long ago. The major advance in present day approaches is that contemporary techniques allow us to explore certain problems with unprecedented precision. Some of the questions which are central to this growing field of research are: How do we remember? Of what are we conscious? What is the relationship of the unconscious to the conscious and of attention and emotion to consciousness? How is consciousness transformed, and what are the psychophysiological concomitants of alterations in consciousness? The techniques and approaches which are currently being brought to bear on these questions include those of electrophysiology, neurochemistry (including pharmacology and endocrinology), cybernetics, and cognitive psychology.

The present volume is intended to represent the best available theory, research, and speculation in areas related to the psychobiology of consciousness. All the techniques mentioned above are included in one or more of the chapters, and different authors have dealt with the same basic questions in different ways. The book is not, however, meant to be exhaustive. Many important investigators are absent for lack of space or other reasons and some highly relevant areas such as sleep and dreams are insufficiently represented. In mitigation we note that this is but an emerging branch of the biobehavioral sciences. The time is not yet ripe for a definitive compilation and the material in this volume is best viewed as work in progress. It is virtually certain that many currently held opinions will undergo extensive modification as we learn more about the brain and consciousness.

This book is divided into seven major sections, which are not mutually exclusive though each has a different focus. The first section is concerned with general issues in the study of consciousness in psychobiological perspective and contains chapters by R. J. Davidson and K. Pribram. Both authors are concerned with a number of similar issues including distinctions between the conscious and unconscious and the relationship of attention to consciousness. These chapters pose a number of central problems in this area of inquiry which reappear throughout the book.

The subsequent chapters are grouped in terms of the general investigative approach of the authors. The second section is concerned with chemical approaches to the study of consciousness and includes chapters by Antelman and Caggiula, and Routtenberg. The former are concerned with the neurochemistry of coping responses to stress and relate their basic research on relationships between neuroregulators and stress to certain disorders of consciousness such as schizophrenia. Routtenberg grapples with the neurochemistry and neuroanatomy of memory and remembering and relates consciousness to a specific neural system which is characterized by redundancy and related to output processes. Other approaches to the understanding of cerebral redundancy have been contributed by Pribram and John (see below).

The third section of the book presents electrophysiological approaches to the study of consciousness. John's chapter describes his work on endogenous evoked response concomitants of information retrieval and challenges strict locationist views of brain function. Buchsbaum and Gershon review a variety of recent data on electroencephalographic concomitants of individual differences in subjective stimulus intensity. They relate these individual differences to genetic factors and personality characteristics.

The chapters in this section illustrate how electrophysiological techniques can be employed to examine empirically the neural substrates of conscious phenomena. These procedures, particularly when used in conjunction with biochemical and behavioral techniques, offer much promise for future research.

The fourth section is concerned with cognitive and developmental approaches to the study of consciousness. Pope and Singer invoke basic information processing concepts in characterizing our waking stream of consciousness. In addition, they consider the role of the body and kinesthetic feedback in the modulation of cognitive processes. Finally, they relate resulting concepts to recent work on brain lateralization. Izard has extended some of his classic work on emotions to younger children and has presented a developmental scheme relating emotion to consciousness. As part of his project, Izard characterizes developmental shifts from the point of view of conscious experience.

Section five presents cybernetic and systems approaches to the study of consciousness. Powers has related certain aspects of a hierarchical control theory to purpose, volition, and intentionality. He challenges certain long held assumptions in behavioral psychology concerning relationships between stimulus and response and illustrates why, from a control theory perspective, the consideration of consciousness is not only interesting, but necessary. Tart presents a scheme which

considers eleven major subsystems involved in the construction of consciousness. He also develops the concept of a discrete state of consciousness and illustrates how it can be stabilized and destabilized. Tart's
system is similar to Powers's in that he illustrates the interdependence
of and feedback loops among the various subsystems of consciousness,
but it differs in that Tart's system is not hierarchical but rather horizontal
or lateral. It appears as if these two models are equipped to handle different aspects of consciousness.

The sixth section is concerned with the psychobiology of transformations of consciousness. J. M. Davidson reviews our knowledge of the
physiological bases of sexual experience and presents a psychobiological
model of the orgasm as an altered state of consciousness. Schuman
presents an overview of psychophysiological research on meditation
and grapples with the important question of whether the physiological
correlates which have been observed are necessary concomitants of
meditation practice. Mandell presents an original model of the neural
circuitry involved in religious or mystical experience, with emphasis on
the vital role of biogenic amines.

The seventh and last section is concerned with philosophical issues
in the study of consciousness in biological perspective. Globus reviews
some of his previous writings on the mind-brain identity thesis and then
considers how the intentionality of the scientific observer interacts with
the nature of his observations.

Although the factors cited at the beginning of this Introduction have
served to redirect scientific attention to internal processes, it has to be
admitted that these developments do not necessarily imply an essential
role for consciousness. In fact, a number of recent workers (e.g., Nisbett
& Wilson, 1977) have suggested that most of our cognitive activity proceeds in the absence of consciousness. While it seems to be the case that
actual processing of information often occurs largely unconsciously, the
products of information processing sequences are available for conscious
report. The distinction is discussed by Routtenberg in the context of the
memory function. Moreover, in addition to the capacity for conscious
representation of the external world we also possess the ability (some
would say need), to consciously represent our internal milieu including
our self-concept (see e.g., Epstein, 1973).

A number of authors in this volume have attempted to come to
grips with distinctions between the conscious and the unconscious and
have asked the question "When do we become conscious?" We are
continuously experiencing moment-to-moment fluctuations in the degree to which we are conscious of both input impinging upon us as well
as output emanating from us (Pope & Singer, this volume). Are there
periods during which we tend to be more conscious than in others?

What do these situations share in common? These are some of the questions which many of the present authors ask and attempt to answer including R. J. Davidson, Pribram, Globus, and Powers.

The science of consciousness is still in its embryonic stage and the phenomena it purports to study are often ill-defined and not fully agreed upon. The adoption of a psychobiological perspective provides a firm foundation upon which we can build. Evidence from a variety of domains seems to indicate that the most informative categorical schemes for behavior and experience are those which emerge from an understanding of the underlying biological architecture of the nervous system. Luria has argued for the adoption of a kind of biological factor analysis where complex behavioral events are broken down into their underlying subcomponents which depend upon different functional systems of the brain. For example, the sequence involving the decision to pick up an object with one's hand, and the subsequent action, depends upon a number of different brain systems which are called into play at different points throughout the unfolding of the behavior. Damage to one of these systems would selectively impair a particular feature of the sequence (Luria, 1973). This type of analysis invites investigators to make certain types of distinctions among behaviors and experiences which they otherwise might not be disposed to make.

Finally, an additional advantage of the psychobiological perspective is that it can speak to *mechanism*. Such an approach can begin to answer questions concerning how certain effects are taking place. An example from the area of hypnosis research illustrates this point nicely. When a subject is hypnotized and given a suggestion of analgesia, he can plunge his hand into a bath of circulating ice water and keep it immersed for a period of time which is significantly longer than in the normal waking state. In addition, the subject will often claim that he experiences no pain whatsoever (Hilgard & Hilgard, 1975). How are such alterations of conscious experience brought about? Are the sensory signals from the periphery being blocked prior to reaching higher levels of the neuraxis? Or is the afferent information proceeding in an unimpeded fashion to the cortex, with the subject simply responding differently to that input? Using signal detection methodology and brain evoked potentials, a number of workers have collected data supportive of the latter hypothesis (see review by Davidson & Goleman, 1977).

The single assumption which the present authors share is the importance of the psychobiological approach. All agree that in some very critical ways, the mind depends on the brain. Many subscribe to the identity thesis which states that the mind and brain are one and the same entity and only descriptive linguistic convention or observer position determine whether the phenomenon is described in terms of brain or mind. Others do not take a firm position on this philosophical issue. In addition to the chapter by Globus in the present volume, readers specifically interested in this issue are urged to consult a recent volume entitled *Consciousness and the Brain* (Globus, Maxwell, & Savodnik, 1976).

What unites the approaches of each of the authors is the recognition of the need to consider biological variables in any attempt to understand complex behavioral phenomena. Long ago William James emphatically suggested (at the beginning of his *Principles of Psychology*), that the brain was the organ of behavior and went so far as to suggest that the whole remainder of the *Principles* was but a footnote to this central thesis. We are essentially psychobiological beings and when we manipulate our behavior we are also changing our brains. Thus, for example, when we generate an image of a red apple, we are activating our occipital cortex while when we generate a kinesthetic image we activate the brain's motor region (Davidson & Schwartz, 1977). The most complete picture of behavioral as well as experiential phenomena must, we believe, come from the simultaneous consideration of biological and psychological domains. Thus the hypnotic suggestion is apparently altering the manner in which the subject responds to or interprets an unchanged afferent input. In addition to this example from the vitally important area of selective attention, numerous additional examples could be provided which illustrate how the psychobiological perspective stressed in this book can elucidate aspects of mechanism.

Finally, in attempting to lay a basis for a psychobiology of consciousness, this book faces (and only partially overcomes) two major obstacles which stem from the impossibility either of defining consciousness objectively or of recording its manifestations directly as distinct from those of behavior. On the one hand there is the danger of sinking into vague theorizing. We wish to advance beyond the kind of nebulous and vague speculation which characterizes much of the writing on consciousness by scientific as well as popular authors. The optimistic belief that a scientific revolution has *already* taken place, from which is emerging a successful application of Western scientific methodology to problems of consciousness, engenders an impatience in many writers who tend to ignore the questionable nature of the present evidence. As a result they may be tempted either to leap over the immense lacunae in our knowledge and arrive at conclusions supported more by ardent hopes than solid evidence; or else content themselves with vague generalities.

Opposite this Scylla of nebulousness and lack of critical judgment lies the Charybdis of hypercaution. This second obstacle represents the temptation to preserve scientific integrity the easy way—by avoiding data and interpretations which cannot be fitted into paradigms, models, and terminology generally acceptable to the scientific community, and limiting oneself to behavioral data. If we followed this route consistently, the result would be another treatise of physiological psychology, and we would fail to fulfill the promise and aim of this book: to make progress toward a newer paradigm.

The chapters differ widely with respect to the ratio of data to speculation with some heavily skewed toward the presentation of findings from an empirical research program and others presenting virtually exclusively, speculative arguments. As editors we encouraged such speculation since we believe it is critically needed in this developing area, so long as it is constrained by attention to whatever relevant data might exist. Such a mandate runs counter to the normal predilections of most competent scientists and most (or all) of our authors experienced some difficulty with it. Our hope and belief is, that the speculative accounts in a number of the chapters will serve to stimulate research activity in the areas covered. We also trust that the speculative and theoretical discussion in this volume will provide new contexts or at least different ways of viewing the data which are being generated in the areas of research which impinge on consciousness and psychobiology.

At this juncture it seems most reasonable to assume that attempts to study psychophysiological concomitants will be more fruitful when directed at the study of the underlying "structure" of conscious experience rather than the actual moment-to-moment content. What we mean by structure is the cognitive or feeling state which pervades a given moment of consciousness and which colors its content but is independent of it. Thus the thought "there goes a black cat" can be fearful or joyful depending on the mode of information processing in the affective domain. Furthermore, it can be filled with quite specific detail about the features of the cat, or it can be a more vague and general idea, depending upon the cognitive structure or style of the individual. This concept of structure is closely related to that of state of consciousness (Tart) but also to the Piagetian information-processing structures (Piaget, 1976). It differs from the latter in that, as discussed by R. J. Davidson, we are or can become conscious of this structure. We regard the desirability of concentrating on structure rather than on content as a matter of simple strategy, given the present state of the art and take no firm position on the ultimate possibility of achieving a biological explication of the content of consciousness. However, it is tempting in this regard to favor the negative viewpoint of S. Kety:

> how long would it take a biochemist or 100 biochemists to differentiate the brain of a Republican from that of a Democrat? "In the case of the brain, the biological disciplines have made and will continue to make remarkable pro-

gress toward understanding its structure, its metabolism its functional inter-relationships, and the mechanisms which underlie behavior. . . . But in the area of information, content, and experience, stored as it is in the complex interrelationships of 13 billion neurons, biology is extremely pretentious if it thinks that it can unravel them by means of its tools. There will, no doubt, some day be a biochemistry or a biophysics of memory—but not of memories." (cited in Kety, 1978)

If the psychology of consciousness is to enter the established realm of neurobehavioral science, it will have to grapple with the issue of animal models. This is because the study of mechanisms must either depend on noninvasive methods of assessing human neural activity or find ways to make animal experimentation relevant to human consciousness. The former alternative, though capable of providing much information given the availability of adequate technology, is severely constrained as to the questions it can deal with; the latter involves such intractable problems as the existence and nature of animal consciousness (see Griffin, 1976), and the extrapolation of findings from species to species. While findings derived or developed in animal research must always be checked—with whatever methodology is available—on humans, progress in the biology of human consciousness will often continue to depend on these animal findings.

A comparative reading of Antelman and Caggiula's chapter and that of Mandell can illustrate and illuminate this matter most effectively. Both chapters approach stress-induced behavioral abberations from the point of view of neuroanatomical and neurochemical substrates. The resemblance between the behaviors emanating in humans and animals is striking, and the neurotransmitters involved seem to be identical. Is the growing body of neurophysiological and neurochemical research on emotional behavior in animals relevant to normal and pathological observations of consciousness in humans? If so, the psychotherapist's view that depression is the mask that anger wears, and Mandell's reasoned insistence that antidepressants reduce fear and its close relation, anger, via defined limbic brain pathways points the way to a clear use of animal models, since fear and anger-related behaviors and their neural mechanisms can be investigated in animals. Antelman and Caggiula approach this relationship between neural pathways and biogenic amine transmitters on the one hand and psychopathology on the other with a generally behavioristic viewpoint: stress-induced disturbances in amine metabolism are shown to be tied to behavioral aberrations which are similar in stressed animals and schizophrenic humans. A similar neurochemistry is invoked by Mandell to supply a neuromolecular basis for altered states of consciousness, which can be categorized, in our judgmental language system, in many ways—from psychotic thought disorder to mystical ecstasy.

The importance of trying to understand the connection between these two approaches cannot be overestimated. But if "transcendent" experience in humans can be "explained" by neuroanatomical and chemical findings in animals, we may feel led directly to a doctrine of biological reductionism for human behavior in which there is no place for free will and consciousness is an epiphenomenon rather than part of a chain of psychophysical causality. This dilemma will likely occupy the thoughts of psychobiologists for years to come. A glimmering of an answer may be discerned in the connections a number of the authors in this volume have made between cybernetics and psychobiology. Consciousness can be thought of as an extremely complex property of phylogenetically advanced neural organization. While it seems clear from contemporary comparative research that nonhuman primates share with us certain rudimentary features of consciousness (see e.g., Gallup, 1977; Premack, 1976), there have been important changes in brain structure in man compared to his closely related ancestors (Jerison, 1973, 1976). Those areas of the cerebral cortex which have increased in mass relative to the remaining parts of cortex may play a critical role in our conscious experience. Furthermore, this anatomical evolution may have contributed to an overall change in brain organization which allows for consciousness to emerge. Consciousness, in this view, may be thought of as a pattern of neural activity and it is the constraints inherent in that pattern which provide consciousness with its causal potency. Systems theorists have taught us that the organizational properties of a system feedback upon the subcomponents which comprise that system and influence their behavior. Systems are determined by the overall relations among the subcomponents and not by the behavior of the individual parts. At the neuronal level, John and his colleagues (Ramos, Schwartz, & John, 1976; Thatcher & John, 1977) have demonstrated that while single cells in particular brain regions respond with a great deal of variability in response to external stimuli, characteristics of large ensembles of those neurons which individuality display a lack of consistency tend to be much more invariant and predictable. In a similar vein, consciousness may be viewed as a systemic property of large neuronal ensembles acting in concert. The relations which inhere among the subcomponents of this system can be said to exert statistical determinancy over the subcomponents themselves.

Animal models may be extremely useful in providing us with a map of the detailed workings of the parts of the system. It is extremely likely that these components are highly similar if not identical in most vertebrate nervous systems. The critical differences may be in the manner in which these subcomponents are combined and organized. It is here that a broad view of the similarities and differences between human and nonhuman behavior is needed. For example, if we assume that male rats

respond to combinations of exteroceptive plus endogenous neuroendocrine influences by a purely reflex mating behavior pattern, the use of the
same genital, neural, and chemical mechanisms does not preclude the
vital involvement of love and choice in *human* sex. Conscious experience
is certainly dependent on biology; hardly less certainly conscious experience is not "nothing but" biology. However, the residue when biological
mechanisms are subtracted is not necessarily the business of the
psychobiologist. Scientists must and will continue to stress biochemical
and biophysical manifestations of the organism's activity, and the
emerging science of consciousness has the task of identifying those
phenomena emerging from such research which are relevant to conscious experience.

REFERENCES

DAVIDSON, R. J., & GOLEMAN, D. J. The role of attention in meditation and hypnosis: A
    psychobiological perspective on transformation of consciousness. *International Journal
    of Clinical and Experimental Hypnosis,* 1977, *25,* 291–308.
DAVIDSON, R. J., & SCHWARTZ, G. E. Brain mechanisms subserving self-generated imag-
    ery: Electrophysiological specificity and patterning. *Psychophysiology,* 1977, *14,* 598–
    602.
EPSTEIN, S. The self-concept revisited, or a theory of a theory. *American Psychologist,* 1973,
    28, 404–416.
GLOBUS, G. G., MAXWELL, G., & SAVODNIK, I. *Consciousness and the Brain: A scientific and
    philosophical inquiry.* New York: Plenum, 1976.
GALLUP, G. G., JR. Self-recognition in primates: A comparative approach to the bidirec-
    tional properties of consciousness. *American Psychologist,* 1977, *32,* 329–338.
GRIFFIN, D. R. *The question of animal awareness: Evolutionary continuity of mental experience.*
    New York: The Rockefeller University Press, 1976.
HILGARD, E. R., & HILGARD, J. R. *Hypnosis in the relief of pain.* Los Altos, Calif.: William
    Kaufmann, 1975.
JERISON, H. J. *Evolution of the brain and intelligence.* New York: Academic, 1973.
JERISON, H. J. Paleoneurology and the evolution of mind. *Scientific American,* 1976, *234,*
    90–101.
KETY, S. S. The biological substrate of abnormal mental states. *Federal Proceedings,* 1978,
    37, 2267–2270.
LURIA, A. R. *The working brain.* New York: Basic Books, 1973.
NISBETT, R. E., & WILSON, T. D. Telling more than we can know: Verbal reports on mental
    processes. *Psychological Review,* 1977, *84,* 231–259.
PIAGET, J. *The Child and reality: Problems of genetic psychology.* New York: Penguin, 1976.
PREMACK, D. *Intelligence in ape and man.* Hillsdale, N.J.: Erlbaum, 1976.
RAMOS, A., SCHWARTZ, E., & JOHN, E. R. Stable and plastic unit discharge patterns during
    behavioral generalization. *Science,* 1976, *192,* 393–396.
THATCHER. R. W., & JOHN, E. R. *Functional neuroscience, Volume I: Foundations of cognitive
    processes.* Hillsdale, N.J.: Erlbaum, 1977.

2

Consciousness and Information Processing: A Biocognitive Perspective

Richard J. Davidson

1. Introduction

Although the facts and phenomena of consciousness have received attention in various forms in the past, it is only recently that the scientific community and the biobehavioral sciences in particular, have begun to recognize its study as a legitimate, even essential, domain of inquiry. Investigators who have attempted to explore this area of functioning have approached it from a myriad of perspectives, with a heterogeneous array of methods and techniques. The available literature in this area consists largely of a disparate collection of findings with an occasional, loosely woven theory. Most researchers working in areas of the biobehavioral sciences which have bearing on the study of consciousness are often not aware of data in a different, but related area which might be relevant to their investigations.

The major purpose of the present chapter is to attempt to begin an initial organizing and ordering of findings in the psychobiology of consciousness and to present a conceptual and theoretical umbrella under which such data may be subsumed. The chapter begins with a brief historical overview of the study of consciousness in psychology and next proceeds to an examination of the role of biocognitive structures in consciousness and unconsciousness. Major influences on biocognitive structures are discussed along with a consideration of individual differences in styles of information processing and their conscious concomitants. The chapter concludes with a speculative exploration of the possibilities and consequences of enabling normally unconscious processing mechanisms to be consciously perceived.

RICHARD J. DAVIDSON • Department of Psychology, State University of New York, Purchase, New York 10577.

2. A BRIEF HISTORICAL OVERVIEW

At the turn of the century, William James posed a number of fundamental questions with which he felt the newly created discipline of psychology ought to grapple. The understanding of consciousness was at the core of these suggestions. In 1910 James defined the discipline of psychology as "the description and explanation of states of consciousness as such." James was particularly concerned with the relationship of brain to consciousness and in the first chapter of his *The Principles of Psychology* (1890/1950) explains

> the fact that the brain is the one immediate bodily condition of the mental operations is indeed so universally admitted nowadays that I need spend no more time in illustrating it, but will simply postulate it and pass on. The whole remainder of *The Principles* will be more or less a proof that the postulate was correct. (p. 4)

James's writing contained a vast number of brilliant insights concerning the structure and function of various psychological processes such as memory, attention, will, and associative thinking. Unfortunately, however, objective means for studying internal psychological events were quite crude and consequently, little systematic research was performed on the numerous problems which he identified.

Also at the turn of the century, a new school of American psychology was being established whose aim it was to discover the fundamental units of conscious experience. This movement was termed structuralism and is identified most closely with E. B. Titchener who had just come to America from Leipzig, where he had worked in the first laboratory of experimental psychology, created by Wundt. Whereas James was interested primarily in the functional significance of various psychological processes, Titchener and the structuralists were concerned with the identification of the elementary units of conscious experience. The method employed by the latter group was introspection and the goal was to have trained observers report on various attributes of their conscious experience such as the intensity and clarity of an image. The structural approach was both static and a-biological. Not surprisingly, disagreement over the fundamental units of description were frequent and interobserver reliability was typically poor. It soon became apparent that the introspective method was unreliable and a growing disenchantment with the structural approach paved the way for behaviorism, which was soon to banish consciousness as a legitimate area of study.

The rise of the behavioral tradition in psychology can be described as primarily a methodological revolution. Only aspects of behavior which were observable and measurable were legitimate to study. The behavioral Zeitgeist unquestionably contributed enormously to the improvement in the rigor with which psychological problems were approached and helped place psychology on firmer ground with respect to its scientific status. However, as is often characteristic of such movements in science, in its zeal to be more objective and restrict psychological inquiry exclusively to observables, it excluded from consideration certain phenomena, not on empirical grounds but rather, on the basis of methodological requirements.[1] Consciousness, cognition and other internal mental events were the principal phenomena to be banished from the domain of psychological science. The most extreme expression of this view can be found in J. B. Watson's classic behavioristic manifesto (Watson, 1913):

> The time seems to have come when psychology must discard all reference to consciousness; when it need no longer delude itself into thinking that it is making mental states the object of observation. We have become so enmeshed in speculative questions concerning the elements of mind, the nature of conscious content... that I, as an experimental student, feel that something is wrong with our premises and the types of problems which develop from them. (p. 164)

The methodological advances occasioned by behaviorism were truly profound. During the first half of the twentieth century, prior to World War II, behaviorism very much dominated American academic psychology. However, as "behavioral" principles and techniques began to be applied to phenomena more complex than simple key pecking and bar pressing responses, it became apparent that knowledge of environmental contingencies was insufficient to account for the diversity of behavior. New discoveries were emerging from a variety of contexts whose import was that the internal workings of the organism were critical to consider in any complete account of that organism's behavior and experience. For example, during World War II, military personnel were being called upon to monitor radar apparatus which required the maintenance of a vigilant state under relatively monotonous conditions. This stimulated a large body of research on attention and helped to reestablish this process as a core one in understanding behavior. The implication of this general body of findings was that the organism actively participates in adaptation to the environment and *constructs* the universe in which it inhabits. This renewed concern with the inner workings of the mental apparatus was accompanied by increased attention to biological substrates of cognition. There were a number of identifiable factors which were at least partially responsible for the shift in Zeitgeist, away from a behavioral view and toward a more cognitive approach to the

---

[1]As Abraham Maslow once observed, "If all you have is a hammer, you tend to treat everything as a nail."

understanding of complex behavior, particularly the higher mental processes.

2.1. Biological Constraints on Learning Processes

One of the most influential critiques of certain core assumptions in behaviorism emerged from some of the very same animal laboratories in which the principles of reinforcement were first studied. Breland and Breland (1961) were among the first to observe certain phenomena that were difficult to reconcile with classical behavioral thinking. This husband and wife team were students of Skinner and after completing their doctorates at Harvard, decided to try their hand in the circus. They reasoned that their superior knowledge of the factors governing animal learning would enable them to create truly spectacular displays of animal tricks. They soon discovered, however, that not all animals can be taught to perform any trick no matter how many training trials were attempted. These observations implied that certain species may be biologically prepared to emit certain behaviors and to associate certain stimuli with particular responses. Attempts to train organisms to make contra-prepared[2] associations typically did not produce a reliable training effect.

One of the first attempts to approach experimentally the assumption of equipotentiality was in a study performed by Garcia and Koelling (1964). This assumption simply states that an organism can learn to associate any stimulus with any particular response. In a classical conditioning paradigm they paired taste and sound with the occurrence of radiation-induced nausea. Importantly, in this situation the unconditioned response, i.e., nausea, was experienced several hours after the occurence of the stimuli, a very long interval by typical classical conditioning standards. The significant outcome of this study was that only taste and *not* sound became a conditioned stimulus which subsequently elicited an aversive response. The investigators reasoned that there existed a biologically prepared association between taste and stomach sickness. In contrast, the association of sound with stomach sickness was less potent.[3] These data indicate that the organism is not a passive

[2]Contra-prepared is being used in the sense employed by Seligman and Hager (1972). A contra-prepared association is one for which the organism is biologically wired *not* to make. For example, we are presumably contra-prepared to associate pleasure with spiders and snakes (see Ohman, Fredrickson, Hugdahl, & Rimmo, 1976).

[3]Garcia and Koelling first submitted their manuscript to the prestigious *Journal of Comparative and Physiological Psychology*. Significantly, after his tenure as editor of this journal, Estes remarked that his one regret during this time was not accepting the Garcia and Koelling manuscript (Seligman & Hager, 1972).

recipient of stimuli but rather may actively process information through previously existing biocognitive structures. These structures may be said to mediate between the stimulus and response and presumably exert a strong influence on the perception and action of an organism. Later, we shall consider contemporary research which has begun to specify explicitly the mechanisms by which these structures exert their effects.

2.2. Growth of the Developmental-Maturational Perspective

As the problems approached by developmental psychologists became more sophisticated, it became apparent that the developing organism is not a passive recipient of environmental stimuli but is rather an active participant in its own adaptation. The specification of exclusively environmental variables was insufficient in accounting for certain ontogenetic sequences of complex behavior. For example, research on the acquisition of language has indicated that it is unlikely that the child's reinforcement history can account for certain anomolies in the development of correct conjugation for irregular verbs. Thus Slobin (1971) has observed that children typically learn the correct form of irregular verbs such as "came," "broke," and "went" relatively early in their acquisition of language because the utterance of these correct words is highly reinforced by parents. Importantly, however, the correct form of these words drops out of the child's vocabulary as he/she learns the *rule* for conjugating regular verbs. Thus children actually say: "it came off," "it broke," and "he did it" *before* they say "it camed off," "it breaked," and "he doed it." Although these findings do not unequivocably challenge a reinforcement interpretation of the acquisition of language, they have resulted in an increased attention to the dynamic relationship between the environment and the cognitive structures of the persons within it. As these biocognitive substrates change either through maturation over the course of ontogeny or via other means, the same stimulus configuration will produce a different pattern of response. These observations in the developmental area were paralleled by recent data in the perceptual area which provided the necessary foundation for a constructivist view of perceptual processes (see Neisser, 1976).

2.3. Constructive Nature of Perceptual Processes

A fundamental shift in our view of perceptual activity has occurred since the time of Johannes Kepler who, in 1604, compared the process of seeing to a camera with an image of the world focussed on the back of the brain. In commenting on this so-called copy theory of perception, Neisser (1968) has explained that "although this theory encounters insurmountable difficulties as soon as it is seriously considered, it has dominated philosophy and psychology for many years" (p. 204). Research in the past three decades has highlighted the constructivist nature of our perceptual processes. All input arriving over our sensory channels is transformed by the nervous system and is integrated into meaningful percepts. Some of the information in a given stimulus array will be accentuated, other information will be attenuated or even eliminated. The hard-wired architecture of the peripheral sensory apparatus, the inherited functional properties of the central nervous system as well as the learned interpretational matrix (see e.g., Kagan, 1967) all combine to govern the manner in which we perceive and respond to our environment. More detailed descriptions of these processes of their mechanisms will be provided in the second part of this chapter.

2.4. Self-Regulation

The growing recognition of the importance of biocognitive structures in the mediation of our perception of and response to our environments has raised the possibility that changes in behavior and transformations in perception may be brought about by manipulation of the relevant underlying psychobiological processes (see e.g., Davidson, 1978). As Kagan (1967) has suggested in another context, "the essence of learning is more dependent on attentional involvement by the learner than on specific qualities of particular external events" (p. 134). There exist many contemporary examples which embody this conception. The recent emphasis in the behavior therapy area on the modification of *biocognitive* processes exemplifies this trend (e.g., Goldfried & Davison, 1976; Meichenbaum, 1976). Recent data on the self-regulation of physiological processes has suggested that self-induced changes in these substrates have significant effects upon important parameters of behavior and experience. A person exposed to the same stimulus before versus during self-regulated manipulation of an internal physiological response, may perceive and respond to that stimulus in very different ways. Thus, the consideration of external stimulus parameters in the absence of considering the "contour" of underlying biocognitive structures, will provide only an incomplete account of the variables influencing behavior. For example, in the area of cardiovascular self-regulation, Sirota, Schwartz, and Shapiro (1974, 1976) have demonstrated that some subjects, when trained to slow their heart rates in anticipation of receiving a noxious stimulus, indicate that they perceive the stimulus as being less aversive than when raising their heart rates. Thus, simple modification of cardiac rate had important effects upon the perception of pain.

In an entirely different context, Schwartz, Davidson, and Pugash (1976) have demonstrated that training subjects to produce particular patterns of EEG asymmetry which were associated with specific tones the meaning of which they were unaware, has significant effects on their subjective experience while they are attempting to produce the criterion electrocortical pattern. Specifically, when feedback is made contingent on the presence of alpha activity in the right parietal region and its absence in the left, subjects report more verbal thoughts than in the opposite feedback condition—absence of alpha in the right parietal region and its presence in the left. Importantly, subjects also report significantly more visual imagery during the latter versus the former feedback condition. These results again indicate that changes in specific patterns of biological processes are associated with shifts in the relative predominance of particular subjective states and lend further support to the suggestion that shifts in the "central software" will have significant effects upon the quality of perception.

Having briefly surveyed some major factors responsible for the shift in emphasis in the contemporary behavioral sciences, we are now in a better position to turn to our essential concern which is to provide a psychobiological framework in which to study the factors governing human consciousness. Needless to say, any such attempt is bound to be overly simplistic in parts and necessarily incomplete. However, enough data are available to begin this task in the hope that it will encourage others to pursue this problem more systematically in the future.

3. Consciousness, Unconsciousness, and Biocognitive Structures

Any attempt to define consciousness immediately raises certain fundamental problems. A concept of consciousness implicitly connotes the existence of unconscious processes unless one is willing to suggest that all of the external and internal forces which impinge upon us, and are sufficiently strong to evoke some types of neural response, are conscious. A brief introspective excursion and exercise in voluntary attention is all that would be required to convince us of the untenability of this position. As I write this chapter, the kinesthetic feedback from my feet touching the floor is not consciously processed. However, if I now direct my attention to this area of my body, I can gain access to this somesthetic information. Presumably, the afferent feedback from my feet was continually being communicated to higher levels of my nervous system. However, my primary engagement in my writing was sufficiently compelling for me not to be conscious of this kinesthetic afferent feedback.

A scrutiny of our information processing apparatus reveals that a significant amount of our cognitive and affective activity[4] proceeds in the absence of conscious awareness. This unconscious system of information processing is presumably comprised of certain neural structures whose function it is to transform input according to certain rules or algorithms. We often have access (i.e., consciousness) to the products of this sequence of information processing, but rarely are we conscious of the actual process. Certain meditative practices and other techniques for the transformation of consciousness may improve our access to these processes. This issue will be considered in more depth later.

Although many cognitive psychologists have assumed these structures to be relatively static and fixed in the constraints they impose on our cognitive competence (e.g., Kahneman, 1973), recent evidence indicates that with appropriate, intensive practice, the constraints that these structures impose can be significantly modified (e.g., Spelke, Hirst, & Neisser, 1976). However, despite the suggestion of plasticity in these structures, some basic properties, particularly at more peripheral levels of the nervous system, may be relatively enduring. In addition, some consistency within individuals may presumably be found in certain higher order structures. When we speak of individual differences in cognitive or attentional styles, we may be referring to these relatively enduring biocognitive structures which contour information in particular and idiosyncratic ways (see e.g., Shapiro, 1965).

Although our conscious access to the functioning of these structures is limited, it is apparent that some of them have conscious concomitants. The output of these processing structures presumably gets fed to those systems in our brain which are responsible for conscious representation. Thus, the nature of the information of which we are conscious is at least in part a function of certain underlying cognitive structures. A variety of variables can be identified which influence myriad parameters of these biocognitive structures and will be delineated in a subsequent section.

With the above as background, let us begin by elucidating some aspects of unconscious cognitive and affective structures and then review some research on the behavioral and physiological consequences of

[4]This also applies to a whole host of lower-order information processing activities such as homeostatic adjustments of our internal milieu to adapt to changing environmental demands, and the integration of feedback from both our environments as well as our bodies into the ongoing stream of behavior.

such unconscious information processing. This will provide a foundation for our consideration of consciousness and some speculation concerning its possible functional significance within a biological framework.

3.1. The Nature of the Unconscious

One of Freud's most important claims and one that has remained with us most forcefully concerns the prepotency of the unconscious and the effects of unconscious motivation on perception and action. The realm most explored by Freud can be considered the affective unconscious since it was emotions and feelings states with which he was most concerned. This is to be distinguished from the cognitive unconscious (e.g., Piaget, 1973; Rozin, 1976) which will be discussed below. In his classic Chapter 7 of *The Interpretation of Dreams*, Freud (1900/1965) explains how complex thought processes may occur in the absence of conscious awareness and further provides a rationale for why certain material is systematically excluded from consciousness. The dynamic unconscious, for Freud, consisted of a mechanism for actively preventing (i.e., repressing) particular thoughts and feelings from reaching consciousness. It is important to note that while various thoughts themselves were excluded from consciousness, this material nevertheless exerted important influences upon behavior.[5]

It is important to note that the term "unconscious" is here being used in two specific ways: (1) to refer to mental structures (i.e., neural systems or functional units as in Luria, 1966, 1973; see also Thatcher & John, 1977 for a similar usage) which contour and transform both exogenous (from the environment) as well as endogenous (from within the person—this would include both interoceptive, proprioceptive as well as cognitive input) information. Although the specific parameters of these structures exert important influences on conscious processes, they themselves are not normally available for conscious inspection; and (2) to refer to processing activity, action, and/or information transmission in the nervous system which proceeds in the absence of conscious awareness. Included in this definition would be reports of creative problem solving where a solution spontaneously emerged after the problem

---

[5]Erdelyi (1977) has recently commented on the multiple meanings of the term unconscious as employed by Freud. Although it is quite clear that Freud used the term to designate processes other than those repressed and excluded from consciousness, this sense of the term is the one most closely associated with psychodynamic theorists. The distinction between the cognitive and the affective unconscious (both of which may be a function of repression, albeit in different forms) was not made by Erdelyi but is a crucial one in the present context.

had been posed some time before (e.g., Hadamard, 1945). The inference is that the processing required to arrive at a resolution took place unconsciously. Thus, the first usage makes reference to internal mental (i.e., biocognitive) structures which influence behavior but are not themselves observable. The second usage is concerned with observable behavior (either directly or indirectly) of which the subject is unaware.

A variety of methods have been used to study unconscious influences upon behavior and a description of some of the more promising approaches and the findings which have been obtained will provide a more complete understanding of the nature of these unconscious effects. Milton Erickson (1939) the renowned hypnotist, has employed posthypnotic suggestion to unconsciously implant a conflict and then examine its effects upon behavior. In one demonstration, a highly susceptible subject was deeply hypnotized and told that upon awakening he would

> (a) notice Dr. D. searching vainly through his pockets for a package of cigarettes; (b) that he then would proffer his own pack, and (c) Dr. D. absentmindedly would forget to return the cigarettes whereupon the subject would feel very eager to recover them because he had no others. He was further told that (d) he would be too courteous to ask for the cigarettes directly or indirectly but that (e) he would engage in a conversation that would cover any topic except cigarettes although at the time his desire for the return of the cigarettes would be on his mind constantly.

After awakening, the subject offered Dr. D. his cigarettes and became involved in conversation. The content of their talk drifted into the area of travel, whereupon the subject exclaimed that he would derive much pleasure from crossing the Sahara Desert riding comfortably on a *camel*. The subject next told a tale of Syrian folklore in which again a camel played an important role.

Another approach involves the use of a dichotic listening paradigm where different messages are played to each of the two ears. Corteen and Wood (1972) have observed that words which were previously paired with shock and introduced on the unattended channel while subjects are actively shadowing (repeating the message on) the criterion channel elicit an electrodermal response which is significantly larger than in response to neutral words. These effects are obtained with the complete absence of conscious awareness for words on the unattended channel (but see Wardlaw & Kroll, 1976).

These examples both highlight an important feature of unconscious influences on behavior. In the first example, the subject was conscious of the provoking stimulus (i.e., Dr. D. absent-mindedly pocketing his cigarettes) but unconscious of his response and its sources. In the second example, subjects were unconscious of *both* the stimulus and their response. These examples are consistent in that they reveal a certain automaticity in the execution of an unconsciously programmed sequence of behavior. As long as the underlying process and response remain outside of conscious awareness, the probability of modifying the response is likely to be relatively weak.[6]

Some of these issues can be elaborated upon more extensively in a discussion of the cognitive unconscious. In the realm of affective phenomena, we say that individuals may be conscious of both the provoking stimulus as well as of certain aspects of their response and yet remain unconscious of the source and reasons for their response. Similarly in the cognitive domain, subjects may be aware of an initial stimulus as well as the result of a sequence of problem solving operations and yet remain entirely unconscious of the processing activity which gave rise to the solution or decision. Similarly, the notion of repression is applicable to the cognitive domain as well as to the affective. Piaget (1973, 1976) suggests that children at certain ages repress perceptual information in order not to have it interfere and complicate previously existing cognitive structures and the understanding which emerges from them. For example, when a ping-pong ball is forced out from under one's hand on a table, it will travel a certain distance and then return as a function of the backward spin. When children prior to age 6–7 are asked to describe this simple event, they state that first the ball spins forward and then it reverses direction and spins backward. Piaget explains that the child of this age is not conscious of the true state of the ball because this perception would contradict existing conscious concepts (e.g., that a ball will not advance by turning in the opposite direction).

Thus, both Freud and Piaget argue that certain forms of unconscious information processing are adaptive and serve to inhibit disregulatory influences which might emerge if these elements became conscious. In the affective domain, unconstrained id impulses would interfere with our reality testing capabilities while in the cognitive realm two types of effects may be discerned: (1) premature awareness of certain physical events and laws would inhibit the establishment of developing cognitive structures and (2) in adulthood, consciousness of the intermediate processing stages following an event and leading to an action might be distracting and wasteful of our limited amount of processing

---

[6]Thus, the goal of many forms of psychotherapy consists of bringing to consciousness thoughts and feelings which were previously unavailable. This process is thought to allow for conscious restructuring of memory associations and habit patterns from the past. Such restructuring would then presumably influence the manner in which the unconscious structures process information and would in turn result in changes in conscious material (see e.g., Wachtel, 1977). This issue is discussed in more depth in Section 5.

space. The fact that our brains contain no sensory receptors so that we literally cannot have access to how our neurons "feel" provides the rationale for a similar adaptive mechanism. If during the course of my writing I was experiencing a series of impulses in my left premotor region, these sensations might well interfere with my writing activity.[7]

3.2. The Transition to Consciousness

I have suggested above that behavior which is a function of the operations of unconscious structures is largely reflexive and automatic. In an information processing sequence the delineation of situations or points when awareness occurs may help to better understand the functional significance of consciousness (see e.g., Posner & Klein, 1973). When the relatively fixed behavioral programs which our unconscious processing mechanisms are capable of regulating are insufficient to meet various environmental demands, the activation of consciousness becomes more probable. Piaget (1976) explains that "If a well-adapted action requires no awareness, it is directed by sensorimotor regulations which can then automate themselves. When, on the contrary, an active regulation becomes necessary, which supposes intentional choices between two or several possibilities, there is awareness in function of these needs themselves" (p. 41). Active regulation and intentional choice are two central components in Pribram's (1980) characterization of feedforward processes. Feedforward is a term used to describe processing activities which are dedicated to formulating plans and evaluating choices; in short, generating images of future behavior. Pribram suggests that feedforward operations require consciousness.

Feedback, on the other hand, involves the detection and utilization of the consequences of past action for the sake of preservation of homeostasis in the behavioral program. It can be likened to the behavior of a thermostat whose function is to detect changes in ambient temperature and regulate the heat output accordingly. Increases in ambient temperature above a set-point attenuate the heat output; once the heat falls below a certain point, heat output is increased and so on in a self-regulating manner. Instances of this type of feedback mechanism

---

[7]It should be noted that this also provides a biological basis for the persistence of mind/ body or mental/physical dualism. One fundamental difference between the neural organization of the skeletal musculature versus the central nervous system is that kinesthetic afferent feedback arises from the former but not from the latter. Thus, we can feel our bodies but cannot feel our brains. The lack of this sense of feeling from our brains may in part be responsible for our persistence in describing the activities of this organ in terms fundamentally different than is employed in the description of the somatic system.

abound in everyday behavior. For example, when walking over varied terrain, the change in feedback from our muscles when we reach an incline facilitates increased muscular output needed to climb the incline at approximately the same rate of walking. Feedback need not always be produced through the skeletal muscular system. While driving, for example, visual feedback obtained from scanning the road results in probably hundreds of minor adjustments of steering and acceleration every minute. An important characteristic of these feedback operations is the capacity for and likelihood of their occurence in the absence of conscious awareness.[8]

3.3. Some Possible Functions of Consciousness

Each stage in an information processing sequence involves some type of transformation of input from a previous stage or an external source. For example, in the visual system, output from the superior colliculus gets integrated with cerebellar output and may serve to coordinate certain visual processes with movement (e.g., Nauta & Karten, 1970). At the striate cortex, cells have been observed which are tuned to particular spatial frequencies and may be involved in a Fourier-like transformation of this spatial information (Pollen & Taylor, 1974). It has been suggested by a number of workers that the visual system encodes spatial information in this way (Campbell, 1974; Campbell & Robson, 1968). As we ascend the neuraxis and examine more central structures, it seems likely that the types of transformations which are possible tend to increase and at the cortical level, particularly in association regions and "uncomitted" cortex, the flexibility of transformational rules is immense. It is presumably at these highest levels where consciousness may be thought to be involved. This pattern resembles that seen over the course of phylogeny where in lower organisms coding operations are most prominently represented at more peripheral stations in the nervous system and as we ascend the phylogenetic scale, central struc-

---

[8]The Piagetian concepts of assimilation and accommodation may be related to feedback and feedforward and unconscious and conscious information processing systems as these terms have been used here. Assimilation involves the integration of new input into already existing cognitive structures. This type of activity resembles feedback processes where new information is incorporated into an existing cognitive structure and may result in modifications in an ongoing sequence of behavior. According to this formulation, assimilative activities should be associated with less conscious awareness than accomodative ones. During accommodation, existing cognitive structures are transformed in order to encode incoming information which is discrepant with the available processing machinery. Such accomodative processing is similar to feedforward operations which involve the restructuring of constraints on information processing systems.

tures assume more of these coding functions (Jerison, 1976; Muntz, 1971).

One function of consciousness is to transform and restructure information as well as information-processing structure themselves. The role of consciousness in the transformation of information is not unique since various structures at lower levels of the neuraxis transform input without the benefit of (or hindrance from) consciousness. The restructuring operations of consciousness may be unique in two specific ways: (1) These types of operations at lower neural levels may be more fixed and hard-wired. Given a particular type of input, only a specified number of coding operations may be performed on that input. However, at a conscious level, the number and diversity of possible transformational schemes may be virtually limitless; (2) it may only be through conscious information processing that unconscious biocognitive structures may be transformed. This again is analogous to feedforward operations which are dedicated to changing the constraints on a particular processing system and thus altering its structure.

The restructuring capabilities of consciousness are well illustrated in a discussion by Piaget (1976) on the application of the notion of catharsis to information processing systems. In the affective domain (i.e., psychoanalysis), catharsis refers to an awareness of emotional conflicts and a reorganization which enables the conflicts to be overcome. Piaget suggests that a similar process occurs in the cognitive domain where information from unconscious memory structures gets recycled into consciousness and then reencoded in a new form in memory. Piaget (1976) describes an experiment in which children were shown a series of six rulers arranged in decreasing size which they were permitted to look at briefly but not to manipulate. One week later the children were asked about what they had seen and Piaget describes a number of types of responses which were elicited such as "a few small sticks all equal," "large-medium, small trios, etc." and others. After six months (and without having been shown the model again), 74% of the children actually *improved* in the accuracy of their recall of this event. Piaget suggests that what was encoded in this situation was a scheme of seriation and not the actual objects which were presented. Over the course of the six months, this scheme was presumably recycled between the cognitive conscious and unconscious and became restructured in the process.

The second major function of consciousness which I would like to mention briefly is not wholly independent of the first and has to do with the role of consciousness in gaining access to subprograms in the cognitive unconscious (see Rozin, 1976). The nature of these subprograms (or adaptive specializations according to Rozin) particularly for lower organisms, is that they are hard-wired into specific behavioral sequences.

For example, in some species of honey bees, after having discovered a food source, a bee can encode certain cues which inform it as to its location and distance from the hive. It can then communicate this information to its fellow hive-mates through an incredibly sophisticated dance so that both it and the others from the hive may return to the food. The bee performs these location encoding operations with respect to the sun's position. Since the sun moves across the sky in the course of the day, the bearing taken relative to the sun would be accurate only for a particular time period. However, the bee has the necessary neural machinery to account for the sun's movements and make the necessary adjustments in localizing its food source (see von Frisch, 1967).

The crucial point for the context of this discussion is that the sophisticated and complex computational operations (presumably unconscious) which the honey bee employs to encode the location of food sources is *not accessible* to other domains of the bee's behavior. These cognitive processes are restricted to food-gathering behavior presumably because hard-wired neural circuitry does not permit other systems in the cognitive unconscious access to these processes. One possible function of consciousness is to facilitate access to particular subprograms or structures (subroutines) by other subprograms or structures. This would allow for a greatly expanded range of flexibility in cognitive processing and behavioral output. Rozin (1976) suggests that

> Part of progress in evolution toward more intelligent organisms could . . . be seen as gaining access to or emancipating the cognitive unconscious. Minimally, a program (adaptive specialization) could be wired into a new system or a few new systems. In the extreme, the program could be brought to the level of consciousness, which might serve the purpose of making it applicable to the full range of behaviors and problems. (pp. 256–257)

Despite our status as conscious beings, many of our unconscious structures and processing activities are still not readily available to consciousness. For example, the regulation of autonomic functions is largely performed in absence of consciousness. For some classes of these events, their failure to ascend to consciousness may be traced to two specific factors: (1) conscious intervention in these processing activities may disturb crucial homeostatic functions; and (2) conscious representation of the events may disturb ongoing conscious processes. For example, it would surely be maladaptive if we experienced a little tingle inside of our heads each time our heart beat and conversely, if we had a large degree of control over our cardiovascular functioning, we might alter this system in a way which could be maladaptive for our biological well-being.

It is interesting to consider the recent work in biofeedback from this vantage point. Data are accumulating for different response systems

which suggests that any control gained by making a previously unconscious process conscious through external feedback, does not typically
extend beyond the normal range of variation in the particular response
system in question. Thus, in the area of alpha electrocortical feedback,
recent evidence indicates that subjects cannot generate more occipital
alpha after feedback training than when asked to simply close their eyes
in a dark and quiet environment (Lynch & Paskewitz, 1971; Orne &
Paskewitz, 1974). The control acquired over the course of feedback training enables subjects to turn on and off alpha on command and to reach
baseline levels (i.e., levels of alpha abundance associated with simply
resting with eyes closed) of alpha production. Similarly, in the area of
heartrate biofeedback, Bell and Schwartz (1975) have recently demonstrated that the magnitude of control achieved over the course of
biofeedback training is within the range of heart rate variation as assessed during a variety of daily activities. These findings indicate that
even when control is acquired by artifically arranging for previously
unconscious processes to be made conscious, the range of learned control is typically constrained by the range of normal variation in the particular response system.

The major point which the findings reported above can be interpreted to make is that autonomic functions are largely unconscious, with
little likelihood of conscious manipulation beyond the range of normal
variation. Conscious access to these processes might permit them to be
manipulated in ways which could be biologically hazardous. Thus, little
evidence has been obtained for the manipulation beyond the range of
normal variation of autonomic processes through biofeedback (Blanchard & Epstein, 1978).

3.4. Hemispheric Specialization and the Representation of Consciousness

In the previous section we considered two of the possible functions
of consciousness: (1) restructuring unconscious information processing
structures; and (2) gaining access to normally unconscious subprograms
(or subroutines of the biocognitive unconscious). In the discussion of the
second function, it was suggested that despite our complex neural machinery and our advanced stage of evolution, certain processing activities and functions were still largely inaccessible to consciousness such as
the experience and control of most autonomic functions. It was argued
that the relegation of activities of this type to an unconscious status may
serve an important adaptive function. The purpose of the present section is to present a body of theory and data which tentatively suggest

that the right hemisphere plays a special role in the regulation of some unconscious processes, including the representation of certain visceral activities. The role of the left hemisphere in conscious processing will be considered in light of its important functions in motor control.[9]

Evidence from a variety of domains has supported the contention that the human brain is asymmetrical both structurally (e.g., Galaburda, LeMay, Kempert, & Geschwind, 1978) and functionally (e.g., Dimond & Beaumont, 1974). In addition to the gross morphological asymmetries which have recently been observed (e.g., Galaburda *et al.*, 1978; Wada, Clarke, & Hamm, 1975), some investigators have suggested important differences in the organization of the hemispheres which have important functional consequences. Semmes (1968) has reviewed a variety of data on the sensory and motor capacities of the hands in brain-injured subjects. She demonstrated that the evidence revealed a consistent difference in the organization of each hemisphere, with functions more focally represented in the left and more diffusely represented in the right. For example, it has been found that certain right-sided somatic disturbances occur only when a lesion is present in the postcentral zones of the left hemisphere. Comparable disturbances on the left side, however, appear to arise in the presence of lesions in a much more widespread area of the right hemisphere (Semmes, Weinstein, Ghent, & Teuber, 1960; Teuber, 1962). Similar findings have been obtained in the electrophysiological domain by Shaw, O'Connor, and Ongley (1977). These investigators have demonstrated greater covariance in the EGG among widely distributed loci in the right versus left hemisphere.

Data such as these have led some investigators to propose that the right hemisphere may generally be more involved with nonfocal, incidental and "less conscious" information processing (e.g., Luria & Simernitskaya, 1977). In a recent study on the effects of localized brain lesions on focal (voluntary) versus incidental (involuntary) learning and memory, Luria and Simernitskaya (1977) have found that left temporoparietal lesions resulted in relatively greater impairment in voluntary memory while comparable right hemisphere lesions were associated with greater deficits in incidental memory. In the domain of writing behavior, Luria and his colleagues have shown that left hemisphere lesions result in deficits in consciously executed writing, while right hemisphere lesions impair automatic and nonconscious writing

[9]It should be emphasized that the present analysis is not meant to suggest that all unconscious processing operations are necessarily localized in the right hemisphere. It seems logical to presume that at least certain types of left hemisphere processing may proceed in the absence of consciousness. This may be particularly true of more elementary sensory and perceptual processing. As will soon be discussed, the motor activities controlled by the left hemisphere seem to be of the conscious, voluntary variety.

such as signing one's name (Luria, Simernitskaya, & Tubylevich, 1970; Simernitskaya, 1974). On the basis of these and related data Simer-nitskaya (1974) suggests that "a lesion of the cortical areas of the left hemisphere induces a disturbance in the extensive conscious fulfillment of a psychic function, but does not affect the execution of stable automa-tic operations. . . . The structures of the nondominant hemisphere are involved in accomplishing subconscious levels of automatic integration" (p. 343). A similar argument is presented by Luria and Simernitskaya (1977).

Consistent with the Soviet data on the differential effects of left and right hemisphere lesions on different components of writing behavior is recent evidence on the role of the left hemisphere in the voluntary con-trol of fine motor behavior (e.g., Geschwind, 1975; Kimura & Archibald, 1974). For example, Kimura and Archibald (1974) have observed that patients with unilateral left hemisphere lesions were significantly im-paired relative to patients with comparable right hemisphere lesions on tasks involving the copying of novel hand movements, and this impair-ment was significant for *both* hands. These investigators conclude that their data "support and extend Liepmann's (1908) contention that the left hemisphere has important functions in motor control, not shared by the right hemisphere" (p. 346).

While the data reviewed above seem consistent in indicating that the left hemisphere preferentially controls complex voluntary move-ment, the association of such motor control with the representation of consciousness is less apparent. Such an association arises from a recent body of theory in cognitive psychology although workers in this area have not made the connection between motor control and hemispheric specialization. A number of writers (e.g., Turvey, 1977; Weimer, 1977) have commented upon the importance of motorlike processes in con-scious information processing. By motorlike is meant downstream, effe-rent modulation of afferent input (see e.g., Livingston, 1959; Spinelli & Pribram, 1966, 1967), as well as the generation of plans for action. It is this latter process which may be particularly associated with conscious-ness.

The classical view of the role of the motor cortex in the control of action can be captured by invoking a keyboard metaphor. Each note on the keyboard was thought to be wired to different muscle groups throughout the body and the generation of action simply consisted of "playing" the appropriate sequence of notes. Such a view, however, is untenable in light of recent evidence. Stimulation of the motor cortex with the same stimulus at the same site will elicit different movements depending upon the position of the limb, the state of the organism, etc. (Turvey, 1977). Pribram (1971) has observed that ablation of the motor cortex has little effect on muscle function in particular movements, but greatly disrupts skilled action. These data, combined with the consideration of motor equivalences where very different patterns of action result in the identical achievement (e.g., writing the letter A with one's hand versus foot), have led to the view that what is encoded in the motor cortex are images of actions to be achieved which could be accomplished with a variety of different movements. The generation of such "action images" representing plans for future behavior is precisely what Pribram (1980) has referred to as feedforward. The actions which emerge from such plans are voluntary and nonautomatic and thus are likely to be associated with consciousness. Given the role of the left hemisphere in the control of such action sequences, the link between the left hemisphere and the representation of consciousness is thus suggested.[10,11]

On the basis of the literature reviewed above, an argument was made for the preferential role of the left hemisphere in the formulation of action plans which may be associated with consciousness. The role of the right hemisphere in the mediation of unconscious processing has not been considered in depth. Luria and his colleagues have argued for such a role for the right hemisphere on the basis of lesion data where it was found that right hemisphere lesions selectively impaired automatic behavior, capable of being performed in the absence of conscious awareness (Luria *et al.*, 1970). What additional data may be brought to bear on the suggestion of a preferential role for the right hemisphere in unconscious information processing? Galin (1974) arguing from an entirely different data base has suggested a special role for the right hemisphere in the control of unconscious processes. For example, he hypothesized in 1974 and recently confirmed (Galin, Diamond, & Braff, 1977) that unconscious ideation may be expressed through output modes not preempted by the left hemisphere, and specifically that hysterical symptoms are more frequently left-sided than right-sided.

[10]Interestingly, Bruner (1962), writing in the early sixties prior to the explosion of research on cerebral specialization, used certain metaphors to describe the differences in the two hands which are remarkably consistent with the present discussion of the role of the left hemisphere (right hand) in action. Bruner (1962) stated that "since childhood, I have been enchanted by the fact and the symbolism of the right hand and the left—the one the *doer*, the other the *dreamer*" (p. 2, italics added).

[11]The role of efference in the modulation of conscious experience can be illustrated in an entirely different domain. Festinger and his colleagues (Festinger, Burnham, Ono, & Bamber, 1967) have proposed a motor theory of visual perception which argues that changes in visual perception are a function of shifts in efferent instructions to the eye which are held in a state of readiness for immediate use. With a distorting prism mounted directly on the eye via a contact lens, Festinger *et al.* (1967) demonstrated that by holding afferent input constant and requiring a shift in the pattern of efferent instructions, visual experience would change accordingly. The relevance of these data to hemispheric specialization, however, is at present unclear.

We have recently pursued the study of the role of the right hemisphere in unconscious information processing through an entirely different avenue. Ongoing biological processes such as respiration and the heart beat are normally not in conscious awareness although both are potentially available to consciousness. If indeed afferent feedback from the heart and other visceral processes (e.g., Lacey, 1967; Lacey & Lacey, 1974, 1978) do affect the central nervous system via baroreceptor projections to the nucleus of the tractus solitarius and then up to cortex via the ascending reticular system, then a question may be asked about possible asymmetries in these systems. Specifically, does afferent feedback from the heart have more extensive projections to areas in the right versus left hemisphere? Another possibility resulting in a similar outcome would be if the right hemisphere is more responsive to afferent projections which themselves may be symmetrical. If indeed processing activity is less available to consciousness when it is performed in the right hemisphere, then it might be adaptive for visceral afferent feedback to project asymmetrically to this hemisphere. Such a strategy would preserve "channel space" which is needed for conscious cognitive processing.

Recent evidence on asymmetries in the blood supply to the brain may have some bearing on this question. It appears that, at least in right-handed subjects, there exists an asymmetry in capacity of the vascular beds, with the right hemisphere showing higher values than the left, possibly reflecting a structural asymmetry in the circumference of the carotid arteries (e.g., Carmon, Harishanu, Lowinger, & Lavy, 1972; Oldendorf & Crandal, 1961; Thompson, 1964). Moreover, this asymmetry appears to be related to speech lateralization and handedness. Carmon *et al.* (1972) injected sodium hippurate labelled with radioactive I^{12} into the orbital vein of 85 subjects. Two scintillation detectors were employed to assess gamma irradiation in each hemisphere. The results indicate greater activity over the right hemisphere in the majority of subjects. Importantly, right hemisphere irradiation was significantly higher than left only for subjects with either a right hand or right ear (for verbal material) preference. Left-handed subjects or those with a left ear preference showed the opposite pattern of asymmetry. The existence of such an asymmetry in cerebral vascular dynamics may provide a basis for the suggestion that cardiac activity may have a greater afferent representation in the right hemisphere in right handed subjects.

There exist some neuropsychological data which are also relevant to these suggestions. According to Hécaen (1969), focal lesions of the right

[12]It is important to note that the data on cerebral specialization which are cited in the text apply only to right-handed individuals unless stated otherwise.

hemisphere result in disturbances of the normal sensation of the subject's own body (the body schema), seven times more frequently, on the average, than comparable lesions of the left hemisphere. On the basis of these data and his own clinical observations, Luria (1973) suggested that "the right hemisphere is directly concerned with the analysis of direct information received by the subject *from his own body* and which, it can be easily understood, is much more closely connected with direct sensation than with verbally logical codes" (p. 165).

In an initial attempt to explore empirically some of these issues, we (Davidson, Horowitz, Schwartz, & Goodman, in press) performed a study designed to assess whether the left hand can more accurately track the heart beat than the right hand. If indeed the right hemisphere plays a special role in the analysis of information "received by the subject from his own body" then the left hand may in fact be more accurate in tracking cardiac activity than the right hand.

Twenty right-handed subjects were employed in one experiment divided into three phases. Subjects were initially told that the experiment was designed to explore physiological concomitants of movement. Heart rate was recorded while, in Phase I, subjects were instructed simply to tap with the index finger of either their right or left hands on a circular silver disk, with hand order counterbalanced among phases and among subjects. Subjects were instructed to tap at approximately one tap per second. The time elapsed between the R-spike prior to a tap and the next tap in milliseconds was automatically printed along with the interbeat interval. Phase I was included in order to assess whether subjects, when simply asked to tap voluntarily, would synchronize their left-handed taps more closely with their heart beat than when using their right hands. Subjects tapped 100 times with each hand and were then asked to stop.

During Phase II, subjects were asked to attend as closely as possible, to their heart beats and attempt to tap with either their right or left hand index finger immediately following a heart beat. If subjects began Phase I with their left hands, they began Phase II with their right hands and vice versa. The same measures were obtained in Phase II as in Phase I. Subjects tapped 100 times with each hand before being told to stop.

In Phase III, subjects were instructed to tap only when they were relatively certain of their heartbeat. They were instructed to try as hard as possible to tap only when a beat was detected. Subjects began Phase III with the same hand which began Phase I. The same measures were again obtained and subjects tapped 75 times with each hand prior to being told to stop.

We predicted that subjects would show more accurate tracking with their left hand, particularly during phases II and III. The main depen-

Table I

Means ($\bar{X}$) + Standard Deviations (SD) of Tap Reaction Time (Time since Last R-Spike to Tap) Divided by Interbeat Interval, Separately for Right and Left Hands ($N=20$)[a]

	Phase I		Phase II		Phase III	
	Right	Left	Right	Left	Right	Left
$\bar{X}$	.551	.529	.546	.522	.519	.527
SD	.053	.040	.053	.043	.068	.056

[a]From Davidson, Horowitz, Schwartz, and Goodman (in press).

dent measure employed consisted of the tap reaction time (time since last R-spike to tap) divided by the interbeat interval (IBI). This provided a measure of where in the IBI the tap occurred. More accurate tracking corresponds to tapping earlier in the IBI and is reflected in smaller ratio scores. The results are presented in Table I and indicate that in Phases I and II, the left hand is significantly faster (demonstrates a signif- icantly lower ratio score indicating that the tap occurred earlier in the IBI) than the right hand ($p = .03$ for Phase I; $p = .05$ for Phase II). Interestingly, no significant difference was obtained between the hands in Phase III. These findings indicate that when subjects are either not trying or moderately trying to tap in synchrony with their heart beats, they track more accurately with their left versus right hands. When the subjects are actively trying to attend to their heart beats (possibly, when their heart beats become consciously detectable) and tapping asynchro- nously, this asymmetry is eliminated.

These data are important because they suggest that when the tap- ping response is controlled by the right hemisphere (left hand), taps occur earlier in the IBI than when the tap is controlled by the left hemi- sphere under conditions of either no or moderate trying. The findings are also consistent with, although by no means prove that, cardiac activ- ity may be represented more in the right hemisphere of right-handed individuals. If these findings are confirmed, they would suggest that the right hemisphere may be particularly specialized for the processing of unconscious autonomic activity.

4. Influences on Biocognitive Structures and Styles of Information Processing

In the previous section, we considered the nature of unconscious and conscious information processing and presented data indicating that certain types of cognitive operations may proceed entirely in the absence of conscious awareness. In addition, the term unconscious was also employed to refer to structures within the nervous system which contour (i.e., modulate) information processing and have conscious concomitants but which are themselves not usually available for conscious inspection. These structures play an extremely important role in shaping our conscious experience and in defining who we each are, i.e., individual differences in how the world is perceived. The "contour" of these structures define the constraints on our information processing systems and our self-concept may literally emerge from the habitual patterning of these underlying structures. The organization of these structures presumably forms the basis for certain personality traits (see Davidson, 1978) which in turn are intimately connected with our self-image. Transformations of consciousness involve shifts in the constraints on our information processing which may be mediated by alterations in "contour" of various biocognitive structures. In the present section, major influences on biocognitive structures will be delineated and representative research which highlight these influences will be described. Relationships between underlying biocognitive structures and styles of information processing will also be examined.

4.1. Species Characteristics

Membership in a particular species involves, among other things, a common biological architecture. As members of the human species, for example, we are endowed with certain sensory capabilities which limit our range of sensitivity to particular wavelengths of electromagnetic energy. Other species are wired differently and consequently may be (a) sensitive to sensory phenomena to which we ordinarily do not possess access as well as (b) unable to perceive objects and/or events which we are capable of perceiving. The contouring of incoming information may take place at various levels of the neuraxis. It appears that as we ascend the phylogenetic scale, the ratio of peripheral to central coding changes. At lower levels of phylogeny, the majority of information transformations are accomplished at peripheral levels in the sensory systems, often at the receptor surface itself. For example, in the frog, both visual (e.g., Lettvin, Maturana, McCulloch, & Pitts, 1959) and auditory (e.g., Capranica, Frishkopf, & Neuro, 1973) input are coded at the most peripheral levels. In humans, the analogous types of coding operations are usually performed more centrally. This transition is frequently referred to as encephalization. A fairly direct test of central versus peripheral gating during selective auditory attention has recently been performed by Picton, Hillyard, Galambos, and Schiff (1971). These investigators simultaneously recorded evoked potentials (EP), to clicks in the cochlear nerve (with a needle electrode inserted in the wall of the external auditory meatus) and at the vertex while subjects were instructed to either attend to clicks (and detect an occasional faint click) or ignore the clicks by reading. With attention, there was a significant accentuation of middle components of the EP from the vertex recording but no change in the evoked cochlear response.

The contrast between this type of auditory discrimination in humans versus frogs highlights an important characteristic of constraints of information processing over the course of phylogeny. That many coding operations which in lower species are hard-wired into the architecture of the sensory systems, are cortically mediated in humans, implies a much greater range of plasticity at higher levels of phylogenetic evolution.

These functional differences over the course of phylogeny are presumably the result of major structural changes in the organization of the central nervous system. Jerison (1973, 1976) has shown that the ratio of "uncommitted" to committed sensory cortex increases systematically over the course of phylogeny. The cortical region which has apparently increased most relative to other brain areas is, interestingly, the frontal cortex (Luria, 1973). This region has been implicated in complex planning functions and the generation of voluntary action (see e.g., Luria, 1966; Nauta, 1971; Pribram, 1973). These are the behaviors most likely to be associated with consciousness as explained above.

4.2. Genetic Influences and Individual Differences

Individual variability in basic cognitive competences is frequently robust and often has important conscious concomitants. Some of these individual differences have been found to be at least partially under genetic control while others have not been investigated from this standpoint. A variety of recent evidence has indicated that a number of forms of attentional style are at least partially heritable. For example, Buchsbaum (1974; Buchsbaum & Gershon, 1980) has investigated augmentation/reduction in monozygotic (MZ) and dizygotic (DZ) twins. This dimension reflects the tendency of an individual to either augment or reduce the impact of sensory stimulation (see Petrie, 1967). In previous research Buchsbaum (1976) had found that some individuals show increases in EP amplitude in response to increasing stimulus intensities while other individuals show actual diminution of the EP amplitude in response to very intense versus weak stimulation. These relationships are seen only from secondary and tertiary association regions of the cortex, but not from primary sensory regions (Buchsbaum & Pfefferbaum, 1971). Buchsbaum (1974) has found that MZ twins were significantly more similar than DZ twins on these measures.

Other traits reflecting attentional competence have also been found to be partially heritable. For example, hypnotizability, which is importantly related to competence in selective attention (e.g., Davidson & Goleman, 1977; Davidson, Schwartz, & Rothman, 1976; Graham & Evans, 1977), has been found to be partially under genetic control (Morgan, 1973; Morgan, Hilgard, & Davert, 1970). Perhaps the most significant work to date in this area, however, concerns the neurochemistry of attention (see e.g., Matthysse, 1977) and individual differences in neurochemical variables which may be partially heritable. While it is beyond the scope of this chapter to comment extensively on this literature, one finding is particularly worthy of mention. Buchsbaum and his colleagues (Buchsbaum, Murphy, Coursey, Lake, & Zeigler, 1978) have examined individual differences in an enzyme involved in cathecholamine synthesis, plasma dopamine-beta-hydroxylase (DBH). These investigators have found that high levels of DBH are associated with greater enhancement of the evoked potential to an attended stimulus. In addition, subjects with high DBH also make fewer commission errors on the continuous performance test. Finally, recent animal data has revealed important genetic influences on DBH and other enzymes involved in catecholamine synthesis (Barchas, Ciaranello, Kessler, & Hamburg, 1975).

These findings suggest that important features of information processing structures (i.e., "biocognitive tuning") are genetically influenced. The particular "contours" or settings of these biocognitive structures presumably have significant conscious concomitants. This is especially apparent with the neurochemical data since some of these variables have been found to be significantly associated with schizophrenia (see e.g., van Praag & Bruinvels, 1977).

One final individual difference which has bearing on some of the discussion in Section 2 of this chapter is hemisphericity, or the relative dominance of a left versus right hemisphere information processing mode. Using a particular type of recording montage, EEG measures of hemispheric asymmetry may be recorded and baseline levels of asymmetry may be correlated with aspects of cognitive performance. For example, Furst (1976) has reported "a high correlation (.55) between successful visuospatial performance and relative right parietal EEG activation." We (Davidson, Taylor, & Saron, 1979) have found that parietal asymmetry during a two-minute resting baseline significantly predicts both verbal and spatial performance. Thus, in the same group of subjects ($N = 18$) we found that greater right hemisphere activation

during baseline was associated with more accurate performance in a
tachistoscopic facial recognition task ($r = .414$) while greater left hemisphere activation was associated with greater accuracy in an analogous
word recognition task ($r = .58$). Whether such differences are genetically influenced must await future research. Recent evidence from our
laboratory (Davidson, Schwartz, Saron, Bennett, & Goleman, 1979)
indicates that anterior and posterior measures of EEG asymmetry may
vary independently. In light of these findings, it is tempting to speculate
about the association of differences in hemisphericity in the motor
regions to the ratio of conscious to unconscious action expressed by an
individual. It may be that individuals with predominant right hemisphere
activation in the motor region would be more likely to perform actions
in the absence of conscious awareness than an individual with the opposite pattern. Again, future research is needed in order to examine this
hypothesis.

4.3. Cultural and Social Influences

All brains exist within a cultural and situational nexus which has a
significant impact on aspects of information processing. In the previous
two sections we considered biological influences on cognitive operations,
and in this section we will briefly consider the impact of cultures and
situations on biocognitive functioning. One of the most significant ways
in which a culture and/or situation can influence underlying information
processing structures is through its influence on affective processes as
they interact with both environmental as well as endogenous events. For
example, some cultures place a premium on the standard average awake
state of consciousness and regard any shifts away from this mode as
deviant. Other societies are more tolerant of nonordinary states of consciousness and may even encourage their production.[13]

The effect of these cross-cultural differences in attitude toward
transformations of consciousness might be to influence the readiness of
certain limbic structures to become activated and generate affective
arousal. For example, the presence of hallucinatory phenomena would
evoke fear and anxiety in some cultures and attention, support and
possibly encouragement in others. The anthropologist Wallace (1959)
explains that

> it is likely that in some cultural subgroups in our society the nature and defini-
> tion and response to hallucination entertained by the hallucinator and his

---

[13]For an excellent discussion of the role of culture in shaping reality, the reader is urged to
consult the sociological work of Berger and Luckman (1967).

associates may aggravate or precipitate other mental disabilities in the hallucinating person. Indeed, the mental patient may suffer from added anxiety precisely because of the nature of the definition of hallucinatory experience which he entertained prior to experiencing it himself. Certainly, among hospitalized patients in our society, the attempt to conceal hallucinatory experiences from the staff is both chronic and in one sense realistic: Staff members frequently take a negative view of hallucinations, and hallucinating patients are subject to measures which, from the patient's standpoint, may be punishments (delay in discharge, restriction of privileges, questioning on sensitive issues, subtle contempt, and even ridicule, from both staff and other patients). (p. 58)

Thus the context in which a particular experience is experienced subtly (and sometimes not so subtly) contours the readiness of the underlying affective structures to superimpose certain emotional states over the primary components of the event.[14] It is likely that many of these cultural biases, once encoded, influence an individual's response to certain experiences in an entirely unconscious fashion. One would expect that if a hallucinating person in this culture were asked why he was experiencing fear and anxiety, he would not explain that he has learned to respond in this fashion as a function of his upbringing. Rather, the more likely possibility is that the response would be relatively automatic. A member of a western culture would probably regard hallucinations as intrinsically anxiety provoking.

The role of the cultural context in supplying an interpretive framework for an experience which has measurable physiological effects can be explored through an examination of pain perception. It has long been known that cultural values play a substantial role in the way a person perceives and responds to pain. One of the most dramatic examples of the import of culture on pain is the hook-hanging ritual still in practice in parts of India (Kosambi, 1967). The function of this ceremony is the blessing of children and crops in a series of neighboring villages during a particular period of the year. A member of the social group is chosen to represent the power of the gods (termed a "celebrant") and is paraded from village to village blessing each in turn. What is truly remarkable about this ritual is that steel hooks, which are attached by strong ropes to the top of a special cart, are shoved under his skin and muscles on both sides of his back. During the journey between villages

---

[14]Interestingly, despite the negative view of hallucinatory activity in western culture, the incidence of such experiences during waking thought is not minimal according to available evidence. Foulkes and Fleisher (1975) asked subjects at six randomly determined intervals during a 45 to 60 minute session of relaxed wakefulness to report on their last mental experience before being questioned. They found that hallucinations were reported on 19% of the trials. Of the 20 subjects employed in the Foulkes and Fleisher study, 11 reported instances of genuine hallucinatory imagery.

the celebrant clings to the ropes. However, at the climax of the ceremony in each village, he swings freely attached to the cart only by the hooks embedded in his back. Apparently, from all overt signs and indicators, there is no evidence that the celebrant experiences any pain whatsoever. Moreover, when the hooks are later removed, the wounds heal rapidly without any medicinal treatment other than the application of wood ash and two weeks later, the marks on the celebrant's back are scarcely visible.

Evidence on the influence of culture on subjective experience and physiological processes comes from research performed on ethnic differences in response to pain. Zborowsky (1952) has delineated the differences in response to pain among different cultural groups in America. He characterized Old Americans or Yankees (Protestants of British descent whose parents and grandparents were born in this country) as phlegmatic and matter-of-fact; Jews are seen as expressing concern for the implication of pain; and Italians express a desire for pain relief. Based upon these attitudinal differences in reaction to pain, Sternbach and Tursky (1965) sought to determine whether psychophysical thresholds as well as electrodermal responses to electric shock would differ among these groups. In addition to the three groups enumerated above, Sternbach and Tursky included Irish subjects who were characterized as inhibiting expression of suffering and concern for the implications of the pain. All subjects were local housewives and were matched on age, height-weight ratio, and time since onset of menses on the day of testing.

Interestingly, the groups were not found to differ on the lower threshold, i.e., the intensity of the electrical stimulation when the subject first reported becoming aware of the sensation. Melzack (1973), in commenting upon this and other evidence, suggests that "there is now evidence that all people, regardless of cultural background, have a uniform *sensation threshold*—that is, the lowest stimuli value at which sensation is first reported" (p. 24). Differences did emerge, however, in upper thresholds—the level at which the subject requested that the stimulation be ended. This measure presumably reflects more of the interpretative and less of the sensory aspects of response to pain between the Italian and Yankee and the Italian and Jewish subjects. The Italians were able to withstand shock the least and requested the stimulation to be terminated at intensities lower than any of the other groups, a finding consistent with their attitude toward pain.

In another phase of the experiment subjects were administered relatively strong shocks at intervals of 30 seconds while continuous recordings of palmar skin potential were made. One important characteristic of the skin potential response is the appearance of a diphasic wave form when the subject is exposed to sudden strong stimulation which may gradually become monophasic in the course of habituation. More rapid habituation of the diphasic component is indicative of less responsivity to the stimulus. Sternbach and Tursky (1965) found that the Yankee women showed the most rapid and greatest decrease in the number of these potentials. Again, this finding is consistent with the matter-of-fact attitude of this group toward pain.

Transient situational variables may influence underlying biocognitive structures in a manner similar to cultural effects. However, situational influences are presumably less long lasting. A large number of such variables have been studied under the label of demand characteristics (e.g., Orne, 1959), implicit situational norms and proprieties, and available roles (e.g., Goffman, 1959). The impact of such influences has been carefully examined as they affect hypnotic responsivity (Barber, 1969). In fact, Barber has argued that hypnosis can be thought of as exclusively a function of such antecedent situational variables (Barber, 1972).[15] It is clear that these situational variables can have profound subjective consequences. For example, suggestions of hypnotic analgesia have been found to significantly attenuate overt signs of discomfort and subjective pain in addition to increasing the duration of time an individual can withstand exposure to a painful stimulus (Hilgard & Hilgard, 1975). Recent evidence suggests, as in the cultural effects upon pain sensitivity, that changes are not observed in sensory thresholds, but rather in the more interpretive components of pain responsivity (Davidson & Goleman, 1977).

Although it has not been clear in previous hypnosis research, it would be instructive to examine whether in experiments where subtle situational variables which have measurable behavioral effects are manipulated, subjects are conscious of the influence of such variables. Nisbett and Wilson (1977) have demonstrated that in other social situations, subjects are rarely conscious of this form of influence. Subjects may clearly be aware of their behavior but not of why they are behaving in a particular manner (i.e., of the social influences governing their behavior). Presumably, these influences bias underlying information processing structures and subjects may consciously experience the consequences of such bias. The change in these structures which results in a behavioral change is usually inaccessible to conscious inspection.

---

[15]Although it is tangential to the present line of discussion it is worth noting that Barber's (1972) position on the nature of hypnosis must strain to encompass a variety of recent data on individual differences in hypnotic responsivity (see e.g., Sheehan & Perry, 1976). As is the case for most behavioral traits, the person by situation interaction offers the most complete account of the behavior in question (Bowers, 1973).

5. ON MAKING THE UNCONSCIOUS CONSCIOUS

Throughout this chapter, I have considered a variety of unconscious determinants of behavior. Much of our everyday behavior is significantly affected by internal and external influences of which we are largely unaware. In the discussion on the neural substrates of conscious versus unconscious motor acts, I indicated that the latter may be characterized as exhibiting a certain automaticity. The goal of such an action is not likely to be modified in the course of its execution because of its unconscious status. The modification of the goals of such action (as well as the action itself) most likely await its ascension to consciousness. The apparent success of behavioral techniques in the modification of certain patterns of maladaptive action (e.g., biting one's nails) may arise not simply as a function of the reinforcement contingency but also as a result of bringing a previously unconscious action back into consciousness. The formulation of new goals and the modification of habitual action patterns may be facilitated by conscious involvement; in fact, they may require it although an adequate empirical test for this suggestion may be difficult to achieve.

This example underscores a theme I would like to highlight in this section. The status of various biocognitive structures and information processing activities as unconscious is not invariant, but is probably quite flexible. The boundary conditions which define this flexibility are largely unknown in western psychology for rarely has such a proposition been seriously entertained. In the remainder of this section, I will consider a number of speculative suggestions concerning the consequences and possibilities afforded by making the unconscious conscious.

As has been detailed in the sections above, numerous factors influence the structure of our basic biocognitive mechanisms which in turn exert important control over various aspects of our behavior. Much of the time, these influences go unnoticed. Upon exposure to consistent influences of this nature over a relatively long period of time, it is likely that habitual modes of perceiving and acting will develop, with very little awareness of alternative behavioral possibilities. We often become "overly identified" with those habitual patterns of behavior and consider them to be our "true nature." The perspective which I am presenting here allows for the possibility of becoming conscious of normally unconscious biocognitive structures. Such a process would involve a shift in attentional focus not from external events to internal mental content, but rather to the processing activities themselves. One would be aware at such times of not necessarily the specific content of consciousness, but the manner in which the environment and onself are apprehended. The literature of various meditative traditions is replete with descriptions of this type of process (e.g., Goldstein, 1976; Goleman, 1977). These traditions explain that the perceptual glimpse afforded in the direct conscious awareness of these processing structures and the manner in which they contour incoming information as well as endogenous events retrieved from memory, enables one to gain some perspective on one's own idiosyncratic way of viewing the world. It is thought that this form of insight facilitates the perception that one's own style of information processing is simply *one* way in which reality may be apprehended, but not necessarily *the* way. The consequence of such perception might be to increase one's acceptance of other styles of functioning.

The neural mechanisms governing a process of this sort are a long way from being discovered. However, in light of the previous suggestions concerning the differential role of the left and right hemisphere in conscious and unconscious action, some tentative speculation may be offered. Enabling the unconscious to become conscious would likely not involve an exclusive reliance on the left hemisphere. Rather, it might involve improved interhemispheric communication so that structures in the left hemisphere may be fully informed about processing activities taking place in the right hemisphere.[16] This process might be explored empirically by examining the premotor cortical potential bilaterally as a habitual action is made conscious. It would be expected that the left hemisphere premotor potential would become accentuated as the action became conscious.

The speculative nature of this final section is in part a product of the paucity of data relevant to these issues. Sophisticated and reliable methods are now available for the exploration of basic biocognitive mechanisms in the intact human. The combination of the improved methodology coupled with a conception of psychology broad enough to include consciousness as a legitimate domain of inquiry provides much to look forward to in future research in these areas.

REFERENCES

BARBER, T. X. *Hypnosis: A Scientific approach.* New York: Van Nostrand, 1969.

BARBER, T. X. Suggested ("hypnotic") behavior: The trance paradigm versus an alternative paradigm. In E. Fromm & R. E. Shor (Eds.), *Hypnosis: Research developments and perspectives.* Chicago: Aldine-Atherton, 1972).

BARCHAS, J. D., CINRANELLO, R. D., KESSLER, S., & HAMBURG, D. A. Genetic aspects of

---

[16]The opposite situation, where presumably unconscious activities in the right hemisphere are totally unavailable to the left is seen in split-brain patients.

catecholamine synthesis. In R. R. Fieve, D. Rosenthal & H. Brill (Eds.), *Genetic research in psychiatry*. Baltimore: The Johns Hopkins University Press, 1975.

BELL, I. R., & SCHWARTZ, G. E. Voluntary control and reactivity of human heart rate. *Psychophysiology*, 1975, *12*, 339–348.

BERGER, P. L., & LUCKMANN, T. *The social construction of reality*. New York: Doubleday, 1967.

BLANCHARD, E. B., & EPSTEIN, L. H. *A biofeedback primer*. Reading, Mass.: Addison-Wesley, 1978.

BOWERS, E. S. Situationism in psychology: An analysis and a critique. *Psychological Review*, 1973, *80*, 307–336.

BRELAND, K., & BRELAND, M. The misbehavior of organisms. *American Psychologist*, 1961, *16*, 681–684.

BRUNER, J. S. *On knowing: Essays for the left hand*. Cambridge: Harvard University Press, 1962.

BUCHSBAUM, M. S. Average evoked response and stimulus intensity in identical and fraternal twins. *Physiological Psychology*, 1974, *2*, 365–370.

BUCHSBAUM, M. S. Self-regulation of stimulus intensity: Augmenting/reducing and the average evoked response. In G. E. Schwartz & D. Shapiro (Eds.) *Consciousness and self-regulation: Vol. I: Advances in research*. New York: Plenum, 1976.

BUCHSBAUM, M. S., & GERSHON, E. S. Genetic factors in EEG, sleep and evoked potentials. In J. M. Davidson & R. J. Davidson (Eds.), *The psychobiology of consciousness*. New York: Plenum, 1980.

BUCHSBAUM, M. S., & PFEFFERBAUM, A. Individual differences in stimulus intensity response. *Psychophysiology*, 1971, *8*, 600–611.

BUCHSBAUM, M. S., MURPHY, D. L., COURSEY, R. D., LAKE, C. R., & ZIEGLER, M. G. Platlet monoamine oxidase, plasma dopamine-beta-hydroxylase and attention in a "biochemical high risk" sample. *Journal of Psychiatric Research*, 1978, *14*, 215–224.

CAMPBELL, F. W. The transmission of spatial information through the visual system. In F. O. Schmitt & F. G. Worden (Eds.), *The neurosciences: Third study program*. Cambridge: The M.I.T. Press, 1974.

CAMPBELL, F. W., & ROBSON, J. G. Application of Fourier Analysis to the visibility of gratings. *Journal of Physiology*, 1968, *197*, 551–566.

CAPRANICA, R. R., FRISHKOPF, L. S., & NEUO, E. Encoding of geographic dialects in the auditory system of the cricket frog. *Science*, 1973, *182*, 1272–1275.

CARMON, A., HARISHANU, Y., LOWINGER, E., & LAVY, S. Asymmetries in hemispheric blood volume and cerebral dominance. *Behavioral Biology*, 1972, *7*, 853–859.

CORTEEN, R. S., & WOOD, B. Autonomic responses to shock-elicited words in an unattended channel. *Journal of Experimental Psychology*, 1972, *94*, 308–313.

DAVIDSON, R. J. Specificity and patterning in biobehavioral systems: Implications for behavior change. *American Psychologist*, 1978, *33*, 430–436.

DAVIDSON, R. J., & GOLEMAN, D. J. The role of attention in meditation and hypnosis: A psychobiological perspective on transformations of consciousness. *International Journal of Clinical and Experimental Hypnosis*, 1977, *25*, 291–308.

DAVIDSON, R. J., SCHWARTZ, G. E., & ROTHMAN, L. P. Attentional style and the self-regulation of mode-specific attention: An electroencephalographic study. *Journal of Abnormal Psychology*, 1976, *85*, 611–621.

DAVIDSON, R. J., HOROWITZ, M., SCHWARTZ, G. E., & GOODMAN, D. E. Lateral differences in the synchronization of finger tapping with the heartbeat. *Psychophysiology*, in press.

DAVIDSON, R. J., SCHWARTZ, G. E., SARON, C., BENNETT, J., & GOLEMAN, D. J. Frontal versus parietal EEG asymmetry during positive and negative affect. *Psychophysiology*, 1974, *16*, 202–203.

DAVIDSON, R. J., TAYLOR, N., & SARON, C. Hemisphericity and styles of information processing: Individual differences in EEG asymmetry and their relationship to cognitive performance. *Psychophysiology,* 1979, *16,* 197.

DIMOND, S. J., & BEAUMONT, J. G. *Hemisphere function in the human brain.* New York: Halstead, 1974.

ERDELYI, M. H. Freud's seven plus or minus two senses of unconscious: E pluribus unum. Unpublished manuscript, Brooklyn College of the City University of New York, 1977.

ERICKSON, M. H. Experimental demonstrations of the psychopathology of everyday life. *Psychoanalytic Quarterly,* 1939, *8,* 338–353.

FESTINGER, L., BURNHAM, C. A., ONO, H., & BAMBER, D. Efference and the conscious experience of perception. *Journal of Experimental Psychology,* 1967, *74,* 1–36 (monograph supplement).

FOULKES, D., & FLEISHER, S. Mental activity in relaxed wakefulness. *Journal of Abnormal Psychology,* 1975, *84,* 66–75.

FREUD, S. *The interpretation of dreams.* New York: Avon, 1965. (Originally published, 1900.)

FURST, C. J. EEG α asymmetry and visuospatial performance. *Nature,* 1976, *260,* 254–255.

GALABURDA, A. M., LeMAY, M., KEMPER, T. L., & GESCHWIND, N. Right-left asymmetries in the brain. *Science,* 1978, *199,* 852–856.

GALIN, D. Implications for psychiatry of left and right cerebral specialization: A neurophysiological context for unconscious processes. *Archives of General Psychiatry,* 1974, *31,* 572–582.

GALIN, D., DIAMOND, R., & BRAFF, D. Lateralization of conversion symptoms: More frequent on the left. *American Journal of Psychiatry,* 1977, *134,* 578–580.

GARCIA, J., & KOELLING. R. A. Relation of cue to consequence in avoidance learning. *Psychonomic Science,* 1966, *4,* 123–124.

GESCHWIND, N. The apraxias: Neural mechanisms of disorders of learned movement. *American Scientist,* 1975, *63,* 188–195.

GOFFMAN, E. *The presentation of self in everyday life.* New York: Doubleday, 1959.

GOLDFRIED, M. R., & DAVISON, G. C. *Clinical behavior therapy.* New York: Holt, Rinehart, and Winston, 1976.

GOLDSTEIN, J. *The experience of insight: A natural unfolding.* Santa Cruz, Calif.: Unity Press, 1976.

GOLEMAN, D. J. *The varieties of the meditative experience.* New York: E. P. Dutton, 1977.

GRAHAM, C., & EVANS, F. J. Hypnotizability and deployment of waking attention. *Journal of Abnormal Psychology,* 1977, *86,* 631–638.

HADAMARD, J. *The psychology of invention in the mathematical field.* New York: Dover, 1945.

HÉCAEN, J. Aphasic, apraxic and agnostic syndromes in right and left hemisphere lesions. In P. J. Vinken & G. W. Bruyn (Eds.), *Handbook of clinical neurology* (Vol. 4). Amsterdam: North-Holland, 1969.

HILGARD, E. R., & HILGARD, J. R. *Hypnosis in the relief of pain.* Los Altos, Calif.: William Kaufman, 1975.

JAMES, W. *The principles of psychology.* New York: Dover, 1950. (Originally published in 1890.)

JERISON, H. J. *Evolution of the brain and intelligence.* New York: Academic, 1973.

JERISON, H. J. Paleoneurology and the evolution of mind. *Scientific American,* 1976, *234,* 90–101.

KAGAN, J. On the need for relativism. *American Psychologist,* 1967, *22,* 131–142.

KAHNEMAN, D. *Attention and effort.* Englewood Cliffs, N.J.: Prentice-Hall, 1973.

KIMURA, D., & ARCHIBALD, Y. Motor functions of the left hemisphere. *Brain,* 1974, *97,* 337–350.

KOSAMBI, D. D. Living prehistory in India. *Scientific American,* 1967, *216,* 105.

LACEY, B. C., & LACEY, J. I. Studies of heart rate and other bodily processes in sensorimotor behavior. In P. A. Obrist, A. H. Black, J. Brener, & L. V. DiCara (Eds.), *Cardiovascular psychophysiology*. Chicago: Aldine, 1974.

Lacey, J. I. Somatic response patterning and stress: Some revisions of activation theory. In M. H. Appley & R. Trumbell (Eds.), *Psychological stress*. New York: Appleton-Century-Crosts, 1967.

Lettvin, J. Y. Maturana, H. R., McCulloch, W. S., & Pitts, W. H. What the frog's eye tells the frog's brain. *Proceedings of the Institute of Radio Engineers*, 1959, *47*, 1940–1951.

Liepmann, H. *Drei Aufsatze aud dem Aproxiegebiet*. Berlin: Karger Verlag, 1908.

Livingston, R. B. Central control of receptors and sensory transmissions systems. In J. Field, H. W. Magoun, & V. E. Hall (Eds.), *Handbook of physiology* (Vol. I). Washington, D. C.: American Physiological Association, 1959.

Luria, A. R. *Higher cortical functions in man*. New York: Basic Books, 1966.

Luria, A. R. *The working brain*. New York: Basic Books, 1973.

Luria, A. R., & Simernitskaya, E. G. Interhemispheric relations and the functions of the minor hemisphere. *Neuropsychologia*, 1977, *15*, 175–178.

Luria, A. R., Simernitskaya, E. G., & Tubylevich, B. The structure of psychological processes in relation to cerebral organization. *Neuropsychologia*, 1970, *8*, 13–18.

Lynch, J. J., & Paskewitz, D. A. On the mechanisms of the feedback control of human brain wave activity. *Journal of Nervous and Mental Disease*, 1971, *153*, 205–217.

Matthysse, S. The biology of attention. *Schizophrenia Bulletin*, 1977, *3*, 370–372.

Meichenbaum, D. Toward a cognitive theory of self-control. In G. E. Schwartz & D. Shapiro (Eds.), *Consciousness and self-regulation: Vol. I: Advances in research*. New York: Plenum, 1976.

Melzack, R. *The puzzle of pain*. New York: Basic Books, 1973.

Morgan, A. H. The heritability of hypnotic susceptibility in twins. *Journal of Abnormal Psychology*, 1973, *82*, 55–61.

Morgan, A. H., Hilgard, E. R., & Davert, E. C. The heritability of hypnotic susceptibility in twins: A preliminary report. *Behavior Genetics*, 1970, *1*, 213–224.

Muntz, W. R. A. Sensory processes and behavior. In J. L. McGaugh (Ed.), *Psychobiology*, New York: Academic, 1971.

Nauta, W. J. H. The problem of the frontal lobe: A reinterpretation. *Journal of Psychiatric Research*, 1971, *8*, 167–187.

Nauta, W. J. H., & Karten, H. J. A. general profile of the vertebrate brain, with sidelights on the cerebral cortex. In F. O. Schmidt (Ed.), *The neurosciences second study program*. New York: The Rockefeller University Press, 1970.

Neisser, U. The processes of vision. *Scientific American*, 1968, *219*, 204–214.

Neisser, U. *Cognition and reality*. San Francisco: W. H. Freeman, 1976.

Nisbett, R. E., & Wilson, T. D. Telling more than we can know: Verbal reports on mental processes. *Psychological Review*, 1977, *84*, 231–259.

Ohman, A., Fredrickson, M., Hugdahl, K., & Rimmo, P. A. The premise of equipotentiality in human classical conditioning: Conditioned electrodermal responses to potentially phobic stimuli. *Journal of Experimental Psychology: General*, 1976, *105*, 313–337.

Oldendorf, W. H., & Crandal, P. H. Bilateral cerebral circulation curves obtained by intravenous injection of radioisotopes. *Journal of Neurosurgery*, 1961, *18*, 195–199.

Orne, M. T. The nature of hypnosis: Artifact and essence. *Journal of Abnormal and Social Psychology*, 1959, *58*, 277–299.

Orne, M. T. & Paskewitz, D. A. Aversive situational effects on alpha feedback training. *Science*, 1974, *186*, 458–460.

Paskewitz, D. A., & Orne, M. T. Visual effects during alpha feedback training. *Science*, 1973, *181*, 361–363.

Petrie, A. *Individuality in pain and suffering*. Chicago: University of Chicago Press, 1967.

PIAGET, J. The affective and the cognitive unconscious. *Journal of the American Psychoanalytic Association*, 1973, *21*, 249–261.

PIAGET, J. *The child and reality: Problems of genetic psychology*. New York: Penguin, 1976.

PICTON, T. W., HILLYARD, S. A., GALAMBOS, R., & SCHIFF, M. Human auditory attention: A central or peripheral process? *Science*, 1971, *173*, 351–353.

POLLEN, D. A., & TAYLOR, J. H. The striate cortex and the spatial analysis of visual space. In F. O. Schmitt & F. G. Worden (Eds.), *The neurosciences: Third study program*. Cambridge: The M.I.T. Press, 1974.

POSNER, M. I., & KLEIN, R. M. On the functions of consciousness. In S. Kornblum (Ed.), *Attention and performance IV*. New York: Academic, 1973.

PRIBRAM, K. H. *Languages of the brain*. Englewood Cliffs, N.J.: Prentice-Hall 1971.

PRIBRAM, K. H. The primate frontal cortex—executive of the brain. In K. H. Pribram & A. R. Luria (Eds.), *Psychophysiology of the frontal lobes*. New York: Academic, 1973.

PRIBRAM, K. H. Mind, brain and consciousness: The organization of competence and conduct. In J. M. Davidson & R. J. Davidson (Eds.), *The psychobiology of consciousness*. New York: Plenum, 1980.

ROZIN, P. The evolution of intelligence and access to the cognitive unconscious. In J. M. Sprague & A. N. Epstein (Eds.), *Progress in psychobiology and physiological psychology*. New York: Academic, 1976.

SCHWARTZ, G. E., DAVIDSON, R. J., & PUGASH, E. Voluntary control of patterns of EEG parietal asymmetry: Cognitive concomitants. *Psychophysiology*, 1976, *13*, 498–504.

SELIGMAN, M. E. P., & HAGER, J. *Biological boundaries of learning*. New York: Prentice-Hall, 1972.

SEMMES, J. Hemispheric specialization: A possible clue to mechanism. *Neuropsychologia*, 1968, *6*, 11–26.

SEMMES, J., WEINSTEIN, S., GHENT, L. & TEUBER, H. L. *Somatosensory changes after penetrating brain wounds in man*. Cambridge: Harvard University Press, 1960.

SHAPIRO, D. *Neurotic styles*. New York: Basic Books, 1965.

SHAW, J. C., O'CONNOR, K. P., & ONGLEY, C. O. The EEG as a measure of cerebral functional organization. *British Journal of Psychiatry*, 1977, *130*, 260–264.

SHEEHAN, P. W., & PERRY, C. W. *Methodologies of hypnosis*. Hillsdale, N.J.: Erlbaum, 1976.

SIMERNITSKAYA, E. G. On two forms of writing defect following focal brain lesions. In S. J. Dimond & J. G. Beaumont (Eds.), *Hemisphere function in the human brain*. New York: Halsted, 1974.

SIROTA, A. D., SCHWARTZ, G. E., & SHAPIRO, D. Voluntary control of human heart rate: Effect on reaction to aversive stimulation. *Journal of Abnormal Psychology*, 1974, *83*, 261–267.

SIROTA, A. D., SCHWARTZ, G. E., & SHAPIRO, D. Voluntary control of human heart rate: Effect on reaction ot aversive stimulation: A replication and extension. *Journal of Abnormal Psychology*, 1976, *85*, 473–477.

SLOBIN, D. I. *Psycholinguistics*. Glenview, Ill.: Scott, Foresman, 1971.

SPELKE, E., HIRST, W., & NEISSER, U. Skills of divided attention. *Cognition*, 1976, *4*, 215–230.

SPINELLI, D. N., & PRIBRAM, K. H. Changes in visual recovery functions produced by temporal lobe stimulation in monkeys. *Electroencephalography and Clinical Neurophysiology*, 1966, *20*, 44–49.

SPINELLI, D. N., & PRIBRAM, K. H. Changes in visual recovery functions and unit activity produced by frontal cortex stimulation. *Electroencephalography and Clinical Neurophysiology*, 1967, *22*, 143–149.

STERNBACH, R. A., & TURSKY, B. Ethnic differences among housewives in psychophysical and skin potential responses to electric shock. *Psychophysiology*, 1965, *1*, 241–246.

TEUBER, H. L. Effects of brain wounds implicating right or left hemisphere in man. In V. B. Mountcastle (Ed.), *Interhemispheric relations and cerebral dominance*. Baltimore: The Johns Hopkins University Press, 1962.

THATCHER, R. W., & JOHN, E. R. *Functional neuroscience: Vol. I: Foundations of cognitive processes*. Hillsdale, N.J.: Erlbaum, 1977.

THOMPSON, S. W. Cerebral blood-flow assessment with radioisotope method. *Archives of Neurology*, 1964, *10*, 12–20.

TURVEY, M. T. Preliminaries to a theory of action with reference to vision. In R. Shaw & J. Bransford (Eds.), *Perceiving, acting and knowing*. Hillsdale, N.J.: Erlbaum, 1977.

VAN PRAAG, H. M., & BRUINVELS, J. (Eds.), *Neurotransmission and disturbed behavior*. Utrecht: Bonn, Scheltema, and Holkema, 1977.

VON FRISCH, K. *The dance language and orientation of bees*. Cambridge, Mass.: Belknap Press, 1967.

WACHTEL, P. L. *Psychoanalysis and behavior therapy: Toward an integration*. New York: Basic Books, 1977.

WADA, J. A., CLARKE, R., & HAMM. A. Cerebral asymmetry in humans. *Archives of Neurology*, 1975, *32*, 239–246.

WALLACE, A. F. C. Cultural determinants of response to hallucinatory experience. *A. M. A. Archives of General Psychiatry*, 1959, *1*, 58–69.

WARDLAW, K. A., & KROLL, N. E. A. Autonomic responses to shock-associated words in a nonattended message: A failure to replicate. *Journal of Experimental Psychology: Human Perception and Performance*, 1976, *2*, 357–360.

WATSON, J. B. Psychology as the behaviorist views it. *Psychological Review*, 1913, *20*, 158–177.

WEIMER, W. B. A conceptual framework for cognitive psychology: Motor theories of the mind. In R. Shaw & J. Bransford (Eds.), *Perceiving, acting and knowing*. Hillsdale, N.J.: Erlbaum, 1977.

ZBOROWSKI, M. Cultural components in responses to pain. *Journal of Social Issues*, 1952, *8*, 16–30.

3

Mind, Brain, and Consciousness: The Organization of Competence and Conduct

KARL H. PRIBRAM

The history of psychology in this century can be charted in terms of the issue that dominated each decade of exploration. Early studies on classical conditioning and Gestalt principles of perception were followed subsequently by two decades of behaviorism. In the 1950s information measurement took the stage to be supplanted in the 1960s by an almost frenetic endeavor to catalogue memory processes, an endeavor which culminated in the new concepts of a *cognitive* psychology. Currently, the study of *consciousness* as central to the mind-brain problem has emerged from the explorations of altered and alternative states produced by drugs, meditation, and a variety of other techniques designed to promote psychological growth.

Each of these new departures built upon old foundations but at the same time challenged and changed the dogma that had solidified to identify those foundations. The environmentalism of conditioning was countered by the nativism of Gestalt. The holism of Gestalt was leavened by the operationism of behavior. The peripheralism of S–R behavior theory gave way to the feedbacks of cybernetics and the correlational descriptive functionalism of both became quickly obsolete in the face of the new process oriented structuralism of cognitive psychology.

The purpose of this chapter is to examine the impact that the study of consciousness must make on the conceptions of current structuralism. True to tradition this impact ought to derive from an examination of the structure of consciousness, while at the same time challenging the dogma that has developed to characterize current thought.

KARL H. PRIBRAM • Department of Psychology, Stanford University, Stanford, California 94305.

1. CONSCIOUSNESS AND INFORMATION PROCESSING

At any period in history, the characteristic dogma is ordinarily implicit and therefore must be made explicit if a challenge is to succeed in making modifications. Originally, structuralism took as its model the digital computer and the programs that make it operational (Miller, Galanter, & Pribram, 1960; Pribram, 1960). As such, it is rooted in both the earlier functionalism of behavioral psychology and in information processing. Information is conceived in terms of features or alternatives that describe a situation, and processing proceeds by associations or list structure hierarchies among alternative features. The operations involved in processing are digital. In the computer, they result from switch settings; in the biological brain from convergences of nerve impulses onto a neuronal switching mechanism (e.g., Pitts & McCulloch, 1947; Pribram, 1971, Chap. 4). The refreshing power of this model in the development of a cognitive psychology and of an information processing approach to brain function cannot be denied.

But certain inadequacies remain. The information processing approach cannot account for the richness and immediacy of imaging. Nor does it by itself, handle the problem of meaning, of the semantic deep structure of language. Current cognitive structuralism also does not satisfactorily address itself to the nature of feelings, the emotions and motivations that are the substance of clinical psychology—though a classical cognitive clinical psychology (which takes into account the issues delineated below) exists in the form of the psychoanalytic metapsychology (Pribram & Gill, 1976).

One of the central problems is that an information processing approach based on nerve impulse transmission ignores the vast number of neurons that do not generate nerve impulses (Pribram, 1971, Chap. 1). Such neurons are often without axons but display widespreading dendritic arborizations. They function by hyperpolarization and depolarization to produce graded inhibition or excitation in their immediate surroundings. The retina is made up exclusively of such neurons until the ganglion cell layer is reached. Only here is the digital nerve impulse produced which allows signals to be transmitted over the distance traversed by the optic nerve and tract. The computations that give rise to these digital signals (and, therefore, vision) all occur in the analogue domain via graded interactions in receptor networks of horizontal, bipolar, and amacrine cells. Studies of the analogue interactions occurring in other neural networks (e.g., the olfactory bulb, Rall, 1970, pp. 552–565; Shepherd, 1974; the pyriform cortex, Freeman, 1960) are in the forefront of neuroscience research.

However, the most incisive challenge to current structural cognitive psychology comes from observations on consciousness. The variety of conscious perceptions and feelings are varieties of *states*. Such states are produced by the operation of processes, but operational and process analyses do not reveal much about the states produced. It is this deficiency in structural cognitive psychology that needs redressing and studies of consciousness provide the tools for meeting that need.

This chapter will therefore focus on the problems raised by studies of consciousness with special emphasis on brain mechanisms that can account for its phenomena. As this is not the first time I have written on these topics, the issues are covered here in nature of review and the reader is referred to their more extensive treatment in the original manuscripts. It should be helpful, however, to gather in one presentation the range of profound problems that must be faced in a scientific attempt at understanding what surely is central to any study of *human* psychology.

2. Consciousness and Self-Consciousness

The first question that must be posed is whether the concept "consciousness" is necessary at all for a scientific understanding of man's psychological processes. My answer (Pribram, 1976a) is a definite "yes." Neurosurgeons are constantly faced with making diagnoses of the amount of brain injury based on the patient's ability to make verbal and gestural responses to inquiries. These inquiries mobilize the patient's attention and a second question therefore arises: Are the concepts "consciousness" and "attention" both necessary? James (1901) raised this question and emphasized the relationship between the two concepts almost to the exclusion of the study of "consciousness" from being a fruitful endeavor. He did in the end retain the term in his own deliberations, however. I will here do likewise because, as we shall see, we need to make a distinction between state and process. "Consciousness" refers to states which have contents; "attention" refers to processes which organize these contents into one or another conscious state.

The problem is not a simple one. Consider recent reports of patients who exhibit "blind sight" (Weiskrantz, Warrington, Sanders, & Marshall, 1974). Carefully performed resections of occipital cortex (for hemangioma or aneurism) restricted to the projections from the retina, produce the expected contralateral homonymous hemianopsia. Despite this inability to see, the patients are able to point with a high degree of accuracy to objects located within the blind visual field and often are able to identify the shapes of such objects. When questioned, they stoutly maintain that they are merely "guessing," that they are completely unaware of any basis for making the responses. Yet their "guesses" come to 80% or even 90% correct answers.

Patients with "blind sight" are not the only ones who show this disassociation between instrumental performance and verbal report of introspection. When surgical severance of the cerebral hemispheres is made by cutting the extent of the major intrahemispheric connections (the corpus callosum and anterior commissure), and visual input is restricted to the right hemisphere, right-handed patients can identify objects gesturally and by matching, but verbal report indicates that the left hemisphere has not "seen" the object that has been gesturally identified.

This dissociation between instrumental and subjective report is not limited to instances where lesions separate the functions of one hemisphere from the other. Patients with bilateral resections of limbic structures—the amygdala, hippocampus, or both—demonstrate a similar syndrome (Milner, 1971; Pribram, 1965, pp. 426–459). While completely unable to "recognize" what ought to have become familiar, they nonetheless are able to learn and retain instrumental skills (Sidman, Stoddard, & Mohr, 1968).

Nor is the dissociation shown by the patients merely between verbal and nonverbal report. The difficulty is more profound, although the critical evidence for this is not easily obtained. Nonetheless, in patients with limbic lesions, it has been shown that performance in both verbal and nonverbal (geometric figure completion) recognition tasks can be substantially improved by providing contextual clues (parts of the word or geometric figures) at the time recognition is requested (Warrington & Weiskrantz, 1971).

My interpretation of these observations is that we need to distinguish between levels or at least between alternate states of consciousness. Closely tied in with verbal report, but not completely interdependent with it, is the state of subjective awareness, the state of self-consciousness. Self-consciousness is what we ordinarily refer to as "consciousness" in human discourse but it is not what is of concern in the neurosurgical clinic nor ordinarily in observations of animal behavior. Here instrumental responses are deemed adequate to define awareness.

Philosophers since James (1901) and Brentano (1960, pp. 39–61) have discussed self-consciousness as *the* essential characteristic that "makes man human" (Pribram, 1970). The term Brentano coined was "intentional inexistence" which von Uexkull (1960) shortened to "intentionality." Intentionality is to perception what intention is to action. Intentions and intentionalities may or may not be realized in the objective world. They thus define subjectivity and self-consciousness. I have elsewhere detailed the brain mechanism whereby self-consciousness can be achieved (Pribram, 1976b) and we shall return to this topic shortly. Here the important point is that self-consciousness can be identified and that on the basis of clinical neuropsychological observations self-consciousness is dissociated from other forms of consciousness which do not involve intentions and intentionalities.

3. Consciousness and Feelings

This distinction between ordinary perceptual consciousness and self-consciousness is paralleled by a similar distinction between forms of attention. James discussed the difference between reflex or primary attention and higher order processes (James, 1901). Freud made the process of attention and its neural mechanism central to the development of (self-) consciousness from perception (Freud, 1954; Pribram & Gill, 1976). And I have reviewed the contributions of recent neuropsychological research including those from my own laboratory to the understanding of the brain mechanisms involved in attention (Pribram, 1977; Pribram & McGuinness, 1975). Three major control processes were identified. One, centered on the amygdala, regulates arousal, a phasic response to input. A second, based on the basal ganglia, activates tonic states of readiness to respond. The third, termed the "effort" process, critically involves the hippocampus and coordinates arousal and readiness.

Both phasic arousal (the orienting reaction, distraction), and tonic readiness to respond were shown to be organized as feedback mechanisms. The operation of the hippocampus links these two feedbacks into a parallel process (Isaacson & Pribram, 1976) which feeds forward thus constituting an open (helical) loop rather than a homeostatic feedback mechanism. The resultant "effort" is a "voluntary" control over arousal and readiness that shows many of the characteristics of the cerebellar mechanism which organizes voluntary acts (Pribram, 1971).

The operation of these three brain systems is predicated on neurochemical differences that are currently the center of concerted research endeavor (see review by Pribram, 1977). Best known is the dopaminergic property of the readiness mechanism. Less well understood are the norepinephrinergic and serotonergic interactions involved in phasic arousal. But striking advances are being made in delineating a series of hormonally sensitive receptor brain sites regulated by peptides secreted from the pituitary gland. Among other things, these peptides control the range of comfort tolerated by the organism and the effort he is able to exert in any specific activity. The peptides have been shown to

have morphinelike qualities and the brain sites involved in the regulation of comfort and effort are those known to be specifically sensitive to
morphine. The pituitary peptides controlling comfort and effort are
closely related to or identical with the hormone that controls the adrenal
cortex. Thus a dual mechanism operates in the regulation, one peripheral and one central. This dual mechanism most likely takes the form
of a homeostat; a quantitative central representation of peripheral hormonal activities is set up. Changes in the representation are effected
directly via the connections from sensory input to the brain structures
in which the representations occur. These alterations in representation then elicit changes in the amount of neuropeptides secreted by
the pituitary, changes which also influence the peripheral hormonal
mechanisms.

Note that two of the control mechanisms outlined above delineate
what are ordinarily called emotional (arousal) and motivational (readiness) processes. They thus define the organism's feelings as well as
regulating his perceptions and actions. Note also that when the automatic feedback mechanisms of control become organized into feedforward
operations that a feeling of "effort" based on very real physiological
changes occurs (Pribram & McGuinness, 1975). Thus the organism
"pays" attention and "exerts" his will in the control of his behavior.

This distinction between feedback and feedforward processing is
considered to be the critical one underlying the difference between ordinary perceptual consciousness and self-consciousness (Pribram, 1976b).
The contents of ordinary consciousness involve interests in occurrences
and objects, interests that were described by William James (1901) as
either "terminating within the subject's own body" (emotions) or "going
farther and entering into practical relations with the exciting occurrence
or object" (motivations). The contents of self-consciousness involve intentions and intentionalities, cognitive thought processes that can be
readily distinguished from emotional or motivational feelings, from perceptions of occurrences of objects, and from the behavioral actions that
constitute James' "practical relations" with them.

4. CONSCIOUSNESS AND INFORMATION MEASUREMENT

This distinction between feedback (emotional/motivational) and
feedforward (cognitive) processing was anticipated by Freud's *Project for
a Scientific Psychology* (1954) and in the distinction between primary and
secondary processes (Pribram & Gill, 1976). Not only was the distinction
carefully drawn, but the specific neural mechanisms upon which the
distinction was based were so clearly enunciated that a hitherto murky

aspect of information measurement theory became clarified in the course of studying *The Project*. The term "information" is commonly used in several ways. In ordinary language, information conveys meaning. But in information measurement theory this usage was eschewed in favor of a simple measure of the *number* of alternatives described by the information—thus, the amount of information could be manipulated as a function of the initial uncertainty (also measured as information) reduced by a communication (more information). As the theory of communication developed, it became enmeshed in the theory of control—cybernetics, the study of steering mechanisms based on the operation of feedback processes. Feedback sense error or discrepancy between a setpoint (readiness) and the results of behavioral operations. Feedback mechanisms control these behavioral operations so as to reduce the discrepancy. The term "information" was used to define both the alternatives operating in a communication and the error sensing of control mechanisms.

However, the structure of feedback controls and that of a communication are different. Communications are feedforward operations. Thus, a distinction ought to be made on the basis of whether the term "information" is applied to feedback or feedforward processes. Shannon in his original treatise (Shannon & Weaver, 1949) did in fact make such a distinction. He called the errors processed by feedbacks "bad information" and the alternatives processed by a communication "good information." Later Brillouin (1962) identified the "good information" of alternatives with novelty and thermodynamic measures on the organization of energy called entropy, while Ashby (1960) pointed out that the sensing of error in feedback organizations involves the enhancement of redundancy rather than its reduction. Thus feedback operations maintain alternatives rather than specify or reduce them. These insights were not commonly recognized, with resulting confusion and degradation of the precise meaning of the term "information" as it had originally been set out in information measurement theory.

To summarize the preceding three sections of this chapter, the distinction between feedback and feedforward organization of control mechanisms is critical to an understanding of the distinction between ordinary perceptual consciousness and self-consciousness. Recall that feedforward organizations are constituted of feedbacks joined into parallel processes. Feedforwards thus mesh simultaneous and sequential operations (as, for instance, in list structure processing). Information processing in communication and computer networks is a feedforward process in which alternatives are specified by feedbacks which reduce redundancy, eliminating error and discrepancy. In biological organisms, redundancy reduction by feedback mechanisms is automatic while feed-

forward mechanisms apparently entail effort as when an action is voluntarily "undertaken" or attention is "payed." I have suggested elsewhere
(Pribram, 1976b) that these communications take effort because they
involve the reorganization of the constraints (redundancies) that define
the system thus altering its processing capacity. These reorganizations
of the structure of neural information processing systems are also the
basis for experiencing alternate states of consciousness.

5. CONSCIOUSNESS AND COMPETENCY

Recently experimental psychologists have been especially concerned with the issue of cognitive capacity—the limits on central processing of information (for review, see Broadbent, 1974; Pribram, 1974,
pp. 249–261; 1976b). William James (1901) had already suggested that an
understanding of the limitations of attention and thus of consciousness
would provide the key to intellectual accomplishment. George Miller in
a classical paper (1956) made the point that information processing
capacity was not fixed but depended on how the information had become organized. Grouping or "chunking" allowed a great increment in
the amount of information that could be handled. When this concept is
extended to the organization of the neural system that processes information, a new view (Pribram, 1976b) of the limitations on processing
capacity becomes evident. Ordinarily the brain's capacity is compared to
that of other communication devices, such as telephone systems, in
which channels are fixed. But as George Miller, Eugene Galanter, and I
(1960) pointed out some time ago, this view of the brain is incorrect.
Information processing by the brain is more like that which takes place
in a computer where efficient programming can influence to a remarkable degree the amount of processing that can take place. I have, therefore, suggested (Pribram, 1976b; Pribram & McGuiness, 1975) that we
approach the problem of limits on processing in terms of competence (or
efficiency) rather than in terms of a limit due to a fixed capacity. There is
much evidence that there is enough brain to go around to solve most
problems and experience the world in new ways, provided we are sufficiently competent in efficiently deploying our attentional and intentional
controls to organize the processing capacity. This competency need not
necessarily reside entirely in the attentional process itself. Just as in
computer processing much of the organization of the central processor is
derived from the input to the computer—the program being processed.
But there must be sufficient central organization to allow the program to
work. It is this central competency or bootstrap organization which is
the analogue to the attentional and intentional mechanism we have been
discussing.

In more biological terms, one can conceive of the limitations on information processing either as due to a fixed and limited capacity or due to a limited but flexible competency which, by reorganization, can overcome the limitations. A fixed capacity is like a crustacean exoskeleton while a flexible competency is more like a vertebrate endoskeleton which can adjust more readily to the demands of the input. Competency may not be limitless, but its limits are continuously challenged by renewed attentional and intentional effort (remember when the four-minute mile was a record?). Competence, not capacity, characterizes human consciousness as the recent "greening" of American consciousness has indicated. Alternate states are characterized not only by changes in what is perceived but also in the amount of information that is processed.

6. CONSCIOUSNESS AND PERCEPTION

Up to now this chapter has focused on the attentional and intentional control processes that make consciousness possible. Current advances in neuroscience also contribute to our understanding of the nature of the contents of consciousness. What we are aware of, what we feel and perceive, derives only in part from the organization of the input to our senses. Brain organization, as we have already touched on with respect to how much we can be aware of, is also critically involved.

The physical dimensions of what we are aware of are usually reduced to differences in spatial and temporal configurations. We are, therefore, inclined to look at brain organization in similar terms. To some considerable extent this approach is successful. The input from the eyes reaches one part of the brain, the input from the ears, another. The timing of nerve impulses (as, for instance, measured by interresponse intervals) is considered to be an important mechanism in the coding of neural information. But recently, both in physics and in brain physiology (Bohm, 1971, 1973; Pribram, 1966, pp. 165–187; 1971; 1976c; Pribram, Nuwer, & Barron, 1974, pp. 416–467) the limitations of explanations in the space/time domain have been faced. In physics, with respect to levels of organization other than those covered by classical mechanics (e.g., the levels of nuclear and quantum physics and also the macro universes to which the special theory of relativity is addressed) paradoxes appear when explanations are formulated in the space/time domain. These paradoxes are described in terms of the principles of complimentarity (Bohr, 1966) and uncertainty (Heisenberg, 1959). In brain physiology, paradox also appears. Despite the exquisitely detailed organization of neuroanatomical structures and exquisitely sensitive neurophysiological timing arrangements, large lesions of brain tissue which disrupt spatial continuity and grossly disturb brain electrical activity, often fail to have any demonstrable effect on awareness and behavioral performance.

In brain science, therefore, it has become accepted that information becomes distributed over a reach of tissue and that replication accounts for the protection against damage. What remains at issue is the extent of brain over which the spread of information occurs and the mechanism of spread. Elsewhere (Pribram 1966, 1971, 1974, 1976c; Pribram, Nuwer, & Baron, 1974) I have argued that optical information or image processing is as potent a model in accounting for the distribution of information as is digital computer processing for the operations of control mechanisms. Here, a brief review of the main points at issue can be helpful in providing an opportunity for presenting some recently acquired data and discussing their relevance to the problem of conscious awareness.

There are basically only two ways by which information could be distributed in the brain. One way would be by virtue of more or less random interconnections. Most computer models of neural nets are predicated on such connectivity. However, as noted earlier, brain organization is highly structured, not random. The structure is one of essentially parallel pathways from receptor surface to cortex which characteristically converge to some extent onto a one-way station, only to diverge in reaching the next. These parallel pathways are crossed at each level (from receptor through way stations to cortex) by networks of neurons whose connectivity is primarily perpendicular to the pathways, neurons which often have no, or only very short and highly arborized, axons. The work of such horizontal networks is therefore, as noted earlier, accomplished by graded local potential changes (Freeman, 1975; Rall, 1970; Shepherd, 1974) rather than by action potentials.

As the ubiquitous horizontal networks of primarily dendritic connectivities operate in the analog mode, it seems plausible to compare their function to that of *lenses* in optical information processing systems. This comparison suggests that the parallel nerve impulse transmitting pathways from receptor to cortex are organized as are the *light paths* in the optical system. Just as in the use of the digital computer model, the *organization* of the information processing mechanism is being modeled—not its realization in the hardware of computers and lens systems or the wetware of the brain.

Optical information processing technology has developed several methods for producing and storing distributed information which are called holography. These methods were originally devised (Gabor, 1948) in mathematical form in order to enhance the resolution of electron microscopy. They have since been found to be useful tools whenever high resolution of images, especially in depth (i.e., in three dimensions) is called for.

The distribution of information in optical systems is delineated mathematically by a spread function which describes what actually happens to the information in the image being processed. The image becomes blurred. However, the blurring is an orderly process which takes each point of information and distributes it in successive arcs much as ripples in a pond are formed by the impact of a pebble. Since there are many points of information in an image, the arcs intersect forming interference patterns. These patterns can be stored and with the appropriate method (the inverse of the transform that had originally been used to distribute the information) the image can be reconstructed. The stored distributed representation is called a hologram, and the process holography, because from each part of the representation the whole can be reconstructed.

The hypothesis that information is distributed in the brain by a process whose organization is like that of holography comes readily from the foregoing considerations. If the horizontal networks of neural interconnections function somewhat as do the lenses of optical information processing systems, then the possibility exists that the distribution of information in the brain is accomplished by virtue of holographic principles (Pribram, Nuwer, & Baron, 1974).

The evidence to date supports this hypothesis, but in a very special sense only. As noted in the earlier publication, two mechanisms at least can be formulated to accomplish the necessary transformation. One involves the storage of information and this possibility has as yet not been put to test. The other depends on the successive transformations of input by the functions of the horizontal networks of neurons we have been discussing. Recordings from single cells in the input systems can be used to analyze those transformations that have occurred in the network by the time that particular cell is reached. In the visual system such analyses have shown that the mathematical formulations which define holography, usefully, describe the transformations occurring in the visual mechanism.

But one major restriction must be recognized in this use of the holographic model. Each cell in the system, by virtue of the size of its receptive field, is tuned to a limited bandwidth of the spectrum of spatial frequencies (the frequency of occurrence of relative light and dark over space which is analogous to the frequency of occurrence of waves of sound in time in audition). Thus, within each receptive field information becomes distributed by the holographic transformation (which is described by spatial frequency). However, each receptive field subtends only a few degrees of visual angle and our initial purpose in using the model was to explain the distribution of information over considerably greater reaches of brain tissue.

The resolution of this dilemma which has been faced by neural holographic theory since its inception (Pribram, 1974) comes from the development of a special type of optical hologram called the composite or multiplex hologram (for a description see Leith, 1976). This holographic process was derived from work in radioastronomy (Bracewell, 1965) where information is gathered in the holographic (spatial frequency) domain in segments or strips and then integrated into a highly detailed three-dimensional whole during image reconstruction.

The composite or multiplex hologram is in many ways simpler than the original more global form. The earlier version necessitated coherent light (produced by a laser beam or monochromatic light source) for its formation and for image reconstruction. This constraint does not apply to multiplex holography which can be performed with ordinary white light. The composite hologram has the additional advantage that three-dimensional *movement* can be captured and reconstructed.

Many of the receptive fields of the cells of the visual cortex have the shape of strips, elongated ovals or rectangles (Spinelli, Pribram, & Bridgeman, 1970). The discovery that such cells were tuned to specific orientations (Hubel & Wiesel, 1962) has ordinarily been interpreted as an indication that the cells were "detecting" the orientation of lines as features of the input. However, the output of each cell is, as we have seen, sensitive to spatial frequency (and often also to movement and direction of movement). It is, therefore, more appropriate to view the output of the cell as representing an integral of spatial frequency, orientation of a strip, movement and direction—an integral mathematically and functionally similar to that produced when a multiplex hologram is illuminated.

The question immediately arises as to what brain process corresponds to the illumination of the composite optical hologram. Much of the work of my laboratory over the past fifteen years has been devoted to delineating the control over input processing which is exercized by remote brain structures such as the association cortex (see review by Pribram, 1974). Changes in receptive field properties and recovery functions have been demonstrated and the anatomical pathways by which these effects are mediated have been traced. Behavioral experiments have linked these control processes to selective attention, intentional behavior, and the ability to make discriminative and delayed responses. Either through such control operations or by way of abstraction (or both) the integrative, imaging properties of the multiplex neural hologram can become realized.

Mathematically the multiplex neural hologram can be thought of as a matrix of cells whose sensitivities, spatial frequency, orientation, color, movement, and direction are represented by vectors. Multivariate matrices have the advantage that they represent occurrences rather than space/time organizations whose limitations were noted earlier and have been extensively discussed by Whitehead (1958), although space/time dimensions can be derived from them. Each vector relationship can in theory be abstracted from them and realized separately (e.g., the derivation of size constancy from spatial frequency (Campbell & Robson, 1968) or the integration into an image can be performed by the neural control operations. In a very real sense the separate derivations are complementary as they are in quantum mechanics where frequency (i.e., momentum) and orientation (location) are never completely specified in one and the same analysis. Research is now being addressed to specifying the conditions under which, and the neural mechanisms by which, various abstractions can occur or image integration takes place.

One of the properties of image processing by holography is that the image which is reconstructed is projected into space away from the holographic storage medium. A series of elegant experiments by von Bekesy (1967) has demonstrated that biological sensory processes behave in a similar fashion by virtue of the horizontal networks of interconnections described earlier in this presentation. Von Bekesy showed both mathematically and by experimental demonstration that projection results from inhibitory interactions within the horizontal network to produce an effect similar to that produced by stereophonic audio systems. The source of the sound is projected away from the speakers when the phase relationships between the frequencies emitted is properly adjusted. Von Bekesy worked with spatial frequency and showed, for instance, that the perception of tactile stimulation would be projected into the space between when two arms or fingers were stimulated.

These experiments and the holographic model (mathematical and optical) help to explain how a brain process can give rise to an image which is experienced as remote from the representational mechanism and even the receptor surface which is involved in the construction of the image. The contents of consciousness (what we are aware of) are thus experienced apart from the brain apparatus (holographic and control) that organizes those contents from its inputs. Mind and brain are separate except in this special relation to each other.

7. Consciousness and Mind

Gilbert Ryle (1949) has pointed out that the term "mind" is derived from minding, attending. The analysis presented in this essay supports Ryle's derivation: minding, attending is a control operation that organizes the holographic process of image construction, the content of mind. Images can be experienced when the process is engaged by sensory input or from memory. We have focused on visual imagery but auditory imagery, which constitutes verbal thought, and haptic or kinesthetic imagery, which enhances mechanical "know how" and even gustatory images are formed in a similar fashion (von Bekesy, 1967). Mind is the sum of the content of psychological perceptual processes such as vision, audition, etc. Mind, so defined, is an emergent property of information processing by the brain much as wetness is an emergent property of the appropriate organization of hydrogen and oxygen into water, and gravity is an emergent property of the organization of matter into interacting masses. Strictly speaking, in all these instances it is inappropriate to locate the emergent in any constituent part of the organized whole, although colloquially we are apt to talk about the earth's gravitational force without referring to other masses on which such a force might be exerted. It is this mode of speaking which identifies consciousness with brain processes without specifying the contribution of sensory input. As Whitehead (1958) suggested, mind is more appropriately conceived of as a property extending throughout the natural universe—with this important caveat, however, that a brain, perhaps a human brain, must be minding. There cannot be mind without minding.

Recently (for review see Dimond & Beaumont, 1974) a good deal of interest has been aroused by the finding that when the cerebral hemispheres are separated by surgical severance of the commissures that ordinarily connect them, that information processing occurring in one hemisphere appears to be inaccessible to the other. When such surgery is performed in man, two separate minds seem to coexist, one verbal— the other instrumental in its operations. Only the verbal hemisphere has so far been shown to produce intention and intentionality and, thus, self-consciousness. This suggests that meta operations of feedforward mechanisms such as those of transformational grammar must be critical in organizing linguistic competence.

These, and some of the observations detailed earlier in this paper, have raised once more other philosophical issues of the relationship between brain and mind. Most physiologists such as Sherrington (1941), Penfield (1975), Eccles (1970), and Sperry (1976, pp. 163–179) have opted for a cleancut dualism. Sherrington, Eccles, and Sperry have proceeded further in stating that mind can act on brain directly. They have not specified, however, what they mean by mind, nor by what mechanism mental organization can influence brain function.

Behavioral psychologists and biologists when they have not entirely eschewed mental operations, have by and large used the information measurement and information processing approach to the brain-mind problem used in this essay. The brain's wetware is akin to the hardware of computers and optical systems. Mental operations are akin to programs and image constructions. A systems approach distinguishes between hardware and software—between reductive analysis on the one hand and conventional construction on the other (Pribram, 1965). Dualism is thus affirmed but in a practical, pragmatic fashion rather than as an epistemological impasse. Furthermore, the mechanisms of interaction between brain and mind are being clearly specified in terms of information measurement and processing operations, mechanisms which do not belie the distinction between subjectivity and objectivity, but rather enhance it. As we have seen, subjectivity is a function of self-consciousness whose structural organization is feedforward rather than feedback.

Science pursues knowledge by observation and experimentation. As such it addresses problems that have been posed and clarified by philosophical analysis. The most recent surge of basic scientific activity in what were heretofore philosophical pastures has been in the behavioral, brain, and information sciences. In this essay we have been grazing, munching, and processing the results of these activities especially as they relate to the problem of consciousness. I believe the evidence attests to the fact that science can address the problem successfully and that we do indeed know a great deal that we did not know only a few decades ago. What is accomplished by such knowing is that a new set of questions at a much more precise (sometimes microstructural, often mathematical) level of inquiry can now be asked. In short our consciousness has been expanded both in breadth and in depth—spatial terms that do injustice to our enhanced feeling for the occurrences which are composed by and compose consciousness.

REFERENCES

ASHBY, W. R. *Design for a brain.* New York: Wiley, 1960.

BOHM, D. Quantum theory as an indication of a new order in physics. Part A. The development of new orders as shown through the history of physics. *Foundations of Physics,* 1971, *1*(4), 359–381.

BOHM, D. Quantum theory as an indication of a new order in physics. Part B. Implicate and explicate order in physical law. *Foundations of Physics,* 1973, *3*(2), 139–168.

BOHR, N. *Atomic physics and human knowledge.* New York: Vintage Press, 1966.

BRACEWELL, R. *The Fourier transform and its applications.* New York: McGraw-Hill, 1965.

BRENTANO, F. The distinction between mental and physical phenomena. In R. M. Chisholm (Ed.), *Realism and the background of phenomenology.* New York: The Free Press, 1960.

BRILLOUIN, L. *Science and information theory.* New York: Academic, 1962.

BROADBENT, D. E. Division of function and integration. *Neurosciences study program, III.* New York: The M.I.T. Press, 1974.

CAMPBELL, F. W., & ROBSON, J. G. Application of Fourier analysis to the visibility of gratings. *Journal of Physiology,* 1968, *197,* 551–566.

DIMOND, S. J., & BEAUMONT, J. G. *Hemisphere function in the human brain.* New York: Wiley, 1974.

ECCLES, J. C. *Facing reality.* New York, Heidelberg, Berlin: Springer-Verlag, 1970.

FREEMAN, W. J. Correlation of electrical activity of prepyriform cortex and behavior in cat. *Journal of Neurophysiology,* 1960, *23:* 111–131.

FREEMAN, W. *Mass action in the nervous system.* New York: Academic, 1975.

FREUD, S. Project for a scientific psychology. Appendix in *The origins of psychoanalysis, letters to Wilhelm Fliess, draft and notes 1887–1902.* New York: Basic Books, 1954.

GABOR, D. A new microscopic principle, *Nature,* 1948, *161,* 777–778.

HEISENBERG, W. *Physics and philosophy.* London: Allen and Unwin, 1959.

HUBEL, D. H., & WIESEL, T. N. Receptive fields, binocular interaction and functional architecture in the cat's visual cortex. *Journal of Physiology,* 1962, *160,* 106–154.

ISAACSON, R. L., & PRIBRAM, K. H. (Eds.), *The hippocampus:* Vol. I: *Neurophysiology and behavior.* New York: Plenum, 1976.

JAMES, W. *The principles of psychology.* London: Macmillan, 1901.

LEITH, E. N. White light holograms. *Scientific American,* 1976, *235(4),* 80.

MILLER, G. A. The magical number seven, plus or minus two, or some limits on our capacity for processing information. *Psychological Review,* 1956, *63*(2), 81–97.

MILLER, G. A., GALANTER, E., & PRIBRAM, K. H. *Plans and the structure of behavior.* New York: Henry Holt, 1960.

MILNER, B. Interhemispheric difference in the localization of psychological processes in man. *British Medical Bulletin,* 1971, *27(3),* 272–277.

PITTS, W., & MCCULLOCH, W. S. How we know universals. The perception of auditory and visual forms. *Bulletin of Mathematical Biophysics,* 1947, *9,* 127.

PRIBRAM, K. H. A review of theory in physiological psychology. Reprinted from *Annual Review of Psychology,* Vol. II, 1960, 1–40.

PRIBRAM, K. H. Proposal for a structural pragmatism: Some neuropsychological considerations of problems in philosophy. In B. Wolman & E. Nagle (Eds.), *Scientific psychology: Principles and approaches.* New York: Basic Books, 1965.

PRIBRAM, K. H. Some dimensions of remembering: Toward a neuropsychological model of memory. In J. Gaito (Ed.), *Macromolecules and behavior.* New York: Academic, 1966.

PRIBRAM, K. H. What makes man human. New York: American Museum of Natural History, 1970 James Arthur Lecture.

PRIBRAM, K. H. *Languages of the brain: Experimental paradoxes and principles in neuropsychology.* Englewood Cliffs, N.J.: Prentice-Hall, 1971.

PRIBRAM, K. H. How is it that sensing so much we can do so little? In F. O. Schmitt & F. G. Worden (Eds.), *The neurosciences study program, III,* Cambridge: The M.I.T. Press, 1974.

PRIBRAM, K. H. Problems concerning the structure of consciousness. In G. Globus, G. Maxwell, & I. Savodnik (Eds.), *Science and the mind-brain puzzle.* New York: Plenum, 1976. (a)

PRIBRAM, K. H. Self-consciousness and intentionality: A model based on an experimental analysis of the brain mechanisms involved in the Jamesian theory of motivation and emotion. In G. E. Schwartz & D. Shapiro (Eds.), *Consciousness and self-regulation, advances in research,* Vol. I, New York: Plenum, 1976. (b)

PRIBRAM, K. H. Holonomy and structure in the organization of perception. Proceedings of the Conference on Images, Perception and Knowledge, University of Western Ontario, May 1974, 1976. (c)

PRIBRAM, K. H. Peptides and protocritic processes. In L. H. Miller, C. A. Sandman, & A. J. Kastin (Eds.), *Neuropeptide inflences on the brain and behavior.* New York: Raven, 1977, pp. 213–232.

Pʀɪʙʀᴀᴍ, K. H., & Gɪʟʟ, M. M. *Freud's 'project' re-assessed.* New York: Basic Books, 1976.

Pʀɪʙʀᴀᴍ, K. H., & McGᴜɪɴɴᴇss, D. Arousal, activation and effort in the control of attention. *Psychological Review,* 1975, *82(2),* 116–149.

Pʀɪʙʀᴀᴍ, K. H., Nᴜᴡᴇʀ, M., & Bᴀʀᴏɴ, R. The holographic hypothesis of memory structure in brain function and perception. In R. C. Atkinson, D. H. Krantz, R. C. Luce, & P. Suppes (Eds.), *Contemporary developments in mathematical psychology.* San Francisco: W. H. Freeman, 1974.

Rᴀʟʟ, W. Dendritic neuron theory and dendro-dendritic synapses in a simple cortical system. In F. O. Schmitt (Ed.), *The neurosciences: Second study program.* New York: The Rockefeller University Press, 1970.

Rʏʟᴇ, G. *The Concept of mind.* New York: Barnes & Noble, 1949.

Sʜᴀɴɴᴏɴ, C. E., & Wᴇᴀᴠᴇʀ, W. *The mathematical theory of communication.* Urbana, Ill.: University of Illinois Press, 1949.

Sʜᴇᴘʜᴇʀᴅ, G. M. *The synaptic organization of the brain—An introduction.* New York: Oxford University Press, 1974.

Sʜᴇʀʀɪɴɢᴛᴏɴ, C. *Man on his nature.* New York: Macmillan, 1941.

Sɪᴅᴍᴀɴ, M., Sᴛᴏᴅᴅᴀʀᴅ, L. T., & Mᴏʜʀ, J. P. Some additional quantitative observations of immediate memory in a patient with bilateral hippocampal lesions. *Neuropsychologia,* 1968, *6,* 245–254.

Sᴘᴇʀʀʏ, R. W. Mental phenomena as causal determinants in brain function. In Gordon G. Globus, Grover Maxwell, & Irwin Savodnik (Eds.), *Consciousness and the brain.* New York: Plenum, 1976.

Sᴘɪɴᴇʟʟɪ, D. N., Pʀɪʙʀᴀᴍ, K. H., & Bʀɪᴅɢᴇᴍᴀɴ, B. Visual receptive field organization of single units in the visual cortex of monkey. *International Journal Neuroscience,* 1970, *1,* 67–74.

Pᴇɴꜰɪᴇʟᴅ, W. *Mystery of the mind.* Princeton: Princeton University Press, 1975.

ᴠᴏɴ Bᴇᴋᴇsʏ, G. *Sensory inhibition.* Princeton: Princeton University Press, 1967.

ᴠᴏɴ Uᴇxᴋᴜʟʟ, J. In R. M. Chisholm (Ed.), *Realism and the background of phenomenology.* New York: The Free Press, 1960.

Wᴀʀʀɪɴɢᴛᴏɴ, E. K., & Wᴇɪsᴋʀᴀɴᴛᴢ, L. Organizational aspects of memory in amnesic patients. *Neuropsychologia,* 1971, *9,* 67–73.

Wᴇɪsᴋʀᴀɴᴛᴢ, L., Wᴀʀʀɪɴɢᴛᴏɴ, E. K., Sᴀɴᴅᴇʀs, M. D., & Mᴀʀsʜᴀʟʟ, J. Visual capacity in the hemianopic field following a restricted occipital ablation. *Brain,* 1974, *97(4),* 709–728.

Wʜɪᴛᴇʜᴇᴀᴅ, A. N. *Modes of thought.* New York: Capricorn Books, 1958.

4

Stress-Induced Behavior: Chemotherapy without Drugs

Seymour M. Antelman and Anthony R. Caggiula

The effects of stress on behavior can be grouped into three general categories: (1) mild stress can induce or potentiate a variety of behaviors such as eating, aggression, and sexual behavior; (2) more severe stress may disrupt behavior by making it repetitive, less finely tuned to the environment and stereotyped; (3) severe stress can also totally suppress behavior. These effects of stress, which have been reported to occur in virtually all species, including man, may represent an attempt by the organism to reduce or eliminate the deleterious effects of the stress. In this sense, these behaviors represent a form of self-therapy.

This chapter deals with evidence derived from both the experimental animal and human clinical literature which suggests that these behavioral responses to stress involve the activity of brain catecholamine-, and particularly, dopamine-containing systems, and their interaction with other neurotransmitter systems such as norepinephrine and serotonin.

Finally, the behavioral consequences of stress and their adaptive or coping function are discussed within the context of several human clinical disorders such as depression, autism, and schizophrenia.

Adaptive or coping responses to stress may be seen at all levels of biological functioning. For instance, at a molecular level, the stress represented by an invading microorganism will trigger a variety of immunological responses in the lymphoreticular system which are designed to isolate and destroy the foreign substance. Such adaptive responses represent, in a very real sense, a form of self-therapy.

These immunological responses provide us with one example of how the organism attempts to protect itself from the adverse effects of a stress by removing the stressor. There is, however, another type of

SEYMOUR M. ANTELMAN • Department of Psychiatry, University of Pittsburgh, School of Medicine, and Western Psychiatric Institute and Clinic, Pittsburgh, Pennsylvania 15260. ANTHONY R. CAGGIULA • Departments of Psychology, and Pharmacology, University of Pittsburgh, Pittsburgh, Pennsylvania 15260.
Research was supported by PHS grants MH24114 and RSDA MH00238 (to S.M.A.) and MH16581 (to A.R.C.).

coping response which is designed to alter the organism in such a way as to coexist with the stress. Sickle cell trait is an example of the latter. At a more molar level, hormones may play an important role in the body's resistance to stress. Here again, two types of adaptive or coping mechanisms have been suggested: syntoxic steroids (e.g., glucocorticords), which create conditions promoting coexistence with the stressor, and catatoxic steroids (e.g., ethylestrenol and spironolactone), which act to destroy toxic substances and thereby remove the stressor (Selye, 1974).

The preceding examples represent only a few of the multitude of physiological processes which can be viewed as adaptive or coping responses through which the organism attempts to maintain homeostatic balance when confronted with specific or nonspecific stress. In this chapter, we hope to show that many of the behaviors exhibited by animals and man during stress can be thought of in the same way. That is to say, stress induces a variety of behavioral responses which represent an attempt, by the organism, to reduce or eliminate the deleterious effects of the stress. In this sense, these behaviors represent a form of self-therapy.

We will document the range of behaviors which frequently accompany some forms of mild stress and are believed to result from the general activational properties of the stress. These will include eating, aggression, sexual behavior, and other biologically significant behaviors. We will also discuss the consequences of more severe or prolonged stress. These include aberrant patterns such as repetitive or stereotyped behaviors in animals and stereotyped behavior and thought patterns in humans suffering from clinical disorders such as autism and schizophrenia. For each of these responses to stress, we will suggest a common neurochemical basis which involves interactions among several transmitter systems, with brain dopamine playing a central role.

1. STRESS-INDUCED BEHAVIOR

In this section, we will first document the link, in both animals and humans, between stressful or activating circumstances and behaviors such as eating, sex, and aggression. We will then suggest a neurochemical basis for stress-induced behaviors.

1.1. Eating

A relationship between stress and feeding behavior has been observed in a wide variety of species under both natural and experimental conditions.

Under natural conditions, feeding is often associated with bouts of fighting or sexual behavior and is presumably the result of the activation produced by these latter behaviors. In birds, where these effects are best documented, eating has been reported during boundary disputes in the prairie horned lark (Pickwell, 1931), both the great and blue tit (Tinbergen, 1937; Hinde, 1952), the avocet (Makkink, 1936), the turkey (Raber, 1948) and the zebra finch (Morris; 1954), among others. Sporadic eating during a series of copulations has also been seen in the wild rat (Barnett, 1958).

In the laboratory, feeding or food-related behavior has been observed under a variety of circumstances, all of which share the common element of stress or activation. For example, Tugendhat (1960a) noted that the thwarting, and presumed frustration induced by covering the food dish with a transparent plate, increased subsequent feeding in the three-spined stickleback. This same investigator (Tugendhat, 1960b) also discovered that electric shock elevated the number of completed feeding bouts per unit time in the stickleback while decreasing the total amount of time spent eating.

Very similar findings have been reported for the activating effects of electric shock on mammalian feeding behavior. For instance, mild shock will induce overeating in both deprived and sated rats, while eating is suppressed by more intense shocks (Sterritt, 1962; 1965). In those animals that did eat in response to shock, eating was reduced between trials. Collectively, these data point to the importance of both intensity and time factors in determining the effects of stress on behavior (Fentress, 1973; 1976). Compatible findings have been reported by Strongman (1965), who found that, while very brief pulses of shock facilitated feeding in rats, longer shocks actually decreased this behavior. An association between electric shock and feeding behavior in rats has also been demonstrated by Siegal and Brantley (1951) and by Ullman (1951; 1952). Recently, Colavita (personal communication) has observed voracious eating in cats after shuttle-box avoidance testing.

Although the studies using electric shock clearly suggest a link between stress and feeding behavior, it is difficult to dissociate, and therefore assess, the contribution of physical pain, which is almost invariably induced by this procedure. Furthermore, this method provides little opportunity for a more detailed analysis of the relationship between activation and feeding since, for example, shock cannot be applied either continuously or chronically without eliciting incompatible behaviors such as freezing or escape responses. The disadvantages of shock, as applied to the study of feeding behavior, may account for the fact that, although some animals ate in response to shock in the Sterritt studies, total eating (including shocked and unshocked periods) was never any greater, and, in some instances, it was significantly less than in un-shocked controls.

There is another type of activating stimulus which has also been found to induce feeding, but which is not encumbered by the disadvantages referred to above. In 1973, while conducting an unrelated experiment, Antelman and Szechtman discovered that a mild pinch applied to the tail of a rat would induce eating in the presence of food. This is an unusually reliable response which typically begins within a few seconds of pinch onset and lasts until its removal (Antelman & Szechtman, 1975; Antelman, Szechtman, Chin, & Fisher, 1975). If goal objects other than food are available during the pinch, the animal's response changes accordingly. Thus, tail-pinch applied in the presence of a tube containing milk or other palatable fluids will induce drinking (Antelman, Rowland, & Fisher, 1976), whereas the same stimulus will result in sexual behavior in the presence of a receptive female (Shaw, Caggiula, Antelman, & Greenstone, unpublished data), and maternal behavior when rat pups are present (Sherman, Fisher, & Antelman, unpublished data). In the absence of goal objects, tail-pinch stress will typically induce nail-pulling or nail-biting behavior (Rowland & Antelman, 1976).

As a model of stress-induced eating, the tail-pinch procedure overcomes many of the problems associated with electric shock. Perhaps most importantly, eating induced by tail-pinch is definitely not a pain-dependent phenomenon. Indeed, when tail-pinch is made painful, the eating which results is harried and fragmented and not at all normal-appearing. By contrast, with a mild pinch properly applied, the animal shows no trace of annoyance or aversion and the resulting eating appears normal in every respect. A second obvious advantage of tail-pinch relates to its reliability in inducing feeding. Since its discovery, several thousand animals have been tested in our laboratories using the tail-pinch/feeding paradigm, and the incidence of eating obtained has been close to 100%. Finally, tail-pinch can produce considerable hyperphagia and obesity, which is similar in several respects to the stress-induced overeating seen in humans (Rowland & Antelman, 1976). For example, finickiness is observed in both the rat and human models (Rowland & Antelman, 1976; Antelman, Rowland, & Fisher, 1976). When food is unavailable, stress also induces responses other than eating in both animals and humans (Antelman, Szechtman, Caggiula, & Rowland, 1975; Glucksman, 1972).

Tail-pinch probably represents nothing more than a mildly stressful stimulus to the organism. If this is the case, then eating should also be seen in response to other mild stressors. It is not surprising, therefore, that eating has also been reported to accompany auditory stimulation (Kupferman, 1964) and is often observed in the laboratory immediately after handling.

Coprophagy, or the eating of excrement by animals is often associated with stressful circumstances. Both we (Antelman, unpublished data) and others (Valenstein, 1976) have observed this behavior in rats during tail-pinch, and it is a common problem among primates in captivity (Hill, 1966). Although coprophagy was often observed in rhesus monkeys reared in enclosed isolation, it was seldom seen in control animals (Mitchell, Ruppenthal, Raymond, & Harlow, 1966). Moreover, the frequency of coprophagy was directly correlated with the extent of isolation stress, showing the greatest incidence the longer, the earlier, and the more severe the captive situation. Isolation of rhesus monkeys has also been reported to produce hyperphagia and also polydipsia of a standard laboratory diet (Miller, Mirsky, Caul, & Sakata, 1969).

Feeding in rats and/or cats has also been reported to accompany other types of activating or stressful circumstances such as deprivation of paradoxical sleep (Dement, 1969), or treatment with low doses of sodium pentobarbital (Jacobs & Farel, 1971) which produces an activated (i.e., desynchronized) cortical EEG pattern.

In addition to the ability of activating or stressful circumstances to induce eating in the intact animal, they are also able to promote recovery of ingestive behavior following brain damage. For instance, in rats made aphagic and adipsic by lateral hypothalamic lesions, mild tail-pinch applied several times a day induced sufficient drinking of sweetened milk to sustain these animals until they recovered the ability to eat spontaneously (Antelman & Rowland, 1975; Antelman, Rowland, & Fisher, 1976). Acute application of a painful clamp to the tails of aphagic cats likewise induces eating (Teitelbaum & Wolgin, 1975; Wolgin, Cytawa, & Teitelbaum, 1976). Similar phenomena have also been observed when tail-pinch stress was applied to rats with either hypothalamic islands (Ellison, Sorenson, & Jacobs, 1970) or 6-hydroxydopamine-induced lesions of the nigrostriatal bundle (Marshall, Richardson, & Teitelbaum, 1974; Antelman, Szechtman, Chin, & Fisher, 1975).

The ability of stressful or activating stimuli to induce feeding in animals has a striking parallel in the human clinical literature. It has long been recognized that the stress associated with traumatic emotional events may contribute to overeating in some obese individuals. Bruch, who perhaps more than any current-day investigator has focused our attention on the importance of emotional factors in overeating, has characterized the weight gain associated with such behavior as "reactive obesity" (Bruch, 1957, 1973). This type of overeating and weight gain is frequently observed after a traumatic experience, such as the loss of a loved one. Although the precipitating stressors vary in kind from individual to individual, they often result in anxiety or depressive reactions which can be diminished by eating (Bruch, 1957, 1973). The use of overeating to allay emotional states is not limited to extreme circumstances.

It may also occur in response to everyday frustrating experiences, as is well illustrated in the following remarks of an unhappy young woman cited by Bruch (Bruch, 1973): "Sometimes I think I'm not hungry at all. It is that I am just unhappy in certain things—things I cannot get. Food is the easiest thing to get that makes me feel nice and comfortable." Although this woman was able to control her eating during the day when surrounded and comforted by other people, she had considerable difficulty at night when she was alone and tense. In speaking of this she stated: "I think that I am ravenously hungry and I do my utmost not to eat. My body becomes stiff in my effort to control my hunger. If I want to have any rest at all—I've got to get up and eat. Then I go to sleep like a newborn baby."

This type of eating pattern is very similar to the "Night Eating Syndrome" described by Stunkard (1955) in some of his patients. This syndrome, which is characterized by hyperphagia and insomnia at night followed by morning anorexia, occurs during stressful periods in life and is diminished by their resolution. In addition to the foregoing clinical examples, a relationship between stress and eating by some individuals has also been observed under more controlled experimental conditions (Meyer & Pudel, 1972; Leon & Chamberlain, 1973a; see Herman & Polivy, 1975 for a possible explanation of some inconsistencies in this literature).

The foregoing represents some of the parallels which suggest a common process in both animals and humans underlying the organism's behavioral response to stress. Other parallels between the animal model and human behavior, including the effects of drugs in stress-related eating, will be discussed when we return to this topic in a later section of this chapter.

1.2. Sexual Behavior

Many of the same types of stressful stimuli which induce feeding also result in copulatory behavior. This was explicitly noted by Morris (1954, p. 271) in his description of the mounting of a nearby female by a male zebra finch during a fight with another male: "The first time displacement mounting was seen, it occurred at the point at which displacement feeding was seen on other occasions." Sexual activity associated with fighting has also been described in the cormorant (Tinbergen, 1951) and avocet (Makkink, 1936). The wide variety of activating conditions which can precipitate sexual behavior in the wild is nicely illustrated by Bergman (1946), who described such behavior in turnstones during the passing of a boat or airplane, a sudden hail storm, or a fight with an enemy.

Within the somewhat more restricted context of laboratory research, Beach (1942) was one of the first to suggest that general activation could raise the level of sexual excitability. In discussing factors which may be involved in the generation of sexual excitement in male animals, he wrote: "We have found that a male rat, sluggish after repeated contacts with non-receptive females, can sometimes be aroused to renewed copulatory activity if he is batted sharply about the cage by the experimenter." Stone and Ferguson (1940) similarly observed that a sluggish male rat not copulating with one female, could often be induced to do so by the novelty of being presented with another female. This same effect, which is presumably due to activation, has also been produced by abruptly removing and replacing the original female (Beach, 1942).

Such early work illustrates two of the three principal types of laboratory studies which have related sexual behavior to activating or stressful conditions: (1) the effects of electric shock or similar stimuli, (2) the effects of exciting the male by handling or novelty, and (3) the effects of frustration.

A number of studies in recent years has examined the influence of electric shock on different aspects of male sexual behavior. These studies, which derived from the original and independent observations of Barfield and Sachs (1968) and Caggiula and Eibergen (1969), have demonstrated that electric shock applied to either the back or the tail can increase the percentage of naive adult male rats copulating on their first sex test (Caggiula, 1972; Caggiula & Eibergen, 1969), and also accelerates the rate of copulation in experienced males (Barfield & Sachs, 1968; Caggiula & Vlahoulis, 1974; Sachs & Barfield, 1974). Moreover, shock has been shown to be extremely effective in increasing the number of prepuberal male rats copulating (Goldfoot & Baum, 1972), and the rate of mounting behavior in aging males (Sharma & Hays, 1974), as well as in eliciting copulation in persistently noncopulating adult males (Caggiula & Eibergen, 1969; Crowley, Popolow, & Ward, 1973; Malsbury & Pfaff, 1975). Finally, a previously ineffective auditory stimulus was shown to activate mating behavior in noncopulators after being paired with back shock (Crowley et al., 1973).

As was the case for feeding, stress can also serve a "therapeutic function in temporarily restoring copulatory activity that had been suppressed by certain types of brain damage. Thus, tail pinch can induce copulation and ejaculation, in a stimulation-bound manner, in males not copulating after receiving intraventricular injections of 6-hydroxydopamine (6-OHDA) a neurotoxin that selectively destroys brain catecholamine-containing pathways" (Caggiula, Shaw, Antelman, & Edwards, 1976; Shaw et al., unpublished data).

Handling of the male, or stimulus novelty, has also been found effective in activating or reactivating sexual behavior. Repeated handling (i.e., picking the rat up and putting him down twice/min) can temporarily reverse the decline in sexual vigor that occurs as a function of age (Larsson, 1963). Handling of 20- to 24-month-old males in these experiments resulted in copulatory performance every bit as vigorous as that shown by 5- to 6-month-old males, and significantly greater than that of nonhandled controls.

The so-called Coolidge Effect is yet another instance of the energizing influence of activation on male copulatory behavior. This effect refers to the resumption of copulation by a male sexually sated on a particular female (satiation being arbitrarily defined as the passage of a given amount of time without copulation) when a novel female is introduced (Bermant, Lott, & Anderson, 1968; Fisher, 1962; Wilson, Keuhn, & Beach, 1963). There's been considerable variability with respect to the degree of rejuvenation which occurs when this procedure is used in the rat, but, with one exception (Fisher, 1962), the upper limit seems to be about two additional ejaculations. The effect is much stronger in ungulates such as the ram (Beamer, Bermant, & Clegg, 1969) and the bull (Schein & Hale, 1965). The bull will typically achieve a maximum of ten ejaculations before becoming "sated." However, by repeatedly replacing the cow each time the bull allows 30 min to elapse without mounting, he may go through as many as seven cows (i.e., an astonishing 70 ejaculations) before retiring.

Thwarting may also serve to facilitate sexual behavior. If, in the midst of copulation, the female rat is removed from the arena and remains separated from the male for longer than the normal interval between intromissions, fewer intromissions will be needed to achieve ejaculation (Larsson, 1956). This "enforced interval" effect has been interpreted by some (Sachs & Barfield, 1974) as an example of frustration-induced facilitation of sexual behavior, although other interpretations are possible. This frustration hypothesis might also explain the facilitative effects on subsequent copulation of permitting a male rat to mount a female that does not allow intromission, because of a surgically closed vagina (Hård & Larsson, 1968).

Before concluding this subsection, several other examples of stress-induced sexual activity should be briefly noted. Calhoun (1962) in his now classic studies on the effects of overcrowding on the Norway rat, mentions several occasions when a male that had just attacked another male, exhibited sexual behavior. He also describes an example of a female who displayed such behavior following a succession of aggressive encounters. Sexual activity apparently precipitated by generally arousing events has also been described in primates by several early investigators. One (Kempf, 1917) reported that when a pair of monkeys

Figure 1.   Early example of tail-pinch induced sexual behavior in humans. Mauron, The Cully Flaug'd (Eighteenth-century illustration for *Fanny Hill*).

shows no tendency to copulate, the introduction of a third, sexually inactive monkey often prompts an immediate initiation of copulation by the original pair. A second observer (Bingham, 1928) noted that his silent but visible presence was sufficient to trigger "quick demonstrations and frequent renewals of sexual relations" in a pair of black apes. Finally, male dogs and chimpanzees confronted with fear-producing stimuli may exhibit erection and even ejaculation (Beach, 1947).

It is difficult to find well-documented instances of activation-induced (or potentiation of) sexual behavior in humans, although the nonscientific literature abounds with such examples (e.g., Hollander, 1972 and see Figure 1).

1.3. Aggression

Relative to feeding and sexual behavior, there have been few systematic field studies of aggression occurring as a result of activation. Rather, as we have already seen, the stress associated with aggression more often serves as a trigger for other stress-induced behaviors. Among the limited observations that have been reported are those of van Lawick-Goodall (1968) on aggression, which appeared to be caused by frustration. She noted, for instance, that chimpanzees often behaved aggressively when an artificially provided supply of bananas became depleted and also when a grooming partner stopped grooming.

In contrast to the dearth of observations on wild animals, a considerable number of experimental studies has demonstrated a link between stress and aggressive behavior. Many of these have employed the shock-induced fighting technique first described by O'Kelly and Steckle (1939). In its most commonly used form, this technique involves shocking paired animals (Ulrich, Hutchinson, & Azrin, 1965), although the effects of shock on single animals have also been studied (Azrin, Hutchinson, & Sallery, 1964). Although shock is usually delivered to the feet through a grid floor, fighting has been reported with back-shock and tail-shock as well (Ulrich & Azrin, 1962). Other stimuli such as tail-pinch and heated floors are also effective (Ulrich, 1966). Collectively, these stimuli have induced fighting responses in paired rats, cats, snakes, monkeys, mice, hamsters, chickens, and turtles (Ulrich et al., 1965). Similar aggressive reactions have also been observed between species (Ulrich et al., 1965).

Although all these studies mentioned thus far have employed painful stimuli as a means of inducing aggression, pain does not appear to be a critical factor in obtaining this response. Thus, we have recently observed (Antelman, unpublished observations) that precisely the same tail-pinch pressure, which induces eating without the slightest sign of aversion when rats are pinched singly, results in aggression when they are paired. It has also been demonstrated that a variety of animals, including pigeons (Azrin, Hutchinson, & Hake, 1974), rats (Thompson & Bloom, 1966), squirrel monkeys (Azrin et al., 1963), and cats (Cole & Shafer, 1966) show a marked increase in aggressive behavior when switched from a reinforcement schedule to extinction. This is typically interpreted as an example of frustration-induced aggression (Moyer, 1968).

Other "stress factors" which have been shown to induce aggression include isolation (Valzelli, 1969), sudden changes in the environment, confinement in small spaces (Clark, 1962), overcrowding (Calhoun, 1962), morphine withdrawal in addicted rats (Boshka, Weisman, & Thor, 1966), and REM sleep deprivation (Morden, Conner, Mitchell, Dement, & Levine, 1968).

In humans, frustration has frequently been identified as a source, or at least a major contributor to the display of some forms of aggressive behavior (Bandura, 1973). More recently, Konecni and others have presented an impressive array of evidence suggesting that nonspecific activation may be an important factor both in the initiation and in the psychological consequences of aggression. Human subjects who were first angered by the insults of a confederate and then given the opportunity to physically hurt (by administering electric shock) the confederate, would exhibit significantly less *subsequent* aggression toward that annoyer, when compared to appropriate control groups (Doob & Wood, 1972; Konecni, 1975; Konecni & Doob, 1972). In this type of situation, the annoyance raises the level of autonomic activation (as measured by systolic or diastolic blood pressure) which is reduced when the target of the insult can hurt the annoyer (Baker & Shaie, 1969; Gambaro & Rabin, 1969; Hokanson & Shetler, 1961). Using this paradigm, nonspecific arousal can increase aggression if it is associated with the appropriate cognitive label. That is, activating stimuli (i.e., complex tones, loud auditory stimulation) led to an increase in aggression (more shocks were delivered by the subject) only in subjects that had been annoyed [compared to soft, simple tones or to loud, complex stimuli given to subjects that had not been annoyed (Konecni, 1975)].

1.4. Neuropharmacology of Stress-Induced Behavior

A considerable amount of leverage has been gained in our efforts to identify the function of stress-related behavior and its relevance to human clinical disorders by the result of an extensive series of pharmacological studies on tail-pinch behavior. These studies suggest some striking parallels between the neurochemical mechanisms underlying tail-pinch behavior (TPB) and those which may enable both animals and humans to respond to stress.

1.4.1. Involvement of Brain Catecholamines

The initial studies in this series concentrated on the brain catecholamines (CA), norepinephrine (NE), and dopamine (DA), since some TP-induced behaviors, such as gnawing and licking, bore a strong resemblance to stereotyped patterns observed following large doses of

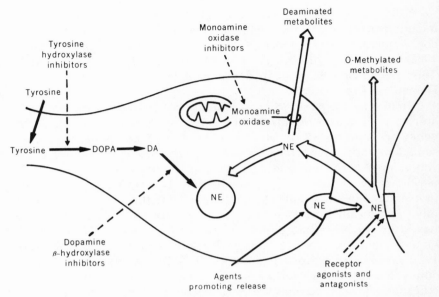

Figure 2.   Schematic diagram of a catecholamine synapse. The biosynthetic pathway for NE and the probable sites of action of the various types of drugs mentioned in the text are shown. The same relationships apply for DA-containing neurons, except that DA is not β-hydroxylated (from Antelman & Caggiula, 1977a).

the CA-releasing agent, amphetamine (see Figure 2).

We began by determining the effects of the butyrophenone neuroleptic, haloperidol, in doses which are thought to antagonize both NE and DA receptors (Janssen, 1967). Within this dose range, haloperidol reduced the incidence of TP eating to approximately 50% of control without causing an apparent debilitation of the animals (Antelman, Szechtman, Chin, & Fisher, 1975). A similar finding has recently been obtained with tail-shock-induced copulation (Antelman, Herndon, Caggiula, & Shaw, 1975). To determine whether this finding was due to blockade of either NE or DA receptors, we used receptor antagonists thought to be specific to each of these CA. Phentolamine and sotalol, presumed α- and β-NE antagonists, respectively, failed completely to block either TP eating or tail-shock copulation, even at high doses. Similar findings for TP eating have since been obtained with other NE antagonists, phenoxybenzamine and D, L–propranolol (Antelman & Black, unpublished observations). In contrast, when we tried the specific DA-receptor blocking agents, spiroperidol and pimozide, significant attenuation was obtained for both TP eating (Antelman, Szechtman, Chin, & Fisher, 1975) and tail-shock-induced copulation (Antelman, Herndon,

Caggiula, & Shaw, 1975). These data have been confirmed by ourselves and others using a variety of neuroleptics (Antelman & Szechtman, unpublished observations; Sahakian & Robbins, 1977; York, Lentz, & Love, 1976).

Although our data are consistent with the hypothesis of DA involvement in TPB, caution must be observed in interpreting the effects of neuroleptics, since it has been proposed that they may merely reflect the inability of an animal to perform a given task (Fibiger, Carter, & Phillips, 1976). It seems unlikely, however, that this stricture applies to our data. In fact, when the effects of neuroleptics are plotted as a function of individual TP trials, a response sequence strongly reminiscent of the pattern which accompanies extinction of a rewarded response is seen. Thus, neuroleptics are least likely to produce an attenuation of TPB on the first trial (Antelman, Szechtman, Chin, & Fisher, 1975; Sahakian & Robbins, 1977). It is only on subsequent trials that the behavior is significantly depressed, a pattern of decline which cannot be ascribed to the time course of the drug. There was actually a partial, though transient, reversal of the neuroleptic depression which tended to take place on trial three or four. Such a partial restoration of behavior is characteristic of the "spontaneous recovery" which is known to occur during extinction.

Despite our contention that the effects of neuroleptics on TPB are not explicable in terms of a drug-induced performance deficit, the reader may yet be skeptical on this point. In order to further satisfy our own apprehensions relative to this issue, we determined the effects of the anxiolytics, diazepam and chlordiazepoxide, on TP-induced eating. When acutely administered at high doses, these drugs have considerable sedative properties. Our results indicated that neither diazepam, in doses up to 5 mg/kg, nor chlordiazepoxide, in doses as high as 50 mg/kg, attenuated TPB to the slightest degree. Instead, they actually produced a marked reduction in the pressure required to induce the response. Although prone and markedly sedated, animals treated with these agents rose up at the slightest touch of the tail, paradoxically showing intense emotional behavior (characterized by loud vocalizing), and began to eat voraciously (Antelman & Szechtman, unpublished observations). Most recently, Robbins, Phillips, and Sahakian (1977) have found an increase in amount eaten during TP with chlordiazepoxide.

Although a fair amount of evidence has been gathered implicating DA, and more specifically the nigrostriatal DA system (NSDA) (see Figure 3; Antelman & Caggiula, 1977), as a key element in TPB, virtually all of it has been indirect, relying on the effects of receptor antagonists, synthesis inhibitors, and lesions. It is only fair to ask whether DA agonists have any effects on TPB. Up to a point, a facilitation might be

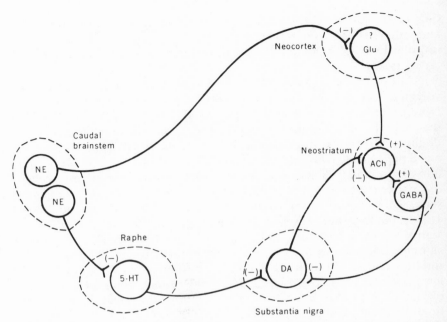

FIGURE 3.   Schematic diagram depicting two of the known pathways through which NE could influence the DA activity of the nigrostraiatal system. Abbreviations: Ach = acetylcholine; 5-HT = serotonin; GABA = γ-aminobutyric acid; Glu = glutamate (from Antelman & Caggiula, 1977a).

expected to occur. In fact, this is exactly what does occur. In a recent experiment, we found that amphetamine (at 0.5 and 2.0 mg/kg) and methylphenidate (at 5.6 mg/kg), both of which act to release DA, significantly increased the eating rate of tail-pinched animals (Antelman, Caggiula, Edwards, & Rowland, 1976; Antelman, Caggiula, Black, & Edwards, 1978). This finding is all the more remarkable since we also found that the same doses of these compounds produced considerable, and in the case of methylphenidate, complete anorexia when administered without TP.

1.4.2. Involvement of Brain Serotonin

Although we have emphasized the importance and perhaps primacy of the nigrostriatal DA bundle in relation to stress-induced behavior (using TPB as a model), this system does not exist in a vacuum. For example, evidence has recently been obtained in our laboratory (Kennedy, Antelman, & Edwards, submitted) which implicates brain serotonin (5HT)-containing systems in TPB and further suggests its possible interaction with DA.

In our studies, we observed a significant reduction in the incidence of TP-induced eating in animals that had received 5-hydroxytryptophan (5HTP), the immediate precursor of 5HT. Since 5HTP loading can be expected to increase brain 5HT somewhat indiscriminately (i.e., in neurons that normally do not contain 5HT) (Fuxe, Butcher, & Engel, 1971), additional experiments were conducted using the precursor amino acid, tryptophan, which provides a more physiological means of increasing 5HT by restricting its formation to neurons normally containing the transmitter (Aghajanian, 1973; Aghajanian & Asher, 1971). When tryptophan was given in combination with drugs which prevent the rapid metabolism of 5HT by monoamine oxidase (called type A MAO inhibitors) dose-dependent decreases in TP eating were obtained (Kennedy et al., submitted). By contrast, when the metabolism of 5HT was not prevented, either because tryptophan was given alone or because it was combined with a type B MAO inhibitor (which is not thought to act on 5HT), TP eating was relatively unaffected. Additional experiments, employing treatments which interfere with 5HT synthesis or reuptake, produced a pattern of results consistent with the hypothesis that increasing 5HT activity suppresses TP eating (see Antelman & Caggiula, 1977 for a more thorough discussion of these data).

1.4.3. Interactions between 5HT and DA

The demonstration that TPB is sensitive to manipulations of both brain 5HT and DA raises the question of whether evidence for a 5HT-DA interaction can be obtained with our TP paradigm. We have so far addressed this question in two ways. First, we have attempted to establish whether a synergism could be obtained by combining largely ineffective doses of a neuroleptic with doses of a tryptophan treatment (including a type A MAO inhibitor, clorgyline) which themselves are also ineffective in attenuating TPB. Conversely, we have also sought to determine whether the attenuation of TPB observed following the administration of a maximally effective dose of the DA-receptor antagonist could be significantly reversed by interfering with 5HT function.

The results of these experiments indicate that both effects can be obtained. In the first instance, we found that 0.062 mg/kg of the DA receptor blocking agent, spiroperidol, which failed to significantly block TP eating (animals continued to respond on 95% of postdrug trials), reduced TP responding to 55% of control levels when combined with 100 mg/kg of tryptophan and 2 mg/kg of clorgyline. When administered alone, the tryptophan-clorgyline combination only marginally affected the response, reducing it to 90% of control levels.

The coupling of PCPA, the 5HT synthesis inhibitor (administered in a dose of 100 mg/kg per day for four consecutive days), with 0.25 mg spiroperidol produced precisely the opposite results of the previous experiment. Whereas spiroperidol, given with the PCPA vehicle, reduced responding down to 13% of control levels, the addition of PCPA significantly reinstated the behavior to 64% of control. By itself, PCPA significantly reduced the mean latency to begin TP-induced eating (Kennedy et al., submitted).

The results of these two experiments indicate that 5HT and DA interact reciprocally in the mediation of stress-induced behavior. Moreover, since PCPA did not completely reverse the influence of spiroperidol, this may suggest that the role of 5HT in TPB is secondary to that of DA. The recent indication from the work of Fibiger and Miller (1976) that there may be projections from the dorsal raphe area, where many 5HT neurons originate, to the zona compacta of the substantia nigra (which contain the cells of the nigrostriatal DA system), provides a possible anatomical basis for our findings.

1.4.4. Possible Interactions between NE and DA

We have already suggested that brain NE-containing systems may also modulate the influence of DA on stress-related behavior (Antelman & Caggiula, 1977). This hypothesis first arose from some early observations on TP-induced feeding. Although all available evidence indicates that this response depends on the nigrostriatal bundle, TP results in an increased release of cortical NE (Antelman, Szechtman, Chin, & Fisher, 1975). While this effect on NE could merely have been an epiphenomenon, unrelated to the behavioral response, other data implied that this was not the case. For instance, treatment with FLA-63, a drug which blocks the synthesis of NE by inhibiting the enzyme dopamine-β-hydroxylase, produced a significant prolongation of the TP response (Antelman, Szechtman, Chin, & Fisher, 1975). That is to say, although the TP response is normally largely stimulation-bound, meaning that it begins shortly after pinch onset and terminates with its cessation, FLA-63 caused the response to extend significantly beyond the removal of the pinch. Viewed in another way, FLA-63 can be said to have retarded the extinction of the tail-pinch response. The reader may recall that this is precisely the opposite of what is found with DA-receptor antagonists, which actually seemed to precipitate extinction of the TP response. These results suggest the possibility that NE may normally exert a regulatory influence on the nigrostriatal DA system (and perhaps on other DA pathways as well) during stressful situations, serving to keep responses related to this system within certain limits. In the absence of this regulatory influence [a situation which occurs when a dopamine-β-hydroxylase inhibitor (DBHI) like FLA-63 is administered],

DA is more likely to react to a stressful situation by overresponding in an uncontrolled fashion. According to this view, interference with NE activity will, during sufficiently activating conditions, potentiate "DA-dependent" behaviors while under relatively nonactivating or even less stressful circumstances, it will not affect, or may depress the same behaviors (Antelman & Caggiula, 1977). A corollary of this hypothesis is that depression of NE activity may either prevent or counteract the effects of interfering with the function of DA-containing neurons. This suggests that selective interference with, or damage to, DA-containing neurons may result in greater functional impairment of the organism during stressful circumstances than similar damage which is also accompanied by a substantial interference with brain NE. Much of the recent work in our laboratories has dealt with the above proposition and it is to this that we now turn.

Our initial approach to the question of whether interfering with NE activity could overcome the effects of impairing DA function has involved mainly the coupling of DBHIs and neuroleptics during both stressful (tail-pinch) and nonstressful (ad lib) feeding tests (Antelman & Black, submitted). The DBHIs which have been used are FLA-63 (Svensson & Waldeck, 1969) and methimazole, which is slightly less potent than FLA-63 but without the peritoneal irritating effects of the latter (Stolk & Hanlon, 1973). Haloperidol has been the primary neuroleptic used to attenuate both ad lib and TP-induced feeding behavior. Figure 4 depicts the results of one experiment done with methimazole and haloperidol. At doses of 25 and 50 mg/kg, methimazole significantly reversed the attenuating influence of haloperidol on TPB when the two drugs were combined. A lower dose of methimazole, 12.5 mg/kg, failed to modify the effect of haloperidol. Since the equivalent of 12.5 mg/kg has been reported to produce a 50% inhibition of DBH, while 25 and 50 mg/kg respectively resulted in approximately 60% and 80% DBH inhibition (Stolk & Hanlon, 1973), this may suggest that the enzyme must be inhibited by at least 60% before stress can effectively reverse the behavioral concomitants of DA-receptor blockade. An almost identical pattern of results was obtained when FLA-63 was combined with haloperidol.

The results of these experiments seem to suggest that inhibiting the synthesis of NE (or possibly some other β-hydroxylated amine) can indeed reverse the effects of DA-receptor blockade on TPB. However, quite a different outcome is obtained when a nonstress feeding situation is used. We observed the effect of haloperidol or haloperidol plus either FLA-63 or methimazole on an ad lib, four-hour feeding test in undeprived rats. In order to further minimize the activating properties of the situation, the animals (housed on a natural day-night cycle) were tested

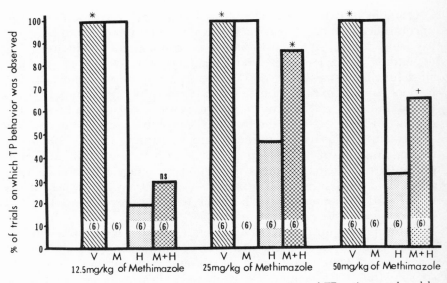

FIGURE 4.   A DBHI (methimazole) reverses the attenuation of TP eating produced by haloperidol. All statistical comparisons made with haloperidol. ( ) = N; *p <.001 + p <.005; V = vehicle; H = haloperidol (0.4 mg/kg); M = methimazole (from Antelman & Caggiula, 1977b).

in the afternoon, prior to their period of maximal activity. Although haloperidol (0.4 mg/kg) significantly suppressed (but did not completely eliminate) ad lib feeding just as it had TP eating, neither FLA-63 (10 mg/kg) nor methimazole (50 mg/kg) showed even the slightest tendency toward reversing this suppression. Thus, the ability of these compounds to counteract the influence of neuroleptics appears related to the activating or stressful properties of the environment. These data also provide support for our hypothesis that NE regulates, rather than inhibits DA (Antelman & Caggiula, 1977), since a simple disinhibitory influence of DBHIs on DA might be expected to result in at least a partial tendency to counter the suppressive influence of haloperidol in the ad lib feeding situation. The postulated regulatory influence of NE on DA may be the raison d'être for the ability of DBHIs to reverse the behavioral deficits of neuroleptics. That is, although such an influence may be in the organism's best interests so long as the nigrostriatal DA system is intact, its continued presence when this system is impaired may actually be deleterious to the organism, by preventing a maximal response to stressful stimuli.

Recently, we have extended our DBHI-neuroleptic paradigm to another stress-induced behavior, i.e., shock-induced aggression, (Antelman, Caggiula, & Black, submitted). Once again, the data clearly indicated that treatment with an NE-synthesis inhibitor significantly overcame the attenuating effects of DA-receptor blockade during stress.

In reflecting on all of the complex pharmacological relationships which have briefly been touched upon in this chapter, and more recent work in our laboratory suggesting that the interaction between NE and DA may also involve acetylcholine (Ach), it seems appropriate to conclude that the neurochemical basis of TPB involves interactions among DA, NE, 5HT, Ach and ?.

1.5. Parallels between Stress-Induced Behaviors in Animals and Humans

We have recently suggested that tail pinch-induced feeding in animals may provide a reasonable model for studying stress-induced behavior in humans (Antelman & Caggiula, 1977). Some of the parallels which led us to this proposal have already been presented in preceding sections of this chapter. We would now like to briefly review several others which strengthen the suggestion that the information provided by the tail-pinch paradigm and its pharmacological substrates may be of considerable value in understanding the neurochemical basis of stress-induced behavior in humans.

It has frequently been observed that people who overeat and become obese are overly responsive to a wide range of stimuli, not just those associated directly with eating (Glucksman, 1972; Schacter, 1965). Moreover, when presented with food, the eating behavior of these individuals tends to be stimulus-bound (Glucksman, 1972; Schacter, 1965), and they show an increased incidence of other oral behaviors or sexual behavior when prevented from eating by strict dieting (Glucksman, 1972; LeMagnen, 1976). These three characteristics, i.e., hyperreactivity to stimuli, stimulus-bound eating, and substitutability of behavior, have all been previously described as prominent features of TPB.

It is also well known that obese individuals have trouble becoming satiated after the ingestion of a given quantity of food (Stunkard, 1967) or after artificial expansion of the stomach by inflating an intubated balloon (Stunkard, 1967). An exact parallel to this can be seen with TPB. Animals will ingest significantly more sweetened milk in one "sitting" (i.e., up to 20 cc) when receiving continuous TP than would be expected during a period of spontaneous eating (Rowland & Antelman, 1976).

Finally, stress-related overeating in humans and TP eating in rats show similar responses to certain anorectic agents. Whereas amphetamine is purported to be ineffective against emotionally-related overeating in humans (Innes & Nickerson, 1970), fenfluramine is thought to be the anorectic of choice in this type of situation (Silverstone, 1975). We have analagous data in the TP situation (Antelman, Caggiula, Black, & Edwards, 1978). Here too, amphetamine (in otherwise anorectic doses) fails completely to suppress TP eating. On the contrary, as we mentioned in an earlier section, the rate of TP eating is actually significantly enhanced by amphetamine and its congener, methylphenidate. In contrast to these results, TP was wholly ineffective in counteracting fenfluramine anorexia.

1.6. Possible Function of Stress-Induced Behavior

In previous sections of this paper we have demonstrated, by example, the ubiquity with which stress-induced behavior is encountered in both animals and humans. We would now like to discuss the possible functions served by the behaviors that are seen during stress and their relevance to clinical disorders.

Several lines of evidence suggest that the behaviors seen during stress may serve an adaptive, coping function.

For example, Bruch (1973) and others (Glucksman, 1972; Hamburger, 1951) have presented a considerable amount of evidence to suggest that many obese, stress-related overeaters tend to eat when emotionally tense, or during other unpleasant states such as depression, and eating is reported to diminish or prevent these states. The coping function which eating appears to serve under these circumstances may not be characteristic of obesity *per se*, since it is not easily obtained in controlled laboratory experiments which do not distinguish between stress-related overeating and the many other types of obesity (Herman & Polivy, 1975; McKenna, 1972; but see Leon & Chamberlain, 1973b). It should also be pointed out that eating in response to emotion or stress is not restricted to obese individuals.

Observations remarkably similar to Bruch's in their import have been made in the course of experiments involving TP or related manipulations. For example, rats are largely unresponsive to being pricked by a needle if the painful stimulus is applied during a TP-induced eating bout, whereas the same stimulus produces vocalization and escape if the animal is prevented from eating (Antelman & Rowland, unpublished data). Similarly, the loud squealing and other signs of distress which normally accompany repeated tail-shock of sexually naive male rats will suddenly disappear when the shock results in copulation with a receptive female. Again, the vocalization can be reinstated by preventing the behavior (Caggiula, unpublished data).

The above examples suggest that one way of understanding the response to stress in both humans and animals is within an adaptive or coping context. That is, the response may actually function to reduce the adverse psychological and, at least in some instances, even biochemical consequences of the stress. The reinstatement of biochemical homeostasis has been well illustrated by experiments dealing with shock-induced aggression. For example, a number of studies has found that animals shocked alone show changes in ACTH (Conner, Vernikos-Danellis, & Levine, 1971), blood pressure (Williams & Eichelman, 1971), NE turnover (Stolk, Conner, Levine, & Barchas, 1974), and cyclic AMP levels (Eichelman, Orenberg, Seagraves, & Barchas, 1976) which differ in either direction or order of magnitude from those observed when the same shock occurs in the presence of a partner against which aggression is possible.

2. Stereotypy as a Consequence of Stress in Animals and Humans

Up to this point we have been focusing on the ways in which stressful circumstances can induce behavior and the possible function of that behavior. However, it has probably already occurred to the reader that stress can often disturb or even suppress these same behaviors. Thus, although eating is often precipitated under conditions of reactive depression, it tends to be inhibited during endogenous depression (Beck, 1973). Likewise, sex can be induced by stress, but it is also well known that some forms of impotence are associated with severe anxiety and emotional stress (Kaplan, 1974). One important variable determining whether a particular behavior is induced or suppressed relates to the intensity and/or duration of the stress (Fentress, 1973, 1976). For instance, as already mentioned, while eating in rats is induced by mild, brief shocks, it is actually suppressed by increasing shock intensity (Sterritt, 1962, 1965) or duration (Strongman, 1965). Similarly, TP-induced eating is best obtained with mild pressure, and while the behavior will occur with more intense, painful pinches, it becomes fractionated and appears less normal. In general, while mild stress may induce a variety of behaviors, the behavior of the organism under conditions of severe or prolonged stress may actually become less finely tuned to the environment, more repetitive, and even autonomous, or it may be completely suppressed. Since we have already discussed the first outcome of stress (i.e., the induction of behavior) in considerable detail, we will move to a consideration of the disruptive effects of stress.

2.1. Stereotypy

An almost universal response to moderate or prolonged stress, which can be found throughout the animal kingdom and as a component in a number of human behavioral disorders, is the emergence of stereotypies. In the present context, stereotypy refers to ". . . repetition of an invariant pattern of certain movements having no observable goal" (Hutt & Hutt, 1965). We shall see later that stereotypy can also describe distortions in thought patterns and emotions. The particular form it takes tends to be uniform and invariant for a given species, at least below the level of the squirrel monkey (Randrup & Munkvad, 1974). More variable (i.e., idiosyncratic) patterns are usually only seen in animals higher in the phylogenetic scale.

2.1.1. Animal Data

In lower animals, stereotypies are most frequently seen under conditions of confinement. For example, hens placed in small, laying cages may show head-shaking tics which diminish significantly when they are transferred to larger enclosures. Large carnivores, such as lions and tigers, can be seen in any zoo to pace repeatedly when confined to cages, while bears, in addition, show repeated upward swinging of the head (Levy, 1944). Monkeys reared in isolation often exhibit nonnutritive sucking and rhythmic rocking movements (Berkson, 1967; Mason, 1968), and chimpanzees similarly treated may display over 30 different stereotyped patterns including rocking, swaying, eye-poking, head-rolling, and limb-posturing (Berkson, 1967).

The stereotypies just described are not unique to confinement, nor does confinement *per se* seem to be the critical variable. Rather, it appears that the activation produced by the confinement, perhaps combined with the severe restrictions imposed on possible alternative behavioral responses to stress, may be responsible for the stereotyped patterns. This is suggested by observations that the incidence of stereotypies in restricted chimpanzees was substantially increased by the introduction of novel stimuli and also when they were placed in a novel situation (Menzel, 1963).

Some of the most elegant examples of stereotypies occurring in response to activating or stressful circumstances have been reported by Fentress (1976). These examples also provide some insight into the possible function of these behavior patterns. In one, a caged Cape hunting dog at the London Zoo had developed a stereotyped figure eight pacing pattern. When a chain was placed across the pattern in an attempt to prevent the behavior, the animal simply relocated its path to avoid the chain and continued to pace. This adjustment occurred only when its movements were relatively slow. However, when excited by external disturbances, the animal resumed its former pattern and frequently tripped over the chain before learning to jump it consistently. After observing several months of this new jumping pattern, Fentress lowered the chain to the ground. Once again, activation altered the behavior and caused a reversion. That is, when undisturbed, the animal resumed the earlier figure eight pacing pattern but when external disturbances occurred, it reverted back to the pattern of jumping as if the chain were still raised. Similarly, voles kept in small cages developed movement stereotypies around water spouts that protruded into their cages. These jumping and weaving behaviors disappeared when the spouts were removed, but reappeared when the animals were disturbed, even in the absence of the spouts.

These examples well illustrate the invariant nature of stereotyped behavior patterns triggered by stressful environments, and in so doing, point up an important relationship. The inflexibility of the stereotyped response makes it less attuned to environmental changes. To the extent that stimulus changes call for new responses, the persistence of these stereotyped patterns makes them at best nonadaptive and often maladaptive.

At this point, the reader may wonder how a behavior which is obviously nonadaptive, when considered within the framework of the organism's effective interactions with its external environment, can be considered to serve an adaptive or coping function when viewed as a response to stress. It is precisely this apparent paradox which may be a key to understanding many aberrant behavior patterns seen in animals, as well as the symptoms characteristic of human clinical disorders such as autism or schizophrenia.

If the stressful, environmental stimuli which trigger the stereotyped behavior pattern represent a level of sensory input or activation beyond the organism's normal or preferred level of functioning, then the behavior itself may be adaptive by serving to control or even reduce the input. The reader will recall that this same argument was advanced earlier when stress-induced behaviors were discussed. It also appears to be true for stereotypies. That is to say, the execution of rapid, stereotyped movements leads to a reduced sensitivity to sensory input. The behavior becomes autonomous in that it is less responsive to the stimuli that originally triggered it, and less easily disrupted by both peripheral or proprioceptive inputs (Fentress, 1976). Thus, the invariant nature of the response is, at one and the same time, both nonadaptive (i.e., inflexible in the face of a complex, changing environment), and adaptive (reducing intolerable levels of stimulation). It should be pointed out that in a relatively simple, stable environment, the invariant nature of the response will be minimally disruptive.

2.1.2. Autism

Stereotyped behaviors also appear in the symptoms of some human clinical disorders, and many of the principles discussed above with respect to animal behavior also seem to apply here. Stereotypies are prominently displayed by autistic children, and it appears that these patterns may, in fact, function to maintain relatively constant levels of sensory input. Autism was originally described by Kanner in 1943. Among the primary pathological features of this disorder are: (1) "a profound withdrawal from contact with people," (2) "an anxiously obsessive desire for the maintenance of sameness," and (3) preoccupation with objects (Kanner, 1943). According to some (but not all) theorists, autistic children are in a relatively continuous state of high arousal. For example, the Hutts (1969) reported that the EEG was predominantly characterized by low voltage, fast, desynchronized activity in comparison to both normal controls and institutionalized children diagnosed with other psychiatric disorders. Autists frequently keep to the periphery of the room and exhibit marked gaze aversion, two behaviors which are often used to minimize social contact in humans and may thereby reduce the stress or activation associated with such contact. Animals show very similar behaviors. For example, rats will show gaze aversion during aggressive encounters, and this has been interpreted as reducing the stress associated with such encounters (Chance, 1962). Similarly, gaze aversion inhibits threat displays of rhesus monkeys (Exline, 1971).

The stereotypies exhibited by autistic children are seen at several levels of functioning, including speech and cognitive, as well as motor performance (Rutter, 1971). For example, the same string of words may be recited endlessly. Cognitively, an autistic child may become fixated on the same subject for years, apparently thinking of little else. In addition, hand waving, jumping, huddling, rocking, twirling, toe stepping, and other motor behaviors are endlessly repeated.

These stereotyped patterns seen in autistic children have also been interpreted as functioning to reduce the stress associated with high levels of arousal, or by actually blocking novel sensory input (Hutt, 1975). Bouts of stereotypy which tend to occur in novel situations, are accompanied by bursts of desynchronous EEG and heart rate arrhythmia, and the termination of such bouts is often associated with a greater rhythmicity of both heart rate and EEG (suggesting reduced arousal; Hutt & Hutt, 1970). Prolonged periods of stereotypy may themselves produce increased rhythmicity of EEG patterns. This suggestion derives from a study of blind, retarded children by Stone (1964). Intense, highly rhythmic stereotypy was associated with a generalized slowing of the EEG pattern and waves characteristic of drowsiness. According to Hutt and Hutt (1970):

> In autistic children, stereotypies may subserve a similar, arousal reducing function, by producing repetitive, endogenous stimulation. The prolonged and intensive bouts of stereotypy would have the qualities of sleep-producing stimuli in normal subjects. . . . Such monotonous stimulation may have the additional effect of blocking novel, sensory input.

Thus, it appears that some of the behavioral symptoms of autism may be viewed, at least in part, as a type of self-therapy whereby the organism modifies physiological processes in response to, and as a way of combating the pathological stress associated with this disease. As we will suggest below, these physiological changes may involve activity in identifiable neurochemical systems.

2.1.3. Schizophrenia

Stereotypies are also commonly found in the schizophrenias and may include repetitive, fixed thought patterns, invariant associative responses to widely different stimuli, and stereotypies of movement, posture, writing, and speech (Bleuler, 1950). One particularly enlightening example of an extreme stereotyped thought pattern was mentioned by Bleuler (1950) who referred to a "catatonic physician who invariably and unfailingly prescribed the identical medicament for each and every disease regardless of its nature."

Although there is little specific evidence directly linking stereotypies in schizophrenics to a stress-related, coping function, this function has been strongly implicated in the wider range of symptoms which characterize this disease.

A considerable amount of evidence suggests that schizophrenia is associated with high levels of arousal (Kornetsky & Eliasson, 1969; Shakow, 1971), as exemplified by significantly reduced alpha waves and an excess of low voltage, fast activity in the EEG (Abemson, 1970). This state of overactivation, which is especially true of chronic patients, has been characterized as resulting from an increased and indiscriminant preoccupation with the sensory environment, an inability to distinguish figure from ground, relevant from irrelevant (Shakow, 1971). This extreme attention to ordinarily disregarded details of "existence" may reflect an underlying dysfunction in sensory processing or filtering mechanisms. An especially vivid and articulate example was provided by a former mental patient who described her own illness (McDonald, 1960):

> The mind must have a filter which functions without our conscious thought, sorting stimuli and allowing only those which are relevant to the situation in hand to disturb consciousness.... What had happened to me... was a breakdown in the filter and a hodge-podge of unrelated stimuli were distracting me from the things which should have had my undivided attention.... By the time I was admitted to the hospital I had reached a stage of "wakefulness" when the brilliance of light on a window sill or the color of blue in the sky would be so important it could make me cry. I had very little ability to sort the relevant from the irrelevant. The filter had broken down. Completely unrelated events become intricately connected in my mind.

Many of the symptoms of schizophrenia may be viewed not only as a product of this perceptual disorder, but also as a coping response designed to minimize its impact. One way in which schizophrenics achieve this is by avoiding or reducing a primary source of stimulation, i.e., social contact.

Since schizophrenic individuals are particularly sensitive to the stress of interpersonal contact (Roberts, 1977), there is a marked tendency to withdraw. This may be done in various ways, such as by minimizing conversation, maintaining a fixed gaze, keeping one's eyes closed, and hiding (Silverman, 1969). The coping nature of these responses is indicated by the tendency on the part of some schizophrenics to show greater tolerance of sensory isolation than normal subjects (Harris, 1959) and to even prefer such conditions (Meehl & Cromwell, 1969). Moreover, Venables and Wing (1962) have demonstrated a positive correlation between physiological arousal level in schizophrenic men and social withdrawal.

In a prospective study designed to identify the development pattern of schizophrenia by following "high risk" children of chronic schizophrenic mothers, Mednick and Schulsinger (1968) concluded that the thought disorder in this disease is a consequence of the individual's attempt to control the stress associated with his perception of his social environment. The thinking of irrelevant thoughts serves as a means of deflecting threatening, emotion-laden environmental stimuli for the preschizophrenic.

The notion that schizophrenics attempt to compensate for sensory overload receives indirect support from recent findings that, relative to normals or patients suffering from bipolar affective disorders, schizophrenics show a reduction in their average evoked response (AER) to increasing intensities of visual stimulation (Buchsbaum, 1975). The AER is believed to be an electrophysiological index of sensory responsiveness and there is some evidence to suggest that the tendency to reduce AER amplitude is accompanied by an increase in the individual's ability to withstand sensory overload and pain (Buchsbaum, 1975).

Some of the symptoms shown by schizophrenics, particularly those which appear to insulate the individual from his environment, are strongly reminiscent of those previously discussed as being characteristic of autistic children who also seem to be suffering from overarousal. While we must certainly be careful not to draw the parallel between autism and schizophrenia too closely, there are other similarities which suggest that in both instances many of the symptoms represent defensive reactions which allow the organism to cope with stress. The reader should be reminded that for both animals and children suffering from autism, the appearance of stereotypy is related to the stress associated with novel environments, and can be viewed as a method for reducing that stress. It may be that the stereotypy seen in schizophrenia serves a similar function. This suggestion is further supported by the observation that in both autism and schizophrenia, there appears to be a desire for sameness, and a tendency to avoid new situations (i.e., neophobia; Kanner, 1943; Shakow, 1971).

2.1.4. Neuropharmacology

We had previously shown that a variety of stress-induced behaviors depend to a large extent on the integrity of brain DA-containing systems. Since stereotypies represent a more extreme response to stress and, like stress induced behaviors, can be viewed as serving a coping function, we may ask whether they have a similar neurochemical basis. The answer, which applies to both animals and humans, is *yes*. Much of the evidence to support this comes from work with stimulants like amphetamine.

Among their myriad actions, amphetamine and similar drugs such as cocaine and methylphenidate, have the ability to release NE and DA from presynaptic neurons. It is quite clear now that the DA-releasing actions of amphetamine are critical for many of its behavioral effects, which range from mild activation at low doses to stereotypy and even psychosis at high doses and/or with prolonged usage (Randrup & Munkvad, 1974; also see Costa & Garattini, 1970; Snyder, 1974).

For example, high doses of amphetamine have been demonstrated to produce stereotypy in virtually every species tested (Randrup & Munkvad, 1974). Stimulant-induced stereotypies may also be seen in humans, although here they tend to be much more idiosyncratic than in lower animals. One anecdote commonly told is that of a group of amphetamine users who were arrested after driving around the same block of buildings several hundred times.

Large doses of amphetamine taken over relatively long periods of time produce a psychosis which is in many ways indistinguishable from paranoid schizophrenia (Snyder, 1974). This psychosis, which also appears to be dependent on DA, as does schizophrenia itself (Snyder, 1974; Snyder, Banerjee, Yamamura, & Greenberg, 1974), is often preceded by stereotypies characterized by a compulsion to disassemble and, less frequently, reassemble, televisions, radios, clocks, etc. (Ellinwood, 1969).

The role of DA in these phenomena is strongly suggested by the findings that amphetamine stereotypy in animals, amphetamine psychosis in humans, and schizophrenia itself can all be antagonized by drugs which share the common element of having DA receptor-blocking properties (Meltzer & Stahl, 1976; Snyder, Banerjee, Yamamura, & Greenberg, 1974). Conversely, stereotypy and/or a schizophreniclike psychosis can be induced by DA agonists such as l-dopa, cocaine, and apomorphine, as well as by amphetamine (Meltzer & Stahl, 1976; Snyder, 1974). In addition, both l-dopa and amphetamine have been found to exacerbate schizophrenic symptoms where the disease already exists (Angrist, Sathananthan, & Gershon, 1973; Janowsky, El-Yousel, Davis, & Sekerke, 1973).

As would be expected from our hypothesis, stress can also exacerbate schizophrenia, and this effect can be at least partially reversed by neuroleptic treatment. In one particularly striking example, several investigators (Brown, Binley, & Wing, 1972; Vaughan & Leff, 1976) have reported a strong relationship between relapse rate in the 9 months following discharge among schizophrenic patients and the type of family setting to which they were returned; 51–58% if the family was judged to be high on "expressed emotion" but only 13–16% if the families were rated low on this measure of potential stress to the patient. Moreover maintenance chemotherapy was particularly effective in "protecting" patients in the high stress homes but was of little value in low stress environments.

The foregoing suggests that there may be a very close correspondence between the neurochemical processes involved in stress-induced behavior, stimulant-induced stereotypies, and some of the symptoms, including stereotyped patterns of thought and behavior, shown by autists and schizophrenics. They all seem to involve increased functional activity of brain DA (although not necessarily in the same DA-containing systems or to the same degree), a hyperarousal manifested by (or as a consequence of) increased sensory responsiveness, and behaviors which function to protect the organism from the stress associated with the arousal. These relationships are well illustrated by some of the time-dependent changes seen following amphetamine in both lower animals and humans. The early effects of amphetamine tend to be an increased alertness to sensory stimuli which has been reported for rats (Randrup & Munkvad, 1974), cats, and monkeys, as well as humans (Ellinwood, 1969). This gives way to stereotypy. With the onset of stereotypy, the organism becomes relatively insensitive to its environment. For example, in one experiment measuring the effects of d-amphetamine (10 mg/kg) on bar-pressing for avoidance of electric foot shock, Randrup and Munkvad (1974) report that

> the drug takes effect gradually.... Right after the injection the rat works rather normally following the rate of lever-pressing required by the schedule; then the rate increases out of proportion to the schedule and the rat goes into a stereotyped phase with very quick continuous lever-pressing; in this phase it also performs continuous sniffing, licking or biting. Then follows a phase in which the rat responds only when receiving the shock, and finally the operant behavior breaks down completely. The rat then sits sniffing and licking the bars of the cage floor, although these give shock continuously. This process may also be seen as a gradual decrease of the influence of environmental factors (shocks and schedule of avoidance) on the behavior. In the last phase the behavior is shaped only by the amphetamine effect, the rat performs the same stereotyped behavior as it does in the home cage. This might perhaps be regarded as "autistic behavior." (p. 1)

A similar progression of hyperalertness, followed by stereotypies increasing in their narrowness, and eventually by a state of being oblivious to the environment, is commonly seen during chronic amphetamine intoxication (Ellinwood, 1969).

3. WHY DOPAMINE?

Throughout this chapter, we have time and again emphasized the importance of dopamine in various aspects of stress-related behavior. The reader may well ask, why dopamine?

To begin to answer this question, we must briefly review current thinking on the function of this transmitter system. There are actually several DA-containing systems which have been identified and are currently under study. We have already referred to the largest and most thoroughly examined of these, the nigrostriatal system (NSDA). As was stated earlier, this system appears to modulate the organism's behavioral responsiveness to its sensory environment. Activating this system by low doses of drugs such as apomorphine or amphetamine, increases the organism's responsivity to its environment (Randrup & Munkvad, 1974). Conversely, interfering with this system, through the use of DA receptor antagonists or chemically specific lesions, reduces the organism's ability to respond to sensory stimuli and, in extreme cases, may even cause an almost total neglect of its environment (Meltzer & Stahl, 1976; Marshall et al., 1974). This system seems ideally suited to play a major role in the organism's coping response to stress for several reasons. First, its location suggests a key role in the gating of sensory-motor function in that its target area, the neostriatum, is an area of convergence of input from all areas of the cortex, as well as from the non-specific thalamic nuclei (and thus indirectly from the reticular formation) (Krauthamer, 1975; Ungerstedt, 1974).

Second, this system shows a remarkable capacity to compensate for a variety of insults. For example, in Parkinson's disease, which is known to be a consequence of degeneration of the nigrostriatal DA system, symptoms do not become clinically manifest until the system is largely destroyed (Hornykiewicz, 1975). This is believed to be due to an increase in the activity of remaining neurons (Hornykiewicz, 1975). Compensation can be seen even when the symptoms of Parkinsonism are already manifest. For instance, it is well known that stress can induce ambulation even in the most severely crippled patients (Schwab, 1972). Similarly, compensation of this system to the extrapyramidal effects of neuroleptics is also observed after chronic treatment, and may reflect both an increase in the activity of presynaptic neurons as well as postsynaptic supersensitivity (Hornykiewicz, 1975).

In contrast to the apparent ability of the nigrostriatal DA system to maintain normal behavioral functioning, even in the face of severe insult, another major DA pathway, the mesolimbic system, seems ill suited to this purpose. This is suggested by our own observations (Antelman, Eichler, & Fisher, 1977; Eichler & Antelman, in preparation) that tolerance fails to develop to the suppressive influence of neuroleptics on self-stimulation of the nucleus accumbens, a terminal region of the mesolimbic system. Turnover of DA in the nucleus accumbens similarly failed to show any evidence of tolerance to neuroleptics (Scatton, Glowinski, & Julou, 1976). The apparently poor compensatory ability of this system suggests that it might also be slow to adapt or adjust to stress. As such, it might be a more likely candidate for those disorders involving prolonged, extreme responses to stress, such as schizophrenia. The prolonged and exaggerated response of this system to stress in indicated by the finding that 72 hours of food deprivation produces a very marked increase in self-stimulation rates from nucleus accumbens electrodes which continue to grow for at least 3 weeks (Antelman et al., 1977; Eichler & Antelman, in preparation). The suggestion that the mesolimbic system in involved in schizophrenia is supported indirectly by evidence indicating that tolerance fails to develop to the antipsychotic effects of neuroleptics. A further indication of the differential response to stress of the two DA systems in provided by the recent finding of Thierry, Tassin, Blanc, and Glowinski (1976) that electric foot shock produced significant changes in indices of DA turnover in the nucleus accumbens, but not in the striatum.

In light of the possibility that stress-related disorders such as schizophrenia might involve nonstriatal DA systems, we may ask whether the presumed function of these systems bears any relationship to the symptoms of this illness. It should be remembered that schizophrenic symptoms have been characterized, at least in part, as a consequence of, or reaction to a state of sensory (and emotional) overload. The individual seems unable to focus attention and filter out irrelevant stimulation, thoughts and emotions. Recently, Matthysse (1977a,b) has summarized evidence which suggests that DA systems in the brain may indeed control shifts in the focus of attention and that excessive DA activity could lead to the attentional deficts of schizophrenia. He bases his argument on analogies with the motor effects of manipulating nigrostriatal DA. As we have already stated, stereotyped behavior produced by DA agonists or by prolonged stress represent repetitions, inflexible motor patterns which are less attuned to stimulus change. Matthysse argues that "If dopaminergic agonists were to produce similar mental effects, one might expect inability to withdraw attention from the stimulus or idea on which it is focused" (Matthysse, 1977b). The analogy is that if NSDA is involved in a filtering or selective attention function with respect to motor control, then perhaps the same principle applies to other DA systems for other spheres, i.e., cognitive and emotional. For example, the mesolimbic DA system, with its connections to limbic forebrain areas traditionally linked to emotional and motivational functions, may be ideally situated to regulate the degree to which particular emotions gain ascendancy and compel the individual's attention.

Evidence in support of this hypothesis comes mainly from the pharmacological literature (see Matthysse 1977a,b for a review). For example, in animals DA agonists such as amphetamine and apomorphine produce attitudinal as well as motor stereotypies, and excessive fixation of attention is also seen after amphetamine overdose in humans. On the other hand, neuroleptic treatment is particularly effective in reducing the imperative nature of obsessive thoughts and emotions in schizophrenic patients. Spohn et al., (cited in Matthysse, 1977a) found that chronic schizophrenics tested on a battery of psychological tests, during double-blind treatment with chlorpromazine or a placebo, showed a decrease in physiological indices of arousal under the drug condition. Perhaps more interestingly, they also showed a reduction of "excessive attention to focal objects."

To summarize, evidence has been presented to suggest that two major DA-containing systems in the brain may be involved in various aspects of the animal response to activation or stress. The nigrostriatal system, because of its location and ability to readily compensate, may be more importantly involved in acute, behavioral responses to stress. On the other hand, the mesolimbic system is more likely to reflect the effects of prolonged stress. In both instances, a failure to compensate completely may trigger behavioral responses which are designed to complement the coping process by removing the stress. The relationship being proposed between DA activity and stress-related behaviors is not an uncommon one when considered within the broader framework of biological systems that are homeostatically regulated.

Although the major neurochemical emphasis of this chapter has been on DA, we have already indicated that stress-related behavior involves interactions with other transmitter systems as well, such as NE and 5HT (Antelman & Caggiula, 1977a,b). While these interactions have been discussed in some detail as they relate to stress-induced behavior in animals, they also have implications with respect to the treatment of stress-related human disorders. For example, we have previously suggested that interference with NE activity will, under activating conditions, potentiate "DA-dependent" behaviors, while under less stressful circumstances, it will not affect or may even depress the same behaviors (Antelman & Caggiula, 1977a). In regard to schizophrenia, this hypothesis leads to the following two predictions. First, those individuals being treated with specific DA receptor-blocking agents should be able to withstand environmental stresses better than those patients receiving neuroleptics which have substantial NE-blocking properties as well. Second, the extent to which a given neuroleptic does or does not induce extrapyramidal side effects may be as much a function of its antiadrenergic properties as of any anticholinergic effects that it may possess.

4. Summary

We have attempted in this chapter to show that many of the organism's responses to stress can be viewed as an effort to treat itself. That is, depending on its intensity and duration, stress may activate a variety of behavioral responses in animals and humans ranging from increases in feeding, sex, and aggression when the stress is mild, to stereotypy when the stress is more intense or prolonged. A common, and very critical feature of many of these responses is the apparent ability to reduce some of the adverse consequences of the stress. Since many of the behavioral responses to stress have been shown to depend on the integrity of brain DA-containing systems (as well as on their interaction with 5HT, ACh and NE-containing pathways), the coping function of stress-related behavior may very well act to complement the self-regulating features of these neurochemical systems.

Acknowledgment

We very much appreciate the invaluable assistance of Dolores M. Shirk.

REFERENCES

ABENSON, M. H. EEGs in chronic schizophrenia. *British Journal of Psychiatry*, 1970, *116*, 421–425.

AGHAJANIAN, G. K. Discussion: Localization, uptake and metabolism of serotonin. In J. Barchas & E. Usdin (Eds.), *Serotonin and behavior*. London: Academic, 1973.

AGHAJANIAN, G. K., & ASHER, I. M. Histochemical fluorescence of raphe neurons: Selective enhancement by tryptophan. *Science*, 1971, *172*, 1159.

ANGRIST, B., SATHANANTHAN, G., & GERSHON, S. Behavioral effects of l-dopa in schizophrenic patients. *Psychopharmacologia*, 1972, *27*, 249.

ANTELMAN, S. M., & CAGGIULA, A. R. Norepinephrine-dopamine interactions and behavior. *Science*, 1977, *195*, 646. (a)

ANTELMAN, S. M., & CAGGIULA, A. R. Tails of stress-related behavior: A neuropharmacological model. In: I. Hanin & E. Usdin (Eds.), *Animal models in psychiatry and neurology*. Oxford & New York: Pergamon, 1977. (b)

ANTELMAN, S. M., & ROWLAND, N. E. Hyperphagia in normal rats and recovery of behavioral deficits in rats with lateral hypothalamic lesions: Stress-induced effects related to the nigrostriatal dopamine system. *Psychosomatic Medicine*, 1975, *37(1)*, 81.

ANTELMAN, S. M., & SZECHTMAN, H. Tail pinch induces eating in sated rats which appears to depend on nigrostriatal dopamine. *Science*, 1975, *189*, 731–733.

ANTELMAN, S. M., HERNDON, J. G., CAGGIULA, A. R., & SHAW, D. H. Dopamine receptor blockade: Prevention of shock-activated sexual behavior in naive rats. *Psychopharmacological Bulletin*, 1975, *11*, 45.

ANTELMAN, S. M., SZECHTMAN, H., CHIN, P., & FISHER, A. E. Tail pinch-induced eating, gnawing and licking behavior in rats: dependence on the nigrostriatal dopamine system. *Brain Research*, 1975, *99*, 319.

ANTELMAN, S. M., SZECHTMAN, H., ROWLAND, N. E., & CAGGIULA, A. R. Tails of eating, drinking, sex and maternal behavior: A nigrostriatal dopamine story. *Society for Neuroscience Abstracts*, 1975 (396), 254.

ANTELMAN, S. M., CAGGIULA, A. R., EDWARDS, D. J., & ROWLAND, N. E. Tail pinch stress reverses amphetamine anorexia. *Neuroscience Abstracts*, 1976, *2*, 845.

ANTELMAN, S. M., ROWLAND, N. E., & FISHER, A. E. Stress-induced recovery from lateral hypothalamic aphagia. *Brain Research*, 1976, *102*, 346.

ANTELMAN, S. M., SZECHTMAN, H., CHIN, P., & FISHER, A. E. Inhibition of tyrosine hydroxylase but not dopamine-β-hydroxylase facilitates the action of behaviorally ineffective doese of neuroleptics. *Journal of Pharmacy and Pharmacology*, 1976, *28*, 66.

ANTELMAN, S. M., EICHLER, A. J., & FISHER, A. E. Site specific effects of chronic neuroleptic administration on brain-stimulation reward. *Procedings of the XXVII Congress of Physiological Sciences 12*, 1977, 687.

ANTELMAN, S. M., CAGGIULA, A. R., BLACK, C., & EDWARDS, D. J. Stress reverses the anorexia induced by amphetamine and methylphenidate, but not fenfluramine. *Brain Research*, 1978, *143*, 580–585.

AZRIN, N. H., HUTCHINSON, R. R., & HAKE, D. F. Pain-induced fighting in the squirrel monkey. *Journal of Experimental Analysis of Behavior*, 1963, *6*, 620.

AZRIN, N. H., HUTCHINSON, R. R., & HAKE, D. F. Attack, avoidance and escape reactions to aversive shock. *Journal of Experimental Analysis of Behavior*, 1967, *10*, 131–148.

AZRIN, N. H., HUTCHINSON, R. R., & SALLERY, R. D. Pain-aggression toward inanimate objects. *Journal of Experimental Analysis of Behavior.* 1964, *7*, 223.
BAKER, J. W., & SCHAIE, K. W. Effects of aggression "alone" or "with another" on physiological and psychological arousal. *Journal of Personality and Social Psychology,* 1969, *12*, 80–86.
BANDURA, A. *Aggression: A social learning analysis.* Englewood Cliffs, N.J.: Prentice-Hall, 1973.
BARFIELD, R. J., & SACHS, B. D. Sexual behavior: Stimulation by painful electric shock to the skin in male rats. *Science,* 1968, *161,* 392.
BARNETT, S. A. 1958, Physiological effects of "social stress" in wild rats: I. Adrenal cortex. *Journal of Psychosomatic Research,* 1958, *3,* 1.
BEACH, F. A. Analysis of factors involved in the arousal, maintenance, and manifestation of sexual excitement in male animals. *Psychosomatic Medicine,* 1942, *4,* 173–198.
BEACH, F. A. 1947, A review of physiological and psychological studies of sexual behavior in mammals. *Physiological Reviews,* 1947, *27,* 240–307.
BEAMER, W., BERMANT, G., & CLEGG, M. Copulatory behavior of the ram, Ovis aries II: Factors affecting copulatory satiation. *Animal Behavior,* 1969, *17,* 706–711.
BECK, A. T. *The diagnosis and management of depression.* Philadelphia: The University of Pennsylvania Press, 1973.
BECK, A. T., WARD, C. H., MENDELSON, M., MOCK, J. E., & ERBAUCH, J. K. Reliability of psychiatric diagnoses: 2. A study of consistency of clinical judgements and ratings. *American Journal of Psychology,* 1962, *119,* 351–357.
BERGMAN, G. Der Steinwalzer, Arenaria i. interpres (L.) in seiner Beziehung zur Umwelt. *Acta Zoologica Fennica,* 1946, *47,* 1.
BERKSON, G. Abnormal stereotyped motor acts. In J. Zubin & H. F. Hunt (Eds.), *Comparative psychopathology—animal and human.* New York: Grune & Stratton, 1967.
BERMANT, G., LOTT, D., & ANDERSON, L. Temporal characteristics of the coolidge effect in male copulatory behavior. *Journal of Comparative Physiological Psychology,* 1968, *65,* 447–452.
BINGHAM, H. C. Sex development in apes. *Comparative Psychology Monographs,* 1928, *5,* 1–161.
BLEULER, E. *Dementia praecox or the group of schizophrenias* (J. Zinkin, Trans.). International University Press, New York, 1950.
BOSHKA, S. C., WIESMAN, H. M., & THOR, D. H. A technique for inducing aggression in rats utilizing morphine withdrawal. *Psychological Record,* 1966, *16,* 541–543.
BROWN, G. W., BINLEY, J. L. T., & WING, J. K. Influence of family life on the course of schizophrenic disorders: a replication, *British Journal of Psychology,* 1972, *121,* 241–258.
BRUCH, H. *The importance of overweight.* New York: Norton, 1957.
BRUCH, H. *Eating disorders.* New York: Basic Books, 1973.
BUCHSBAUM, M. Average evoked response augmenting/reducing in schizophrenia and affective disorders. In D. X. Freedman (Ed.), *Biology of the major psychoses: A comparative analysis.* New York: Raven, 1975, pp. 129–142.
CAGGIULA, A. R. Shock-elicited copulation and aggression in male rats. *Journal of Comparative Physiology,* 1972, *80,* 393.
CAGGIULA, A. R., & EIBERGEN R. Copulation of virgin male rats evoked by painful peripheral stimulation. *Journal of Physiological Psychology,* 1969, *69,* 414.
CAGGIULA, A. R., & VLAHOULIS, M. Modifications in the copulatory performance of male rats by repeated peripheral shock, *Behavioral Biology,* 1974, *11,* 269.
CAGGIULA, A. R., SHAW, D. H., ANTELMAN, S. M., & EDWARDS, D. J. Interactive effects of brain catecholamines and variations in sexual and non-sexual arousal on copulatory behavior of male rats. *Brain Research,* 1976, *111,* 321.

CALHOUN, J. B. The ecology and sociology of the norway rat. *Public Health Service Publication No. 1008*, U.S. Department of Health, Education, and Welfare, 1962.

CHANCE, M. R. A. An interpretation of some agonistic postures: the role of 'cut-offs' acts and postures. *Symposium of the Zoological Society of London*, 1962, *8*, 71–89.

CONNER, R. L., VERNIKOS-DANELLIS, J., & LEVINE, S. Stress, fighting and neuroendocrine function. *Nature*, 1971, *234*, 564.

COSTA, E., & GARATTINI, S. *Amphetamines and related compounds*. New York: Raven, 1970.

CROWLEY, W. R., POPOLOW, H. B., & WARD, O. B., JR.. From dud to stud: Copulatory behavior elicited through conditional arousal in sexually inactive male rats. *Physiology and Behavior*, 1973, *10*, 391–394.

DOOB, A. N., & WOOD, L. Catharsis and aggression: Effects of annoyance and retaliation on aggressive behavior. *Journal of Personality and Social Psychology*, 1972, *22*, 156–162.

EICHELMAN, B., ORENBERG, E., SEAGRAVES, E., & BARCRAS, J. Social setting: Influence on the induction of brain cAMP in response to electric shock in the rat. *Neuroscience Abstracts*, 1976, 860.

ELLINWOOD, E. H. Amphetamine psychosis: A multidimensional process. *Seminars in Psychiatry*, 1969, Vol. 1, No. 2 (May), 208–226.

ELLINWOOD, E. H., JR. Behavioral and EEG changes in the amphetamine model of psychoses. In E. Usdin (Ed.), *Neuropsychopharmacology of monoamines and the regulatory enzymes*. New York: Raven, 1974.

ELLISON, G. D., SORENSON, C. A., & JACOBS, B. L. Two feeding syndromes following surgical isolation of the hypothalamus in rats. *Journal of Comparative Pysiological Psychology*, 1970, *70*, 173–180.

EXLINE, R. V. Visual interaction: The glances of power and preference. In J. K. Cole (Ed.), *Nebraska Symposium on Motivation*, 1971.

FENTRESS, J. C. Development of grooming in mice with amputated forelimbs. *Science*, 1973, *179*, 704–705.

FENTRESS, J. C. (Ed.), *Simpler networks and behavior*. Sunderland, Mass.: Sinauer Assoc., 1976.

FIBIGER, H. C., & MILLER, J. J. Raphe projections to the substantia nigra: A possible mechanism for interaction between dopaminergic and serotonergic systems. *Neuroscience Abstracts*, 1976, *2*, 487.

FIBIGER, H. D., CARTER, D. A., & PHILLIPS, A. G. Decreased intracranial self-stimulation after neuroleptics or 6-hydroxydopamine: Evidence for mediation by motor deficits rather than by reduced reward, *Psychopharmacology*, 1976, *47*, 21–27.

FISHER, A. E. Effects of stimulus variation on sexual satiation in the male rat. *Journal of Physiological Psychology*, 1962, *55*, 614–620.

FUXE, K., BUTCHER, L., & ENGEL, J. DL-5-hydroxytryptophan induced changes in central monoamine neurons after decarboxylase inhibition. *Journal of Pharmacy and Pharmacology*, 1971, *23*, 450.

GAMBARO, S., & RABIN, A. I. Diastolic blood pressure responses following direct and displaced aggression after anger arousal in high- and low-guilt subjects. *Journal of Personality and Social Psychology*, 1969, *12*, 87–94.

GLUCKSMAN, M. L. Psychiatric observations on obesity. *Advances Psychosomatic Medicine*, 1972, *7*, 194.

GOLDFOOT, D. A., & BAUM, M. J. Initiation of mating behavior in developing male rats following peripheral electric shock. *Physiological Behavior*, 1972, *8*, 857.

GRAHAME-SMITH, D. G. Metabolic compartmentation of brain monoamines. In R. Bahzas & J. E. Gremer (Eds.), *Metabolic compartmentation in the brain*, New York: Wiley, 1971. (Second ed.).

GRAY, D. F. *Immunology: An outline of basic principles, problems and theories concerning the immunological behavior of man and animals.* New York: American Elsevier, 1970. (Second ed.).

HAMBURGER, W. W. Emotional aspects of obesity, *Medical Clinics of North America,* 1951, *35,* 483.

HÅRD, E., & LARSSON, Effects of mounts without intromission upon sexual behavior in male rats, *Animal Behaviour,* 1968, *16,* 538–540.

HARRIS, A. Sensory deprivation and schizophrenia, *Journal of Mental Science,* 1959, *105,* 235–237.

HERMAN C. P., & POLIVY, J., Anxiety, restraint and eating behavior, *Journal of Abnormal Psychology,* 1975, *84,* 666–672.

HILL, C. A. Corprophagy in apes. *International Zoo Yearbook,* 1966, *6,* 251–257.

HINDE, R. The behaviour of the great tit (parus major) and other related species. *Behaviour Supplement,* 1952, *2,* 1.

HOLLANDER, X. *The Happy Hooker.* New York: Dell, 1972.

HOKANSON, J. E., & SHETLER, S. The effect of overt aggression on physiological arousal level. *Journal of Abnormal and Social Psychology,* 1961, *63,* 446–448.

HORNYKIEWICZ, O. Brain monoamines and parkinsonism. In B. D. Bernard (Ed.), *Aminergic hypotheses of behavior: Reality or cliche?* NIDA Research Monograph Series 3, Maryland, 1975, pp. 13–21.

HUTT, S. J. An ethological analysis of autistic behavior. In H. M. Van Pragg (Ed.), *On the origin of schizophrenia psychoses.* Amsterdam: De Erven Bohn, B.V., 1975.

HUTT, C., & HUTT, S. J. Effect of environmental complexity upon stereotyped behaviours in children, *Animal Behaviour,* 1965, *13,* 1–4.

HUTT, C., & HUTT, S. J. The biological study of childhood autism. *Journal of Special Education,* 1969, *3,* 3–11.

HUTT, C., & HUTT, S. J. Stereotypies and their relation to arousal: A study of autistic children. In S. J. Hutt & C. Hutt (Eds.), *Behavior studies in psychiatry.* Oxford: Pergamon, 1970.

INNES, I. R., & NICKERSON, M. Norepinephrine, epinephrine, and the sympathomimetic amines. In L. S. Goodman and A. Gilman (Eds.), *The pharmacological basis of therapeutics.* New York: Macmillan, 1970, p. 477.

JACOBS, B. L., & FAREL, P. B. Motivated behaviors produced by increased arousal in the presence of goal objects. *Physiology and Behavior,* 1971, *6,* 473–476.

JANSSEN, P. A. J. The pharmacology of haloperidol. *International Journal of Neuropsychiatry,* 1967, *3,* 10.

JANOWSKY, D. S., EL-YOUSEL, M. K., DAVIS, J. M., & SEKERKE, H. J. Provocation of schizophrenic symptoms by intravenous methyl-phenidate. *Archives of General Psychiatry,* 1973, *28,* 185–191.

KANNER, L. Autistic disturbances of autistic contact. *Nervous Child,* 1943, *2,* 217–250.

KAPLAN, H. S. *The new sex therapy.* New York: Bruner/Mazel, 1974.

KEMPF, E. J. The social and sexual behavior of infrahuman primates with some comparable facts in human behavior, *Psychoanalytic Review,* 1917, *4,* 127–154.

KORNETSKY, C., & ELIASSON, M. Reticular stimulation and chlorpromazine: An animal model for schizophrenic overarousal. *Science,* 1969, *165,* 1273–1274.

KRAEPELIN, E. *Dementia praecox and paraphrenia.* Edinburgh: E. and S. Livingstone, 1919.

KRAUTHAMER, G. M. Catecholamines in behavior and sensorimotor integration: The neostriatal system. In A. J. Friedhoff (Ed.), *Catecholamines and behavior,* Vol. 1. New York: Plenum, 1975, pp. 59–87.

KONECNI, V. J. Annoyance, type and duration of postannoyance activity and aggression: The "cathartic effect". *Journal of Experimental Psychology,* 1975, *104,* 76–102.

KONECNI, V. J. & DOOB, A. N. Catharsis through displacement aggression. *Journal of Personality and social Psychology*, 1972, 23, 379–387.

KUPFERMANN, I. Eating behavior induced by sounds. *Nature*, 1964, 201, 324.

LARSSON, K. Conditioning and sexual behavior in the male albino rat. *Acta Psychological Gothoburgensia*, 1956, 1, 1–269.

LARSSON, K. Non-specific stimulation and sexual behavior in the male rat. *Behaviour*, 1963, 20, 110–114.

VAN LAWICK-GOODALL, J. Behavior of free-living chimpanzees of the Gombe Stream area. *Journal of Experimental Psychology*, 1968, 40, 175.

LEFF, J. P. Life events and maintenance therapy in schizophrenic relapse. *British Journal of Psychiatry*, 1973, 123, 659–660.

LE MAGNEN, J. Stress et obésité. *La Recherche*, 1976, 7, 777.

LEON, G. R. & CHAMBERLAIN, K. Emotional arousal, eating patterns and body image as differential factors associated with varying success in maintaining a weight loss. *Journal of Consulting and Clinical Psychology*, 1973a, 40, 474–480.

LEON, G. R., & CHAMBERLAIN, K. Comparison of daily eating habits and emotional states of overweight persons successful or unsuccessful in maintaining a weight loss. *Journal of Consulting and Clinical Psychology*, 1973b, 41, 108–115.

LEVY, D. M. On the problem of movement restraint: Tics, stereotyped movements, hyperactivity. *American Journal of Orthopsychiatry*, 1944, 14, 644–671.

MAKKINK, G. F. An attempt at an ethogram of the European Avocet (Recurvirostra avosetta L.) with ethological and psychological remarks. *Ardea*, 1936, 25, 1.

MALSBURY, C. W. & PFAFF, D. W. Neural and hormonal determinants of mating behavior in adult male rats. A review. In L. V. DiCara (Ed.), *Limbic and autonomic nervous system research*. New York: Plenum, 1975.

MARSHALL, J. F., RICHARDSON, J. S., & TEITELBAUM, P. Nigrostriatal bundle damage and the lateral hypothalamic syndrome. *Journal of Comparative Physiological Psychology*, 1974, 87, 808–830.

MASON, W. Early social deprivation in the nonhuman primates: Implications for human behavior. In D. C. Blass (Ed.), *Environmental influences*. New York: Rockefeller Foundation & Russell Sage Foundation, 1968, pp. 70–100.

MATTHYSSE, S. W. The role of dopamine in schizophrenia. In E. Usdin, D.A. Hamburg, & J. D. Barchas (Eds.), *Neuroregulators and psychiatric disorders*. New York: Oxford University Press, 1977a, pp. 3–13.

MATTHYSSE, S. W. Dopamine and selective attention. In E. Costa & G. L. Gessa (Eds.), *Nonstriatal dopamenergic neurons*. New York: Raven Press, 1977b, pp. 667–689.

MCDONALD, N. Living with schizophrenia. *Canadian Medical Association Journal*, 1960, 82, 218–221.

MCKENNA, R. J. Some effects of anxiety level and food cues on the eating behavior of obese and normal subjects. *Journal of Personality and Social Psychology*, 1972, 22, 311–319.

MEDNICK, S. A., & SCHULSINGER, F. Some premorbid characteristics related to breakdown in children with schizophrenic mothers. In D. Rosenthal & S. S. Kefy (Eds.), *The transmission of schizophrenia*. London: Pergamon, 1968, pp. 267–291.

MEEHL, M. M., & CROMWELL, R. L. The effect of brief sensory deprivation and sensory stimulation on the cognitive functioning of chronic schizophrenics. *Journal of Nervous and Mental Disease*, 1969, 148, 586–596.

MELTZER, H. Y., & STAHL, S. M. The dopamine hypothesis of schizophrenia: A review. *Schizophrenia Bulletin*, 1976, 2, 19–76.

MENZEL, E. W. The effects of cumulative experience on responses to novel objects in young isolation-reared chimpanzees. *Behaviour*, 1963, 21, 1–12.

MEYER, J. E., & PUDEL, V. Experimental studies on food-intake in obese and normal weight subjects. *Journal of Psychosomatic Research*, 1972, *16*, 305.

MILLER, R. E., MIRSKY, I. A., CAUL, W. F., & SAKATA, T. Hyperphagia and polydipsia in socially isolated rhesus monkeys. *Science*, 1969, *165*, 1027–1028.

MITCHELL, G., RUPPENTHAL, G. C., RAYMOND, E. J., & HARLOW, H. F. Long term effects of multiparous and primiparous monkey mother rearing. *Child Development*, 1966, *37*, 781–791.

MORDEN, B., CONNER, R., MITCHELL, G., DEMENT, W., & LEVINE, S. Effects of rapid eye movement (REM) sleep deprivation on shock-induced fighting. *Physiology and Behavior*, 1968, *3*, 425–432.

MORRIS, D. The reproductive behaviour of the zebra finch (Poephila guttata), with special reference to pseudo female behaviour and displacement activities. *Behaviour*, 1954, *6*, 271.

MOYER, K. E. Kinds of aggression and their physiological basis. *Committee in Behavioral Biology*, 1968, *2*, 65–87.

NG, L.K.Y., CHASE, T. N., COLBURN, R. W., & KOPIN, I. J. Release of ^{3}H-dopamine by 5-L-hydroxytryptophan. *Brain Research*, 1972, *45*, 499.

O'KELLY, L. W., & STECKLE, L. C. A note on long enduring emotional response in the rat. *Journal of Psychology*, 1939, *8*, 125.

PICKWELL, G. B. The prairie horned lark. *Transactions of the Academy of Science of St. Louis*, 1931, *27*, 1.

RABER, H. Analyse des Balzverhaltens eines domestizierten Truthahnes (Meleagris), *Behaviour*, 1948, *1*, 81.

RANDRUP, A., & MUNKVAD, I. Pharmacology and physiology of stereotyped behavior. In S. Kety & S. Matthysse (Eds.), *Catecholamines and their enzymes in the neuropathology of schizophrenia*. *Journal of Psychiatric Research*, 1974, *11*, 1.

ROBBINS, T. W., PHILLIPS, A. G., & SAHAKIAN, B. J. The effects of chlordiazepoxide on tail-pinch induced eating in rats. *Pharmacology, Biochemistry, and Behavior*, 1977, *6*, 297–303.

ROBERTS, E. The γ-aminobutyric acid system and schizophrenia. In E. Usdin, D. A. Hamburg & J. D. Barchas (Eds.), *Neuroregulators and psychiatric disorders*. New York: Oxford University Press, 1977, pp. 347–357.

ROWLAND, N. E., & ANTELMAN, S. M. Stress-induced hyperphagia and obesity in rats. A possible model for understanding human obesity. *Science*, 1976, *191*, 310.

RUTTER, M. The description and classification of infantile autism. In D. W. Churchill, G. D. Alpern, & M. K. DeMyer (Eds.), *Infantile autism*. Springfield, Ill.: Thomas, 1971.

SACHS, B. D., & BARFIELD, R. J. Copulatory behavior of male rats given intermittent electric shocks: Theoretical implications. *Journal of Comparative and Physiological Psychology*, 1974, *83*, 607.

SAHAKIAN, B. J., & ROBBINS, T. W. Isolation rearing enhances tail pinch induced oral behavior in rats. *Physiology and Behavior*, 1977, *18*, 530.

SCATTON, B., GLOWINSKI, J., & JULOU, L. Dopamine metabolism in the mesolimbic and mesocortical dopaminergic systems after single or repeated administrations of neuroleptics. *Brain Research*, 1976, *109*, 184–189.

SCHACTER, S. Obesity and eating. *Science*, 1965, *161*, 751.

SCHEIN, M. W., & HALE, E. Stimuli eliciting sexual behavior. In F. Beach (Ed.), *Sex and behavior*. New York: Wiley, 1965, pp. 440–482.

SCHWAB, R. S. Akinesia paradoxica. *Electroencephalography and Clinical Neurophysiology*, 1972, *31*, 87–92.

SELYE, H. *Stress without distress*. Philadelphia: Lippincott, 1914, 171.

SHAKOW, D. Some observations on the psychology (and some fewer, on the biology) of schizophrenia. *The Journal of Nervous and Mental disease*, 1971, *153*(5), 300–316.

SHARMA, O. P., & HAYS, R. L. Increasing copulatory behavior in ageing male rats with an electrical stimulus. *Journal of Reproduction and Fertility*, 1974, *39*, 111–113.

SIEGAL, P. S., & BRANTLEY, J. J. The relationship of emotionality to the consummatory response of eating. *Journal of Experimental Psychology*, 1951, *42*, 304–306.

SILVERMAN, J. Percephial and neurophysiological anaogues of "experience" in schizophrenic and LSD reactions. In D. V. S. Sankar (Ed.), *Schizophrenia: Current concepts and research*. New York: PJD Publications, Ltd., 1969, pp. 182–208.

SILVERSTONE, T. Anorectic drugs. In J. T. Silverstone (Ed.), *Obesity: Pathogenesis and management*. Acton, Mass.: Publishing Sciences Group, 1975, p. 193.

SNYDER, S. Catecholamines as mediators of drug effects in schizophrenia. In F. O. Schmitt & F. G. Worden (Eds.), *The neurosciences: Third study program*. Cambridge, Mass.: M.I.T. Press, 1974, pp. 721–732.

SNYDER, S. H., BANERJEE, S. P., YAMAMURA, H. I., & GREENBERG, D. Drugs, neurotransmitters and schizophrenia. *Science*, 1974, *184*, 1243.

STERRITT, G. M. Inhibition and facilitation of eating by electric shock. *Journal of Comparative Physiological Psychology*, 1962, *55*, 226.

STERRITT, G. M. Inhibition and facilitation of eating by electric shock, III. *Psychonomic Science*, 1965, *2*, 319–320.

STOLK, J. M., & HANLON, D. P. Inhibition of brain dopamine- hydroxylase- activity by methimazole. *Life Sciences*, 1973, *12*, 417.

STOLK, J. M., CONNER, R. L., LEVINE, S., & BARCHAS, J. D. Brain norepinephrine metabolism and shock induced fighting behavior in rats: Differential effects of shock and fighting on the neurochemical response to a common footshock stimulus. *The Journal of Pharmacology and Experimental Therapeutics*, 1974, *190*(2), 193–209.

STONE, A. A. Consciousness: altered levels in blind retarded children. *Psychosomatic Medicine*, 1964, *24*, 14–19.

STONE, C. P., & FERGUSON, L. W. Temporal relationships in the copulatory acts of adult male rats. *Journal of Comparative Psychology*, 1940, *30*, 419–433.

STRONGMAN, K. T. The effect of anxiety on food intake in the rat. *Quarterly Journal of Experimental Psychology*, 1965, *17*, 255–260.

STUNKARD, A. J. The night-eating syndrome. *American Journal of Medicine*, 1955, *19*, 78.

STUNKARD, A. J. Obesity. In Freedman & Kaplan (Eds.), *Comprehensive textbook of psychiatry*. Baltimore: Williams & Wilkins, 1967.

SVENSSON, T. H., & WALDECK, B. On the significance of central noradrenaline for motor activity: experiments with a new dopamine-β-hydroxylase inhibitor. *European Journal of Pharmacology*, 1969, *7*, 278.

TEITELBAUM, P., & WOLGIN, D. Neurotransmitters and the regulation of food intake. In W. H. Gispen, T. B. Greidanus van Wimersma, B. Bohus, & D. deWied (Eds.), *Progress in brain research*. Amsterdam: Elsevier, 1975.

THIERRY, A. M., TASSIN, J. P., BLANC, G., & GLOWINSKI, J. Selective activation of the mesocortical DA system by stress. *Nature*, 1976, *263*, 242–243.

THOA, N. B., EICHELMAN, B., RICHARDSON, J. S., & JACOBOWITZ, D. 6-hydroxydopa depletion of brain norepinephrine and the facilitation of aggressive behavior. *Science*, 1972, *178*, 75.

THOMPSON, T., & BLOOM, W. Aggressive behavior and extinction-induced response-rate increase. *Psychonomic Science*, 1966, *5*, 335–336.

TINBERGEN, N. Ueber das Verhalten Kampfender Kohlmeisen (Parus m. major L.). *Ardea*, 1937, *26*, 22.

TINBERGEN, N. *The study of instinct.* Oxford: Claredon Press, 1951.

TUGENDHAT, B. The normal feeding behavior of the three-spined stickleback (Gasterosteus aculeatus). *Behavior,* 1960a, *15,* 284–318.

TUGENDHAT, B. The disturbed feeding behavior of the three-spined stickelback: I electroshock is administered in the food area, *Behavior,* 1960b, *16,* 159–187.

ULLMAN, A. D. The experimental production and analysis of a "compulsive eating symptom" in rats. *Journal of Comparative Physiological Psychology,* 1951, *44,* 575–581.

ULLMAN, A. D. Three factors involved in producing "compulsive eating" in rats. *Journal of Comparative Physiological Psychology,* 1952, *45,* 490–496.

ULRICH, R. E. Pain as a cause of aggression. *American Zoology,* 1966, *6,* 663.

ULRICH, R. E., & AZRIN, N. H. Reflexive fighting in response to aversive stimulation. *Journal of the Experimental Analysis of Behavior,* 1962, *5,* 511.

ULRICH, R. E., HUTCHINSON, R. R., & AZRIN, N. H. Pain-elicited aggression. *Psychological Record,* 1965, *15,* 111.

UNGERSTEDT, U. Brain dopamine neurons and behavior. In F. O. Schmitt & F. G. Worden (Eds.), *The neurosciences:* Third study program. Cambridge, Mass.: The M.I.T. Press, 1974, pp. 695–703.

VAUGHAN, C. & LEFF, J. P. The influence of familial and social factors in the course of psychiatric illness. *British Journal of Psychiatry,* 1976, *129,* 125–137.

VALENSTEIN, E. S. Stereotyped behavior and stress. In T. Serban (Ed.), *Psychopathology of human adaptation.* New York: Plenum, 1976.

VALZELLI, L. Aggressive behavior induced by isolation. In S. Garattini & E. B. Sigg (Eds.), *Aggressive behavior.* New York: Wiley, 1969.

VENABLES, P. H., & WING, J. K. Level of arousal and the subclassification of schizophrenia. *Archives of General Psychiatry,* 1962, *7,* 114–119.

WILLIAMS, R. B., & EICHELMAN, B. Social setting: Influence on the physiological response to electric shock in the rat. *Science,* 1971, *174,* 613–614.

WILSON, J. R., KUEHN, R. E., & BEACH, F. A. Modification in the sexual behavior of male rats produced by changing the stimulus female. *Journal of Comparative and Physiological Psychology,* 1963, *56,* 636–644.

WOLGIN, D. L., CYTAWA, J., & TEITELBAUM, P. The role of activation in the regulation of food intake. In D. Novin, W. Wyrwicka, & G. Bray (Eds.), *Hunger: Basic mechanisms and clinical applications.* New York: Raven, 1976, pp. 179–191.

5

Redundancy in the Nervous System as Substrate for Consciousness: Relation to the Anatomy and Chemistry of Remembering [1]

ARYEH ROUTTENBERG

One day, when we lived in Kent, I was carving a sculpture in the open air, and someone came up to me and said, "What do you do all this for—such hard work and what use is it?" I could have told him that it's the growing use of our senses for non-practical and unimmediate purposes which makes us different from animals—that to a cow a clump of green grass and buttercups is something to eat, not to contemplate. But, he walked away. (Henry Moore, cited in Müller, 1976, p. 53)

1. INTRODUCTION

My task in this chapter is to relate the conscious experience of remembering to the physical and chemical mechanisms of brain cells involved in memory formation. No one will deny, to be sure, that such an enterprise is ultimately necessary. It is, however, clear that with currently available information the best that can be accomplished is to lay the groundwork for, or to outline the various directions of an approach to this problem. The present effort, then, is an attempt to bridge the gap, by providing a specific, testable neurobiological mechanism of consciousness that may be applied at each level of analysis involved in the study of the chemistry of memory.

The hypothesis to be proposed grows out of a comparison between

[1]This manuscript was prepared while the author was at the Institute of Pharmacology in Zürich and was supported by "THE ROCHE FOUNDATION for Scientific Exchange and Biomedical Collaboration with Switzerland." I wish to thank Dr. Joseph Huston for helpful discussion. I am grateful to Ellen Routtenberg and Betty Wells for assistance in preparing the manuscript.

ARYEH ROUTTENBERG • Departments of Psychology and Biological Science, Northwestern University, Evanston, Illinois 60201.

the remarkable anatomical localization which can be demonstrated with regard to memory consolidation processes, on the one hand, and the apparent redundancy that has been demonstrated in mammalian central nervous systems, on the other. In order to resolve this problem, I have suggested, therefore, that redundancy is, in fact, two sides of the same coin: that there exist within particular brain regions two processes, one which can be termed unconscious, the other conscious. The former is an obligatory input processing system; the latter a modulating output system. The former is involved in the consolidation of memories, the latter memory retrieval. Although there are several different broad implications to this hypothesis, in the present chapter the focus of attention will be on the relationship of this hypothesis to memory and its anatomical and biochemical basis.

But, what is memory? It seems reasonable to refer to the neurophysiological postulate of memory formation proved by Hebb, who stated that "When an axon of cell A is near enough to excite a cell B and repeatedly and persistently takes part in firing it, some growth process or metabolic change takes place in one or both cells, such that A's efficiency, as one of the cells firing B, is increased" (Hebb, 1949, p. 63).

In this chapter, then, we will consider memory to be the neurological and metabolic activity consequent to inputs, which engenders activity in the cerebrum leading to some more or less permanent alteration. In brief, memory has as its substrate an input-dependent residue following synaptic transmission. In one section of this chapter, I shall discuss the potential sites within specific brain regions where these residues may be engendered, and in a later section, the candidate molecules which may, in fact, be the residues themselves.

It is of more than historical interest to those of us who perceive that considerable progress has been made in our study of the mechanisms of memory to recall that the essential concepts with which we are working are not very different from those of the Russian neurophysiologist, the father of modern Russian neurophysiology, Professor Ivan Sechenov, who in 1863 was able to see that there were two processes involved in memory. Sechenov saw activity in the brain as a first step in the production of a material organization prerequisite to the formation of memory. He noted: "It is obvious that the nervous apparatus undergoes an increasingly profound change with each new influence encountered; between two successive influences these changes are retained by the nervous apparatus for a more or less considerable time. The capacity of retention must be inborn and, consequently, has its source in its material organisation" (Sechenov, 1965, pp. 68–69).

From a historical point of view, then, it is clear that our *conception* of the mechanisms of memory is not dissimilar from that initially proposed by Sechenov. It is clear, however, that since Sechenov's time we have gained a considerable amount of information concerning the structure and material substance that compose the nerve cells, as well as the interrelationships, both electrophysiological and biochemical, among nerve cells (see Schmitt, Dev, & Smith, 1976, for review). In this context a growing body of research on the anatomy and biochemistry of memory can be more clearly understood, particularly in the sense that it integrates well with our knowledge of the cell biology of nervous system function (e.g., Rosenzweig, & Bennett, 1976). It is these consequences of research of the past few decades that will enable the presentation of a more detailed view of the mechanisms of memory.

2. Localization of Memory Consolidation Function

In this section I wish to discuss work carried out in our laboratory that indicates that stimulation of restricted brain sites has a profound effect on learning and memory. On the face of it, it would appear that such findings would conflict with the view of redundant brain processes (to be discussed in Section 3) and the general theoretical approach proposed by John in this volume. According to these views there exists extensive redundancy in the central nervous system and, therefore, no necessity for a particular neuron in the processing of information. The paradox, then, is how does one obtain such localized effects on memory, if such a process is redundantly organized? Presumably, localized anatomical manipulations should have little impact on this extensively redundant system. As mentioned earlier, an attempted resolution to this problem is the main theme of this chapter since it may provide both a deeper understanding of the mechanisms of memory, and also assist in relating such mechanisms to the experience of remembering.

In order to appreciate the nature of this paradox, we shall begin by taking a look in this section at the data and the extent of localization which we have achieved. In the next section I will discuss some of the evidence which indicates that considerable redundancy exists in the central nervous system. In subsequent sections I shall present the hypothesis that consciousness is derived from presumed redundant neural circuits. Finally, applications of the hypothesis to memory processes and macromolecular coding will be provided.

The modern study of memory consolidation followed the lines initiated by Duncan (1949), using electroconvulsive shock (ECS) following learning. This procedure, while implicating such seizure-prone structures as the hippocampus (Routtenberg, Zechmeister, & Benton, 1970), as well as amygdala, in memory consolidation processes is still not sufficiently specific from an anatomical point of view. Thus, since the whole cerebrum is disorganized by ECS, it does not indicate the special importance of any particular cytoarchitectural region within brain structures. There were suggestions in the earlier work by Glickman (1958), Olds and Olds (1961), and Goddard (1964), using local brain stimulation techniques, which implicated certain brainstem and limbic structures in memory formation. On the basis of these early leads we began then to study memory from the anatomical point of view in the hope that this would provide a basis for a biochemical understanding of memory processing.

Following the suggestion of Kesner and Doty (1968), we began exploration of the amygdala. In collaboration with Elaine Bresnahan, then, I studied the effect of electrical brain stimulation on a simple learning situation, the so-called and often-used one-trial passive avoidance situation. It is curious that this learning situation requires, in fact, more than one trial, and, based on observation of the animals, is not quite passive in character. On the first trial the animal is placed on a platform and allowed to descend. It receives an aversive shock for doing so. This the animal does not particularly like and appropriately registers his distress. Not being totally foolish, it climbs back up onto the platform. Unfortunately the rat descends from the platform within the next 1–2 min. Finding that the floor of the apparatus is still quite intolerable, the rat climbs back up to the safety of the platform. He withdraws and remains steadfastly on the platform. This, then, is the one-trial portion of the learning situation. There are a few animals that do indeed require only one trial to learn. These are no doubt the more cynical of the rodents we deal with. There are, however, the majority of rodents who will require more than one trial, and a few that require as many as four or five trials before they finally give up, as it were. It is probably the hopelessly idealistic ones that require so many trials.

In order to equalize for these pecularities of inclination, we instituted a 2-min learning criterion. This criterion is designed so that all of the animals have in fact learned the situation. It should be pointed out that this differs from most "one-trial" experiments because in most studies the animal after descending from the platform and receiving the aversive shock is immediately removed from the apparatus. This is one trial, I suppose, but defined by the experimenter's preconception of the animal's learning ability. The one-trial procedure, it should be admitted, has the virtue of providing a similar physical stimulus to each of the animals, but has the unfortunate consequence that one has not equated for levels of original learning among subjects. In sum, in the present experiments animals are required to achieve a criterion of learning so that the brain manipulations, e.g., electrical stimulation, local chemical injection, are performed on roughly the same degree of original learning.

The next day, 24 hr after reaching the learning criterion, the animal is placed on the platform and remains there, presumably remembering the aversive event of yesterday. I have been able, indeed, to convince biochemists that the animal, in fact, remembers. This is perhaps a bold statement for a psychologist, but it is difficult to avoid since the animal remains on the platform for a 3-min retention test. I suppose that it may only be stated, rigorously speaking, that in this situation the animal demonstrates adequate retention performance. It would be a strain for some to imagine that the rat probably *knows* that were it to descend it would receive an aversive footshock.

As briefly mentioned earlier, the animal is not quite passive on the platform. It peers down at the grid floor which has delivered the painful footshock experience so unmercifully 24 hr previously. The animal will also at times pace back and forth on the platform, looking down, then withdrawing his nose, then putting his nose again over the edge of the platform very close to the grid, his whiskers moving back and forth at the characteristic frequencies (Welker, 1964). It is quite a remarkable performance for an animal that is supposed to be passive.

The majority of animals (> 95%) remain on the platform for the 3-min retention test period. We consider animals who do so to have perfect retention.

It is important to emphasize that we have no delusions concerning the generality of the training task. It is not a perfect mirror of learning or a general reflection of the process of memory, and it is not a simple learning task as it would at first perhaps appear. Unfortunately such complexity is not reduced by seeking other approaches to the study of learning, i.e., other learning tasks. If one uses other tasks, one is then faced with a different set of complex interactions, which, given our present state of ignorance, probably means that such an endeavor may not be fruitful. In this way, then, the author excuses himself on the question of the use of other learning tasks. The learning task that we use then is nonspecific in the sense that a variety of component processes are learned and remembered. It is specific, however, in the sense that the learning is finally based on an aversive experience, which requires that the animal withhold a particular response, i.e., stepping down from the platform.

Using this situation, we have studied the effects of brain stimulation delivered during learning at restricted brain loci on retention of the task measured 24 hr later. Encouraged by results of Goddard (1964), we proceeded to study the amygdala from an anatomical point of view. Since there are several cytoarchitectural regions of the amygdala (Valverde, 1965), we asked the question, are there particular nuclear groups within the amygdala which when electrically stimulated show any effects on memory? When we initiated these studies we were not certain whether brain stimulation would disrupt or facilitate retention. We, therefore, instituted a 5-day retention testing sequence, evaluating retention performance in a 3-min test situation for the 5 days after learning. If there were facilitatory effects, this would be observed over a 5-day period, since we had determined that control unstimulated animals begin to descend on days 2–5 after learning. It has generally been the case, however, that in the paradigm we have used brain stimulation disrupts retention performance.

To our surprise, Dr. Bresnahan and I (1972) found quite localized disruptive effects of stimulation in the amygdala. Indeed, we determined that the medial nucleus of the amygdala, in contrast to lateral, basal and cortical nuclear regions, led to disruptive effects on retention performance. In these experiments, animals were stimulated only during the learning trial and only when they were on the platform. When they descended onto the grid floor, they did not receive brain stimulation. This was done for practical reasons to prevent potential electrical current interaction between footshock and brain stimulation. We used, in fact, mild brain stimulation current levels, unilaterally, which did not produce any behavioral or electrophysiological signs of seizures, yet we could obtain disruption of retention performance 24 hrs later. Thus, animals that received unilateral medial amygdala stimulation during learning, descended during retention from the platform in less than 3 min. Operated controls and animals that received amygdala stimulation in other than the medial nucleus showed little or no retention disruption.

Of particular significance was the localization of the disruptive effect to the medial nucleus of the amygdala. It should be emphasized that we had no particular bias with respect to the medial nucleus of the amygdala. The data simply pointed to this structure. McDonough and Kesner (1971), using somewhat different techniques, in fact, suggested that memory disruptive effects might be localized to the medial nucleus of the amygdala. We suggested initially that medial amygdala plays an important role in modulating memory mechanisms. The broader anatomical significance of this finding, however, was not fully appreciated until we began to study other brain loci using a similar paradigm. Despite our lack of bias, it is worthwhile mentioning that such localization did provide the initial data that suggested an interesting overlap between the sites of memory disruption and the sites of brain stimulation reward (Routtenberg, 1975a,b).

In the last few years, in addition to the involvement of the medial nucleus of the amygdala in memory mechanisms (Bresnahan & Routtenberg, 1972), we have implicated other cytoarchitecturally defined nuclear groups in certain brain regions. Thus, we have found that low-level stimulation of substantia nigra, pars compacta, but not substantia nigra, pars reticulata, provokes retention disruption (Routtenberg & Holzman, 1973). This finding has been confirmed by Fibiger and Phillips (1976). We have also discovered that stimulation of the medial or sulcal prefrontal cortex of the rat (Leonard, 1969) influence retention performance while dorsal prefrontal areas are ineffective (Santos-Anderson & Routtenberg, 1976). Finally, we have found that stimulation of the medial forebrain bundle, particularly its lateral aspect, produces a retention disruption effect (Bresnahan & Routtenberg, 1976). Taken together these results indicate quite localized consequences of electrical brain stimulation on retention performance and suggest that only certain brain loci within a brain region may play a role in the memory consolidation process. It is clear, therefore, that not all electrical brain stimulation will produce disruptive effects.

Recently we have begun to study the effects of posttrial intracranial chemical injection on behavior in an effort to provide more precise anatomical information by chemically manipulating pathways, implicated in memory consolidation, at sites of synaptic transmission. Kim and Routtenberg (1976) have shown, for example, that picrotoxin blockade of the descending GABA system, which postsynaptically inhibits substantia nigra neurons (Precht & Yoshida, 1971), produced a 90% disruption of retention performance. This effect was dose dependent. Interestingly, a 500 ng dose of picrotoxin was less effective than the 50 ng dosage of picrotoxin which we found to be most effective. Thus, Kim and I showed that GABA terminals on substantia nigra cells which are presumed to have their origins in caudate nucleus and globus pallidus are involved in retention performance. When these GABA synapses are blocked after learning by picrotoxin there is disruption of retention performance. It is clear, then, that intracranial chemical injection of specific synaptic transmitter manipulating compounds are likely to be of great value in providing further anatomical localization and specificity with regard to memory disruption effects.

The broader view of these results suggests the hypothesis that during learning, specific brain regions are physiologically active, and this activity contributes to memory consolidation. If this activity is disrupted by 60 Hz electrical stimulation or by chemical injection of synaptically active or inhibiting compounds, then retention performance is disrupted. One may say, then, that electrophysiological activity in a certain set of brain regions is necessary for providing for memory consolidation. The possibility exists, indeed, that biochemical alterations in these pathways is important for providing for the metabolic or growth mechanisms of which Hebb spoke, or the material substance suggested by Sechenov. We have, it would appear, a basis for selecting certain pathways which could be part of the Hebbian cell assembly. Thus, these localized effects in certain cytoarchitectural loci and particular pathways appear to be quite impressive. In the next section, however, we shall consider the problem of redundancy in the nervous system which, if true, seems to raise an important paradox with respect to the localized effects so far described.

3. Redundancy of the Central Nervous System

If we are to understand the broader significance of the precise localization seen with brain stimulation techniques, it is necessary to integrate these data with the concept of redundancy and related empirical findings. It is a striking fact that, in considering data gathered from several different points of view, the general principle emerges that lesions of the mammalian central nervous system, whether produced by physical or chemical means, typically require destruction of more than 90% of a given structure to be effective in producing a behavioral impairment. It is worth considering a few particular examples of this generalization.

Redundancy has been dramatically illustrated by the results of Galambos, Norton and Frommer (1967), who studied the effects of lesions of the optic tract on visual performance of cats. They were unable to find any impairment in visual flux discrimination or pattern discriminations (e.g., 9 vs. 6), even when greater than 90–95% of the entire optic tract was destroyed. This surprising result seems difficult to understand in relation to current concepts of processing of visual information by the visual system (Hubel & Wiesel, 1977). How is it possible that the great majority of the entire optic tract system which conveys visual impulses from the retina photoreceptors through the bipolar cells and ganglion cells, interwoven with amacrine and horizontal cells, providing a mosaic of information for the processing of lateral geniculate neurons, is so unnecessary? How can destruction of so much material in the optic system produce so little consequence? Galambos et al. (1967) discuss the possibility that vision both requires and can function with the support systems buried deep within the brainstem. It is clear, whatever the interpretation, that it is not necessary to have much of the visual system intact in order to achieve adequate visual discrimination performance.

Of particular interest in this study was their demonstration that while 90% destruction of the optic tract had no effect, deterioration of performance was observed when over 90% of the optic tract was destroyed (Norton, Galambos, & Frommer, 1967). Thus, there exists evidence that a very small percentage, perhaps only less than 5% of the total optic tract, is necessary for the performance of the visual task. With less than 5% of the system it is no longer possible for visually-guided performance to be accurate.

It is possible that the holographic model, discussed by Dr. Pribram (this volume) may be related to these data. Essentially, when one destroys more and more of the optic system, one is obtaining a degraded image or degraded visual picture; but one is not obliterating the picture. Thus, one is simply obtaining an increasingly "noisy" picture, yet visual information remains until the last bit of tissue is removed.

Another example from a different field in neuroscience illustrates the generality of redundancy in the CNS. Nottebohm, Stokes, and Leonard (1976) have provided an elegant series of studies of the neural mechanisms involved in the control of the specific song patterns in canaries. They have found that the song pattern depends on particular nuclear groups and a circuit connecting them, finally, to the syrinx, the organ involved in song production. While the integrity of the caudal hyperstriatum ventrale is crucial for the production of the specific song pattern, if only a portion is destroyed, no major impairment occurs in the patterning or repertoire of the particular songs of this bird. Total destruction of this region, however, produced severe deficits in song production. It is not unreasonable to presume, then, that the neural mechanisms subserving the maintenance of the song patterns of the canary are highly redundant and that not all neurons located in the hyperstriatum are essential for song production. It would appear, then, that a subset of these neurons may be considered necessary. This study is particularly important with regard to the model to be discussed since it is a clear example that redundancy may be demonstrated in individual nuclear groups.

The role of catecholamines in brain function is well documented (e.g., Usdin & Snyder, 1973). What has emerged in the study of the role of catecholamines and the pharmacology of behavior is that the assessment of catecholamine involvement in behavioral activity such as feeding, avoidance, learning, and intracranial self-stimulation (Wauquier & Rolls, 1976) is hampered by the apparent redundancy of the catecholamine system. The blossoming of catecholamine research has been in part related to the effectiveness of drugs which specifically destroy catecholamine neurons and terminals. The neurotoxin, 6-hydroxy-dopamine, selectively destroys dopamine containing cells of the sub-nigra (Ungerstedt, 1971) and leads to a reduction in dopamine in its terminal field in the neostriatum. But, more than 90% reduction in dopamine levels in the neostriatum must be achieved in order to obtain effects on locomotor activity, feeding, and self-stimulation. Thus, the dopaminergic nigro-neostriatal system appears to have a redundant organization as does the caudal hyperstriatum of the canary, and as does the optic tract system of the cat.

One final example of redundancy is worth mentioning not only because of the quantitative data available but because it relates directly to the problems of memory mechanisms discussed in this chapter. In particular it has been shown that if protein synthesis inhibition of greater than 90% is present immediately after learning, a degrading effect on long-term memory can be demonstrated (Barondes, 1970, p. 747). What is particularly relevant about this finding to the present scheme is that one can inhibit brain protein synthesis up to 85–90% using cycloheximide or anisomycin (Squire & Becker, 1975; Squire, St. John, & Davis, 1976) without having any effect on memory. In these cases, then, the animal possesses protein synthetic machinery in its brain which is reduced to a mere 10–15% of its former self. Yet this animal is fully capable of producing long-term memories. It seems rather remarkable that this memory process can occur in such an inhibited system. Nonetheless this has been repeatedly demonstrated. It has also been repeatedly demonstrated that when this protein synthetic inhibition is greater than 90% there is a deterioration of long-term memory. Only with protein synthetic inhibition of this magnitude can one demonstrate these effects.

Thus, we have four different illustrations of the fact that severe deterioration of particular systems within the CNS will have little effect on behavioral endpoints. When deterioration exceeds 90% of the total capacity of the system, then, behavioral deterioration, e.g., pattern vision, song patterning in birds, catecholamine dependent functions, protein synthesis, and long-term memory is manifest. The fact that this redundancy appears in a variety of behavioral systems and different neurobiological endpoints adds generality to the view that redundancy is a concept which requires recognition in any general view of brain function. The question then is, how can one have both anatomical specificity as demonstrated in our brain stimulation experiments along with this high degree of redundancy?

4. REDUNDANCY AS A NEUROBIOLOGICAL SUBSTRATE OF CONSCIOUSNESS

In this section I wish to propose a neuronal model of consciousness which may be applied to the paradox raised in the previous section.

I wish to emphasize, too, that the present proposal is set forth in response to the call for a renewed nonmentalistic approach to the neurobiology of consciousness (Sperry, 1969, 1970, 1976). Before setting down the details of this model, it is worthwhile to quote the general arguments presented.

Sperry (1969) first notes that

> Most behavioral scientists today, brain researchers in particular, have little use for consciousness. From the objective experimental standpoint, it is difficult to see any place in the material brain process for the likes of conscious experience. Most investigators of cerebral function will violently resist any suggestion that the causal sequence of electro-physico-chemical events in the brain could in any way be influenced by conscious or mental forces . . . Whatever the stuff of consciousness, it is generally agreed that it does not interact back causally on the brain's electrophysiology or its biochemistry. (Sperry, 1969, pp. 532–533)

In contrast to this prevailing view, Sperry suggests that "the conscious phenomena of subjective experience do interact on the brain process exerting an active causal influence" (Sperry, 1969, p. 533).

In somewhat greater detail, Sperry suggests something of the process involved:

> It is the emergent dynamic properties of certain of these higher specialized cerebral processes that are interpreted to be the substance of consciousness. . . . It must detect the overall qualities of different kinds and different species of cerebral process and respond to these as entities rather than to their individual cellular components. . . . The brain process must be able to detect and to react to the pattern properties of its own excitation. (Sperry, 1969, p. 534)

Finally, Sperry indicates the goal of his proposal:

> Exactly how these properties of the brain mechanisms operate remains to be determined . . . to determine exactly the precise features of circuit design by which cerebral activity produces its conscious effects remains . . . a central challenge for the future. One merely hopes at this stage that future experimental and intellectual efforts, if focused within the guidelines of the present hypothesis, will be more effective than if directed on the assumption that mind is just an epiphenomenon. (Sperry, 1970, p. 590)

I believe that the facts of redundancy documented earlier provide for a specific mechanism of consciousness. I propose, therefore, that redundancy in brain is in fact a reflection of two complementary, similarly functioning systems present in each cytoarchitectural region. One system is the information processing system, and the other sytem is an output monitoring one. I shall refer to the first as System I and the second, System II. System I operates on the input; System II determines the output. In terms of John and co-workers, System I is exogenous, System II endogenous. In terms of Skinner, System I is elicited, System II, emitted. In neurobiological terms (Schmitt et al., 1976) System I is essentially axodendritic, axosomatic or orthograde, both chemically and electrophysiologically. System II is essentially dendro-dendritic, dendro-somatic, dendro-axonal or retrograde, both chemically and electrophysiologically.

Consider the dynamic properties of the proposed organization. Inputs to System I are processed with Huselian propriety (Hubel & Wiesel, 1977). But such processing leads to the influence of a second set of neurons embedded within the feature detector, System I, network. Whether System I is allowed to proceed is determined by the consequences of System II activity. System I allows for efficient sorting and coding of information; System II decides whether the coding should proceed to the next station. Our experience and wisdom is embedded within the activity of System II; our precise knowledge within System I. Finally, memory consolidation occurs within System I; information retrieval or simply, remembering, within System II.

The reader may now appreciate that the proposed formulation in the present paper is an attempt to answer the call made for more specific neurobiological mechanisms related to consciousness. The present model specifically applies presumed redundant neural circuits to a function: consciousness. One may use different terms from input-output monitoring to self-awareness to describe this function. But the essential point to be made here is that there exists sufficient redundancy in nuclear groups to provide for self-regulating systems, *mechanistically conceived,* which form the substrate of consciousness.

In order to place the model in a less poetic framework, it is worthwhile to consider one potential synaptic organization of the model as depicted in Figure 1. According to this model, inputs are applied to System I and the processing of these inputs is then regulated by System II, following signals from System I to System II. The nature of these interactions should be considered synaptic in the sense of Shepherd (1979), but it is not necessary at this point to be more specific. Since it is not made explicit in Figure 1 it is necessary to point out that there is sufficient negative feedback, to enable the organism to leave a System I–System II interaction at one brain locus and move to the next stage of processing.

The model in Figure 1 shows different brain regions where this organization occurs. In the context of the specific brain regions involved in memory documented in the present chapter, we may consider structures such as the medial nucleus of the amygdala, the substantia nigra, pars compacta, and the medial frontal cortex as important anatomical sites. Input processing by System I in the frontal cortex, for example, is then modulated by System II. If appropriate conditions are met, System I of frontal cortex provides a set of inputs to System I of the substantia

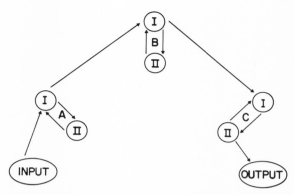

FIGURE 1. Proposed model of consciousness, which presumes that neural circuits within a brain region, previously considered redundant, serve two separate functions, labeled System I and System II (see text). These systems interact via local circuits. Interplay among brain regions (A: medial nucleus of the amygdala; B: frontal cortex; C: nigroneostriatal system) is also indicated. Both types of interactions are discussed further in the text.

nigra for processing. If these conditions are not met, then the processing terminates or is dumped into another routine ("subconscious"). In this model, then memory consolidation occurs as a consequence of activation of System I. Memory retrieval is *provided for* if the sequence of structures depicted in Figure 1 is engaged and System II activity in each structure gives the "enable" signal. Retrieval failure may occur, then, in the presence of memory consolidation. Such a situation would occur when System I activity is engaged, while System II activity is not.

In previous theoretical treatments of the mechanisms of memory (Routtenberg, 1971, 1975a) I have suggested that there exists a modulating control of the state of the system engaged. This modulation is reflected in hippocampal activity, i.e., hippocampal synchronization ("theta") which reflects input processing activity (System I) and hippocampal desynchronization which reflects output processing activity (System II). This system then has some influence in determining whether System I or System II is predominantly active at a given point in time.[2] The hippocampus, then, may be important in determining the brain state of the organism in the sense that System I or System II activity may be engaged. (Hippocampal state may in part be determined, in current neurobiological thinking [Bloom, 1973], by peptide neuromodulators.)

Dissociations of retrieval processes from awareness may occur

[2]For certain reasons related to the history of reticular formation, System I and System II were previously referred to as output and input, respectively (Routtenberg, 1968, 1972). It seems reasonable at this juncture to adopt the more conventional designation of System I processing inputs and System II processing outputs.

when hippocampal activity is in one mode and System I–System II activity in particular brain structures is in the other mode. Thus, for example, retrieval without awareness may occur when the hippocampus is in the synchronization mode of System I while amygdala, frontal cortex and substantia nigra are still in the System II retrieval mode. Conversely, phenomena such as "tip-of-the-tongue" may occur when the hippocampus is in the desynchronization mode, System II retrieval mode, but certain brain structures are still in the System I mode.[3] Such dissociations lead to temporary retrieval failure. It should be noted that the application of the hippocampal mechanism to the modulation of System I–System II interaction allows for an independent assessment of the proposed schema. This, then, reduces some of the circularity in the present theory and provides an approach toward the differential measurement of each system's activity. It suggests, for example, that consciousness exists when activity of System II neurons throughout the neuraxis is coincident with hippocampal desynchronization. An intriguing report by Beninger, Kendall, and Vanderwolf (1974) suggests that rats can demonstrate "self-awareness" when they engage in behaviors which typically are associated with either hippocampal theta or hippocampal desynchronization. In this regard, then consciousness or the ability to "self-report" is likely in either hippocampal state, suggesting that it is the congruence between that hippocampal state and the activity of nonhippocampal neurons coherent with that state that represents the condition of consciousness.

Given this description of the model, how might we understand the facts of redundancy discussed earlier? In the four cases of redundancy considered in the previous section, some form of lesion to the central nervous system was used. Assuming that such manipulations affect System I and System II equally, it can be concluded that more than 95% of each must be destroyed in order for impairment to occur. Another way to look at this is that impairments in behavior only occur when either System I or System II is totally removed. The partial destruction of one System will not cause impairment, if a portion of the other remains.

---

[3]What we are dealing with in the tip-of-the-tongue phenomenon addresses quite a broad and fundamental issue: the boundary between consciousness and the unconscious. Tip-of-the-tongue items are poised in the latter state ready to be released into the former state. But, items that exist in memory storage, nonetheless, may exert their influence without being retrieved, i.e., entering into consciousness. Items that are retrieved may occur without clear reference to the stored item that formed the basis of that retrieval. The task of psychoanalysis, for example, is to enable some coherence between that which is stored and that which is retrieved. The retrieval without reference to storage leads to the feeling of "Why did I say (or do) that?" Storage without subsequent retrieval can manifest itself in various gradations: repression, suppression, forgetting, "tip-of-the-tongue."

Given the nonselective nature of those lesions, it is likely, then, that some portion of both systems is still capable of functioning.

It is clear from these considerations, that the stimulation techniques we have used must be disrupting a considerable proportion of both systems. In fact, it seems necessary to conclude that nearly all of both systems is disrupted. Another possibility, however, may be suggested, which does not require that every neuron in both System I and System II be altered by our localized brain manipulations. Rather, it seems possible that the electrical stimulus, however finally localized, is disrupting the physiological activity involving the *interaction between* System I and System II. Thus, only those elements that mediate the interaction itself may be important. In modern neurobiological terms, the stimulation disrupts the *local circuit* mechanism (Schmitt *et al.*, 1976) in any brain region. A lesion, it may be suggested, cuts some circuits while leaving others intact, or, at least, capable of functioning.

One analogy to support this speculation comes from the split brain patient (Sperry, 1966). Here both the perceptual capability of the right hemisphere (System I) and the language capacity of the left hemisphere (System II) are intact, but the fibers which allow the two to interact have been cut. Thus, one may consider the section of the callosum as a special case in which the functioning of two systems which normally interact is separated by a long axon tract.[4] Thus, callosotomy severs all of the axons responsible for the interaction.

Within nuclear groups, however, we are not so fortunate to be able readily to split the two functions. The close proximity of System I and System II in spatial terms means that lesions of a particular brain structure must be almost total to destroy both the relation between System I and System II and the systems themselves. I suggest, however, that our electrical stimulus or chemical injection is capable of achieving a disruption of System I–System II interactions, in the same way, that callosotomy disrupts hemispheric associations.[5,6]

It is conceivable that there are in fact two types of cells differing anatomically which form the substrate of System I and System II, respectively. If they do not differ anatomically, they may differ in some chemical way. A potential example of this may be derived from recent work of ours on memory (Morgan & Routtenberg, 1977). We have been

[4] I am grateful to Dr. Samuel Feldman for making this point.
[5] The disruption occurring in the two cases is, however, quite different. Thus, local brain stimulation would alter the functioning of one particular System I–System II interaction. Callosum section, on the other hand, is conceived of as separating communication among several different System I axons projecting to several different System II cells of the other hemisphere.
[6] The present model bears certain similarities to the "modular-distributional" system pro-

studying the consequences of posttrial angiotensin-II injection into the caudate nucleus on retention performance using the same procedures as discussed earlier (Kim & Routtenberg, 1976). We have found that angiotensin injections into the dorsal portions of the caudate nucleus are quite effective in disrupting retention tested 24 hr later. However, injections into the ventral caudate nucleus are ineffective. It is unlikely that this effect is related to spread up the cannula to the overlying cerebral cortex since angiotensin injection into the overlying cerebral cortex itself is without effect. These results are interesting in relation to the role of peptides in memory, since it points to a role for the octapeptide, angiotensin II, in mnemonic processes. Relevant to the present discussion is the possibility that System I cells and System II cells of the caudate nucleus differ in their biochemistry, for example, with respect to their ability to produce or respond to angiotensin. Thus, it is conceivable that System I cells process information in the presence of exogenous angiotensin, i.e., they are unaffected by angiotensin. On the other hand, System II cells of the caudate nucleus may be sensitive to the high levels of angiotensin which were injected into the caudate. In such a case the angiotensin might be important for the regulation of the cell's own activity, i.e., System II cells secrete angiotensin in the microenvironment, or are influenced by angiotensin by synaptic mechanisms as proposed in Figure 1. In either case it seems reasonable to propose that, if System I and System II cells show little anatomical difference, that they may nonetheless show specific differences from a biochemical point of view.

If biochemical differences underly the difference between System I and System II cells and if such a difference plays some role in the formation of memory, it would be of interest to determine what biochemical events occur which are uniquely related to the memory process. Thus, we may assume that memory consolidation is brought on by activation of System I cells, but that the capacity to retrieve that which is stored occurs as a consequence of biochemical changes which are engendered in or related to System II cells. If so, then it will be interesting to determine what biochemical events are unique to the memory consolidation process and those unique to the retrieval or remembering process. Having achieved such a differentiation, it would be possible to define, using cytochemical methods, the nerve cells which function in each System. Since we are quite far from this goal at present, it will be well to determine whether current information on the biochemistry of memory may be potentially useful for achieving these distinctions.

---

posed by Mountcastle (1979, p. 22). If the columns or modules form part of System II, then their interactions would involve "pericolumnar inhibition . . . a powerful mechanism for the functional isolation of active columns from their neighbors" (p. 37). Thus, System

5. BIOCHEMISTRY OF MEMORY

With regard to the extensive literature on experience and its effects on brain biochemistry, the reader is referred to several excellent reviews (Glassman, 1969; Horn, Rose, & Bateson, 1972, Dunn, Entingh, Entingh, Gispen, Machlus, Perumal, Reese, & Brogan, 1974, p. 679; Rosenzweig & Bennett, 1976). It is, however, necessary to review briefly certain findings to emphasize the research strategies which have been taken recently in my laboratory.

It should be acknowledged at the outset that the philosophical and empirical guidelines in this field have been set forth in the pioneering work of Hydén over the past two decades (Hydén, 1967, p. 243). There have been certain reservations concerning the interpretation of these results and their particular significance (e.g., Glassman, 1969). It is clear, however, that Hydén has made a significant contribution to the field in terms of the specific empirical approaches used and the general strategy of this research area as it has subsequently been used by most investigators in this field.

In my own laboratory, using this approach, we have been studying glycoproteins (Routtenberg, George, Davis, & Brunngraber, 1974) and phosphoproteins (Routtenberg, Ehrlich, & Rabjohns, 1975) as possible molecular species whose alteration may play some role in memory (see Routtenberg, 1979, for review).

We have been studying glycoproteins in relation to memory because it has been demonstrated that these macromolecules exist in high concentrations in the synaptic complex. Thus, it has been demonstrated by several EM cytochemistry studies (Rambourg & Leblond, 1967; Bondareff, 1967; Cotman & Taylor, 1974) that the synaptic junction possesses high concentration of glycoproteins. This conclusion is also supported by biochemical data (Brunngraber, Dekirmenjian, & Brown, 1967). Thus, it is conceivable then that glycoproteins play a role in memory consolidation and they do so by altering the synaptic junction mechanism in ways that are not yet known. Since certain glycoproteins are attached to the membrane and exist in part on the outside of the

---

II may be composed of columns, modules, lamellae or islands (Collier & Routtenberg, 1977).

These modules function within a larger structure, e.g., visual cortex, and are essentially replicated local circuits. Replication of modules, then, may be considered a potential mechanism for the redundancy proposed in the present chapter.

Mountcastle notes that a module's function may be determined by the neighboring module's activity *and* the influence of extrinsic modules from other structures. This concept of "distributed systems" is similar to the second order interaction of System I in structure A with System II in structure B.

membrane in the extracellular space of the synaptic junction, it is conceivable that they play some role as a transmitter receptor or as has been proposed by Barondes (1970b, p. 272) that they play a role in intercellular recognition.

In an initial study of whole brain glycopeptides, we were unable to demonstrate any effects of training on brain biochemistry. Thus, Holian, Brunngraber, and Routtenberg, (1971) using whole brain preparations of glycopeptides found no changes in levels of hexosamine, NANA, fucose or ^{14}C-glycosamine incorporation into glycopeptides (DPM/ng hexosamine). In a more recent study separating particular protein moieties with gel electrophoresis using a specific glycoprotein label, ^{3}H-fucose, we were able to demonstrate that particular protein bands in particular locations were altered following the training experience (Routtenberg et al., 1974). These results were encouraging, demonstrating the feasibility of finding restricted changes in particular proteins using techniques which were specific with respect to the anatomical location, the subcellular components studied, and the molecular moieties observed. It is interesting that in these experiments we have found that the most significant changes have occurred in the caudate nucleus, a region which we have implicated in our brain stimulation experiments and our chemical injection studies. The possibility that the nigro-neostriatal system plays some role in the memory consolidation process is certainly enhanced, then, when we can demonstrate both with electrical stimulation, chemical injection and biochemical techniques that this system consistently demonstrates an involvement in memory-related processes.[7]

We have recently begun to study the role of phosphoproteins and memory, since it has been shown that an endogenous phosphorylation system exists in synaptic membrane preparations (Ueda, Maeno, & Greengard, 1973). In addition, it has been shown that cyclic AMP stimulates the phosphorylation of certain membrane proteins (Ueda et al., 1973). This result has suggested the intriguing hypothesis that cyclic AMP, which is thought to play a significant role in synaptic transmission (Bloom, 1973), may cause an immediate and selective change in the phosphate content of membrane proteins. These alterations then link electrophysiological activity to biochemical alterations.

We have begun to study the effects of learning in this preparation and have discovered that the phosphoprotein of 47,000 m wt first described by us (Ehrlich & Routtenberg, 1974; Routtenberg & Ehrlich, 1975) is in fact altered as a consequence of learning (Routtenberg et al., 1975). The other phosphoproteins are not altered to the same extent. These results are intriguing. They suggest that only specific protein components within the synaptic plasma membrane may play a role in memory.

[7]See Morgan and Routtenberg (in press).

Further, we have shown that these occur predominantly in the caudate nucleus and are seen only poorly in the cerebral cortex and cerebellum (Routtenberg, 1976). Taken together, then, these two molecular species of the membrane, the glycoproteins and phosphoproteins, have been implicated in learning (cf. Routtenberg, 1979, for review).

What significance, then, can be attributed to these molecular events, with respect to System I and System II cells? Is it possible, for example, that only half of the nerve cells, roughly, demonstrate biochemical alteration? That the other half, to preserve information processing ability, is biochemically unaltered, so as to *resist contamination of past events*. Such an organization would enable one to have one's memory retrieval and a clear head too!

This view may help to understand why biochemical alterations in nerve cells have not been striking. If the crucial biochemical changes which form the residual, which is the material substance of memory, occurs in the local circuits, but *not in other synaptic connections*, then only a proportion of the synaptic membranes studied chemically would be altered. More to the point, proteins existing in both types of cells would migrate similarly in our electrophoretic experiments, but only a certain proportion of them would be altered.

It is important to emphasize, then, from a methodologic point of view, that our experiments are not as yet capable of achieving an answer to this problem because we now dissect particular brain regions and study their chemistry. In the context of the major hypothesis, we would be studying both System I and System II cells. Thus, the failure to observe large differences, even when effects have been reported, could be related to the absence of the biochemical process under study in at least half of the cells studied, thereby diluting the specific activity, i.e., incorporated isotope/milligram *relevant* membrane protein.

6. Conclusion

The present chapter sets forth an hypothesis concerning the neurology of consciousness which states that this process occurs as a consequence of self-monitoring activity in individual nuclear groups throughout the neuraxis. While the verbalization of awareness of this process may be related to language centers in the human cerebral cortex, the self-monitoring process occurs in cerebral cortex of nonhuman vertebrates as well.

This hypothesis was offered, in part, to provide an answer to the presumed redundancy which exists in the central nervous system. Thus, what has been assumed to be redundant is, in fact, a self-monitoring process whose function may escape detection in the information processing type of tasks that are often used to assess the consequences of brain injury.

In a phylogenetic perspective it is difficult to say whether Henry Moore's cow is conscious of or contemplates the grass it is about to consume. One may infer, however, that the circuitry which establishes human consciousness is not absent in other animals. Whether local circuits present in animals confer on them characteristics of thought previously reserved for humans cannot be stated. The present model is compatible, however, with the notion that there are certain sacred cows of human capacity, e.g., language, which *may* be achieved by nonhumans (Gardner & Gardner, 1969).

In a developmental-ontogenetic perspective the present scheme offers a potential model for the development of consciousness and self-awareness in humans. Briefly stated, these qualities emerge as the local circuits linking System I and System II develop. There is little question that the number of synaptic interactions follows a developmental course (Aghajanian & Bloom, 1967), which, at least, in part, could represent a source of local circuit interactions. As Schmitt *et al.* (1976) have pointed out, the neurons which form part of the local circuit develop *after* the long-axon systems which presumably are more rigidly determined.

REFERENCES

AGHAJANIAN, G. K., & BLOOM, F. E. The formation of synaptogenesis junctions in developing rat brain: A quantitative electron microscopic study. *Brain Research,* 1967, *6,* 716–727.

BARONDES, S. H. Brain glycomacromolecules and interneuronal recognition. In F. O. Schmitt (Ed.), *The neurosciences, second study program.* New York: The Rockefeller University Press, 1970. (a)

BARONDES, S. H. Multiple steps in the biology of memory. In F. O. Schmitt (Ed.), *The neurosciences, second study program.* New York: The Rockefeller University Press, 1970. (b)

BENINGER, R. J., KENDALL, S. B., & VANDERWOLF, C. H. The ability of rats to discriminate their own behaviors. *Canadian Journal of Psychology/Revue Canadienne de Psychologie,* 1974, *28,* 79–91.

BLOOM, F. E. Dynamic synaptic communication: Finding the vocabulary. *Brain Research,* 1973, *62,* 299–305.

BONDAREFF, W. An intercellular substance in rat cerebral cortex: Submicroscopic distribution of ruthenium red. *Anatomical Record,* 1967, *157,* 527–536.

BRESNAHAN, E., & ROUTTENBERG, A. Memory disruption by unilateral, low-level, subseizure stimulation of the medial amygdaloid nucleus. *Physiology and Behavior,* 1972, *9,* 513–525.

BRESNAHAN, E., & ROUTTENBERG, A. Passive avoidance retention disruption as a result of unilateral, low-level medial forebrain bundle stimulation during learning. Unpublished manuscript, Evanston, Ill.: Northwestern University, 1976.

BRUNNGRABER, E. G., DEKIRMENJIAN, H., & BROWN, B. D. The distribution of protein-bound N-acetylneuraminic acid in subcellular fractions of rat brain. *Biochemical Journal*, 1967, *103*, 73–78.

COLLIER, T. J., & ROUTTENBERG, A. Entorhinal cortex: Catecholamine flourescence and Nissl staining of identical Vibratome® sections. *Brain Research*, 1977, *128*, 354–360.

COTMAN, C. W., & TAYLOR, D. Localization and characterization of concanavillan A receptors in the synaptic cleft. *Journal of Cell Biology*, 1974, *62*, 236–241.

DUNCAN, C. P. The retroactive effect of electroshock on learning. *Journal of Comparative and Physiological Psychology*, 1949, *42*, 32–44.

DUNN, A., ENTINGH, D., ENTINGH, T., GISPEN, W. H., MACHLUS, B., PERUMAL, R., REESE, H. D., & BROGAN, L. Biochemical correlates of brief behavioral experiences. In F. O. Schmitt & F. G. Worden (Eds.), *The neurosciences—Third study program*. Cambridge, Mass.: The M.I.T. Press, 1974.

EHRLICH, Y. H., & ROUTTENBERG, A. Cyclic AMP regulates phosphorylation of three protein components of rat cerebral cortex membranes for thirty minutes. *FEBS Letters*, 1974, *45*, 237–243.

FIBIGER, H. C., & PHILLIPS, A. G. Retrograde amnesia after electrical stimulation of the substantia nigra: Mediation by the dopaminergic nigroneostriatal bundle. *Brain Research*, 1976, *116*, 23–33.

GALAMBOS, R., NORTON, T. T. & FROMMER, G. P. Optic tract lesions sparing pattern vision in cats. *Experimental Neurology*, 1967, *18*, 8–25.

GARDNER, R. A., & GARDNER, B. T. Teaching sign language to a chimpanzee. *Science*, 1969, *165*, 664–672.

GLASSMAN, E. The biochemistry of learning: An evaluation of the role of RNA and protein. *Annual Review Biochemistry*, 1969, *38*, 605–646.

GLICKMAN, S. E. Deficits in avoidance learning produced by stimulation of the ascending reticular formation. *Canadian Journal of Psychology*, 1958, *12*, 97–102.

GODDARD, G. V. Amygdaloid stimulation and learning in the rat. *Journal of Comparative and Physiological Psychology*, 1964, *58*, 23–30.

HEBB, D. O. *The organization of behavior, a neuropsychological theory*. New York and London: John Wiley & Sons, Inc., Chapman & Hall, 1949.

HOLIAN, O., BRUNNGRABER, E. G., & ROUTTENBERG, A. Memory consolidation and glycoprotein metabolism: A failure to find a relationship. *Life Sciences*, 1971, *10*, 1029–1035.

HORN, G., ROSE, S. P. R., & BATESON, P. P. G. Experience and plasticity in the central nervous system. *Science*, 1973, *181*, 506–514.

HUBEL, D. H., & WIESEL, T. N. Functional architecture of macaque monkey cortex. *Proceedings of the Royal Society*, London, 1977, Series B. *198*, 1–59.

HUBEL, D. H. The architecture of macaque monkey visual cortex. Grass Foundation Lecture, Society for Neuroscience, Toronto, Ontario; 1976.

HYDÉN, H. RNA in brain cells. In G. C. Quarton, T. Melnechuk, & F. O. Schmitt (Eds.), *The neurosciences—A study program*. New York: The Rockefeller University Press, 1967.

JOHN, E. R., Chapter 6, this book, 1980.

KESNER, R. P., & DOTY, R. W. Amnesia produced in cats by local seizure activity initiated from the amygdala. *Experimental Neurology*, 1968, *21*, 58–68.

KIM, H.-J., & ROUTTENBERG, A. Retention disruption following post-trial picrotoxin injection into the substantia nigra. *Brain Research*, 1976, *113*, 620–625.

LEONARD, C. M. The prefrontal cortex of the rat. I. Cortical projections of the mediodorsal nucleus. II. Efferent connections. *Brain Research*, 1969, *12*, 321–343.

McDONOUGH, JR., J. H., & KESNER, R. P. Amnesia produced by brief electrical stimulation of amygdala or dorsal hippocampus in cats. *Journal of Comparative and Physiological Psychology*, 1971, *77*, 171–178.

MORGAN, J., & ROUTTENBERG, A. Angiotensin injected into the neostriatum after learning disrupts retention performance. *Science, 1977, 196,* 87–89.

MORGAN, D. G., & ROUTTENBERG, A. The incorporation of intracranially injected ³H-fucose into electrophoretically separated glycoproteins of the neostriatal P₂ fraction. II. The influence of passive avoidance training. *Brain Research, 180,* in press.

MOUNTCASTLE, V. B. An organizing principle for cerebral function: The unit module and the distributed system. In F. O. Schmitt & F. G. Worden (Eds.), The neurosciences—Fourth study program. Cambridge: The M.I.T. Press, 1979.

MÜLLER, G. (Ed.). *Expo Henry Moore,* Zürich: Zürcher Forum, 1976.

NORTON, T. T., GALAMBOS, R., & FROMMER, G. P., Optic tract lesions destroying pattern vision in cats. *Experimental Neurology, 1967, 18,* 26–37.

NOTTEBOHM, F., STOKES, T. M., & LEONARD, C. M., Central control of song in the canary, serinus canarius. *Journal of Comparative Neurology, 1976, 165,* 457–486.

OLDS, M. E., & OLDS, J. Emotional and associative mechanisms in rat brain. *Journal of Comparative and Physiological Psychology, 1961, 54,* 120–129.

PRECHT, W., & HOSHIDA, M., Blockage of caudate evoked inhibition of neurons in the substantia nigra by picrotoxin. *Brain Research, 1971, 32,* 229–233.

RAMBOURG, A., & LEBLOND, C. P., Electron microscope observations on the carbohydrate-rich cell coat present at the surface of cells in the rat. *Journal of Cell Biology, 1967, 32,* 27–53.

ROSENZWEIG, M. R., & BENNETT, E. L. (Eds.). *Neural mechanisms of learning and memory.* Cambridge: The M.I.T. Press, 1976.

ROUTTENBERG, A. The two-arousal hypothesis: Reticular formation and limbic system. *Psychological Review, 1968, 75,* 51–80.

ROUTTENBERG, A. Forebrain pathways of reward in Rattus norvegicus. *Journal of Comparative and Physiological Psychology, 1971, 75,* 269–276.

ROUTTENBERG, A. Memory as input-output reciprocity: An integrative neurobiological theory. *Annals of the New York Academy of Science, 1972, 193,* 159–174.

ROUTTENBERG, A., Significance of intracranial as pathway for memory consolidation. In P. B. Bradley (Ed.), *Methods in brain research.* New York: John Wiley & Sons, 1975, 453–474. (a)

ROUTTENBERG, A. Intracranial self-stimulation: Catecholamine brain pathways and memory consolidation. In J. K. Cole & T. B. Sonderegger (Eds.), *Nebraska symposium on motivation,* Lincoln, Neb.: University of Nebraska Press, 1975, 161–182. (b)

ROUTTENBERG, A. Doubts about the locus coeruleus role in learning and the phosphorylation mechanism it engages in cerebellum. *Nature, 1976, 260,* 79–80.

ROUTTENBERG, A. Anatomical localization of phosphoprotein and glycoprotein substrates of memory. *Progress in Neurobiology, 1979, 12,* 85–113.

ROUTTENBERG, A., & HOLZMAN, N. Memory disruption by electrical stimulation of substantia nigra, pars compacta. *Science, 1973, 181,* 83–86.

ROUTTENBERG, A. & EHRLICH, Y. H., Endogenous phosphorylation of four cerebral cortical membrane proteins: Role of cyclic nucleotides, ATP and divalent cations. *Brain Research, 1975, 92,* 415–430.

ROUTTENBERG, A., ZECHMEISTER, E., & BENTON, C. Hippocampal activity during memory disruption of passive avoidance by electroconvulsive shock. *Life Sciences, 1970, 9,* 909–918.

ROUTTENBERG, A., GEORGE, D., DAVIS, L. & BRUNNGRABER, E. Memory consolidation and focusylation of crude synaptosomal glycoproteins resolved by gel electrophoresis: A regional study. *Behavioral Biology, 1974, 12,* 461–475.

ROUTTENBERG, A., EHRLICH, Y. H., & RABJOHNS, R. R. Effect of a training experience on phosphorylation of a specific protein in neocortical and subcortical membrane preparations. *Federation Proceedings, 34,* No. 3, March, 1975.

SANTOS-ANDERSON, R. & ROUTTENBERG, A. Stimulation of rat medial or sulcal prefrontal cortex during passive avoidance learning differentially influences retention performance. *Brain Research,* 1976, *103,* 243–259.

SCHMITT, F. O., DEV, P. & SMITH, B. H. Electronic processing of information by brain cells. *Science,* 1976, *193,* 114–120.

SECHENOV, I. M. *Reflexes of the Brain.* Cambridge: The M.I.T. Press, 1965.

SHEPHERD, G. M. *The synaptic organization of the brain.* (2nd ed.) New York: Oxford University Press, 1979.

SKINNER, B. F. *The behavior of organisms: An experimental analysis.* New York: Appleton-Century-Crofts, 1938.

SPERRY, R. W. Brain bisection and consciousness. In J. C. Eccles (Ed.), *Brain and conscious experience.* New York: Springer-Verlag, 1966, p. 298.

SPERRY, R. W. A modified concept of consciousness. *Psychological Review,* 1969, *76,* 532–536.

SPERRY, R. W. An objective approach to subjective experience: Further explanation of a hypothesis. *Psychological Review,* 1970, *77,* 585–590.

SPERRY, R. W. Changing concepts of consciousness and free will. *Perspectives in Biology and Medicine,* 1976, *20,* 9–19.

SQUIRE, L. R. & BECKER, C. K. Inhibition of cerebral protein synthesis impairs long-term habituation. *Brain Research.* 1975, *97,* 367–372.

SQUIRE, L. R., ST. JOHN, S. & DAVIS, H. P. Inhibitors of protein synthesis and memory: Dissociation of amnesic effects and effects on adrenal steroidogenesis. *Brain Research,* 1976, *112,* 200–206.

UEDA, T., MAENO, H. & GREENGARD, P. Regulation of endogenous phosphorylation of specific proteins in synaptic membrane fractions from rat brain by adenosine 3′,5′-monophosphate. *Journal of Biological Chemistry,* 1973, *248,* 8295–8305.

UNGERSTEDT, U. Stereotaxic mapping of the monoamine pathways in the rat brain. *Acta Physiologica Scandinavica,* 1971, *Suppl. 367,* 1–48.

USDIN, E. & SNYDER, S. (Eds.). *Frontiers in catecholamine research.* New York: Pergamon Press, 1973.

VALVERDE, F. *Studies on the piriform lobe.* Cambridge: Harvard University Press, 1965.

WAUQUIER, A., & ROLLS, E. T. (Eds.). *Brain-stimulation reward.* Amsterdam and New York: North-Holland/American Elsevier, 1976.

WELKER, W. I. Analysis of sniffing of the albino rat. *Behavior,* 1964, *22,* 3–4.

6

Multipotentiality: A Statistical Theory of Brain Function—Evidence and Implications

E. Roy John

Most contemporary theories of brain function, strongly influenced by anatomical tradition, conceive of relatively discrete localization of sensory and motor function. In conditioning, new movements constitute the responses learned to the conditioned stimulus or signal for the behavior. As a logical consequence of the assumption that sensory perception is mediated by a localized sensory system and that movement is controlled by a localized motor system, most theories of learning are "connectionistic." That is, they assume that the crucial event that takes place in learning is establishment of a pathway between the nerve cells in the brain that respond to the sensory cue and the nerve cells that control the learned response (Gerard, 1961; Hebb, 1949; Konorski, 1967). Memory of what was learned is composed of the connections newly established or facilitated during learning. Remembering consists of activity in these special pathways. Responses are determined by such activity.

Many objections can be raised against such theories (John, 1972). From the psychological viewpoint, they emphasize stimulus–response learning of the sort epitomized by operant conditioning and offer little insight into observation learning, gestalts, or insightful learning. They do not deal with cognitive processes, with thinking about how to solve problems. They treat learning as a type of reflex. Many adverse effects of such learning theories can be found within psychology itself and in the educational and therapeutic practices that society has constructed based on belief in certain psychological theories.

E. Roy John • Department of Psychiatry, New York University Medical Center, New York, New York 10016. The original research reported herein was supported by grants from USPHS, National Science Foundation, and Health Research Council of the City of New York and was carried out in collaboration with many colleagues, especially Messrs. F. Bartlett, J. Grinberg-Zylberbaum, Drs. K. Killam, D. Kleinman, A. Ramos, E. Schwartz, M. Shimokochi and S. Sutton.

From the neuropsychological viewpoint, generations of physiological psychologists have tried and failed to localize these hypothetical
connections by lesion experiments, in which it is attempted to eradicate
memories by destroying specific brain regions or cutting particular
pathways (Lashley, 1950). As long as the specific sensory input pathways and final motor output pathways are spared, such experiments
have been unsuccessful. Apparent successes abound in the literature,
but careful analysis has always indicated that the apparent memory
deficit was in fact due to a loss of sensory acuity, a decrease in motivation, an inability to maintain attention, and many other unspecific
causes rather than to the destruction of a specific memory (for reviews,
see John, 1967; 1972).

Further obstacles to such theories of localization of learning, and of
localization of brain function in general, are posed by innumerable experiments that show that when massive brain damage, which normally
causes severe loss of some functional capacity when inflicted in a single
step, is inflicted in multiple stages, little or no functional deficit ensues
(Stein, Rosen, & Butters, 1974). It seems as though the first lesion in
such multiple-stage procedures constitutes a stimulus toward the reorganization of function and the compensation of deficit, so that the subsequent lesion no longer interferes with function. Such paradoxical and
contradictory effects of sparing of functions after multiple-stage lesions
have long been known and have been demonstrated with such dramatic
findings as the retention of pattern vision after the complete removal of
the striate cortex (Dru, Walker, & Walker, 1975) or the retention of
consciousness after the massive destruction of the brain stem reticular
formation (Adametz, 1959). Normally, animals subjected to these operations in one stage would be blind (in the first example) or comatose (in
the second example). Similar phenomena in everyday life are provided
by the commonplace observation of substantial or complete recovery of
function after a stroke that is initially devastating in its effects. Often,
such patients show no permanent deficits, even though the blood ves-
sels in the brain occluded by the stroke remain blocked. In one recent
dramatic example, neither hemiplegia nor hemianopsia resulted in a
mature patient after complete hemispherectomy years after a head injury suffered in childhood (Damásio, Lima, & Damásio, 1975).

Finally, neurophysiological studies providing direct observation of
the activity of single nerve cells in the brain show that the responses of a
neuron to a sensory stimulus are extremely variable and unreliable, that
many different neurons respond to any stimulus, that many different
stimuli can affect any neuron, and that neurons often discharge spontaneously for no apparent cause (for a review, see John, 1972). If re-

membering consists of firing in a pathway that stands for a memory, how is firing of a neuron due to a familiar event distinguished from firing due to a novel event distinguished from firing due to spontaneous discharge? Neurons are effusively responsive, often unresponsive or refractory, noisy, unreliable reporters.

Thus, on psychological, neuropsychological, and neurophysiological grounds, the theory of extreme localization of brain functions in general and of learning in particular seems suspect. It is highly unlikely that memory consists of the establishment or facilitation of a specific neural pathway in which firing constitutes remembering.

Impressed by these shortcomings, various theorists in the past have proposed that brain functions are not localized but are anatomically distributed. Perhaps the best known of these theorists, Karl Lashley (1931), proposed what he called the "law of equipotentiality," by which he expressed his belief that many different regions of the brain could carry out the same functions. Lashley's views, although provocative and controversial, did not prevail for several reasons. Certain experiments in contemporary neurophysiology have shown great precision in the extraction of certain features about the external environment by specific "feature extractor cells" (Hubel & Wiesel, 1962) or about the position of particular muscles by cells in the motor system (Mountcastle, 1967, pp. 393–408; Mountcastle & Powell, 1959). This impressive demonstration of functional specificity on the input and the output sides has tended to reinforce beliefs in localization of function and discreteness of informational representations. At the same time, real-life experience provides all too many examples of persons who have suffered localized brain damage due to stroke, other diseases, or injury and have shown permanent functional deficits.

A series of experiments that I have carried out during the last 25 years has led me to propose a different theory, which is called the *statistical configuration theory* (John, 1972). This new theory offers a way to reconcile the localizationist and nonlocalizationist views of brain function. Statistical theory proposes that sensory information is diffusely available to most if not all brain regions and that movements can be initiated from a wide variety of structures. Information is represented not by activity in a specific neuron or a selected pathway, but by the average temporal pattern of firing in anatomically extensive populations of neurons. The activity of any neuron—whether we consider representation of sensory information, control of movement, or participation in other functions—is significant only insofar as it contributes to the average behavior of the ensemble, to the statistical process. The difference between brain regions is not "all-or-none" qualitative mediation of specific sensory, motor, or other functions, but the "graded" quantitative representation of different functions, each with its characteristic local "signal-to-noise" ratio.

This formulation has both theoretical and practical implications. On the theoretical level, if information is anatomically distributed in a statistical fashion, then consciousness must also be distributed diffusely in a statistical fashion (John, 1976, pp. 1–50). Conscious awareness cannot be mediated by the activity of a single self-conscious "I" neuron but must arise as a consequence of a statistical, cooperative process in a population of neurons. The physical consequences of cooperative, orderly activity in neural ensembles must generate subjective experience. These consequences are not predictable from the properties of the constituent neurons of the ensemble. The whole is more than merely the sum of its parts. Subjective experience cannot, therefore, be attributed to activity in any specific cell or set of cells that monitor the activity of sensory "reporters."

Further, if experiences are the average temporal patterns of activity shared by extensive ensembles, memories of those experiences must similarly be represented by comparable shared temporal patterns in neuronal populations. That is, if a memory or a thought cannot be represented by activity in a specific pathway because activity in that pathway has no uniqueness, then memory must be represented by a process that reproduces the distinctive effects of the actual experience within the neuronal ensemble, namely, its average temporal pattern.

On the practical level, suppose that the difference between anatomical regions were in fact *quantitative*, with different relative representation of various functional systems producing different local signal-to-noise ratios for different sensory, motor, or other processes, rather than *qualitative*, so that activity of a cell in a region stands for a specific sensory event or some specific function. Then, the problem of the remediation of brain damage or dysfunction would become the question of gaining useful access to information with a poor signal-to-noise ratio in intact brain regions. This prospect is radically different from the dismaying task of building pathways that did not exist before and may be impossible to establish. Worst of all, the conviction that function is localized leads to a prophecy that is all too often self-fulfilling: "since damage has caused loss of this function, it is irremediable." With this viewpoint, treatment must be directed to reconciling and adapting the patient to the deficit, not to the recovery of function.

Let us consider the experimental data from which the statistical configuration theory was derived. In an attempt to achieve radioactive labeling of the hypothetical neural pathways established during learning, I spent several years studying the uptake of radiotracer chemicals by the brain. The substances that I used were so actively utilized in brain metabolism that it was not possible to identify specific pathways with sufficient resolution. As an alternative, some years later, one of my colleagues and I devised a functional analogue of the radioactive tracer procedure, a "physiological tracer" (John & Killam, 1959; 1960). The method was simple but effective: a flash or click at a specified repetition rate was defined as the conditioned stimulus for a new behavioral response. Electrodes chronically implanted in multiple regions of the brain (we conventionally now use 34 electrodes) monitored the electrical rhythms appearing in different anatomical structures. Electrical waves *at the frequency* of the repetitive stimulus were called *labeled rhythms*, which reflected the response to the tracer stimulus (TCS).

In the naive animal, labeled rhythms appeared in only a few brain regions when a visual TCS was presented. These regions primarily corresponded to the classical notions of the visual system. As conditioning was carried out and a new behavioral response was established to the TCS, the labeled rhythms became far more widespread, appearing in brain regions where they were previously absent or faint. Thus, as an animal learned that a stimulus was meaningful, the stimulus came to affect many portions of the brain.

We observed a fascinating phenomenon when the animal (cat) was awaiting presentation of the next signal, during the intertrial intervals. Various regions of the brain, especially so-called non-sensory-specific regions, displayed very pronounced electrical rhythms at the tracer frequency. Such activity dominated the inter-trial period during certain stages of learning. Often, the appearance of "bursts" of these frequency-specific waves was accompanied by spontaneous performance of the conditioned response, as if the cat were rehearsing its previous experiences. Many other workers observed similar phenomena. (For reviews, see John, 1961, 1967, 1971, pp. 199–283; Thatcher & John, 1977.)

When we trained cats to make two differentiated behavioral responses, $CR_1 + CR_2$, to two discriminated frequencies of tracer stimuli (for example, a light flickering at 1/sec [TCS_1] or at 5/sec [TCS_2]), another intriguing fact was noted. If the cat committed an error and performed CR_1 to TCS_2, some regions of the brain displayed frequencies as if TCS_1 were present. Conversely, if CR_2 were erroneously performed to TCS_1, electrical waves appeared at the frequency of TCS_2. Similarly, if a neutral test stimulus were introduced into the random sequence of TCS_1 and TCS_2, at a frequency between the two tracer frequencies (say, 3/sec), generalization often occurred. The conditioned response (CR) to be subsequently performed could often be predicted because the frequency of the electrical waves in some brain regions corresponded to that of TCS_1 or TCS_2, and the behavior appropriate to that tracer frequency then occurred (Bartlett, John, Shimokochi, & Kleinman, 1975; John, 1972; John, Bartlett, Shimokochi, & Kleinman, 1975; John & Killam, 1959, 1960).

Since these incongruous rhythms observed in certain brain regions actually disagreed with the frequency of the physical stimulus but corresponded to the frequency of the *absent* stimulus appropriate to the subsequent behavior, it became obvious that a portion of the electrical activity recorded from the brain while sensory stimuli were being evaluated must be released from memory. We called these released electrical processes *endogenous* or *readout* activity.

About 1960, special-purpose computers became available that were capable of constructing an accurate picture of the actual waveshape of the brief oscillation in the voltage of the EEG caused by presentation of a sensory stimulus. These computers operated by averaging a number of samples of the EEG, each sample taken during a precisely defined time interval after the occurrence of the stimulus, to extract the typical or average waveshape of the response "evoked" in the brain by the incoming information. With the use of such "average evoked response" (AER) computers, it soon became apparent that each different type of sensory signal evoked a characteristic waveshape of AER in different brain regions.

As soon as average response computers became available, we began to study the amplitudes and waveshapes of AERs produced by various signals in different brain regions, as the animals learned that each signal had a specific meaning, serving as discriminative stimuli for differentiated conditioned responses. Such studies showed that, as learning proceeded, AERs appeared in regions which showed little response to the stimulus previously, confirming our prior observations on the anatomical distribution of labeled rhythms. Of greater interest was the observation that as a signal acquired meaning, a new long latency component appeared in the AER waveshape from most structures, in the interval from 60 to 300 milliseconds after the occurrence of the stimulus. The pattern of these late components differed for stimuli with different meanings (Bartlett *et al.*, 1975; John, 1961, 1967, 1971, 1972; John *et al.*, 1975; John & Kleinman, 1975; Morrell, 1961; Thompson, Patterson, & Teyler, 1972).

Analogous to our earlier findings with labeled rhythms, we found that during behavioral errors to one TCS, the AER waveshapes from some regions resembled the waveshapes usually elicited by the other TCS, which would have been the appropriate cue for that behavior (John, Ruchkin, Leiman, Sachs, & Ahn, 1965; Ruchkin & John, 1966). In studies of differential generalization, when the cat performed one or another CR to a neutral test stimulus, the AER to the test stimulus displayed the waveshape characteristic of the response to the cue appropriate for that performance (John, Shimokochi, & Bartlett, 1969). It proved possible to write pattern recognition programs for a computer that analyzed the evoked-response waveshape elicited by each presentation of a test stimulus and to predict with very high accuracy which behavioral response would be forthcoming in each trial (Bartlett, John, Shimokochi, & Kleinman, 1975; John, 1972; John, Bartlett, Shimokochi, & Kleinman, 1973). Thus, it became apparent that the AER actually contained two different processes: a relatively short-latency ("exogenous") process reflecting the encoding of the physical sensory stimulus, and a relatively long-latency ("endogenous") process reflecting the release of information from memory that was the interpretation or meaning attributed to the incoming information. The generalization experiments, in which the test stimulus had *no* meaning, showed that the system established in brain during a learning experience could produce an accurate facsimile of a previous event, released from storage in memory. These released facsimiles, illustrated in Figure 1, could be observed in many different brain regions (John, Shimokochi, & Bartlett, 1969).

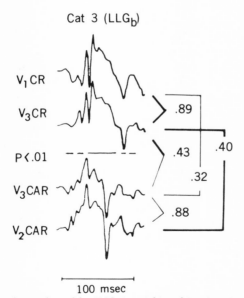

FIGURE 1.   Top: Waveshape elicited by TCS_1 in trial resulting in correct performance of CR_1. Bottom: Evoked-potential waveshape elicited by TCS_2 in trial resulting in correct performance of CR_2. Second and third waveshapes are both elicited by neutral test stimulus TCS_3. *Second* waveshape is average response to TCS_3 from trials in which differential generalization resulted in CR_1. Note similarity to *upper* waveshape. *Third* waveshape is average response to TCS_3 from differential generalization trials resulting in CR_2. Note similarity to *lower* waveshape. Numbers at right are correlation coefficients between indicated waves. (Data from John, Shimokochi, & Bartlett, 1969.)

An important line of closely related evidence comes from studies primarily carried out on human subjects and is particularly important in assessing the likelihood that these released electrical patterns actually correspond to the activation of specific memories, because it has been possible to establish unequivocally that there is a subjective correlate to the appearance of these released potentials. These studies show that when an *expected* event does not occur, a cerebral potential appears at a latency similar to that of potentials usually evoked by the expected stimulus. Evoked potentials elicited in man by absent events have been reported (Barlow, Morrell, & Morrell, 1967; Klinke, Fruhstorfer, & Finkenzeller, 1968; Picton, Hillyard, & Galambos, 1973; Riggs & Whittle, 1967; Rusinov, 1959; Sutton, Tueting, Zubin, & John, 1967; Weinberg, Grey-Walter, & Crow, 1970; Weinberg, Grey-Walter, Cooper, & Aldridge, 1974). Similar findings in the cat were reported by John (1963, pp. 243–282). These cerebral events, termed *readout* or *emitted* potentials, have been interpreted by Weinberg *et al.* (1974) to reflect the generation of processes corresponding to the memory of past or imaginary stimuli.

After reaching the conclusion that both exogenous and endogenous processes were reflected in the evoked response, we devised methods to separate and quantify the relative amounts of each of these processes that contributed to the AERs recorded from different places in a brain (Bartlett & John, 1973). Since our cats made occasional errors, AERs were available from trials in which either of the two behaviors, CR_1 or CR_2, was performed to each of three stimuli (TCS_1, TCS_2, or the neutral generalization stimulus). Thus, AERs were available for a total of six different stimulus–response contingencies. Sets of simultaneous equations were constructed in which AERs obtained from the same brain structure under different contingencies were added and subtracted like terms in algebraic equations. Carrying out these simple operations in a computer, it was possible to solve the sets of equations for the exogenous processes representing the different stimuli and the endogenous processes representing the different meanings attributed to the stimuli. These solutions consisted of actual pictures of waveshapes that were the residuals obtained as a result of the algebraic procedures carried out on the AERs. Since each stimulus and each response could be included in several different, independent equations, it was possible to get several independent examples of each of these residuals. The accuracy of the computation could then be checked by quantifying the similarity between residuals representing the same process. This quantification was accomplished by computing the so-called correlation coefficient, which is the most commonly used method to assess similarity.

This technique was successful in revealing the existence of processes within the AER that could be separated to provide reproducible

CAT I8 L LG b

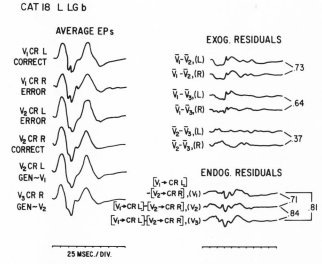

25 MSEC./DIV.

FIGURE 2. Lower right: Endogenous Residuals. The three waveshapes illustrated below this heading represent three independent estimates of the same endogenous processes. *Independent* means obtained by performing the same algebraic operations on three different bodies of data. Ignore labels to left of waves; numbers to right are correlation coefficients. (Data from Bartlett & John, 1973.)

examples of relatively "pure" exogenous and endogenous processes. Three pictures of the same endogenous process, obtained by calculations performed on three independent bodies of data, are shown in Figure 2.

Once we had ascertained the feasibility of separating exogenous and endogenous processes in a reproducible fashion, this operation was carried out on thousands of AERs computed from many different anatomical structures in dozens of cats. The contributions of the exogenous and endogenous process to the AERs in a particular anatomical region were averaged across all the different examples available from all the cats in our study, to provide a value characteristic of that region of the brain. The average contribution of endogenous processes was then plotted versus the average contribution of exogenous processes to the AER of each structure, separately for data from visual and auditory signals (Bartlett & John, 1973; Bartlett *et al.*, 1975). The final result of this computation is shown in Figure 3.

It was remarkable that these points fell along a straight line if semilogarithmic graph paper was used. This finding showed that the logarithm of the endogenous contribution ("memory") to the evoked potential in a brain region was proportional to the amount of the

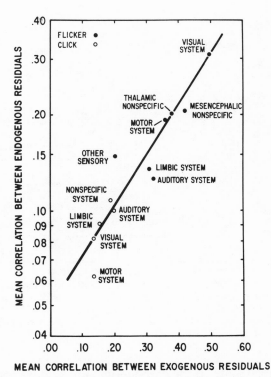

FIGURE 3.   Average contribution of endogenous processes plotted versus average contribution of exogenous processes to different systems. Average was computed across different anatomical structures within each of these functional systems and across many cats for each structure. Open circles are data from experiments using auditory cues; closed circles are data from experiments using visual cues. (Data from Bartlett, John, Shimokochi, & Kleinman, 1975.)

exogenous contribution ("sensation") to the activity of that region. This observation has many implications. *First,* note that all regions for which data were available displayed measurable contributions from exogenous processes. This finding shows that specific information about different sensory stimuli is available in all these various brain regions.

Second, note that all regions displayed endogenous processes. The memory of these different events influenced the activity of all these various structures.

Thus, localizationist theories are not accurate. Were they accurate, these processes would be present in only one or a few structures and not in the others. Conversely, the theory of equipotentiality is also wrong. Were it accurate, all brain regions would have the same exogenous or endogenous influences. What the data tell us is that *both* positions are qualitatively correct but quantitatively wrong. Information about sensory events is very widely distributed throughout the brain, but the signal-to-noise ratio varies by more than a factor of 20. Memories about previous sensory experiences are also very widely distributed, but the signal-to-noise ratio varies by a factor of about 10. Presumably, under normal circumstances, the brain relies primarily on the information available from regions with the highest signal-to-noise ratio and does not make use of the same information available elsewhere with poorer reliability. The term *multipotentiality* is a good way to describe this property of the brain. It suggests that any region may contribute to the mediation of a diversity of functions but does not imply that different regions are functionally equivalent.

Third, note that the points representing auditory data fall on the same line as those representing visual data—there is a general relationship between sensation and memory represented by the *slope* of that line. The involvement of a region in memory about an event is proportional to its involvement in representing the actual event, and the slope of the line shows that the constant of proportionality is the same whether the event be in the visual or the auditory modality. This finding makes excellent intuitive sense. It suggests that for the neurons in a region to participate in the memory of input to the brain, they must be affected by that input. Further, the more they are affected, the more they will participate. Most theories about the *chemistry* of memory storage agree that there must be an early phase, mediated by reverberatory activity in neural networks, that leads to a later, stable phase after "consolidation" of memory, and that somehow the chemical compounds involved in long-term storage must be the result of processes activated during the early phase (John, 1967; 1970, pp. 335–342). Thus, it would seem that the lawful relationship revealed by the data is probably a reflection of the influence of the experience on the chemical reactions mediating the storage of the memory.

It was necessary to rule out the possibility that these widely distributed AER phenomena arose from the electrical fields generated by more localized neuronal activity. Although this possibility could be excluded on several bases, it was desirable to examine the actual neuronal activity associated with these processes. Accordingly, my colleagues and I devised a chronically implanted movable microelectrode that could be moved very slowly through the brain of a cat, while the animal was performing these various behavioral responses, and permit us to observe the effects of these stimuli on the activity of simple neurons and small groups of neurons. After sufficient study of cells in a particular region, the microelectrode could be moved to a deeper region. Thus, it was possible to construct maps of the neuronal activity correlated with the AERs in many different electrode positions in the same animal. These direct observations showed that the neuronal activity was indeed widespread, confirming the AER findings. As expected, every cell we observed showed highly variable responses to single presentations of any stimulus, much more reliable average responses to repeated stimulation, different average firing patterns to different stimuli, and a high level of spontaneous activity. We found cells in different brain regions that showed very similar average firing patterns to the same stimulus. A few cells were found that displayed a facsimile property, producing the same average firing patterns during generalization to a novel stimulus as normally shown during correct response to the conditioned stimulus (John & Morgades, 1969b,c; Ramos, Schwartz, & John, 1976c). As our methods became more precise, we succeeded in showing that there seemed to be two different classes of cells: "stable" cells, which primarily participated in exogenous processes, and "plastic" cells, which participated in endogenous processes (Ramos, Schwartz, & John, 1976a,b,c). The two kinds of cells were found intimately interrelated in every region we studied. The results of our studies of neuronal activity supported the statistical formulation. The information appeared to be represented by the average temporal pattern of firing in the population of neurons, and not by the reliable all-or-none firing of any single neuron or activity in a special pathway built by learning and unique to some past experience.

Thus, a great deal of evidence has been gathered that is compatible with the statistical theory, all of it based on inferences drawn from the observation of correlations between electrophysiological phenomena and behavior. Those observed correlations did not validate the theory; they simply were compatible with it. I realized that a far more direct evaluation of the theory could be accomplished. It was possible to construct patterns of electrical pulses that would simulate certain aspects of the observed electrophysiological activity and to use these patterns to stimulate different brain regions directly. Obviously, such stimulation could at best produce average temporal patterns of activity within masses of neurons that simulated features of the observed activity but that could not possibly produce selective activation of precisely the neural pathways postulated by connectionistic theory to mediate performance of the conditioned response. To rule out this possibility even more unequivocally, it was decided to use two different electrical patterns for the stimulation of each region, each pattern simulating the activity observed during the performance of one of two differential conditioned responses. Accordingly, cats were trained to perform CR_1 or CR_2 to two different visual tracer stimuli, $VTCS_1$ and $VTCS_2$. They were next trained to perform the same two responses to two different auditory tracer stimuli, $ATCS_1$ and $ATCS_2$. $VTCS_1$ and $ATCS_1$ were flashes and clicks at repetition rate 1, while $VTCS_2$ and $ATCS_2$ were flashes and clicks at repetition rate 2. After these discriminations had been highly overtrained in each cat, different brain structures were stimulated with bursts of high-frequency electrical pulses at either repetition rate 1 or repetition rate 2. In almost every structure examined, examples were obtained of the *immediate* performance of the conditioned response appropriate to the repetition rate, as soon as the electrical stimuli were tested. The most impressive generalization from peripheral to central input was obtained by the use of electrical stimulation of the reticular formation, which produced uniformly high levels of accurate discrimination (John & Kleinman, 1975).

The cats were next trained to high accuracy levels using brain stimuli to any one of several regions. When this training had been achieved, conflict studies were carried out in which brain stimuli at one repetition rate were delivered concurrently with visual or auditory stimuli at the contradictory second repetition rate. Parametric studies were carried out exploring the effects of systematically increasing the current intensity of the brain stimuli. In every cat, we found that as the strength of the electrical stimulation was increased (equivalent to increasing the signal-to-noise ratio in the neuronal population), the brain stimulus controlled the behavioral outcome almost completely. However, this was uniformly true only for the reticular formation, while other brain regions showed varying effectiveness (Kleinman & John, 1975).

Finally, electrical stimuli were divided anatomically, so that part of the pattern was delivered to one brain region while the remainder of the pattern was delivered to another brain region or via visual or auditory input. In most of such combinations, the cat performed appropriately to the timing of the total signal delivered to the brain, in spite of the fact that different parts of the signal were delivered to different brain regions (John & Kleinman, 1975). Electrophysiological studies made during these "distributed input" experiments suggested that the integration was accomplished by a system including the cortex and the non-sensory-specific thalamus (John, 1976).

Thus, electrophysiological studies of labeled rhythms and AERs produced by tracer stimuli led to the conclusion that learning is mediated by an anatomically distributed neuronal network, which has the capability of reproducing a facsimile of the response usually caused by an absent but familiar cue. Quantitative studies of these endogenous facsimile processes showed that they, as well as exogenous processes directly reflecting the sensory stimulus, were present in a constant proportion in different brain regions, but with differing absolute amounts from region to region. Studies of cellular activity led to the conclusion that the statistical properties of cell firing in extensive neuronal populations represent both the exogenous and the endogenous processes. This conclusion supported the formulation of a statistical theory of information processing by the brain and led to the prediction (1) that brain stimulation could elicit previously learned behavior from many regions with differential behavior determined by the temporal pattern but not the region stimulated; (2) that such brain stimuli could preempt decision when contradicting sensory cues, if the signal-to-noise ratio were sufficiently high and, (3) that anatomically separated portions of a temporal pattern would be functionally integrated. All of these predictions were strongly confirmed by the evidence.

Science proceeds by the gathering of observations, which lead to the formulation of a theory, which in turn leads to predictions of how to control the observed phenomena. If such control is achieved, the theory is supported, not proved, because today's accepted theory may be demolished by tomorrow's observation. Nonetheless, the findings described in this paper strongly support statistical theory and are difficult if not impossible to reconcile with connectionistic theory and with theories postulating strict localization of function.

These findings have certain practical implications beyond those discussed in the first portion of this paper. The problems of remediation of brain damage appear in quite a different light from the viewpoint of statistical theory. The crucial problem in rehabilitation after brain damage becomes how to gain functional access to essential information that is present in intact regions of the brain but with a signal-to-noise ratio below the threshold that the brain has *learned* to utilize. Remediation of "cortical" or central" sensory deficits, motor impairment, and possibly cognitive deficits in learning disability, retardation, and senile deterioration may be within our means to achieve if the proper use is made of conditioning, biofeedback, pharmacotherapy, or even direct stimulation techniques. The possible reversibility of every type of brain dysfunction should be systematically challenged with such approaches, whether the dysfunction be congenital, traumatic, disease, or metabolic in etiology.

Equally important, these findings and a host of others produced by other researchers in the field show clearly that sensory, perceptual, and cognitive processes can be measured from the electrophysiological activity produced by the brain. Many of the findings described herein have their counterpart in EEG or AER phenomena that have been found in human subjects. A vast body of literature, some of it from our laboratories, shows that AERs in humans reflect not only neuropathology but sensory acuity, perceptual constancies, expectations about anticipated events, and cognitive operations performed upon stimuli (Regan, 1972; John, 1977). For example, Grinberg-Zylberbaum and I have found that the AER waveshape recorded from certain regions of the scalp changes when the same vertical line is perceived as the letter *l* or the number *1*. In other regions, a characteristic waveshape can be observed when a particular letter of the alphabet is presented, whether the letter be large or small (John, 1976).

We realized the potential diagnostic value of the quantitative, differential profiles of brain function that could be provided by such measurements. Under the sponsorship of the RANN (Research Applied to National Needs) program of the National Science Foundation, my colleagues and I undertook to develop an automatic computer technology for the rapid evaluation of sensory, perceptual, and cognitive functions as reflected in the electrophysiological test battery, which is computer-administered and provides over 285,000 measures elicited during a wide variety of conditions devised to challenge different aspects of brain function. These measures have already been shown to be sensitive indicators of abnormality in various forms of neuropathology, senile deterioration, and learning disability (John, Karmel, Prichep, Ahn, & John, 1977; pp. 291–337; John, 1977; John, Karmel, Corning, Easton, Brown, Ahn, John, Harmony, Prichep, Toro, Gerson, Bartlett, Thatcher, Kaye, Valdes, & Schwartz, 1977; John, Prichep, Ahn, Brown, Easton, Karmel, Thatcher, & Toro, 1978, pp. 585–592; Karmel, Kaye, & John, 1978, pp. 141–198). We expect the differential diagnostic profiles provided by this technique to be extremely useful in selecting and evaluating the therapeutic measures used with the individual patient.

REFERENCES

ADAMETZ, J. H. Rate of recovery of functioning in cats with rostral reticular lesions. *Journal of Neurosurgery*, 1959, *16*, 85–97.

BARLOW, J. S., MORRELL, L., & MORRELL, F. Some observations on evoked responses in relation to temporal conditioning to paired stimuli in man. *Proceedings International Colloquium on Mechanisms of Orienting Reactions in Man*. Bratislava-Smolence: Slovak Academy of Sciences, 1967.

BARTLETT, F., & JOHN, E. R. Equipotentiality quantified: The anatomical distribution of the engram. *Science*, 1973, *181*, 764–767.

BARTLETT, F., JOHN, E. R., SHIMOKOCHI, M., & KLEINMAN, D. Electrophysiological signs of readout from memory. II: Computer classification of single evoked potential waveshapes. *Behavioral Biology*, 1975, *14*, 409–449.

DAMÁSIO, A. R., LIMA, A., & DAMÁSIO, H. Nervous function after right hemispherectomy. *Neurology*, 1975, *24*, 89–93.

DRU, D., WALKER, J. P., & WALKER, J. B. Self-produced locomotion restores visual capacity after striate lesions. *Science*, 1975, *187*, 265–266.

GERARD, R. W. The fixation of experience. In J. F. Delasfresnaye, A. Fessard, R. W.

Gerard, & J. Konorski (Eds.), *CIOMS symposium on brain mechanisms and learning.* Oxford: Blackwell, 1961.

Hebb, D. O. *The organization of behabior: Neuropsychological theory.* New York: Wiley, 1949.

Hubel, D. H., & Wiesel, T. N. Receptive fields, binocular interaction and functional architecture in the cat's visual cortex. *Journal of Physiology* (London), 1962, *160*, 106–154.

John, E. R. Higher nervous functions: Brain functions and learning. *Annual Review of Physiology,* 1961, *23*, 451–484.

John, E. R. Neural mechanisms of decision making. In W. S. Fields & W. Abbot (Eds.), *Information storage and neural control.* Springfield, Ill.: Charles C Thomas, 1963.

John, E. R. *Mechanisms of memory.* New York: Academic Press, 1967.

John, E. R. Summary: Symposium on memory transfer AAAS. In W. L. Byrne (Ed.), *Molecular approaches to learning and memory.* New York: Academic, 1970.

John, E. R. Brain mechanisms of memory. In J. McGaugh (Ed.), *Psychobiology.* New York: Academic, 1971.

John, E. R. Switchboard versus statistical theories of learning and memory. *Science,* 1972, *177*, 850–864.

John, E. R. A model of consciousness. In G. Schwartz & D. Shapiro (Eds.), *Consciousness and self regulation: Advances in research,* Vol. 1. New York: Plenum, 1976.

John, E. R. *Functional neuroscience.* Vol. 2: *Neurometrics: Clinical applications of quantitative electrophysiology.* Hillsdale, N.J.: Erlbaum, 1977.

John, E. R., & Killam, K. F. Electrophysiological correlates of avoidance conditioning in the cat. *Journal of Pharmacology and Experimental Therapeutics,* 1959, *125*, 252.

John, E. R., & Killam, K. F. Electrophysiological correlates of differential approach–avoidance conditioning in the cat. *Journal of Nervous and Mental Disease,* 1960, *131*, 183.

John, E. R., & Kleinman, D. Stimulus generalization between differentiated visual, auditory and central stimuli. *Journal Neurophysiology,* 1975, *38*, 105–1034.

John, E. R., & Morgades, P. P. A technique for the chronic implantation of multiple movable micro-electrodes. *Electroencephalography and Clinical Neurophysiology,* 1969, *27*, 205–208. (a)

John, E. R., & Morgades, P. P. Patterns and anatomical distribution of evoked potentials and multiple unit activity elicited by conditioned stimuli in trained cats. *Communications in Behavioral Biology,* 1969, *3*, 181–207. (b)

John, E. R., & Morgades, P. P. Neural correlates of conditioned responses studies with multiple chronically implanted moving microelectrodes. *Experimental Neurology,* 1969, *23*, 412–425. (c)

John, E. R., Ruchkin, D. S., Leiman, A., Sachs, E., & Ahn, H. Electrophysiological studies of generalization using both peripheral and central conditioned stimuli. *Proceedings of 23rd International Congress of Physiologic Sciences* (Tokyo), 1965, *4*, 618–627.

John, E. R., Shimokochi, M., & Bartlett, F. Neural readout from memory during generalization. *Science,* 1969, *164*, 1519–1521.

John, E. R., Bartlett, F., Shimokochi, M., & Kleinman, D. Neural readout from memory. *Journal of Neurophysiology,* 1973, *36*, 893–924.

John, E. R., Bartlett, F., Shimokochi, M., & Kleinman, D. Electrophysiological signs of the readout from memory. *Behavioral Biology,* 1975, *14*, 247–282.

John, E. R., Karmel, B. Z., Corning, W. C., Easton, P., Brown, D., Ahn, H., John, M., Harmony, T., Prichep, L., Toro, A., Gerson, I., Bartlett, F., Thatcher, R., Kaye, H., Valdes, P., & Schwartz, E. Neurometrics: Numerical taxonomy identifies different profiles of brain functions within groups of behaviorally similar people. *Science,* 1977, *196*, 1393–1410.

John, E. R., Karmel, B. Z., Prichep, L., Ahn, H., & John, M. Neurometrics applied to the quantitative electrophysiological measurement of organic brain dysfunction in children. In C. Shagass (Ed.), *Psychopathology and brain dysfunction.* New York: Raven Press, 1977.

JOHN, E. R., PRICHEP, L., AHN, H., BROWN, D., EASTON, P., KARMEL, B., THATCHER, R., & TORO, A. Neurometrics: Quantitative electrophysiological analysis for diagnosis of learning disabilities and other brain dysfunctions. In D. Otto (Ed.), *Multidisciplinary perspectives in event-related brain potential research.* Washington, D.C.: U.S. Government Printing Office, EPA 600/9–77–043, 1978.

KARMEL, B. Z., KAYE, H., & JOHN, E. R. Developmental neurometrics: The use of quantitative analysis of brain electrical activity to probe mental function throughout life-span. In A. Collins (Ed.), *Minnesota symposia on child psychology: Vol. 11.* Hillsdale, N.J.: Erlbaum, 1978.

KLEINMAN, D., & JOHN, E. R. Contradiction of auditory and visual information by brain stimulation. *Science,* 1975, *187,* 271–273.

KLINKE, R., FRUHSTORFER, H., & FINKENZELLER, P. Evoked responses as a function of external and stored information. *Electroencephalography and Clinical Neurophysiology,* 1968, *26,* 216–219.

KONORSKI, J. *Integrative activity of the brain.* Chicago: University of Chicago Press, 1967.

LASHLEY, K. Mass action in cerebral function. *Science,* 1931, *73,* 245–254.

LASHLEY, K. In search of the engram. *Symposium of the Society of Experimental Biology,* 1950, *4,* 454–482.

MORRELL, F. Effect of anodal polarization on the firing pattern of single cortical cells. *Annals of New York Academy of Science,* 1961, *92,* 860–876.

MOUNTCASTLE, V. B. The problem of sensing and the neural coding of sensory events. In G. C. Quarton, T. Melnechuk, & F. O. Schmitt (Eds.), *The neurosciences.* New York: The Rockefeller University Press, 1967.

MOUNTCASTLE, V. B., & POWELL, T. P. S. Neural mechanisms subserving cutaneous sensibility, with special reference to the role of afferent inhibition in sensory perception and discrimination. *Bulletin Johns Hopkins Hospital,* 1959, *105,* 201–232.

OTERO, G., HARMONY, T., & RICARDO, J. Polarity coincidence correlation coefficient and signal energy ratio of ongoing EEG activity. II: Brain tumors. *Activitas Nervosa Superior,* 1975, *17,* 120–126.(a)

OTERO, G., HARMONY, T., & RICARDO, J. Polarity coincidence correlation coefficient and signal energy ratio of ongoing EEG activity. III: Cerebral vascular lesions. *Activitas Nervosa Superior,* 1975, *17,* 127–130. (b)

PICTON, T. W., HILLYARD, S. A., & GALAMBOS, R. Cortical evoked responses to omitted stimuli. In M. N. Livanov (Ed.)., *Major problems of brain electrophysiology.* Moscow: USSR Academy of Sciences, 1973.

RAMOS, A., SCHWARTZ, E., & JOHN, E. R. An examination of the participation of neurons in readout from memory. *Brain Research Bulletin,* 1976, *1,* 77–86. (a)

RAMOS, A., SCHWARTZ, E., & JOHN, E. R. Evoked potential-unit relationships in behaving cats. *Brain Research Bulletin,* 1976, *1,* 69–75. (b)

RAMOS, A., SCHWARTZ, E., & JOHN, E. R. Stable and plastic unit discharge patterns during behavioral generalization. *Science,* 1976, *192,* 393–396. (c)

REGAN, D. *Evoked potentials in psychology, sensory physiology and clinical medicine.* New York: Wiley, 1972.

RIGGS, L. A., & WHITTLE, P. Human occipital and retinal potentials evoked by subjectively faded visual stimuli. *Vision Research,* 1967, *7,* 441–451.

RUCHKIN, D. S., & JOHN, E. R. Evoked potential correlates of generalization. *Science,* 1966, *153,* 209–211.

RUSINOV, V. S. Electroencephalographic studies in conditioned reflex formation in man. In

M. A. B. Brazier (Ed.), *The central nervous system and behavior.* New York: Josiah Macy, Jr. Foundation, 1959.

Schwartz, E., Ramos, A., & John, E. R. Single cell activity in chronic unit recording: a quantitative study of the unit amplitude spectrum. *Brain Research Bulletin,* 1976, *1,* 57-68.

Stein, D. G., Rosen, J. J., & Butters, N. (Eds.). *Plasticity and recovery of function in the central nervous sytem.* New York: Academic, 1974.

Sutton, S., Tueting, P., Zubin, J., & John, E. R. Information delivery and the sensory evoked potential. *Science,* 1967, *155,* 1436-1439.

Thompson, R. F., Patterson, M. M., & Teyler, T. J. The neurophysiology of learning. *Annual Review of Psychology,* 1972, *23,* 73-104.

Thatcher, R., & John, E. R. *Functional neuroscience,* Vol. 1: *Foundations of cognitive processes.* Hillsdale, N.J.: Erlbaum, 1977.

Weinberg, H., Grey-Walter, W., Cooper, R., & Aldridge, V. J. Emitted cerebral events. *Electroencephalography and Clinical Neurophysiology,* 1974, *36,* 449-456.

Weinberg, H., Grey-Walter, W., & Crow, H. H. Intracerebral events in humans related to real and imaginary stimuli. *Electroencephalography and Clinical Neurophysiology,* 1970, *29,* 1-9.

7

Genetic Factors in EEG, Sleep, and Evoked Potentials

Monte S. Buchsbaum and Elliot S. Gershon

1. Introduction

Are mental characteristics or their disorders inherited? An increasing body of data on adoptees, twins, and families argues convincingly that genetic effects are important in the transmission of neurophysiological variables, psychiatric illness, and personality traits. The pertinent question for neuroscientists has become: What is inherited, and through what kinds of mechanisms do genetic and experiential factors interact in the central nervous system?

The genetics of both structural and functional characteristics of the CNS are especially difficult to study in man. Not only does the CNS geneticist face the usual problems in human genetics (e.g., long generation time, impossibility of experimental crosses), but the CNS, unlike fingerprints or blood enzymes, cannot be directly observed or biopsied. Autopsy material from families tested on behavioral measures before death is impractical, and detection of subtle wiring errors might require experimental neuroanatomic techniques inapplicable to autopsy material. Recording of electrical activity of the brain from the scalp, however, may be an important approach to the mechanisms behind behavior-genetic effects in man. EEG can be recorded completely noninvasively and can reflect alertness, hemispheric asymmetry, and levels of arousal or sleep. Further, with the advent of computer average-evoked-potential techniques, specific sensory events can be studied and possibly localized. The supposition that EEG, sleep, and evoked potential techniques might be useful in genetic studies is supported by the preliminary findings discussed in this article; we hope to stimulate psychophysiologists and geneticists to more intense future collaboration by the strengths and peculiarities of these reports. We have limited this

Monte S. Buchsbaum and Elliot S. Gershon • Biological Psychiatry Branch, Division of Clinical and Behavioral Research, National Institute of Mental Health, Bethesda, Maryland 20205.

article to direct studies in man of central neurophysiological variables; interactions of these variables with biochemical characteristics, personality, and psychiatric disorders have been reviewed elsewhere (e.g., Rosenthal, 1970; Fuller & Thompson, 1960).

2. The Electroencephalogram—Resting and Response Measures

2.1. Visual Observations of Twin EEG

Spontaneous EEG in a resting subject shows a complex mixture of frequency ranging from very slow (1–2 Hz) to fast (30 Hz and above); certain frequencies, especially those in the 8- to 12-Hz range (alpha), dominate at irregular intervals, almost replacing other frequencies. Individual differences in predominant frequencies are quite apparent on visual inspection and appear to be stable individual characteristics. The remarkable similarity of spontaneous EEG in monozygotic (MZ) twins was among the earliest features of the EEG to be noted by the Davises (1936) and Loomis, Harvey, and Hobart (1936a,b). Visual inspection suggested an analogy to the facial features of identical twins to other investigators (Lennox, Gibbs, & Gibbs, 1945). The pronounced similarity of EEG findings was also found in a unique study of eight pairs of identical twins reared apart (Juel-Nielsen & Harvald, 1958).

2.2. Alpha Waves

One of the main features giving MZ twins such great similarity in the previously mentioned studies was the prominence of alpha rhythm. Individuals vary greatly in the amount of time spent producing alpha, with some individual tracings showing little else and other individuals showing almost a complete lack. Alpha prominence appears to be quite a stable individual characteristic. Studying 10 subjects, 2–7 days apart, Fenton and Scotton (1967) reported test–retest reliabilities of 0.91 for percentage of recording time taken up by all waves in the alpha frequency range and 0.91 for their mean amplitude. Vogel (1970) noted in a review of population studies that from 6% to 11% of normal individuals lacked alpha rhythms even with eyes closed. Family studies of parents and siblings of individuals lacking alpha revealed a striking bimodal distribution of percent-time alpha; genetic analysis suggested a simple autosomal dominant mode of inheritance (Vogel, 1970).

The alpha rhythm may also vary in its precise frequency and frequency width. Digital spectral estimates of power at very narrow intervals such as 0.1 Hz often show a band only 0.2–0.4 Hz wide containing power 10 times the level in any other single power estimates. The precise alpha frequency peak may be a stable individual characteristic, although some individuals vary their alpha peak frequency from second to second. Hume (1973) found a higher MZ intraclass correlation (0.75) for mean alpha frequency than for any other EEG or autonomic measure; MZ/DZ (dizygotic) intraclass correlation coefficients were also significantly different. Davis and Davis (1936) noted the appearance of 13-Hz alpha, the highest frequency they ever observed, in both members of a pair of twins. Raney (1939) found alpha frequency to have higher MZ pair correlations ($r = 0.91$) than percent alpha (in some leads as low as $r = 0.67$). Examination of frequency spectra (see below in Section 2.5 for explanatory comments) in MZ twins illustrated by Lykken, Tellegen, and Thorkelson (1974) and Dumermuth (1968) suggests that not only the dominant frequency but also the width and shape of the spectral profile within the alpha frequency bands are extraordinarily similar. Peak alpha frequency and kurtosis (or peakedness) of the spectrum alpha peak are also highly heritable (Lykken *et al.*, 1974).

It should be noted that Lykken *et al.* (1974) apparently calculated their spectral estimates on a very long epoch of 3 min. The details of the shape of the spectrum in the vicinity of the alpha peak may be somewhat distorted by the use of such a long epoch since the alpha frequency is not precisely fixed. Further distortions may arise from each abrupt transition into or out of alpha, clearly indicating that EEG's statistical properties vary over time and thus violating the assumption of "stationarity" implicit in spectral analysis. The broad alpha spectral peak may be produced by the operation of several alpha generators of different frequency, a single but wandering alpha pacemaker, or transitional processes, but these three possibilities are not resolved with long epoch spectra. The stability of the alpha pace or the number of pacers might both be genetic characters, which, if assessed separately by tabulating results of spectra or zero-crossing analysis of short epochs (see Section 2.5), might yield indexes with some heritability in DZ twins.

Using an analogue band-pass filter with half-amplitude frequency range of 7.5–13.5 Hz, Young, Lader, and Fenton (1972) estimated alpha power in 17 MZ and 15 DZ adult twins. While MZ twin pairs had an intraclass correlation of 0.52 ($p < 0.05$), the DZ correlation of 0.29 was not significantly different. Percent time alpha and mean alpha amplitude also showed significant intraclass correlations in MZ twins but no significant MZ–DZ differences. These EEG samples were collected during an auditory evoked-response recording procedure, however, so alpha may have been partially blocked. More striking alpha heritability was shown in the study of Lykken *et al.* (1974). They measured alpha as a proportion of total EEG power within a 3-Hz band centered on the peak frequency between 7 and 14 Hz, and they found intraclass correlations of 0.82 in MZ twins and −0.20 in DZ twins (difference, $p < 0.0001$).

2.3. Alpha Blocking

The alpha wave pattern is diminished or even completely blocked by sudden sensory stimuli, perhaps via ascending reticular activating system influences on underlying pacemakers in the thalamus (Lindsley & Wicke, 1974). Brief light flashes are commonly used experimentally to study alpha blocking. In normal adults, the alpha rhythm is initially diminished to less than 50% amplitude in about 3 cycles (250–300 msec) and remains at less than 50% amplitude for 6–12 cycles (0.6–1.2 sec; Milstein, Stevens, & Sachdev, 1969). With successive trials, the latency of blocking increases and the duration of blocking decreases (Milstein *et al.*, 1969) frequently reaching a stable level after 20–30 trials (Fenton & Scotton, 1967). Individuals are consistent in being slow or fast alpha blockers; Fenton and Scotton reported test–retest correlations of 0.69 and 0.96 for mean blocking duration for the 1st through 25th and the 26th through 60th flash stimuli, respectively (delivered only when a prominent alpha rhythm was present). MZ twins have more similar durations of alpha blocking (intraclass correlation 0.58 over all 60 trials) than DZ twins ($r = 0.30$) or unrelated individuals ($r = 0.19$), although comparison between MZ and DZ twins did not reach statistical significance (Young & Fenton, 1971). Examining the first 5 or the last 35 trials separately yielded the highest MZ correlations, and lumping the first 25 trials produced the lowest, suggesting that habituation rate might be heritable; this was not tested, however.

2.4. Beta Waves

These low-amplitude ($1–10\mu V$), fast (13–30 Hz) waves appear in alerted subjects (e.g., when alpha is blocked) and those individuals with low percent time alpha. Using frequency spectra, Lykken *et al.* (1974) found the proportion of power in the beta band (13–19.9 Hz) to be extremely similar in MZ twins (intraclass $r = 0.82$) and much less similar in DZ twins ($r = 0.15$). Among all of the EEG frequency bands studied by Young *et al.* (1972), only beta (13.5–26 Hz) showed a statistically significant difference between the intraclass correlations in MZ twins (0.90) and DZ twins (0.56). This finding may be due to the greater stability of beta amplitude across time within subjects. Beta amplitude (12.5–17.5 Hz as analyzed with analogue filters by Matousek & Petersen, 1973) showed a lower coefficient of variation over consecutive 10-sec epochs (0.11–0.15), whereas, as expected, alpha showed the highest (up to 0.28). Further, Young *et al.* (1972) collected their EEG sample during auditory stimulation, which may have blocked alpha, perhaps minimizing expression of the alpha phenotype.

Vogel (1970) regards the appearance of regular 16- to 19-Hz waves maximal at the occiput and blocked by eye opening as being a quick variant of alpha. This infrequent finding (approximately 0.5% of adults) appeared to show an autosomal dominant mode of inheritance in the examination of EEG pedigrees in the families of 22 quick alpha probands. Power spectra in Dumermuth's (1968) twins indicate that where a distinct beta peak appears, it appears at almost exactly twice the frequency of the alpha activity in both twins, suggesting a relationship to underlying alpha pacemakers.

2.5. Complete Power Spectra

Spectral analysis techniques allow us to calculate the variance in a signal such as the EEG for specific frequencies such as alpha or beta. The numerical techniques used to estimate the variance at each frequency step are called *power spectral techniques* since the variance at each frequency is equivalent to the electrical concept of power (voltage squared is proportional to power). These techniques free the EEG investigator from having to make visual subjective judgments on the basis of examining the paper record. Normally, a series of power estimates from low to high frequencies, often in frequency steps of 1 Hz or less, are calculated over short epochs of EEG (1–10 sec). Thus, a profile of power content at each frequency is generated.

Comparison of EEG power spectra in MZ twins (Dumermuth, 1968; Lykken *et al.*, 1974) makes it apparent why EEG similarities were noted so easily by early investigators depending only on visual inspection; the spectra in twins appear as similar as their facial profiles. Quantitative analysis shows MZ twins' spectra to resemble each other 96% as much as an individual resembles his own on another session. In contrast, DZ twins seemed no more similar than unrelated pairs. Similarly, for power estimates of delta, theta, alpha, and beta, intraclass correlations in DZ pairs were negligible (−0.01, −0.03, −0.20, and 0.15, respectively). Similarly, Young *et al.* (1972) found low intraclass correlations for the three lower frequency bands with no statistically significant difference between DZ and unrelated pairs.

This MZ–DZ difference also appears in evoked-potential studies and is discussed below.

3. Sleep

3.1. Normal Sleep

Human sleep has been divided into rapid eye movement (REM) sleep and non-REM sleep. REM sleep is associated with rhythmic conjugate eye movements, a mixed-frequency EEG, and very low-amplitude EMG; perhaps most importantly, it is the stage of sleep in which dreaming occurs. Non-REM sleep has been divided into stages based on the predominant EEG characteristics. There are stable differences between individuals in total sleep time, REM latency, proportion of slow-wave

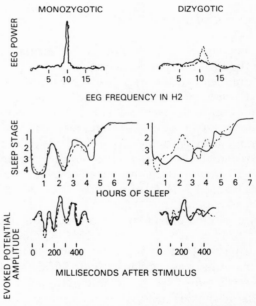

FIGURE 1. Similarity of electrophysiological measures in MZ and DZ twins; each pair is shown as a solid and a dotted line. Above: EEG power spectra in twins showing precise alignment of alpha peak in MZ pair and showing DZ pair differing in alpha markedly (adapted from Lykken *et al.*, 1974). Middle: Time course of sleep stages throughout the night showing regular rhythmic shifts synchronized in MZ pairs but not DZ pairs (adapted from Zung and Wilson, 1966). Below: Visual evoked potentials, again showing great MZ similarity (adapted from Dustman and Beck, 1965).

EEG sleep, and presumably in other parameters of sleep (Mendelson, Gillin, & Wyatt, 1977). Analysis of differences in concordance on these parameters between MZ and DZ twins can demonstrate which of the parameters of sleep are under genetic control. A study of four MZ and two DZ twin pairs revealed some resemblance in sleep latency, total sleep time, percentage of REM time, and percentage of time spent in the various stages of sleep. Because of the lack of statistically significant MZ–DZ differences in concordance, genetic control could not be confirmed. However, examination of the mean all-night sleep EEG and REM patterns shows striking similarities between MZ twins but not DZ twins in sequencing and timing of sleep stage changes (Figure 1). This finding suggests that the same kind of genetic effects noted in waking EEG may be appearing here.

3.2. Narcolepsy

This disorder is characterized by sleep attacks, cataplexy (sudden loss of tone in voluntary muscles), and often accessory symptoms of hypnagogic hallucinations, sleep paralysis, and disrupted nocturnal sleep. The majority of patients have REM onset either at the time of sleep onset or within 11 minutes of sleep onset, whereas in normal persons REM onset is approximately 90 minutes after sleep onset (Rechtschaffen, Wolpert, Dement, Mitchell, & Fisher, 1963). Patients with REM onset at the same time as sleep attacks are referred to as REM narcoleptics. In these patients, a disorder in the regulation of REM is thought to be the underlying pathophysiological event (Rechtschaffen et al., 1963; Mendelson et al., 1977).

Narcolepsy is a familial disorder (Daly & Yoss, 1959; Imlah, 1961; Krabbe & Magnussen, 1942). In the families of patients with REM narcolepsy, both narcolepsy and other disorders of excessive sleep (DES) have been described (Bruhova & Roth, 1972; Kessler, Guilleminault, & Dement, 1974). Direct examination of ill relatives has not been reported, so it is not known if a disorder of REM accompanies the more mild sleep disturbances. A multifactorial genetic model applied to the family history data of Kessler et al. (1974) was compatible with a single genetic diathesis underlying both DES and REM narcolepsy (Leckman & Gershon, 1976), with REM narcolepsy a more severe and rarer form of the disorder. That is, the liability to sleep disorders is conceived as a continuous variable with additive genetic and environmental components. The genetic component is polygenically transmitted. When the amount of liability in an individual is greater than a threshold value, DES occurs, and when it is greater than a second (higher) threshold value, REM narcolepsy occurs. Although this liability is observable only through the familial transmission of these disorders, a corollary of the continuous liability hypothesis is that a continuous physiological measure that reveals vulnerability exists that corresponds to liability and that may be directly evaluated in any individual. For example, a REM latency of 10 min might indicate narcolepsy, 20 min DES, and 30 min normality. If disordered REM control is this physiological manifestation of liability, then the same physiological abnormality of disordered REM control should be found in the DES relatives of REM-narcoleptic patients.

4. EVOKED POTENTIALS

4.1. Waveform Similarity

Evoked potentials (EPs) vary greatly in size and shape from person to person, and these individual differences in EP shape are reproducible over time (Dustman & Beck, 1963). As with EEG, EPs have almost identical shape in identical twins. Figure 2 illustrates the great across-twin-pair variation and within-twin-pair similarity in 33 pairs of identical twins. Shape similarity has been measured by calculating product–moment correlation coefficients between the ordinates of EP waveforms recorded from twin pairs. Thus, the values of the EP at each post-stimulus sample time for each twin form a pair (X and Y) for entry into a product–moment correlation coefficient calculation. Typically, 100 or more such points make up an EP waveform, sampled at intervals of 1–4 msec: the correlation coefficient so calculated is usually Z-transformed to yield a *waveform similarity score*. Groups of MZ and DZ twins can then be compared by t test. Since the triphasic $P100$–$N140$–$P200$ complex appears fairly clearly in most individuals at about the same latency, the waveform similarity score between unrelated individuals' AERs is about 0.5. This index of EP similarity is quite sensitive to changes in peak latency (since minor shifts in latency in two curves may cause high and low values to be paired) but insensitive to amplitude variation across the whole EP. Note that the correlation coefficient cannot be interpreted as the usual correlation between MZ twin measurements but is useful as a measure of between-pair differences.

Dustman and Beck (1965) first reported significantly higher correlations between visual EPs in MZ twin pairs (0.82–0.74) than in pairs of unrelated individuals (0.61–0.53). Higher correlations in MZ than in unrelated pairs of visual EPs were also found by Osborne (1970) and Young

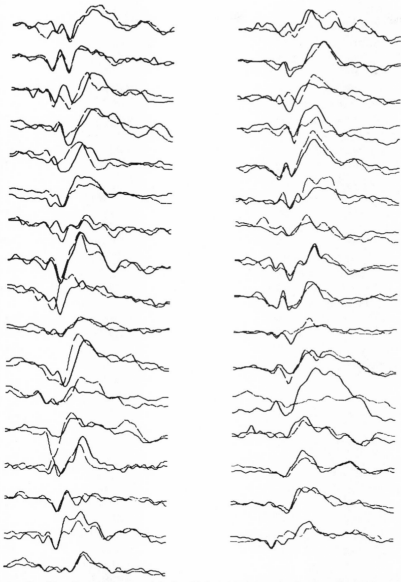

Figure 2. Visual evoked potentials for 80 foot-lambert stimulus for 33 adult MZ pairs with one twin shown as a solid line and one as a dotted line. Individuals vary widely both in amplitude and waveform but are remarkably similar within twin pairs. Whole components may appear in both members of one pair but disappear in both members of another pair, a problem in calculating heritability on peak latencies especially.

et al. (1972), with DZ twins being intermediate in value. Only frontal (F4) visual EPs showed significant MZ–DZ differences, but mean correlational differences were similar across leads (Lewis, Dustman, & Beck, 1972). Similar findings were reported for auditory and somatosensory EPs from several leads, although somatosensory MZ correlations did not differ significantly from those found in unrelated pairs (Lewis *et al.*, 1972). They suggest that the greater apparent heritability of visual EPs may result from the fact that small changes in electrode placement at the occiput affect visual EP waveforms little, whereas small displacements at C3 may alter somatosensory EPs more. Vertex (Cz) is also insensitive to small variations in electrode position and is therefore a good location for genetic studies.

Lewis and Beck (1970) report that MZ pair similarity appears to increase (C4) or remain constant (O2) from childhood to adulthood, whereas similarity in unrelated pairs diminishes for the 0–110 msec EP segment. Correlations in this time segment from these leads are probably primarily influenced by *P*40, *N*70, and *P*95, all thought to have a neurogenic "probable origin" rather than originating from extracranial sources (see maps in Allison, Matsumiya, Goff, & Goff, 1977). While eye blink artifacts might be more widespread in children (Eisengart & Symmes, 1971), this kind of artifact and its topographical distribution diminishes with age. Thus, the pattern of increasing heritability with age seems to suggest that eye movement artifacts are not the major source of EP heritability.

4.2. EP Latency

Examination of Figure 2 indicates that peaks of the EP have latencies no more than a few msec apart in most identical twin pairs. However, component identification is ambiguous in some pairs, especially for *P*100, which might be identified as an early 80-msec or late 120- to 130-msec component in several pairs. We used the rules that (1) *N*140 was the lowest negative point between 100 and 160 msec and that *P*200 and *P*100 were the first major positive components following or preceding *N*140. Attempting to identify analogous components in both members of a twin pair, we obtained test–retest reliabilities for *P*100, *N*140, and *P*200 of 0.56, 0.44, and 0.45, respectively. Heritabilities of 0.53, 0.25, and 0.41 for *P*100, *N*140, and *P*200, respectively, were observed. Using similar peak identification rules, Rust (1975) also found the same ordering of peak heritabilities for the auditory EP—*P*100(*P*2L), *P*200(*P*3L), *N*140(*N*2L)—although his reliabilities were somewhat higher (0.7–0.9).

4.3. EP Amplitude

As can be seen in Figure 2, amplitude as well as general waveshape is very similar in identical twins. Amplitude appears to be a stable individual characteristic, with test–retest reliabilities of 0.7–0.9 reported by a number of workers (Buchsbaum, 1976; Rust, 1975; Soskis & Shagass, 1974). Using line length (summing absolute differences between successive digital values) calculated over specified time intervals to assess amplitude, Lewis *et al.* (1972) compared adult MZ and DZ twin pairs. For visual, auditory, and somatosensory stimuli, frontal (F4) leads showed significantly higher MZ than DZ intraclass correlations for components later than the first 66 msec. For visual EPs, the time band 112–176 msec and 178–300 msec for the occipital lead also showed significant MZ–DZ differences. For these time bands, probably including peaks $P95-N140$ and $P200-N250-P300$, we calculated heritabilities of 0.57 and 0.46 on these data (Holzinger's heritability index; see discussion in Rosenthal, 1970). However, these significant heritabilities arise primarily from the high MZ intraclass correlations. Examination of Lewis *et al.*'s Table II (1972) shows MZ intraclass correlations in the 0.6–0.8 range, with DZ correlations generally 0.2–0.0 and rarely statistically different from zero. No DZ intraclass correlation was significantly different from the unrelated-pair intraclass correlation, whereas 14 out of 21 MZ correlations were different either from the DZ or the unrelated pairs or both.

Using the line length or perimeter measure to estimate amplitude in the visual EPs in our sample of MZ and DZ twins (Buchsbaum, 1974), we obtained a pattern of intraclass correlations similar to that of Lewis *et al.* (1972). The calculated heritabilities of 0.63 and 0.33 for our time bands 116–152 msec and 168–248 msec were quite comparable with the 0.57 and 0.46 heritabilities of Lewis *et al.* (1972) on time intervals close to if not identical with theirs. It might be agreed that the line length measure would be especially inflated in subjects with high amounts of EMG contamination, and that genetic effects might reflect situational electromyographic artifacts, not CNS genetics. However, the finding of equal or higher heritabilities using each successive point of the EP (Buchsbaum, 1974), a technique that should yield poorer heritabilities in the presence of EMG noise, argues against this.

Area integration and peak-to-trough measurement techniques have also yielded significant EP amplitude heritability.

Significant heritabilities for visual EP amplitude were also obtained in a twin study by Buchsbaum (1974). Using integrated area within three timebands, 76–112, 116–152, and 168–248 (corresponding to components $P100$, $N140$, and $P200$ commonly identified in vertex evoked-potentials), it was found that MZ twins showed significant intraclass correlations but that DZ twin intraclass correlations were negligible or negative (Buchsbaum, 1974). Heritabilities of 0.41, 0.46, and 0.39 for $P100$, $N140$, and $P200$ were calculated. Using peak-to-trough measures on peaks $P100$, $N140$, and $P200$ as identified by visual inspection, Buchsbaum calculated heritabilities of 0.35 and 0.52 for $P100$–$N140$ and $N140$–$P200$. In auditory EPs, Rust (1975) also found higher heritability for $N140$–$P200$ (his $N2$–$P3$) than $P100$–$N140$ (his $P1$–$N2$), although his heritability estimates were as high as 86%. Rust concluded that there was very strong evidence for genetic influence on the amplitude of the EP, with "no evidence at all for an environmental effect in these components." However, Rust's estimation of heritability was based on a purely additive genetic model. Since the data were collected in MZ twins, heritability would be overestimated if dominance, epistasis, or dominance interactions involving several loci were involved (Crow & Kimura, 1970).

We have already noted that results from EEG spectral analysis, sleep records, and EPs have all shown MZ intraclass correlations to be quite high and DZ correlations to be low or negligible. If the MZ correlation is more than twice the DZ correlation, it indicates that additive genic variance does not account for the heritability. The implication of such data is that the variable is indeed under genetic control but that the mechanism of inheritance is complex. Under this circumstance, assigning a single number to represent heritability is not very useful.

We have already noted in EEG studies of family pedigrees (Vogel, 1970) that alpha predominance and frequency appear to be inherited as an autosomal dominant. Parent–offspring correlations are informative about the presence of dominance variance, since dominance variance enhances the sibling–sibling correlation but not the parent–offspring correlation. In our study (Gershon & Buchsbaum, 1977) of certain EP parameters discussed below, parent–offspring correlations approximately equaled sibling–sibling correlations. suggesting that multiloci interactions are producing the similarity in MZ twin pairs.

If several loci are responsible for the expression of EP characteristics, the probability of DZ twins' having these N loci identical by descent is $(1/2)^n$, whereas the probability for MZ twins is 1. If, for example, the EP phenotype resulted from a four-locus interaction, nearly all ($15/16$) of DZ twins would be dissimilar. Disassortative mating is another possibility for producing great MZ and no DZ similarity, since the parents of DZ twins would be more dissimilar than by chance alone, thus reducing the DZ pair's chances of being similar. However, disassortative mating is an uncommon phenomenon, and assortative mating for high-voltage alpha waves (Dieker, 1967) and for EP parameters (Gershon & Buchsbaum, 1977) has been observed. Lykken *et al.* (1974) have suggested that initial differences between DZ twins may be enhanced by the formation of complementary personalities, perhaps especially in areas of stress coping. While MZ twins are indubitably alike, DZ twins may be more often compared and contrasted by parents, magnifying minor differences, Lykken theorizes. If one twin habitually takes charge, arousal-sensitive measures such as EEG, sleep, and EPs may be affected, creating disparity. Clearly, more family and pedigree studies are needed to resolve the issue fully.

4.4. Response to Stimulus Parameters

EPs have been shown to change with differences in simple stimulus characteristics such as intensity or frequency as well as more complex psychological aspects of attention selectivity, novelty, and uncertainty. Since performance on many perceptual and cognitive tasks shows a genetic influence, (e.g., Fuller & Thompson, 1960) we might expect EP parameters also to show genetic influence. If this could be demonstrated, we would have increased confidence that genetic influence on a functional neurophysiological characteristic, rather than merely variations in the spatial orientation of certain anatomic features, was being measured.

4.4.1. Stimulus Intensity

EPs to visual stimuli generally increase in amplitude with increasing stimulus intensity up to some intermediate intensity and then level off or even decrease (Buchsbaum, 1976); individual differences are extremely prominent. The rate of increase in amplitude with increasing stimulus intensity for an individual can be measured as the slope of a straight line fit to the EP amplitude and stimulus intensity data; thus high slopes are indicative of great increases in amplitude with increasing stimulus intensity, and negative slopes would be indicative of actual decreases in amplitude with increasing intensity. EP amplitude–intensity slopes appear to be stable over time (test–retest correlations ranging from 0.6 to 0.8; Buchsbaum, 1974; Soskis & Shagass, 1974; Stark & Norton, 1974). Individual differences in EP amplitude–intensity slope for the $P100-N140$ component have been associated with monoamine enzyme activity levels (Buchsbaum, Landau, Murphy, & Goodwin, 1973), personality characteristics such as sensation seeking (Zuckerman, Murtaugh, & Siegel, 1974) and psychiatric diagnoses of schizophrenia (Landau, Buchsbaum, Carpenter, Strauss, & Sacks, 1975), affective illness (Borge, 1973; Buchsbaum et al., 1973), and alcoholism (Coger,

Dymond, Serafetinides, Lowenstam, & Pearson, 1976; von Knorring, 1976; Ludwig, Cain, & Wikler, 1977).

In adult MZ and DZ twins, we observed heritabilities of the amplitude–intensity slope for P100 or P100–N140 ranging from 0.51 to 0.68, depending on the exact technique of EP measurement (Buchsbaum, 1974). These significant heritabilities arose almost entirely from the MZ twin-pair similarities, however, and DZ intraclass correlations were almost uniformly near zero. In data collected on the families of normal controls and psychiatric patients with affective disorders we (Gershon & Buchsbaum, 1977) noted similar intraclass correlations in the offspring–offspring (0.30) and sibling–sibling (0.29) comparisons—both higher than the correlations observed in DZ twin pairs. However, since the amplitude–intensity slope was significantly elevated in the patients with affective illness and their relatives, the increased variance along with sampling from the extremes of the population distribution may explain the higher observed correlations. Assortative mating (individuals and their spouses having similar amplitude–intensity slopes) was also observed (intraclass $r = 0.32$).

It may be of interest that amplitude–intensity slopes and latencies for peak N140 alone do not show zero DZ correlations. For the mean deviation measure, the amplitude–intensity slope for N140 (116–152 msec) for DZ twins was about half that for MZ twins (0.28 versus 0.60, $p < 0.05$). Thus, the N140 peak, specifically associated with selective attenuation effects in many EP studies (e.g., Schwent, Snyder, & Hillyard, 1976) may be more likely to be under single locus or additive polygenic control, as opposed to complex interaction between loci.

4.4.2. Contrast Effects

For both visual and auditory stimuli; there is a tendency to judge a stimulus of a particular intensity as more intense when it is preceded by a weaker stimulus and less intense when it is preceded by a stronger stimulus. The term *contrast effects* has been used to refer to this modulation of perceived stimulus intensity, and it has also been investigated as *time error* (e.g., Holzman, 1954), *context effects* (e.g., Ellis, 1972; Tempest, McRobert & Bryan, 1965), and *anchor effects* (Boardman, Aldrick, Reiner, & Goldstone, 1959). We have observed an EP analogue of the contrast effect for the P200 component (Buchsbaum, Silverman, Henkin, & Pfefferbaum, 1971); when a stimulus is preceded by a weaker stimulus, its AER amplitude tends to increase, and conversely, when a stimulus is preceded by a stronger stimulus, its AER amplitude tends to decrease. Individuals who show large EP contrast effects tend to maximize stimulus differences and to be less influenced by irrelevant contextual cues of starting position and stimulus sequences. In a battery of psychophysical judgment tasks where subjects were required to match a standard intensity stimulus with a variable one, most subjects showed a tendency to be influenced by the starting position in a series of intensity judgments. Subjects underestimated the intensity of a variable stimulus in comparison to a standard on trials of descending intensity and overestimated on ascending trials. Individuals with high EP contrast effects appeared able to overcome such starting-position bias, perhaps because of their perceptual tendency to contrast adjacent stimuli. The correlation between differences between descending and ascending series of trials on the alternate binaural loudness balance and the EP contrast measure was -0.61 for $N140$ and -0.52 for $P200$. The EP contrast effect seems not entirely due to sensory end-organ fatigue as it is minimized by modifications in the regularity and/or complexity of stimulus presentation that leave simple fatigue effects unchanged (Buchsbaum *et al.*, 1971).

Visual AER contrast effects were studied by comparing AERs to flashes of medium intensity preceded by either a dim or a bright flash presented at a 1-sec interstimulus interval. Stimuli were presented in the intensity sequence dim, medium, bright, medium, dim, medium.... EEG was recorded from vertex, and amplitude EP was calculated as described elsewhere for the four intensity experiment (Buchsbaum, 1974).

The AER amplitude for the medium flash preceded by a dim flash minus the AER amplitude for the medium flash preceded by the bright flash was a contrast score; high values indicated a contrast effect. The contrast effect was largest for peak $P200$ measured either as peak-to-trough $N140$–$P200$ or as an area between 168 and 248 msec following stimulus onset (see Buchsbaum, 1974, for measurement technique and stimulus description). Between 70% and 95% of groups of normal volunteers show positive contrast effects for $P200$. Test–retest reliability studies of AER contrast scores over 2–4 weeks for peak $P200$ in the vertex lead yielded intraclass correlations of 0.39 ($p < 0.01$, $n = 128$). A sample of 34 adult MZ twin pairs described elsewhere (Buchsbaum, 1974) had intraclass correlations of 0.49; the 34 DZ twins had a correlation of $-.01$ ($p < 0.05$). As before, the pattern of MZ intraclass correlations being much greater than DZ correlations appears here with contrast effects.

4.5. EP Asymmetry in Twins

Hemispheric asymmetry of EPs was studied in MZ and DZ twins using sinusoidally modulated light at 10 Hz as the stimulus and recording from right and left occipital leads. EPs were averaged and amplitude measured by fitting Fourier coefficients for 10 Hz (sinusoidal frequency) and 20 Hz. The 20-Hz response may reflect responses to stimulus alterations, since the light becomes bright and then dims 10 times per second for a total of 20 stimulus alterations and a possible 20 "stimuli," counting both "on" and "off" responses. The absolute value of the difference in amplitude between left and right occipital EPs showed MZ ($r = 0.67$) significantly higher than DZ ($r = 0.22$) intraclass correlations for the 20-Hz term. Thus the absolute extent of amplitude asymmetry seems to be heritable. It is noteworthy, however, that MZ twins showed mirror-image asymmetry; of one twin had left occipital EPs larger than right, his co-twin tended to have right occipital EPs larger than left. This finding is demonstrated in intraclass correlations in MZ twins that used the signed (not absolute-value) left–right differences; MZ twins had an intraclass r of -0.47 ($p < 0.05$). This finding of mirror-image asymmetry is consistent with the EEG data of Raney (1939), who found that 12 of 17 MZ twin pairs showed occipital alpha EEG amplitude greater on the right side in one twin and on the left side in the other. Mirror imaging is also seen in handedness and in ectodermally derived tissues, such as hair whorls (see Nagylaki & Levy, 1973). The appearance of apparent heritability of EP asymmetry in twins must therefore be interpreted cautiously and may reflect the developmental factors related to the twinning process rather than genetic influence on EPs.

5. Anatomic Features and Electrophysiology

Peripheral factors such as head shape or skull thickness must be considered as one possible source of the genetic similarity observed in electrophysiological twin studies. Similar head shapes might bring particular cortical areas more directly under the bony landmarks used to place EEG electrodes, producing a genetic effect of trivial interest. However, investigations by Dustman and Beck (1965) demonstrated that selecting subjects on the basis of similar cephalic index did not yield at all similar EP waveforms. We found no relationship between cephalometric roentgenographic measures of skull thickness and any EP amplitude measure (Buchsbaum, Henkin, & Christiansen, 1974).

Central structural differences are known to influence EP waveforms, however. Such wiring differences as disorganization of nondecussated optic fibers in human albinos produce fairly striking EP waveform differences (Creel, Witkop, & King, 1974). Crossed pathways are intact, so that on binocular visual stimulation, albinos' EPs are symmetrical. However, if one eye is covered, a dramatic reduction in EP amplitude and even the disappearance of components are seen on the side receiving nondecussated optic fibers. The reduced ipsilateral connections in albinos are associated not only with disorganized lamina in the geniculate but with auditory system abnormalities as well. It has been hypothesized that the retinal pigments provide some mechanism of genetic control over axonal growth in this system (Creel *et al.*, 1974). Other links between behavior variables and skin melanin include interactions between catecholamines and regulation of the tyrosine–melanin biosynthetic pathway (see Robins, 1974; Baron, 1976) proposed as a possible basis of schizophrenia. Differential environmental interactions also appear: rearing in impoverished versus enriched environments differentially affected visual EPs in albino rats (Edwards, Barry, & Wyspianski, 1969). Thus the relationship between albinism, its varying tyrosinase enzymatic deficiencies, and anatomical development of the CNS may be especially instructive in the search for links between abnormalities in brain biochemistry and behavior.

Genetic variation in the cortical sulcal pattern may also be important for EPs. Electrophysiological evidence has increasingly indicated that, at least in animals, sulci lie at boundaries between cortical convolutions that have functional significance; Campos and Welker (1976) suggested that individual intraspecies differences in sulcal pattern "reveal real differences in orientation, relative size and location of different but adjacent functional projections." Genetically controlled differences or similarities in sulcal pattern might be the source of the remarkable electrophysiological similarities in monozygotic twins and perhaps even relate to the similarities in perceptual processing.

The finding that human cerebral hemispheres exhibit many types of structural asymmetry between the left and right sides (see review by Levy, 1975), as do cortical EPs, also suggests a functional–structural relation that may help explain genetic variation. Here again, simple Mendelian rules for the inheritance of handedness seem not to apply; sex of the proband and possibly recurrent environmental factors also appear to influence the determination of handedness and of cortical dominance.

6. ELECTROPHYSIOLOGY, GENETICS, AND CONSCIOUSNESS

The studies that have been reviewed here indicate that the EEG and EP parameters that are related to changing levels of consciousness (e.g., sleep) and to the processing or inhibition of sensory signals coming into the CNS all show wide individual differences that are at least partly under genetic control. EP changes have been particularly related to attention, novelty, and surprise, and thus, in a sense, they reflect input of sensory information to consciousness. Indeed, filtering or coping with the tremendous information overload that the human eye, ear, and other sense organs can dump upon the CNS may be one of the major functions of the cerebral cortex. Individual differences in these characteristics would then appear to produce a different consciousness of the external environment, each person biasing his admission or rejection of sensory signals in various stages of central processing.

The importance of this selectivity in human consciousness was early recognized by the James brothers (appropriately for this section on genetics). William James, in *Principles of Psychology*, noted that "each of us literally chooses by his way of attending to things what sort of a universe he shall appear to himself to inhabit." (p. 402) The same emphasis on selectivity is stressed by Henry James in his preface to *The Spoils of Poynton* in describing how he obtained the idea for a story from "a mere floating particle in the stream of talk" and explained "Life being all inclusions and confusion and art being all discrimination and selection." (p. 120)

This selectivity can be excessive, leading to a sensorially impoverished consciousness; indeed either too much or too little sensory input can be stressful. Not only may sensory deprivation lead to permanent sensory damage in developing animals, but in adults, sensory deprivation (see review by Suedfeld, 1975; Zubec, 1973) or sensory overload (Gottschalk, Haer, & Bates, 1972; Ludwig, 1972; Lipowski, 1975; Miller, 1960) may be associated with psychiatric symptoms. Modulatory mechanisms have been postulated that act as a "sensoristat" to increase or decrease incoming sensory information as needed to maintain optimum arousal of the organism (e.g., Zuckerman, Murtaugh, & Siegel, 1974). The EP phenomenon of augmenting–reducing discussed above might be indicative of the operation of such a mechanism. Why should such wide individual differences in perceptual mechanisms apparently under genetic control be present in the populations we study? Three possible explanations are suggested. First, we may be examining a population in evolutionary transition, with selection for a new pattern creating temporary heterogeneity. Second, behavioral polymorphism in the population may confer some survival benefits on the group as a whole. Thus, for example, augmenting in the EP has been correlated with high scores on the Zuckerman Sensation Seeking Scale (Zuckerman *et al.*, 1974) indicative of disinhibition and risk taking. These characteristics as well as their opposites may be valuable in a small proportion of the population and may be maintained genetically in heterozygotes. Third, the individual differences may reflect selection for different perceptual characteristics at some time and place in the past, with mixing occurring in the present environment.

Clearly, different ecological requirements have quite different levels of sensory input; the quiet uniformity of the northern tundra at twilight contrast with the cacophony of noises and colors in a tropical rain forest. Genetic selection for different "settings" on the sensoristat might yield the genic diversity we observe in the populations we test. Similarly, the demands of night-time vigilance might select different patterns and percentages of sleep stages. Environmental stimuli can be responded to during sleep, and EP amplitude may even increase (Buchsbaum, Gillin, & Pfefferbaum, 1975). This perceptual ability has important evolutionary significance for responding to predators, the presence of prey, or crying infants.

Evolutionary transition, adaptive polymorphism, and ecologically tuned perceptual filtering may all produce individual differences that in a given environment may range from adaptive to maladaptive. Compounding the individual problem could be new genetic combinations of several perceptual traits, each valuable in certain settings but pathological in impact on combination. This viewpoint, expressed also by Bleuler (1976) on the basis of clinical experience, is as yet highly speculative: whether speculativeness itself is a pathological or adaptive trait will require further investigation.

REFERENCES

ALLISON, T., MATSUMIYA, Y., GOFF, G. D., & GOFF, W. R. The scalp topography of human visual evoked potentials. *Electroencephalography and Clincal Neurophysiology*, 1977, 42, 185–197.

BARON, M. Albinism and schizophreniform psychosis: A pedigree study. *American Journal of Psychiatry*, 1976, 133, 1070–1072.

BLEULER, M. An approach to a survey of research results on schizophrenia. *Schizophrenia Bulletin*, 1976, 2, 356–357.

BOARDMAN, W. K., ALDRICK, R. C., REINER, M. D., & GOLDSTONE, S. The effect of anchors upon apparent length. *Journal of Genetic Psychology*, 1959, 61, 45–49.

BORGE, G. F. Perceptual modulation and variability in psychiatric patients. *Archives of General Psychiatry*, 1973, 29, 760–763.

BRUHOVA, S., & ROTH, B. Heredofamilial aspects of narcolepsy and hypersomnia. *Archives Suisses di Neurologie Neurochirurgie et Psychiatrie*, 1972, 110, 45–54.

BUCHSBAUM, M. S. Average evoked response and stimulus intensity in identical and fraternal twins. *Physiological Psychology*, 1974, 2, 365–370.

BUCHSBAUM, M. S. Self-regulation of stimulus intensity: Augmenting/reducing and the average evoked response. In G. E. Schwartz & D. Shapiro (Eds.), *Consciousness and self-regulation*. New York: Plenum, 1976.

BUCHSBAUM, M. S., SILVERMAN, J., HENKIN, R. I., & PFEFFERBAUM, A. Contrast effects on the auditory evoked response and its relation to psychophysical judgments. *Perception and Psychophysics*, 1971, 9, 379–384.

BUCHSBAUM, M. S., LANDAU, S., MURPHY, D., & GOODWIN, F. Average evoked response in bipolar and unipolar affective disorders: Relationship to sex, age of onset and monoamine oxidase. *Biological Psychiatry*, 1973, *7*, 199–212.

Buchsbaum, M. S., Henkin, R. I., & Christiansen, R. L. Age and sex differences in averaged evoked responses in a normal population with observations on patients with gonadal dysgenesis. *Electroencephalography and Clinical Neurophysiology*, 1974, *37*, 137–144.

Buchsbaum, M. S., Gillin, J. C., & Pfefferbaum, A. Effect of sleep stage and stimulus intensity on auditory average evoked responses. *Psychophysiology*, 1975, *12*, 707–712.

Campos, G. B., & Welker, W. I. Comparisons between brains of a large and small hystricomorph rodent: Capybara, hydrochoerus guinea pig, cavia; Neocortical projection regions and measurements of brain subdivisions. *Brain, Behavior and Evolution*, 1976, *13*, 243–266.

Coger, R. W., Dymond, A. M., Serafetinides, E. A., Lowenstam, I., & Pearson, D. Alcoholism: Averaged visual evoked response amplitude-intensity slope and symmetry in withdrawal. *Biological Psychiatry*, 1976, *11*, 435–443.

Creel, D., Witkop, C. J., Jr., & King, R. A. Asymmetric visually evoked potentials in human albinos: Evidence for visual system anomalies. *Investigative Ophthalmology*, 1974, *13*, 430–440.

Crow, J. F., and Kimura, M. *An introduction to population genetics theory*. New York: Harper & Row, 1970.

Daly, D. D., and Yoss, R. E. A family with narcolepsy. *Proceedings of the Staff Meetings of the Mayo Clinic*, 1959, *34*, 313–320.

Davis, H., & Davis, P. A. Action potentials of the brain. *Archives of Neurology and Psychiatry*, 1936, *36*, 1214–1224.

Dieker, H. Untersuchungen zur Genetik besonders Regelmabiger hoher Alpha-Wellen im EEG des Menschen. *Humangenetik*, 1967, *4*, 189–216.

Dumermuth, G. Variance spectra of electroencephalograms in twins. In P. Kellaway & I. Petersen (Eds.), *Clinical electroencephalography of children*. New York: Grune and Stratton, 1968.

Dustman, R. E., & Beck, E. C. Long term stability of visually evoked potentials in man. *Science*, 1963, *142*, 1480–1481.

Dustman, R. E., & Beck, E. C. The visually evoked potential in twins. *Electroencephalography and Clinical Neurophysiology*, 1965, *19*, 570–575.

Edwards, H. P., Barry, W. F., & Wyspianski, T. O. Effect of differential rearing on photic evoked potentials and brightness discrimination in the albino rat. *Developmental Psychobiology*, 1969, *2*, 133–138.

Eisengart, M. A., & Symmes, D. Effect of eye blink on the visual evoked response in children. *Electroencephalography and Clinical Neurophysiology*, 1971, *31*, 71–75.

Ellis, H. D. Adaptation-level theory and context effects on sensory judgments: Perception or response? *Perception*, 1972, *1*, 101–109.

Fenton, G. W., & Scotton, L. Personality and the alpha rhythm. *British Journal of Psychiatry*, 1967, *113*, 1283–1289.

Fuller, J. L., and Thompson, W. R. *Behavior genetics*. New York: Wiley, 1960.

Gershon, E. S., & Buchsbaum, M. S. A genetic study of average evoked response augmentation/reduction in affective disorders. In C. Shagass, S. Gershon, & A. J. Friedhoff (Eds.), *Psychopathology and brain dysfunction*. New York: Raven, 1977.

Gottschalk, L. A., Haer, J. L., & Bates, D. E. Effect of sensory overload on psychological state changes in social alienation-personal disorganization and cognitive–intellectual impairment. *Archives of General Psychiatry*, 1972, *27*, 451–457.

Holzman, P. S. The relation of assimilation tendencies in visual, auditory and kinesthetic time-error to cognitive attitudes of leveling and sharpening. *Journal of Personality*, 1954, *22*, 375–394.

Hume, W. I. Physiological measures in twins. In G. Claridge, S. Canter, & W. I. Hume (Eds.), *Personality differences and biological variations: A study of twins*. New York: Pergamon, 1973.

Imlah, N. W. Narcolepsy in identical twins. *Journal of Neurology, Neurosurgery and Psychiatry*, 1961, *24*, 158–160.

James, H. *The art of the novel*. Scribners: New York, 1962.

James, W. *Principles of psychology*. Holt: New York, 1890.

Juel-Nielsen, N., & Harvald, B. The electroencephalogram in uniovular twins brought up apart. *Acta Genetica et Statistica Medica*, 1958, *8*, 57–64.

Kessler, S., Guilleminault, C., & Dement, W. C. A family study of 50 REM narcoleptics. *Acta Neurologica Scandinavica*, 1974, *50*, 503–512.

von Knorring, L. Visual averaged evoked responses in patients suffering from alcoholism. *Neuropsychobiology*, 1976, *2*, 233–238.

Krabbe, E., and Magnussen, G. On narcolepsy. I: Familial narcolepsy. *Acta Psychiatrica Neurologica*, 1942, *17*, 149–173.

Landau, S. G., Buchsbaum, M. S., Carpenter, W., Strauss, J., & Sacks, M. Schizophrenia and stimulus intensity control. *Archives of General Psychiatry*, 1975, *32*, 1239–1245.

Leckman, J. F., & Gershon, E. S. A genetic model of narcolepsy. *British Journal of Psychiatry*, 1976, *128*, 276–279.

Lennox, W. G., Gibbs, E. L., & Gibbs, F. A. The brain-wave pattern, an hereditary trait. *Journal of Heredity*, 1945, *36*, 233–243.

Levy, J. A review of evidence for a genetic component in the determination of handedness. *Behavior Genetics*, 1975, *6*, 429–453.

Lewis, E. G., & Beck, E. C. Cerebral evoked response similarity in monozygotic, dizygotic, and unrelated individuals. *Proceedings, 78th Annual Convention, APA*, 1970, 181–182.

Lewis, E. G., Dustman, R. E., & Beck, E. C. Evoked response similarity in monozygotic, dizygotic and unrelated individuals: A comparative study. *Electroencephalography and Clinical Neurophysiology*, 1972, *32*, 309–316.

Lindsley, D. B., & Wicke, J. D. The electroencephalogram: Autonomous electrical activity in man and animals. In R. F. Thompson & M. M. Patterson (Eds.), *Bioelectric recording techniques—Part B: Electroencephalography and human brain potentials*, Vol. 1-B. New York: Academic, 1974.

Lipowski, Z. J. Sensory and information inputs overload: Behavioral effects. *Comprehensive Psychiatry*, 1975, *16*, 199–221.

Loomis, A. L., Harvey, E. N., & Hobart, G. Electrical potentials of the human brain. *Journal of Experimental Psychology*, 1936, *19*, 249–279. (a)

Loomis, A. L., Harvey, E. N., & Hobart, G. Brain potentials during hypnosis. *Science*, 1936, *83*, 239–241. (b)

Ludwig, A. M. "Psychedelic" effects produced by sensory overload. *American Journal of Psychiatry*, 1972, *128*, 114–117.

Ludwig, A. M., Cain, R. B., & Wikler, A. Stimulus intensity modulation and alcohol consumption. *Journal of Studies of Alcohol*, 1977, *38*, 2049–2056.

Lykken, D. T., Tellegen, A., & Thorkelson, K. Genetic determination of EEG frequency spectra. *Biological Psychology*, 1974, *1*, 245–259.

Matousek, M., & Petersen, I. Frequency analysis of the EEG in normal children and adolescents. In P. Kellaway & I. Petersen (Eds.), *Automation of clinical electroencephalography*. New York: Raven, 1973.

Mendelson, W. B., Gillin, J. C., & Wyatt, R. J. *Human sleep and its disorders*. New York: Plenum, 1977.

Miller, J. G. Information input overload and psychopathology. *American Journal of Psychiatry*, 1960, *116*, 695–704.

MILSTEIN, V., STEVENS, J., & SACHDEV, K. Habituation of the alpha attenuation response in children and adults with psychiatric disorders. *Electroencephalography and Clinical Neurophysiology*, 1969, *26*, 12–18.

NAGYLAKI, T., & LEVY, J. "The sound of one paw clapping" isn't sound. *Behavior Genetics*, 1973, *3*, 279–292.

OSBORNE, R. T. Heritability estimates for the visual evoked response. *Life Sciences*, 1970, *9*, 481–490.

RANEY, E. T. Brain potentials and lateral dominance in identical twins. *Journal of Experimental Psychology*, 1939, *24*, 21–39.

RECHTSCHAFFEN, A., WOLPERT, E. A., DEMENT, W. C., MITCHELL, S. A., & FISHER, C. Nocturnal sleep of narcoleptics. *Electroencephalography and Clinical Neurophysiology*, 1963, *15*, 599–609.

ROBINS, A. H. Skin melanin pigmentation in schizophrenia. *Journal of Psychiatric Research*, 1974, *10*, 239–246.

ROSENTHAL, D. *Genetic theory and abnormal behavior*. New York: McGraw-Hill, 1970.

RUST, J. Genetic effects in the cortical auditory evoked potential: A twin study. *Electroencephalography and Clinical Neurophysiology*, 1975, *39*, 321–328.

SALZMAN, L. F., KLEIN, R. H., & STRAUSS, J. S. Pendulum eye-tracking in remitted psychiatric patients. In L. C. Wynne, R. L. Cromwell, & S. Matthysse (Eds.), *The nature of schizophrenia*. New York: Wiley, 1978.

SCHWENT, V. L., SNYDER, E., & HILLYARD, S. A. Auditory evoked potentials during multichannel selective listening: Role of pitch and localization cues. *Journal of Experimental Psychology*, 1976, *2*, 313–325.

SOSKIS, D. A., & SHAGASS, C. Evoked potential tests of augmenting-reducing. *Psychophysiology*, 1974, *11*, 175–190.

STARK, L. H., & NORTON, J. C. The relative reliability of AER parameters. *Psychophysiology*, 1974, *11*, 600–602.

SUEDFELD, P. The clinical relevance of reduced sensory stimulation. *Canadian Psychological Review*, 1975, *16*, 88–103.

TEMPEST, W., McROBERT, H., & BRYAN, M. E. The estimation of relative loudness. In D. E. Commins (Ed.), *Proceedings of the Fifth International Congress on Acoustics*. Liege: Thone, 1965.

VOGEL, F. The genetic basis of the normal human electroencephalogram (EEG). *Humangenetik*, 1970, *10*, 91–114.

YOSS, R. E., & DALY, D. D. Narcolepsy. *Medical Clinics of North America*, 1960, *44*, 953–968. (a)

YOSS, R. E., & DALY, D. D. Narcolepsy. *Archives of Internal Medicine*, 1960, *106*, 168–171. (b)

YOUNG, J. P. R., & FENTON, G. W. An investigation of the genetic aspects of the alpha attenuation response. *Psychological Medicine*, 1971, *1*, 365–371.

YOUNG, J. P. R., LADER, M. W., & FENTON, G. W. A twin study of the genetic influences on the electroencephalogram. *Journal of Medical Genetics*, 1972, *9*, 13–16.

ZUBEK, J. P. Behavioral and physiological effects of prolonged sensory and perceptual deprivation: A review. In J. E. Rasmussen (Ed.), *Man in isolation and confinement*. Chicago: Aldine, 1973.

ZUCKERMAN, M., MURTAUGH, T., & SIEGEL, J. Sensation seeking and cortical augmenting–reducing. *Psychophysiology*, 1974, *11*, 535–542.

ZUNG, W. W. K., & WILSON, W. P. Sleep and dream patterns in twins: Markov analysis of a genetic trait. In J. Wortis (Ed.), *Recent advances in biological psychiatry*. New York: Plenum, 1967.

8

The Waking Stream of Consciousness

KENNETH S. POPE AND JEROME L. SINGER

The importance of a psychological study of man's consciousness was affirmed by no less a psychologist than Ivan Pavlov:

> Psychology, in so far as it concerns the subjective state of man, has a natural right to existence; for our subjective world is the first reality with which we are confronted. (Pavlov, 1927 p. 329)

And the importance of the biological perspective in an understanding of man's psychological experiences was argued by no less a student of consciousness than William James:

> Bodily experiences, therefore, and more particularly brain-experiences, must take a place amongst those conditions of the mental life of which Psychology need take account. *The spiritualist and the associationist must both be "cerebralists,"* to the extent at least of admitting that certain peculiarities in the way of working of their own favorite principles are explicable only by the fact that the brain laws are a codeterminant of the result.
>
> Our first conclusion, then, is that a certain amount of brain-physiology must be presupposed or included in Psychology. (James, 1890/1950, p. 5)

In this chapter, we will discuss both psychological and biological aspects of the normal, waking stream of consciousness. Most studies of thinking focus upon the outcome of a thought process, the solution of an arithmetic or concept-formation problem, or the retrieval of specific memories. Yet one of the chief characteristics of human thought is its continuous nature, so effectively captured by writers like James Joyce, Saul Bellow, and Virginia Woolf.

1. WILLIAM JAMES: CHARACTERISTICS OF CONSCIOUSNESS

Let us begin with some basic descriptive characteristics of the stream of thought itself. William James formulated five fundamental characteristics that still serve as valuable touchstones.

KENNETH S. POPE • Director of Psychological Services, Gateways Hospital and Mental Health Center; 1891 Effie Street, Los Angeles, California 90026. JEROME L. SINGER • Department of Psychology, Yale University, New Haven, Connecticut.

1. "Every thought tends to be part of a personal consciousness." James's initial emphasis is on the subjective nature of thought: each thought has an individual person to whom the thought belongs. Thoughts do not lead some sort of mysterious, impersonal, independent life of their own outside the individual mind, nor does a particular person's thought intrude directly into anyone else's mind. Thought invariably flows through the channel of the individual mind.

2. "Within each personal consciousness, thought is always changing." James stressed here the uniqueness of each moment of our waking life. The state we are in now will never and can never recur. The biological perspective becomes significant here. The nervous activity of the brain, which accompanies each moment of consciousness, serves constantly to modify the brain itself—and the effects are cumulative! "Every brain state is partly determined by the nature of this entire past succession." Our experience of thought at any given moment is influenced by the history of our experience of thought.

3. "Within each personal consciousness, thought is sensibly continuous." James then developed the central metaphor of his chapter: thought flows; it is a stream passing through the mind; it is not a series of discontinuous, static segments tied together. Changes in the mental state do not involve absolute breaks.

James also discussed variations in the clarity and vividness of consciousness. Each mental state seems to involve a primary focus and also to include a vague fringe area. These fringe areas, while not receiving our full attention, nevertheless help shape the ongoing stream of thought. Virginia Woolf, one of the early stream-of-consciousness novelists, supported this view:

> Life is not a series of gig lamps symmetrically arranged; but a luminous halo,
> a semi-transparent envelope surrounding us from the beginning of con-
> sciousness to the end. (Woolf, 1925/1953, p. 154)

4. "Thought always appears to deal with objects independent of itself." Thought seems to have a representational nature. It points beyond itself to particular objects, or ideas, or other content matter. Our normal waking thinking is not directly about thought itself but rather about that to which the thoughts refer. This point makes the important distinction between our thoughts and their content or referents, between, for example, the thought of a chair and the chair itself.

5. "Thought is interested in some parts of these objects to the exclusion of others, continuously choosing from among them." The external environment alone furnishes a multitude of stimuli to which the person can attend at any given moment—and yet only some of these actually become a part of the stream of thought:

One of the most extraordinary facts of our life is that, although we are besieged at every moment by impressions from our whole sensory surface, we notice so very small a part of them.... Yet the physical impressions which do not count are *there* just as much as those which do, and affect our sense organs just as energetically. Why they fail to pierce the mind is a mystery. (James, 1890/1950, p. 225)

The process is not dichotomous; that is to say, it is not simply a matter of attending or not attending to a particular object—there are degrees of attending:

The phenomenon of selective attention and of deliberative will are of course patent examples of this choosing activity. But few of us are aware how incessantly it is at work in operations not ordinarily called by those names. Accentuation and Emphasis are present in every perception we have. (James, 1890/1950, p. 284)

2. THE VARIETY OF CONSCIOUS EXPERIENCE

In considering the normal, waking stream of consciousness, we need to keep in mind not only those qualities outlined by James but also that the phenomenon seems marvelously varied. This variety is both represented in the arts and reported by individuals who describe the flow of their own experience. In films, it has been represented as a halting verbal diary narrated by the individual (*Taxi Driver*), as including purely visual images of other people (*Face to Face, Buffalo Bill and the Indians*), as a private running commentary on what is being spoken during social conversation (in both *Strange Interlude* and the brilliant takeoff on it in *Animal Crackers*), as involving brief flashbacks (*Spellbound*), anticipations of the future (*Midnight Cowboy*), or purely imaginary figures (*Juliet of the Spirits*).

The novels incorporating and portraying the stream of consciousness—reaching from the present back to Dorothy Richardson, James Joyce, Gertrude Stein (a student of William James), and Virginia Woolf—likewise convey the varied nature of conscious experience, of which we will give three examples. In *The Eye of the Storm*, Patrick White, awarded the Nobel Prize for literature in 1973, depicts the blending of both unpleasant emotions from a recent meeting with her mother and the long-term memories or dreams as they are experienced by a young daughter as she walks down a stairway:

Dorothy de Lascabanes was in fact stumbling down the stairs: dreams she remembered in which she was trampling recently-hatched nestlings swam into the actual waters of the sacrificial platypus. So she was trampled and lurched. In the hall she found herself pushing at what? the only opposition was a void: and guilt, tenderness, desire, lost opportunities. She must never

forget *Mother is an evil heartless old woman.* If you did forget, Basil would
remember, himself Mother's only equal at driving the knife home. (White,
1973, p. 73)

In the same novel, a nurse "sees" her wishes and fears while she goes
about bathing a very old patient:

What am I living for? The nurse crimped her forehead. One rabbit-blow
might finish the party. Then she would run away, never set eyes on this
house again, never see Col. Snow, or anyone, run till she arrived at some
long, empty beach, and still running, by now miraculously out of her clothes,
fall into the shallow foam, the bubbles fizzing and filling wherever there was
entry, soothing wherever she was physically bruised or mentally troubled.
(White, 1973, p. 79)

In a passage of *Ulysses,* James Joyce presented the stream of consciousness as a mix of plans, realizations, speculations, memories, and associations:

Better not stick here all night like a limpet. This weather makes you dull.
Must be getting on for nine by the light. Go home. Too late for *Leah, Lily of
Kilarny.* No. Might be still up. Call to the hospital to see. Hope she's over.
Long day I've had. Martha, the bath, funeral, house of keys, museum with
those goddesses, Daedalus' song. Then that brawler in Barney Kiernan's.
Got my own back there. Drunken ranters. (Joyce, 1961, p. 380)

That the flow of consciousness is a phenomenon of almost infinite
variety—as opposed to theories in which the mind is described as occupied primarily with forming realistic images of the outside world and
performing rational, task-oriented operations on those images—finds
support also in first-person narrations of the flow of consciousness.
Pope (1978) asked people to "think aloud" and to record their streams of
consciousness in the absence of any experimental tasks—subjects simply
reported whatever was going through their minds during several reporting periods. The following tape-recorded excerpts exemplify some of the
diversity:

I'm looking at my coat now. I got it from—uhm—Hadassah. And there's
this great Jewish lady there that was uh, oh, I'm thinking about this tie that I
had. Oh now I'm thinking of a tie of my grandfather's. I'm thinking about the
day that my grandfather died. I was at junior high and (name) walked into
the office. I was in the office and I was crying and I didn't really care if he, if
he cared I was crying. Uhm.

Water and scotch, scotch with water, with ice, with uh soda, with soda
on the side, uh wine, beer, uh vomit, nausea, headaches, uhm aspirin. No
Doz, Tums, uh Tums, little metal cases with railroad pictures on them and
uh, uh the trains into clouds of smoke and dust and the paintings in the Fogg
Art Museum and fog also, and uhm California and uhm California and uhm
P. G. Wilthouse in G's and Little Orphan Annie. . . .

I can see that those two screws on the side are eyes and the light switch itself is a nose. I'm looking at the doorknob. I'm looking at this tape and I'm thinking that the carbon on it looks like a poster. Now, which, well, I'm thinking of the poster of *Pal Joey*. I was in *Pal Joey*. Uhm, there were a lot of gay people in the show. I don't want to think about that anymore. I'm looking at the light switch again, the light socket. It seems, it seems that whenever I don't want to think about something I look at a light socket.

The thud in my head matches people walking, the sound of people walking across the floor. There's a piece of floor that looks like a fish. Paula has some fish. No, I wonder if she's going to take them home. My mother seems to get lonely. The tape doesn't stick too well. I hate looking at people. I keep listening to the sound upstairs. Somebody said "hail!" She ought to go to a class this morning. (Name)'s probably given me her cough. She should have gone to the doctor. I had a dream that I had a two-room double. I might have swore that I have one now. I'll probably have a good time next year. (Name) and I get along very well. The room feels like it's shaking. People don't seem to give this girl a rest. It sorta kind of sounds like someone's swinging on a swing. Jungle Jim. I remember the time I fell off the swing at home. It was the time I broke my ankle. I had a pain behind my left eye. It feels like I have something in it.

The analyses of these reports showed that for most of the time, the stream of thought was not involved in the immediate situation and rational process but rather primarily oriented toward long-term memory and future fantasy. This picture of the mind differs from the more present-focused, orderly models often generalized from experiments emphasizing convergent experimental tasks or static, discrete aspects; from the presentations of textbooks on thinking (Bourne, Ekstrand, & Duminowski, 1971; Johnson, 1955), which ignore or say little about the stream of consciousness and imagination, or of books on personality (Mischel, 1971) or on adolescence (Seidman, 1960), which say so little about imagination or fantasy; and even from some psychoanalytically oriented approaches, which seem to relegate "primary process" to childhood, mental illness, and dreams and to imply that the well-analyzed, mature mind is generally engaged in purposeful, directed, secondary-process thought, except for brief lapses and "regressions."

In fact, reports of the stream of consciousness like those quoted above may, through their reliance on a verbal, sequential mode of report, tend to underrepresent the less verbal, logical processes. There was, for instance, much greater discontinuity indicated in the flow of thought when subjects simply recorded nonverbally whenever there was a "shift" in their streams of thought (during periods when the stream of consciousness was not reported verbally) than within the verbal reports of "thinking aloud" (both when the subject himself or herself indicated the shifts and when independent judges working with transcripts of the reports reliably indicated the shifts). Indeed, on the average there occurred about five times as many shifts of thought in the nonverbal periods of report than there were in comparable periods of "thinking aloud." The evidence, both from the arts and from psychological investigation, suggests, then, that the normal, waking stream of consciousness is a phenomenon of great variety.

3. A BASIC MODEL

How can we account for the behavior of the flow of consciousness? Having specified some fundamental descriptive characteristics, can we formulate some principles concerning, for example, why a particular item or idea appears in consciousness, preoccupies thought for a while, then drops out of awareness, perhaps reappearing seconds, days, or years later? The following model, presented elsewhere (Pope & Singer, 1977) in detail and with experimental evidence, attempts to specify some determinants of the stream of consciousness. Here we present them briefly.

3.1. The Mind as Activity

The mind appears to be not so much a static storage bin or a blank slate as an organ that seems to be constantly in process, handling different forms of information. The wealth of material reaching the human organism through the various senses at any one time is fairly great; from this sometime immensity, the salient and relevant information must be abstracted, put to use immediately when necessary, and kept alive and available in useful form for the future. The mind is, as Neisser (1972) put it, "a vast array of stages, activities, and processes at every level" (p. 237).

3.2. Sensory Input

As mentioned above, this continuously functioning organ, the mind, is dependent to some extent on the information it is able to extract from moment to moment from the external environment. Characteristics of sensory functioning, then, can exert a shaping and regulating influence on what reaches consciousness from those stimuli available in the environment. "No two animals or people live in exactly the same world, for no two are precisely identical in sense perception" (Kalmus, 1952, p.

64). Aside from abnormal functioning, the sensory system of each individual may vary in what Petrie (1967) calls "perceptual reactions"; the
subjective experience of the sensory environment may be characterized
as reducing or augmenting what is perceived.

3.3. A Continuum of Consciousness

The awareness of the individual, of course, is not restricted to the
sensory information that is being received from the environment at any
given moment. Rather, the mind might be conceived as operating within
a continuum of consciousness that runs from the public to the private.
At the most public end of the continuum, are the physical stimuli from
the surrounding world, which are generally capable of consensual validation. further along the continuum are the interoceptive and proprioceptive stimuli from within the physical body itself; this stimulation,
while not open to direct visual observation, is nevertheless usually capable of physical measurement. Further still are the more sophisticated
organizational and coding activities of the mind, particularly the complex matching of these exteroceptive, proprioceptive, and interoceptive
stimuli to relatively recent stimulation held in short-term memory. Deeper into the internal dimension are the rehearsal and replay activities
from long-term memory. Hearing a few notes of an old song, unpacking
an old piece of clothing, or smelling the aroma of a kind of food not
enjoyed since childhood may flood the mind with long-out-of-
consciousness thoughts from our childhood or youth. Perhaps most
private on this continuum is that material from long-term memory and
fantasy that is several steps of associations removed from that which
was originally triggered by an external stimulus.

3.4. Attention: The Ability to Screen and Select

The normal, waking stream of consciousness is not a "blooming,
buzzing confusion," a chaotic blur of simultaneous awareness encompassing all of the continuum. Attention seems to regulate what sort of
stimulation finds its way into the stream of consciousness at a given
moment. Hernandez-Peon (1956) demonstrated the ability of a more
salient external stimulus to block out, in great part if not totally, the
nerve impulses from another, less salient stimulus. In fact, stimuli from
any part of the continuum are capable of preoccupying attention at the
expense of less salient stimulation from the same or other parts of the

continuum. Thus, a particularly exciting conversation may cause us to continue to be unaware of signals from our body indicating lunchtime; or a vivid memory of an exciting novel or a fantasy about a future meeting with someone may make us oblivious of the traffic as we cross the street.

Attention exerts a dual control: not only over what is appearing in consciousness at present but also over what consequently passes into short- and long-term memory (against which future incoming stimuli will be matched). As Penfield asserted:

> All the things that a man can call to mind, and all the skills a man can use, were established with materials that once formed a part of his awareness, that appeared in the stream of consciousness. There is no evidence, so far as I am aware, that any of the things he ignored are stored away—at least not in any available form—in the central nervous system. Thus, a man, in selecting what he will attend to, selects what is to be preserved not only in the sequential record of experience but in the numerous mechanisms of the brain. (Penfield, 1969, p. 166)

3.5. A Bias Favoring Sensory Input

Generally, salient or important material from the external, public segments of the continuum seem to receive priority in processing. Adaptive purposes in the human may be served by what Rapaport (1960) termed a "permanent gradient towards external cathexis." This cathexis helps us to avoid the numerous potential hazards involved in navigating through the environment: we note the "Walk" and "Don't Walk" signs, the open windows in high buildings, and sharp objects whenever they appear in our path.

Moreover, limited channel capacity for processing material may help to explain this bias toward sensory input. To the extent that our waking life involves moving around and receiving stimulation from the environment, the more private material simply has less opportunity to appear, less ability to find "free" channel space within the mind. There is considerable evidence, for instance, that visual imagery caused by external stimulation shares the same processing pathways as private, internally generated imagery (Antrobus, Singer, Goldstein, & Fortgang, 1970; Atwood, 1971; Brooks, 1974; Segal & Fusella, 1970). Thus, the sensory perception of the active, waking person is likely to monopolize much of the available channel space. Furthermore, we undoubtedly train ourselves to ignore much of our private stimulation, much as we learn not to notice the nose on our face or the hundreds of twitches and gurglings of our active bodily machinery.

3.6. Predictable, Dull, or Barren Environments: An Opportunity for Private Processing

Fantasies, imaginative anticipations, and very private material from long-term memory seem to occur with much greater frequency in predictable, dull, or barren environments: in bland waiting rooms, sitting by the phone after being placed on "hold," or lying still in bed waiting for sleep to come. Evidence has been found for this phenomenon in laboratory experiments (Antrobus, Singer, & Greenberg, 1966; Drucker, 1969), field studies and interviews (Csikszentmihalyi, 1974), and investigations into the nature of hallucinations (West, 1962).

3.7. The Matching Function

Having a gun put to our head would qualify as an exciting environmental event, and spending several days in a sensory-deprivation chamber would strike most of us as dull. There are, nevertheless, considerable individual differences concerning what constitutes exciting or dull environmental stimulation. More is involved than a simple quantitative measure of input (Fiske & Maddi, 1961). At this point, the notion of a central executive function and optimal levels of stimulation (Hebb, 1955) becomes useful. There is considerable evidence (Anokhin, 1969; Rescorla, 1969; Shepard, 1975; Sokolov, 1969;) that a major function of the mind is creating images of schemes. The organism, then, steers its way through the environment by schematizing its experiences into at least some relatively simple categories or rubrics, then elaborating further on these through encoding processes that allow not only an image (not necessarily visual) of the status quo but also anticipations of future patterns of stimulation (Miller, Galanter, & Pribram, 1960; Neisser, 1967, 1972; Pribram, 1971; Tomkins, 1962, 1963). The degree to which environmental stimulation plays a key role in these plans or presents difficulty in terms of recognizability or predictability further defines the salience of the environment and particular aspects of the environment. The overall "image" (of the way things are, should be, can be), which is to a great extent influenced by the individual's history of experience and his ability to schematize, process, or incorporate current stimulation into

that image, is a powerful determinant of what makes a given environment "dull" or "exciting" for a given individual.

3.8. The Affects

The influence of the matching function on what attracts the attention of the individual and subsequently reaches consciousness can be
sharpened by reference to the affects, which are, we will maintain here,
the chief motivational system. Izard and Tomkins (1966) proposed that
personality be viewed as a complex organization of five interacting systems: homeostatic, drive, affect, cognitive, and motor. The first two are
primarily related to biological maintainance, reproduction, and regulation of the body, while the latter three are more influential in social
interaction and the higher human functions. The emotions, which serve
to motivate the individual, are themselves aroused by the mind's information processing of material from the environment or the memory
system:

> With respect to density of neural firing or stimulation, then, the human being
> is equipped with affective arousal for every major contingency. If internal or
> external sources of neural firing suddenly increase he will startle, or become
> afraid, or become interested, depending on the suddenness of increased
> stimulation. If internal or external sources of neural firing reach and maintain
> a high, constant level of stimulation he will respond with distress or anger,
> depending on the level of stimulation. If internal or external sources of neural
> firing decrease he will probably laugh or smile with enjoyment, depending
> on the suddenness of decrease of stimulation . . . stated another way, such a
> set of mechanisms guarantees sensitivity to whatever is new, to whatever
> continues for any extended period of time, and to whatever is ceasing to
> happen, in that order. (Izard & Tomkins, 1966, p. 88)

3.9. Current Concerns, Unfinished Business, and Unresolved Stress

Individuals may show a special sensitivity to unfulfilled plans or
insufficiently processed stimulation. Thus, there seems to be increasing
evidence that recurring thoughts or dream contents are related to current unfinished business, current concerns and unresolved immediate
stresses (Breger, Hunter, & Lane, 1971; Klinger, 1971; Lewin, 1916;
Singer, 1975). This process—the tendency for consciousness to be filled
with thoughts of tasks initiated but as yet uncompleted, plans set in
motion but as yet far from execution, actions taken quite recently that

were inadequate or incorrect, deadlines in work assignments still to be met, etc.—has obvious adaptive value: "Since fantasy content is normally adrift, it provides continuous reminders of concern other than those [one] is working on which [one] needs to bear in mind" (Klinger, 1971, p. 356). Furthermore, particular events or perceptions may be recognized as of such overwhelming importance that they may generate strong demands for processing and keep drawing attention until this processing is completed. Particularly if this sort of stimulation is extremely aversive—for instance, a severe automobile accident or the death of a loved one—these thoughts may be experienced as intrusive and preempting the ability to think effectively of other matters (Antrobus, Singer, & Greenberg, 1966; Horowitz, 1975; Horowitz & Becker, 1971).

3.10. Sets toward Internal or External Processing

In addition to the factors mentioned so far, long- and short-term sets toward the processing of conscious experience seem to exert strong influence over the material that occupies the normal, waking stream of consciousness. Factor-analytic studies (Huba, Segal, & Singer, 1976; Giambra, 1974; Segal & Singer, 1976; Singer & Antrobus, 1963, 1972; Starker, 1974) suggest three general and stable patterns of daydreaming: one characterized as guilty–dysphoric, another as distractible, and a third associated with Positive Content, Vivid Imagery, and Planful Fantasies. Insofar as an individual is given to one or another of these patterns of consciousness, he or she has in a sense become habituated to approaching the search of internal material with a view toward organizing it in these styles.

To the idea of a fairly consistent, long-standing, habitual approach to processing private and external material can be added the notion of temporary, situation-specific strategies or sets. Miller (1972) demonstrated the measurable differences between the mental sets involved in listening to a prose passage with a view toward scientific problem-solving and with a view toward simply experiencing the prose. Similarly, Klinger (1974) has analyzed the temporary sets adopted for solving a manual puzzle, solving a logic problem, reverie, and quasi-hypnagogic thought and has identified differences between the set for problem-solving ("operant thought") and that for non-problem-solving ("respondent thought").

3.11. Structural Characteristics of the Stimuli

Another possible influence on the stream of consciousness is the form of the material. The emergence of material from memory, the visual images formed by random arrangements of furniture or scenery, the sound and accent of a rush of words—certain of these may reflect particular properties of structure of "good gestalten" that will attract the attention and encourage further rehearsal and replaying of the material. An example of this quality in the extreme is Mark Twain's short story in which each successive person is driven mad by the little phrase "Punch, brothers, punch with care; punch in the presence of the passenjare!", an inane jingle about trolley car conductors of which each person who hears it cannot rid his mind until he has finally told someone else about it.

The model sketched above attempts to touch on some of the factors that influence the normal, waking stream of consciousness. In summary, it seems that the mind is an organ of activity, process, and ongoing work. The screening processes of attention direct consciousness to areas of a continuum that runs from sensory input, toward which humans seem to be favorably biased, to images and fantasies drawn from long-term memory. The less the environment offers novel, salient, or unpredictable stimulation, the more the mind seems to turn to the private areas of the continuum—guided in large part by the chief motivational system, the affects. Each individual possesses a wealth of private material that is available for appearance in the stream of consciousness. What material actually reaches the stream seems to be influenced by current concerns, unfinished business, and unresolved stress. Two additional factors influencing the direction in which consciousness flows from moment to moment are the long- and short-term sets toward internal or external processing and the structural characteristics of the available stimuli.

4. THE ACTIVITIES OF MIND AND BODY

The model outlined above can be greatly refined by attending to some biological aspects of the individual. Each person who is aware of an ongoing stream of thought has a living, physical body. This body constantly assumes a posture, is always immobile or physically active to some degree. These aspects seem to bear rather directly on the waking stream of consciousness.

Rorschach (1942) noted that people who tended to be less active overtly seemed to engage more in fantasy life, to have active imaginations. In looking at inkblots, people who showed restrained physical movement gave more M responses; that is to say, they reported seeing more human figures in motion among vague patterns on the cards. It was Heinz Werner who first followed up on this observation. In support of his sensory–tonic theory of perception and his notion that the body's tonicity was the dynamic link between muscular activity and perception, Werner (1945) examined data from retarded children that demonstrated that the endogenous mentally retarded who were generally more controlled or phlegmatic in motility showed significantly more Rorschach M responses and lower thresholds for stroboscopically or tachistoscopically presented motion than did the hyperkinetic, exogenous mentally retarded.

Meltzoff, Singer, and Korchin (1953) continued this line of investigation and demonstrated that persons who were required to inhibit motility by means of a slow-writing task showed a subsequent increase in their perception of human-movement responses in the Rorschach. Persons who showed numerous M responses were also better able to inhibit writing speed. Singer, Meltzoff, and Goldman (1952) found that M responses increased after subjects were required to "freeze in place" for a period of time. Subsequent studies (Singer, 1960; Singer & Brown, 1977) indicated that persons who show more M responses are likely to be able to inhibit motility, show more deliberation in problem solving, are less active during solitary enforced waiting periods, are less likely to use gestures while defining verbs in an interview, or, in the case of mental patients, are less likely to be described by nurses or attendants as overactive on the wards. Other studies, with children (Singer, 1973), showed that children who lead an active fantasy life can sit still for longer periods of time than children who do not fantasize much and who pay relatively little attention to stimulation from the private areas of the continuum.

Taken as a whole, the studies described above offer considerable evidence that physical motion and attention to private material bear an inverse relationship: physical activity, whether as a long-term habitual trait or as a temporary state, seems to be associated with reduced preoccupation with internally generated stimulation.

Several studies have also demonstrated the effect of posture on thought processes. Kroth (1970) found that people who were reclining rather than sitting could free-associate with greater freedom, spontaneity, and general effectiveness. Morgan and Bakan (1965) found, in a memory study, that earlier and more memories occurred when people were in a reclining rather than a sitting position. Segal and Glickman (1967) reported that people were much less likely to recognize an external signal (the projection of a picture at the fixation point where they were imagining a specific scene) while lying than while sitting.

These effects of posture seem to apply also to the normal stream of consciousness. In a study referred to previously (Pope, 1978), people reported their flow of consciousness using either a "thinking-aloud" or a key-press procedure. Three variables were of central importance: the number of shifts of thought, the number of present-centered thoughts (as opposed to thoughts focused primarily on material drawn from long-term memory or fantasy), and the cumulative duration of time during each reporting period spent engaged in present-centered thinking. These variables were established both through the subject's own report (either oral or key press) and through the reliable judgments of independent raters working with transcripts of the thinking-aloud reports. Here are a few examples of thought segments judged to be present-centered:

> "It's hot in here."
> "There's a hair sticking in my pants."
> "My throat hurts."
> "I need new shoes."
> "Thinking about my button on my sleeve, I've been sort of fooling with and slightly hurt my finger."
> "This floor is stone."

Here are some segments judged to be not primarily focused on the present situation:

> "I can sort of see myself in a room writing papers but I'm not thinking about it much."
> "I just had an image of a-a—you know—a sixty-year-old businessman walking—you know—back and forth in his office, sweating about some business deal that's going to be made, reading a tickertape."
> "I'm thinking about sex. I heard on the radio once that a young person's mind has a sexual thought every one or two minutes."
> "I had a car accident over Christmas vacation."
> "Thinking about (name) and (name) who were at the party and how (first person's) father is dying."
> "On the road outside Davenport Photo, a man at Ceraphano's telling me that clip-ons will not work."

Posture produced consistent effects: when subjects were in a reclining rather than a standing or walking posture, they reported fewer shifts of thought, fewer present-centered thoughts, and less cumulative duration of time spent with consciousness focused on the present. Sitting showed an intermediate effect. A sitting posture, and even more a lying position, seems to require less scanning of the environment than standing or walking postures. If we do not need to attend to it in order to navigate through it, or if we are not facing the accustomed perspectives but rather are lying staring at the blank ceiling or closing our eyes, the environment may become much less salient, may intrude much less often on our ongoing flow of consciousness.

5. THE STREAM OF CONSCIOUSNESS AND BRAIN ACTIVITY

In the last 15 years, systematic investigations into eye activity while the individual is awake have produced a useful indicator of conscious activity and of some of the underlying activity of the brain. Experimental studies suggest that the waking stream of consciousness in the individual with eyes open is generally associated with reduced eye movement (Antrobus, Antrobus, & Singer, 1964; Klinger, Gregoire, & Barta, 1973; Marks, 1972; Singer & Antrobus, 1965; Singer, Greenberg, & Antrobus, 1971). These findings support the notion that the eyes seek to fix themselves on a bland stimulus or to "go out of focus" in order to reduce the processing of externally derived stimulation and to leave channel space for internally generated imagery. Holland and Tarlow (1975) found that "the blink rate is low when information in memory is being operated on" (p. 405) and hypothesized that "since the blackout period of the blink produces a rapid change in visual level, blinking disrupts those cognitive processes utilizing display areas accessible to visual input, which include operational memory and the visual imagination" (p. 401).

The tendency for the eyes to seek a bland, nondisruptive field in order to process internal material seems particularly strong in the social or dyadic situation. The presence of another person, especially another person's face, seems to be the most significant stimulus in our environment, a rich source of information (Ekman, Friesen, & Ellsworth, 1971; Izard, 1971; Tomkins, 1962). Indeed, the presence of another person in the environment—even when that person is silent, motionless, and noninteractive—produces more shifts of thought and a greater emphasis on present-oriented thought in the stream of consciousness (Pope, 1977). In an interactive dyadic situation, then, it should be difficult to engage in extended reflection without shifting one's eyes to a blank wall or a neutral stimulus, a phenomenon borne out experimentally (Meskin & Singer, 1974).

That the brain has differential specialization of function in the left and right hemispheres for processing different types of cognitive material adds to our understanding of eye activity, the stream of consciousness, and the underlying brain processes. Since the eyes are related neuroanatomically to the contralateral side of the brain, right eye-shifts should be related to verbal or quantitative processing, and logical or analytic thought, while left eye-shifts should reflect visual–spatial, emotional, and fantasy processing (Bogen, 1969; Gazzaniga, 1967; Bakan, 1969, 1971). Moreover, the convergences of clinical observation (Day, 1967), split-brain experiments (Gazzaniga, 1967; Bogen, 1969, Sperry, 1973), perceptual studies (Kinsbourne, 1971, 1973), and personality, social, and problem-solving research (Bakan, 1969, 1971; Harnad, 1972; Kocel, Galin, Ornstein, & Merrin, 1972; Morgan, McDonald, & MacDonald, 1971) all point to the possibility that eye shifts during reflective thought may represent: (a) the particular content, visual–spatial or verbal–quantitative; or (b) the habitual style of the individual.

A rather elaborate experiment (Rodin & Singer, 1976) sought to investigate the interaction of a number of these influences. Subjects sat facing the experimenter and were asked a number of questions requiring either verbal or spatial reflective thought. At times, a confederate was sitting to the left or right of the experimenter. Subjects were either of normal weight or overweight—the work of Rodin (1973) has suggested that obese persons may have a different thinking style from normals and may be much more vulnerable to and dependent upon external cues and stimulation. The results illustrated the previously mentioned tendencies for contralateral eye-shifting both as a habitual individual trait and also as something influenced by the particular cognitive process (verbal–mathematical or visual–spatial). Furthermore, the obese subjects indicated significantly less visually oriented daydreaming on the questionnaires. They tended to show much more right-shifting during questions involving verbal or quantitative content and while the confederate was seated toward their left. During visual-content questions, the obese subjects sometimes tended to close their eyes altogether. Taken as a whole, the results suggest that eye activity, particularly shifting and blinking, can reveal aspects of the stream of consciousness. The behavior of the eyes may reflect habitual tendencies of the individual, the immediate cognitive demands, and the nature of the immediate visual environment.

A recent, rather elaborate experiment by Rosenberg (1977) has pursued further the implications of the studies by Singer, Greenberg, and Antrobus (1971) and the Meskin and Singer (1974) and Rodin and Singer (1976) researches just cited. This investigation examined the tracking movements of the participants' eyes when they were confronted by a screen across which bands of stripes were moving continuously either from left to right or from right to left. The subjects were assigned mental tasks such as counting, word definition, or reciting the lyrics (verbal content) of a song, all of which involve verbal–sequential processes presumably related to activity of the left hemisphere. They also were assigned tasks involving visualization and spatial representation or other presumably right-brain-hemisphere functions, for example, picturing an outdoors scene, visualizing specific shapes, or singing subvocally the *melody* of a popular song. They also were required to combine some of the tasks, for example, counting while visualizing an outdoor scene, or singing subvocally both the melody and the words of a song.

Results indicated that despite the natural "pull" of the stripes that produced the optokinetic nystagmus reflex, there was consistently less tracking movement of the eyes when the stripes were moving from left to right and when subjects were processing visual images or melodies, presumably right-hemisphere functions. The greatest amount of eye-tracking movement occurred for the verbal–sequential thought activities when stripes moved left to right; presumably carrying on private left-hemisphere functions enhanced the leftward drift of the eyes. When presumably left-hemisphere and right-hemisphere thoughts were carried out in combination, eye-tracking scores were intermediate between the high tracking associated with verbal–sequential and the low scores associated with the visualization or melody activities. When the stripes were moving in the contrary direction, right to left, there was some increase in the leftward optokinetic nystagmus movements when subjects engaged in presumably right-hemisphere, visual, or parallel-processing activities, but the effect was smaller, suggesting that private visual activity involves both gating out of external cues and left shifting of the eyes. Daydreaming as measured by specific tasks or by questionnaires about predispositional tendencies was strongly linked to reduced eye-tracking particularly of left-to-right moving stripes and also to the apparent capacity to adjust more extensively to changing environmental configurations. Apparently, practiced daydreamers learn to "tune in or out" of situations or to allow for leftward drift of the eyes when this doesn't interfere with the development of vivid private experience.

In general, the experiments on ocular activity and direction suggest subtle but important links between basic psychophysiological processes and the content and vivid awareness of material represented in the stream of consciousness. Most daydreaming involves some visual imagery (Singer, 1975a, b), and visual representations or the more holistic, parallel structures of private fantasy are governed by right-hemisphere processes. Conscious involvement in daydreams would appear to involve the gating out of complex environmental information, a leftward shift of eyes.

6. Fantasy, Emotion, and Visual Imagination

The evidence suggests that not only visual–spatial and fantasy processes but also the emotional processes are specialized right-hemispheric functions (Schwartz, 1974; Schwartz, Davidson, & Maer, 1975). We will conclude this chapter with some speculation on why these functions may be grouped together in one hemisphere.

The notion is this: visual–spatial imagery tends, as a parallel-processing system, to deminiaturize events and present them in their full immediacy. As events become encoded into language (whether verbal or mathematical), they become abstracted and lose their immediate impact on our experience; as a result, they become less emotional events, make less cogent demands, and tend not to present the vivid here-and-now challenge for processing stimulation that Tomkins argues is the basis for affects. As Bruner notes, "Once language becomes a medium for the translation of experience, there is a progressive release from immediacy" (Bruner, 1968, p. 407).

The process of visual–spatial imagination is limited to the immediate present: a visual representation lacks the grammar to say "was" or "will be," to indicate past or future; it follows and embodies the course of events as if they are happening now.

The great mathematician and physicist S. M. Ulam, inventor of the Monte Carlo methods for studying problems too complex to be fully defined and explained only by a complete system of equations, and a member of the Los Alamos team, described this difference quite vividly. The difference between mathematical and physical thought seems to be fundamentally a difference between left- and right-hemispheric functions:

> The feeling for problems in physics is quite different from purely theoretical mathematical thinking. It is hard to describe the kind of imagination that enables one to guess at or gauge the behavior of physical phenomena. Very few mathematicians seem to possess it to any great degree. (Ulam, 1976, p. 147)

Ulam went on to describe the immediacy and impact of the visual imagination involved in thinking about physics:

> Very soon I discovered that if one gets a feeling for no more than a dozen other radiation and nuclear constants, one can imagine the subatomic world almost tangibly, and manipulate the picture dimensionally and qualitatively, before calculating the more precise relationships. (Ulam, 1976, p. 148)

The translation of these movements into linguistic or mathematical symbols involves a considerable miniaturization and loss of emotional impact:

> . . . and remarked to him about my surprise that $E = MC^2$—which I of course believed in theoretically but somehow did not really "feel"—was, in fact, the basis of the whole thing and would bring about a bomb. What the whole Project was working on depended on those few little signs on paper. (Ulam, 1976, p. 157)

In light of the close relationship between visual–spatial imagination and actual perception (Antrobus, Singer, Goldstein, & Fortgang, 1970; Atwood, 1971; Brooks, 1967; Segal & Fusella, 1970) and the obvious crucial survival value of the latter, both may be given priority in processing, both in terms of initial immediacy and impact and also in terms of introduction into and availability within the memory system (Bower, 1972; Luria, 1968; Paivio, 1971). As potent stimuli, both in terms of immediate attention and recognition and also in terms of vivid, effective memory retrieval, the material from these processes may then constitute prime triggers of the affect system discussed earlier.

We are suggesting, therefore, that the elicitation of emotion from the right hemisphere may not be a function of a "location" or specialization of that hemisphere but rather that the *cognitive* operations of vivid visual or auditory imagery re-create *contexts* that make emotional responses more *appropriate* or more easily *retrievable* (Singer, 1974). There are indications that when individuals assume body postures or role-play occurrences from earlier in their lives, long-unrehearsed memories of childhood recur along with strong emotion. It is possible that even without gross bodily or external contextual cues, the generation of vivid private imagery may enhance the retrieval of other experiences along with the appropriate emotional reactions to such settings.

In the last days of the 1976 election campaigns, both President Ford and Jimmy Carter "broke down emotionally," that is, showed tears when they returned to their hometowns. One might surmise that despite the remarkable self-control these campaigners showed in the grueling months before, they might have revealed a comparable loosening of control and reversion to a more childlike (in our society) emotional response if they had been asked earlier to visualize in detail a hometown-return scene. Psychotherapeutic approaches that emphasize specific body postures (e.g., reclining on a couch in psychoanalysis, assuming certain postures in Gestalt or primal-scream therapy) or that draw heavily on vivid imagery associations all seem to elicit more intense emotional reactions.

In effect, then, the stream of thought by its very wide-ranging nature, its potential for vivid imagery or for playing in visual form with new possibilities, seems to open the way for experience of strong and varied emotional reactivity. Demands of day-to-day adaptation to particular physical or social environments may preclude allowing focal attention to be directed toward such private processes and the possible loss of "emotional control" that could follow. We all learn to lose ourselves in watching television, to talk to people on CB radios, or to read newspapers or magazines lest we become too aware of the many bits of unfinished business, the pleasant or unpleasant memories, or the anticipations that are so easily evoked if we drift along on our *own* stream of consciousness. Perhaps, however, we have gone too far in seeking external substitutes and have lost some of the rich variety and emotional sense of self and liveliness that is available in the drifting currents of our own consciousness.

REFERENCES

ANOKHIN, P. K. Cybernetics and the integrative activity of the brain. In M. Cole & I. Maltzman (Ed.), *Handbook of contemporary Soviet psychology*. New York: Basic Books, 1969.

ANTROBUS, J. S., ANTROBUS, J. S., & SINGER, J. L. Eye movements accompanying daydreaming, visual imagery, and thought suppression. *Journal of Abnormal and Social Psychology*, 1964, *69*, 244–252.

ANTROBUS, J. S., SINGER, J. L., GOLDSTEIN, S., & FORTGANG, M. Mindwandering and cognitive structure. *Transactions of the New York Academy of Sciences*, 1970, *32*, 242–252.

ANTROBUS, J. S., SINGER, J. L., & GREENBERG, S. Studies in the stream of consciousness: Experimental enhancement and suppression of spontaneous cognitive processes. *Perceptual and Motor Skills*, 1966, *23*(2), 399–517.

ATWOOD, G. An experimental study of visual imagination and memory. *Cognitive Psychology*, 1971, *2*, 290–299.

BAKAN, P. Hypnotizability, laterality of eye-movements and function brain asymmetry. *Perceptual and Motor Skills*, 1969, *28*, 927–932.

BAKAN, P. The eyes have it. *Psychology Today*, 1971 (April), 64–68.

BOGEN, J. E. The other side of the brain. *Bulletin of the Los Angeles Neurological Societies*, 1969, *34*, 135–162.

BOURNE, L. E., EKSTRAND, B. R., & DUMINOWSKI, R. L. *The Psychology of Thinking*. Englewood Cliffs, N.J.: Prentice-Hall, 1971.

BOWER, G. Mental imagery and associative learning. In L. Gregg (Ed.), *Cognition in learning and memory*. New York: Wiley, 1972.

BREGER, L., HUNTER, I., & LANE, R. W. *The Effect of stress on dreams*. New York: International Universities Press, 1971.

BROOKS, L. R. The suppression of visualization by reading. *Quarterly Journal of Experimental Psychology*, 1967, *19*, 289–299.

BRUNER, J. S. The course of cognitive growth. In P. C. Wagon, & P. N. Johnson-Laird (Eds.), *Thinking and reasoning*. Baltimore: Penguin, 1968.

CSIKSZENTMIHALYI, M. *Flow: Studies of enjoyment*. PHS Grant Report N. R01 HM 22883–02, 1974.

DAY, M. E. An eye-movement indicator of type and level of anxiety: Some clinical observations. *Journal of Clinical Psychology*, 1967, *23*, 428–441.

DRUCKER, E. Studies of the role of temporal uncertainty in the deployment of attention. City University of New York unpublished doctoral dissertation, 1969.

EKMAN, P., FRIESEN, W. V., & ELLSWORTH, P. *Emotions and the human face: Guidelines for research and a review of findings*. New York: Pergamon, 1971.

FISKE, D. W., & MADDI, S. R. *Functions of varied experience*. Homewood, Ill.: Dorsey Press, 1961.

GAZZANIGA, M. S. The split brain in man. *Scientific American*, 1967, *217*, 24–29.

GIAMBRA, L. Daydreaming across the life span: Late adolescent to senior citizen. *Aging and Human Development*, 1974, *5*, 116–135.

HARNAD, S. Creativity, lateral saccades and the nondominant hemisphere. *Perceptual and Motor Skills*, 1972, *34*, 653–654.

HEBB, D. O. Drives and the central nervous system. *Psychological Review*, 1955, *62*, 243–253.

HERNANDEZ-PEON, R., SCHERRER, H., & JOUVET, M. Modification of electrical activity in the cochlear nucleus during "attention" in unanesthetized cats. *Science*, 1956, *123*, 331–332.

HOLLAND, M. K., & TARLOW, G. Blinking and thinking. *Perceptual and Motor Skills*, 1975, *41*, 403–406.

HOROWITZ, M. Intrusive and repetitive thought after experimental stress. *Archives of General Psychiatry*, 1975, *32*, 1457–1463.

HOROWITZ, M. J., & BECKER, S. The compulsion to repeat trauma. *Journal of Nervous and Mental Diseases*, 1971, *153*, 32–40.

HUBA, G., SEGAL, B., & SINGER, J. L. The consistency of daydreaming styles across samples of college male and female drug and alcohol users. *Journal of Abnormal Psychology*, 1977, *86*, 99–102.

IZARD, C. *The face of emotion*. New York: Appleton-Century-Crofts, 1971.

IZARD, C. E., & TOMKINS, S. S. Affect and behavior: Anxiety as a negative affect. In C. Spielberger (Ed.), *Anxiety and behavior*. New York: Academic, 1966.

JAMES, W. *The Principles of psychology*, Vols. 1, 2. New York: Dover, 1950. (Originally published, 1890.)

JOHNSON, D. M. *The psychology of thought and judgment*. New York: Harper, 1955.

JOYCE, J. *Ulysses*. New York: Modern Library, 1961.

KALMUS, H. Inherited sense defects. *Scientific American*, 1952, *186*, 64–70.

KINSBOURNE, M. The control of attention by interaction between the cerebral hemispheres. Paper presented at the Fourth International Symposium on Attention and Performance, Boulder, Colo., 1971.

KINSBOURNE, M. The control of attention by interaction between the cerebral hemispheres. In S. Kornblum (Ed.), *Attention and performance*, Vol. 4. New York: Academic, 1973.

KLINGER, E. *Structure and functions of fantasy*. New York: Wiley, 1971.

KLINGER, E., GREGOIRE, K. L., & BARTA, S. G. Physiological correlates of mental activity: Eye movements, alpha, and heartrate during imagining, suppression, concentration, search and choice. *Psychophysiology*, 1973, *10*, 471–477.

KLINGER, E. Utterances to evaluate steps and control attention distinguish operant from respondent thought while thinking out loud. *Bulletin of the Psychonomic Society*, 1974, *4*, 44–45.

KOCEL, K., GALIN, D., ORNSTEIN, R., & MERRIN, E. L. Lateral eye movement and cognitive mode. *Psychonomic Science*, 1972, *27*, 223–224.

KROTH, J. A. The analytic couch and response to free association. *Psychotherapy: Therapy, Research, and Practice*, 1970, *7*, 206–208.

LEWIN, K. Die psychische Tätigkeit bei der Hemmung von Willensvorgangen und das Grundgesetz der Assoziation. *Zeitschrift für Psychologie*, 1916, *77*, 212–247.

LURIA, A. R. *The mind of a mnemonist*. New York: Basic Books, 1968.

MARKS, D. Individual differences in the vividness of visual imagery and their effect on function. In P. Sheehan (Ed.), *The function and nature of imagery*. New York: Academic, 1972.

MELTZOFF, J., SINGER, J. L., & KORCHIN, S. J. Motor inhibition and Rorschach movement responses: A test of sensory–tonic theory. *Journal of Personality*, 1953, *21*, 400–410.

MESKIN, B., & SINGER, J. L. Daydreaming, reflective thought and laterality of eye movements. *Journal of Personality and Social Psychology*, 1974, *30*, 64–71.

MILLER, G., GALANTER, E., & PRIBRAM, K. *Plans and the structure of behavior*. New York: Holt, 1960.

MILLER, T. Some characteristics of two different ways of listening. Unpublished doctoral dissertation, New York University, 1972.

MISCHEL, W. *Introduction to personality.* New York: Holt, Rinehart, and Winston, 1971.

MORGAN, A. H., McDONALD, P. J., & MacDONALD, H. Differences in bilateral alpha activity as a function of experimental task, with a note on internal eye movements and hypnotizability. *Neuropsychologia,* 1971, *9,* 459–469.

MORGAN, R., & BAKAN, P. Sensory deprivation hallucinations and other sleep behavior as a function of position, method of report, and anxiety. *Perceptual and Motor Skills,* 1965, *20,* 19–25.

NEISSER, U. *Cognitive psychology.* New York: Appleton-Century-Crofts, 1967.

NEISSER, U. Changing conceptions of imagery. In P. W. Sheehan (Ed.), *The function and nature of imagery.* New York: Academic, 1972.

PAIVIO, A. *Imagery and verbal processes.* New York: Holt, Rinehart, and Winston, 1971.

PAVLOV, I. P. *Lectures on conditioned reflex,* W. H. Gantt. London: Martin Lawrence, 1927.

PENFIELD, W. Consciousness, memory, and man's conditioned reflexes. In K. H. Pribram (Ed.), *On the biology of learning.* New York: Harcourt, Brace, 1969.

PETRIE, A. *Individuality in pain and suffering.* Chicago: University of Chicago Press, 1967.

POPE, K. S. The flow of consciousness. In K. S. Pope & J. L. Singer (Eds.), *The stream of consciousness: Scientific investigations into the flow of human experience.* New York: Plenum, 1978.

POPE, K. S., & SINGER, J. L. Some dimensions of the stream of consciousness: Towards a model of ongoing thought. In G. E. Schwartz & D. Shapiro (Eds.), *Consciousness and self-regulation: Advances in research,* Vol. 2. New York: Holt, Rinehart & Winston, 1978.

PRIBRAM, K. H. *Languages of the brain.* Englewood Cliffs, N.J.: Prentice-Hall, 1971.

RAPAPORT, D. The psychoanalytic theory of motivation. In M. R. Jones (Ed.), *Nebraska Symposium on Motivation.* Lincoln: University of Nebraska Press, 1960.

RESCORLA, R. A. Conditioned inhibition of fear. In N. J. Mackintosh & W. K. Honig (Eds.), *Fundamental issues in associative learning.* Halifax, Nova Scotia: Dalhousie University Press, 1969.

RODIN, J. Effects of distraction on the performance of obese and normal subjects. *Journal of Comparative and Physiological Psychology, 1973, 83,* 68–78.

RODIN, J. & SINGER, J. L. Thought and obesity. *Journal of Personality,* 1976, *44,* 594–610.

RORSCHACH, H. *Psychodiagnostics.* Berne: Hans Huber, 1942.

ROSENBERG, B. *Visual responsiveness during different types of mental activity.* Unpublished doctoral dissertation, Yale University, 1977.

SCHWARTZ, G. E. Hemispheric assymmetry and emotion: Bilateral EEG and lateral eye movement. Paper presented at the 82nd Annual Convention of the American Psychological Association in New Orleans, August 31, 1974.

SCHWARTZ, G. E., DAVIDSON, R. J., & MAER, F. Right hemisphere lateralization for emotion in the human brain: Interactions with cognition. *Science,* 1975, *190,* 286–288.

SEGAL, S. J., & FUSELLA, V. Influence of imaged pictures and sounds on detection of auditory and visual signals. *Journal of Experimental Psychology,* 1970, *83,* 458–464.

SEGAL, S. J., & GLICKMAN M. Relaxation and the Perky effect: The influence of body position and judgments of imagery. *American Journal of Psychology,* 1967, *60,* 257–262.

SEGAL, B., & SINGER, J. L. Daydreaming, drugs and alcohol in college students: A factor analytic study. *Addictive Behaviors,* 1976, *1,* 227–235.

SEIDMAN, J. M. *The adolescent: A book of readings, revised.* New York: Holt, Rinehart, and Winston, 1960.

SHEPARD, R. N. Form, formation, and transformation of internal representation. In R. Solso (Ed.), *Information processing and cognition: The Loyola Symposium.* Hillsdale, N.J.: Erlbaum, 1975.

SINGER, J. L. The experience type: Some behavioral correlates and theoretical implications. In M. R. Rickers-Ovsianking (Ed.), *Rorschach psychology.* New York: Wiley, 1960.

SINGER, J. L. *The child's world of make-believe.* New York: Academic, 1973.

SINGER, J. L. Daydreaming and the stream of thought. *American Scientist,* 1974, *2,* 417–425.

SINGER, J. L. Navigating the stream of consciousness: Research in daydreaming and related inner experience. *American Psychologist,* 1975a, *30,* 727–738.

SINGER, J. L. The inner world of daydreaming. New York: Harper & Row, 1975.

SINGER, J. L., & ANTROBUS, J. S. A factor analysis of daydreaming and conceptually related cognitive and personality variables. *Perceptual and Motor Skills,* 1963, Monograph supplement 3-V17.

SINGER, J. L., & ANTROBUS, J. S. Eye-movements during fantasies. *AMA Archives of General Psychiatry,* 1965, *12,* 71–76.

SINGER, J. L., & ANTROBUS, J. S. Daydreaming, imaginal processes and personality: A normative study. In P. Sheehan (Ed.), *The function and nature of imagery.* New York: Academic, 1972.

SINGER, J. L., MELTZOFF, J., & GOLDMAN, G. D. Rorschach movement responses following motor inhibition and hyperactivity. *Journal of Consulting Psychology,* 1952, *16,* 359–364.

SINGER, J. L., GREENBERG, S., & ANTROBUS, J. S. Looking with the mind's eye: Experimental studies of ocular motility during daydreaming and mental arithmetic. *Transactions of The New York Academy of Sciences,* 1971, *33,* 694–709.

SINGER, J. L., & BROWN, S. The experience-type: Some behavioral correlates and theoretical implications. In M. C. Rickers-Orsiankina (Ed.), *Rorschach Psychology.* New York: Krieger, 1977.

SOKOLOV, E. N. The modeling properties of the nervous system. In M. Cole & I. Maltzman (Eds.), *Handbook of contemporary Soviet psychology.* New York: Basic Books, 1969.

SPERRY, R. W. Lateral specialization of cerebral function in the surgically separated hemispheres. In F. J. McGuigan & R. A. Schoonover (Eds.), *The Psychophysiology of thinking.* New York: Academic, 1973.

STARKER, S. Daydreaming styles and nocturnal dreaming. *Journal of Abnormal Psychology,* 1974, *83,* 52–55.

TOMKINS, S. *Affect, imagery, and consciousness,* Vols. 1, 2. New York: Springer, 1962, 1963.

ULAM, S. M. *Adventures of a mathematician.* New York: Scribner's Sons, 1976.

WERNER, H. Motion and motion perception: A study of vicarious perception. *Journal of Psychology,* 1945; *19,* 317–327.

WERNER, H. *The comparative psychology of mental development.* Chicago: Follett, 1948.

WEST, L. J. A general theory of hallucinations and dreams. In L. J. West (Ed.), *Hallucinations.* New York: Grune and Stratton, 1962.

WHITE, P. *The eye of the storm.* New York: Avon Books, 1973.

WOOLF, V. Modern fiction. In V. Woolf, *The Common Reader.* New York: Harcourt, Brace, 1953. (Originally published, 1925.)

9

The Emergence of Emotions and the Development of Consciousness in Infancy

Carroll E. Izard

The conceptual framework for this chapter is differential emotions theory (Izard, 1959, 1960, 1971, 1972, 1977; Tomkins, 1962, 1963). The theory assumes a limited set of discrete fundamental emotions, each having unique motivational properties that derive from the distinct quality of consciousness resulting from the activation of the specific emotion. The neural substrate, phenomenological quality, and facial expression of a fundamental emotion are encoded in the genes, but learning and experience account for the majority of the causes and complex behavioral consequences of emotions. The emotions constitute the principal motivation system for human beings, and the emotions interact with each other and with perceptual and cognitive processes to form a virtually limitless number of motivational phenomena that characterize the adult personality.

Emotions are seen as motivational phenomena that give impetus and directedness to perceptual and cognitive processes and to motor acts. Emotion is assumed to be always present in ordinary consciousness, giving it a particular experiential quality and maintaining its purposeful flow. At no time of life is this more evident than in infancy and early childhood.

An increasing number of developmental psychologists are recognizing emotions as important motivational/experiential phenomena. This recognition has led to some investigations of the effects of affective experiences on children's subsequent behavior (e.g., Rosenhan, Underwood, & Moore, 1974) and on the problem of integrating affect and cognition in empathic and altruistic behavior (Hoffman, 1975). Yet, most developmental research continues to focus on perceptual, cognitive, or motor development without considering the emotion experiences in any systematic way.

CARROLL E. IZARD • Department of Psychology, University of Delaware, Newark, Delaware 19711.

There is still a prevailing tendency to view emotions in terms of disrupting and disorganizing phenomena or as the negative consequences of the interruption of ongoing sequences of behavior (e.g., Mandler, 1975). As a result, relatively little attention has been given to the organizing and guiding functions of emotions, though these were ably discussed 30 years ago (Leeper, 1948).

One reason that many scientists do not give emotion such a critical role in consciousness is their reluctance to recognize the ubiquitous interest in novelty and change displayed by human beings from birth as an emotion. Several investigators (e.g., Wolff, 1965; Fantz, 1966; Kagan, 1971) have observed the manifestations of interest in infants and have used the term descriptively without conceiving of it as an affective-motivational system. Others have described similar concepts, like *aroused intention*, which Bruner (1974) conceives of as a key factor in organizing skilled actions in infants. Breger (1974) is an exception, for like Tomkins and Izard, he sees interest as an emotion as "primary" as sadness, anger, or fear. Once interest is conceived of as an emotion, we have an explanation for the focusing and selectivity of attention that characterizes focal awareness and for the directedness of approach and exploratory behavior from birth. All the empirical research on attention and visual tracking in infancy is consistent with this position.

One might argue that selective attention in early infancy is in part reflexive. This may be so, in that the young infant is less capable of voluntary effort to sustain attention to a given stimulus in the face of competing ones than is a 6- or 12-month-old. This does not mean that the attentional responses in early infancy are unmotivated or nonemotional or that reflexlike responses to novelty and change cannot include emotional responses. Interest, or any emotion, as Darwin (1872) suggested, may be regarded in part as a highly complex reflex. In the course of normal development, such a complex reflex comes more under voluntary or self-control and less under stimulus control.

When an affect other than interest achieves awareness (e.g., physical distress), consciousness and the resources of the individual are appropriately redirected. The exploration motivated by interest gives way temporarily to activities (e.g., a cry for help) relevant to the dominant emotion experience (e.g., distress).

1. BIOLOGICAL PROCESSES, EMOTIONS, AND CONSCIOUSNESS

In his essay on the evolution of mind, the geneticist Edmund Sinnott (1966) reviewed the robust evidence for the innately programmed directedness in biological mechanisms and in the organism as a whole.

He argued that the directedness that is an integral part of biological structures and processes is felt ("as by something like a kinesthetic sense") and that consequently "psychical life is the sense of being consciously oriented towards ends" (p. 153). He maintained that the feeling of being oriented or drawn toward some end gives rise to the sensation of desiring or wanting to achieve that end. He concluded that the subjective experiences of wants, desires, and their opposites are emotions.

Although Sinnott made no effort to deal with emotion concepts in a specific or technical way, the thrust of his thinking is consistent with differential emotions theory and is supported at least in part by theorists and investigators like Spitz (1959, 1965) and Emde, Gaensbauer, and Harmon (1976).

Sinnott's idea that an emotion experience is the awareness of basic biological directedness that characterizes neurophysiological systems and the organism as a whole has parallels not only in differential emotions theory but in various concepts relating to intrinsic motivation and psychological growth. For example, there is an easy parallel between Sinnott's idea and Elkind's (1971) notion that "intrinsic growth forces" generate seeking behavior in the infant and child. Further, Piaget and Inhelder (1969) made it very clear that affect is assumed to be the motive force for cognitive and intellectual development: "There is no behavior pattern, however intellectual, which does not involve affective factors as motives" (p. 158). Thus, in Piaget's theory, the cognizance or consciousness of objects and their relations develops as a function of affective experience.

The central thesis of the present paper is that consciousness develops and realizes its highly complex organization as a function of the emergence of emotions. The arguments and evidence relating to this proposition range from impressions based on extensive clinical experience and clinical investigations to theoretical conceptions of basic relationships between affects and cognitive development and a small but growing number of clever and well-designed experiments.

The term *affect* refers both to drives (physiological needs) and to fundamental emotions (those with preprogrammed expressions). It is recognized that drive states may play a significant role in consciousness in the first few weeks of life, but even in this period, emotions amplify the drive signals and add urgency to the need state. For example, signals stemming from a state of hunger or pain become effective by activating efferent messages that produce the facial expression of distress and the crying response. When the neonate cries, the proprioceptive and cutaneous impulses from the patterned facial movements flood the central nervous system and produce a distress experience that dominates consciousness, and the way the distress takes over the whole baby suggests that infantile consciousness is truly affective in nature. Aside from critical physiological need states in emergency conditions, emotion experiences, relatively independent of drives, function as the principal organizing and motivational conditions in consciousness. The emotion experiences are always conscious, but emotion-eliciting or emotion-related imagery and thoughts may be a part of unconscious processes that influence consciousness. Of course, such emotion-eliciting imagery and ideas become more influential as they achieve awareness by activating the related emotions.

1.1. Infant Consciousness as Affective Experiences

The development of the emotion–perception–cognition relationships of consciousness, like the development of the individual as a whole, is a function of genetically programmed structures, the maturation of biological mechanisms, and learning resulting from person–environment interactions. In early infancy preprogrammed affective responses accomplish the information-processing and communicative functions of consciousness that are later sophisticated by the perceptual and cognitive systems. During this period (the first few weeks of life), internal stimulation (information) usually takes precedence over external stimulation.

Among the first contemporary scientists to recognize the predominance of affects in the newborn's consciousness was Spitz (1959, 1965). Spitz maintained that in the early weeks of life, most of the sensory data received in consciousness come from interoceptors and proprioceptors, both internal sources of stimulation that contribute to affective experience. Perceptual development has not proceeded far enough to provide consciousness with a wide array of peremptory inputs from the surround, and it will still be some months before there will be any evidence that cognitive development has resulted in acquired images or any form of memory that might compete with or modify the affective signals. Thus, the first structures of consciousness are essentially affective in nature, and it is by means of affective experiences and expressions that the infant first relates to the objects and persons in the surrounding world.

A number of other investigators support the idea that consciousness in early infancy is primarily affective experience. Stechler and Carpenter (1967) maintained that it is primarily affect by which the infant derives meaning from person–environment interactions. Escalona (1968) suggested that a variety of stimulus conditions differ for 4-week-old infants only in how they make them feel. Sroufe (1976) described the infant "not as a perceptive being, not as a cognitive being, but as a human being that experiences anxiety, joy, and anger and that is connected to its world in an emotional way" (p. 1). Taking a position on the importance of the emotions in human motivation very similar to that of Tomkins (1962) and Izard (1971), Sroufe went on to describe affective life as "the meaning and motivational system which cognition serves" (p. 1). The empirical investigations of Emde, Gaensbauer, and Harmon (1976) support Spitz's (1959, 1965) position that the emergence of a particular affect functions as an "organizer of the psyche," describes a "new relational factor in development," and heralds a "new mode of functioning" (pp. 8-9).

Haviland (1976) has argued convincingly that users of infant intelligence scales base their assessment of awareness and comprehension in large measure on the infant's expressions of affects. The fact that the examiner's judgments of affect are typically intuitive and unsystematic may partially account for the long-term unreliability and poor predictive validity of infant scales.

1.2. Affect–Perception–Cognition Relations and Levels of Consciousness

An affect-dominated consciousness is highly adaptive for the infant. The infant's survival depends on attracting the attention of the caregiver. The distress cry is a compelling signal for help, and it typically communicates the need for a change in stimulation.

The emotion of interest, whose activation threshold is relatively high in the neonate, is nevertheless crucial in gradually effecting the change from the predominantly receptive mode of consciousness structured by interoceptive and proprioceptive stimulation to a perceptive-cognizing consciousness that explores and eventually differentiates objects, persons, and relationships.

The smile of joy, evident in the early weeks of life, invites yet another kind of interaction from the caregiver and other persons in the social context. The smile tends to elicit from the caregiver a particular type or level of stimulation and to maintain a positive quality in the affective interchange.

The experiential component of interest, joy, and distress, interacting periodically (and in some measure cyclically) with the feelings initiated by drive signals, constitutes consciousness at its first level of organization. These affective-experiential modes may be regarded as the predominant structures of consciousness and their expressions as the manifestations of the operations of consciousness in early infancy.

The concept of developmental levels of consciousness is analogous to, though not necessarily synchronous with, the concept of phases or stages as applied to other aspects of development or to the individual as a whole. Biologists have recognized for a long time that individual development is not simply a matter of the young and small getting older and bigger. The single fertilized cell that begins human life does not produce a person simply by growing larger; it differentiates and multiplies, giving rise to cells with totally different functions and increasing the qualitative complexity of life. In a somewhat analogous fashion, the emergence of new emotions in the course of the first year of life brings new and qualitatively unique sensibilities and motivates the development of higher levels of organization in consciousness.

The concept of stages of development has been given considerable impetus by the work of Piaget and his colleagues (e.g., Piaget, 1976; Piaget & Inhelder, 1969). According to Piaget, the level of development of biologically determined modes of functioning sets the stage for cognitive development. As the biological functions develop through maturation and person–environment interactions, changes occur in behavioral structures. Differential emotions theory assumes that the biologically determined modes of functioning most critical to organized consciousness and to perceptual and cognitive development are the emotions. In a dynamic sense, emotions motivate, hence precede, changes in cognitive structures and action sequences. This assumption is generally consistent with the theory of Piaget, for he assumes that "affectivity constitutes the energetics of behavior patterns whose cognitive aspect refers to the structures alone" (Piaget & Inhelder, 1969, p. 158).

The terms *stage* and *level* as used here do not imply that development occurs in discrete or disjunctive steps. Levels overlap, and many of the underlying processes of growth are more continuous than suggested by the term *stage* (Flavell, 1971; Kagan, personal communications, 1976). The levels of consciousness to be discussed in the following sections emerge at different times, but ultimately they coexist.

2. THE EMERGENCE OF EMOTIONS AND CHANGES IN CONSCIOUSNESS

Consciousness, like all other organismic phenomena, develops in a more-or-less regular fashion in accordance with underlying neurophysiological and psychological principles. It develops and changes like all other living systems. Changes occur both in the basic sensibility/awareness (consciousness) of the individual and in the contents and operations of consciousness. The emergence of discrete emotions, governed primarily by maturational processes, increases the scope of sensibility/ awareness. The development of affective-perceptual modes and affective-cognitive organizations or structures (Izard, 1977), produced by interaction of maturation and learning, increases the complexity of the contents and operations of consciousness.

The idea of looking at consciousness, in terms of maturational and developmental processes, and beginning the study at birth pose some problems. Three types of data can be collected in studies of consciousness: psychophysiological and biochemical measures, behavioral and expressive signals such as facial expressions, and verbal self-reports. Combining data of either of the first two types with the third type offers the possibility of developing sound inferences about the contents and operations of consciousness. For example, a particular pattern of electromyograchic (EMG) activity in specified facial muscles combined with self-reports of feeling irritated and annoyed strongly supports the inference that experiential anger is prominent in consciousness (Schwartz, Fair, Greenberg, Mandel, & Klerman, 1976). Similarly, nonverbal signals of blushing, head lowering, and gaze aversion combined with self-reports of feeling overexposed and inept support the inference that consciousness was at least momentarily dominated by the heightened self-awareness that occurs in shame. Sometimes data from either of the first two classes permit a reasonably good inference about states or processes in consciousness, but the case is usually much stronger when these can be shown to be consistent with systematic self-report data.

Inferences about consciousness in the preverbal infant have to be based on psychophysiological and biochemical data and nonverbal signals. One might well take the position that it is better to make no inferences about consciousness or subjective experience in early infancy, but it may well be that something very fundamental about the ultimate character of consciousness takes place during this critical period of development.

Three kinds of processes are involved in the growth and development of consciousness and in establishing its structures and operations. These processes can be described as sensory-affective, affective-perceptual, and affective-cognitive. The development of consciousness is conceptualized here primarily in terms of these three processes. Each of these three processes is, in turn, relatively more prominent in successive periods of infancy. However, the emergence or relative prominence of a new process does not exclude from consciousness the type of process that was preeminent earlier. Indeed, after all three processes have developed, each of them can and does continue to operate in consciousness with varying frequency, depending on the overall growth and development of the individual and particular person–environment interactions. For this and other reasons, the term *level* is preferred to the term *stage*, with *level* having as its primary referent a type of process in consciousness. In a sense, the three processes that characterize different levels of consciousness continue to have a degree of independence in consciousness, but in the well-integrated personality, they interact and combine harmoniously.

Early infancy offers the best possibility for studying the emergent character of these three processes and for investigating how emotions are linked to each other and to thought and action. Maturational and experiential factors bring these processes to a high degree of interrelatedness, so that ultimately, in adult consciousness, there is generally smooth interaction of the emotional, perceptual, cognitive, and action systems. Sensory-affective, affective-perceptual, and affective-cognitive processes characterize consciousness and its structures and operations in varying degrees during the first year of life. Periods in which these processes are predominant may be considered levels in the developmental organization of consciousness. The three types of processes that figure in the development of consciousness may also correspond to levels of consciousness and complexity of conscious operations in the adult.

The development of a system of differentiated emotions is intrinsically related to the three processes of consciousness, and certain emotions play critical roles in changing the relative prominence of, say, sensory-affective processes (wherein affective experience circumscribes consciousness) and affective-cognitive processes (wherein imagery, thought, and memory are joined with affect in innumerable structures and orientations that provide organization and meaning to conceptions of self and world).

Since differential emotions theory holds that the cortical integration of sensory feedback from a particular facial pattern generates a specific emotion experience, the presence of a universal or pancultural expression permits us to infer the presence of the corresponding emotional experience. By this criterion, the emotions of interest, enjoyment, distress, disgust, and perhaps startle are present at birth. Interest is indicated by an alert, attentive face with increased muscle tonus, enjoyment by the smiling face, distress by the crying face, and disgust by downturned corners of the mouth and a forward thrust (ejection movement) of the tongue. Their presence at birth does not mean that their relationship with antecedent conditions and consequent actions are fully developed. Their thresholds for activation, their sensitivities to various sources of stimulation (activators), and their ranges of intensity change with the growth and development of the individual. Thus, a sudden change in stimulation (e.g., a loud sound) may elicit startle in early infancy and fear in the toddler.

It is hypothesized that the neural substrates of the other fundamental emotions (anger, contempt, fear, shame/shyness, and guilt) are innate but that a period of maturation is required before they can be expressed and experienced. The role of person–environment interactions in the emergence of these emotions is little understood. It is not known whether shame or shyness, for example, emerges as a function of interactions between maturation and experience or appears full-blown at a certain age simply because of biological growth processes and the relevant incentive event. While existing evidence does not settle this issue, it suggests that maturation is the dominant factor and that discrete emotion experiences first achieve consciousness in qualitatively distinct forms that remain invariant over the life span. Eibl-Eibesfeldt's documentary films of greeting behavior and initial interactions between strangers of many different cultures frequently include the gaze-aversion and head-lowering components of the shame expression. The apparent universality or transcultural nature of expressions, which also holds for anger, contempt, and fear, suggests innate determinants. Sackett (1966) has clearly demonstrated that fear in rhesus monkeys is under biological control and that only maturation is required for its emergence. Once an emotion emerges, however, person–environment interactions and learning can link one emotional experience to another and any emotional experience to a wide variety of antecedent conditions and subsequent responses (Izard, 1971).

The experiential distinctiveness and specific motivational properties of emotional experiences provide the basic selectivity, organization, and directedness that characterize consciousness. The invariance of the fundamental emotional experiences guarantees the essential continuity of consciousness (including awareness of self) that prevails despite a number of developmental discontinuities like those studied by Kagan (1971). Interestingly, the one continuity found in Kagan's follow-up study of 10-year-olds involved emotion. Four-month-olds who exhibited the "smile of assimilation" in response to facial configurations were more reflective (on measures of the reflective-impulsive dimension) than those who did not show the "smile of assimilation" at four months (Kagan, personal communication, 1976). The original study (Kagan, 1971) showed that infants who smiled more frequently tended to focus and sustain attention for longer periods of time. This finding seems consistent with Birns and Golden's (1972) finding that the amount of "pleasure" shown in performance on the Cattell and Piaget Object Scales at 18 months of age was predictive of Stanford–Binet intelligence scores at age 3.

2.1. Sensory-Affective Processes: Consciousness Level I

Consciousness in early infancy is primarily a function of drive (physiological need or physical distress) signals and signals from the affect of interest, the most frequently experienced affects in the first weeks of life. The capacity for disgust, enjoyment, and startle is also present in the early weeks of life, but disgust in this period is a relatively rare response to distasteful substances in the mouth, the neonatal smile is more a neurophysiological reflex than a volitional psychological or social phenomenon (Emde, Gaensbauer, & Harmon, 1976), and startle is a gross response to a sudden increase in stimulation.

The sensory-affective processes of Level I are devoted primarily to the survival of the infant, and they respond mainly to changes in broad classes of stimulus conditions. The sensory data from tissue deficits in the neonate have little competition from outside sources of stimulation, and they achieve awareness with immediacy and regularity in the healthy infant. Once in awareness, the physical distress causes the infant to cry. The physical distress signals completely dominate consciousness, and because of the lack of competing signals and stored information in consciousness, the whole infant is caught up in the physical distress experience and responses to it. Anyone who has cared for an infant will readily testify to the fact that the squalling baby is a single-minded being. The infant's one purpose is to bring about a change in the pattern of stimulation, and this is accomplished by attracting the attention and services of the caregiver.

Thus, in the first few weeks of infancy, the affect of physical distress and its expression, crying, are primarily in the service of physiological needs and the business of survival. At this level, consciousnesss is more receptive to inner events and processes than to external ones, and the distress threshold is lower for interoceptive signals than for exteroceptive ones. In Spitz's view, the infant cannot be distressed by perceptions of the outer world since the young infant is essentially a preperceptual being protected from external stimulation by a "stimulus barrier." Spitz (1959, 1965) argued that in the early weeks of infancy, sensory data result in "reception" rather than perception. The assumption that the sensory data received by the young infant result only in "sensory-affective impressions" rather than in percepts is generally supported by other investigators who view the neonate as a preperceptual affective being (e.g., Breger, 1974).

Exactly when the infant is capable of perception in the sense of obtaining an image or percept of an object is not known, but there can be little doubt that in the first days of life, distress (and a distress-dominated consciousness) is far more a function of interoceptive signals than of sensory data emanating from the environment. Nevertheless, distress contributes significantly to the development of awareness of self. Distress expression followed repeatedly by caregiver ministrations constitutes the infant's first opportunity to experience a relationship between events: crying and activities that relieve distress. These events eventually become discriminated as self- and other-initiated activities, the first phase of self–other differentiation. Ferguson (1971) made a similar argument.

If distress were the only emotion present in Level I, consciousness in early infancy would be even more dominated by internal signals than is actually the case. Fortunately, the emotion of interest is present, and it serves to focus and maintain attention to sources of external stimulation. Interest-sustained attention is essential in obtaining percepts and in learning to discriminate objects and persons. For example, interest in the human face brings about the change from indiscriminative to discriminative smiling by 4–5 months of age, and this change has very important implications for social development.

Evidence for the existence of the emotion of interest in early infancy comes from the work of a number of different investigators of attention, although none of them has dealt explicitly with interest as an emotion (see Greenberg, 1977, for a review). The evidence supports the notion that interest adds selectivity and directedness to sensory processes.

Interest serves several adaptive functions in the life of the infant. First, it motivates the infant to attend to various sources of stimulation. This function of interest is probably more important in tuning and focusing receptors for external stimulation. Internal sources of stimulation, such as the tissue deficits involved in physiological needs, can become sufficiently strong and disturbing to inhibit interest in external events and to recruit the affect of distress and the cry for help. Fear in response to external objects would not be adaptive at this age since fear would make such peremptory demands on the infant that the vital internal signals would be gated out.

External sources of stimulation are innumerable and ever-changing, and it would not be possible or adaptive for the infant to give equal attention to all of them. Interest provides the necessary selectivity of attention that is required for the development of distinctively different sensory impressions and ultimately for the development of percepts and concepts.

The work of investigators of attention in infants supports, at least indirectly, the notion that the emotion of interest is present at birth and plays a significant role in selective attention and in laying the groundwork for perceptual development. Wolff (1965) studied the development of attention in young infants as part of a larger study that involved observing 10 bottle-fed infants 30 hours a week for several weeks in the natural environment of their home. In addition to keeping a running record of the infants' behavior, he set up a number of quasi-experimental conditions and observed the infants' responses to various stimuli. Wolff defined the attentive state as "a general disposition to respond adaptively to selected elements in a consistently changing environment" (P. 815). To say that the attentive state is characterized by the emotion of interest seems consistent with Wolff's observation, since he elaborated his definition of the attentive state as the "time when the infant can be *intermittently 'interested'* in a task like visual pursuit" (p. 816, latter italics added).

Wolff presented evidence supporting the idea that the attentive state during alert inactivity is not a wakefulness of necessity—one that Klietman (1963) identified as a result of negative affective signals such as those from hunger, pain, and cold—but one that meets the criterion of wakefulness of choice. Wolff believes, however, that the alert-inactive state of the neonate cannot be characterized by volition or voluntary motor actions and that it is not appropriate to speak of the state as full consciousness. If Wolff is correct, the reaching and grasping movements of neonates as demonstrated by Bower (1971) would have to be considered reflexive.

The idea that the motivational condition for the attentive state is the emotion of interest, a function of the somatic system, is supported indirectly by Wolff's finding that attentive states in periods of alert activity are independent of visceral stimulation such as from hunger and stooling. In fact attentive states were more likely to occur after feeding or stooling. He concluded that absence, rather than presence, of significant visceral stimulation is the necessary condition for alertness in the neonate. Brody and Axelrod (1970) drew a similar conclusion.

Evidence for the potency of the emotion of interest in maintaining focal awareness was obtained in an experiment in which Wolff moved a pencil back and forth across the infant's visual field just at the moment when the baby was falling asleep. The results show that the presentation of an interesting nonperemptory visual stimulus can significantly prolong the attentive state and delay sleep. In this fashion, the attentive state was prolonged for an average of 19 minutes in the first week of life and for an average of 34 minutes in the fourth week. As Tomkins (1962) has noted, intense interest or excitement, though typically over much more complex affairs than a moving pencil, can cause insomnia in the adult.

The work of Fantz (1965) on visual perception during the first weeks of life also supports the premise that the emotion of interest motivates and selectively focuses attention on external sources of stimulation:

> The young infant appears to see things because he explores his surroundings with his eyes, gazing in the direction of various objects or parts of the room and on occasion looking for a longer period in a particular direction, as if something of particular *interest* had caught his attention. (p. 793, italics added).

Fantz's carefully controlled experiments showed that infants are aware of certain differences in forms and patterns from birth. More importantly, using mean fixation time as a dependent measure, he showed that infants exhibited significantly different preferences among the visual stimuli. Infants showed strong preferences for more complex patterns throughout the early months of life. Although Greenberg (1977) has found that visual preference and complexity are not linearly related (i.e., patterns can be too "complex" to hold attention), Fantz is probably correct in suggesting that the adaptiveness of interest in complexity is in attracting attention to objects of potential importance to the infant. And in terms of differential emotions theory, object discriminations consist initially of awareness of differences in intensities or durations of interest arousal.

Lewis (1969) obtained some data that showed that in older infants, stimuli consisting of scrambled facial features tended to attract relatively more attention than stimuli consisting of regular faces. However, regular faces elicited more smiles and vocalizations across all age groups. He explained the apparent preference of older infants for scrambled facial features in terms of their relationship to existing or emergent schemas. Kagan's (1970) research with stimuli consisting of regular and scrambled facial features led him to a similar conclusion. Lewis and Kagan assume that during the early months of life, regular faces, which are closest to the emergent schemas, elicit the most attention but that in older infants in whom the facial schema is well developed, rearrangements of that schema will elicit more attention. One might also conjecture that the older infants' relatively longer fixation times for the scrambled facial features are a result of complexity-elicited *interest*, which motivates exploration that leads to the resolution of uncertainty or the assimilation of complexity.

Bower (1971) interpreted his and Ball and Tronick's (1971) finding of defensive reactions to an approaching object as evidence that the neonate "expects a seen object to have tactile consequences" (Bower, 1971, p. 4). He regarded the infant's response to grasping a "virtual object" (shadow) as surprise following a misexpected event. Whether or not Bower was correct in inferring expectancy and surprise in the neonate, his data strongly suggest that a startlelike movement pattern is in the infant's repertoire at birth. The startle response in the neonate may be simply a result of a sudden increase in stimulation independent of expectations or cognitive processes. As Tomkins (1962) suggested, a function of the surprise or startle response is to clear consciousness and the information-processing channels of the nervous system and to ready the individual for responses appropriate to the new situation.

While some of the data considered in this section suggest that the young infant makes considerable progress in differentiating objects in the environment, Spitz (1965) was probably correct in assuming that in early infancy, "affect and percept are the same." That is, the infant's awareness of differences and its preferences (or differential attention-focusing) are based on affective changes in consciousness rather than on any sort of psychophysical differentiations that are obviously beyond the young infant's capacity. Thus, the infant looks at one stimulus configuration longer than at another because it arouses and sustains more interest or less distress, and whatever difference exists in the infant's consciousness is a difference in quality or level of affect. Similarly, the infant senses some difference in conditions that elicit interest and conditions that elicit distress by virtue of the difference in the quality of the elicited affect.

Thus, initially, the infant's "preferences" and other indexes of differential responding are based more on the effects of different emotion experiences or qualities of consciousness than on discrimination of the physical properties of stimuli. The apparent discriminative responses in young infants (e.g., the social-stimulus response bias) are adaptive in that they strengthen mutual attachment and spark positive emotional communication and interchange. The infant's predisposition to respond preferentially to certain stimuli (e.g., the human voice and face) is rooted in evolutionary history.

2.2. Affective-Perceptual Processes: Consciousness Level II

It is probably sometime during the second quarter of the first year of life that interest-sustained attention to novelty and change leads to the ability to discriminate objects based on specific features or physical characteristics, originally attended to as novel aspects of objects. These kinds of differentiations mark the emergence of percepts and launch the critical processes involved in perceptual development.

The prototype of infant percepts is the human face or the critical set of facial features that Spitz (1965) has referred to as the facial gestalt and that consists of the region including the forehead, eyes, and nose. The infant responds to this gestalt as a sign in the second month of life, when it elicits or increases interest and sustains attention. Beginning in the third month of life, this gestalt moving toward the baby's face elicits the social smile, which Spitz (1959) considered "conscious, reciprocal communication" (p. 18). Still, the percept to which the infant responds is rudimentary in the sense that the response is to a sign or a class of objects rather than to a specific object or person; that is, the infant smiles at any face or any moving stimulus with the critical facial features.

A study by La Barbera, Izard, Vietze, and Parisi (1976) showed that 4- and 6-month-old infants discriminated between the smile of joy and the anger expression and between joy and neutral expressions, though not between anger and neutral expressions. The data were considered consistent with the postulate that the neurophysiological system underlying a particular discrete emotion becomes functional as that emotion becomes adaptive in the life of the infant (Izard, 1971). The recognition of joy by the infant, particularly when it produces a reciprocal joy expression, facilitates the recurrence of the joy experience and positive affective interchanges between the infant and the caregiver. The failure of infants in the first half year of life to recognize the anger expression (discriminate it from a neutral expression) is also adaptive in that it screens from consciousness a stimulus for negative affective experience, which in turn could contribute to a negative affective exchange between the infant and the social environment.

The emergence of the social smile and the discrimination of the joy expression help set the stage for a new level of consciousness. In the earlier weeks of life, awareness of differences among objects is dependent mainly on differences in level of aroused interest. Smiling in response to the human face heralds the beginning of the processes involved in relating affects to social percepts and in distinguishing social and nonsocial stimuli. Now, an external social-stimulus configuration can elicit a positive affective experience distinct from the interest previously elicited by social and nonsocial stimuli alike.

The perceptual development that occurs at an increasingly rapid rate after the emergence of the social smile is greatly facilitated by the experiences gained by the infant when sensory–affective processes were dominant. The awareness of differences based on changes in level or quality of affect has laid the foundations for percepts or schemas that along with their affective component constitute the structures of consciousness. This supposition is consistent with Spitz's (1965) view that perception proper is predicated on apperception, which in turn is a function of experiences provided by affective interchanges with persons and objects in the environment.

The growth of consciousness would be highly limited if it remained dependent on a limited set of affects to regulate changes in consciousness in relation to external events and to facilitate the processes involved in perceptual discrimination. The variety of emotions that eventually emerge, their numerous interactions and patterns, and their relative independence of biological cycles or rhythms provide the basis for a virtually infinite set of changes in consciousness and hence great freedom of affect–percept and ultimately affect–concept relationships.

Affective-perceptual processes, the discrimination of objects through differential affective response to object-specific features, are facilitated by the capacity for surprise in response to misexpectation and the new emotion of anger. Surprise and anger play critical roles in the growth of consciousness and the development of its structures.

Charlesworth (1969) has provided an excellent review of the literature on surprise. He has also offered a definition of surprise and has discussed its functions in consciousness and cognitive development. Charlesworth noted that early accounts of consciousness held that any disruption of ongoing activities produced a heightened awareness and an effort to restructure existing cognitive structures. Charlesworth saw surprise as performing a similar function.

In distinguishing surprise from the orienting reflex and response to novelty, he held that surprise is a result of a misexpected object or event. The orienting reaction and the response to novelty are the result of unexpected events rather than misexpected ones. In defining surprise in this fashion, Charlesworth made it dependent on a level of cognitive development at which the infant can form expectations or assumptions. Although Charlesworth did not consider response to novelty an affect, the distinction he drew between the response to novelty and the response to the misexpected event is described in differential emotions theory as part of the distinction between the emotions of interest and of surprise.

In viewing surprise as an affective response to the misexpected, Charlesworth believed that he was dealing with a basic idea common to the well-known models developed by Miller, Galanter, and Pribram (1960) and Anokhin (1959). These investigators, along with some later ones (e.g., Hunt, 1965; Singer, 1974), suggested that a mismatch between incoming information and stored information results in emotion responses that initiate processes that tend to restructure the old information. Berlyne (1960) has also placed a great deal of emphasis on the importance of this kind of epistemic conflict between incoming and stored information in the development of intelligence. In Berlyne's system, however, such conflict is viewed as a determinant of curiosity (a concept that has much in common with the concept of interest-as-emotion), which facilitates the reduction of conflict and the consequent reinforcement of curiosity behavior.

Charlesworth (1969) attributed to surprise many of the characteristics that differential emotions theory assigns to interest. He suggested that surprise increases arousal (providing a dynamogenic element in cognitive processes) and instigates and directs attention to the object or event eliciting the surprise:

> In conclusion, the surprise reaction can be viewed as consisting of a number of complex stimulus-producing responses that may serve to mediate, cue, arouse, instigate, "illuminate" and reinforce a variety of other responses that ultimately contribute to changes in existing cognitive structures. (p. 308)

Whether or not Charlesworth was correct in attributing these characteristics to surprise, there can be little doubt that the emergence of surprise reflects certain changes in consciousness and its structures. The infant's ongoing consciousness, directed largely by the emotion of interest, now has a new alternative in the capacity to experience surprise. In terms of differential emotions theory, the principal function of surprise is to clear the information-processing channels of the nervous system for the possibility of a different affective experience and for different affective-perceptual processes. In Level II of consciousness, surprise may be followed by heightened interest, sadness, anger, or disgust. Thus, surprise resets consciousness, and the resulting affect gives directedness to subsequent perceptual activity.

As with all other emotions, the emergence of anger not only provides a new experience in consciousness, it motivates a variety of responses. Up to this point, distress, except for infrequent disgust experiences, has been the only negative affect, and responses to it were confined mainly to the crying response that signals the caretaker for help. Now, restraining or frustrating conditions may elicit anger and motivate responses that attempt to remove the restraints or barriers. Such responses are the infant's first nonreflexive motor acts that reduce negative affect through the direct manipulation of objects. Actions that successfully remove restraints or circumvent barriers increase the sense of separateness of self and other and foster conceptions of self as causal agent.

Earlier in life, the infant, in the face of frustration and negative affect, could only cry for help. The removal of the barrier was through acts of the caregiver. With the emergence of anger, the tendency to act directly on restraints or barriers is increased. As a result, the self-as-agent is experienced as being in opposition to (and as different from) the barrier. Such experiences provide part of the framework for developing self-conceptions and self-awareness.

Although, on the average, the 6-month-olds in the study of La Barbera *et al.* did not discriminate the anger expression, some 5-month-old infants produce an anger expression that meets the essential criteria established by cross-cultural research with adults (Parisi and Izard, 1977). Since neither this study nor the preceding one was longitudinal, it is not possible to say whether production and recognition of the anger expression emerge sequentially or concomitantly.

During this period, the infant's capacity for enjoyment has increased, and clear indications of the expression of joy are now observable. Thus, perceptual processes can now relate to six different emotions—interest, enjoyment, surprise, sadness, anger, and disgust—and to various interactions or patterns of these. In the absence of pain, high-need states, or other conditions that elicit distress or anger, interest remains the dominant factor in consciousness. Interest supports an even greater selectivity of perception in this period, and a greater variety of objects are capable of sustaining longer periods of focal attention. Despite the increased selectivity and durability of attentional processes, the infant still has not developed strong emotional attachments to persons or objects. The infant has no sense of ownership or possession. A favorite toy can be removed from the infant's grasp with little or no negative emotion, and any negative emotion that appears can be quickly dissipated by the substitution of another object. The lack of strong emotional attachments extends even to the infant's mother or principal caregiver. Up until about the age of 6 months, separation or loss of the mother is not severely detrimental, and the infant readily accepts affection and care from anyone. It seems reasonable to infer that the infant's lack of strong emotional attachments reflects an absence of memory or the ability to store and retrieve the affective-cognitive structures that give specific meaning to different objects within a class.

2.3. Affective-Cognitive Processes: Consciousness Level III

The emergence of two new emotions provides the experiential–motivational conditions for the third level of consciousness, which leads to a new level of awareness of self, of other persons, and of self–other interchanges. This new level of consciousness is manifested through the development of intense and durable emotional attachments and relationships. The new emotion of shyness facilitates the development of self-awareness and self-identity, but increased self-identity comes at the cost of a sense of vulnerability. The new emotion of fear functions to protect the vulnerable self, particularly through strengthening interpersonal affective ties.

The occasions for feeling shame or shyness begin to occur with some regularity when the infant can discriminate self from other and familiar (e.g., mother) from stranger. Typically, it is when the infant is called upon to relate to a stranger that shyness manifests itself. Through the experience built up by innumerable affective interchanges with caregivers, the infant becomes adept at relating effectively to familiar persons. The infant has a repertoire of responses that facilitate such relating. When the infant is faced with the problem of relating to a stranger, the familiar stimuli for positive affective exchange are absent or different, and the infant may sense an awkwardness or ineptitude. The resulting heightened awareness of self and of self-as-inept or incapable constitutes the experience of shame or shyness. In the ensuing months and years, the heightened consciousness of self that is fostered by shame and shame anticipation serves to clarify and delimit self-images and self-conceptions and to support the development of competencies and skills that increase self-esteem and reduce the likelihood of shame.

The emotion of fear facilitates the development of perceptual processes and cognitive structures that make it possible to assess danger situations and to protect the self from harm. Beginning around the seventh to the ninth month of life, the infant responds with fear and avoidance responses to situations that earlier elicited only sadness or no negative emotion at all. Certain stimulus configurations can cause fear to dominate consciousness and direct behavior without any experiences with these situations that would suggest that the fear experience and avoidance behavior are based on learning. Gibson (1969) concluded that the perception of a safe surface in contrast to a potentially dangerous drop-off appears early in evolution and early in the ontogenetic development of the human being, with little if any learning required for its development. Emde, Gaensbauer, and Harmon (1976) concluded that the fear of strangers that is manifested under certain circumstances in the third quarter of the first year of life is far more a function of maturational processes than of learning. Bowlby (1973) described a number of "natural clues" for fear and suggested that these and their derivatives account for a considerable proportion of the fear situations in infancy and early childhood. The increasingly mobile infant may now experience fear in a number of situations, but the adaptiveness of fear as motivation for avoidance or escape is assured by a new level of locomotor ability, which increases rapidly between 9 and 15 months of age.

The fear experience serves a positive function as well as a protective or defensive one. As Eibl-Eibesfeldt (1971) observed, fear motivates flight to another. In the growing infant, fear often motivates flight to the principal caregiver. Thus, fear strengthens the attachment of the infant to the caregiver, and for the first time, the infant begins to develop proximity-maintaining activities in relation to the caregiver and other familiar persons in the social environment.

The increased sensibility/awareness resulting from the emotions of shyness and fear greatly increases the number of specific objects within classes that are discriminated and take on special meaning. With the strengthening of the infant–caregiver relationship, attachment to a variety of objects, places, and conditions also emerges. Separation from or loss of caregiver can now activate fear as well as distress and may result in severely detrimental effects on the infant. Even separation from a favorite toy may elicit fear or other negative emotions.

The last quarter of the first year of life offers innumerable opportunities for the development of new structures in consciousness. The increased variety of affects and affective interactions with the environment hasten cognitive development through increasing sensitivity to a wider range of objects, persons, and situations. The sensory-affective and affective-perceptual processes that predominated earlier laid the groundwork for the development of imagery and symbolization. By means of mechanisms and processes not yet understood, the coming and going of affective experiences in relation to the coming and going of affect-eliciting objects and eventually the continuation of the affect in the absence of the object lead to the development of an image of the object and a valuation of it. Through a similar process, symbols become associated with affect-eliciting objects, and the acquisition of language begins.

With the emergence of language, affective-cognitive development increases at an astronomically rapid pace. Linkage of symbols and ideas with affects or combinations of affects form the affective–cognitive organizations or structures that characterize adult consciousness.

3. SUMMARY

If one thinks of consciousness as a complex array of sensations, affects, percepts, and concepts or as a stream of thought and feeling, then obviously the infant in the first weeks of life is not characterized by such consciousness. To be sure, the infant possesses a sensibility/awareness that might be considered the core of consciousness or consciousness proper, but one cannot infer that the neonate has anything like percepts or images based on sensory input and information processing. The neonate's sensory-perceptual system has not yet developed to a point where such percepts or images can be obtained.

There is the possibility that some types of images are innate, as Freud (1936/1959) and Jung (1936/1959) assumed, but assumptions about such images are controversial and unsupported by any kind of data. Present evidence suggests that consciousness in the neonate consists primarily of affective experiences devoid of images and symbols.

The infant's subjective experiences consist of the experiential component of the affects that characterize its existence. The infant responds to its own bodily needs with emotion, and it relates to objects and persons in its surround through affective expression. Thus, the study of the development of consciousness entails the study of the emergence of emotions and the processes whereby emotions lead to perceptual and cognitive processes. While affective processes such as hunger and other physiological needs play a role in such phenomena as sleep–wakefulness cycles, the emotions are the affects most intricately involved in the development of consciousness. Even in the early weeks of infancy, when physiological needs seem to play such a prominent part in the infant's life, these needs typically produce the affect of distress, and it is the distress cry that communicates a need to the caregiver and, at least indirectly, effects a change in stimulation and the quality of consciousness. The repeated squencing of affective experience, affect expression, appearance of caregiver, and change in quality of consciousness lays the foundation for a number of important developments, including sense of self as causal agent.

The development of consciousness is conceived of as a function of the emergence of discrete emotions and the development of relationships between affective experience on the one hand and sensory, perceptual, and cognitive processes on the other. Level I of consciousness is characterized primarily by sensory-affective processes. Awareness is essentially affective experience, and changes in awareness are a function of changes in the quality and intensity of affects. Affective responses occur mainly in relation to objects as global entities or to objects as a class capable of eliciting a particular quality or intensity of affect.

In Level II, consciousness consists primarily of affective-perceptual processes. The development of sensory organs and the strengthening of the emotion of interest enable the infant to focus and maintain attention not only to objects but to their unique features. Thus, awareness can now change as a function of changes in intensities or duration of affective experience in relation to specific objects within a class. The emergence of the capacity for surprise in response to misexpectation and of the new emotion of anger plays a critical role in the affective-perceptual processes in Level II. Surprise serves a resetting function in consciousness, and the anger experience and the behavior it motivates add a new element, self-effected changes in the environment, to the growing sense of self as causal agent.

The emergence of shame/shyness and fear provide the experiential/motivational conditions for Level III of consciousness, which leads to a new level of awareness of self, of other persons, and of self–other interchanges. Shyness increases awareness of self but brings with it a sense of vulnerability. Fear motivates escape behavior and flight to the caregiver, thus strengthening attachment. The increased sensibility/awareness resulting from the emotions of shyness and fear fosters the development of additional affect–concept relations.

The level of consciousness achieved by the end of the first year of life offers innumerable opportunities for the development of affective-cognitive relations that eventually become the predominant structures of adult consciousness. The increased variety of affects greatly increase sensitivity to a wider range of objects, persons, and situations, and the number of affect–percept and affect–concept relations increase rapidly. Sometime in the second half of the first year of life, affective experience in relation to an object achieves some independence of direct sensory contact with the object, and by some unknown process, the object is eventually imaged or symbolized. In a similar fashion, and with much greater facility in the second year of life, symbols become associated with objects, language is acquired, and affective-cognitive development increases at an astronomical pace.

REFERENCES

ANOKHIN, P. K. New data on the functional heterogeneity of the reticular formation of the brain stem. *Zhurnal Vysshei Nervnoi Deyatel'Nosti Imeni I. P. Pavlova*, 1959, *9*, 489–499.

BALL, W., & TRONICK, E. Infant responses to impending collision: Optical and real. *Science*, 1971, *171*, 818–820.

BERLYNE, D. E. *Conflict, arousal, and curiosity*. New York: McGraw-Hill, 1960.

BIRNS, B., & GOLDEN, M. Prediction of intellectual performance at three years from infant test and personality measures. *Merrill-Palmer Quarterly*, 1972, *18*, 53–58.

BOWER, T. G. R. The object in the world of the infant. *Scientific American*, 1971, *225*, 30–38.

BOWLBY, J. *Attachment and loss*, Vol. 2: *Separation, anxiety, and anger*. New York: Basic Books, 1973.

BREGER, L. *From instinct to identity: The development of personality*. Englewood Cliffs, N.J.: Prentice-Hall, 1974.

BRODY, S., & AXELROD, S. *Anxiety and ego formation in infancy*. New York: International Universities Press, 1970.

BRUNER, J. S. The organisation of early skilled action. In M. P. M. Richards (Ed.), *The integration of the child into a social world*. Cambridge, England: Cambridge University Press, 1974.

CHARLESWORTH, W. The role of surprise in cognitive development. In D. Elkind & J. Flavell (Eds.), *Studies in cognitive development*. London: Oxford University Press, 1969.

DARWIN, C. R. *The expression of emotion in man and animals*. London: John Murray, 1904. (Originally published, 1872.)

EIBL-EIBESFELDT, I. *Love and hate: The natural history of behavior patterns*. New York: Holt, Rinehart, and Winston, 1971.

ELKIND, D. Cognitive growth cycles in mental development. In J. K. Cole (Ed.), *Nebraska Symposium on Motivation*, 1971, *19*, 1–31.

EMDE, R., GAENSBAUER, T., & HARMON, R. *Emotional expression in infancy: A biobehavioral study*. New York: International Universities Press, 1976.

ESCALONA, S. *The roots of individuality*. Chicago: Aldine, 1968.

FANTZ, R. L. Visual perception from birth as shown by pattern selectivity. *Annals of the New York Academy of Sciences*, 1965, *118*, 793–814. Also in L. J. Stone, H. T. Smith, & L. B. Murphy (Eds.), *The competent infant*. New York: Basic Books, 1973.

FANTZ, R. L. Pattern discrimination and selective attention as determinants of perceptual development from birth. In Aline H. Kidd & J. L. Rivoire (Eds.), *Perceptual development in children*. New York: International Universities Press, 1966, pp. 143–173.

FERGUSON, L. R. Origins of social development in infancy. *Merrill-Palmer Quarterly*, 1971, *17*, 119–137.

FLAVELL, J. H. Stage-related properties of cognitive development. *Cognitive Psychology*, 1971, *2*, 421–453.

FREUD, S. Inhibitions, symptoms, and anxiety. In J. Strackey (Ed.), *The standard edition of the complete psychological works of Sigmund Freud*, Vol. 20. London: Hogarth Press, 1959. (Originally published, 1936.)

GIBSON, E. J. *Principles of perceptual learning and development*. New York: Appleton-Century-Crofts, 1969.

HAVILAND, J. Looking smart: The relationship between affect and intelligence in infancy. In M. Lewis (Ed.), *Origins of intelligence*. New York: Plenum, 1976.

HOFFMAN, M. L. Developmental synthesis of affect and cognition and its implications for altruistic motivation. *Developmental Psychology*, 1975, *11*, 607–622.

GREENBERG, D. J. Visual attention in infancy: Processes, methods, and clinical applications. In I. C. Uzgiris & T. Weizmann (Eds.), *The structuring of experience*. New York: Plenum, 1977.

HUNT, J. McV. Intrinsic motivation and its role in development. In D. Levine (Ed.), *Nebraska Symposium on Motivation*. Lincoln: University of Nebraska Press, 1965.

IZARD, C. E. Positive affect and behavioral effectiveness. Unpublished manuscript, Vanderbilt University, 1959.

IZARD, C. E. Personality similarity and friendship. *Journal of Abnormal and Social Psychology*, 1960, *61*(1), 47–51.

IZARD, C. E. *The face of emotion*. New York: Appleton-Century-Crofts, 1971.

IZARD, C. E. *Patterns of emotions: A new analysis of anxiety and depression*. New York: Academic, 1972.

IZARD, C. E. *Human emotions*. New York: Plenum, 1977.

JUNG, C. G. The archetypes and the collective unconscious. In *Collected works*, Vol. 9, Part I. Princeton, N.J.: Princeton University Press, 1959. (Originally published, 1936.)

KAGAN, J. *Change and continuity in infancy*. New York: Wiley, 1971.

KLEITMAN, N. *Sleep and wakefulness*. Chicago: University of Chicago Press, 1963.

LA BARBERA, J. D., IZARD, C. E., VIETZE, P., & PARISI, S. A. Four- and six-month-old infants' visual responses to joy, anger, and neutral expression. *Child Development*, 1976, *47*, 535–538.

LEEPER, R. W. A motivational theory of emotion to replace "emotion as disorganized response." *Psychological Review*, 1948, *55*, 5–21.

LEWIS, M. Infants' responses to facial stimuli during the first year of life. *Developmental Psychology*, 1969, *1*, 75–86.

MANDLER, G. *Mind and emotion*. New York: Wiley, 1975.

MILLER, G. A., GALANTER, E., & PRIBRAM, K. H. *Plans and the structure of behavior*. New York: Holt, 1960.

PARISI, S. A., & IZARD, C. E. Five-, seven-, nine-month-old infants' facial responses to twenty stimulus situations. Unpublished paper, 1977.

PIAGET, J. *The grasp of consciousness: Action and concept in the young child*. Cambridge, Mass.: Harvard University Press, 1976.

PIAGET, J., & INHELDER, B. *The psychology of the child*. New York: Basic Books, 1969.

ROSENHAN, D., UNDERWOOD, B., & MOORE, B. S. Affect moderates self-gratification and altruism. *Journal of Personality and Social Psychology*, 1974, *30*, 546–552.

SACKETT, G. P. Monkeys reared in isolation with pictures as visual input: Evidence for an innate releasing mechanism. *Science*, 1966, *154*, 1468–1473.

SCHWARTZ, G. E., FAIR, P. L., SALT, P., MANDEL, M. R., & KLERMAN, J. L. Facial muscle patterning to affective imagery in depressed and nondepressed subjects. *Science*, 1976, *192*, 489–491.

SINGER, J. L. *Imagery and daydream methods in psychotherapy and behavior modification*. New York: Academic, 1974.

SINNOTT, E. W. *The bridge of life*. New York: Simon & Schuster, 1966.

SPITZ, R. A. *A genetic field theory of ego formation: Its implications for pathology*. New York: International Universities Press, 1959.

SPITZ, R. A. *The first year of life*. New York: International Universities Press, 1965.

SROUFE, A. Emotional development in infancy. Unpublished paper, Institute of Child Development, University of Minnesota, 1976.

STECHLER, G., & CARPENTER, G. A viewpoint on early affective development. In J. Hellmuth (Ed.), *The exceptional infant*, Vol. 1. Seattle: Special Child Publications, 1967.

TOMKINS, S. S. *Affect, imagery, consciousness*, Vol. 1: *The positive affects*. New York: Springer, 1962.

TOMKINS, S. S. *Affect, imagery, consciousness*, Vol. II: *The negative affects*. New York: Springer, 1963.

WOLFF, P. H. The development of attention in young infants. *Annals of the New York Academy of Sciences*, 1965, *118*, 815–830.

10

A Systems Approach to Consciousness

WILLIAM T. POWERS

1. INTRODUCTION

The nature of consciousness will still be a mystery by the time this essay ends. We are concerned here with an approach, not an arrival. To some readers it may seem, for the first three quarters of the essay, that the approach begins unnecessarily far out in left field, but I hope that by the end, it will be seen that I have backed off so far in order to come at the subject from a new direction. Bear with me. The systems approach sometimes requires developing a lot of detailed groundwork before one can hazard any generalizations.

In applying the systems approach to anything as complex as a higher organism, the chief problem facing the theorist is that of finding a manageable level of generality—analyzing the whole system into units that are neither so detailed as to overwhelm one's limited ability to comprehend large assemblies of elements, nor so general that nothing surprising can possibly emerge from the final synthesis. Much of the controversy over consciousness has arisen, I believe, because of the gulf that lies between these two extremes. A neurologist deals with billions of tiny elements—neurons—and interactions that hold between only a few of them at a time. The humanistic psychologist deals with the brain as a single lump, and with interactions among global properties of that brain in a world of other brains. It is not surprising that there is a lack of common ground between these approaches.

2. SOME GENERALITIES ABOUT THE SYSTEMS APPROACH

The systems approach, as I use it, grew out of the hardware world, not out of biology, but it was developed for the same reasons it is needed in biology. When technologists began building complex electronic systems, they found it impossible to understand their own creations at the individual component level and, of course, unprofitable to describe

---

WILLIAM T. POWERS • 1138 Whitfield Road, Northbrook, Illinois 60062.

them only at the user's-manual level. An intermediate level of description, the block diagram, developed along with the complexity of electromechanical systems.

A block diagram describes a model of a physical system in terms of the major functions that, when assembled, constitute the whole system. Each block is intended to stand for a subsystem, not an abstraction, but the description of each block is given in the abstract. As a simple example, if two neural signals, f_1 and f_2, converged on a single neuron, and if the outgoing frequency of impulses that resulted was proportional to the weighted sum of the incoming frequencies, this arrangement would be drawn as a block with two inputs and one output, described by the equation

$$f_{\text{out}} = k_1 f_1 + k_2 f_2$$

The describing equation is abstract in the sense that it is a mathematical idealization and omits any description of the physical means by which this relationship is brought about. Yet, the meaning of the block diagram is not abstract; behind it is always supposed to be a physical device, located in space, which accounts for the described relationship. The arrows indicating inputs and outputs are not meant simply to lead the eye along a path through the diagram; they are intended to be schematic representations of physical pathways along which flow real neural signals. Block diagrams do not show sequences of transient events, as in the flowchart of a computer program, but fixed relationships among physical subsystems, as in a representation of the computer itself.

When a collection of such blocks has been defined, one has the pieces from which working models can be constructed. The output of one block can be connected to the inputs of other blocks. *Every* way of connecting such blocks will do *something*; that is, the behavior of any assembly will follow from the input–output rules governing each individual block and from the structure of interconnections. As was discovered early in this game, the behavior of a whole asembly is by no means self-evident in the properties of the individual blocks; it is not so much a matter of the whole's being greater than the sum of its parts as of the whole's being an entity *different from* the sum of its parts. When apples and walnuts are assembled into a system, one gets not the sum of apples and walnuts but Waldorf salad.

Every way of connecting building blocks results in *some* whole-system properties. Thus, the question of how to interconnect the blocks is of a different category from the question of what the blocks are. Even after one has properly identified a set of blocks and has verified that each block corresponds with an identifiable physical unit and that the functional description of the block is correct, one must still find an organization of the blocks that will reproduce the phenomena of interest. That organization cannot be found in the detailed description of how the blocks work. It can be found only in the structure that results from interconnecting the blocks in a particular way.

One of the most important discoveries of the systems approach, in retrospect, was the finding that the properties of a whole system are nearly independent of the properties of the building blocks that comprise it. Any simplistic notions of physical determinism had to be abandoned before the first electronic digital or analogue computer was constructed. The entities that proved important to understanding a large system were the functional blocks, but not the internal construction of those blocks. There is an infinity of different ways to build a physical device that is to perform according to a given functional description.

An elementary function could be designed to sum three signals, f_1, f_2, and f_3, and to represent the sum as a single output signal, f_4. This could be accomplished by a three-way convergence on a single summing element, or it could be accomplished in two stages; first, f_1 and f_2 are added together to produce a signal f_{2a}, and then f_{2a} and f_3 are added together to produce an output signal f_4. In this case, the time lag would distinguish the two internal constructions, but it would not distinguish a third alternative in which f_1 and f_3 are the two signals added together at the first stage especially if the remaining signal, whichever it is, passes through a time-delay element too.

The laws that govern the behavior of a complex system, therefore, are not the laws that govern the individual components of that system. The laws governing the individual components contain no statements about how those components shall be interconnected, nor do they impose any limits on possible interconnections (other than setting the number of *all possible* interconnections). Furthermore, there is no possible way to analyze a given system property into a *necessary* set of component properties, because any given system property could be brought about through assembling components in an immense variety of ways. Those ways are equivalent at the system level but not at the component level.

Not only are system properties independent of the laws governing individual components of the system, but they are independent of the *kinds* of physical elements involved. Once a function such as summation has been identified, it no longer matters to a system description whether the summation is done by neurons, by transistors, by vacuum tubes, or by fluid flow through channels cut in plastic blocks. The only essential aspect of the physical components is that they be able to create the relationship called summation between some set of input quantities and an output quantity.

Once the structure of a system is given, of course, and once the actual physical components have been identified, there is complete harmony between the system description and the component description. Given the structure, the behavior of the whole is seen as consistent with the behaviors of all the components. But the structure must be given; it is not enough to state the properties of the components. Structure is not a property of any one component; it is a property only of an assembly of components, just as temperature and pressure are properties only of an assembly of molecules or atoms.

The systems approach has therefore shown us very clearly that there is a hiearchy of laws of nature. The higher-level laws are not simply sums or averages of lower-level laws; they are laws that transcend lower-level laws and that cannot be described without introducing structural rules that have no meaning at the lower level of description (Brown, 1969; Pattee, 1973). We should not be surprised to find that this is true in biology; it is certainly true in physics. For example, conservation laws are laws of structure and cannot be found in the laws governing the movements of masses. When two elastic solids collide, their movements can be analyzed into accelerations due to forces generated by physical deformations and the spring constants of the materials involved. These laws say nothing about conservation of momentum, but conservation of momentum is found to hold true for *all* collisions of masses having *any* elastic properties. The nature of the physical interactions that actually took place during a collision cannot be deduced from an observation that momentum has been conserved, although when those details are known, they prove to be entirely consistent with conservation of momentum. The systems approach to organisms, therefore, has revealed only what has been a commonplace in physics for centuries.

The properties of an assembly of components structured in a particular way are consequences of laws of structure not effective at the component level. But there is no reason to stop there. Once a structure exists, and its properties are derived, that whole structure may become a component in a higher-level structure made of many such substructures. New laws of structure, one might guess, will come to light. But here the mind tends to boggle; Why would not such "structures of structures" be expressible simply in terms of a more complex statement of the same structural laws? It is very tempting to make a distinction once and for all between components and structures, creating not a hierarchy of laws but a simple dichotomy.

In principle, there is no reason that nature should not leave us with a dichotomy. But there is really no difficulty in imagining another level of structural law, when it is realized that the "component" level of laws is really a structural level, too, relative, say, to the laws of subatomic physics or quantum mechanics. Thus, it is equally true that in principle, there is no reason that nature should stop with a dichotomy, especially since it does not seem to have done so in the world described by physicists.

The systems approach itself is not limited to any particular number of hierarchical levels; it is simply a process of analysis of something into components that are individually describable, and then synthesis into structures that interconnect those components. Sometimes, this process results in discovery of a new level of laws, and sometimes, it simply expands the scope of levels already found. There is, however, no way to predict in advance which will happen; that is up to nature, not the analyst.

The systems approach, therefore, is not just an analysis of organisms that lies halfway between holistic concepts and molecular concepts. It is a method through which any number of intermediary stages can be constructed, as many as necessary to link both ends of the spectrum, if they are linkable. It is, thus our best hope for reconciling mechanistic approaches to (or avoidances of) the subject of consciousness with the intuitive approaches that seem for now to exist in a different universe of discourse.

3. A Particular System Model

For what seems a long time (considering the progress I have made), I have been focusing on a particular set of laws of structure and their implications for behavioral science: the laws that govern the organization of functions known as a *negative feedback control system*. The applicability of these laws to an understanding of organisms was noticed at the outset of cybernetics; indeed, feedback control was the core concept from which Wiener (1948) developed most of his thinking on this subject. The fact that I have not gone on to the kinds of complexity and diversity that have characterized cybernetics since those early days probably marks me as backward, but I have been convinced that the concept of feedback control is exceptionally important and that its potential as an organizing principle has not been fully appreciated in the behavioral sciences. Others have noted and used the concept of negative feedback; many have. For the most part, however, the uses of these concepts have been limited and have been strongly conditioned by older concepts of cause and effect. Even in engineering psychology, where the methods of control system analysis have been applied to studies of tracking behavior for well over 20 years, the organism itself is still usually represented in block diagrams as a simple input–output or stimulus–response device, a "transfer function" that reduces, at low frequencies, to a single constant of proportionality. In a few instances (e.g., Kelley, 1968) the analysis has gone farther than that, several hierarchical levels of control being proposed for some peripheral neuromuscular systems, but generally there has been no concerted attempt to see what the concept of feedback control means when contrasted with the fundamental assumptions under which most of behavioral science still operates.

It is that level of analysis to which I have devoted my efforts (Powers, Clark, & McFarland, 1960; Powers, 1973). The interpretations that come out of a control-system analysis of behavior seem to point toward new approaches to many subjects, particularly two subjects of interest here, awareness and volition, with which behavioral science has dealt largely by avoiding the real issues. Like Nasrudin, behavioral science has been looking for its house key under a handy streetlight, not because it was lost there but because the light is better there.

There are many ways to order a discussion of control theory, but for present purposes, it will be profitable to start with a phenomenon that has puzzled behavioral scientists as long as there has been such a subject.

3.1. Control Theory and Stabilized Consequences

William James (1890) is credited with pointing American psychology toward the laboratory, where, as some say, psychology lost its mind. It certainly lost the concept of purpose. But in his introduction to *The Principles of Psychology,* James insisted in several different ways that the one distinguishing feature of living organisms was their ability to keep reaching a fixed aim by employing variable means. He was saying that living organisms demonstrate purpose, not blind reactions to external forces.

John Dewey (1896/1948), writing at the same time, saw that the reflex arc could not be characterized in terms of lineal cause and effect; it is a closed circle with no beginning and no end. Both Dewey and James, had they had the tools, could easily have gone on from there to found cybernetics, for the phenomena of purpose and the kind of organization that involves a closed circle of cause and effect are key elements of control theory. The rudiments of control-system analysis were available; James Clerk Maxwell had analyzed mechanical control systems (governors) in 1868. Unfortunately, no Norbert Wiener came forth to save scientific psychology its 11-decade pursuit of a different cause–effect model, by seeing how the organizational principles that apply to governors also permit the existence of purposive systems in a universe of physical laws. Simple determinism, involving external causation of behavioral acts, won the day.

But the phenomena that have always suggested inner purpose refused to disappear. All such phenomena can be characterized in one general way: they involve stabilized consequences of variable actions. Let us pause for a few definitions.

An *action* will be taken to mean some measure of behavior that appears to be unaffected by interfering environmental circumstances: at the lowest level of analysis, a train of neural signals entering a muscle could be called an action of the nervous system. It is usually possible to find more global measures: an applied force, a velocity of a limb, and so on. The main criterion is that an action should be attributable to the organism alone, either because there is nothing present that can interfere with it or because, for whatever reason, potential interferences are, in fact, ineffective.

We need to define a comparable quantity in the environment, a quantity we will call a *disturbance*. This is a measure of some physical variable that can vary or be fixed independently of what the behaving organism does. Gravity is a ubiquitous disturbance.

A *consequence* is technically defined for this discussion as a physical variable (or a set of them) that is a joint function of action and disturbance. The posture of an animal, for example, results from the combination of muscle forces with forces due to gravity, all acting on the masses of the body through the geometric linkages of the skeleton, according to the appropriate laws of mechanics. In general, a given action and a given disturbance will be found to have many identifiable consequences; they jointly affect physical variables of many kinds.

Consequences of action and disturbance that are not joint functions of both are taken as alternative measures of action or disturbance; the term *consequence* would not be used, even though it would be permitted in ordinary discourse. I shall say *joint* consequences to emphasize this special definition.

The great majority of the phenomena that are commonly called *behavior* can be analyzed as joint consequences of an action and a disturbance (or the resultant of several disturbances, which is what *the disturbance* will generally mean). They are not, however, identifiable with *all* joint consequences. A randomly selected joint consequence would, in general, be affected just as much by unpredictable variations in the environment as by variations in an organism's actions; there would be no *repeatable* pattern to the joint consequence unless the environment and the organism precisely repeated their separate patterns. In order for a joint consequence to show enough general repeatability to be recognized as behavior in a normally variable environment, there must be a special relationship between action and disturbance: whatever the disturbance, the action must adjust so that the joint consequence repeats.

This requirement has, of course, been noticed, and there have been qualitative explanations offered for the fact that it is so often met. One is the *compensatory response* explanation: the mechanical effects of a disturbance are accompanied by sensory effects that alter the behavior in just the way that cancels the mechanical effects. But like all such analyses that do not employ the principles of control theory, it fails when put to the quantitative test even in simple cases. Consider a person holding an arm out straight ahead, the finger being held within 5 mm of a target for 30 sec, with a net load of 10 kg referred to the wrist. The muscle forces acting upward will nearly cancel the force due to gravity, 98 n. How nearly? The average acceleration of the arm must be such that the arm moves by no more than 5 mm in 30 sec; by the relationship

$$s = \tfrac{1}{2}at^2,$$

we find the maximum acceleration to be 1.11×10^{-5} me/sec^2, or about one millionth of a gravity. The compensatory response explanation requires the nerves and muscles to retain an accuracy of calibration some four orders of magnitude better than the best that is ever measured; it is flatly untenable.

In this case, we have an action (upward force due to muscles) canceling the effects of a disturbance (downward force due to gravity) to create a stabilized joint consequence (arm position, the second integral of the acceleration of the moving mass). This is precisely the situation to which control theory applies. A model is easily constructed and is worth a brief look as preparation for what follows.

First, there must be a sensor that detects the current state of the consequence to be stabilized, arm position, the sensor representing that state as a signal, y. Next there must be a comparator that generates an error signal, e, that is proportional to the difference between the actual state as sensed and a reference state, y_0 (usually supplied in the form of another signal, inside the system as a whole), letting the proportionality constant be unity, we have $e = y_0 - y$. Finally, the error signal enters an output actuator, which produces a degree of action proportional to the amount and sign of error signal; in this case, we call the action f, the upward force, and assume that $f = ke$, k being a constant of proportionality having units of force per meter of error.

To finish the closed loop, we have to add the effects of the action together with the effects of the disturbance to create a state of the stabilized consequence (or, more conveniently, its representation, y). The acceleration, a, of the arm in the $+y$ direction is net force divided by mass, or $(f - mg)/m$, or $f/m - g$ (g is the acceleration due to gravity). Thus $a = f/m - g$. We have three system equations:

(1) $e = y_o - y$
(2) $f = ke$
(3) $\ddot{y} = f/m - g$

The acceleration, a, corresponds to the second derivative of y-position, or $\ddot{y}$ (the double dot signifies the second derivation with respect to time).

This set of equations can be solved as a system; the solution is *not* correct. The solution predicts some kind of endless sinusoidal oscillation, which we observe does *not* occur in the real case. Thus, a system analysis is not better than any other kind; it does not automatically give right answers if the model is not basically correct. One must still attend to nature and ask, when the model doesn't work, *why* it doesn't work.

In this case, it doesn't work because we have left out friction and all other effects that create (or simulate) a drag proportional to the velocity of a movement. We have modeled, in effect, a mass suspended on a perfect spring. To make the model work, all that is needed is to introduce into one of the equations a term involving the first time derivative of y, which may amount only to changing the part of the system description that pertains to the physical properties of the environment through which the feedback occurs. When that change is made, the model is given another degree of freedom in the form of the coefficient of a *damping* term. That coefficient can then be adjusted to make the predicted behavior match actual behavior quite nicely. This has been done so often that I won't bother to repeat it here. (See, for example, Stark, 1968 or Maxwell, 1868/1965.)

The only aspect of the solution of interest here is the fact that, with sufficient damping present, there is a steady-state condition predicted. If there is a steady-state condition, all the derivatives will become zero, meaning that $\ddot{y}$ becomes zero in Eq. 3. Making the appropriate substitutions from Eqs. 1 and 2, this produces

(4) $0 = k(y_o - y)/m - g$

or

$$y_o - y = mg/k$$

In this equation there are two parameters pertaining to the behaving system, y_o (the setting of the reference signal) and k (the output force per unit error). The parameter k indicates the amount of steady-state change in output force that results from a steady disturbance-caused deviation of arm position and so corresponds roughly to the sensitivity factor that must be accurately calibrated in the compensatory response model. In this control model, as can be seen, the only requirement on k

is that it be *large enough*. For $y_0 - y$ to be less than .005 meter, and with $mg = 98$ N, k must be at least 1.96×10^4 (i.e., 20 N/mm). If k were then *doubled*, the result would be that the error, $y_0 - y$, would be *halved*. "Compensation" requires the accurate balancing of large opposing effects; control requires only high sensitivity to error. The actual sensitivity can vary over a wide range without any significant effect on the observable results. Thus, the control model works both qualitatively and quantitatively, without requiring impossible precision of the neuromuscular system.

This extremely brief run through a control analysis has been meant only to give the general idea, and especially to show how the subject of *perception* enters the picture almost without being noticed. Whatever a control system controls, it must sense. Thus, it is often the case that one cannot tell what is being controlled without finding out, somehow, what is being sensed. It is this close relationship of perception to control that creates the appearances misinterpreted for so long as a direct stimulus–response, input–output, cause–effect relationship between external events and behavioral actions.

3.2. Control Theory and Causation

According to the control model, stabilized consequences are stabilized because they are sensed and compared with a reference. An indication of the error is used to cause the very output that opposes the error. Disturbances tending to alter the stabilized consequence are not directly sensed but are sensed only through the resultant small deviations of the stabilized consequence, that is, departures of the signal representing it from the reference signal representing the target state. A system with very high error sensitivity (k in Eq. 4) makes large changes in its output before a disturbance has affected the stabilized consequence by more than a small amount; those changes of output are opposed to the effects of the disturbance simply because they are opposed to the sign of the error, however the error is caused. As a result, the effects of output actions on the consequence are seen to be balanced, at all times, against the effects of any disturbance.

The rub is that this balancing of action against disturbance can be seen *only* in terms of the stabilized consequence, the joint effect of action and disturbance that is being sensed and controlled. If control is effective, that consequence will not vary appreciably, and since it does not, *it will fail to show significant correlations with either action or disturbance.* The traditional statistical approach cannot reveal controlled consequences.

The observer who is trying to find out *why* a given action follows upon, or accompanies, a given independent environmental occurrence must be completely aware of the possibility that control is involved; if he is not, he is very likely to fall into the trap that nature has baited for us. The appearance created by control behavior is that the organism simply *mediates* between disturbance and action. Since both disturbance and action may affect the stabilized (joint) consequence through delayed, indirect, and nonlinear paths, and since more than one disturbance may be acting, the fact that action is continuously canceling the net effects of disturbances on some stabilized consequence is not transparently self-evident. What *is* evident is that action bears some regular relationship to disturbance. In terms of effects on a properly defined stabilized consequence, that relationship is quantitative and precise *opposition*, but even in terms of direct measures, more than a chance correlation between action and consequence will be seen. Adding to the clear existence of such relationships the *absence* of any clear relationship to the stabilized consequence (because it *is* stabilized), we have a situation guaranteed to lead the uninformed observer astray. A sudden disturbance will lead, a fraction of a second later, to a sudden change of action; a continuing disturbance to a steady bias of action; a varying disturbance to covarying actions. The appearance is that of a cause–effect relationship.

The conclusion into which we are enticed by that painted hussy is that the organism must be sensing the disturbance; that the disturbance is a stimulus that acts on the nervous system to *make* it produce the variations of action that are observed. That picture places the organism between disturbance and action, as a mediating input–output device that converts the former into the latter. One could write transfer functions describing that relationship to the sixth decimal place—and still have it wrong.

Suppose that by a stroke of luck comparable to the birth of Norbert Wiener, someone had appeared on the scene in about 1869, someone who was aware of Fechner's work in about 1860 on the psychophysics of perception and also of Maxwell's analysis of mechanical control systems, and who was capable of putting the two schemes together. The model that would have resulted would, of course, have been not electromechanical but neuromechanical; that is of no consequence. The important thing is that the model would have shown a way in which a system could have an internal reference, with respect to which it *controlled what it sensed*. It would have been realized from the start that there could be *apparent* cause–effect relationships seen in behavior that were illusions as convincing and as incorrect as the optical illusions with which psychologists were to become so preoccupied.

Had that theoretical advance occurred, it would have been impossible to argue, as influential biologists, neurologists, and behaviorists were to do for the next century, that behavior is necessarily controlled by events impinging on the organism. When half a century later Watson stood contemplating the bird in his hand struggling to get back into the bush, he would not automatically have rejected the appearance of goal direction as illusory, and he would not have been struck by the unfortunate insight that all responses could in principle be predicted on the basis of stimuli. That would have been a fine insight if Watson had been studying systems that were *not* control systems, but that case had already been handled some centuries before when the physical sciences rejected animism. Although Watson had at least a chance to launch the scientific study of *animate* systems, he missed it.

Another outstanding chance to found cybernetics early came in 1938 (there were several others between). In that year, B. F. Skinner found that when organisms were given the means to control their own food inputs, they learned the required behaviors far more rapidly than had ever been seen before. To Skinner, however, the significant fact was not the strong tendency of changes in action to counter the effects of disturbances on food inputs but the fact that specifying the way in which action affected consequence (the schedule of reinforcement) had very reliable effects on the actions that came to be performed. Skinner's ambition was control of the animal's behavior, not understanding of the animal's control of the inputs that mattered to *it*. With that emphasis, coupled with the *a priori* assumption that a proper theory of behavior had to leave all causes in the environment, Skinner missed his chance. We will always be in his debt for his discovery of operant conditioning and the equally important phenomenon of shaping, but it is too bad that he does not also have the credit for introducing control theory to psychology. Operant conditioning demonstrated the first organismic control behavior that was well enough instrumented to permit systematic deduction of the laws of negative feedback; it was not interpreted that way.

It fell to Norbert Wiener to recognize the similarity between the structure of servomechanisms being designed by technologists and the structure of neuromuscular systems. But by this time, the mid-1940s, the concept of behavior as a consequence of external circumstances had developed a stranglehold on thinking in nearly every field that aspired to the adjective *scientific*. Even though Wiener and his immediate successors saw all of the major implications of control theory with regard to goal seeking and purpose (Buckley, 1968), they were unable to shake off that last concept of cause and effect. Wiener (1948) drew a diagram of a control system that shows an input coming in from the left and an output leaving to the right, with *internal* feedback serving to make the output a more reliable function of the input. The fact that the input he was talking about was really the reference signal and that neuroanatomically it came from centers higher in the brain and *not* from sensory receptors seems to have been missed, perhaps by Wiener himself and certainly by scores of others who have re-created the organization of that fateful diagram in the literature all during the past 30 years. The general relationship among action, disturbance, and consequence that we have been examining, although repeatedly approximated, has for all practical purposes remained unknown.

I don't wish to argue *ad hominem*, but there comes a point when recognition of ordinary human frailty can be important. I think there is a very good reason for the almost universal failure to recognize the basic implications of control theory. The result of such recognition by any person with two neurons to rub together would have been the realization that the basic cause–effect relationship assumed for an analysis of "irritable tissue" had been in error from the start. To visualize the consequences if that were true would be to imagine the skyscrapers of New York going down like dominoes. Scarcely a single "fact" about organisms would remain intact. So what do human beings do when they realize that a train of thought is leading toward disaster? They think about something else.

3.3. Control Theory and Purpose

For the first 40 years of its existence as a science, psychology was billed as the study of consciousness. Introspection was a legitimate tool. The idea that people and perhaps some animals were purposive was widely accepted; each person could examine his own experiences and see plenty of examples of actions directed toward preselected goals. Even after behaviorism came on the scene and preempted the term *scientific psychology*, there were many diehards who knew that purpose was a fundamental aspect of human organization but couldn't justify this belief scientifically. The result was a deep split between "hard" and "soft" studies of human nature.

The basic cause of this split was a mistaken concept of cause and effect, coupled with the naive epistemology that goes with it. The main argument against purpose or intentionality as a factor in shaping behavior was that physical determinism made no room for inner direction of behavior, regardless of the weight of circumstantial evidence. The basic organization of the nervous system seemed fairly well understood; stimuli affected sensory nerves, which sent signals to higher centers, which relayed them and elaborated on them and eventually sent them outward in patterns that excited the muscles, thus producing what we recognize as behavior. Without realizing it, those who offered this picture were assuming more than neurologists could know.

All that neurologists knew then about the structure of the nervous system (and most of what is known even now) consisted of the general concepts of synaptic transmission, a few highly localized relationships, and some of the main pathways of neural signal flow. In an approximate way, some crudely defined units of behavior such as "movements" of limbs were known to arise when specific areas of the brain were "excited." Superimposed on the facts known about the components of the nervous system was an *assumed structure*, which combined the components into a model that would support a preselected cause–effect organization. As I pointed out in the beginning, assembling components into a structure introduces laws peculiar to the structure. In this case, the law was exceedingly simple: output is a function of input.

Many exceptions to the general input–output flow were found as neurological investigations continued. Both excitation and inhibition occurred; neural pathways were found that provided shortcuts from input to output at many levels lower than the cortex, and pathways were found from outputs back to inputs both inside and outside the system. Of particular interest to us are the discoveries of the many stages in *output* processes where *inputs* enter with a sign opposite to "commands" from higher centers, resulting almost universally in negative feedback and cancellation of most of the so-called command signal. It is possible—and as time goes on, more and more strongly advisable—to abandon the old input–output structure and to adopt a control-system structure for models of the central nervous system.

That structure provides a place for inner purposes. They can be identified functionally as reference signals, signals that specify to a given control system what level of its inner representation to bring about and maintain. A variable reference signal specifies corresponding variations in the controlled consequence being sensed and represented. A fixed reference signal specifies a static condition of the inner representation, although not necessarily a static condition of external physical variables (rates, velocities, and sequences can easily be represented as steady signals: consider *amplitude* and *phase*).

This change in the structure assumed for the brain changes all interpretations of the meanings of signals in the brain, particularly the outbound signals that used to be thought of as stages in the relaying of patterns from the cortex to the muscles. Now, they are seen as error signals, determined in part by reference signals from higher centers but determined just as strongly by disturbances tending to alter controlled consequences. There are no patterns high in the cortex that are relayed intact to the muscles. The patterning of behavior takes place on the input side.

As a result of this change in assumed structure, we arrive at a new concept of the meaning of *purpose*. A purpose is not an intended *action* but an intended *consequence* of action. Furthermore, in the final analysis, it is an intended state of an inner representation of that consequence— an intended state of a perception. With all the work currently going on in neurophysiological laboratories, following the lead of Hubel and Wiesel (1965), and with the addition of just a little common sense, we should begin to suspect that the world of perception that is experienced is constructed by computers at various levels in the brain, that *all* we experience is an inner representation, a signal that is an unknown function of unknown variables that no one can sense directly. When Hubel and Wiesel found neurons that responded preferentially to certain visual objects such as edges or oriented lines, how did they know what the electrode recordings corresponded to? By looking with their own eyes at the test stimulus, of course. What they found is not a neural correlate of an external object but a correlation between an electronic data display and a *subjective perception*. They were comparing two ways of looking at neural signals. They were no more able to peek past their retinas and see what was really causing those electronic or neural "meter readings" than is anyone else.

If we admit that the world we perceive is, at best, a *function of* external stimuli and not those external stimuli themselves, the concept of purpose can be defended against all traditional criticisms. The philosophers of behaviorism at the turn of the century objected to the idea of purpose because they took purpose to mean (a) intended *outputs* and (b) predetermined future consequences of present acts. If they could show that an output was "caused by" some external event (i.e., depended on it in a regular way), there was no need to introduce purpose as a second cause of the same actions. And, if an organism intended for a certain consequence of its actions to occur, they argued, how could failure to achieve those results be explained? *Predetermination* to them meant predestination, in the sense that a spring-powered watch that is not wound is predestined to stop running. Since no given act has precisely the same future consequences twice in a row, went the objection, there is no way for an act to be intentional in the sense of having a predestined result in the future.

Control theory bypasses all those arguments by identifying purpose with the specification of *reference levels for inputs*. There is no prediction of the future involved; the organism simply acts at all times in the direction that will oppose the present-time error. When disturbances arise or external conditions change in any (reasonable) way, actions adjust quite automatically and by understandable mechanisms to continue opposing error. It is not as if a single spasmodic action had to produce a predestined future consequence. The control system is always right there, continually altering its actions to keep the sensed consequence what it is intended to be (one level of sensed consequence could be a steady approach toward some final relationship).

3.4. Control Theory and Volition

One of the main reasons for rejecting the idea that *any* inner phenomenon could shape behavior was very practical. According to the cause–effect model that was thought to be required by physical determinism, it should be possible to study the way behavior depended on external conditions and eventually to achieve the ability to predict and control behavior through manipulations of external circumstances. "Prediction and control" was the slogan of science. Since a great many people wished to study organisms in a scientific manner, it would obviously have been inconvenient to believe that organisms contained *internal* causative agencies that could not be manipulated by an external experimenter. It became fashionable to assume that if any internal causative agency existed, it would behave lawlessly or, as a favorite pejorative had it, "capriciously." The unthinkability of capriciousness was taken as its refutation.

This point of view was unwittingly supported by the proponents of purpose; somehow the argument came to be not a factual dispute about internal causation but a philosophical argument about free will versus mechanistic determinism. As a result, the intellectual debates concerned the last chapter of a book, the main bulk of which had not yet been written. As we shall see, the most likely analysis of internal causation does not support the concept of either mechanistic external determinism *or* "free will" (whatever that is).

The reference signal given to a control subsystem tells that subsystem how much of its perception to want to perceive; the error is the *want*. In a *hierarchical* control-system model, the reference signal reaching a system of level n is a function of the error signal in a system of level $n+1$; variation of the lower-level reference signal is the means by which the higher-level system controls its own representation of reality. At each higher level, says the model, the representations that are controlled are invariants abstracted (neurally, not verbally) from the next lower level of representations. Therefore, for all practical purposes, the environment of a system at a given level consists of the neural representations that are under control by systems of the next lower level. The higher-level system acts on that environment by emitting reference signals into it (for the lower-level systems); the organism learns through experience what reference signals must be emitted in order to control any representation with which it is concerned.

This model shares at least one major capacity with its modeler: a concern with control. I have always thought it odd that a science dedicated to prediction and control omitted both capacities from its models of human beings.

The term *volition* belongs to the world of common sense, primarily because science has recoiled from it. Common sense, however, occasionally turns out to have found the right answer while science pursues the complex consequences of erroneous assumptions. Now that we know of a way in which inner purposes and intentions can exist, it is not a long step to see how the general phenomena called *volition* could be allowed, once again, to exist.

To say that one has performed an act volitionally is to say that there is no immediate external cause for the act. The situation is not that simple, however. An act at one level of description is only a means at the next higher level. I may say that I volitionally extended my arm and be quite convinced that there was an internal predetermination to perform just that act; yet, in a larger context, I can see that the goal of catching a falling vase, together with the geometry of the prevailing external circumstances as perceived, made that act and no other mandatory. To catch the vase, I had to get my hand under it, and nowhere else.

This has always been the main point of confusion about volition, even for common sense. Any action is at the same time an *intended goal*, continuously achieved, and a *variable means* adjusted according to the requirements of higher-order goals and external disturbances. The degree of volition one senses depends on whether he is focusing on the intended action (as the goal state of a perception of action) or on the higher-order *reason* for the action, the higher-order goal served by the action. When attention is on the higher-order goal, the lower-level action is sensed as *output;* when attention is focused on the intentional nature of lower-level action, the same action is sensed as an *input,* a perceived and controlled consequence of an output of still lower level (say, "effort").

The control model shows that all these interpretations are correct; there is no contradiction. In fact, these commonsense descriptions have an uncanny congruence with the structure that arises out of a control-system model. The control model elucidates the commonsense descriptions, by showing how one and the same behavior can seem both volitional and dictated by circumstances. The behavior of any control system—that is, the output it generates—is always governed by precisely those two considerations, acting jointly: the inner goal, which determines the level to which the perception will be brought and maintained, and external circumstances, which determine the amount and direction of the action needed at any given moment to keep perception in that goal state. Behavior is not directed by inner volition alone or by external circumstances alone: it is a joint consequence of *both*. The specific states of stabilized consequences of actions cannot be explained in terms of external circumstances; the details of action cannot be explained in terms of the inner goal. We are dealing with a system in which both of these considerations operate *at the same time*. Either–or cause–effect thinking is totally inadequate to handle this phenomenon. For control theory, it's a piece of cake.

The structure of our lower levels of control organization does not seem to us to be our own structure but rather the structure of the world of direct experience. One has to extend a hand to catch a falling vase because that is the way the outside world, not the nervous system, works. For that reason, we tend not to recognize the same means–ends relationships at these lower levels; we externalize them. Often we do this just by omitting the statement of the goal that is involved. One says, "I ducked because he took a swing at me," as if taking a swing, through some law of nature, could cause someone else to duck. In fact, one would not duck unless doing so served to keep some perception at the intended level: the perception of being hit, perhaps, at the reference level of *zero*. Under unusual circumstances, which ought to be enlightening but usually aren't, one may select a different reference level for the same perception; a small amount of being hit (a movie stuntman) or even a large amount (a person intending to prove that he is impervious to pain or above being bullied).

This omission of the implicit goal from discussions of cause and effect makes relationships between disturbances and actions appear to be cause–effect laws that work just as behavioral scientists have been assuming that the nervous system works. I strongly suspect that it is this commonsense model of lower-level actions that is behind the initial scientific models. It takes a rather strange set of circumstances to cause a person to say, "I couldn't get out of the classroom because the teacher was looking right at me" and then add," . . . and I didn't want to leave while she was looking at me." When the goal *is* specified, it seems superfluous to mention; it goes without saying. Unfortunately, it also goes without *thinking*, which is the main problem here.

I should mention another reason for omitting implicit goals, one that is at least more defensible (and seemed final in 1913). *Any* cause–effect relationship can be described in terms of an implicit goal: the negatively charged pith ball moved because a negatively charged rod approached it, and the pith ball didn't want to be touched by the rod. Even the most exhaustive examination of pith balls and charged rods, however, will fail to reveal the structure of a control system. Therefore, attributing goals to this system is simply a blunder. All that happens can be explained in terms of direct interactions between the entities involved (and a little unavoidable magic—"fields"). Inanimate objects almost never possess the internal structure necessary to permit purposive behavior. One *should* omit hypotheses concerning inner goals when such goals are ruled out.

3.5. Ultimate Purposes

Anyone who proposes a hierarchical model has to realize, sooner or later, that he has a problem: the highest level. As long as one can remain comfortably in the middle or lower reaches of such a model there is no conceptual difficulty, but the model is not limited in the upward direction as it is in the downward direction. There is a temptation to achieve closure, to settle on some way of topping off the structure, even if one doesn't know how to.

I don't know how to; perhaps that admission is as important a part of this model as the parts that have been positively proposed. I am refusing to fish for some way to make the whole structure complete just to lend support to a philosophical prejudice (I tried it once, in my last book, and the discussion got so fuzzy as to be useless).

What can be said about the higher levels is mostly negative. We *do not* know the basis on which the highest-level goals are set. We are *incapable* of tracing them to any specific external circumstances, particularly not present-time circumstances. We can offer some reasonable conjectures about how biochemical and genetic factors enter, particularly in connection with learning, but we can *by no acceptable scientific means* show that those factors are "ultimate" determinants, not in any sense. It is time to stop trying to make everything fit 19th-century ideas of physical determinism, which are based on little more than an allergic reaction to religion. The upper regions of human organization are a mystery that we have barely begun to approach; we will never understand them on the basis of a jab-and-jerk model of behavior.

4. CONSCIOUSNESS

As long as behavioral science worked under the assumption that the brain is simply a link in the chain from sensory input to motor output, subjective perception, memory, and feelings of volition and intention had to be treated as epiphenomena. Like the lights on the front panel of a computer, such phenomena of consciousness informed the observer about what was going on but had no influence on the operation of the system. To "be scientific" about behavior meant, largely, to *redefine* subjective phenomena, finding words that would permit one to deny internal causes and assert external ones. Calling every action a *response* was just one such semantic ploy.

This denial of an active role to consciousness has, of course, created a gulf between scientific psychology and the common sense of laymen. Probably as a defensive measure against commonsense criticism, there has grown up an unspoken attitude that seems detectable whenever behavioral scientists get together to talk about behavior. If it were put into words, it might sound something like this:

> Sometimes it seems that organisms seek goals, want things, decide things, and act spontaneously. But you and I know that such appearances are illusions, because we know that natural laws of physics and chemistry are behind all such appearances. In ordinary affairs, we use ordinary language for convenience, but when we want to speak as scientists, we have to put metaphysical nonsense aside. If laymen criticize our scientific descriptions, that is only because of leftover superstitions, beliefs, and sloppy habits of thought from their primitive past. We scientists do not have any superstitions, beliefs, or sloppy habits of thought, especially since such things do not really exist in the first place. And if you won't call attention to my consciousness, I won't call attention to yours.

As I tried to show earlier, the systems approach brings out the clear existence of laws of structure that cannot be traced to, or deduced from, laws of physics and chemistry. For three-quarters of this essay, I have been trying to show that one particular systems approach, control theory, offers strong grounds for denying that the brain simply mediates between events affecting the senses and subsequent behavioral actions. Now, the argument can be carried to its logical conclusion: the phenomena of consciousness can no longer be dismissed by mutual agreement and must be studied as causative phenomena just as real as the physical events that are involved in behavior.

4.1. Causative Factors in the Brain

While it is not yet possible to trace reference signals to the highest level of the brain's control hierarchy, certain generalizations can be defended even without knowing the architecture of the higher levels. The main working hypothesis concerns relationships between levels.

A control hierarchy involves a hierarchy of perceptions— representations of higher-and-higher-order invariants constructed on the raw material of lower levels. It also involves a hierarchy of adjustable purposes: reference signals that specify to a given control system whether it is to keep its perception at a minimum, intermediate, or maximum level. As we have seen, the action performed by a given system (that is, the lower order reference signal or, for first-order systems only, the motor signal) reflects both the setting of a reference signal received from higher systems and the presence of disturbances that tend to alter the perceptual signal being controlled by the given system. For a fixed reference signal from above, the action is determined by disturbances; for a disturbance-free lower-order environment, the action is determined by the higher-order reference signal. We are concerned for now with this latter case, in which no significant disturbances are present and actions at the level of interest result primarily from the settings of reference signals.

Consider a control system that senses and controls one dimension of a repetitive pattern, say tapping out a steady rhythm on a tabletop with one finger. To implement a speed-of-tapping control system, there must be a perceptual device that reacts not to each tap but to the average rate of tapping; the output part of the system must respond to error by varying the speed with which the reference signal for finger position is switched back and forth between "up" and "down." If the rate is sensed at the "slow" end of the perceptual scale, and if the reference signal is set at a magnitude corresponding to "fast," the resulting error signal should cause the output function to increase its speed of alternation of position-reference signals. If the system is sufficiently sensitive to error, it will come to a steady-state condition with the sensed rate of tapping matching the steady reference signal, the sensed rate being in the form of a steady signal also.

This control system needs no external stimulus to keep the tapping going; it needs only a steady value of reference signal, supplied from higher systems. The behavior is "spontaneous," in that there is no series of environmental events that could be said to cause the individual tapping events, in any one-to-one way. If a disturbance occurred—say, the ambient medium were changed from air to cold molasses—the changes in reference signal for finger position might become more exaggerated and might advance in phase, and that change in the output pattern could be said to have been externally caused, even though the final result is thereby kept from being affected. But the central consequence, the controlled rate of finger-tapping as perceived, must be considered to have its immediate cause inside the person doing the tapping.

In any specific instance of a control phenomena, it makes no difference whether the controlled quantity is a static or a dynamic condition: the immediate cause of the phenomenon, in the absence of significant disturbances, must be attributed to the next higher level of organization, further removed from the external environment.

Even when disturbances are taken into consideration, the same kind of role is found for higher-order systems. A change of output in response to a disturbance always occurs so as to resist changes of the affected perception away from some given reference level, determined by a higher-order system. The response to a disturbance depends not on the disturbance alone, but on where the perceptual signal is relative to its reference level (above or below) and the effect of the disturbance relative to that reference level.

In a search for the causes of any given action, the control model thus always takes us farther from the periphery and into levels involving higher and higher orders of invariants constructed by the nervous system. The direction toward ultimate causes is not back toward the sensory inputs but in exactly the opposite direction, deeper into, or higher into, the hierarchy.

Somewhere in that hierarchy, we must eventually find all that is experiencable, and that includes not only representations of the physical and the physiological environments but relationships among elements of the environment, structures of logic concerning those relationships, abstract principles by which programs of logical thought are directed, and systems concepts that allow us to represent collections of principles in terms of models. In short, we must sooner or later come across *every object of experience*. Every time we ask why a given perception is controlled, the *why* will become *how* a higher-order perception is controlled. The ultimate model of the nervous system will be a model of our entire structure of purposes, and identically a model of the world on which we act to carry out those purposes. The whole will be a model of experience, everything to which a person can attend whether he refers to it as being inside or outside himself.

Clearly, the causes of behavior cannot be understood until we understand this entire structure, which I assume to be the structure imposed by the organization of the brain. It is not possible, in these terms, to speak of "the" cause of anything a person does; any attempt to find such causes leads inevitably to the necessity of understanding the entire hierarchy and its interactions with that world outside that we have barely begun to deduce. The laws of the external reality, as they affect us, are inextricably interwoven with the laws of structure that reside in our brains and mark us as human.

4.2. Ultimate Causes

We are not born with this inner structure completed. It grows, and takes on its adult form through decades of incessant interactions with the external world. When we fail to control perceptions of various types, either because we have not yet constructed those invariants or because we have not yet stumbled across a means, the failure has many consequences that affect us through routes other than the senses. To take a simple case, if we do not learn to control the efforts, tastes, sounds, movements, sequences, and relationships involved in eating, we suffer direct physiological effects that would occur even if all our senses were numbed. Somewhere inside us, there is a link between these unsensed effects and the way the hierarchy of control changes and grows. And inherent to this link, there must logically be some specification of the *proper* states of the physiological variables involved. That specification is certainly not acquired by an individual during his lifetime. It must have developed over countless thousands of years, through slow processes of genetically preserved change. It is not subject to present-time manipulation.

If there can be any ultimate determinant of the way we learn to think and act, it must be in this set of inherited specifications for the state of the physical organism that calls for no change in behavioral organization. When these specifications are not met, the result is change—change of the very structure that is the hierarchy we have been discussing. I have called these specifications *intrinsic reference levels,* and I have viewed the process of change as a kind of metacontrol system that alters structure as its means of controlling what it senses. Our highest purposes have to do with continuing to be human.

To some, this invocation of physiological variables may come as a relief—finally, we are back to physics and chemistry! But I don't think we can afford to be as simplistic as that. What we are talking about is *organization,* not components; we are talking about the same kind of organization of stored information that can make us grow kidneys and fingerprints. The physics and chemistry of DNA and RNA provide us with a model of only the tape and the tape recorder (more or less); they do not explain the origin or the evolution of the message. We may be dealing here with the highest-order invariants of all. The "state of the physical organism" can mean anything from the pH of the bloodstream to the elegance of a solution to a conflict. I am not willing to put any restrictions on the subject matter to which intrinsic reference levels might refer. Laws of structure are involved, and we know very little about the number of levels of structure that have laws of their own.

4.3. The Nature of Consciousness: Point of View

There is one fact about the nervous system that is very easy to forget, or ignore. The nervous system we know about through sensory experience bears practically no relationship to the nervous system we use in our theories. The nervous system of naive perception is a gray blob, which under a microscope becomes a mass of separate blobs and filaments. We see no organization there; we imagine it. We have pieced together a mental model of events in that gray blob, trimming, rearranging, and adding to the mental model until it behaves more or less as our instruments and logic combined report real brains to behave.

Somewhere in that gray blob, we must conclude, is the mental model of the gray blob. We don't know anywhere *else* it might exist. We deal, perforce, with what von Foerster (1974) has called a "recursive system." The system, as his students have put it, computes that it is computing. The experience experiences itself.

This bothers me. Something has been left unsaid, or unthought, or unnoticed. I think the problem lies not in our models but in a certain attitude toward models, one that encourages us to follow our own logic once around the loop and then forget to follow it around again. What is a "recursive system"? It is first of all *an idea about systems*. More: it is, for those who think about it, an *object of experience*, just as much as a toenail is, although it does not share the same space in which toenails exist. To think about recursive systems, or nervous systems, or control theory, or any conceptual scheme at all requires that someone adopt a particular structured point of view toward lower-order experiences.

That is what bothers me: the fact that there is always a point of view, and that it is structured. What is it that can adopt, and abandon, points of view? Where do we find it in this hierarchical model of perception and control of perception?

The answer is that we do not find it there. We do not yet have a model that can reproduce this phenomenon I call *point of view*. The structure that is involved in any given point of view is the acquired structure of the brain; that much is not hard to fit in. But the brain, once organized, contains *all* points of view possible to it, even those not currently operative. Moreover, points of view can shift up and down in the hierarchy suggested by this model; one may become a configuration-recognizer and may after a while become a relationship-recognizer. Yet there could be no relationships, such as "next to," if the lower levels were not still faithfully constructing the configurations that are related. Something moves. Something that is not yet represented in the model.

5. CONCLUSIONS

If these explorations have led me anywhere, it has been to a vivid sense of my ignorance. Control theory, I believe, turns us around and pushes us off in a new direction, and leads us to see how little progress toward understanding our own existence we have really made in the past 300 years. It does not allow us to see very far ahead in that new direction.

It does do something of value, however, by forcing us to look at ordinary experience as evidence of our own structure as much as evidence about an external reality. When thinking about hierarchical levels of perception, one is forced to move his point of view upward (or whatever the direction is) merely to try to comprehend the currently operative structure that gives form to the current, or just previous, point of view. It forces us to experience this phenomenon in action rather than just constructing words or block diagrams about it. It pins the label *model* on our models, which otherwise we would be inclined to accept without thinking as truths about a hypothetical external world.

Most important to me, it leads almost inevitably to the realization that the objects of experience, from the "concrete" to the "abstract," are indeed *objects of* experience, phenomena moving in and out of the field of experience so effortlessly and easily that we scarcely see any significance in their comings and goings. Yet, I think those comings and goings constitute a higher-level fact that is at least as important as the specific items that come and go. A relationship, such as the distance from your eyes to the page you are reading, does not come from anywhere when you notice it or go anywhere when you are tired of noticing it. It appears in experience when one adopts the point of view of a relationship-perceiver. Perhaps the signal was there all along; under some circumstances involving several levels of hierarchically related control tasks, the signal *has* to be there all along, even when not being experienced.

It would be gratifying to know how to test this phenomenon of point of view. If it exists, it must have effects; it is not there merely for the amusement of a passive occupant. I think I know of one way, and I am slowly getting organized to try it. Even though this is still just an idea, it may be worth mentioning so that others so inclined might poke around in this direction, too.

Point of view seems to me to involve both what we call *awareness* and what we call *volition*. Furthermore, for reasons that will probably not stand the light of day, I have a suspicion that awareness and volition are closely related to all the manifestations of *change of organization*. These thoughts lead to the idea of constructing some multileveled control experiments (experiments concerning control, that is) in which subjects are encouraged, asked, or underhandedly forced to concentrate on one of the hypothetical levels of perception involved, enough to drive the others out of immediate attention, much as a reader concentrating on the meanings of a string of words may fail to realize that all the *t*'s are taller than any of the *a*'s. If awareness has the properties of something that can move from one point of view to another, and if it is intimately or even necessarily involved in the process of reorganization, the parameters of control ought to become variable at the level where the current point of view is located. It is not excessively difficult to monitor a few basic parameters of control, such as sensitivity, phase shift, and RMS (root-mean-square) error on a continuous basis, and I have succeeded in doing this for some simple two-level (supposedly) control tasks. It will not be easy to prove that the control system in effect is multileveled and not just complex, but I think there are some ways involving simultaneous application of different kinds of random uncorrelated disturbances and others involving looking at reaction times. At any rate, this project seems worth pursuing, since I don't know of any other scientific approach that might reveal some *property* of consciousness. I will report on the results in due course, if I am not too old by the time there are any.

REFERENCES

BROWN G. S. *Laws of form.* Oxford: Blackwell's, 1969.

BUCKLEY, W. *Modern systems research for the behavioral scientist.* Chicago: Aldine, 1968.

CAMPBELL, D. T. "Downward causation" in hierarchically organized biological systems. In T. Dobzhansky & F. J. Ayala (Eds.), *The problem of reduction in biology.* London: Macmillan, 1973.

DEWEY, J. *The reflex arc concept in psychology,* In W. Dennis (Ed.), *Readings in the history of psychology.* New York: Appleton-Century-Crofts, 1948, pp. 355–365. (Originally published, 1896.)

HUBEL, D. N., & WIESEL, T. N. Receptive fields and functional architecture in two non-striate visual areas of the cat. *Journal of Neurophysiology,* 1965, *28,* 228–289.

JAMES, W. *The principles of psychology.* New York: Holt, 1890.

KELLEY, J. R. *Manual and automatic control.* New York: Wiley, 1968.

MAXWELL, J. C. On governors. In *The scientific papers of James Clerk Maxwell, Vol. 2.* New York: Dover, 1965, pp. 105–120. (Originally published, 1868.)

PATTEE, H. H. *Hierarchy theory.* New York: Braziller, 1973.

POWERS, W. T. *Behavior: The Control of Perception.* Chicago: Aldine, 1973.

POWERS, W. T., CLARK, R. K., & McFARLAND, R. L. A general feedback theory of human behavior, Parts I and II. L. V. Bertalanffy & A. Rapoport (Eds.), *General Systems: Yearbook of the Society for General Systems Research.* Ann Arbor, Mich.: Society for General Systems Research, 1960, pp. 63–83.

STARK, L. *Neurological Control Systems.* New York: Plenum, 1968.

VON FOERSTER, H., and students. *Cybernetics of Cybernetics.* Urbana: University of Illinois Biological Computer Laboratory, 1974.

WIENER, N. *Cybernetics.* New York: Wiley, 1948.

11

A Systems Approach to Altered States of Consciousness

Charles T. Tart

1. Introduction

In more than 15 years of observing and researching the phenomena termed *altered states of consciousness*, I have been repeatedly impressed with the incredible range of phenomena encompassed by that term and with the high degree of unrelatedness of most of these phenomena. Hundreds of people have given me reports of radical alterations in the functioning of their consciousness, not only about such relatively familiar things as the changes caused by sleep and dreaming or by strong emotional states, but about changes associated with more exotic techniques, like various meditations, hypnosis, marijuana intoxication, intoxication with major psychedelic drugs, mediumistic trance states, out-of-the-body experiences, a variety of idiosyncratic states that seem to be unique to given persons, states that seem to be socially shared by groups of practitioners of particular spiritual disciplines, and experiences of that category that we vaguely label *mystical experiences.*

As a field of science, we have thousands of miscellaneous bits of data. A few pieces here and there relate to each other, but most pieces seem to have little relation to any others. Although I have researched some of the above states fairly extensively, it gradually became apparent that my own and others' researches were mainly adding more interesting but unrelated pieces to this already scrambled picture, so beginning around 1970, I decided to temporarily move away from the rather safe role of experimentalist and take up that of theoretician in order to make some sense of this area. The result has been the creation of a theoretical framework or paradigm, a systems approach to altered states of consciousness, that, to my general knowledge, makes most of the data hang together in a sensible pattern.

This systems approach is primarily a psychological framework, for my first requirement was that the framework should fit the experiences

Charles T. Tart • Department of Psychology, University of California, Davis 95616.

people report. This makes it a fairly complex approach, but fidelity to experience is more important than conceptual simplicity. A general systems approach can also be applied to purely neurophysiological data, of course, ignoring the psychological components, and some of the most advanced work on neural functioning is beginning to fall into a systems approach. Ultimately, the study of how the systems conceptualized from psychological experiential data fit with those conceptualized from neurological data will shed much light on the traditional mind–body question. This systems approach has been presented in full in my *States of Consciousness* (Tart, 1975a), and this chapter is a brief overview of some of its major features. The researcher who finds this approach useful for his own problems should consult the book for details.

Because of the inherent range and complexity of the data associated with altered states of consciousness, the systems approach is a complex, multidimensional one. While I am attracted to the elegance of approaches that try to find one or two major variables to account for various altered states, I have not found one that begins to account fully for the richness of the phenomena. Note, too, that this is a new approach and has not yet been applied in detail, although my students and I are working on a comprehensive review of the literature to see exactly how well the systems approach fits.

For the philosophically inclined, my systems approach to consciousness is holistic and could be termed an emergent, dualistic, interactionist approach. Consciousness, as experience, emerges from the system properties of both basic awareness and neural action. It is dualistic in that the analytical principles for discovering lawfulness in awareness and consciousness are of a different nature than those governing neural action and must be studied on their own level. It is interactionist in that basic awareness actively influences neural functioning and vice versa: awareness and neural functioning partially pattern each other.

2. CONSTRUCTED NATURE OF ORDINARY CONSCIOUSNESS

One of the main outcomes of my observations and studies of *altered* states of consciousness has been to make me aware of how ignorant we are of the nature of our ordinary state of consciousness. In particular, there are two major, *implicit* operating assumptions, used by almost all ordinary people and almost all scientists, that seriously hinder our understanding of both our ordinary state and altered states.

The first assumption is that our ordinary state of consciousness is somehow "natural," that it simply is the way consciousness ought to be.

One effect of this assumption is to make the phenomena reported in altered states seem odd or unusual. Many of the phenomena we routinely experience in our ordinary state are just as odd and unusual, but because they are familiar, we don't pay much attention to them. The second assumption, related to the first, is that our ordinary state of consciousness is "normal," that it is the "best" or "optimal" possible organization of consciousness. The consequence is that all altered states are implicitly viewed in a biased manner as being somehow inferior or pathological. Even the editors of this book, in putting "altered states of consciousness" into a different section from "states of consciousness" may be unwittingly demonstrating this kind of bias. The data of modern psychology show quite clearly, to the contrary, that our ordinary state of consciousness is a *construction*, not a given, and a *specialized* construction that in many ways is quite arbitrary. Thus, many of the values associated with it are quite arbitrary and culturally relative.

Figure 1 illustrates a concept I call the *spectrum of human potentialities*. Simply by being born human beings, we possess a certain kind of body and nervous system operating in accordance with physical laws governing us and the environment. Thus, there are a very large (although certainly less than infinite) number of potentials, thousands of potentials, which *could* be developed in us. Each of us is, however, born into a particular culture, and the culture may be viewed as a group of people who recognize the existence of only some of these potentials and have decided that some of those they recognize are "good" and thus to be developed, while others are "bad" and thus to be discouraged. Thus Culture A in Figure 1 reinforces certain human potentialities to be developed and deliberately blocks others. A different culture, Culture B, makes different selections from the spectrum of human potentials. Some overlap those of culture A, others are totally different. Each culture is apt to view the other as peculiar, savage, quaint, or evil. Both cultures remain ignorant of a large number of potentials. Of those potentials either not actively encouraged through ignorance or actively rejected by a given culture, some may remain potentially available for development later in life; others (running a four-minute mile, for example) disappear as potentials if not developed early enough in life.

Looking just at Culture A for the time being, we could say that a human being comes into the world with a basic capacity for attention or awareness and with a given biological/neurological structure. Basic awareness cannot be adequately defined verbally, for it is a given behind the more specialized operations that constitute verbal logic. It is important phenomenologically to distinguish basic awareness from specific mental contents, as there seem to be important variations in the degree

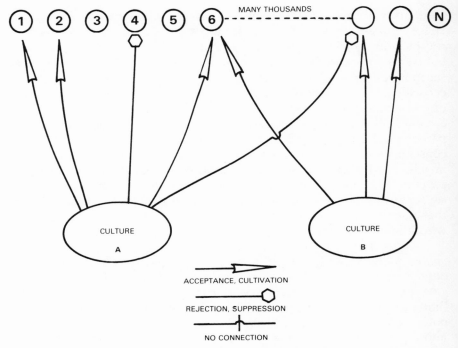

FIGURE 1. Spectrum of human potentials.

to which people experience awareness as distinct from content across various altered states, and it is also quite important theoretically, for reasons discussed elsewhere (Tart, 1975a).

Figure 2 shows the enculturation process schematically. I have put the basic capacity for awareness on the left, and I assume that this is a natural attribute of all adequately developed human beings. Then, we have various fixed, biological structures that *must* develop if a person is to function as a full-fledged human being. These are such things as a capacity for language. Then, we can further distinguish the fixed structures that *may* develop if the proper encouragement or freedom is found within a given cultural matrix. Here, we would include the idea of *archetypal experiences,* as Carl Jung used the term. These are vital psychological experiences that happen to some people and seem to have a relatively common form across cultures, even though cultural diversity would not lead us to predict this commonality. Finally, what may be the most distinctly human category are the large number of potential, *programmable* structures, capacities, skills, habits, personality traits, etc., whose nature and content are determined entirely by the developmental process occurring within a specific cultural matrix. Thus, all human beings may develop some kind of language, but whether it is Chinese or French is determined by the specific cultural matrix a person develops in.

Our capacities, then, develop not in isolation but under two major kinds of pressures, namely, cultural pressures and the limits set by physical laws as we interact with the physical world around us. Other random factors also intervene. Cultural pressures mean that in addition to the basic capacity for awareness, some of the spectrum of human potentials is selected out for active development or inhibition. The end result of the long developmental process is that a much smaller number of the human potentials than were available at birth are finally fixed in a relatively enduring form to produce the adult state of "normal" consciousness, a characteristic and habitual patterning of mental (and consequent behavioral) functioning that adapts the individual, more-or-less successfully, to survive in his culture's *consensus reality*, those aspects of physical and social reality that the culture has defined as important.

Our ordinary (I shall drop *normal* to avoid the value implications) state of consciousness, then, at a given moment, is a small selection of structures, activated by the deployment of attention/awareness and other kinds of psychological and physiological energies. This small en-

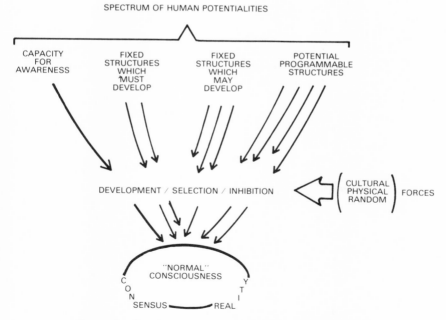

FIGURE 2.   Enculturation: fixed and programmable potentials.

semble is the momentary manifestation of a much larger selection of enculturated structures that are readily available within our ordinary state of consciousness. These structures constitute such things as arithmetic skills, driving skills, appropriate emotional reactions to various situations, and linguistic structures.

Within the structure of our ordinary state of consciousness, we have *partial* voluntary control of awareness; that is, we have some, but far from total, control of which structures we shall deploy awareness to, with consequent activation of those structures. If someone says "Two plus two equals ?," we immediately think of *four*. The control exerted by the external stimulus situation has deployed our awareness in a way to activate structures carrying information about arithmetical skills, even though they were not activated a moment ago. Enculturation, however, also builds up large numbers of emotional and cognitive constraints to ensure a reasonable degree of conformity with the values of the consensus reality of the culture. Thus, either it never occurs to us to think or have experiences about certain kinds of things, or such thoughts are actively blocked because of conditioned emotional associations. In examining a variety of "spiritual development" and psychological growth systems, I am struck by the common emphasis on increasing the ability to deploy attention *at will*, overcoming cultural conditionings and emotional blocks. The limitations imposed by culturally shared assumptions are particularly important for the development of the psychological sciences, for if we do not develop the ability to recognize the assumptions that limit us and our colleagues (see, for example, Tart, 1975b, for a presentation of some of these assumptions), we may build sciences with a kind of pseudovalidation, based on never examining certain premises and phenomena.

3. States of Consciousness

If we consider that many of the human potentials that are developed or inhibited by a particular culture are directly relevant to what we can experience, we can also view Figure 1 as a spectrum of *experiential* potentialities. Culture A, then, by making a certain selection, has effectively patterned experience along certain lines and restricted it from certain other lines. Culture B, in making a different selection, has given a different experiential patterning to the everyday experience of its members.

Now, instead of labeling the two foci "Culture A" and "Culture B," we could substitute "State of Consciousness A" and "State of Consciousness B," and thus illustrate that the ordinary state of consciousness for two different cultures is different in important ways. We can use this same analogy to clarify one of the two basic ideas underlying the concept of a *state* of consciousness, namely, that, *within the same individual*, State A may represent a selection of potentialities available to him or her that gives a certain range of experience, perhaps his or her ordinary state of consciousness, but State of Consciousness B is a different selection focus[1] that results in an overlapping but importantly different selection of available potentials. Thus, State B is an "altered state or consciousness" with respect to State A.

If a person, in his ordinary state of consciousness, is not happy but believes that some gratifying potentials for experience or functioning are potentially available to him if he could somehow radically reorganize his mind, we can understand the motivation for his wanting to experience altered states of consciousness. Many people in our culture are not happy with the flow of life in their ordinary state of consciousness: the range of experience *within* their ordinary state is not satisfying. Sometimes, this is a neurotic dissatisfaction, sometimes an existential dissatisfaction of the more successful members of our culture. Although all the human potentials that a person was born with are probably not available in adulthood, after we have gone through the enculturation process, a number of valued, latent potentials may indeed be available if we could somehow make a different selection, "alter" our *state* of consciousness over and above just trying to find a part of the range of ordinary consciousness that is satisfying.

4. MAPPING EXPERIENCE

Because the terms *state of consciousness* and *altered state of consciousness* are used so imprecisely to cover so many different things and not only in popular usage but frequently in scientific usage—an important aspect of the systems approach is clarifying exactly what is meant by a *state*. *State* certainly is *not* identical with whatever the momentary content of consciousness happens to be, the way the term is all too frequently used: it refers to far-ranging, radical, important changes in mental functioning.

One way of clarifying the concept occurs if we use the procedure of mapping experience. A useful way of keeping track of an object's or an individual's movements in physical space is to set up some kind of coordinate system, that is, to identify the important dimensions along

---

[1]While my emphasis here is on the particular potentials selected, the manner in which they are organized is also very important and will be emphasized later.

which movement can occur and then, at various times, measure where the object or individual is with respect to each coordinate. Three dimensions suffice to cover movements in physical space, and by comparing three-dimensional coordinates at various times, we can tell whether changes occurred and measure velocity, acceleration, etc. Similarly we can, in principle, map a person's position in *experiential space* at any time if we identify and define the important dimensions of experience along which quantitative variation occurs and devise means of measuring them. We might define a dimension of "rationality," for example, and give a person a brief problem every X minutes and then score the rationality of his answer. Relaxation, as a second example, might be assessed by self-report. In practice, of course, experience is frequently complex enough so that only multidimensional mapping would be adequate to get the full flavor of it, but sometimes, a few dimensions are adequate for given observations.[2]

For simplicity, assume that two dimensions would be adequate for a given problem. Then, for a specific example, let one dimension be ability to visualize or hallucinate, ranging from a low of a person reporting that his visual imagery is well nigh undetectable to him versus a high of a visual imagery being as intense and vivid as ordinary visual perception. Let a second dimension be "rationality," the ability to think in terms of consensus reality "sense," ranging from a low where bizarre, irrational ideas occur to a high where practically all thought processes reflect what is sensible in terms of a person's particular culture. Now we can draw a map for these dimensions, as in Figure 3. Note carefully that what we are mapping is selected characteristics of the *contents* of consciousness at given moments.

Suppose, in *working with a single individual*, that on 28 temporally successive occasions we measured both his degree of rationality and his ability to visualize associated with 28 different contents of consciousness. For each measurement, we put a circle on the grid defined by Figure 3. Suppose we obtained the results shown, namely, that our measurements obviously fall into three rather discrete areas or clusters (I have drawn a dotted line around them for convenience), and do *not* fall anywhere else in this two-dimensional space even with additional observation. We have taken a kind of time-lapse photograph of aspects of

---

[2]I have emphasized the mapping of experience here, but the same kind of mapping procedure could be used with other classes of variable, such as behavioral observations or physiological measurements. We might use behavioral or physiological dimensions to supplement or replace some experiential dimensions, for example, using basal skin resistence as a measure of activation/relaxation rather than asking a subject to rate his degree of activation/relaxation. The interrelationships of experiential, behavioral, and physiological mappings are of great interest.

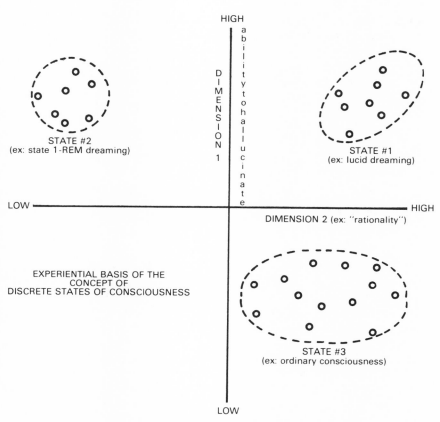

FIGURE 3.   Mapping experience.

the contents of consciousness. This kind of mapping, done implicitly, is behind the basic concept of states of consciousness. Done consciously and precisely, it is the operation for defining *states* for scientific work. *States* are temporal clusterings of the content and organization of consciousness. That is, we have many data that suggest that experience falls into several discrete clusters, and that there are important changes in functioning within various clusters, so to fully understand experience and behavior, it is important to know which cluster, which state of consciousness a person is in at a given time.

For the particular example shown in Figure 3, we have two universally known and one rather exotic state of consciousness. The cluster in the lower-right-hand corner of the graph, where rationality ranges from moderate to very high, while ability to visualize ranges from somewhat low to fair, is, for most people, the ordinary state of consciousness.

The cluster in the upper-left-hand corner, where ability to visualize is quite high but rationality is often quite low, is, for most people, the state of nocturnal dreaming usually associated with a Stage 1–REM (rapid eye movement) physiological state. In a dream, we experience a visual world around us that seems almost as real as ordinary visual perception. It is much more intense than our usual waking-state visual images. The bizarreness of many dream sequences indicate that the degree of rationality is generally quite low.

In the upper-right-hand corner of the graph, we have a state characterized by high ability to visualize but also a high degree of rationality; this is what has been described as lucid dreaming (Van Eeden, in Tart, 1969). This is a special type of dream, usually following an ordinary dream, in which a person suddenly "wakes up" in the sense that he suddenly remembers his identity, realizes that he is actually asleep, is able to think quite logically about his situation (including the apparent impossibility of feeling perfectly awake and lucid while simultaneously realizing that he is dreaming), but nevertheless still finds himself in a (hallucinated) dream world. That is, his visual "images" (from a waking perspective) look to him like ordinary visual perceptions although he is *in* the dream world; yet, if he surveys his internal mental functioning, it seems to have the same logicality, lucidity, and coherence as his ordinary waking state.

This mapping procedure is quite important in the systems approach: the presence or absence of a given state of consciousness for a given individual must ultimately be ascertained by an experiential mapping of the dimensions of experience. If, after repeated study, we find that particular experiences, behaviors, or physiological measures are invariably associated with being in a certain cluster, given a full-scale experiential mapping, then we may end up using a smaller number (as few as one) of these factors to indicate the presence of a given state, but this is an operation of convenience only. We may, for example, come to believe that if we see a Stage 1 EEG and REM pattern, then a person is in the state we call *dreaming*. This may be a highly reliable criterion for a given person, but *dreaming* is defined psychologically as being a certain kind of experiential space determined by full mapping and is not *defined* as present because a Stage 1–REM pattern exists.[3]

As mentioned earlier, multidimensional mapping is necessary to

---

[3] I emphasize the psychological–experiential approach here, but this systems approach can be readily used with different emphasis, such as the convergent operations strategy advocated by Stoyva and Kamiya (1968), where dreaming would be defined as present *if* a Stage 1–REM pattern was present *and* reports from the awakened sleeper fit psychological criteria of "dreamlike." Given such a definition of the occurrence of dreaming, research would then go on to elucidate other aspects of it.

clearly describe and define most states of consciousness. Indeed, Figure 3 is not really an adequate map for separating ordinary dreaming from lucid dreaming: for purposes of clarity, I put ordinary dreaming entirely in the upper-left-hand quadrant of the map, but many people often experience long sequences in their ordinary dreams that proceed according to consensus reality, "rational" standards. For many such people, mapping over time on these particular two dimensions would yield data points extending all the way over to the upper-right-hand quadrant of the graph from the upper-left-hand quadrant, so lucid dreaming could not be reliably distinguished from ordinary dreaming on this dimension. By adding a third or an n dimension on which lucid dreaming is always distinguished from ordinary dreaming (for example, continuity with waking-state memories), the three- or n-dimensional map would show ordinary dreaming as quite distinct from lucid dreaming. Given the complexity of various altered states in terms of current knowledge, one of our main tasks is actually to carry out the necessary multidimensional mapping of these states to establish exactly how they are quantitatively and qualitatively different from one another and where they overlap on given dimensions. Initial selection of mapping dimensions will be crude and "intuitive," but techniques such as factor analysis will refine them.

Note carefully that this kind of mapping allows for changes *within* clusters: no state of consciousness is static. Within our ordinary states, we think about different topics, carry out different kinds of actions, have different kinds of fantasies, etc., and yet it all falls within a range, within a cluster that we call our ordinary state of consciousness.

5. Discrete States of Consciousness

The kind of experiential mapping of Figure 3 conveys the idea of different levels of functioning of particular human potentials in different states. Imagery, for example, may be much more or less intense in one state than in another. The idea could be further extended to include qualitative changes, going abruptly from so low as to be undetectable to high enough to be strongly present, and so bring in the first major change that is part of the definition of an altered state, namely, a different selection of human potentialities compared to the baseline state, the appearance or disappearance of potentialities across states. What the kind of mapping of Figure 3 does not convey, however, is the *organizational* qualities of states of consciousness, the gestalt or *system* properties. A different set of human potentialities is not just lying around to become accessible to consciousness; rather, as in our ordinary state, there are determinations of transitions from one potential structure to another, and certain kinds of sequences of experiences are much more likely to occur than others—that is, there is organization. When we discuss stabilization of states of consciousness later, we shall see how this organization constitutes the system.

Figure 4 is another way of representing a state of consciousness that illustrates the organizational qualities more clearly. Each of the various geometric figures represents particular human potentialities or structures that are available in that state, and the interconnecting lines represent the likely interaction routes or the probable sequential attention and information flows between these particular potentials. For the time being, look only at the structures interconnected by the heavy lines, which form a roughly rectangular pattern in this case, and ignore the structures connected by the lighter lines. In a given state of consciousness, a per-

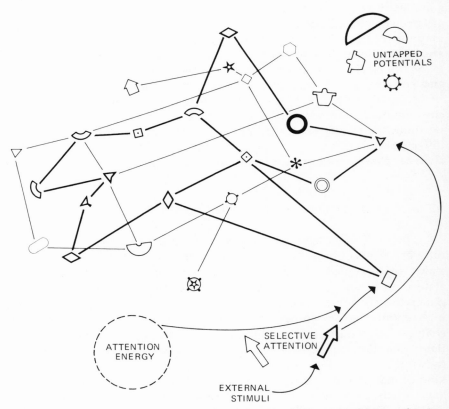

FIGURE 4. Representation of a d-SoC as a configuration of structures/subsystems forming a recognizable pattern. Light lines and circles represent *potential* interaction and potentialities/structures/subsystems not used in the baseline d-SoC.

son receives stimuli from the environment, processes them in selective ways to incorporate their information content, and then has conscious experiences that have a certain pattern or organizational quality to them.

As in the experiential mapping of Figure 3, Figure 4 is really a time-lapse diagram. Awareness is clearly present in only a few of the available structures for this state of consciousness at any one moment, but as we map its activation of various structures, the flow of experiences through time, we would map out the habit patterns, the probable experiential flow routes that give us the "shape" or "feel" of that state of consciousness.

In order to rescue the terms *states of consciousness* and *altered states of consciousness* from the slipshod use into which they have fallen and to provide more precise terms for scientific use, my systems approach proposes to use the terms *discrete state of consciousness* (d-SoC) and *discrete altered state of consciousness* (d-ASC). The states we talk about are *discretely* different from one another: they involve not only qualitative shifts in the selection of human potentials available and quantitative shifts in the level of other potentials, but a shift in the organizational style imposed on these potentials. We may formally define a d-SoC *for a given individual* as a unique *system* or configuration of psychological structures or subsystems. These structures (grouped into subsystems for convenience) show some quantitative and some minor qualitative variation in the way in which they function (process information, shape experience, etc.) within a d-SoC, but the structures or subsystems and their awareness/energy pattern of interactions comprise a system with a recognizable identity. Further, the operations of these structures and subsystems interact with one another and stabilize each other's functioning by various kinds of stabilization processes (discussed below), so that the *system*, the d-SoC, maintains its overall identity and patterning of functioning despite a wide range of variation in input from the environment.

The psychological realities I am attempting to encompass in this definition involve the fact that although we have a wide range of experiences (indeed, our experiences are never exactly the same) in our ordinary state, we nevertheless implicitly classify it as a given state and would not confuse it, say, with dreaming or being drunk. When lecturing, I often ask people whether they would seriously like to contend that rather than actually being there, they are dreaming *right then* about listening to me and will wake up at home in bed in a few minutes. No one of thousands I have asked has ever seriously contended this with me.

When I ask them *how* they can be sure they are in their ordinary waking state and not dreaming, their answers fall into either or both of two categories. Some people check whether certain specific potentials are available; for example, one person might say he had checked his memory to see if there was continuity back as far as he cared to search, found that there was, and since this continuity is characteristic of his waking state but not of his dreams, he used this as a sufficient guideline to tell him he was awake and not dreaming. Other people may say that they do not check the specifics of their experience but, in a sense, scan the whole *pattern* of their experience rapidly and have the holistic, gestalt recognition that the pattern of their experience is the pattern of their waking state, not the pattern of a dream state. Thus, a d-SoC is a recognizable pattern of particular human potentials/conscious experiences. In terms of methodological consequences for understanding any d-SoC, then, we have both to investigate the structure of its subsystems and components in a molecular way and to continually investigate the way in which they interact and the gestalt, *system* qualities that arise from this interaction.

If you will return your attention to Figure 4 and look at the structures connected by the light lines now, this is what is meant by a discrete *altered* state of consciousness. While some structures or potentials that were involved in the baseline d-SoC are still functioning in the new pattern, some of them are not. Some new potentials are now activated, and the overall organizational style, the pattern of the system is different, depicted as a roughly star-shaped configuration for this illustration. We have a radical reorganization of both the selection of structures making up consciousness and the pattern of flow of awareness and experience between these available potentials.

The differences between any two d-SoCs, then, exist not only on a molecular level, but also in terms of their emergent system properties. By analogy, we might take an automobile apart, temporarily throw away some parts, add a few other parts (corresponding to latent potentials) from elsewhere, and put it together into an airplane. While we can certainly trace some things in common between an automobile and an airplane, their overall styles of motion through space are radically and importantly different.

It is important to note that the adjective *altered* is only descriptive for scientific purposes. When we pick any one d-SoC as our baseline, then all other d-SoCs become d-ASCs with respect to it, but there is no implication that an "altered" d-SoC is better or worse than any other. Valuation must not be confused with description.

At our present level of knowledge, this systems approach to defining d-SoCs has been mainly applied to what are commonly recognized as radical reorganizations of consciousness, such as dreaming, lucid dreaming, hypnosis, and drug intoxication. I am convinced that *strong* emotional states also constitute d-ASCs; I have particularly developed this analysis for sexuality elsewhere (Tart, in press). It is also possible to apply the concept of d-SoCs on a much finer level to variations within our ordinary d-SoC, and these themes have also been developed elsewhere (Tart, 1975a).

6. Individual Differences

Although we do not currently have sufficient data to get very specific, my observations have convinced me that there are enormous individual differences between people in the configuration and potential selection of their ordinary d-SoC as well as in d-ASCs that look like the same states across individuals at first glance. Social conventions and lack of full communication of experiences make these differences difficult to notice without systematic inquiry. But in general, when doing an experiential mapping for two persons, we may find the situation shown in Figure 5.

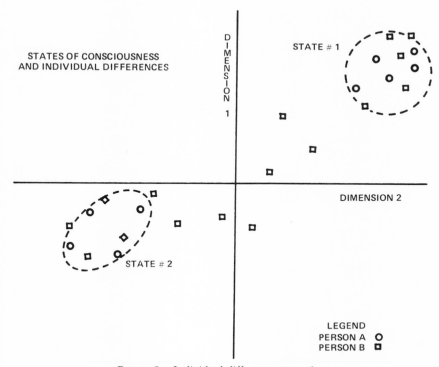

Figure 5.   Individual differences mapping.

Here, on the two dimensions of our mapping, Person A's data points, represented by the circles, show two discrete clusterings of experiences, suggesting that he functions in two d-SoCs at various times. Person B, however, shows experiences (plotted by the trapezoids) not only within the two clusters that defined two d-SoCs for Person A but also for the range in between. For Person B, we have only one d-SoC, but a wide range. Describing him as being in d-SoC 1 or d-SoC 2 when he happened to be functioning within that part of his repertoire would be very misleading, for we have only quantitative variation within one d-SoC.

The systems approach deals first with individuals, and we need detailed mapping of the experiential spaces of individuals before making generalizations across individuals. In practice, of course, the generalizations, based largely on incomplete and implicit mappings, have already been made, giving us state names like *hypnosis* that are in common use. Thus, we are forced to speak in generalities, given our present state of knowledge, but our main research task for the future is accurate delineation and specification of individual differences in various d-SoCs.

7. Major Subsystems of Consciousness

The d-SoC or system is the overall organization of all other components, of subsystems and energies. The system has emergent properties not predictable from component properties. Any system can be analyzed into subsystems, these subsystems into subsubsystems, etc., as long as the knowledge base is useful for such division and is empirically useful. Ultimately, we come down to the level of more atomistic structures and basic activating energies, such as attention–awareness.

The above discussion has been rather abstract, so let me indicate briefly the direction that increased specificity moves in. The systems approach currently distinguishes eleven different major subsystems of consciousness, each of which undergoes important, sometimes radical alterations (qualitative and quantitative) of functioning across the range of known d-ASCs. the identification of these subsystems at this time is primarily a matter of a convenient grouping of related psychological functions, but as our knowledge increases, we shall undoubtedly further subdivide some of these subsystems and probably arrange component structures in new groupings, as well as more thoroughly understand the neurological substrates of each.

A brief listing of each major subsystem and an idea of some of its variations follow:

1. *Exteroception:* Included here are the classical sensory systems—sight, hearing, etc.—for perceiving the physical environment around us.

2. *Interoception:* Here are the sensory receptors for perceiving what is happening in our own bodies: position, muscle tension, internal discomfort, pain, etc.

3. *Input Processing:* This subsystem comprises the many innate and learned structures that nonconsciously process sensory information from both the exteroceptors and the interceptors and pass on a small abstraction of the total incoming information to awareness in the form of consensus-reality acceptable percepts. Drastic changes can take place in input processing in various d-ASCs, ranging, at one extreme, from a total elimination of perceived sensory input (leading to one kind of analgesia, e.g.) to the feelings of greatly increased elaboration, organization, and richness of perception associated with psychedelic drug–induced states. Perceptual changes probably almost always occur in input processing rather than in the functioning of the exteroceptors and interoceptors *per se.*

4. *Memory:* This subsystem comprises the many ways in which past information is stored and drawn on for perceiving, evaluating, emoting, etc. In various d-ASCs, we may get changes, like memories becoming more or less available and state-specific memory.

5. *Sense of Identity:* This subsystem takes a certain aspect of experience and makes it *my* experience, thus giving it priority for processing and activating various emotional reactions. Drastic changes can occur across various d-ASCs, from an expansion of this ego sense to include others or the world around us, to its diminution to the point where there is just experience, with no personal quality to it at all.

6. *Evaluation:* This subsystem includes various cognitive processes, taking information about ongoing situations, comparing it against previous experiences, values, etc., and making a decision as to what to do. Although much current research is focused on differences between evaluative processes apparently associated with the right and the left hemispheres of the brain, and although there obviously seem to be shifts in right–left dominance in various d-ASCs, even more radical effects can occur, such as state-specific knowledge and state-specific logic.

7. *Subconscious:* This subsystem includes the many processes identified by Freud as unconscious, especially those that are actively repressed, as well as any other processes that we cannot be directly aware of but that we infer must exist from their effects on our overt behavior or conscious experience. In various d-ASCs, the "boundary line" between conscious and subconscious processes may change, so that what was unconscious (and so only inferred) may become a directly conscious experience in some d-ASCs, and vice versa.

9. *Emotions:* This subsystem includes our various emotions, which are a kind of evaluation of experience. We know a good deal about some

of the neurophysiological substrates of this system, compared to most of the other major subsystems. In various d-ASCs, changes can range from experiencing new emotions that are not available in the ordinary d-SoC to major changes in what kind of stimuli or experiences will or will not trigger various emotions.

9. *Space–Time Sense:* This rather overlooked subsystem provides an implicit background to experience: most of our experiences do not just happen to us, they are experienced in a certain spatiotemporal context. In the various d-ASCs, perceptions of the way space is arranged, its magnitude, and the rate or style of time passage may be drastically altered.

10. *Motor Output:* This subsystem comprises the effector routes whereby we voluntarily control our physical body. This also is a subsystem where we have a fair knowledge of the neurophysiological substrates. In various d-ASCs, there may be an experiential (and sometimes behavioral) diminution or enhancement of strength, different feedback feelings resulting from operating the musculature, etc.

11. *Latent Functions:* In various d-ASCs, people sometimes report that entirely novel experiences become available, demonstrating the existence of ordinarily latent subsystems that are temporarily activated, in addition to quantitative and qualitative changes in the above-mentioned subsystems.

8. STABILIZATION OF DISCRETE STATES

When we begin to fully appreciate the complexity and range of functioning of our ordinary d-SoC, much less that of various d-ASCs, the question naturally arises as to what keeps this incredibly complex system functioning in such a stable manner. Indeed, it is a wonder how blithely we overlook this amazing property of any d-SoC; its stability in spite of change. In our ordinary d-SoC, for example, people talk to us and almost all of their communications are different in content from any preceding one; emotions come and go, life is full of surprises, and yet, by and large, our experience of our mental functioning remains within a familiar experiential space that we call our "ordinary" state. From the point of view of the systems approach, any complex system must have various stabilization processes functioning in order to maintain its stability. Indeed, a reasonable degree of stabilization is highly adaptive. It is easy to speculate that our remote ancestors who went into a mystical state at the sight of a strange movement in the brush and "tripped out" on the strangeness of it all did not live to reproduce, for the saber-toothed tigers came out of the brush and ate them. Our ordinary d-SoC is a tool for coping with the environment, especially the consensus reality we live in. A good tool should maintain its function in spite of changes and difficulties, and both our ordinary d-SoC and the various d-ASCs we have some scientific knowledge about do show fair to good degrees of stability.

I have identified four major ways of stabilizing the system of a d-SoC, analogous to the way cultures control the activities of their members. In order to ensure that someone is a "good citizen" we can (1) keep him busy with activities of the sort good citizens engage in; (2) reward him when he carries out these socially valued activities; (3) punish him if he engages in undesirable activities, ideally conditioning the punishment mechanisms into his consciousness so that he starts feeling anxious and guilty if he even thinks about engaging in undesirable activities; and (4) eliminate, as much as possible, opportunities for engaging in socially disapproved-of activities.

The first major process for stabilizing a d-SoC is what I call *loading stabilization*, keeping a person's mental activities heavily occupied with things considered socially good and useful. This means that there is little or no surplus attention–awareness to act as psychological energy that might activate undesired structures or initiate processes that might destabilize the ordinary d-SoC, and the loading simultaneously patterns mental activity along lines approved of in the person's consensus reality, thus reinforcing earlier conditionings. Don Juan, the Yaqui man of knowledge, told Carlos Castaneda that the ordinary, repeated, day-to-day activities of people keep their energies so bound within these particular patterns that it keeps them from becoming aware of nonordinary realities.

In addition to the loading stabilization from the consumption and patterning of thoughts by social interaction, our body provides another major source of loading stabilization: it is a range of familiar sensations that is impinging on us almost constantly as a result of ordinary body moment.

There are two types of *feedback stabilization*, positive and negative. Various structures monitor the activity of other structures and subsystems within a d-SoC and either augment such activities when they are within desired ranges for maintaining the integrity of the system of the d-SoC or inhibit them if they start to go beyond these limits. Positive and negative feedback may have experiential correlates in terms of feeling good or bad, but they are far more general processes.

Limiting stabilization refers to processes of nonlinear, extreme negative feedback, whereby activity beyond a certain range in various structures and subsystems is so strongly inhibited that it becomes impossible. Extreme emotions, for example, can initiate the transition to a d-ASC by disrupting the ability of the baseline d-SoC. One of the effects of tranquilizing drugs seems to be so blunting the range of affective responses, for example, that they do not allow emotions to go beyond a certain point and thus stabilize the baseline d-SoC. Some kinds of psychopathology, incidentally, may be looked upon as disorders created by inadequate stabilization of the patient's ordinary d-SoC, a line of thought which needs further development.

The importance of these various stabilization processes will become more clear as we consider the opposite process, disrupting the stability of a d-SoC in order to induce a d-ASC.

9. INDUCTION OF A DISCRETE ALTERED STATE

If we look through the psychological and anthropological literature for information about processes that have been known to produce radical alterations in consciousness, we find ourselves faced with an incredibly large (and possibly limitless) number of techniques that have been used by some people sometime somewhere to induce d-ASCs. Ingesting drugs, dancing, listening to another's words, singing, fasting, rubbing a stone around and around in a circle, breathing exercises, etc., have all acted as induction techniques. From the point of view of the systems approach, however, all these various induction techniques seem to consist of two basic psychological/physiological operations that, if successful, induce d-ASCs in a three-stage process.

The first basic induction operation is *disrupting* the stabilization of the baseline d-SoC. If we can identify particular stabilization processes, we can apply psychological or physiological pressures to disrupt them directly, or we can indirectly disrupt a d-SoC by pushing various psychological functions, structures, and subsystems to and beyond normal limits of functioning. We can try to disrupt particular subsystem functionings by overloading them with stimuli, depriving them of the (patterning) stimuli necessary for their stable operation, giving them anomalous stimuli that can't be processed in habitual ways, or deliberately withdrawing attention awareness from them as a way of deenergizing them.

The induction process is illustrated in Figure 6. Here, the analogy is used of a d-SoC's being like a stable configuration of various-shaped blocks (various structures, interconnected in a certain pattern) in a gravitational field (the stimulus environment we live in). The left-most drawing shows the baseline d-SoC. The several blocks drawn below the line indicate subconscious functions, which also seem to be affected by induction processes, although our information is scanty here. As the first step of induction, we apply various kinds of disrupting forces, and the second panel of Figure 6 shows the baseline d-SoC pushed to the limits of its stability, although it has not lost its basic integrity, its basic pattern, yet.

Like any well-engineered system, our ordinary d-SoC is multiply stabilized. A number of the kinds of stabilization processes discussed above go on simultaneously. Thus, in an induction process, the disrupting forces may directly interfere with one or more stabilizing processes, but if they do not interfere with some others, it may be impossible to induce a d-ASC. The person may experience some quantitative change *within* the baseline d-SoC, such as feeling more relaxed or focusing more strongly on a verbal induction procedure, but basically, no other important changes occur: the system (d-SoC) moves faster or slower, but the pattern holds its basic shape. This way of considering induction resolves apparent paradoxes involved in work with psychoactive drugs: the *physiological* action to a drug may indeed disrupt certain processes on a physiological level and even produce some psychological changes, but other psychological/physiological processes that are *not* disrupted may still produce sufficient stabilization to prevent disruption of the pattern/ integrity of the system. Additional disruption, in the form of psychological factors, then determines whether or not the drug actually succeeds in inducing a d-ASC or not. Experienced marijuana users, for example, can frequently "turn off" the effects of the drug at will (Tart, 1971).

The second major induction operation is applying what I call *patterning forces* or stimuli, psychological and physiological pressures to

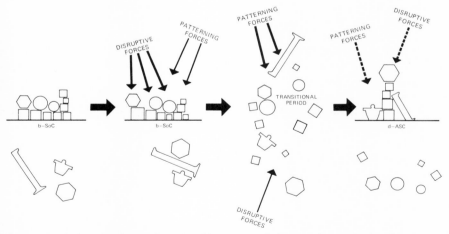

FIGURE 6.   Induction of a d-ASC. The abbreviation "b-SoC" indicates the baseline states of consciousness that we start from.

restructure consciousness in the pattern of the desired d-ASC. I mention patterning forces at this point, before we have reached the stage of major disruption, as disrupting and patterning forces are often applied simultaneously in induction procedures: patterning forces may simultaneously act as disrupting forces on the baseline d-SoC.

If the disrupting forces are successful, we get the situation shown in the third panel of Figure 6, a transitional *period* (it is important not to call this a transitional "state" if we do not want to confuse the issue) in which consciousness is temporarily unorganized. People often describe this time as a "blank period," or "I must have fallen asleep for a minute," or "dreamlike" activity that is not recalled well, etc. Given that the person *is*, in many important ways, his d-SoC, there obviously is a problem in collecting experiential data here, for our observer has temporarily left the scene! Some meditation disciplines, which aim toward the development of a relatively independent portion of consciousness that is detached from ordinary functioning, offer important research possibilities for gathering data here.

The disruption of patterning, of integrated functioning, that occurs during this transition period accounts for the "gaps" in the mapping of experience shown in Figures 3 and 5. Quantitative variations in intensity of functioning along various dimensions (experiential, behavioral, physiological) occur within the baseline d-SoC; then, we have this temporary breakdown, and some of the originally available functions suddenly become active again but at quantitatively (or qualitatively) different levels of activity. The fact that we apparently have levels/combinations of functioning for various structures/subsystems that can *not* occur must reflect something about the basic nature of both biologically given and culturally constructed structures/subsystems. Not only does this base nature sets limits on what kinds of d-SoCs are possible, but the detailed study of these limits, the intellectually extrapolatable but not observed d-SoCs, should reveal a great deal about the basic nature of the human mind and organism.

It is also important to note that like any other human function, the transition from one d-SoC to a d-ASC can be learned very well and automated, so that it can happen very quickly and almost unnoticeably.

The patterning forces and stimuli become all-important during this transitional period, for it is they that determine how the temporarily destructured consciousness will re-form. The disruptive forces may still play a role in maintaining the transitional period, especially if the baseline d-SoC is "overlearned," as is the ordinary d-SoC for most of us, and so has a strong tendency to automatically re-form from any transitional period.

If induction is successful, the patterning forces result in the reorganization of consciousness into the desired d-ASC, as shown in the fourth panel of Figure 6. Now, some psychological structures that were part of the baseline d-SoC are temporarily latent, others are below the threshold of consciousness but may have indirect effects, some that were *sub*conscious to the baseline d-SoC are now part of the d-ASC, and the overall organization of available structures has a different pattern.

When d-ASCs are first being experienced by a person, it may be necessary to maintain the patterning forces as ways of stabilizing the d-ASC, and perhaps to maintain the disruptive forces to prevent the recurrence of the baseline d-SoC, but with practice, many of the d-ASCs we have some knowledge about develop their own internal stabilization processes.

How transitions from one d-SoC to a d-ASC are learned is an important research question about which we have very few data at present, but clearly they can be learned. A classic example is that the neophyte marijuana user usually has to be taught how to "get stoned," how to get into the d-ASC associated with marijuana use. He may ingest what are, by later standards, enormous quantities of the drug for several sessions and yet experience no major alteration in his consciousness. But "with a little help from his friends," with the application of psychological forces that help disrupt stabilization of his ordinary d-SoC and help pattern the d-ASC, he not only learns to make the transition but from then on is able to make the transition to being stoned with a much smaller amount of the drug (Tart, 1971). Indeed, he may be able to make the transition to being stoned with marijuana from which all the THC has been chemically extracted.[4] While it is conventional to (deprecatingly) call this a "placebo response," it will probably be more fruitful for research to see it as a learned skill and to try to discover how it is learned.

To briefly concretize the process of induction, consider the process of falling asleep. One lies down in a dark, quiet room, away from others. This immediately removes several major sources of loading stabilization. One is not functioning in a consensus-reality environment, interacting with other people, which would load one's consciousness and pattern it heavily. One no longer has the physical environment to cope with, so the environmental sensory patterning and the kinesthetic feedback and patterning from moving one's body is gone. Indeed, by lying still and relaxing, one's kinesthetic receptors adapt out, so the body literally dis-

---

[4]I assume he actually reaches the same d-ASC as that reached when THC is active in the body on the basis of current knowledge, that is, crude, global reports from subjects. It may very well not be the same d-ASC when more sophisticated data collection can be carried out. An especially interesting research problem is exactly what aspects of drug-associated d-ASCs can occur only when the drug is active in the body and what essentially identical aspects can be produced by purely psychological means.

appears as a source of patterning and loading stabilization. Further, one takes an attitude of nothing's being important (the best way to *fail* to go to sleep is to *try* to go to sleep); that is, one gives up the usual striving, goal-directed attitude that works well in one's ordinary d-SoC. This process effectively withdraws much attention–awareness energy from various structures. Particularly, by not having a goal to try to get to, various positive and negative feedback stabilization systems are relaxed: if there is no goal, there's no need to monitor whether various structures and subsystems are functioning in the proper range.

All of the above act to (gently) disrupt the stability of the baseline d-SoC. Then that factor we call tiredness, the physiological need to sleep, acts both as a further disrupting force and as a patterning force, and one goes on into various sleep states. The balance of forces is important here: if one's tiredness is extreme, he may fall asleep on his feet without having to go through the other induction procedures. On the other hand, if one is not at all tired, he can go through the other induction procedures and sleep will not result.

Deinduction, the process of returning from a d-ASC to the baseline d-SoC, is the reverse of the induction process. Disrupting stimuli break down the integrity of the d-ASC, and a transitional period results during which the patterning forces then reorganize the temporarily disorganized condition of one's mind back into the baseline d-SoC. The baseline d-SoC is usually the ordinary state, which, being tremendously overlearned, means that one has innumerable patterning forces working to structure it. The deinduction process has not been studied very extensively, simply because we tend to take it for granted.

10. METHODOLOGICAL CONSEQUENCES OF THE SYSTEMS APPROACH

A primary function of a scientific theory is organizational: starting from a mass of data, one wants to get a conceptual system that organizes it, relates it, makes "sense" out of it. This is a primary function of my systems approach to d-ASCs now. to organize the chaotic data in this field. In terms of my overall understanding from years of research, the systems approach does this quite well. My students and I are currently working on the specifics of this kind of organization. A scientific theory must also go beyond making sense of and organizing data, though, and must have predictive capabilities. Although the systems approach does lead to testable predictions, I have not emphasized this aspect, as I think it is premature. Our specific knowledge about the experiential, behavioral, and physiological parameters of most d-ASCs is still so sketchy at this time that large-scale descriptive research is far and away our biggest need. The systems approach does have a variety of methodological consequences for how one goes about such research, however, so let us look at some of the major ones.

Perhaps the prime methodological consequence of the systems approach for me, although it was not my intention while developing the approach, is the way it draws attention to things that we too readily take for granted, such as (1) the stabilization of our ordinary d-SoC and various d-ASCs; (2) the value judgments implicit in the common use of the term *normal consciousness;* (3) the shared biases that we have, even in the scientific community, because of our sharing a certain consensus reality and the need to recognize these biases and to see if they can be overcome (see Chapter 2 in Tart, 1975b); (4) the crucial importance of the concepts of basic awareness and attention; (5) the cogency of the mind–body problem—since drastic changes in experienced mind–body relationship happen in various d-ASCs, this is not just a verbal issue to be left for philosophers (see Chapter 3 in Tart, 1975b); and (6) the limitations of our language in dealing with many of the important phenomena of d-ASCs.

Second, the systems approach emphasizes the importance of the detailed study of *individuals.* One must carry out detailed mapping of the experiential spaces of given individuals to see just how specific concepts of various d-ASCs work for them and how they don't. One then goes on to map the experiential space for various d-ASCs for individuals *in detail,* asking questions about the main features of each d-ASC, the induction procedures that produce it, the deinduction procedures, the nature of the stabilization processes and their limits, the actual advantages and uses of particular d-ASCs for specific tasks, the real disadvantages or hazards of specific d-ASCs for specific tasks, whether there are depth dimensions to various d-ASCs (see Tart, 1972a; 1975a), etc. When this kind of detailed, individual data has been collected, then comparisons across individuals will tell us if common state names are really warranted or whether they create more confusion than clarity.

A third consequence of the systems approach is the way it highlights the importance of researching the basic subsystems and structures comprising consciousness and the basic nature of awareness and psychological/physiological "energies." The concept of psychological energies is unfashionable, yet they are often immediate experiential realities to people experiencing various d-ASCs (and often in our ordinary d-SoC) and are useful conceptual tools, but we have never dealt adequately with them. The variations in subsystem and structure functioning across various d-ASCs can highlight the identity and functioning of particular subsystems, especially if their functioning is relatively implicit in our ordinary d-SoC. Studying d-ASCs gives us an advantage of the sort embodied in the old dictum that the abnormal teaches us about the normal. The study of subsystems and structures, as the components of consciousness, must, however, be balanced by remembering that there are emergent, system properties of a d-SoC that must be studied in themselves, as they are not derivable from knowledge of the components alone.

A fourth major methodological consequence of the systems approach stems from the conceptualization that d-SoCs are *mulitply* stabilized. From this idea, it follows that applying any one (or even several) induction *procedure* to a person does not guarantee that a d-ASC will result. Whether a d-ASC results in a given instance *must* be determined by appropriate experiential/ psychological/ behavioral/ physiological mapping, by the *actual presence of criterion variables*. This requirement is particularly important to note because a common bias toward overvaluing physical, easily observable variables and rejecting experiential ones has led to a number of experiments where the presence of a d-ASC has been *equated* with carrying out the induction procedure. Thus, if a psychoactive drug has been administered in a high dosage, the d-ASC associated with that drug is present, or if a hypnotic induction procedure has been carried out by the hypnotist, the subject's responses are considered those of a hypnotized person, etc. These are clearly inadequate and misleading procedures, even if they give the appearance of "objectivity": it is certainly easy to get 100% reliability among observers as to whether an experimenter has read out a set of words labeled a *hypnotic induction technique*, but the subject may not have become at all hypnotized.

Finally, the highlighting of the cultural relativity of our ordinary d-SoC and the biases and limits conditioned into it provide a background for a proposal I made some years ago (Tart, 1972b) for the development of state-specific sciences. Although space does not allow the development of the concept here, it recognizes that the *essence* of scientific method (as opposed to the particular *products* of science that we tend to identify with science) is an emphasis on disciplined observation, theorizing, prediction, and full communication with colleagues about each of these processes. The area of interest this procedure is applied to may be an aspect of the external, physical world or it may be various experiential phenomena. By applying this very useful knowledge-refining method, science, in only one d-SoC, the ordinary one for our culture, we have shared consensus-reality limits and biases on our observations, our style of thinking, our style of prediction, and our style of communication that impose real limits on scientific progress. Many experiencers of various d-ASCs have reported that there are state-specific perceptions, state-specific logics, state-specific communications, and state-specific memories unique to a particular d-ASC. If the basic scientific method outlined above is used in a disciplined way *within* a particular d-ASC, we will get a unique view of things and will be able to develop a science that is practiced in that particular d-ASC. Such state-specific sciences, although they will be difficult to develop, will give us unique and important understandings of various kinds of human experiences and functionings. These understandings will be complementary to our ordinary d-SoC understanding and so will allow us to greatly broaden our knowledge. They may be the only way to adequately understand some human experiences, for example, the value changes derived from "mystical" experience (Tart, 1975b). This kind of development will take us beyond the study of d-ASCs as a curiosity to be studied from the point of view of our ordinary d-SoC and, by utilizing d-ASCs, will allow us to develop and profit from a broader selection of our human potentials.

References

Stoyva, J., & Kamiya, J. Electrophysiological studies of dreaming as the prototype of a new strategy in the study of consciousness. *Psychological Review*, 1968, *75*, 192–205.

Tart, C. (Ed.). *Altered states of consciousness: A book of readings*. New York: Wiley, 1969.

Tart, C. *On being stoned: A psychological study of marijuana intoxication*. Palo Alto, Calif.: Science & Behavior Books, 1971.

Tart, C. Measuring the depth of an altered state of consciousness, with particular reference to self-report scales of hypnotic depth. In E. Fromm & R. Shor (Eds.), *Hypnosis: Research developments and perspectives*. Chicago: Aldine/Atherton, 1972, pp. 445–477. (a)

Tart, C. States of consciousness and state-specific sciences. *Science*, 1972, *176*, 1203–1210. (b)

Tart, C. *States of Consciousness*. New York: Dutton, 1975. (a)

Tart, C. (Ed.). *Transpersonal psychologies*. New York: Harper & Row, 1975. (b)

Tart, C. Sex and drugs. In K. Blum (Ed.), *The social meanings of drugs: Principles of social pharmacology*. New York: Basic Books, (in press).

12

The Psychobiology of Sexual Experience

Julian M. Davidson

1. Introduction

A rich and complexly interwoven matrix of psychosocial and physiological variables influence those transformations of consciousness that we label *sexual*. Much more than for other "instinctive" behaviors, sexual activity manifestly involves a set of unique physiological correlates, interacting with a highly prized array of subjective experiences. The physiological, behavioral, and experiential events undergo slow shifts of intensity and quality as well as sharp transformations from one "state" to another. Furthermore, this is a realm of human experience directly accessible to all and obviously essential to the preservation of the species. For these reasons, sexual phenomena are of great potential interest to students of psychophysiology and can provide unique and important models for psychobiological research.

This chapter presents a preliminary analysis of known phenomena that are potentially relevant to the construction of these models. My strategy will be to discuss pertinent knowledge of sexual physiology in the context of how the physical events might conceivably be related to the "subjective" phenomena of erotic experience. This approach has not yet been pursued systematically in the literature, yet it is a necessary prerequisite for the development of a sexual psychobiology devoted to solving problems of human sexuality as well as to advancing the emerging science of human consciousness.

The chapter first establishes major aspects of the biological bases of sexual behavior, by outlining findings from animal research, before considering human sexuality. First sexual arousal is considered and later, the psychophysiology of orgasm. Unfortunately, only the discussions dealing with animals are firmly based on established research findings. For reasons to be discussed in the next paragraph, the rest of the text is laden with more-or-less speculative inferences arising out of a very small data base. Such speculations, though out of place in more ad-

ULIAN M. DAVIDSON • Department of Physiology, Stanford University, Stanford, California 94305.

vanced fields of research are, I believe, necessary in an area such as this, which is still in the early stages of a very retarded development.

Unfortunately, the peculiar ambivalence of our attitudes to sex have resulted in the paradox that though this area of human experience receives intense and incessant attention in literature, the arts, and popular culture, it has been very little investigated by experimental scientists. Thus, we have only slight and superficial knowledge of the relevant biology. Past investigations on sex have consisted mostly of behavioral-psychological or social science studies on the one hand and of anatomical-physiological ones on the other. Psychophysiological relationships are usually mentioned only *en passant* or are simply (and often wrongly) assumed to be obvious. Thus it is that we know little of the extent to which the known physiological events (and others yet undiscovered) of sexual arousal and orgasm are integral to the experience. Further, we know even less about the ways in which conscious processes can determine physiological events, including those that are essential for reproduction, like ejaculation and ovulation.

But apart from the lack of research effort, there are various other obstacles to the successful study of the physiological bases of human sexual experience. One that deserves mention at the outset is the lack of any scientifically acceptable phenomenology in this area. This seems surprising when we consider the ubiquity of these experiences and the vast amount of writing that has been devoted to the topic of sex. The psychophysiologist, therefore, has the problem of relating the great variety of sexual experiences to physiological events in the absence of accepted descriptive terms for these experiences.[1]

1.1. The Evolutionary Background: Animal Sexual Behavior

The situation in humans is in direct contrast to the study of sexual behavior in animals, in which well-defined end points are available. The potential relevance of data from animals arises from the fact that the basic physiological principles involved in sexual-reproductive function (though not the details) are essentially similar in all mammals. But since the information from the rich animal literature is sometimes taken to represent the biological basis of human sexuality, it is important at the

---

[1]A more basic problem relates to the definition of *sex* itself. I shall not attempt such a definition but will try to avoid some ambiguity by referring to *copulatory behavior* when dealing with animal mating and confining use of the term *sexuality* to human sexual experience, broadly defined to include sexual inclinations, preferences, and attitudes (see also Beach, 1979).

outset to warn the reader against promiscuous extrapolation of animal data. This point will be elaborated at the end of the next section.

Some major features of the animal literature will now be briefly summarized; missing primary references can be found in Beach (1948), Young (1961), Davidson (1972, 1977), and Bermant and Davidson (1974). The literature is concerned almost entirely with the more covert neural, hormonal, and environmental factors that regulate and control copulatory and related behavior, rather than with the overt physiological events during sexual activity.

1.1.1. Hormones

The removal of androgenic hormones by castration or other means results in a decline or disappearance of sexual activity in males of all the mammalian species that have been studied and in some nonmammalian species. The rate of decline, if not also the final base level, is, however, extremely variable within and between species. Replacement therapy with androgen maintains or restores the behavior and is necessary also for the differentiation of the internal and external genital apparatus in early development and its subsequent growth and maintenance. This requirement for androgen includes the morphological features necessary for intromission in some species, probably including the baculum or penile bone, as well as other features whose behavioral function is unclear, like the cornified papillae or spines on the glans penis of various species (Zarrow & Clark, 1968). Androgen is also necessary for the development and growth of the accessory sexual glands, including those that provide the bulk of the semen, but apparently these glands have no necessary role in sexual behavior. Specific electrophysiological effects on the penile innervation have not yet been demonstrated (see Section 1.1.3).

In female mammals, gonadal hormones play a similarly important role in the control of sexual behavior. "Courtship" behavior (i.e., sexual solicitation), as well as receptivity to the male, is not found in ovariectomized mammals. Estrogen plays a ubiquitous role as the major and vital endocrine factor, making possible the expression of female sexual behavior. This influence weakens significantly only in some primates. Progesterone is also important in many species, though its effects vary in different species and in some conditions it may be inhibitory. Ovarian hormones act more rapidly on female copulatory behavior than does androgen in the male, and the decline of behavior patterns after gonadectomy is more rapid in females. Though androgen can stimulate female sexual behavior, this reaction is probably due to conversion to estrogen within the animals. Only in rhesus monkeys has a plausible case been made for a unique role of androgen (of adrenal origin), but it is still controversial (references in Davidson, Gray, & Smith, 1978, pp. 61–81).

1.1.2. Brain

Copulatory behavior can be activated in rats and monkeys by electrical stimulation of several areas of the brain, as well as by peripheral application of electrical shock, presumably operating via some widespread arousal mechanism (Sachs & Barfield, 1974). Destruction of specific brain areas can affect sexual behavior in quite specific fashion. Thus, medial preoptic lesions essentially eliminate copulation in male rats, cats, dogs, and rhesus monkeys. The operation apparently does not eliminate genital reflexes, including erection, in cats and dogs, and even masturbatory activity has recently been found to continue in rhesus monkeys, which cease to mate following destruction of the medial preoptic region (Slimp, Hart, & Goy, 1978). This area of the brain was also reported to be a "nodal point" for electrical stimulation of erections by intracranial electrodes in squirrel monkeys (McLean & Ploog, 1962). In female animals, too, sexual behavior is eliminated by hypothalamic lesions, but the critical area in rats is slightly more posterior than in the male—the anterior hypothalamic-ventromedial region (Singer, 1968). Experiments on effects of brain lesions in both sexes on heterotypical behavior (i.e., mounting in females, lordosis in males) provide rather convincing support for a "neural sexual dimorphism" in rats (Modianos, Flexman, & Hitt, 1973). The data indicate the existence of spatially separate cerebral mechanisms for the expression of masculine and feminine sex behavior, homologous between the sexes.

Inhibitory mechanisms are also believed to be present in the brain, but much confusion surrounds this concept. Certain changes in the behavior of male monkeys showing the "Kluver-Bucy" syndrome after temporal lobectomy have been widely described as being indicative of "hypersexuality." Later, more focal lesions in limbic structures centering on the amygdala were reported to release cerebral inhibition of sexual behavior in cats and several other species and to reinforce the concept of hypersexuality. As discussed in the next section, there is considerable doubt whether these operations do indeed *specifically* enhance sexual behavior. More recently, however, several investigators have shown that small lesions in the midbrain strikingly decrease the normally very stable postejaculatory refractory period, thus increasing the frequency of copulation in male rats (Barfield, Wilson, & McDonald, 1975). In females of this species, certain forebrain lesions, particularly in the septum, enhance sexual receptivity, and septal lesions also facilitate mating in the male (Nance, Shryne, & Gorski, 1974). A variety of reflexes "utilized" in copulatory behavior (e.g., erections and motor responses) still function in spinally sectioned animals of both sexes, and it is believed that the brain exercises an overall inhibitory control over them (Beach, 1967). Investigation of inhibitory processes in sexual behavior are relevant to any understanding of the phenomena of initiation and refractoriness in sexual behavior. Evidence from experimental analysis in the rat suggests that the latter probably involves both decreases in an arousal process and increases in an active inhibitory one. The area has been ably discussed by Sachs and Barfield (1976).

Very little is known yet about central nervous system correlates of sexual activity, but some data are available from electrical recordings during mating or artificial genital stimulation. However, the hypothalamic activation noted in the female rat might be related to mating-induced pituitary hormone release (see 1.1.4.) rather than the mediation of behavioral responses (see Blake & Sawyer, 1972). More recently, fluctuations in hippocampal theta activity and cortical spindling have been correlated with behavioral events during mating in both male and female rats (Kurtz, 1975; Kurtz & Adler, 1973). These data were interpreted as yielding evidence for cerebral mechanisms underlying sexual satiety.

1.1.3. Peripheral Nervous System

Investigation of the involvement of the peripheral nervous system during sexual activity has been quite limited. Thus, our knowledge of sympathetic and parasympathetic control of erection and ejaculation has hardly advanced since the classical studies of Semans and Langworthy in cats (1938).

There has been little electrophysiological work on afferent input from the genitals. Cooper and Aronson (1974) have measured neural traffic with microelectrodes and single neuron recordings in afferent nerves in response to tactile stimulation of the glans in cats. They could find no difference in the peripheral nervous activity between normal and castrated animals. Some evidence was obtained that the central reception of stimuli applied to the penis is affected by androgen, namely, enhancement of cortical evoked potentials in intact compared with castrated cats (Cooper, 1969). In the female rat, it does appear that ovarian hormones can affect the function of peripheral nerves in a biologically meaningful way. Several laboratories have demonstrated that estrogen extends the genital sensory field of the pudendal nerve (see Pfaff, Diakow, Zigmond, & Kow, 1974), and similar effects have been shown to occur spontaneously at the time of estrus (Adler et al., 1977). The utility of such a mechanism would be to allow for increased (lordotic) responsiveness to the mounting male, whose initial penile thrusts make contact with the perivaginal area, activating skin receptors. Interestingly, these kinds of effects are not limited to the genital area: estrogen also extends receptive fields of the facial nerve in rats (Bereiter & Barker, 1975).

1.1.4. Neuroendocrinology

Gonadal hormones apparently act on sexual behavior via effects both on the brain and on genital tissues. In the male, the primacy of cerebral action is demonstrated most dramatically by the implantation of crystalline hormones in castrated rats and the resulting restoration of complete patterns of mating behavior (Davidson, 1966). The most effective area of implantation is apparently the medial preoptic region. Presumably, receptors for this action of androgen would be present in highest concentrations in this area, though the data suggest their presence also in other areas of the hypothalamus (Smith, Damassa, & Davidson, 1977). Hormone implantation studies in female cats, rats, hamsters, guinea pigs, and rabbits have provided evidence of brain loci for the behavioral actions of estrogen and progesterone. The most precise localization achieved to date indicates a ventromedial hypothalamic site for the action of estrogen on the sexual receptivity of rats (Barfield & Chen, 1977). Thus, both the hormone implant and the lesion studies indicate that different though contiguous areas of the brain are involved in the mediation of masculine and feminine sex behavior in both sexes. Isotopically labeled androgen and estrogen are selectively accumulated in a variety of hypothalamic and limbic system regions of the brain, and no differences between their distribution patterns have yet been found. However, it is not yet possible in this kind of research to differentiate between receptor mechanisms or cells concerned with sexual behavior and those related to other effects of gonadal hormones, such as "feedback" regulation of gonadotropin secretion and regulation of nonsexual behavior patterns (e.g., maternal and aggressive).

There are high hopes that the study of the molecular actions of hormones on brain cells, beginning with the isolation of receptors, will provide answers to the problems of behavioral endocrinology (McEwen, Denef, Gerlach, & Paplinger, 1974). Much research is currently being devoted to the hypothesis that aromatization to estrogen is a necessary step in the action of androgen on brain-behavior mechanisms, particularly in rats (Naftolin, Ryan, & Petro, 1972). Another rapidly growing body of literature is concerned with the role of biogenic amines. These investigations have not yet succeeded in tackling the immensity of the problem of demonstrating specific relationships between specific amines (norepinephrine, dopamine, or serotonin, primarily), specific nerve cells, and specific behavioral mechanisms.

Hormone release in response to mating has been studied in a variety of species. The most obvious case of a clear-cut effect is in "reflex ovulators," for example, in cats and rabbits. In these and some other mammalian species, large increases in the release of gonadotropic hormones (particularly luteinizing hormone, LH) from the pituitary are seen following coitus in the female and are obligatory for ovulation (release of the ovum). Pigeons, doves, and other ovian species ovulate in response to auditory or visual communication between the sexes. Even in a spontaneously ovulating species—the rat, for example—gonadotropin release can be demonstrated for approximately an hour after mating, and it can lead to normal ovulation even if the spontaneous LH release is blocked (Davidson, Smith, & Bowers, 1973). In rats and other species, mating-induced prolactin release is essential for normal pregnancy. There is evidence, albeit largely indirect, for the release of oxytocin during mating in both and male and female sheep (Fitzpatrick, 1966a,b). Increased LH and/or testosterone release has been reported in several species following copulation or sexual arousal from exteroceptive stimuli, though the data are somewhat inconsistent (see Södersten, Damassa, & Smith, 1977).

1.2. From Animal Behavior to Human Sexuality

There is no doubt that the behavioristic-mechanistic approach has paid off handsomely in producing a body of knowledge about the physiological determinants of animal sexual behavior. The temptation for undiscriminating extrapolation of this information to humans makes it important to stress the change in vantage point as we move from studying animal to human species.

It is not meaningful to evaluate human sexual behavior, as we do that of animals, in terms of the achievement of certain mechanical responses, except for the procreative function. Instead, the focus is on the attainment of a cognitive state: the conscious perception of sexual satisfaction. This state depends on a combination of experiences perceived as originating in the experiencer's body and in that of the sexual partner. Obviously, large inter- and intraindividual variations exist both in the relative importance attributed to these two components and in their individual qualities. Also contributing to the variance in sexual experience are differences in the emphasis that the individual may place on different stages of arousal and on orgasm versus arousal, a matter of personal preference that is receiving particular attention in the current efforts to understand women's sexuality and its dysfunctions. Regarding the interpersonal component, again tremendous variability exists— from the violent imposition of sexual attentions on an unwilling partner to the reciprocal satisfactions of a mutual love relationship. Thus, the private nature of human sexual experience, its great variability, and the lack of an appropriate language to describe its elements all increase the difficulty of establishing the relevant biological variables.

Given these caveats, why be concerned with animal data? First, it is a well-established article of faith that biological mechanisms involved in human behavior can generally be traced "backwards" to other mammalian species. The reproductive function of sexual behavior applies equally to human and infrahuman species, and they share many features of reproductive biology and the anatomy and physiology of copulation. If we differ from animals primarily by virtue of our level of awareness, we must never forget that our "higher consciousness" is grafted onto an animal body. That body is much closer to the gorilla's than the gorilla's body is to that of many other mammals. Since most of the experimental work required to elucidate the relevant physiology can be performed only on animals (for primarily ethical reasons), knowledge of animal sex behavior still must provide the background if not the basis for understanding human sexual biology.

2. PHYSIOLOGY, SENSATIONS, AND CONCEPTS OF SEXUALITY

2.1. The Physiology of Sexual Arousal

At this point, it is necessary to describe briefly the main physiological changes in *preorgasmic* human sexual behavior, before discussing their relationship to the sexual experience. Details and some references for most of the phenomena to be mentioned can be found in Masters and Johnson (1966), though systematic quantitative data on adequate samples of subjects are seldom available. Furthermore, the phases of sexual response described by these authors are not sharply delineated, constant, or even clearly established by objective criteria but are only convenient approximations of the sequence of events. We will distinguish five classes of physiological effects during sexual activity. The first three are well-known "overt" responses and are mentioned only in outline.

I. First are autonomically mediated changes in the genitals and surrounding regions as well as internal sexual tissues—the reproductive tract of both sexes and the accessory sexual glands that open into the tract. Among *vascular* changes, the generalized vasocongestion in the pelvic region (including both genital and surrounding tissues) is of primary interest. Specific phenomena of importance, however, include penile and clitoral erection and testicular and vaginal vasocongestion. These occur early—at the beginning of the so-called excitement phase, according to Masters and Johnson's classification. Genital vasocongestion has more recently been studied by more sophisticated plethysmographic methods in both sexes. Increased vaginal blood flow includes the development of the "orgasmic platform" in the "plateau phase" described by Masters and Johnson (1966). Vasocongestion of the ovary has also been described (Danesino & Martella, 1976). *Secretory* effects include vaginal "lubrication," which is a transudate from the vaginal walls; there are also occasional drops secreted from Bartholin's gland. The latter effect has a parallel in the male's preejaculatory emission of drops of a mucoid semen, possibly coming from Cowper's gland. This reportedly occurs during the plateau phase with a timing similar to that of the Bartholin secretion (Masters & Johnson, 1966). *Muscular* changes include tensing and thickening of the scrotum and elevation of the testes, expansion and distension of the vagina and elevation of the uterus. In general, these changes in the sex-related tissues begin promptly with the onset of stimulation and tend to increase progressively with arousal until the stage of orgasm.

II. In a second class are autonomically mediated extragenital effects. These tend to begin later than the genital ones and are clearly present only in the "plateau" phase. Most prominent are sympathetically mediated facilitation of respiratory and cardiovascular reactions: increases in the rate of respiration, heart rate, and blood pressure. There are also widespread increases in peripheral blood flow, but these have not been extensively described. Masters and Johnson (1966) emphasized the "sex flush," a vasocongestive reaction of the skin originating in the epigastrium and spreading, in the later stages of sexual activity, to cover sometimes very large areas of the body. They reported that the sex flush occurs in 25% of males and 75% of females studied, but (by their admission) conditions in their studies were not necessarily typical. Vasocongestion commonly affects the breasts and produces nipple erection in both sexes. Occasional observations of blood flow in other peripheral extragenital tissues have been made (see Zuckerman, 1971), but no clear-cut pattern of events has been established.

III. The third class of physiological effects relates to the somatic musculature. There is an overall increase in muscle tension beginning in the early stages ("excitement phase") and leading to "semispastic contractions of facial, abdominal and intercostal musculature." During the "plateau phase" (Masters & Johnson, 1966, pp. 286, 290), rhythmic movements of the body take on a seemingly reflex pattern.

Many of the physiological events that fit under the above three headings are common to other emotional or stress responses, but more than for other emotional behaviors, there are aspects that are specific to sexual arousal, particularly the genital responses and the marked vasodilation in certain extragenital tissues. Thus, though more quantitative and detailed investigations are needed, there is a generally accepted pattern of *overt* events in sexual arousal, that is, those readily accessible to noninvasive means of recording. Our knowledge of the *covert* events in humans is, however, minimal: it is discussed under the headings of neural and endocrine phenomena.

IV. While the *neural* control of erection and ejaculation is assumed to be similar in humans and other mammals, the existing experimental data boil down to very few studies in animals and on humans with neural lesions, mostly at the spinal level in the human subjects. Ejaculation is apparently controlled by sympathetic innervation, while erection is predominanatly parasympathetic, albeit with a secondary component of cholinergic sympathetic fibers (Tarabulcy, 1972). Even less is known about cerebral mechanisms: most of the reports tend to be of rather anecdotal nature. Heath (1972), one of the few individuals who have felt justified in implanting chronic electrodes in the brains of mental (or other) patients, reported penile erection during electrical stimulation of the septum, an area found to respond in like manner in the squirrel monkey (McLean & Ploog, 1962). In the female squirrel monkey, clitoral erection is reportedly produced by stimulation of similar limbic brain regions (Maurus, Mitra, & Ploog, 1965).

In an ethically as well as scientifically questionable attempt to deal with deviant sexuality in men, Roeder (1966) has destroyed the ventromedial nucleus of the hypothalamus. The claims of specific "cures" for the sexual problems of his patients have not yet been adequately evaluated. Various pathologic or traumatic brain lesions have been associated with sexual disorders, and these often seem to involve the limbic system, a finding that is in accord with the animal data (see Epstein, 1973). The Klüver–Bucy syndrome is believed by some to occur in humans subjected to temporal lobectomy (Terzian & Dalle-Ore, 1955; Blumer, 1970). There are reports of compulsive masturbation after surgery, and this kind of phenomenon has been related to the evidence of "hypersexuality" alleged to follow temporal lobe lesions in some animal species. Unfortunately, the interpretation of the animal data in terms of specificity for sexual behavior has been widely questioned, and the changes noted may in fact be due to non-sex-related changes, such as visual agnosia with consequent failure to recognize sexual objects and territories and the tendency to engage in stereotyped behaviors (Valenstein, 1973). It should also be noted that though some of the reported human cases involve females, there are no data on "hypersexuality" related to brain lesions in female animals.

V. As to the endocrine system, investigators have almost invariably looked for changes in hormone levels some time after rather than during sexual activity, presumably because of expectations derived from the animal literature (see Section 1.1.4.) and because most hormones respond with some delay to stimulation. There are a variety of clinical reports on ovulation induced by coitus in women (references in Jochle, 1973). This apparently atavistic vestige of reflex-ovulating species may occur regularly, if at all, only in highly stressful or other unusual circumstances. Recent attempts to demonstrate coitus-induced elevated levels of the gonadotropic hormones that are responsible for triggering ovulation in normal women or men have failed (Davidson & Trupin, 1975, pp. 13–20; Stearns, Winter, & Faiman, 1973). Steroid hormones have not been studied in the female, but earlier data suggesting that sexual activity stimulated testosterone release in men (Anon., 1970; Fox, Ismail, Love, Kirkham, & Loraine, 1972) were not corroborated in the investigations on larger numbers of subjects, cited above, or after masturbation (Shirai, Matsuda, Mitsukawa, Nakamura, & Yonezawa, 1974).

Adrenal hormones have been investigated, and an increase in circulating epinephrine has been reported during sexual arousal induced by an erotic film (Levi, 1969). This effect is a manifestation of sympatheticoadrenal activation and is not specific for sexual stimulation. Adrenocortical hormones are apparently not affected by sexual arousal (Kling, Borowitz, & Cartwright, 1972).

It is believed that the posterior pituitary hormone, oxytocin, is released during coitus in the human female. This phenomenon is of particular interest because of the dual stimulatory action of this peptide hormone on the milk-releasing cells of the breast and on uterine contractions. Unfortunately, only a few scattered observations exist relating to milk release from the nipples in lactating women (see Fitzpatrick, 1966b), and no systematic data have apparently been published yet on circulating oxytocin levels. Yet, this mechanism could be the key to understanding some aspects of orgasmic psychophysiology and is the subject of further discussion in Section 3.

2.2. Sexual Dualism

2.2.1. Dualism in Animal and Human Sexuality

Given the information on physiological events associated with sexual activity, what is established about psychophysiological relationships? Surprisingly little. The physical manifestations of sexual behavior seem to proceed on a path parallel to the unique stream of consciousness that comprises sexual experience, but for all we know, the two sets of processes could be quite separate. Presumably because of the difficulty we have in understanding this relationship, theorists, clinicians, and laboratory investigators have adopted a frankly dualistic approach to human sexuality. Thus, our thinking in this area is dominated by the concept that sexuality consists of two separate functional categories, one directly observable in terms of physical events, and the other basically experiential and private, though its existence is inferred and its extent may be measured by reference to behavioral events. It will be instructive to look briefly at the various ways in which this type of dualistic conceptualization has been expressed in the analysis of both human and animal sexual behavior without claiming strict analogies between all of the dichotomies used. While the major emphasis is initially on the male, the discussion is soon extended to include both sexes.

In the *animal* literature, male sexual behavior is often thought of as consisting of an arousal mechanism and a copulatory, or intromission–ejaculatory, mechanism (Beach, 1956). Though motivational constructs like arousal cannot be directly assessed, indirect methods of measurement include tests of maze running or bar pressing, etc., with receptive females as reward. In mating tests, it is generally assumed that arousal is reflected in latency to onset of copulatory or precopulatory behavior or frequency of mounting when the consummatory responses of intromission and ejaculation are prevented. Copulatory mechanism variables, on the other hand, are those related to successful completion of mating behavior patterns, primarily the time and the number of copulatory events required for ejaculation. Erection, though seldom studied directly, can be inferred in small animals from observation of the behavioral patterns accompanying intromission, and ejaculation is likewise inferred from its characteristic behavioral concomitants.

Some limited progress has been made in the attempt to define separate physiological bases for arousal and copulatory mechanisms. For example, destruction of the medial preoptic region of the brain seems to suppress sexual arousal in a variety of species without suppressing the capacity for erection and ejaculation (Hart, 1974). Yet, as mentioned above, this brain region has been regarded as a key area for the electrical stimulation of erection in primates. This apparent inconsistency is a reflection of the inadequacy of our knowledge of sexual neurophysiology.

In *humans*, the classical clinical analysis of male sexual behavior sets up the duality; libido versus potency. *Libido* has to do with sexual interests, drive, or motivation, while *potency* generally refers to capacity for erection and ejaculation. This dichotomy resembles that of the arousal–copulatory mechanisms from the animal literature, but with some inevitable differences. Thus, the arousal–copulatory categories are defined in terms of behavioral responses, while in humans it is possible to assess the arousal function—libido—directly from verbal report of the conscious experience of sexual desire. To this extent, libido is more accessible to investigation than the arousal mechanism in animal research, because though behavior can be "objectively" quantified, the relationship between sexual behavior and the construct of arousal depends on inference.

Another duality that relates the arousal–copulatory and the libido–potency classifications is reflex–nonreflex. Because of their stereotypic nature, male and female copulatory patterns in many animal species appear to resemble a set of reflexes, and this impression is confirmed by the retention of a variety of components of the mating pattern following complete spinal section. For the human male, erection and ejaculation—the manifestations of potency—have to be regarded as reflex responses in that they are largely involuntary, stimulus-bound behaviors, though the stimulus may be cognitive. In addition, men with spinal cord lesions may show the spontaneous pelvic thrusting associated with reflexive erections. Since there is no sensation or motor control of these events in the paralyzed human, they clearly exemplify the ways in which automatic reflexive acts are built into willed behavior patterns in sexual (as in other) behavior.

A final duality comes into view when we consider sexual behavior from the neuroanatomical perspective, that is, central versus peripheral control. Each of the previously mentioned dualities can be regarded as depending on the distinction between cerebral activity and peripheral nervous-spinal regulation. Although investigators are aware of the hierarchical regulation of reflex responses at all levels of the nervous system, there is a strong tendency to relegate the reflex "copulatory mechanism" phenomena to the periphery (genitospinal circuits) and the more "psychological" aspects of sex to the brain. This dichotomy arises from the belief that intentional and complex behaviors connected with conscious motivations are "in" the brain. Its scientific rationale derives from the maintenance of various sexual reflexes after spinal section and the failure of peripheral denervation or anesthetization to abolish sexual behavior.

We see, then, that the adoption of dualistic concepts of sexuality is a common device for dealing with the difficulties of comprehending psychophysical interactions in sex. Now we shall consider the extent to which these concepts are justified.

2.2.2. Validity of the Dualistic Concepts

In this section, I attempt to show that though the dualistic approach is heuristically advantageous, it is conceptually unsatisfying. Let us first briefly explore each of the three polarities that originated primarily from the animal literature and then concentrate on the example of libido–potency, which is the most relevant to our concerns. The arousal–copulatory dichotomy, useful in psychobiological research, is now being revealed as a somewhat misleading oversimplification. Thus, the putative "arousal mechanism" has been regarded in more recent writings as influencing more than just the initiation of behavior (Cherney & Bermant, 1970; Sachs & Barfield, 1976). Likewise, if sexual arousal in humans is manifested as the conscious urge to initiate sexual activity, simple introspection tells us that this same urge is not different from that which continues to be present during the activity.

The reflex–nonreflex (or voluntary-involuntary) distinctions also cannot be considered exclusive polarities. Thus, erection and ejaculation can, to an extent that varies greatly between individuals, be brought under voluntary control. Sexual responses, like respiration and many other human functions, can fluctuate between greater and lesser degrees of "reflexiveness." Thus, as awareness shifts—spontaneously or with the conscious deployment of selective attention—the level of control over sexual responses shifts, too.

The rigid distinction between central and peripheral mechanisms is also hard to maintain in the light of accumulating experimental data. Thus, for example, animals with anesthetized or denervated penes will mount receptive females, but when not reinforced by genital input, the mounting behavior rapidly declines or disappears (Carlsson & Larsson, 1964). Furthermore, sexual reflexes, though organized at the spinal level, are importantly influenced by input from the brain (see Beach, 1967; McLean & Ploog, 1962). Behavioral events reflecting both arousal and copulatory mechanisms can be manipulated in animals by brain lesions and peripheral or central electrical stimulation, as well as by changing environmental conditions or levels of genital sensory input (Sachs & Barfield, 1976). Thus, there are multiple controls for different components of sexual behavior operating at different levels of the neuraxis.

These questions about the validity of the experimentalists' categorizations of arousal–copulation mechanisms, reflex-voluntary behaviors, and central-peripheral control provide a fitting introduction to a critical consideration of the libido–potency dichotomy and its potential usefulness for human sexual psychophysiology. Can the various known physiological events during sexual experience be related individually either to libido or to potency; and is this duality any more valid than the others just discussed? Of the known physiological phenomena, those most relevant to potency are the mechanisms responsible for erection, as well as the neuromuscular events during ejaculation (to be discussed in Section 3). However, as noted earlier, erection (in males *and* females) is only one specific (albeit unique) case of the general vasocongestion affecting the pelvic region. Thus, penile erection and therefore potency pertain to a wider cluster of physiological events rather than being an isolated mechanism functioning alone to facilitate the biologically essential act of insemination. The relationship between pelvic vasocongestion and similar changes in extragenital tissues is unclear, but presumably libido relates to both of them, yet no known physiological event is essential to libido.

At this point, we have to recognize that, though *potency* is a term that is used only in relation to male sexuality, the concept can also be legitimately applied to women. As we have seen, potency depends on vascular events that have close analogies in the female sexual response. Unlike in the male, reproductive function in the female is not dependent on potency, yet the full experience of sexual arousal and orgasm may be equally dependent on potency in both sexes. In studying female sexual responses, Campbell (1976) noted that the first sign of sexual arousal (in the absence of tactile stimulation) was a tingling in the clitoral area, presumably signifying increased blood flow. The appearance of vaginal transudate ("lubrication") within seconds of an arousing stimulus (Masters & Johnson, 1966) also speaks to the rapidity of the vascular response (Geer & Quartararo, 1976). The initial blood-flow increase and tingling presumably also apply to the male. Is libidinous experience invariably associated with such physical sensations? This question beckons us to return to a deeper exploration of the libido–potency dichotomy.

Earlier, doubt was expressed regarding the traditional analysis of arousal/libido as relating to events that occur prior to the initiation of sexual activity, and of potency as coming into play only after that point. This suggests that the two are discrete entities. However, potency is not normally conceivable without libido, since the "reflex" responses of erection and ejaculation are dependent on prior excitation, that is, sexual arousal.[2] Whether normal libido is possible without potency in individuals with an intact nervous system—that is, in the presence of

---

[2]The phenomena of nocturnal erection and emission do not invalidate this statement, since they occur during an altered state of consciousness (rapid-eye-movement sleep) and since in most cases we do not know their experiential correlates, if any (Kinsey *et al.*, 1953).

functioning neural connections from the genitals to the central nervous system—is also open to question. Some alleged cases of impotence with intact libido (in senescent or otherwise impotent men) may simply reflect low sexual arousal, with the memory of sexual pleasure or social expectations producing the desire for sexual activity. Thus, the possibility of "mislabeling" libido results from the complex roles played by sexual activity in human society (see below). But if libido without potency is hard to understand, the rarer situation of potency without libido (the ability of the male to perform sexually without anticipatory or consummatory pleasure) is even more difficult to explain.

Let us consider briefly two specific ways in which the systems interact at the level of conscious experience. The first of these involves the recognition of potency or its absence. If, for whatever reason, there is a real or imagined failure of potency, the resulting expectation of future failure can not only further reduce potency but also inhibit libido. The same sequence can occur in females experiencing problems that arise from failure of lubrication or other events related to inadequate physiological response. Similarly, the expectation of optimal potency can engender a feeling of self-confidence that may enhance libido by increasing openness to hedonic experience.

The second interaction is a ubiquitous mechanism that occurs in all sustained successful sexual acts. It seems that at the level of the genital (and other erotogenic?) sensory receptors, if not also at the level of cerebral mechanisms afferent to these tissues, there is a kind of positive feedback mechanism whereby the activation of potency (read: sexual response) enhances sexual arousal (read: libido). Genital stimulation produces sexual arousal, and the resulting vasocongestion involves a change in sensitivity of response to subsequent stimuli, with consequently increased afferent input conveying pleasurable sensations from the genital tissue (Campbell, 1976, p. 60). Parallels may exist in other erotogenic tissues, particularly the female breast. It is important to point out that this cascading reaction can originate either from tactile stimulation or from purely cognitive arousal, as in the case of fantasy or exteroceptively induced erection. Although direct measurements have not yet been taken, changes in threshold and/or intensity/rate of responding to stimuli could be studied at the level of genital tissue. But stimulation-induced enhancement of erotic responsiveness could also be a function of central nervous changes or both central and peripheral ones. As in other areas of behavior, we can not tell whether the experiential events of sexual arousal are related more to efferent output to the genitals, or afferent input to the CNS, or both equally. The experimental investigation of these mechanisms should be feasible, at least in animal models.

2.2.3. Concluding Statement

We are led to conclude, then, that libido and potency are closely correlated in the overwhelming majority of normal (i.e., nonpathological) situations involving sexual behavior in *both* sexes. They should be regarded not as two distinct elements reflecting independant physiological mechanisms but rather as two sides of the same coin of sexuality. Regarding them as exclusive entities is a misleading product of our common dualistic nonsolution to the body–mind problem.

Yet, the critique of sexual polarities should not obscure the fact that these concepts have heuristic value *and* underlying physiological bases. Rather such a critique should serve to emphasize the dangers arising from the uncritical use of these concepts. In the clinical area, these dangers include the treatment of apparently physical sexual problems without concomitant counseling or psychotherapy and the failure to utilize pharmacologic or other physical approaches for apparently psychogenically based conditions.

2.3. From Sexual Sensations to Sensational Sex

2.3.1. Sexual Sensations and Sexual Emotion

If, in organizing concepts about sexuality into pairs of functional categories, we run the danger of creating imaginary, mutually exclusive polarities, we can escape the worst consequences of this dilemma by thinking in terms of a dynamic interacting system. This theme, which pervades many of the discussions in this chapter, is congruent with the systems approaches used by Tart (Chapter 11) and Powers (Chapter 10) in considering the phenomena of consciousness as a whole.

Let us now return to our central question about the relationship between physiological events and sexual experience. At this point, I shall not attempt to deal with sexual experience in terms of *states* of consciousness nor to analyze the cognitive events that make up the *content* of consciousness. It will be simpler to start by asking how "simple" sexual perceptions may relate to physiological events and the whole sexual experience in ways that are (up to a point) direct and obvious.

A major debate throughout the history of the psychology of emotions has centered on this problem of the relationship between bodily feelings and emotional experience. The James–Lange theory—that all emotions consist of the experiential response to the perception of physiological changes that are generated by emotion-arousing stimuli— is almost a century old. Already at the turn of the century, Sherrington

(1900) found that "emotional behavior" was not eliminated after complete transection of the cervical spinal cord in dogs. Since then, similar criticisms relating to the independence of emotions from peripheral perceptions in humans have been advanced, and the work of Cannon (1927) and Bard (1928) seemed to have finally demolished the theory. Yet, it keeps reappearing in different forms (e.g., Pribram, 1976; Schachter, 1975), and though few psychophysiologists today accept the unadulterated James–Lange view that emotions are "nothing but" perceptions of these events, it is also not reasonable to suppose that the physical sensations are mere epiphenomena of emotional experience.

A major problem with any James–Lange type of theory is that it can account for the variety of emotional experiences only by demonstrating a separate set of perceptible physiological responses for each emotion. This has not yet been successfully accomplished, despite numerous attempts in the earlier literature (Arnold, 1945; Ax, 1953; Funkenstein, 1956) and more recent progress, for instance, in delineation of the facial characteristics of emotions (Ekman, Friessen, & Ellsworth, 1972) and various psychophysiological parameters. It would seem, however, that the case of sexual emotion is ideally suited to a James–Lange type of formulation, in that various aspects of the sexual response are so obviously unique and distinguishable from those of other emotional situations. Because of the dual function of genital sensory receptors mentioned earlier, it becomes possible to view the experience of sexual activity in terms either of (a) a direct emotional response to mechanical genital stimulation; (b) the response to endogenous sensations arising from vascular engorgement, as in the case of exteroceptive fantasy-induced arousal; or (c) most logically, both together.

Of course, the relatively great specificity of sexual sensations does not prove their essential role in sexual experience; it only makes this a more reasonable hypothesis than is the case for other emotions. Furthermore, the alternative centrally oriented view of emotions developed by Cannon (1927)—that the physical events are the result rather than the cause of emotional experience—can also be reconciled with the James–Lange view in the case of sexual experience. The dual role of the sexually responding tissues as receptors and effectors makes it possible to view physical sensations in sex simultaneously as cause *and* effect. The extent to which this argument might apply to other emotions merits exploration, but this is beyond the scope of the present chapter.

A challenge to the James–Lange type of interpretation seems to come from the well-documented observations that sexual activity and response are not necessarily dependent on the integrity of the genitals or their neural connections. Much evidence from animal research shows that denervation of the genitals by nerve section or anesthetization does not suppress sexual arousal, as measured for instance by mounting in rats (Adler & Bermant, 1966; Carlsson & Larsson, 1964). In humans, there is the evidence that paraplegic subjects in which genital sensory input to the brain is absent, just as in the operated animals, are capable of sexual arousal (Money, 1960). These considerations do not quite settle the issue, because quite obviously, genital sensation has a vital role in sexual experience under *normal* conditions. They do suggest that both in animals and in humans, other mechanisms can take over in the absence of the relevant nervous connections and/or that sexual arousal may be associated more with efferent commands from the CNS than with afferent information. Furthermore, the extent to which sexual experience under these unusual conditions resembles the normal situation is not clear. So, if we limit our consideration to the normal situation, how far can we get in defining the role of sexual sensations?

2.3.2. The Transactional Nature of Sexual Experience

Nothing is more obvious than that genital input and associated stimuli cannot alone begin to account for the richness and variety of human sexual experience. Clearly, in this (as in other) contexts, it is not the "raw feel" that is of greatest importance. The sensory data are subject to processing (which I shall call *interpretation*) to such a degree that the same input can be converted—between and with individuals—into vastly different experiences. Now, an important point to realize is that the interpretation of sensory input is a two-way street: cognitive events not only are influenced by raw sensations but in turn influence the extent and quality of their *reception*, for instance, by deploying selective attention. Relevant examples are the sensory loss in orgasm and the transformation of painful to pleasurable stimuli at the height of sexual arousal (see Section 3.3.5.). Sexual experience must therefore be viewed as a continuous transaction between the sensory and the cognitive.

Sexual sensations are analyzed and assigned values in terms of such scales as pleasure/unpleasure, exciting/routine, acceptable/unacceptable, and safe/dangerous. This attribution of value, in fact, involves even the actual decision about whether an experience is sexual or not, for if sexual sensations are not merely the result of *genital* stimulation, what are their anatomical limits? The entire body surface is covered with potentially erogenous zones, and their relative valency is defined by cultural and individual experience. Whether a touch, scratch, or bite is or is not interpreted as sexual has less to do with any physical properties of the stimulus than with the cognitive operation based on information from other sensory modalities and from a whole complex of relevant past experience. This point is well exemplified by the cases of women who could experience orgasm from the stimuli of stroking the eyebrows, pressing on the teeth, or even in the absence of any sensory stimulus (Kinsey, Pomeroy, Martin, & Gebhard, 1953, p. 490). But rare examples are not needed to make the point that the differentiation between sensuous and sexual experience involves a *cognitive* act.

In the process of sensory interpretation, an important element is the interface between sexual experience and the rest of the individual's life. Attitudes relating to the value, significance, and role of sex in the satisfaction of life goals are an integral part of the experience, spring from it, and in turn influence its progress. The personal and interpersonal mingle in the cognitive act of sex: the experience is therefore greatly influenced by preferences as to the sexual and other personal characteristics of the desired partner. These preferences undoubtedly depend on both biological and social influences exerted during ontogeny, as well as on possible genetic factors (Money & Ehrhardt, 1972).

Furthermore, if sensory input is not sexual or pleasurable until it is cognitively interpreted as such, so also the construction of attitudes and preferences is in part the product of a previous history of sexual sensations, albeit colored by other experiences. The sexual experience is not merely the sum total of sensory and cognitive input; rather, both are engaged in a continuously reverberating transaction, the results of which affect proximal as well as future events.

To this point, the discussion has stressed sensory input from tactile stimulation and the responses of "erogenous" tissue. The James–Lange theory, however, concerns autonomic responses in general. It is not clear to what extent the pattern of autonomically mediated, extragenital responses in sexual arousal differs from that of other emotional behavior (though the Kinsey report emphasized the uniqueness of the high degree of peripheral vasodilation). Nevertheless, the relevance of nonspecific visceral changes (such as increased cardiac and respiratory activity) in the total sexual experience need not be denied.

The major modern version of emotional psychology arising from the James–Lange approach is the theory of Schachter (1975), which views emotional experiences as engendered by the cognitive interpretation of the perception of events resulting from autonomic nervous activation. In their classic experiment, for instance, Schachter and Singer (1962) demonstrated that an injection of epinephrine could result in emotional experience, but whether anger or euphoria was felt depended on the presence of a confederate in the experimental room who acted euphorically or angrily. While this work precipitated many similar experimental results (London & Nisbett, 1974), subsequent criticism and research suggest that greater physiological specificity can or will be found, for instance, if patterning of multiple physiological responses (Schwartz,

1975) rather than individual events is considered. Certainly, contextual influences usually need not be invoked to *define* an emotion as sexual because of the specificity of the physiological responses, particularly genitopelvic phenomena. Since, however, cognitive influences do play an important role in determining the quality of sexual experience, we may look to this body of experimentation and theory for support in constructing a suitable model to express the significant influence of "interpretation."

Unfortunately, little can yet be said about the relative importance of specific sexual activation and the general nonspecific interoceptive events in sexual experience, or about the relationship between either of these and the cognitive processes that may direct the form of the sexual emotion triggered by feedback from bodily sensations. Cognitive activation can precede or succeed tactile or exteroceptive sexual stimulation, but presumably the two types of physiological response—genital and nonspecific autonomic—are linked in a relatively invariant sequence of events, at least if Masters and Johnson's descriptions of the human sexual response are correct. It would be of considerable interest to compare the physiological events in normal circumstances to those in the (unfortunately rare) cases of fantasy-induced orgasms without tactile stimulation. Recordings should also be obtained in sleeping subjects prone to nocturnal emission or in the allegedly common cases of female orgasm during sleep (Campbell, 1976).

Some fair portion of the individual variance in sexual experience must derive from the relative importance of cognitive factors vis-à-vis the "raw feel" of genital sensation. Perhaps the differences might be correlated with the intensity or pattern of autonomic activation. A relevant model comes from the unlikely source of the psychology of anxiety. There is a fair amount of evidence to support the view that persons suffering from anxiety may be differentiated into those for whom somatic manifestations play a major role and those for whom somatic symptoms are much less important than the perception of "mental" stress (Davidson & Schwartz, 1976; Tyler, 1976). If the inter- and intraindividual variation in sexual experience may be similarly analyzed, it might provide useful insights into normal and dysfunctional sexuality.

Thus, we see that though physical sensations are a vital part of sexual experience, they have little meaning and significance on their own, but only as essential components of the system of cognitive-physical interactions. Failure of sexual sensation can hamper or prevent sexual experience, but this can be caused by physical or "psychological" influences. Furthermore, failure of the sensory apparatus can be overcome by apparent psychological "adjustments." Excellent examples may be the reported phantom orgasms of paraplegics and quadriplegics

(Money, 1960) or, less dramatically, the phantom uterine contractions of some hysterectomized women (Masters & Johnson, 1966, p. 118). Here, the cerebrally encoded experience becomes independent of the presence of the peripheral tissue. How such experiences compare with those of neurally intact individuals is still a matter of some conjecture.

3. ORGASM AS AN ALTERED STATE OF CONSCIOUSNESS (ASC)

Little has been said so far about orgasm, which is the most psychophysiologically interesting component of sexual behavior. In this section, I consider the advantages of viewing orgasm as an ASC and summarize our all-too-meager knowledge of its characteristics. I hope to demonstrate both the appropriateness of using orgasm as a model in the psychobiology of conscious states and the poverty of our knowledge in this area. These two assertions, if valid, lead to a third: that herein lies an excellent opportunity for research.

As was pointed out in Chapter 1, our knowledge of the psychobiology of consciousness is still in an embryonic state, primarily because of the lack of established, definitive psychophysiological correlations. Even more than sleep states, orgasm presents unique and specific manifestations in the realms of both psychology and physiology. As a model system, it has the practical advantages of being entirely natural, harmless (to say the least), and potentially available in all healthy human subjects, and of being possible to elicit reproduceably under standard laboratory conditions. Its utilization as the subject of scientific investigation is limited only by taboos that appeared (albeit with undue optimism) to have been overcome by the classic studies of Masters and Johnson (1966), conducted well over a decade ago.

What justification is there for classifying orgasm as an ASC? First, it qualifies by the simplest definition (see Chapter 1) as a qualitative departure from usual experience easily recognized by the experiencer as such. Obviously, there are immense individual differences, but all orgasms share *some* of the criteria commonly found in full-blown ASCs. These include changes in exteroception and interoception and in the senses of space, time, and identity, as well as strong emotions and great changes in motor output (see Tart, Chapter 11). While most are short-lived, in some individuals orgasms can be prolonged, and (particularly in women) multiple orgasms can occur in rapid succession, stretching over a relatively long period of time.

Tart (1975 and Chapter 11) discusses the conditions that are conducive to the "induction" of ASCs in general under the rubric of two sets of forces. The first are those that tend to produce disruption or destabilization of the existing state of consciousness, such as drugs or any intense physiological procedure—for example, exhaustion, extreme excitation, or other stresses—or removal of normal stabilizing stimuli. The second group comprises patterning forces that tend to substitute an ASC for normal basal states. The latter commonly involve processes of relaxation, as in sleep, meditation, and hypnosis, in which there is reduction of exteroceptive and (presumably) interoceptive sensory input.

"Destabilizing" conditions occur in the case of orgasm. These include intense physical stimulation, exercise, rhythmic motion, and focused attention, all of which tend to disrupt the normal state of consciousness and stop the internal dialogue that is a condition of its maintenance. Major physiological changes that operate here include vasomotor and muscular events and, generally, strong autonomic nervous system activation (see below), which resemble destabilizing events for many other ASCs (see Tart, Chapter 11). The capacity to "let go" of inhibition and of self-consciousness is necessary to some extent for orgasm (Lowry & Lowry, 1976, p. 205), as it seems to be for "mystical" (and other) ASCs (Davidson, 1976).

There are, however, "patterning forces" in orgasm that are quite unique to the sexual situation. Thus, in induction of orgasm, as in other ASCs, there is a combination of relatively nonspecific conditions that disrupt the normal state of consciousness as well as a set of specific conditions (like tiredness in sleep) that orient the organism toward this specific state of consciousness.

3.1. Psychological Phenomena

For an experience, generally of notable intensity, that most humans have thousands of times throughout a lifetime, it is rather amazing how little we have to say about it. Kinsey, Pomeroy, Martin, and Gebhard (1953, p. 628) remarked, "few persons realize how they behave at . . . orgasm, and they are quite incapable of describing their experiences in any informative way." Nevertheless, we must try to identify the recognizable commonalities in the orgasmic experience. In a recent study, Vance and Wagner (1976) submitted to independent qualified "judges" brief descriptions of orgasms collected from groups of men and women. The judges were unable to determine the sex of the participants from their descriptions, showing the close resemblance of the orgasmic experience in men and women, a point also stressed by Lowen (1965, Chapter 11).

The terms included in the Vance and Wagner study (perhaps because of instructions or editing by the investigators?) were relatively concrete, unlike the metaphoric allusions found in literary sources. In the 48 statements reported were many repeated themes, which can be classified into (a) sensations referred to the body and (b) those that are not overtly physical. In the former category, one finds, first, terms relating to general muscular sensations, such as muscular spasm or rigidity and "tightening inside" (Masters and Johnson described the initiation of female orgasm as an experience of "stoppage" or suspension, as in the second stage of labor). Second, various localized physical sensations were described, such as throbbing in the temples, stomach vibration, hot or cold feelings in the genitals and elsewhere, expanding feelings in the pelvis leading to release of tension, and genital or anal contractions. Third were less localized sensations, such as light-headedness, dizziness, and the desire to sigh; and such sensory phenomena of various modalities as tingling, fluttering, buzzing, tickling, and pulsating and occasionally visual phenomena, for example, spots in front of the eyes.

In the second category (b) are found general mood changes, including those clearly recognizable as changes in conscious state. These included, first, such banal experiences as tiredness, release of tension, or sleepiness and some negative manifestations in a few subjects, such as anxiety in the buildup to orgasm. Other mood changes reported were euphoria and peacefulness, as well as experiences clearly belonging in the category of ASCs, such as loss of control (with spontaneous movement in some cases), loss of contact with the environment, apparent lapses of consciousness, and the sensation of being "immersed" in the present or "in limbo," and such hallucinationlike experiences as visualization of lights becoming patterns of color.

Of course, it is the more extreme orgasmic experiences (when, in Hemingway's phrase, "the earth shakes") that are of particular interest in the present context. Terms frankly reminiscent of other ASCs were, however, less frequent, either because they are in fact rarer or because they are more difficult to describe ("ineffable"). Conditions predisposing to these occurrences have not been studied, and one would like to know the role of such factors as the quality of the sexual relationship, the level of libido, and the capacity to "let go." Extreme ASCs in sex are probably facilitated by drugs such as cannabis (see Tart, 1971). From an examination of Tart's and Laski's (1961) data, Greeley (1974) suggested that coitus "often" triggers mystical experience. Indeed, the mystics sometimes describe their transcendental experiences in language that has strong sexual connotations, a good example of which is the description by Saint Teresa of Avila of the vision of an angel plunging a great golden spear into her body. A quotation from Greeley (1974, p. 93) expresses well one view of the relationship between sexual and mystical experience:

It is not unreasonable to believe that under some circumstances sexual orgasm can trigger an ecstatic experience. Intercourse does de-automatize
somewhat our ordinary reality orientation. It does take us out of ourselves; it
is an experience of passionate unity; it is . . . a temporary inertia in fundamental life forces. While it is not the same kind of experience as mystical
ecstasy . . . the two experiences are similar enough that it is not surprising
that one could lead to the other.

In the Oriental tradition (especially Taoism and Tantric Hinduism
and Buddhism), prolonged intercourse without ejaculation is used to
induce mystical experience (see Scharfstein, 1973, pp. 108–110). Intromission is maintained for hours and, reportedly through breath control
as well as contraction of penile and anal muscles, the aim of "temporary
and simultaneous arrest of breath, thought and semen" is achieved, with
the resulting "inexpressible experience of unity" (Garrison, 1964, pp.
114–115). Although the Tantric tradition is a very ancient one, sexual
techniques form only a small and unorthodox segment of the rich
pantheon of mystical practices originating in Indian–Chinese religions.
Nevertheless, the relationship between sex and mysticism is more than
trivial.

Apart from orgasm's having been used extensively to induce mystical states and the similarities between aspects of these experiences discussed above, there are other analogies. For instance, there is the resemblance between the condition of sensory loss in orgasm and the state
of total detachment from the environment achieved in the deep state of
meditation known as *samadhi*. Individual descriptions of orgasms that
are reminiscent of accounts of mystical experiences are to be found in
Hite (1976), Laski (1961), and Lessing (1962). It may not be coincidental
that this random selection from the existing literature consists of three
books by female authors. I suspect (without systematic evidence) that
women are more prone to such experience than men.

3.2. Physiological Phenomena

The known physiological events during orgasm may be divided into
autonomically mediated changes and those involving skeletal (voluntary) muscle. Both classes of effect involve genital and nongenital structures. They are well described by Masters and Johnson (1966) and are
outlined here only briefly.

Genital changes are, of course, more striking in the male, where
orgasm is presaged by increased penile rigidity, which precedes the
throbbing contractions leading to ejaculation–seminal emission. The latter phenomenon is a complex, autonomically and somatically controlled

mechanism; it is discussed in more detail later, as are other physiological phenomena of interest. In the female, there are involuntary contractions of the "orgasmic platform" (lower third of vagina) caused by the same skeletal muscles (bulbocavernosus, etc.) that in male orgasm contract to produce seminal expulsion. Also common to both sexes is a peak of intense genital vasocongestion followed by rapid detumescence, that is, removal of blood and tissue fluid from the genital area. These involve interesting shifts in autonomic nervous function that are considered later.

Though few data are available, major uterine contractions apparently occur only during orgasm. Contractions during arousal in addition to increases in intensity during orgasm have been stressed by some authors (Fox & Fox, 1971) but not by others (Masters & Johnson, 1966). The nature and meaning of changes in uterine pressure during coitus have been debated in relation to mechanisms of sperm transport, both in animals and in humans. It has been hypothesized that an "insuck" of semen by positive cervical-uterine action occurs in the human, though contrary evidence is presented by Masters and Johnson (1966). The latter work was criticized by Fox and Fox (1971), and some observations were presented indicating that a positive intrauterine pressure recorded during coitus changes to a negative pressure immediately after orgasm. Such a sequence of events would be appropriate to the occurrence of "insuck", but clearly female orgasm is not necessary for fertilization, and there is no evidence that it increases the probability of conception.

Of greater relevance to the present discussion, however, are observations from both animal and human research that the posterior pituitary hormone, oxytocin, is released during coitus and thus may be responsible for orgasmic contractions of the uterus. This hormone, apart from its effects in the uterus, produces milk ejection in the suitably prepared mammary gland; in fact, observations of lactating animals and women do show that milk may be "let down" during coitus (Fitzpatrick, 1966b; Fox & Knaggs 1969). Oyxtocin release is part of a neuroendocrine reflex whose afferent arm may come from suckling *or* genital tract stimulation. This reflex is activated both in sexual activity and in childbirth, and oxytocin plays a role in the later stages of labor. It is not known if this reflex is a general phenomenon during female orgasm or if it is related to other CNS changes that are integral to the experience. Postcoital release of anterior pituitary hormones in various animal species is of central importance for reproduction (see Section 1.1.4); the possibility of copulation-induced ovulation in humans remains problematic.

The sounds accompanying human coitus have been described by Pomeroy (1967), and the emission of sounds as a correlate of orgasm in animals and humans has been discussed by Fox and Fox (1971). Although their review cited some evidence from studies on female animals, the occurrence of orgasmic events in infrahuman females is still not established. More recently, the emission of a supersonic "song" has been shown to be an invariable sequel to ejaculation in the male rat (Barfield & Geyer, 1975). Most recently, spectrographic analysis of human coital sounds showed that they intensified in women with the approach of orgasm when they assumed a rapid regular rhythm not found in the male (Hamilton & Arrowood, 1978).

Information on CNS changes during orgasm would, of course, be of great psychophysiological interest. Scalp EEG recordings have not yet revealed any consistent, replicated findings of interest (but see Section 3.3.6). The only available intracranial data of interest are those of Heath (1972), who recorded spike and slow-wave activity in the septum (and related areas) of one mental and one epileptic patient just before and during orgasm. Citing other evidence from electrical self-stimulation and injection of acetylcholine in the septal region in his patients, Heath connected this finding with the occurrence of pleasure reactions, in analogy to the experimental animal data on "rewarding" self-stimulation of the brain.

The extragenital autonomic changes do not seem to differ much between the sexes. Toward orgasm, there is increasing sympathetic dominance, with peaking of heart rates and blood pressure as well as the "sex flush," which may eventually cover extensive areas of the body. Rarely, fainting may occur, presumably because of decreased blood flow to the brain. Phenomena related to respiration include gasping or breath holding and groaning, sobbing, crying, or even laughing and the sounds mentioned earlier. Most dramatic and mysterious in origin are the sudden changes in autonomic balance. In the body as a whole, there is a precipitous shift, as the active phase of orgasm comes to an end, from massive sympathetic activation to parasympathetic dominance with general physical quiescence (see Section 3.3.6).

Extragenital skeletal-muscle effects are prominent in both sexes (Kinsey et al., 1953; Masters & Johnson, 1966). Apart from the obvious pelvic thrusting, there may be twitching of legs, mouth, and arms; total body rigidity with jerks, convulsions, and heaves; pointing of toes; abdominal contraction, tongue protrusion, staring or tight closing of the eyes, etc. In both sexes there are synchronous rhythmic contractions of the anal sphincter and other muscles of the pelvic floor (bulbocavernosus, transverse perineals, external anal sphincter, etc.). They participate in ejaculation in the male and possibly in the postorgasmic reversal of vasocongestion in both sexes (Sherfey, 1972).

In women, there are some interesting similarities between the experiential and physiological manifestations of orgasm and those of two other vital reproductive states: parturition and lactation. Newton (1973) analyzed Grantly Dick Read's reports (1949) on hundreds of "natural childbirths" and noticed many similarities to sexual excitement as regards breathing and vocalization; uterine, cervical, abdominal muscle, and central nervous system reactions; sensory perception; and emotional response. She also mentioned clitoral engorgement as occurring in labor. In lactation, too, uterine contractions, nipple erection, emotional phenomena, and other events point to a close correlation with the coital experience. The neuroendocrine reflex involving oxytocin release has been reported to occur in all three. Newton concluded that the orgasmic experience is less "specific" in women than in men. To the extent that there are experiential similarities between those conditions, the investigation of the oxytocic reflex could be a fruitful approach to the study of psychophysiologic relationships in orgasm, the major concern of the rest of this chapter.

3.3. Psychophysiological Relationships

It is hardly necessary to detail a number of experiential components of orgasm that are quite obviously related to physical events. Thus, the release from tension is connected with the relaxation of skeletal muscle, and sensations of heat and cold are probably related to changes in blood flow. We are more concerned with the major changes of mood and, in fact, state of consciousness, in regard to which no direct relationships to sensory reception are obvious. One way to tackle this problem is by attempting to relate qualitative and quantitative variations in experience to the known physiological events.

3.3.1. Individual Differences

Quantitatively speaking, is there a direct relationship between the extent of known physiological and experiential phenomena? Masters and Johnson (1966) issued a warning (p. 137) against the arbitrary presumption that the magnitude of physiological events defines that of the experience. Yet, these authors and others do suggest the existence of such relationships: in the female, for uterine and vaginal contractions and vasocongestion; in the male, for semen volume (Masters & Johnson, 1966, p. 216); and in both sexes for various genital and extragenital reactions (Campbell, 1976, and personal communication). In the aging male, for instance, a diminished experience of orgasmic intensity may be related to a progressive weakening of the penile muscles, with concomitantly weaker contractions.

These statements are based on anecdotal reports, however, and do not clarify which aspects of the orgasmic experience may be correlated with the physiology.

The experience of satisfaction or pleasure from orgasm is not necessarily tied to the *magnitude* of known physiological responses, and this statement has been said to apply even to the lowest common denominator of orgasmic experience: release from tension (Singer, 1973). "Satisfaction" can be in large part a function of the numerous psychosocial and environmental variables relevant to the sexual act. If these are held constant, however, is a more satisfying experience accompanied (or caused) by more intense physiological changes? Unfortunately, the laboratory conditions necessary for physiological measurement are not the most conducive to the normal range of psychological response in sexual activity.

Apparently, however, a considerable amount of physiological variance *is* encountered in the laboratory. Campbell and co-workers (1976 and personal communication) have studied 617 coital and masturbatory orgasms from 23 men and 57 women, though the results have been reported only in an abstract at this time. The intraindividual variation in physiological events was much smaller than the interindividual variability. Thus, changes in respiratory patterns varied greatly between subjects: some showed extreme hyperventilation at different stages of orgasm and others showed apnea or no change, but there was a strong tendency for a given pattern to be retained on different occasions within one subject. While Campbell stated that recorded magnitude of response (muscular and vascular) in genital and extragenital tissues is directly related to the perceived "magnitude" of orgasm, there is no information on interindividual comparisons. Perhaps the more subtle and important experiential parameters may relate more to the pattern than to the amplitude of physiological response. We must conclude that beyond the general impression that quantitative correlations exist, little understanding of psychophysiological relationships is to be gained at this time from existing information on overall *quantitative* correlations. *Qualitative* variations in orgasm have been discussed widely, primarily as regards the female. Before discussing these, however, let us see if some progress can be made by considering possible mechanistic relationships between some orgasmic phenomena.

3.3.2. Mechanisms of Orgasm

Regarding causal relationships between physiological events and the experience of orgasm, the literature contains statements such as "orgasm is a sensation caused by contraction of the smooth muscles of the internal sexual organs and the striated muscles of the perineum and pelvic floor, coinciding with seminal emission and ejaculation proper" (Tarabulcy, 1972). The belief that muscular contractions in either sex *trigger* the central psychophysiological experience of orgasm is not uncommon and not unreasonable, but they could equally be *caused* by the experience. If not, what causes the contractions?

One view (Sherfey, 1972, p. 74) is that orgasm in physiologically triggered in both sexes by a stretch reflex mechanism in which the stimulus comes from vasocongestive distension in the genital tissues and that the response is vigorous contraction of the perineal-genital muscles, which expel blood trapped in the venous plexuses. This author believes that the expulsion of blood "creates" the orgasmic sensations.

Masters stated that the relevant sensations in the male are derived from seminal expulsion (Masters & Johnson, 1966, p. 212), while also holding (Masters, 1960) that "actual orgasmic experiences are initiated in both sexes by similar muscle components." Yet, in describing the female orgasmic experience, Masters and Johnson (1966) delineated three stages: first a sensation of "stoppage" (akin to "bearing down" in labor), then a flow of warmth from the pelvis over the body, and then contractions leading to throbbing sensations. The first two stages of the female orgasmic experience therefore *precede* the pelvic muscle contractions (which expel semen in the male).

In fact, these authors stated explicitly that the "sensation" of orgasm begins 2–4 sec before "she responds physiologically" (p. 118). They further remarked that in subjects for whom the increase in tension is great, there is an initial muscle spasm *before* the rhythmic contractions, which "parallels the subjective report of orgasm." This spasm is, however, stated to occur during the *third* stage. It is compared to the first stage of male ejaculation 2–4 sec before the appearance of semen at the urethral meatus (see below). This stage carries with it the sensation of ejaculatory inevitability rather than the actual experience of orgasm, which can be delayed beyond this stage.

Obviously, there is no clarity, not only about what actually causes orgasm but also about when it begins or ends, that is, which coital events may be defined as truly orgasmic (see also Kinsey *et al.*, 1953, pp. 627–628.)

If several clinical reports that claim that female orgasm can occur in the absence of contractions of vaginal and pelvic floor muscles (Singer, 1973, p. 66ff) are to be believed, the present emphasis on these contractions would seem inappropriate. This phenomenon has not, however, been demonstrated under controlled conditions. If perception of pelvic muscular activity is essential for orgasm, we might ask what are the intervening mechanisms between these contractions and the experience? What role is played by direct perception of other muscular, vascular, respiratory, and/or other overt physiological events? And what about the more covert physiological processes of which we may not be consciously aware? These kinds of questions can, of course, be asked about any emotional experience but seldom with the immediacy and the richness of specific physical and experiential events as in orgasm. Though no answers are available, the situation may be further illuminated by a more detailed consideration of the male.

The relationship between ejaculation–emission and orgasm presents the psychophysiological dilemma in most dramatic form. Under normal conditions, ejaculation has two major experiential correlates: the orgasmic ASC on the one hand and the rapid decline in sexual arousal, followed by refractoriness to subsequent sexual stimulation on the other. These are very different events and should be separated in considering the question of psychophysiological correlations. Similarly, ejaculation consists of two processes: seminal emission into the penile urethra, caused by contractions of the accessory sexual glands; and ejaculation proper, caused by penile muscles. These differ in neural control, the former being sympathetic (smooth muscle) and the latter somatic (skeletal muscle). We may first ask whether ejaculation proper (i.e., the expulsion of semen through the penile urethra) is necessary for either of the two events?

Certain drugs such as the hypertensive agent guanethidine and α-adrenergic blockers can result in nonejaculatory orgasms (Shader, 1972). These drugs apparently produce retrograde ejaculation—that is, seminal expulsion into the bladder—because they inhibit the normal contraction of the internal bladder sphincter. The subjective experience of orgasm is retained, however, so that actual passage of semen through the penile urethra is not necessary for it. The retention of orgasmic capacity in some postpubertal castrates for periods long after semen-producing glands have atrophied is further evidence on this score (Bremer, 1959; Money, 1961). Now, the neural events controlling expulsion of the semen are presumably intact in retrograde ejaculation and are likely also in the castrates, though no semen is present. These neural events and not the actual seminal emission therefore seem to be what is important experientially.

Second, we may ask whether the contractions of the skeletal muscles of the penis and the pelvic floor are essential for the orgasmic experience. Relevant information has recently become available from observations on "multiorgasmic" men. Robbins and Jensen (1976) have reported multiple nonejaculatory orgasms (analogous to those experienced by multiorgasmic women) in 14 men. Penile contractions were present in each orgasm, but only the final one in each series was accompanied by emission and loss of sexual arousal. There is a question about the quality and intensity of the preejaculatory orgasms, and they have been described as "miniorgasms" in a popular magazine (Petersen, 1977). B. Campbell (personal communication) has studied these men (some of whom were middle-aged) physiologically. The cardiovascular and respiratory changes and the contractions of the muscles of the pelvic floor recorded from intra-anal transducers during nonejaculatory orgasms were not different from those recorded during normal male ejaculation.

It appears that with training (M. Fithian, personal communication), men can differentially inhibit the (sympathetically innervated) mechanism of seminal emission while retaining the (somatically innervated) "ejaculatory" contractions. Accompanying those pelvic muscular contractions that are found in both sexes, the orgasmic experience of ASC is retained (or may be enhanced?), but not the subsequent loss of arousal and refractoriness. It is a reasonable guess that the same general psychophysiological process occurs in the cases of "Karezza" (Stockham, 1896), Tantric Yoga (Garrison, 1964), Taoist practices (Chang, 1977), and the nineteenth-century Oneida community in New York state, although the subjective effects very likely differ in intensity in the different situations.

3.3.3. Hypothesis of the Bipolar Origin of Orgasm

Does all this lead us to any understanding of the psychophysiology of orgasm? My conclusion is that some very interesting implications follow from the twin observations that (a) seminal emission *invariably* entails sexual satiety and (b) synchronous contractions of pelvic skeletal muscle without emission are accompanied by *orgasmic experience without satiety*. Note that in each case, a unique peripheral nervous function is tied to a unique experiential phenomenon. Could it be that there are common central nervous origins for each pair of events?

It seems reasonable, in fact, to postulate that some process related to activity of the muscles of emission is responsible for sexual refractoriness, while a separate process related to activity of the somatic musculature of the pelvic floor correlates with the experience of an ASC. As a working hypothesis, at least. I propose that neural elements involved in emission simultaneously fire centrifugally ("downwards") to eject semen from the accessory glands and centripetally ("upwards") to suppress sexual arousal. The latter may be regarded as a change of mood state or appetitive condition as distinct from the "high" state of complete orgasm. Similarly, the neural mechanism for ejaculation proper may be thought to consist of a centrifugal component, which causes the skeletal muscle contractions, and a centripetal one, which triggers the major experiential events of orgasm (i.e., the ASC). It is not unreasonable to assume that the latter may begin before the muscular contractions, which would fit with statements by Masters and Johnson (see above). Nothing can be said as yet about the location or nature of the putative neural "center(s)," which triggers the bipolar reactions when excitation from the preceding events of sexual arousal crosses the orgasmic threshold. Figure 1, which presents this "bipolar hypothesis" diagrammatically, depicts these centers in the form of an "organ of or-

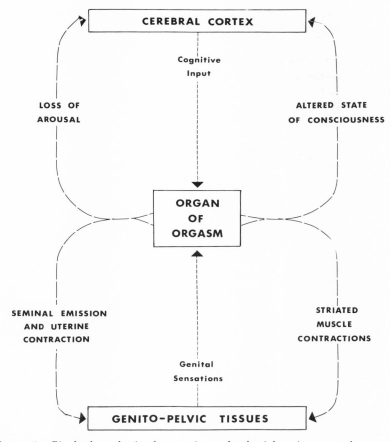

FIGURE 1. Bipolar hypothesis of orgasmic psychophysiology in men and women.

gasm." The hypothesis can be tested experimentally. For instance, information relevant to the loci of these mechanisms may come from study of the sites of action of the drugs that differentially affect different components of orgasm.

While I am proposing two "bipolar" neural mechanisms to explain the two correlations—emission–loss of arousal and ejaculatory contractions–ASC—this does not imply that other mechanisms are not also operating. The scheme does not, for instance, negate a possibly important role for a James–Lange type of sensory feedback from the events of emission or ejaculation. Certainly, the transactional interplay between sensory input and emotion must operate in orgasm just as it does in arousal. Apart from the obvious ways in which this is so, it applies to the idea expressed by Komisaruk (1979) that proprioceptive afferent activity from somatic (skeletal) and visceral (smooth) muscles may intensify orgasmic experience.

The hypothesis is speculative—necessarily so, in the absence of experimental work. It may appear to depend too much on evidence that is still rather sparse about multiple orgasms in males, and this is a key issue, though other arguments will be presented. As yet, no comparisons exist of the experience of preejaculatory and ejaculatory orgasms, and these may well be somewhat different. The hypothesis would not, however, be disproved if the preejaculatory experiences were merely "miniorgasms," so long as they could be distinguished as discrete alterations of state—experientially as well as physiologically.

It is also important to stress that the relationship of seminal emission to loss of arousal applies only when emission is complete. It is common knowledge that drops of semen often "leak" during nonorgasmic sexual activity. Likewise, significant amounts of semen are "emitted" in multiorgasmic males before the final ejaculatory orgasm, at which point the seminal emission is completed, with concomitant loss of arousal (Hartman & Fithian, 1978). Perhaps the "interim" emissions are associated with slight transient decreases in arousal but not with a true refractory period.

Implicit in the proposed mechanism is the assumption that the orgasmic vascular decongestion is related to the emission processes rather than to the pelvic skeletal muscle contractions. Though the extension of the hypothesis to women is considered only in the following section, it should be recalled at this point that these contractions have been regarded as causing pelvic decongestion in the female (Sherfey, 1972). That view is not consistent with the bipolar hypothesis. However, the contractions may contribute to decongestion in both sexes, only if accompanied by loss of arousability in the presence of the neural process of emission. In fact, the vasocongestion is apparently parasympathetically induced in both sexes, and the most reasonable assumption is that it is reversed by the sympathetic process that also triggers emission in the male (Geer & Quartararo, 1976; Stilwell, 1976). Since, as discussed in Section 2, the vascular changes in the genitals are tied to perceived sexual arousal in a reverberating feedback relationship, the massive sympathetic outflow of orgasm can be regarded as involved in three major interrelated events in the male: emission, genital decongestion, and loss of arousal and arousability. The last of these is the least understood physiologically, but it surely also has both central and peripheral components.

There is no intention to create a falsely sharp dichotomy between the interrelated experiences of arousal and orgasm. Thus, the intensity of the orgasmic state of consciousness is very likely related to, and in part determined by, the degree of sexual arousal that precedes it. On the other hand, sexual arousal does not seem necessary for *emission*, as in the cases of nocturnal emission, emission produced by electrical stimulation of the penis in nonaroused men (Sobrero, 1965), electroejaculation via peripheral or brain stimulation in many species, and the spontaneous daily seminal emissions of rodents (Orbach, 1961). In these cases, and in that of anxiety-produced premature ejaculation in humans, the bipolar hypothesis would predict that though emission does not abolish arousal (because the subject may not be aroused!), it decreases arousability (see Whalen, 1966). Thus, following emission, it can be assumed that the male cannot be aroused by sexual stimuli for a period of time, regardless of the level of arousal before the event.

In addition to the lack of preceding arousal, much evidence attests to the fact that seminal emission can occur without pleasure (see Singer, 1973, p. 126) and, in fact, with little or none of the major experiential features of orgasm. Furthermore, the converse (orgasmic experience without emission) has often been reported. Thus, drugs affecting the autonomic nervous system can differentially influence the two parameters (Shader, 1972). Physiological-experiential correlative studies would be helpful in showing what physiological components are missing in these cases. Emission without the ASC component is found, in addition to the cases mentioned in the last paragraph, in morphine withdrawal (Gebhard, 1965, cited in Beach, Westbrook, & Clemens, 1966). Such cases must often have to do with the situation that sympathetic dominance (as in the case of anxiety) can decrease erectile capacity while facilitating ejaculation. When this situation results in a premature ejaculation (particularly before intromission), little skeletal muscle activity is present. Kinsey, Pomeroy, and Martin (1948, p. 160) described a type of male orgasm in which there is little or no evidence of body tension or buildup of arousal, and penile throbs may be limited to the urethra, so that semen seeps out without forcible ejaculation. This kind of orgasm was found to occur in a high proportion of older males and (without emission) in 22% of the preadolescent cases on which these investigators were able to obtain data. From their comment that "climax passes with minor aftereffects," one would assume that in this type of orgasm, there is little alteration of consciousness. This information supports the relatedness of the ASC system with pelvic skeletal-muscle contraction and high levels of preceding arousal. A similar situation was observed by Sobrero (1965), who produced seminal emission in schizophrenic males and others with infertility problems by applying a vibrating cup to the glans penis. This procedure appeared to result in few or no full erections, and only 5 of the 45 subjects reported "orgasmic feelings."

The physiological mechanisms operating when orgasm is experienced in the absence of seminal emission are of great relevance but are not well understood. The best-established cases result from genital stimulation in prepubertal boys (Kinsey, Pomeroy, & Martin, 1948) and treatment with phenothiazines and other drugs affecting catecholamine metabolsim. The former situation is probably simply due to immaturity of the semen-producing glands. A not dissimilar situation is that of postcastrational sexual activity (see Section 3.1.3). As to the drug effects, these have been studied, particularly with the antiadrenergic agent thioridazine and similar drugs, which, as mentioned in Section 3.3.3., not infrequently produce retrograde emission into the bladder. This effect is hypothesized to result from failure of closure of the internal bladder sphincter (Shader, 1972), a necessary part of the sympathetically controlled series of smooth muscle contractions in emission. That loss of arousability is not apparently affected by these drugs in men—or in rats (Beach et al., 1966)—is consistent with the hypothesis of a separate, centripetal neural mechanism for this effect, which need not be disturbed simply because the path of semen expulsion has been misdirected by a peripheral mechanism.

Beach et al. (1966) related several such situations in men to observations of animals where seminal emission is separated from the behavioral sequelae of ejaculation. They commented (p. 759) that "the simple discharge of seminal fluid does not, in and of itself, account for all of the behavioral changes which normally follow an ejaculation resulting from genital stimulation." The postejaculatory refractory period in animals is a useful model of decreased arousal, and because of the difficulties of human experimentation, animal data on the effects of drugs, brain manipulations, etc., on refractory periods can aid in evaluation of the proposed relationship of emission to arousability, even if such animal data are hardly relevant to the ASC aspect of orgasm.

3.3.4. The Varieties of Female Orgasm

Psychological–medical thinking in this area was dominated for most of the century by the Freudian concept of vaginal versus clitoral orgasms. It was claimed that stimulation of these two genital "substrates" resulted in physiologically and experientially different types of orgasm, the capacity to experience which was related to different stages of psychosexual maturity. This idea took a severe blow with the publication of Masters and Johnson's work (1966). They claimed that it was not possible to differentiate orgasms in terms of mode of stimulation, since all show similar physiological responses. Furthermore, it was claimed (and is now generally accepted) that essentially all orgasms require stimulation of clitoral sensory receptors, either directly by touch or indirectly by pulling on surrounding (including vaginal) tissues. The idea is supported by the fact that the vaginal wall has few nerve endings, while the clitoris is richly innervated.

The problem with Masters and Johnson's monistic view of orgasm, however, is that it is based primarily on anatomical-physiological responses. In more recent years, there has been something of a rebound from their view with the realization that regardless of possible invariance of physiological response, important experiential differences may result from the manner (including the site) of sexual stimulation. Thus, several authors have supported the plurality of female orgasmic experience without denying the position of Masters and Johnson on the universal and primary role of clitoral sensory receptors. In a sociopsychological study, Fisher (1973, p. 313) has suggested that vaginal orgasms (i.e., those resulting from penile intromission) are, in fact, less "ecstatic" because of the lesser degree of total body excitation involved. According to the questionnaire data of Hite (1976) based on several thousand respondents, most women described "vaginal orgasms" as more diffuse than clitoral ones (i.e., those without intromission), and they felt (along with Masters and Johnson, 1966) that clitoral stimulation produces more "intense" orgasms. Of course, the advantage of immediate direct feedback in autoerotic stimulation has to be weighed against the considerable advantages of intercourse, including the possibility of greater body stimulation from coitus, affecting the number of receptors activated. Probably more important are the interpersonal factors that may lead to profoundly different experiences resulting, for example, from clitoral masturbation on the one hand and coitus with a sensitive lover on the other.

In an intriguing book on human sexuality, Singer (1973) has proposed three types of female orgasm: a "uterine," a "vulval," and a "blended" (intermediate) type, while holding with Masters and Johnson that all types involve clitoral stimulation, directly or indirectly. Although the factual basis of Singer's speculative analysis is mostly unstated or tentative, it derives support from various clinical reports, and he proposed a unique set of orgasmic psychophysiologic correlations that are, in fact, amenable to experimental validation. A complete description of the differences among the three proposed forms of female orgasm is being presented here since they include some rather complex and possibly fanciful psychophysiological mechanisms. Some of Singer's points, however, are most relevant to this discussion.

The "uterine" orgasm is produced, Singer claims, by deep intravaginal penile thrusting with the female pelvis motionless, producing cervical and/or uterine "jostling" and resulting peritoneal stimulation. This is said to activate an autonomic reflex, one response to which is laryngeal displacement with apnea. The "vulval" orgasm, which results primarily from clitoral-vulval stimulation, is presumed to lack this component of uterine-peritoneal activation of visceral reflexes. Though uterine contractions are present, they are presumed to be less strong, but there are strong vaginal and pelvic floor contractions in the vulval orgasm. Such contractions *may* be absent in the uterine orgasm, and Singer cites several clinical reports of orgasm without noticeable contractions of the "vaginal platform," the experiential (ASC-like) nature of which have not been reported (see below). Of particular interest, however, is the claim that satiation and loss of sexual arousal are not necessarily present in the vulval orgasm but invariably are in the uterine orgasm (Singer, 1973, p. 79). The relationship between loss of arousal and deep vaginal stimulation is confirmed by a careful reading of Hite (1976). Apparently, the women in her sample found that multiple (i.e., nonterminative) orgasm was more likely to follow clitoral stimulation than vaginal coitus. Extensive clinical experience had earlier led the neo-Reichian authority Lowen (1965, p. 217) to the same conclusion.

If Singer's analysis is correct, it presents a striking parallel with the scheme proposed above for the male, in which the autonomic component of orgasm (which results in seminal emission) is related to loss of arousal (refractoriness) and the skeletal muscle contractions are related to the major "elevation" of consciousness (see Figure 1). It is not clear how similar the proposed uterine-induced visceral reflexes are to the male, sympathetically induced, seminal emission response. Yet, it is true that a neuroendocrine reflex, discussed earlier, originates in stimulation of the female genital tract (in animal experiments, cervical probing is used) and has oxytocin release as one of its important efferent components. Animal evidence indicates that oxytocin may also be normally released as a result of coitus in the male, and there are suggestions, albeit poorly substantiated, that it may be involved in seminal emission

(Fitzpatrick, 1966a). But regardless of the possibility of neuroendocrine reflexes in orgasm, the suggestion that uterine contractions may be more intense in terminative orgasm is interesting, since the direct neural control of these contractions is sympathetic, via the hypogastric nerve. This control mechanism corresponds to the sympathetic control of emission in the male by the same nerves, supporting the likelihood of a similar neural mechanism involved in sexual satiation in both sexes. It should be stressed that just as in the male it was the neural mechanism of emission and not emission *per se* that could be related to loss of arousal, so also in the female it is postulated that the neural discharge underlying uterine contractions is responsible for this effect and not the peripheral events. Thus, hysterectomy does not necessarily alter orgasmic capacity. Again, as in the male, a contributory role for afferent input from sensory receptors in muscle need not be ruled out.

It is important at this point to emphasize that the unitary model of female orgasm presented by Masters and Johnson is based on laboratory research, whereas Singer's "pluralistic" ideas have not been tested in the laboratory. Nevertheless, Masters and Johnson paid little attention to experiential as opposed to physiological responses, and it is also entirely possible that more careful data collection and analysis under more varied conditions of laboratory testing would have revealed the specific kinds of physiological and psychological variation proposed by Singer. His views are supported by one laboratory investigator who has noted a quantitatively and qualitatively distinct pattern of uterine activity in the terminative orgasm of one (or more?) multiorgasmic women (Fox, 1976; Fox & Fox, 1971). My guess is that the distinctions between female orgasms will not be absolute, but all will very likely involve *some* contractions of both skeletal and uterine muscle, regardless of the sites of stimulation. Again, in the female, as in the male, it may be the *completeness* of the hypogastric-mediated mechanism that is necessary for loss of arousal/arousability.

All of the possible mechanisms that have been discussed are amenable to experimental validation by simultaneous measurement of myographic, vascular, hormonal, and experiential parameters. This validation should include (among other physiological measurements) assessment of the relative strength of uterine and pelvic muscular contractions in single (terminative) and multiple male and female orgasms, combined with measurements of circulating oxytocin by radioimmunoassay and genital blood flow—noninvasive methods for measurement of which are well developed (Bancroft, 1974; Cohen & Shapiro, 1970; Geer & Quartararo, 1976). Confirmation or denial of the bipolar hypothesis for women will require such laboratory data on sufficient numbers of subjects to derive some assessment of probabilities. In this area, there must be considerable inter- and intraindividual variance, ranging to the extreme cases where orgasmic experience appears independant of the relevant overt physiological apparatus (see Davidson, 1978). Clearly, no statement that a certain kind of stimulus invariably produces a certain kind of experience is consistent with the capacity of some women to have orgasmic experience without any discernible physical stimulation. At any rate, if and when such currently anecdotal phenomena (Kinsey *et al.*, 1953; Masters & Johnson, 1966) are studied in the laboratory, the physiological manifestations of subjects' responses should be most illuminating.

But regardless of whether the different types of female orgasm are real or imaginary, the basic factual differences between male and female orgasm are consistent with application of the "bipolar" hypothesis of orgasmic psychophysiology to both sexes: female orgasm involves pelvic contractions but not seminal emission, and women have the capacity for multiple orgasm (i.e., repeated ASC experiences without intervening periods of sexual refractoriness) to a much greater extent than men.[3] In fact, it is now believed that most mono-orgasmic or anorgasmic women can be trained to be multiorgasmic if they wish (Kline-Graber & Graber, 1975). In these repeated orgasms, all the major physiological responses found in the male are presumably present, except seminal emission. This finding, combined with the indications that some males can show essentially similar repeated orgasmic events if emission is delayed, provides the major support for the bipolar hypothesis.[4]

It should be noted that there is no true counterpart in the female to the experience of emission without the orgasmic ASC in the male, unless the supposed instances of orgasm without vaginal contractions were devoid of the ASC (and not due to vaginal pathology). But the selective absence of the postulated ASC mechanism would pass unnoticed as loss of arousal without orgasm, unless uterine contractions were detected. In

[3]In fact, Sherfey (1972) proposed that women are sexually "insatiable" by nature. Her case is somewhat overstated, for a variety of reasons, including the fact that satiation is more than the absence of physiological refractoriness.
[4]The occurrence of female ejaculation emission (expulsion of fluid from the urethra at orgasm) was described by de Graaf in the seventeenth century and by a few twentieth-century sexologists but is denied by modern authorities. The matter has been reopened in an interesting speculative article published as this chapter was being completed (Sevely & Bennett, 1978). Indeed, the observation that the female prostate may not be entirely vestigial, and the possibility that in some women at least, it may be secretory, potentially removes the last barrier to consideration of the hypothesis that *no* qualitative differences exist between the male and female sexual response. And the phenomenon may be widespread but unnoticed because of the preponderance of vaginal exudate ("lubrication"), as Sevely and Bennett point out. By focusing on urethral emissions, if they exist, research could thus quickly confirm or deny the bipolar hypothesis for the female.

the male, on the other hand, there is the strong expectation that emission will be accompanied by the ASC component. However, the kind of total separation between the two components that can be found in males does not occur in females. At the very least, the proposed formulation of orgasmic psychophysiology provides a working hypothesis in an area in which systematic physiological investigation has hardly commenced. This could be pursued in the laboratory and consequently clarify much that is obscure in male sexual physiology as well as in the relationship between male and female orgasm.

3.3.5. Sensory Loss

In seeking common physiological conditions predisposing both to orgasm and other ASCs, it is of interest to examine the phenomenon of decreased awareness of environmental (including painful) stimuli during sexual arousal. This "sensory loss" reaches its zenith during orgasm, which, for this and other reasons, has been called *le petit mort*. Some form of sensory detachment is common to many ASCs, including the extreme "mystical states" (see Davidson, 1976), and has even been utilized in the attempt to define "altered states of awareness" (Hilgard, 1969). Conversely, the normal or "ordinary" state(s) of consciousness is/are largely dominated by sensory input (see Pope & Singer, Chapter 8). But the phenomenon under consideration seems to be more than just the absence of certain sensory inputs. Lowen (1965, p. 182) has pointed out that the individual does not "become unconscious" but rather "tends to lose consciousness of the self." This is an essential characteristic of mystical experience; its relationship to the physiological condition being considered here is an intriguing question. For, as the following discussion shows, this correlate of orgasm is amenable to experimental study, has at least one relevant animal model, and can provide one approach to exploring the respective roles of central and peripheral mechanisms in orgasmic psychophysiolgy.

Given that it makes no sense to explain the sensory loss during intense orgasmic experiences in terms of low arousal, the alternative is to regard it as a case of selective attention, although it is hard to pinpoint the focus of attention. This model allows us to pose the following physiological question: Is the sensory detachment due to changes in sensitivity at the receptor of primary synaptic level ("peripheral gating") or to some intracerebral block?[5]

---

[5]The two are not mutually exclusive: selective attention may involve failure of *reception* of sensory impulses at the cortical level (as indicated by data on cortical evoked potentials), and centrifugal impulses from the brain can also raise thresholds at peripheral synapses (Harter & Salmon, 1972).

There is a complex relationship between pleasurable and painful reactions to genital stimulation at different stages of sexual activity. Intense genital stimulation in the early phases of sexual arousal and immediately after orgasm are generally painful, while in the immediate preorgasmic phase they are pleasurable, if not, in fact, necessary for triggering orgasm. It is tempting to interpret this sequence of events in terms of local sensitivity shifts in tactile sensory receptors resulting from changes in blood flow (see above), particularly when rapid vascular shifts coincide with equally rapid sensory changes, as occurs postorgasmically. But these changes also coincide with general shifts in conscious state and could be due to CNS changes. This is particularly so where tissues not directly affected by the sexual response are concerned, as in orgasmic sensory loss.

These effects may be related to autonomic mechanisms. For example, Takagi, Takayuki, and Kawasaki (1975) have provided evidence that norepinephrine mediates the spinal analgesic effect of morphine, and Melzack (1973) has suggested that increased sympathetic activation may have an analgesic effect in such cases as absence of pain perception during serious injury (e.g., in soldiers in combat). At the brain level, the pleasure/pain shifts could involve the newly discovered opiate receptors and endogenous opiatelike peptides in the hypothalamic-limbic system (Goldstein, 1976), that is, in brain regions where mechanisms for positive reinforcement ("pleasure centers") are located. As yet, however, no physiological role has been established for the endogenous opiates.

Thus, various quantitative and qualitative shifts in sensory response seem to characterize orgasm, and underlying mechanisms may range from local receptor changes to widespread, centrally controlled organismic reactions that must surely be involved in the more extreme examples of sensory detachment. These mechanisms will very likely prove to be operative also in other varieties of intense emotional experience.

In looking for experimentally testable animal models, we come upon a seemingly analogous phenomenon in the animal behavior literature. Vaginal-cervical stimulation of rats with a glass rod results in lordosis with immobility, accompanied by a marked reduction in sensitivity to painful stimuli (Komisaruk, 1974), perhaps via a "gate control" mechanism (Melzack & Wall, 1965). Crowley, Rodriguez-Sierra, and Komisaruk (1977) also have evidence that the analgesic effect of vaginal stimulation is mediated by norepinephrine. This reflex induces a behavioral response necessary for successful mating (lordosis) while suppressing perception of noxious stimuli, which is also conducive to conception. As discussed above (Sections 1.1.4 and 3.2), stimuli from coital activity precipitate a variety of physiological effects in animals, including release of oxytocin, gonadotropins, and other hormones, and more attention should be devoted to investigating such effects in humans.

The kind of direct somatic-visceral reflex relationship proposed above between genital stimulation on the one hand and sensory loss (and by extension other mood changes) on the other is only one kind of possible mechanistic approach to orgasmic psychophysiology. An alternative kind of mechanism is suggested by the controversial (Elliot, 1974) but influential views of Lacey and Lacey (1974), who emphasized the importance of visceral afferents as mediators of behavioral events in humans. Thus, small decreases in heart rate and blood pressure were found to accompany the shifting of attention to external events, while inner-directed attention ("mental concentration") was correlated with cardiac acceleration. Lacey and Lacey postulated that attentional changes first affect cardiac function; the rise in blood pressure (in the case of internal attention) increases firing in the visceral afferents from activated baroreceptors in the atrial sinus and/or the aortic arch, producing widespread CNS inhibition. Recent electrophysiological studies in animals support the existence of central depressor effects of this kind in animals (Coleridge, Coleridge, & Rosenthal, 1976; Gahery & Vigier, 1974). The extrapolation of these findings to the interpretation of cortical inhibition in orgasmic sensory loss is not more than suggestive, since, for instance, the scale of changes in cardiovascular activity in the Lacey experiments is much smaller than in orgasm. However, this analogy does indicate a possible kind of testable neurophysiological model.

Does orgasmic sensory loss resemble the situation of Komisaruk's rats in lordosis, involving specifically genital afferents, and/or that of the Laceys' humans involving cardiovascular afferents? The answer can not be given until more research data are available, for even basic information on the dynamics of autonomic changes in different subjects during sexual activity has not yet been pursued systematically.

3.3.6. Autonomic Imbalance and Hemispheric Lateralization

The previous discussion of possible autonomic mechanisms in one component of the orgasmic ASC leads now to a consideration of whether overall patterns of autonomic activity such as have been implicated in the induction of other ASCs might serve as triggers of the orgasmic state of consciousness as a whole. Based on Hess's original work, Gellhorn (1967, 1970) developed in the 1950s and 1960s a concept of the relationship of autonomic nervous activity to behavior. High levels of peripheral sympathetic activity were observed to act in concert with cerebral (EEG) activation and high skeletal muscle responsiveness, producing an organismic state termed *ergotropic*, adaptive for emergency and stress situations. On the other hand, stimuli that increase parasympathetic activation were normally associated with such effects as sleeplike EEG activity, low muscle tone, and behavioral quiescence, that is, the *trophotropic* state. The two organismic conditions were thought to be related to the activity of two anatomically separable systems represented at the various levels of the nervous system.

Gellhorn devoted much effort to validating the concept of hypothalamic "tuning," in which this brain area plays a central role in controlling the state of reactivity of the whole central nervous system by shifting the ergotropic-trophotropic balance. Under normal conditions (which for our purposes can be called the ordinary state of consciousness), the two systems show reciprocity in that activating one of them tends to suppress activity in the other. In addition, the peripheral-autonomic and somatic components of the system show congruence, in that both are activated or suppressed together. Imbalances in these systems result when there is a deviation from reciprocity and congruence. Gellhorn's view was that such "imbalances" result from high levels of activation, during which there are paradoxical responses to stimuli with ergotropic stimuli having trophotropic effects and vice versa, or even simultaneous discharges of both systems; and these events provide the physiological basis for various types of psychopathology and altered states of consciousness. In a recent publication, I proposed that so-called mystical experience, such as may arise spontaneously or as a result of meditative and other practices, are (a) precipitated by conditions of autonomic imbalance and (b) may occur in a right-hemisphere–dominated state (Davidson, 1976). It was further suggested that they have nonspecific characteristics shared by other ASCs, but the nature of the specific experience is dictated by cognitive variables, such as beliefs and attitudes resulting from experience and training. I believe that these hypotheses may be applied to the orgasmic ASC, and this idea is examined in the following discussions.

What is the condition of the ergotropic-trophotropic systems during states of high sexual arousal and of orgasm (see Masters & Johnson, 1966; Wenger, Averill, & Smith, 1968)? The early stages of sexual arousal are dominated by the sacral parasympathetics, and though this parasympathetic activation is maintained during increasing arousal as far as the innervation of the blood supply to the pelvis and elsewhere is concerned, the *overall body reaction* shows an increasing sympathetic dominance (high blood pressure, respiration, etc.) in the plateau stage. Correlation between the parasympathetically controlled genital manifestations of sexual arousal (as measured, for example, by erection in the male) and pupillary dilation, as an index of overall sympathetic activation, has been demonstrated in a variety of studies (Zuckerman, 1971). Thus, two interesting phenomena are found in the preorgasmic stages: a change in autonomic balance from early to late arousal and a lack of "reciprocity" between parasympathetic vasodilatory responses in the pelvic (and other) regions and sympathetic cardiorespiratory responses (i.e., simultaneous ergotropic and trophotropic discharges).

At orgasm, there is clearly a switch in *genitopelvic* reactions from parasympathetic to sympathetic domination. In the female, Geer and Quartararo (1976) have recorded genital vasocongestive responses using a vaginal photoplethysmograph and found a dramatic drop in vaginal blood volume at the onset of orgasm, continuing until an upturn after its termination. Thus, apart from the simultaneous discharges that occur in the earlier stages, there is at orgasm a sudden shift in the autonomically controlled blood flow to the genitals, from parasympathetic to sympathetic domination. On the other hand, with the completion of orgasm, there is another total body shift from the ergotropic to the trophotropic state reflected in skeletal muscle and behavioral quiescence.

Gellhorn's thesis that changes in organismic state are characterized by autonomic "nonreciprocity" and "noncongruence" and the suggestion that rapid shifts between conditions of ergotropic or trophotropic dominance are conducive to major alterations in conscious experience (Davidson, 1976) have relevance to the orgasmic ASC. The application of this concept to sexual activity can be examined by relating the sequence of physiological shifts around orgasm to the changes in subjective experience. An asset in such investigations would be the use of Porges's (1976) new method for assessing autonomic balance by the analysis of respiratory influence on heart rate. As yet, no such research has been done, but it seems clear that various changes in autonomic balance, including simultaneous sympathetic-parasympathetic discharges, coincide with the major change in state of consciousness. The overall bodily ergotropic to trophotropic switch, however, is not completed at least until the postorgasmic resolution phase and seems to be a good example of Gellhorn's "rebound phenomenon," whereby strong activation of either system leads to an extreme switch to the opposite one. Clarification of the sequential changes of autonomic balance during different stages of sexual activity should facilitate our understanding of such clinical problems as female anorgasmy and premature ejaculation. It has been contended, for instance, that the latter condition may be caused by acute anxiety-related sympathetic dominance. Since strong sympathetic discharges are, in fact, present in several of the phases of sexual activity, this hypothesis cannot be adequately assessed until we know more about the relationships between activity in different segments of the autonomic nervous system at different phases of sexual responding and what the limiting factors are for maintenance of the normal sequence of events.

The idea is gaining support that the right (or nonlanguage) cerebral hemisphere dominates during ASCs. This idea was pursued for the case of meditative-mystical types of experience by drawing analogies with data on dreaming[6] and other states of consciousness characterized by primary-process thinking and/or simultaneous (holistic) instead of the normal sequential form of cognition (Davidson, 1976).

Orgasm would appear to provide an excellent model for testing this hypothesis of left-to-right switching in ASC, but very few observations are yet available on this subject. Recently, however, Cohen, Rosen, and Goldstein (1976) recorded left and right parietal EEGs from four male and three female subjects during orgasm produced by self-stimulation. In 8 of 12 experiments, they found a statistically significant change in laterality, as indicated by a large increase in EEG amplitude recorded from scalp electrodes over the right hemisphere during orgasm. The alpha rhythm was replaced over the right hemisphere by a wave pattern in the 4-Hz range, with minimal effect on left hemisphere alpha. These findings are decidedly preliminary, and it is not clear that the effects noted necessarily indicate right-hemisphere–dominant activity. Nevertheless, the data do indicate a dissociation between right- and left-hemisphere function in orgasm and suggest the likelihood that further investigation would be fruitful.

Central to our consideration of the role of major physiological changes in the orgasmic ASC is the question of specificity. In the case of mystical experience (Davidson, 1976), it was suggested that the predisposing conditions of autonomic imbalance and of the shift to right-hemisphere–dominated activity were conducive only to an undifferentiated ASC experience that could be manifested in profoundly different ways depending on the relevant cognitive variables ("set and setting"). This view was related to concepts of Schachter (1975, and see Section 2.3.1.) in which cognitive variables, in effect, help to explain extreme emotional variance in the face of apparent (i.e., overt) physiological invariance.

Such a Schachterian analysis of orgasm could be relevant to variations in experiential intensity and quality that depend on the context of the experience. However, orgasm differs from other ASCs in that a set of quite specific physiological events are known. This fact may indicate a

---

[6]More recent research has failed to corroborate the proposed right-hemisphere dominance in dreaming (J. S. Antrobus, H. Ehrlichmann, & M. S. Wiener, personal communication). Perhaps dominance depends on dream content; at any rate, the issue is not yet settled.

basic difference between orgasmic and other ASCs, or it may simply reflect our present ignorance of important specific physiological mechanisms in the majority of nonsexual ASCs. The specific nature of the physiological correlates of orgasm, however, precludes a radical application of the Schachterian viewpoint to the orgasmic ASC: an orgasm is unlikely to be transformed into some other ASC by change of context. In fact, it is the very specificity of the sexual response—pelvic and uterine muscle contractions, seminal emission and other myotonic phenomena, the sequence of vasomotor changes, etc.—that makes this ASC particularly interesting from a psychophysiological point of view.

4. Sex Differences and the Role of Hormones

The question of male–female differences in sexual response has arisen repeatedly in the previous discussions. Now it is time to summarize more systematically the nature and scope of sex differences in the psychophysiology of human sexuality. First, I consider physiological effects and later experiential ones.

4.1. Physiological Differences

The clearest sex differences in sexual response are the presence of seminal emission in the male and of uterine contractions in the female. The differentiation of embryonic Wolffian and Müllerian ducts into the male and female internal genital tissues, respectively, depends upon the presence or absence of the fetal testis, which secretes two "organizing principles": an androgen or androgenlike material, which develops the vas deferens, prostate, and related glands and ducts, and a (nonsteroid) Müllerian inhibiting factor, which suppresses the development of uterus, Fallopian tubes, and related structures. Thus, the major sex difference has to do with anatomic structures whose differentiation from embryonic anlagen is not under the direct influence of genetic factors but is mediated by hormones. If sex differences in general are merely the outcome of anatomic differentiation of peripheral structures, one would expect, for instance, that normally masculinized genetic males with failure of Müllerian inhibiting-factor production or utilization (*herniae uteri inguinale*) would show uterine contractions during sexual activity. Further, virilized ("pseudohermaphroditic") genetic females who had been exposed to androgen in early fetal life would show seminal emission during coitus (see footnote 4). Though there are no data on humans, an animal model of the latter phenomenon is available. Rhesus monkeys treated during pregnancy with androgen and possessed of penislike clitorides can, in fact, show male coital behavior with ejaculation (Goy & Resko, 1972). This finding suggests that intrinsically both sexes share the same central and peripheral nervous mechanisms of the sexual response.

Otherwise, there are no qualitative sex differences in the physiological sexual response that we know of, although Masters and Johnson described some quantitative differences. After studying 350 instances of human sexual response, B. Campbell (personal communication) concluded that records of cardiovascular and pelvic muscular activity as well as respiratory and peripheral blood flow cannot be distinguished on the basis of the sex of the subjects. Despite the disparity in size between the clitoris and the penis, the female genital anatomy includes large internal extensions of the clitoris and other structures homologous to penile tissues (e.g., the crura and the vestibular bulbs), which apparently undergo extensive vasocongestion during sexual arousal (Sherfey, 1972; Stilwell, 1976), as do the labia. As we have emphasized, erection should be regarded as only one special case of pelvic vasocongestion during the sexual response, which in both sexes involves the phallic organ and related structures. Studies on vaginal blood flow during sexual activity show similarities between males and females, possibly even in the case of REM sleep, where erection in the male has its counterpart in increased vaginal blood flow in the female (Cohen & Shapiro, 1970).

The clinical observation that the major sexual disability of men is impotence while in women it is anorgasmy also does not imply a true physiological sex difference. Many cases of the latter can perhaps be regarded in part as failure of the sexual response in general, that is, failure of those physiological changes that are a necessary prelude (or trigger) to orgasm. There must be many cases of supposed anorgasmy in women that in reality are cases of female impotence. The latter condition is not yet adequately recognized in our male-dominated society because it does not preclude coitus, unlike male impotence.

It may be concluded that the only major physiological differences in the sexual response between men and women relate to anatomical differences and to differences in reproductive function—intromission and insemination versus receptivity and conception.

4.2. Psychological Differences and Psychophysiological Correlation

In the past, it was widely believed that there were very considerable differences between males and females in the psychology of sex. It is impressive how these differences seem to be shrinking in recent years when one compares recent data with those of the Kinsey report. This is true, for instance, of the use of masturbation and of sexual fantasy, both of which showed a low frequency in women in the earlier accounts. It is now hard to regard these phenomena as being largely biologically determined, since the changes are very likely a function of our changing sexual culture. There is also the possibility that the earlier results were due to the studies' being inadequately designed (Luria, 1979). This latter consideration may be particularly relevant in the case of susceptibility to visual erotic material, which was thought to be much greater for males (Kinsey *et al.*, 1953). This difference was entirely absent in more carefully performed and recent investigations (Schmidt & Sigusch, 1973).

As to sex differences in the experience of orgasm, there is little to add to the earlier discussion (Section 3.1) of the study of Vance and Wagner (1976), who could not distinguish differences in their collection of written descriptions. That finding becomes less significant, however, to the extent that intense orgasm may share in the essential ineffability of mystical experience (Stace, 1960; Davidson, 1976). There remains the major sex difference of multiple orgasm, which has been discussed earlier. The almost invariable loss of sexual arousal following male orgasm is apparently related to seminal emission. It was suggested that similar neural processes of sexual satiation may, however, be intrinsically present in both sexes, but not activated in cases of female (and the rare male) preterminative multiple orgasms. If that analysis is valid, this striking sex difference, like the others discussed, may also be "reduced" to a matter of genital anatomy. For the male, sexual activity almost invariably entails penile stimulation, the orgasmic response to which is almost inevitably terminative because in the absence of special training, the emission reflex is triggered. Females have greater flexibility in mode of stimulation, and clitoral stimulation, particularly, may bypass the uterus-related reflex mechanism postulated to be involved in loss of sexual arousal (see Section 3.3.4.).

4.3. The Role of Sex Hormones

4.3.1. Sex Difference and the Role of Androgen

In discussing the endocrinology of sexual experience, it is well to begin with a major sex difference, not in physiological or psychological response, but in the endocrinologic regulation of sexuality as a whole. Unlike all animal species, men and women differ in that only the male of our species seems to depend absolutely on the secretions of his gonads for maintenance of libido and potency.

That the two classes of ovarian hormones—estrogenic and progestational—are not essential for libido and potency in women is clear from the lack of serious deficiencies in many or most women after menopause or removal of ovaries. But are women totally "emancipated" from hormonal control, or, as is believed by many clinicians, do adrenal (together with ovarian?) androgens provide the endocrine support as postulated for rhesus monkeys (see Section 1.1.1)? The latter view, though widespread and even plausible, is based on inadequate evidence: sparse data on the reduction of libido by adrenalectomy (a near-terminal procedure) in women with malignant cancer, and superficial clinical reports on stimulatory effects of pharmacologic doses of androgen given to normal or sexually deficient women (see Bermant & Davidson, 1974, p. 240). If the case were established by adequate research, however, it would simplify the concept of the hormonal bases of behavior in that men and women would both be shown to depend on androgenic hormones, albeit originating in different tissues.

For the present, therefore, the only well-established case in human sexual psychoendocrinology is that of the role of androgen in the male, which in fact provides the best model of a natural, phylogenetically ubiquitous, psychoneuroendocrine phenomenon. It is clear that castration is incompatible with normal sexuality in men or males of any other mammalian species studied. While no sophisticated behavioral studies have been performed in human castrates, the mass of anecdotal, clinical, and historical material indicates overwhelmingly that most men have a rapid decline in sexuality after this operation, and there is no evidence that entirely normal function ever remains (Bremer, 1959; Sturup, 1972). Of course, the psychological effects of the knowledge of having been castrated is profound for many men. Sturup, who examined records of thousands of castrates, suggested that the loss of libido derives from the castration-induced loss of potency, though he recognized that the two cannot really be separately evaluated. It can equally be concluded that a decrease in potency may result from decreased libido, and because of the transactional nature of sexual experience, it would be hard to know from the available data which of these effects of castration is primary (see Section 2.3.2.). Progress in understanding the sequence of events would nevertheless be achieved by careful evaluation of the progressive changes in male sexual experience, motivation, and performance (including nocturnal erections) after castration without replacement therapy (in the event this were ethically justified).

Although again, no scientifically adequate experiments had been published, clinical experience with androgen treatment of hypogonadal males is great, and the evidence indicates that the effects of androgen on male sexuality are not "nonspecific" as suggested by Kinsey (see Bermant & Davidson, 1974, p. 237). We have recently performed an intensive double-blind study on four males with hypogonadism secondary to pituitary tumors and two others with primary testicular insufficiency (Davidson, Camargo, & Smith, 1979). Two doses (100 and 400 mg) of a long-acting androgen—testosterone enanthate—or placebo were administered once monthly in random order over a five- or six-month period, and circulating levels of testosterone were monitored at one- to two-week intervals, while extensive information on sexual experience and activity was obtained from daily logs. It was clear from the results that the men responded to testosterone in terms of one or more of the measures of sexuality obtained; the high dose was generally more effective than the low one, and the placebo had little or no effect. The most consistently androgen-responsive measure was total number of erections reported, including nocturnal, coital, masturbatory, and other forms of erection. This measure was closely related to blood androgen levels, at least in five of six subjects, as shown in Figure 2. The delay between plasma testosterone elevations and increased frequency of erection was of the same order of magnitude as the latency from onset of androgen treatment to enhancement of sexual behavior in rats.

What can we learn about the psychobiology of conscious experience from this unique near-total dependence of a natural behavior on one endogenous chemical agent? Of primary interest is the issue of whether the hormone acts peripherally or centrally; that is, is it mediated by cerebral or spinal cells or by sensory receptors and/or their associated nerves in genital or extragenital areas? The animal evidence is quite clear (see Section 1.1.4.) that there is a cerebral (hypothalamic-preoptic) effect of androgen that has a profound effect in the restoration of male sexual behavior in castrated rats, but we cannot exclude additional effects of androgen on the periphery. Hart (1973), working with rats and dogs, has promoted the idea that the spinal cord is also an important site of the behavioral action of androgen. His evidence is based on the response of sexual reflexes to hormone administration in spinally sectioned animals (see below) and intraspinal implantation of androgen in castrates.

In humans there is no experimental evidence relating to the location of sites of androgen action on sex behavior. If it is true that sexual arousal is always accompanied by early changes in the genital tissues, these could depend on hormonal enhancement of the responsiveness of tactile receptors. Published comprehensive studies on the androgen dependency of erection using appropriate controls and objective measures (not verbal reports) do not seem to exist for the human male, though clear results were obtained in a study on one man by Beumont, Bancroft, Beardwood, and Russell (1972). Erection and other sexual reflexes have been shown to be androgen-dependent in studies on spinally sectioned

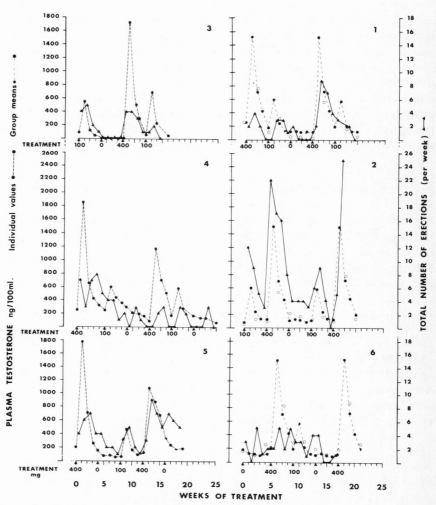

FIGURE 2. Total erections (however elicited, summated for each week and recorded at the midpoint of the week) for all subjects, in relation to testosterone enanthate treatments and plasma testosterone levels. The broken lines in the right-hand panel (Subjects 1, 2, and 6) show mean data for *all* subjects. Individual determinations on these subjects are also shown as open circles.

(Hart, 1968; Hart & Haugen, 1968) and intact animals (Davidson, Stefanick, Sachs, & Smith, 1978). Our data suggested that nocturnal erections were clearly influenced by androgen levels in some hypogonadal males (Davidson et al., 1979). Nocturnal erections cannot be ascribed to exteroceptive stimulation and are not very likely related to erotic arousal from dream experiences, since they occur during REM sleep without necessary relationship to dream content (Fisher, Schiavi,

Lear, Edwards, Davis, & Witkin, 1975). This effect thus appears to be a hormonal sensitization of a centrally induced, spontaneous reflex event. At any rate, it does provide preliminary support at least for the well-established clinical opinion that there is a direct effect of androgen on potency.

There is evidence regarding the importance of peripheral nervous input for sexuality in men, from a study of paraplegics, many of whom can have erections and some of whom can ejaculate, but presumably without tactile sensitivity. Hohmann (1966) argued that the quality of sexual experience in these men is "sentimental," by which he presumably meant that in the absence of genital sensation, a purely "cognitive" kind of satisfaction only is possible. Unfortunately, there are again no adequate data. It is likely that many instances of retention of sexuality in paraplegics may involve incomplete cord lesions. There is also the possibility of "phantom" sexual experience (Money, 1960), which presumably involves responses that remain "encoded" in the truncated central portion of the nervous system. But all this leaves the problem of the site of androgen action in men largely unsolved. It would be most informative to observe the influence of varying hormone levels on sexual behavior and experience in paraplegics.

4.3.2. Do Hormones Influence Orgasm?

It is interesting to note that the evolution of the female's independence from control of sexuality by gonadal hormones was accompanied by another major evolutionary event: the appearance of female orgasm. Though it has often been contended that female orgasm is present in some higher mammals, particularly primates (Chevalier-Skolnikoff, 1973; Lancaster, 1979), there is still little convincing evidence. In fact, it would be hard to imagine what such evidence would look like, since, notwithstanding the successes of ape language teachers, no female chimpanzee has yet been able to tell us whether she had an orgasm. If in the future we were to find out by physiological and behavioral evidence that indeed something akin to orgasm occurs in subhuman primates, there would arise the opportunity to study the relationship of this evolutionary phenomenon to that of the gonadal emancipation of the female. In many primate species, females show a wide distribution of coitus throughout the cycle, and the effects of ovariectomy are considerably more variable in many primates than in other subprimate mammals. The inter- and intraspecific variance in ovarian hormone dependence could thus be correlated with the incidence of the postulated primate orgasm.

Does testosterone have a direct role in orgasm separate from its effects on sexual arousal? This is clearly difficult to determine for at least two reasons. First, orgasm does not occur without previous sexual arousal (though emission does in certain circumstances, as discussed in Section 3.3.3.), so that it is not easy to test the proposition of a direct effect on orgasm separate from effects on arousal. Second, the incompleteness of our knowledge of the physiological phenomena of orgasm and of the relative importance of the different physical events for the experience of orgasm makes it difficult to construct a hypothesis of how hormones might affect the orgasmic process. Nevertheless, in the realm of possibilities, some of which are potentially researchable, several mechanisms are worth considering. As described in Section 3.2, Heath (1972) has reported that specific changes in neuronal function occur in the septal and related brain areas during orgasm. The septum is intimately connected with the preoptic area, and the medial preoptic is the major site of the central action of androgen on behavior in rats and probably other mammalian species (see Sections 1.1.2. and 1.1.4). If Heath is right, action on the septopreoptic or other limbic regions could provide a reasonable central mechanism for a direct effect of androgen on brain processes subserving orgasm.

On the other hand, orgasm depends on continuous input of stimuli from the genitals, and a peripheral action of hormones to maintain genital sensory receptors may be the sum total of hormone involvement in male orgasm. In light of the putative positive feedback mechanism whereby sensory input is enhanced by genital responses in sexual arousal (see Section 2.2.2), orgasmic threshold could be lowered by increased hormone levels via facilitation of the peripheral sexual response. Vasocongestive events—for example, the preorgasmic increased penile stiffening—may participate in the series of events involved in triggering the experience of orgasm. Gonadal hormones—both ovarian and testicular—affect vascular reactivity, perhaps via changes in monoamine oxidase activity with altered response to catecholamines (Bell, 1975). The extent to which this action might suffice to influence sexual arousal and/or orgasm is unknown.

Another possible mechanism involves the genital pelvic musculature or secretory tissue. While androgen in general promotes skeletal muscle growth, it has a particularly powerful effect on muscles of the genital–perineal area, for example, the bulbocavernosus and the levator ani. Certainly, androgen is necessary for maintenance or growth of the (smooth) muscular and secretory tissue of the accessory sexual glands involved in emission and semen production, as well as of the vas deferens and the epididymis. If the strength of contraction of these muscles is a factor in the orgasmic experience, this could provide a relevant site of androgenic action. In the woman, estrogen is the major factor in maintaining uterine structure and function. Again, if myotonic factors are important, we would expect postmenopausal or oophorectomized women to have qualitatively or quantitatively different orgasms than premenopausal women, even though they may not differ in age. As to the male, androgen frequently declines to quite low levels in old men, as does the strength of contractions in ejaculation. Whether the two phenomena are related to each other and to orgasmic experience should be the subject of correlative research, which would be of potential basic as well as clinical importance in relation to problems of geriatric impotence. An essential role for some of the possibilities discussed in this paragraph is inconsistent with the bipolar hypothesis, thus providing one approach to examining its validity. We may conclude that, although we have no definitive information on the role of sex hormones in orgasm, several promising possibilities for future investigation are available.

5. SUMMARY

In this chapter, an attempt is made to construct a psychophysiological approach to the understanding of sexual experience. The chapter describes physiological and psychological events in sexual arousal and orgasm and examines possible relationships between the two groups of phenomena. A model is proposed of a bipolar (centripetal and centrifugal) neural mechanism underlying the experiential events during orgasm. The model links (a) the orgasmic altered state of consciousness to neural activity subserving the synchronous contractions of pelvic skeletal musculature and (b) the loss of arousal to sympathetic neural discharge, which triggers seminal emission in the male and increased uterine activity in the female. The proposition is examined that similar mechanisms of arousal and orgasm apply in both sexes.

Acknowledgments

I am most grateful to Frank Beach for my initial and continuing education in the complexities of the study of animal sexual behavior and its relationship to human sexuality. I also wish to thank Benjamin Sachs, Barry Kamisaruk, and Gary Gray for reading the manuscript and making useful suggestions, and Dorothy Tallentire and Cathy Spruck for aid in its preparation.

REFERENCES

ADLER, N. T., DAVIS, P. G., & KOMISARAK, B. R. Variation in the size and sensitivity of a genital sensory field in relation to the estrous cycle in rats. *Hormones and Behavior*, 1977, *9*, 334–344.

ADLER, N., & BERMANT, G. Sexual behavior of male rats: Effects of reduced sensory feedback. *Journal of Comparative Physiology and Psychology*, 1966, *61*, 240–243.

ANON. Effects of sexual activity on beard growth in man. *Nature* (London), 1970, *226*, 869–870.

ARNOLD, M. Physiological differentiation of emotional states. *Psychological Reviews*, 1945, *52*, 35–48.

AX, A. F. The physiological differentiation between fear and anger in humans. *Psychosomatic Medicine*, 1953, *13*, 433–442.

BANCROFT, J. *Deviant sex behavior: Modification and assessment*. Oxford: Clarendon, 1974.

BARD, P. A diencephalic mechanism for the expression of rage with special reference to the sympathetic nervous system. *American Journal of Physiology*, 1928, *84*, 490–515.

BARFIELD, R. J., & CHEN, J. Activation of estrous behavior in ovariectomized rats by intracerebral implants of estradiol benzoate. *Endocrinology*, 1977, *101*, 1716–1725.

BARFIELD, R. J., & GEYER, L. A. The ultrasonic postejaculatory vocalization and the postejaculatory period of the male rat. *Journal of Comparative Physiology and Psychology*, 1975, *88*, 723–734.

BARFIELD, R. J., WILSON, C., & McDONALD, P. G. Sexual behavior: Extreme reduction of postejaculatory refractory periods by midbrain lesions in male rats. *Science*, 1975, *189*, 147–149.

BEACH, F. A. *Hormones and behavior*. New York: Hoeber, 1948.

BEACH, F. A. Characteristics of masculine sex drive. In M. R. Jones (Ed.), *Nebraska symposium on motivation*. Lincoln: University of Nebraska Press, 1956, pp. 1–32.

BEACH, F. A. Cerebral and hormonal control of reflexive mechanisms involved in copulatory behavior. *Physiological Review*, 1967, *47*, 289–316.

BEACH, F. A. Animal models for human sexuality. In *Sex, hormones, and behavior*. New York: CIBA Foundation, Symposium 62 (new series), Elsevier, 1979.

BEACH, F. A., WESTBROOK, W. H., & CLEMENS, L. G. Comparisons of the ejaculatory responses—Men and animals. *Psychosomatic Medicine*, 1966, *28*, 749–763.

BELL, C. Sexual modification of cardiovascular regulation. In M. Sandler & G. L. Gessa (Eds.), *Sexual behavoir: Pharmacology and biochemistry*. New York: Raven, 1975.

BEREITER, D. A., & BARKER, D. J. Facial receptive fields of trigeminal neurons: Increased size following estrogen treatment in female rats. *Neuroendocrinology*, 1975, *18*, 115–124.

BERMANT, G., & DAVIDSON, J. M. *Biological bases of sexual behavior*. New York: Harper & Row, 1974.

BEUMONT, P. J. V., BANCROFT, J. H. J., BEARDWOOD, C. J., & RUSSELL, G. F. M. Behavioral changes after treatment with testosterone: Case report. *Psychology of Medicine*, 1972, *2*, 70–72.

BLAKE, C. A., & SAWYER, C. H. Effects of vaginal stimulation on hypothalamic multiple-unit activity and pituitary LH release in the rat. *Neuroendocrinology*, 1972, *10*, 358–370.

BLUMER, D. Hypersexual episodes in temporal lobe epilepsy. *American Journal of Psychiatry*, 1970, *126*, 1099–1106.

BREMER, J. *Asexualization*. New York: Macmillan, 1959.

CAMPBELL, B. Neurophysiology of the clitoris. In T. P. Lowry & T. S. Lowry (Eds.), *The clitoris*. St. Louis: W. H. Green, 1976.

CANNON, W. B. The James–Lange theory of emotion: A critical examination and an alternative theory. *American Journal of Psychology*, 1927, *39*, 106–124.

CARLSSON, S. G., & LARSSON, K. Mating in male rats after local anesthetization of the glans penis. *Zeitschrift für Tierphysiologie*, 1964, *21*, 854–856.

CHANG, J. *The Tao of love and sex*. New York: Dutton, 1977.

CHERNEY, E. F., & BERMANT, G. Role of stimulus female novelty in the rearousal of copulation in male laboratory rats (*Rattus norwegicus*). *Animal Behavior*, 1970, *18*, 567–574.

CHEVALIER-SKOLNIKOFF, S. Male–female, female–female and male–male sexual behavior in the stumptail monkey, with special attention to the female orgasm. *Archives of Sexual Behavior*, 1973, *3*, 95–116.

COHEN, H. D., ROSEN, R. C., & GOLDSTEIN, L. Electroencephalographic laterality changes during human sexual orgasm. *Archives of Sexual Behavior*, 1976, *5*, 189–199.

COHEN, H. D., & SHAPIRO, A. Vaginal blood flow during sleep. Paper presented at the 10th annual meeting of the Association for the Psychophysiological Study of Sleep, Santa Fe, N.M., March 1970.

COLERIDGE, H. M., COLERIDGE, J. C. G., & ROSENTHAL, F. Prolonged inactivation of cortical pyramidal tract neurones in cats by distension of the carotid sinus. *Journal of Physiology* (London), 1976, *256*, 635–649.

COOPER, K. K. An electrophysiological study of the effects of castration on the afferent system of the glans penis of the cat. Doctoral dissertation, New York University, 1969.

COOPER, K. K., & ARONSON, L. R. Effects of castration on neural afferent responses from the penis of the domestic cat. *Physiology and Behavior*, 1974, *12*, 93–107.

CROWLEY, W. R., RODRIGUEZ-SIERRA, J. F., & KOMISARUK, B. R. Monoaminergic mediation of the antinociceptive effect of vaginal stimulation in rats. *Brain Research*, 1977, *137*, 67–84.

DANESINO, V., & MARTELLA, E. Modern conceptions of corpora cavernosa function in the vagina and clitoris. In T. P. Lowry & T. S. Lowry (Eds.), *The clitoris*. St. Louis: W. H. Green, 1976.

DAVIDSON, J. M. Activation of the male rat's sexual behavior by intracerebral implantation of androgen. *Endocrinology*, 1966, *79*, 783–794.

DAVIDSON, J. M. Hormones and reproductive behavior. In S. Levine (Ed.), *Hormones and behavior*. New York: Academic, 1972.

DAVIDSON, J. M. The physiology of meditation and mystical states of consciousness. *Perspectives in Biology and Medicine*, 1976, *19*, 345–380.

DAVIDSON, J. M. Neuro-hormonal bases of male sexual behavior. In R. O. Greep (Ed.), *Reproductive physiology II* (*International Review of Physiology*, Vol. 13). Baltimore: University Park Press, 1977.

DAVIDSON, J. M. Gonadal hormones and human behavior. In M. C. Diamond & C. C. Korenbrot (Eds.), *Hormonal contraceptives, estrogens and human welfare*. New York: Academic, 1978.

DAVIDSON, J. M. Gonadal hormones and human behavior. In H. Katchadourian (Ed.), *Sex and its psychosocial derivatives*. Berkeley: University of California Press, 1979.

DAVIDSON, J. M., & TRUPIN, S. Neural mediation of steroid-induced sexual behavior in rats. In M. Sandler & G. L. Gessa (Eds.), *Sexual behavior: Pharamacology and biochemistry*. New York: Raven, 1975.

DAVIDSON, J. M., CAMARGO, C., & SMITH, E. R. Effects of androgen on sexual behavior in hypogonadal men. *Journal of Clinical Endocrinology and Metabolism*, 1979, *48*, 955.

DAVIDSON, J. M., GRAY, G. D., & SMITH, E. R. Animal models in the endocrinology of reproductive behavior. In N. Alexander (Ed.), *Animal models for research on contraception and fertility*, New York: Harper & Row, 1978.

DAVIDSON, J. M., SMITH, E. R., & BOWERS, C. Y. Effects of mating on gonadotropin release in the female rat. *Endocrinology*, 1973, *93*, 1185–1192.

DAVIDSON, J. M., STEFANICK, M. L., SACHS, B. L., & SMITH, E. R. Role of androgen in sexual reflexes of the male rat. *Physiology and Behavior*, 1978.

DAVIDSON, R. J., & SCHWARTZ, G. E. The psychobiology of relaxation and related states: A multi-process theory. In D. I. Mostofsky (Ed.), *Behavior control and modification of physiological activity.* New York: Prentice-Hall, 1976, pp. 339–442.

EKMAN, P., FRIESEN, W. V., & ELLSWORTH, P. *Emotion in the human face.* New York: Pergamon, 1972.

ELLIOTT, R. Further comments on the Lacey hypothesis. *Journal of Personality and Social Psychology,* 1974, *30,* 19–23.

EPSTEIN, A. W. The relationship of altered brain states to sexual psychopathology. In J. Zubin & J. Money (Eds.), *Contemporary sexual behavior: Critical issues in the 1970s.* Baltimore and London: Johns Hopkins University Press, 1973.

FISHER, C., SCHIAVI, P., LEAR, H., EDWARDS, A., DAVIS, D. M., & WITKIN, A. P. The assessment of nocturnal REM erection in the diagnosis of sexual impotence. *Journal of Sex and Marital Therapy,* 1975, *1,* 277–289.

FISHER, S. *The female orgasm.* New York: Basic Books, 1973.

FITZPATRICK, R. J. The neurohypophysis and the male reproductive tract. In G. W. Harris & B. T. Donovan (Eds.), *The pituitary gland,* Vol. 3. Berkeley and Los Angeles: University of California Press, 1966. (a)

FITZPATRICK, R. J. The posterior pituitary gland and the female reproductive tract. In G. W. Harris & B. T. Donovan (Eds.), *The pituitary gland,* Vol. 3. Berkeley and Los Angeles: University of California Press, 1966. (b)

FOX, C. A. Some aspects and implications of coital physiology. *Journal of Sex and Marital Therapy,* 1976, *2,* 205–213.

FOX, C. A., & FOX, B. A comparative study of coital physiology with special reference to the sexual climax. *Journal of Reproduction and Fertility,* 1971, *24,* 319–336.

FOX, C. A., ISMAIL, A. A. A., LOVE, D. M., KIRKHAM, K. E., & LORAINE, J. A. Studies on the relationship between plasma testosterone levels and human sexual activity. *Journal of Endocrinology,* 1972, *52,* 51–58.

FOX, C. A., & KNAGGS, G. S. Milk-ejection activity (oxytocin) in peripheral venous blood in man during lactation and in association with coitus. *Journal of Endocrinology,* 1969, *45,* 145.

FUNKENSTEIN, D. H. Norepinephrine-like and epinephrine-like substances in relation to human behavior. *Journal of Nervous and Mental Disease,* 1956, *124,* 58–68.

GAHERY, Y., & VIGIER, D. Inhibitory effects in the cuneate nucleus produced by vago-aortic afferent fibers. *Brain Research,* 1974, *75,* 241–246.

GARRISON, O. V. *The yoga of sex.* New York: Julian, 1964.

GEER, J. J., & QUARTARARO, J. D. Vaginal blood volume responses during masturbation. *Archives of Sexual Behavior,* 1976, *5,* 403–413.

GELLHORN, E. *Principles of autonomic–somatic integrations.* Minneapolis: University of Minnesota Press, 1967.

GELLHORN, E. The emotions and the ergotropic and trophotropic systems. *Psychological Forschrift,* 1970, *34,* 48–94.

GOLDSTEIN, A. Opioid peptides (endorphins) in pituitary and brain. *Science,* 1976, *193,* 1081.

GOY, R. W., & RESKO, J. A. Gonadal hormones and behavior of normal and pseudohermaphroditic female primates. *Recent Progress in Hormone Research,* 1972, *28,* 707–733.

GREELEY, A. M. *Ecstasy: A way of knowing.* Englewood Cliffs, N.J.: Prentice-Hall, 1974.

HAMILTON, W. J., III, & ARROWOOD, P. S. Copulatory vocalizations of Chacma baboons (*Papio ursinus*), gibbons (*Hylobates hoolock*), and humans. *Science,* 1978, *200,* 1405–1408.

HART, B. L. Alteration of quantitative aspects of sexual reflexes in spinal male dogs by testosterone. *Journal of Comparative Physiology and Psychology,* 1968, *66,* 726–730.

HART, B. L. Reflexive behavior. In G. Bermant (Ed.), *Perspectives on animal behavior.* Glenview, Ill.: Scott, Foresman, 1973.

HART, B. L. The medial preoptic-anterior hypothalamic area and sociosexual behavior of male dogs: A comparative neuropsychological analysis. *Journal of Comparative Physiology and Psychology*, 1974, *68*, 328–349.

Hart, B. L., & Haugen, C. M. Activation of sexual reflexes in male rats by spinal implantation of testosterone. *Physiology and Behavior*, 1968, *3*, 735–738.

Harter, M. R., & Salmon, L. E. Intra modality selective attention and average evoked responses randomly presented patterns. *Electroencephalography and Clinical Neurophysiology*, 1972, *32*, 605–613.

Hartman, W., & Fithian, M. Presented at Western Psychological Association Annual Meeting, San Francisco, 1978.

Heath, R. G. Pleasure and brain activity in man. *Journal of Nervous and Mental Disease*, 1972, *154*, 3–18.

Hilgard, E. R. Altered states of awareness. *Journal of Nervous and Mental Disorders*, 1969, *149*, 68–79.

Hite, S. *The Hite Report*. New York: Dell, 1976.

Hohmann, G. Some effects of spinal cord lesion on experienced emotional feeling. *Psychophysiology*, 1966, *3*, 143–156.

Jochle, W. Coitus-induced ovulation. *Contraception*, 1973, *7*, 523–564.

Kinsey, A. C., Pomeroy, W. B., & Martin, C. E. *Sexual behavior in the human male*. Philadelphia and London: W. B. Saunders, 1948.

Kinsey, A. C., Pomeroy, W. B., Martin, C. E., & Gebhard, P. H. *Sexual behavior in the human female*. Philadelphia: W. B. Saunders, 1953.

Kline-Graber, G., & Graber, B. *Women's orgasm*. New York: Bobbs-Merrill, 1975.

Kling, A., Borowitz, G., & Cartwright, R. D. Plasma levels of 17-hydroxycorticosteroids during sexual arousal in man. *Journal of Psychosomatic Research*, 1972, *16*, 215–221.

Komisaruk, B. R. Neural and hormonal interactions in the reproductive behavior of female rats. In W. Montagna & W. Sadler (Eds.), *Reproductive behavior*. New York and London: Plenum, 1974.

Komisaruk, B. R. The nature of the neural substrate of female sexual behavior in mammals and its hormonal sensitivity: Review and speculations. In J. B. Hutchison (Ed.), *Biological determinants of sexual behavior*. New York: Wiley, 1977.

Kurtz, R. G. Hippocampal and cortical activity during sexual behavior in the female rat. *Journal of Comparative Physiological Pshchology*, 1975, *89*, 158–169.

Kurtz, R. G., & Adler, N. T. Electrophysiological correlates of copulatory behavior in the male rat: Evidence for a sexual inhibitory process. *Journal of Comparative Physiology and Psychology*, 1973, *84*, 225–239.

Lacey, J. I., & Lacey, B. C. On heart rate responses and behavior: A reply to Elliott. *Journal of Personality and Social Psychology*, 1974, *30*, 1–18.

Lancaster, J. B. Sex and gender in evolutionary perspective. In H. Katchadourian (Ed.), *Sex and its psychosocial derivates*. Berkeley: University of California Press, 1979.

Laski, M. *Ecstasy*. Bloomington: University of Indiana Press, 1961.

Lessing, D. *The golden notebook*. London: M. Joseph, 1962.

Levi, L. Sympatho-adrenomedullary activity, diuresis and emotional reactions during visual sexual stimulation in human females and males. *Psychosomatic Medicine*, 1969, *31*, 251–268.

London, H., & Nisbett, R. E. *Thought and feeling*. Chicago: Aldine, 1974.

Lowen, A. *Love and orgasm*. New York: Macmillan, 1965.

Lowry, T. P., & Lowry, T. S. *The clitoris*. St. Louis: W. H. Green, 1976.

Luria, Z. Psychosocial determinants of gender identity, role of orientation. In H. Katchadourian (Ed.), *Sex and its psychosocial derivatives*. Berkeley: University of California Press, 1979.

Masters, W. H. The sexual response cycle of the human female. *Western Journal of Surgery,*

Obstetrics and Gynecology, 1960, *68*, 57–72.

MASTERS, W. H., & JOHNSON, V. E. *Human sexual response.* Boston: Little, Brown, 1966.

MAURUS, M., MITRA, J., & PLOOG, D. Cerebral representation of the clitoris in ovariectomized squirrel monkeys. *Experimental Neurology*, 1965, *13*, 283–288.

McEWEN, B. S., DENEF, C. J., GERLACH, J. L., & PAPLINGER, L. Chemical studies of the brain as a steroid hormone target tissue. In G. Adleman (Ed.), *The neurosciences.* Cambridge and London: MIT Press, 1974.

McLEAN, P. D., & PLOOG, D. W. Cerebral representation of penile erection. *Journal of Neurophysiology*, 1962, *25*, 29–55.

MELZACK, R. *The puzzle of pain.* New York: Basic Books, 1973.

MELZACK, R., & WALL, P. D. Pain mechanisms: A new theory. *Science*, 1965, *150*, 971–979.

MODIANOS, D. T., FLEXMAN, J. E., & HITT, J. C. Rostral medial forebrain bundle lesions produce decrements in masculine, but not feminine sexual behavior in spayed female rats. *Behavioral Biology*, 1973, *8*, 629–636.

MONEY, J. Phantom orgasm in the dreams of paraplegic men and women. *Archives of General Psychiatry*, 1960, *3*, 373–382.

MONEY, J. Sex hormones and other variables in human eroticism. In W. C. Young, (Ed.), *Sex and internal secretions*, Vol. 2 (3rd ed.). New York: Williams & Wilkins, 1961.

MONEY, J., & EHRHARDT, A. A. Man and woman, boy and girl. Baltimore: Johns Hopkins University Press, 1972.

NAFTOLIN, F., RYAN, K. J., & PETRO, Z. Aromatization of androstenedione by the anterior hypothalamus of adult male and female rats. *Endocrinology*, 1972, *90*, 295–298.

NANCE, D. M., SHRYNE, J., & GORSKI, R. A. Septal lesions: Effects on lordosis behavior and pattern of gonadotropin release. *Hormones and Behavior*, 1974, *5*, 73–81.

NEWTON, N. Interrelationships between sexual responsiveness, birth and breast feeding. In J. Zubin & J. Money (Eds.), *Contemporary sexual behavior: Critical issues in the 1970s.* Baltimore and London: Johns Hopkins University Press, 1973.

ORBACH, J. Spontaneous ejaculation in rat. *Science*, 1961, *134*, 1072.

PETERSEN, J. R. The extended male orgasm. *Playboy*, April 1977.

PFAFF, D. W., DIAKOW, C., ZIGMOND, R. E., & Kow, L. M. Neural and hormonal determinants of female mating behavior in rats. In G. Adelman (Ed.), *The neurosciences.* Cambridge and London: The M.I.T. Press, 1974.

POMEROY, W. B. The Masters–Johnson report and the Kinsey tradition. In R. Brecher & E. Brecher (Eds.), *An analysis of human sexual response.* London: Deutsch, 1967, pp.. 111–123.

PORGES, S. W. Peripheral and neurochemical parallels of psychopathology: A psychophysiological model relating autonomic imbalance to hyperactivity, psychopathy and autism. In H. W. Reese (Ed.), *Advances in child development*, Vol. 2. New York: Academic Press, 1976, pp. 35–65.

PRIBRAM, K. H. Self-consciousness and intentionality: A model based on an experimental analysis of the brain mechanisms involved in the Jamesian Theory of motivation and emotion. In G. E. Schwartz & O. Shapiro (Eds.), *Consciousness and self-regulation.* New York: Plenum, 1976.

READ, G. D. Observations on a series of labors with special reference to physiological delivery. *Lancet*, 1949, *1*, 721–726.

ROBBINS, M. B., & JENSEN, G. D. Multiple orgasm in males. In R. Gemme & C. C. Wheeler (Eds.), *Progress in sexology.* New York: Plenum, 1976, pp. 323–328.

ROEDER, F. D. Stereotaxic lesion of the tuber cinereum in sexual deviation. *Confinia Neurologica*, 1966, *27*, 162–163.

SACHS, B. D., & BARFIELD, R. J. Copulatory behavior of male rats given intermittent electric shocks: Theoretical implications. *Journal of Comparative Physiology and Psychology*, 1974, *86*, 607–615.

Sachs, B. D., & Barfield, R. J. Functional analysis of male copulatory behavior in the rat. In J. S. Rosenblatt, R. Hinde, E. Shaw, & C. G. Beer (Eds.), *Advances in the study of behavior.* New York: Academic, 1976.

Schachter, S. Cognition and peripheralist–centralist controversies in motivation and emotion. In M. S. Gazzaniga (Ed.), *Handbook of psychophysiology.* New York: Academic Press, 1975, pp. 529–564.

Schachter, S., & Singer, J. E. Cognitive, social and physiological determinants of emotional state. *Psychological Reviews,* 1962, *69,* 379–399.

Scharfstein, B. S. *Mystical experience.* New York: Bobbs-Merrill, 1973.

Schmidt, G., & Sigusch, V. Women's sexual arousal. In J. Zubin & J. Money (Eds.), *Contemporary sexual behavior: Critical issues in the 1970s.* Baltimore: Johns Hopkins University Press, 1973, pp. 117–144.

Schwartz, G. E. Biofeedback, self-regulation and the patterning of physiological processes. *American Scientist,* 1975, *63,* 314–324.

Semans, J. H., & Langworthy, O. R. Observations on the neurophysiology of sexual function in the male cat. *Journal of Urology,* 1938, *40,* 836–846.

Sevely, J. L., & Bennet, J. W. Concerning female ejaculation and the female prostate. *Journal of Sex Research,* 1978, *14*(1), 1–20.

Shader, R. I. Ejaculation disorders. In R. I. Shader (Ed.), *Psychiatric complications of medical drugs.* New York: Raven, 1972.

Sherfey, M. J. *The nature and evolution of female sexuality.* New York: Random House, 1972.

Sherrington, C. Experiments on the value of vascular and visceral functions for the genesis of emotion. *Proceedings of the Royal Society,* 1900, *66,* 309–403.

Shirai, M., Matsuda, S., Mitsukawa, S., Nakamura, M., & Yonezawa, K. Effects of ejaculation induced by manual stimulation on plasma gonadotropin and testosterone levels in infertile man. *Tohoku Journal of Experimental Medicine,* 1974, *114,* 91–92.

Singer, I. *Goals of human sexuality.* New York: Shocken Books, 1973.

Singer, J. J. Control of male and female sexual behavior in the female rat. *Journal of Comparative Physiology and Psychology,* 1968, *66,* 738–742.

Slimp, J. C., Hart, B. C., & Goy, R. W. Heterosexual, autosexual and social behavior of adult male rhesus monkeys with medial preoptic–anterior hypothalamic lesions. *Brain Research,* 1978, *142,* 105–122.

Smith, E. R., Damassa, D. A., & Davidson, J. M. Plasma testosterone and sexual behavior following intracerebral implantation of testosterone propionate in the castrated male rat. *Hormones and Behavior,* 1977, *8,* 77–87.

Sobrero, A. J. Technic for the induction of ejaculation in humans. *Fertility and Sterility,* 1965, *16,* 765–767.

Sodersten, P., Damassa, D. A., & Smith, E. R. Sexual behavior in developing male rats. *Hormones and Behavior,* 1977, *8,* 320–341.

Stace, W. T. Mysticism and philosophy. Philadelphia: Lippincott, 1960.

Stearns, E. L., Winter, J. S. D., & Faiman, C. Effects of coitus on gonadotropin, prolactin and sex steroid levels in man. *Journal of Clinical Endocrinology and Metabolism,* 1973, *37,* 687–691.

Stilwell, D. Anatomy of the human clitoris. In T. P. Lowry & T. S. Lowry (Eds.), *The clitoris.* St. Louis: W. H. Green, 1976.

Stockham, A. B. *Karezza, ethics of marriage.* Chicago: Alice B. Stockham, 1896.

Sturup, G. K. Castration: The total treatment. In H. L. P. Resnik & M. E. Wolfgang (Eds.), *Sexual behaviors: Social, clinical and legal aspects.* Boston: Little, Brown, 1972, pp. 361–382.

Takagi, H., Takayuki, D., & Kawasaki, K. Effects of morphine, L-dopa and tetrabenazine on the lamina V cells of spinal dorsal horn. *Life Sciences,* 1975, *17,* 67.

TARABULCY, E. Sexual function in the normal and in paraplegia. *Paraplegia,* 1972, *10,* 201–208.

TART, C. T. *On being stoned. A psychological study of marijuana intoxication.* Palo Alto, Calif.: Science and Behavior Books, 1971.

TART, C. T. *States of consciousness.* New York: Dutton, 1975.

TERZIAN, H., & DALLE-ORE, G. Syndrome on Klüver and Bucy reproduced in man by bilateral removal of the temporal lobes. *Neurology,* 1955, *5,* 373–380.

TYRER, P. *The role of bodily feelings in anxiety.* Oxford, England: Oxford University Press, 1976.

VALENSTEIN, E. *Brain control.* New York: Wiley, 1973.

VANCE, E. B., & WAGNER, N. N. Written descriptions of orgasms: A study of sex differences. *Archives of Sexual Behaivor,* 1976, *5,* 87–98.

WENGER, M. A., AVERILL, J. R., & SMITH, D. D. B. Autonomic activity during sexual arousal. *Psychophysiology,* 1968, *4,* 468–478.

WHALEN, R. E. Sexual motivation. *Psychological Reviews,* 1966, *73,* 151–163.

YOUNG, W. C. The hormones and mating behavior. In W. C. Young (Ed.), *Sex and internal secretions,* Vol. 2. Baltimore: Williams & Wilkins, 1961.

ZARROW, M. X., & CLARK, J. H. Ovulation following vaginal stimulation in a spontaneous ovulator and its implications. *Journal of Endocrinology,* 1968, *40,* 343–352.

ZUCKERMAN, M. Physiological measures of sexual arousal in the human. *Psychological Bulletin,* 1971, *75,* 297–329.

13
The Psychophysiological Model of Meditation and Altered States of Consciousness: A Critical Review

Marjorie Schuman

The beginning of knowledge is the realization that interpretation stands for interpretation; the end of knowledge is the decision that interpretation stands for something, or is the interpretation of something.

—Sankara

In recent years, a growing literature has addressed itself to the psychophysiological bases of altered states of consciousness (ASCs). An unprecedented interest in meditation, biofeedback, and other techniques for altering consciousness reflects in part the widespread notion that science has begun to understand the physiological bases of these states. Thus, based on research involving practitioners of Yoga, Zen, or Transcendental Meditation (TM), meditation has been considered a unique psychophysiological state, associated with a distinct configuration of autonomic and electrocortical changes. For example, it has been proposed on the basis of these data that the practice of Transcendental Meditation leads to the experience of a fourth major state of consciousness, distinct from waking, dreaming, and nondreaming sleep (Wallace, 1970).

Major emphasis has been placed on two observations of psychophysiological changes during the meditative state. First, substantial increases in alpha brainwave activity have been observed during the Zazen practice of Zen Buddhist priests (Kasamatsu & Hirai, 1969) as well as in investigations of Yogis (Anand, Chhina, & Singh, 1961) and transcendental meditators (Wallace, 1970; Wallace, Benson & Wilson, 1971). A second major observation concerns changes in alpha blocking response during meditation. Two patterns of response have been reported, apparently varying with the type of meditation: either an absence of alpha blocking to sensory stimuli (Yogic meditation), or a failure of the alpha blocking response to habituate (Zen meditation and TM;

Marjorie Schuman • Department of Psychiatry, University of California at Los Angeles 90024.

Anand *et al.*, 1961; Kasamatsu & Hirai, 1969, pp. 501–514; Wallace, 1970). Taken together, these changes in baseline EEG and electrocortical responsiveness to sensory stimulation have been interpreted to be evidence of a unique meditative state of consciousness.

The question arises as to how these EEG correlates should be interpreted in relation to the psychological state of meditation on the one hand and the neurophysiological basis of consciousness on the other. "Meditation" embraces a wide range of mental as well as physical practices, and it may be somewhat premature to jump to any conclusions about the neurophysiology of *the* "meditative state." In the following discussion, an attempt is made to provide an analysis of some of the behavioral features of meditation and how these might relate to the observed psychophysiological correlates. The literature on meditation is critically evaluated with regard to changes in EEG, changes in arousal, the occurrence of sleep, and attentional phenomena. In addition, meditation is compared and contrasted with related psychological states (relaxation, hypnosis, and alpha biofeedback) in order to examine the conclusion that meditation constitutes a unique state of consciousness. The discussion concludes with an analysis of the psychophysiological model of meditation with regard to the necessary and sufficient conditions for altered states of consciousness to occur.

1. THE MEDITATIVE ASC

Meditation embraces a diverse group of mental and physical practices. It may involve focusing on a mentally generated sound or mantra, as in TM; contemplating an external object; mentally watching the breath; or observing the stream of consciousness. Alternatively, it may be active, as for instance in the flowing movements of t'ai chi ch'uan or the whirling of a Sufi dervish. Although a full discussion of meditation is beyond the scope of this paper (see Goleman, 1977, for an excellent introduction to the varieties of meditation experience), some of the general features may be sketched.

Naranjo (1974, pp. 15–29), for instance, distinguishes three major types of meditation practice: meditations with an external object of focus, meditations with an internal focus (image or thought), and meditations that have no fixed focus. Along similar lines, meditations may be classified (Goleman, 1977) as *concentration* practices and *mindfulness* practices. Concentration involves technques for focusing attention on a particular target and includes the first two categories specified by Naranjo. In contrast, mindfulness simply involves noticing whatever comes into awareness. Different forms of meditation are regarded as resulting in different experiences and/or phenomenological states; Sanskrit, for example, has at least 22 words for different states of consciousness.

One important phenomenological category of experiences induced through meditation includes trancelike states of absorption ("samadhi," "transcendental consciousness") produced through the practice of concentration. Concentration (exemplified in the practice of Yoga) entails becoming perfectly focused to the point where the meditator loses awareness of himself as a subject and becomes totally absorbed in the meditation object. This mode of experience is foreign to normal consciousness and is consequently difficult to communicate, but it is described as a state in which the mind transcends the duality of subject and object; evidently, the meditator experiences sinking into or becoming one with the meditation object, so that there is no longer an experience of being a subject meditating, merely the experience "meditation is." (Samadhi states are discussed somewhat further in the context of trance states in Section 8.) Experience of altered states is also produced through the perfection of mindfulness, a practice in which one learns to continuously observe the contents of consciousness. (The Buddha was said to be able to observe some 10^{21} separate "mind-moments" in the wink of an eye! [Goleman, 1977].) In Zen, for instance, one sits with the intention of just sitting, doing nothing. In this practice, the challenge is to notice thoughts as they come up without allowing them to capture the attention and distract from an awareness of sitting. Ultimately, a state is achieved ("nirvana") in which there is consciousness without subject or object.

Meditation progresses through a sequence of experiences or phenomenological stages. Certain features may be specific to the particular technique practiced, while others may be common to different traditions of meditation practice (cf. D. P. Brown, 1977; Goleman, 1977). It should be emphasized that many of these experiences of altered states are rare and never happen to the majority of meditators (Goleman, 1977). On the other hand, common to all meditation practices and, it would seem, encompassing the variety of experiences that occur during meditation is the goal of *passive awareness*—a state in which the mind becomes still and consciousness transcends thought. *Awareness* describes the focus of attention on the present moment, being with whatever one is experiencing in the here and now; *passive* emphasizes that there is nothing one need *do* in order to experience in this way, merely be receptive and allow the experience to happen. One of the basic tenets of meditation is the notion that passive awareness is a natural, elementary, and direct form of experience that is ordinarily overwhelmed and obscured by the activity of the mind. The purpose of meditation, therefore, is to allow the mind to become quiet and thereby uncover the capacity for this experience.

The state of passive awareness is produced in different ways by different meditation practices. In concentration, one eliminates the distractions of random mind activity; in mindfulness, one seeks to conquer the mind through present-centered awareness. Yet another approach is exemplified in certain types of active meditations, for example Sufi dancing or the "chaotic meditation" of Bhagwan Rajneesh (1976). Here the intent is to create a background of activity against which the experience of inner silence can emerge.

Passive awareness, considered here the *sine qua non* of the meditative ASC, involves a fundamental shift in the frame of reference of experience. Ordinarily, the mind is caught up in its own activity and internal chatter; in the absence of any experience to the contrary, we generally assume this constant mental activity to be both natural and inevitable, and in fact, we tend to identify this mental activity as self or "consciousness." In meditation, one comes to discriminate mental activity as a process added to and apart from direct, conscious experience. In so doing, one transcends the mind and breaks through to another level of awareness. This shift in the frame of reference of experience may be likened to the process of looking in a mirror; in the ordinary scheme of things, our focus is on the images reflected in the glass, but under special conditions we may become aware of the mirrored surface on which the images appear. In a sense, all meditation may be considered a means toward this *transformation* of consciousness—in the terms proposed by Schwartz (1974), an altered *trait* rather than an altered *state* of consciousness.

It is the thesis of this chapter that the meditative ASC can best be understood in terms of the passive awareness of ongoing experience—that is, *the context in which experience occurs*—rather than in terms of any particular experience or psychophysiological state. That is to say, distinct from the particular altered-states phenomena that may be experienced during meditation, the more important aspect of the meditative ASC is seen to be the context or frame of reference in which experience occurs—the *relationship* between the experiencer and his experience (King, 1963). The meditative ASC is thus seen not as a static state but rather as a dynamic process of passive awareness, within which a variety of phenomenological experiences can occur.

A major implication of this view, developed in the body of the chapter, is the idea that the psychophysiological changes observed during meditation reflect changes in *behavior* (including cognitive behavior or mental experience) rather than the meditative ASC *per se*. That is to say, the subject sits in a particular manner, attends to certain things, adopts a certain cognitive set, consciously relaxes, etc., and changes in psychophysiological functioning come about in consequence of these behaviors. The question then becomes *which behaviors or mental processes* during meditation are related to *which psychophysiological changes*.

The substantive issue, here, has to do with the interpretation of the relationship between the psychological states or experiences achieved through meditation, on the one hand, and their psychophysiological correlates, on the other. In the scientific literature on meditation, psychophysiological changes that occur during meditation have been regarded as defining characteristics of a stable meditative ASC. Alternatively, it may be more reasonable to attempt to understand the behavioral significance of each of the various psychophysiological changes that occur, and whether these are in fact necessary or sufficient for the meditative ASC to occur. For example, certain of the psychophysiological phenomena attributed to the meditative ASC may perhaps be more accurately interpreted as correlates of the "relaxation response" (Benson, Beary, & Carol, 1974) elicited during certain sitting meditations. Such a low arousal state may or may not, however, be a *necessary* component of the meditative ASC. Other meditation techniques might be associated with a very different physiology—Sufi dancing, for instance, with physiological changes of exercise—and yet might engender a very similar result in terms of quieting the mind. According to the present view, what defines the meditative ASC is the quality of awareness brought to these ongoing experiences, the context in which they are held, rather than a particular psychophysiology.

It should be acknowledged here that the experience that occurs during meditation (the content of meditation) is not unrelated to the state of consciousness (the context) in which it occurs. On the contrary, meditation techniques are methodologies for producing experiences that may predictably give rise to transformations of consciousness of the sort described here. Moreover, experiences are a reflection of the state of consciousness in which they occur: a transformation in one's sense of oneself-as-experiencer (context) has a considerable impact on the content of experience. Some of these complexities may be handled in part in terms of a systems approach to consciousness (see Tart, 1975) as discussed somewhat further below. For our present purposes, the point is that the psychophysiological changes that occur during meditation may not be intrinsically related to the meditative ASC.

To anticipate the conclusions developed in the pages to follow, the psychophysiological phenomena associated with meditation seem largely accountable in terms of psychological processes that are in no way unique to meditation, for example, changes in arousal and attention. Demonstrating the psychophysiological correlates of meditation is incomplete without answers to certain key questions. Can a comparable low arousal state occur without the cognitive/experiential changes of meditation? Would focusing attention to an extent comparable to that achieved in meditation produce analogous EEG changes in a behavioral context other than meditation?

Insufficient attention has been paid to the subjective phenomena of the meditation experience. Thus, some studies have concerned correlates of mystical states achieved through meditation, whereas others have involved correlates of meditation without regard to the experience or the level achieved. Differences between meditators and the problem of fluctuations in experience over time have been ignored. Undoubtedly, these factors contribute to the observed variability in the psychophysiological correlates of meditation. Moreover, so long as we are attempting to characterize *the* meditative state, variabilities are construed as discrepancies to be resolved, whereas they may, in fact, represent important data in their own right.

According to the present formulation, there is, at the very least, heuristic value in interpreting the psychophysiological changes of meditation as correlates of specific behaviors and experiences in meditation. This conclusion does not necessarily bear upon the question of whether there *exist* discoverable correlates of the "context component" of the meditative ASC (a few speculations about which appear in the concluding portion of the chapter). Simply, it seems unlikely that the complex phenomenology of meditation can be accounted for in terms of a very few (and rather crudely defined) psychophysiological data.

2. EEG CHANGES DURING MEDITATION

Most attempts to characterize the neurophysiological basis of meditation have generated a picture of EEG slowing and enhanced cortical synchrony during meditation, despite a considerable diversity in subjects, meditation techniques, and EEG methodology (see review by Woolfolk, 1975). A composite picture of the progression of EEG changes during a meditation session, derived from studies of Yoga, Zen, and TM, appears to be, first, an increase in the abundance of alpha rhythm in the EEG, with well-organized alpha activity appearing in all leads, especially frontal and central; second, an increase in the amplitude of alpha potentials; third, a decrease in the modal frequency of alpha; progressing to, fourth, the appearance of rhythmical trains of theta waves (5–7 Hz) (Anand *et al.*, 1961; Kasamatsu & Hirai, 1969; Wallace, 1970; Wallace *et al.*, 1971). Not all features, it should be noted, are necessarily found with every technique, in every meditator, or on every occasion.

The general characteristics of this "alpha–theta" meditation EEG may be further illustrated by citing a few of the relevant studies. For example, Anand *et al.* (1961) found prominent and persistent alpha activity with well-marked amplitude modulation in four Yogis practicing Raj Yoga, but they observed no theta activity associated with this type of meditation. Kasamatsu and Hirai (1969) observed a sequence of increased alpha abundance, decreased alpha frequency, and theta activity in a population of Zen meditators, which appeared to develop as a function of proficiency and experience in meditation. Wallace and his co-workers (1970, 1971) found an increase in the regularity and amplitude of alpha activity during TM, with a shift toward theta in some but not all subjects. In a study of another mantra practice, Ananda Marga Yoga, Elson, Hauri, and Cunis (1977) found a pattern of EEG slowing consisting of 50% alpha waves or a predominance of theta activity on a low-voltage mixed background.

As evident in this description, theta activity during meditation is a particularly variable characteristic. To make matters more complicated, when theta activity does occur, in some instances it appears to resemble a drowsy or sleep onset pattern (theta on a mixed low-voltage background), while in others is reported to consist of bursts or trains of high-amplitude (60–100 μV) activity at a relatively constant frequency (Banquet, 1973; Kasamatsu & Hirai, 1969) unlike the typical drowsy pattern. These findings are discussed in depth in Section 6.

A recent study by Hebert and Lehmann (1977) systematically investigated theta activity in a good-sized population of transcendental meditators ($n = 78$) and control subjects. Criterion bursts of generally spindle-form theta activity ($\geqslant 100$ μV, $\geqslant 1$ sec) were observed in 27% of the meditators (never in controls) and tended to occur synchronously in all leads, although frequently occipital alpha continued during a frontal theta burst; highest voltages were generally recorded in the frontal channel. Longer bursts showed intermittent and irregular amplitude modulation and at times were discontinuous and mixed with high-voltage alpha waves. Contrary to the experience of Kasamatsu and Hirai (1969) with Zen meditators, Hebert and Lehmann found no relationship between the frequency of occurrence of theta bursts and the number of months of meditation in a given subject, nor a significant difference in the amount of meditation practice between subjects who showed theta activity and those who did not. Interestingly, moreover, those subjects who showed theta bursts during meditation tended to show similar activity during pre- and post-eyes open baseline periods, although with less frequency than seen during meditation. Criterion theta activity was also observed during a longer period of relaxation recorded presleep in a subgroup of the meditation subjects, but it was never seen in controls. The functional significance of this finding is considered below.

In contrast to the alpha–theta pattern, a second EEG pattern consisting of high-voltage beta waves is sometimes seen during meditation, though not necessarily in lieu of EEG slowing. Thus, Das and Gastaut (1955), in a study of seven practitioners of Kriya Yoga, noted an *acceleration* of the alpha rhythm by 1–3 Hz, with a decrease in amplitude and the appearance of faster (15–30 Hz) components. Toward the end of and after meditation, these authors also noted the reappearance of alpha rhythm, often slower and more widely distributed than at first (7–8 Hz).

A synchronous fast-wave pattern was similarly observed in a spectral analysis of TM by Banquet (1973). Several stages or phases of meditation were observed, with no clear differentiation among them. First, there was a general tendency for an early shift from the basic alpha rhythm (9 Hz, 10–50 μV) to a more pronounced, higher amplitude (70 μV) rhythm, with slowing of frequency in some subjects. Short bursts of high-voltage (up to 100 μV) theta at 5–7 Hz then occurred, simultaneously in all channels or first in the frontal region. Longer rhythmic trains of theta at 60–80 μV usually followed. In a third stage, seen in only four of the meditators, a stable rhythmic beta activity at 20 Hz was seen. This activity was intermittent at first, spindlelike bursts alternating with alpha or theta rhythms, and tended to become continuous on a persistent background of slow frequencies. Reminiscent of the generalized fast activity observed by Das and Gastaut (1955), this activity reached a voltage of 30–60 μV and predominated in anterior channels. Also similar to the findings of Das and Gastaut, the end of meditation was characterized by the return of alpha, persisting in some subjects into the eyes-open postmeditation period.

Both Das and Gastaut (1955) and Banquet (1973) interpreted the fast-wave pattern as a correlate of subjectively experienced mystical or transcendent feelings ("samadhi") during very deep Yogic or transcendental meditation; an apparent exception to this interpretation, however, are the findings of Anand *et al.* (1961), who reported an alpha-wave correlate of presumed samadhi experience. Alternatively, Peper and Ancoli (1977) suggested that there are two distinct meditational styles characterized by these different psychophysiological parameters: fast beta frequencies corresponding to focused, intentional tasks in their view, and alpha–theta corresponding to relaxation-meditation. A similar formulation, proposed by B. B. Brown (1977), is that differences in arousal may distinguish the two meditational styles. Regardless of the specifics, the important point in these interpretations is the suggestion the EEG patterns during meditation relate to specific cognitive and experiential features of meditation rather than a meditative ASC *per se*.

Beyond changes in EEG frequency and amplitude, recent evidence suggests that meditation may be characterized by changes in inter- and intrahemispheric coherence. Orme-Johnson (1977) reported coherence values ≥ 0.8 for 40-sec epochs of EEG activity in theta, alpha, and beta bands in many (and sometimes all) derivations during TM. He regarded this increase in coherence as a correlate of a "low-noise state" of the brain produced during TM, an "EEG signature of the transcendental state." Along somewhat similar lines, Rogers (1976) found significant enhancement of left–right synchrony as a correlate of chanting meditation (Nichiren Shoshu). Rogers interpreted this result as an auditory driving response to a complex auditory stimulus, analogous to the well-known phenomenon of photic driving; she speculated that rhythmic or repetitive elements in a number of meditative and religious practices may function to enhance EEG coherence through a driving mechanism. She also stressed, however, that the phenomenon is complex and is not readily explained as a simple rhythmic response of the brain to rhythmic stimuli. Interestingly, the largest-amplitude rhythmic brain activity in the Rogers study occurred in the 3–8 Hz (theta) band, and in frontal leads, similar to findings in studies of TM.

Measures of phase and coherence may provide particularly meaningful clues as to consciousness or state-related changes during meditation. Adey (1969) suggested in another context that state-dependent EEG effects may be characterized in terms of the probability of Gaussian distributions of EEG amplitude; spindle sleep, for example, is characterized in scalp records by diminished probability of such distributions, indicating increased connectivity between generating elements.

It should be emphasized that not all investigators have been able to confirm the EEG changes of meditation. For example, Bagchi and Wenger (1957) found *no* changes in EEG alpha in comparing meditation and quiet rest in 14 Yogis. Similarly, Tebecis (1975) reported that:

> The EEG changes during TM were rarely as pronounced as previous reports suggest. There was considerable variation between subjects, some displaying no EEG changes at all during TM compared with an equal period of nonmeditation. Any changes that did occur in a particular individual were not necessarily repeated in a subsequent session. (p. 312).

Overall, in fact, these investigators found *no* consistent or significant difference between meditation and nonmeditation, despite a trend toward increased theta and decreased beta, and they concluded that "pronounced and reliable physiological changes do not necessarily occur during TM, as has been claimed." This finding parallels a report by Travis, Kondo, and Knott (1976) that occipital alpha production of transcendental meditators did not change significantly during meditation and did not increase over premeditation baselines as previously reported by Wallace. Brown, Fischer, Wagman, Horrom, and Marks (in press) also found no difference between meditation and eyes-closed relaxation in a population of touch healers doing a variety of (unspecified) individual meditations. These negative results belie the robustness of the EEG correlates of meditation, and they underscore the need for careful phenomenological analysis in unraveling the significance of the EEG data.

Many of the issues related to variability in the correlates of meditation have been reviewed in excellent recent articles by Woolfolk (1975) and J. M. Davidson (1976). To mention a few, methodological considerations including EEG recording technique, measurement, and baseline procedures are critical in the proper evaluation of meditation. Many studies of meditation may also be faulted with a number of design errors that render results equivocal (Tebecis, 1975), including baseline procedures, failure to vary the order of conditions (meditation versus rest), and lack of appropriate controls.

Baseline procedures are of particular importance because baseline EEG tends to vary over the length of an experimental session, so that comparison with premeditation control periods is not necessarily appropriate. As Paskewitz, Lynch, Orne, and Costello (1970) have pointed out with respect to EEG biofeedback paradigms, alpha may increase as a result of disinhibition from influences that block alpha, and it has not been unequivocally demonstrated that meditation actually increases alpha above maximum disinhibited levels.

The issue of appropriate baseline and control procedures is a complex one. First, it is probably not sufficient to compare meditation simply with rest, since relaxation is a skill that is enhanced through repeated practice; on the other hand, the use of experienced relaxation subjects as controls may not solve the problem, since regular relaxation may have ASC-inducing effects of its own. Second, premeditation control periods do not take into account the progressive deepening of relaxation that may take place over time within a session. And third, a further consideration in regard to premeditation baselines is that conditioned psychophysiological changes may occur in anticipation of meditation practice, as for instance occurs among practitioners of autogenic training upon assuming the training posture (Luthe, 1969). The meditator may find it necessary to actively inhibit the development of the meditative state once the usual practice position is assumed, or may find it impossible to do so.

Issues related to EEG measurement have not been sufficiently emphasized in studies of meditation. For instance, broadly defined EEG frequency categories (e.g., alpha defined as 8–12 Hz) do not necessarily reflect homogeneous brain processes. Indeed, multichannel recordings suggest that alpha activity may be determined by three or more semi-independent generators (Lehmann, 1971), clearly implying that differences in electrode placement, filter characteristics, and measurement are relevant to results. B. B. Brown (1977) cited no fewer than 11 separate characteristics—abundance, frequency, amplitude, topographical location, phase, synchrony, variability, reactivity, and burst characteristics of rate of onset, duration, and frequency of occurrence—that must be taken into account and concluded that alpha should be interpreted not as a single brain rhythm but rather as a complex or family of brain frequencies.

These various considerations raise the questions of whether the changes in EEG and other psychophysiological variables attributed to meditation are real and to what extent they may be accounted for in terms of nonspecific relaxation effects. The following discussion examines several factors that influence EEG and that may possibly, therefore, mediate the changes that are observed during meditation.

3. Oculomotor Processes and EEG

One specific behavioral feature of meditation that is of particular importance in the interpretation of the EEG findings is whether the eyes are closed or, if open, "not looking." It has long been known that there is an important relationship between alpha waves and vision. Alpha waves, it will be recalled, are generally most conspicuously associated with the occipital region; they appear in the average subject when the eyes are closed and are blocked when the eyes are opened. An important series of investigations by Mulholland and his colleagues (e.g., Mulholland, 1969, pp. 120–127; Mulholland & Peper, 1971), as well as others, have demonstrated that the efferent oculomotor processes involved in looking (the triad of focusing, accommodation, and convergence of the eye muscles) are the probable major determinants of the presence or absence of alpha in the occipital EEG. Thus, while it is descriptively true that alpha waves are blocked when a subject attends to the environment or when a cognitive process requires effort, the oculomotor hypothesis explains this relationship on the basis that visual mechanisms are an important part of the orienting response. According to this model, occipital cortical activation occurs in association with coordination of the muscular apparatus of the eyes for sensory intake of visual data. Thus, looking blocks alpha, and in the absence of active looking, alpha reappears.

Plotkin (1976) has argued on the basis of EEG biofeedback work that oculomotor behaviors mediate changes in EEG whenever cognitive strategies are successful in producing changes in occipital alpha strength (including, presumably, during meditation). He argued that cognitive processes control alpha only to the extent that they mediate changes in oculomotor functions. One possibility is that when the mind turns inward during meditation, attention is withdrawn from events in the external environment, and visual orienting ceases. It is also interesting to note in this regard that when the eyes are closed, they often turn naturally into an upwardly deviated position, which is known to be associated with occipital alpha. In fact, in some (not all) subjects, alpha can be precisely regulated on or off by the simple expedient of turning the eyes upward (Dewan, 1967). This mechanism may also be relevant to certain spiritual practices in which attention is placed on a point between and slightly above the eyebrows, the so-called third eye; another similar technique stresses concentration on various points at the top of the skull. Possibly, these practices are associated with oculomotor behaviors that mediate the changes in alpha observed during meditation. While this is a plausible explanation of changes in occipital alpha, however, it does not necessarily account for the prominent frontal and central alpha seen during meditation.

An alternative possibility is that oculomotor processes are merely *incidentally* related to more essential cognitive aspects of the meditative ASC. This position has been expounded by Hardt and Kamiya (1976); the oculomotor hypothesis, they have argued, even if true, merely explains how alpha control is made possible physiologically and does not say anything about the specialized states of consciousness in which the requisite oculomotor changes are likely to occur. Hardt and Kamiya further argued that the changes in EEG alpha during alpha feedback (and, presumably, during meditation) occur in two phases. In the first phase, they suggested, alpha increases as a function of eliminating processes that block alpha; in a second phase, there is an increase in alpha above maximum baseline levels, and it is this high alpha state that is associated with the ASC. While this theory potentially circumvents the criticisms of Plotkin and others, it is unfortunately unsupported by any data.

In any case, the significance of changes in eye movements and eye position in meditation is an empirical issue that can be explored in relationship to the hypothesis of Hardt and Kamiya as well as experimental questions such as whether alpha levels during meditation are increased above maximum baseline levels and above levels achieved by instructed oculomotor behaviors ("not looking").

4. MEDITATION AND AROUSAL

A second factor that may mediate the EEG response during meditation is level of arousal. It is well known that the EEG undergoes a predictable sequence of changes in the transition from wakefulness to sleep. These changes are generally held to be a function of changes in arousal along the sleep–wakefulness continuum (e.g., Lindsley, 1952). These facts raise several questions. First, to what extent can the EEG changes during meditation be explained in terms of decreased arousal? And second, to what extent is the low arousal state of meditation psychophysiologically unique?

Woolfolk (1975) has recently reviewed the data on the electroencephalographic and autonomic correlates of Yoga, Zen, and TM. Although there is not, he concluded, a thoroughly consistent or replicable pattern of responses, most of the psychophysiological data support the view that meditation is associated with a low-arousal psychophysiological state. Signs of reduced arousal in meditation may include greater synchronization and slowing of the EEG; lowering of respiratory rate and/or minute volume; some decrease in heart rate (HR); and a decrease in spontaneous electrodermal activity and/or reactivity. Additionally, some studies have found changes indicative of a slowing of energy metabolism, including decreased oxygen consumption, decreased carbon dioxide elimination, and a decline in blood lactate (Fenwick, Donaldson, Gillis, Bushman, Fenton, Perry, Tilsley, & Serafinowicz, 1977; Wallace, 1970; Wallace, Benson, & Wilson, 1971).

To illustrate the research findings to date, the psychophysiological correlates of several types of meditation practice are summarized in Table 1. In general, most (not all) findings are consistent with the low-arousal interpretation. It should be noted, however, that most studies have not statistically assessed the significance of the physiological changes during meditation, and it is additionally unclear whether changes of the observed order of magnitude merit the inference that a change in "psychophysiological state" has occurred.

The lowering of arousal in meditation can be understood as a shift in autonomic balance in the direction of parasympathetic dominance. Inasmuch as peripheral autonomic balance is not independent of central nervous system and skeletal muscle arousal, the implication is that meditation may be characterized in terms of interrelated changes in the autonomic system (decreased sympathetic arousal), central nervous system (enhanced cortical synchrony), and somatic musculature (general body relaxation). A number of authors have described meditation in these terms. For instance, Gellhorn and Kiely (1972) proposed that meditation consists of a shift in the ergotropic (sympathetic)/trophotropic (parasympathetic) continuum to the trophotropic side. Along similar lines, Benson, Beary, and Carol (1974) theorized that the psychophysiological basis of the meditative ASC is an integrated hypothalamic reaction ("the relaxation response") consisting of a shift

TABLE 1
Psychophysiological Correlates of Meditation and Related Practices: Summary of Studies Cited

Type of practice	EEG	Respiration	Heart rate	Electrodermal	Reference
Yoga	No change	Decrease	No change	Increase SRL[a]	Bagchi & Wenger, 1957
Yoga	Alpha (samadhi)	Decrease	Increase	Decrease SRL	Wenger & Bagchi, 1961
Yoga	Beta (samadhi)		Increase (samadhi)		Anand, Chhina, & Singh, 1961
Kriya Yoga (n=7)					Das & Gastaut, 1955
Ananda Marga Yoga	Alpha-theta	Decrease	No change	Increase SRL	Elson, Hauri, & Cunis, 1977
TM	Alpha-theta		Decrease	Increase SRL	Wallace, 1970
TM	Alpha-theta			Increase SRL	Wallace, Benson, & Wilson, 1971
TM				Decrease SRRs[b] / Increase SRR habituation	Orme-Johnson, 1973
TM	Alpha-theta / Beta				Banquet, 1973
TM	Alpha-theta (variable)				Tebecis, 1975
TM, autohypnosis	No difference between groups	Decrease	Decrease	Increase SRL / Decrease SRRs	Walrath & Hamilton, 1975
TM, progressive relaxation	No difference between groups		Decrease		Warrenburg, Pagano, Woods, & Hlastala, 1977
TM, relaxation	No change TM	No change	No change	No change	Curtis & Wessberg, 1976
	Alpha-theta		No change TM		Travis, Kondo & Knott, 1976
Zen	Alpha-theta	Decrease	Decrease		Kasamatsu & Hirai, 1969
Zen				More stable	Goyeckhe, Chihara, & Shimizu, 1972
Zen	Alpha-theta	Decrease	Decrease		Hirai, 1974

[a] SRL = skin resistance level.
[b] SRR = skin resistance response.

toward decreased sympathetic and perhaps increased parasympathetic activity.

Autonomic, central, and skeletal muscle arousal comprise an interlocking system of feedback mechanisms with reciprocal influences, so that changes in one system produce corresponding effects in the others (Gellhorn & Loofbourrow, 1964). That is to say, changes in autonomic balance are seen as correlated with changes in muscle tension, EEG, and behavior on a continuum that ranges from deep sleep to wakefulness to behavioral excitement. Moreover, to the extent that autonomic balance is controlled by the CNS, peripheral autonomic activity can be regarded as an index of central state (Porges, 1976). Despite the close association between somatic, autonomic, and central components of arousal, however, recent evidence suggests that it may be more fruitful to emphasize patterning and specificity in psychophysiological activity (Davidson, 1978). That is to say, arousal is not a unidimensional process, and it is likely that different patterns of activity in various components may occur in different practices.

In an excellent review of this area, Davidson & Schwartz (1976, pp. 399–442) proposed that low-arousal or relaxation states consist of a number of *dissociable* dimensions: cognitive, somatic, and attentional. For example, they pointed out that someone may be physically tired and somatically relaxed and yet be unable to fall asleep because his "mind is racing." This phenomenon implies that it may not be sufficient to characterize meditation simply as a low-arousal state on a unidimensional continuum, nor may it be accurate to suppose it lies somewhere between normal waking consciousness and sleep.

It is reasonably clear from the data summarized in Table 1 that meditation is associated with a decline in autonomic arousal, although minor dissociations are seen among different measures. The central arousal component is less clear-cut. Thus, alpha–theta EEG is interpreted as a sign of reduced cortical arousal, and yet meditation is often accompanied by an experience of enhanced alertness. Along the same lines, meditation (Zen, at least) is associated with increased alpha activity *and* increased attention, in apparent contradiction of the more typical finding that alpha rhythm is inversely related to attention; even theta rhythm in these subjects is coupled with an ability to respond quickly to auditory stimuli while meditating (Kasamatsu & Hirai, 1969), which on the face of it is contradictory to the report of Beatty, Greenberg, Diebler, and O'Hanlon (1974) that theta enhancement is correlated with performance decrement. Clearly, psychophysiological measures alone do not completely specify level of arousal; the significance of an EEG pattern evidently depends on what "state" context it occurs in.

What these data suggest, following the discussion by Davidson and

Schwartz (1976), is that states of consciousness may be characterized only in terms of patterns of somatic-autonomic, cognitive, and attentional factors. In meditation, there is a cognitive or attentional alertness that is not predicted by the pattern of peripheral or even cortical arousal. Gellhorn and Kiely (1972) ascribe this dissociation to sympathetic activity occurring against the background parasympathetic shift; another possible interpretation is proposed by Jevening, Wilson, Smith, and Morton (1975), who inferred from indirect measures that brain blood flow (and therefore, presumably, neural activity) increases during meditation (TM).

Patterns of psychophysiological activity in meditation may be quite specific to particular practices. Goyeche, Chihara, and Shimizu (1972), for instance, published results of a pilot study of psychophysiological differences between Zen concentration and a concentration practice called *cotention*. In the Zen exercise, subjects were asked to concentrate their attention on the muscle sensations arising from their abdominal breathing, and in the cotention exercise, on the muscle sensations of their eyes. Within-subject comparisons were made over a 15-min session consisting of 5-min intervals of Zen, cotention, and simple relaxation randomly ordered across subjects. A trend was found for Zen to produce a greater decrease in heart rate than cotention and to produce a diminution in respiration rate, while cotention produced an increase in respiration rate. While these psychophysiological changes appear to indicate a decrease in arousal during Zen, Goyeche *et al.* also found that the amplitude of abdominal breathing tended to increase and that of thoracic breathing to decrease, a result opposite to the pattern associated with decreases in arousal leading to sleep (Timmons, Salamy, Kamiya, & Girton, 1972). Possibly, attention on the breath may enhance abdominal breathing apart from arousal-related effects. Here again, the significance of a particular psychophysiological change needs to be interpreted within a particular state context.

The importance of patterns of psychophysiological activity is emphasized in a study by Pelletier (1974). Pelletier found, in a case study of a Yogic adept, that states of consciousness could be characterized only in terms of the multiple parameters of EEG, respiratory, and cardiovascular functions. Voluntary control of alpha (increased alpha production) was associated with an increase in respiration rate and a decrease in heart rate with no change in electrodermal response (EDR) or EMG, while increased theta production was associated with a decrease in respiration rate and EMG with no change in HR or EDR. Each pattern of activity was associated with distinct subjective correlates.

A number of studies in the biofeedback area are beginning to define the patterns of covariation and potential dissociation between psychophysiological variables. Thus, we know, for instance, that conditioned EEG changes can occur relatively independently of cardiac and respiratory activity (Beatty & Kornfeld, 1972; Schwartz, Shaw, & Shapiro, 1972), EDR (Suter, Johnson, Franconi, & Smith, 1977), and EMG (DeGood & Chisholm, 1977). Despite the potential dissociability of CNS (EEG) and autonomic variables, deep somatic relaxation tends to be associated with correlated changes in EEG, such as heightened alpha. For instance, DeGood and Chisholm (1977) have shown that frontalis EMG feedback results in a generalized pattern of arousal changes reflected in heart rate and respiration as well as EMG and EEG. Hassett and Schwartz (1975) found a combination of heart rate decrease and alpha "on" elicited more reports of relaxation than other conditions in a 2 × 2 design.

The relative contributions of sympathetic and parasympathetic influences on the various components of the low arousal state in meditation is an interesting, and unanswered, question. Heart rate appears to be parasympathetically influenced and related to somatic components of arousal, whereas phasic electrodermal activity may be sympathetically mediated and related to emotional arousal (Davidson & Schwartz, 1976). A number of predictions may also be derived from the relationship between autonomic activity and attention. For example, Porges (1976) suggested that sustained attention is characterized by parasympathetic influences on autonomic activity (reduced HR and HR variability). Increased parasympathetic activity in meditation would be consistent with the observation that cholinomimetic drugs produce a slowing of thinking (Davis, Hollister, Overall, Johnson, & Train, 1976). While there are no data that address this point, Porges suggested a methodology (the rationale for which is too complex to go into here) for assessing sympathetic and parasympathetic influences through the quantification of respiratory influences on heart rate.

5. Specificity of the Meditative ASC

There are four basic elements, according to Benson, necessary to effect the relaxation response: (1) a mental device (constant stimulus or other technique for shifting from logical, externally oriented thought); (2) a passive attitude; (3) decreased muscle tonus; and (4) a quiet environment. These criteria are rather general and suggest that the relaxation response may be rather nonspecific; according to Benson, it can be elicited through autogenic training, progressive relaxation, hypnotic suggestion, and related practices as well as meditation (Benson, Beary, & Carol, 1974). Such a generalization, however, disregards the diversity among meditation techniques, and in regard to subjective experience, at least, it may be inaccurate to regard Yoga and Zen, much less autogenic training and progressive relaxation, as identical states (Mills & Campbell, 1974).

One way to look at this issue is in terms of a "multiprocess" model of relaxation states (Davidson & Schwartz, 1976). According to this view, low-arousal states consist of specific patterns of somatic, cognitive, and attentional relaxation. The general principle of the multiprocess model is that active generation of behavior in a given mode competes with and inhibits unwanted activity and thereby generates relaxation in that mode; different techniques, therefore, may elicit different components of the relaxation response. TM, for example, utilizing a self-generated verbal mantra, is seen as competing with verbally mediated cognitions, whereas Hatha Yoga would have a relatively greater effect on somatic processes. Thus, meditation can be conceptualized as a family of practices that generate particular patterns of somatic, cognitive, and attentional relaxation, dependent on how effectively the particular technique inhibits ongoing activity in these modes. While certain components of the low-arousal state in meditation may be nonspecific, as Benson suggested (somatic and autonomic components especially), others (cognitive and/or attentional) may at the same time be quite specific.

Some evidence relevant to the comparison of meditation and other low-arousal states has been published in the last few years. By and large, it appears to support the position that the autonomic and somatic components of the relaxation response, at least, are nonspecific and can be elicited with a variety of different techniques. For example, Curtis and Wessberg (1976) compared HR, respiration, and EDR level among transcendental mediators, relaxers with a comparable degree of experience in Jacobson's technique, and inexperienced subjects instructed to sit quietly. No statistically significant differences were found among groups, suggesting that meditation is not distinguishable from relaxation. (However, there were also no significant effects from any of the experimental treatments relative to pre- and postexperimental baselines in this sketchily reported study, which renders these results rather equivocal.) In another study addressing the same questions, Warrenburg, Pagano, Woods, and Hlastala (1977) compared oxygen consumption, heart rate, EMG, and EEG in TM and progressive muscle relaxation; both practices produced a significant degree of relaxation from baseline, including a 4% drop in oxygen consumption, a 1.6-BPM (beats/min) drop in heart rate, and a 3.1-μV decrease in frontalis EMG. There were no significant differences between groups. In yet another study,

Walrath and Hamilton (1975) investigated peripheral autonomic correlates of TM, autohypnosis, and control subjects, all selected for a high susceptibility to hypnosis. Again, it was shown that meditation and hypnosis do not differ from each other, nor from instructed relaxation.

Fenwick, Donaldson, Gillis, Bushman, Fenton, Perry, Tilsley, and Serafinowicz (1977) reexamined the drop in metabolic rate during TM observed by previous investigators. Oxygen consumption in TM and relaxation control groups was measured and related to initial metabolic rate and to subjects' self-ratings as "tense" or "relaxed" during the experimental session. It was found that nonspecific relaxation techniques such as listening to music were as effective as meditation in terms of a slowing of metabolic rate. Interestingly, the percentage of change in oxygen consumption during meditation was comparable in magnitude to the 16% observed by Wallace et. al. (1971) only in a subgroup of subjects self-rated as "tense" (13.5% drop), while "relaxed" subjects showed a much smaller drop, consistent with muscle relaxation and small changes in body posture, which, according to the authors, is of little physiological significance. This finding tends to suggest that the "hypometabolic state" of TM is not due to meditation alone but rather to an interaction between meditation and initial level of relaxation. In additional support of these conclusions, it was also found that the magnitude of change in oxygen consumption was comparable for "good" and "bad" meditations. Further, in a fasting control designed to reduce metabolic rate to the lowest possible level, meditation failed to produce any significant change in metabolic rate.

In a somewhat related study, Michaels, Huber, and McCann (1976) investigated the effects of TM on plasma norepinephrine and epinephrine and could find no evidence of an effect greater than that produced by relaxation. On the other hand, however, Jevening, Wilson, Smith, and Morton (1975) found TM to be associated with a pattern of decrease in hepatic and renal blood flow and an increase in cardiac output that differed from the pattern in resting controls; relaxation controls were not used, however.

While the combined results of these studies clearly undermines Wallace's characterization of TM as a unique hypometabolic state, it should be recognized that this fact does not in itself prove anything about the uniqueness of the ASC associated with TM (or other practices). Correctly understood, the results cited show, first, that the repeated practice of TM does not routinely enable the practitioner to enter a profoundly hypometabolic state and, second, that the relaxation elicited by TM is not unlike that produced by various relaxation techniques or hypnosis. Data relevant to the uniqueness of the EEG characteristics of TM and other meditations are discussed in the next section, and considerations pertinent to the ASC aspects of meditation are detailed in the remainder of the chapter.

In conclusion, the evidence strongly demonstrates that the practice of meditation tends to elicit a low-arousal psychophysiological state. Although the somatic and autonomic correlates of meditation appear to be satisfactorily accounted for in terms of nonspecific relaxation effects, it is possible that meditation may be unique in regard to the cognitive and attentional components of the low arousal state that occurs. Evidence on this point is unclear; there has been little attempt to delineate these components of meditation vis-à-vis correlated psychophysiological changes, despite the fact that these would *a priori* seem to be the more relevant dimensions of the meditative ASC. It should also be emphasized that although it is clear that low arousal is one of the primary behavioral dimensions of meditation, it does not logically follow that meditation can be *equated* with this psychophysiological state. It is not clear at this time which, if any, features of the meditative ASC are linked to the occurrence of which components of the low-arousal state, nor whether any of these is a sufficient condition for its occurrence.

6. EEG, AROUSAL, AND SLEEP

Whether decrements in arousal explain the EEG changes associated with meditation is not clear. As Plotkin has noted (1976), there are at least two dimensions of the variation in alpha with levels of consciousness. On the one hand, the *strength* (amplitude) of the synchronous alpha rhythm diminishes as a correlate of attentional processes and/or increased arousal in the transition to nonsynchronous, low-voltage, fast beta activity. (This desynchronization does not necessarily imply, however, that alpha activity has ceased at the neuronal level [Lindsley, 1952].) On the other hand, a shift in the *dominant frequency* of alpha characterizes the shift toward sleep, with alpha slowing into the theta band. While meditation has been described in terms of both an increase in alpha strength and a decrease in alpha frequency, Plotkin suggested that only the shift in frequency should be regarded as an index of (diminished) arousal. This is an interesting point in light of a recent suggestion that the change in alpha strength (amplitude) may be the more essential feature of meditation (Kamiya, 1975–1976).

A related question concerns the relationship between the EEG changes associated with meditation and the phenomena of sleep. Changes in arousal are generally held to be associated with the functions of the reticular activating system and the sleep–waking continuum (e.g.,

Lindsley, 1952). Covariations in EEG, EMG, and certain aspects of respiration activity occur along this dimension. For example, amplitudes of abdominal and thoracic respiratory movements covary with shifts in arousal and level of muscle tension as a subject falls asleep (Timmons, Salamy, Kamiya, & Girton, 1972), and there is a marked and sudden drop in frontalis EMG coincident with the alpha–theta transition (Budzynski, 1972; Sittenfeld, Budzynski, & Stoyva, 1976). Of additional interest in this context is the fact that certain psychological changes occur predictably as a consequence of low arousal with a variety of practices, for example, in autogenic training (Luthe, 1969) or when EMG levels fall to sufficiently low levels in the course of frontalis biofeedback training (Budzynski, Stoyva, & Adler, 1970). These changes—notably a decline in organized, secondary-process thinking and the appearance of progressively more free-associative, primary-process types of cognition—are similar to the hypnagogic period between sleep and waking.

The possibility that EEG and psychological phenomena associated with meditation might be accounted for in terms of sleep-onset phenomena in a low-arousal state was recently brought into particularly sharp focus by a report in *Science* by Pagano, Rose, Stivers, and Warrenburg (1976). These investigators reported that experienced practitioners of TM spend up to 40% of the meditation period in stages II, III, and IV sleep, with no significant difference between meditation and nap sessions. In agreement with these findings, Younger, Adriance, and Berger (1973, p. 99) reported that a group of eight TM subjects spent half of a typical meditation in waking alpha, slightly less asleep, and the remainder alert. Also along similar lines, Fenwick and colleagues recently reported that experienced judges could not evaluate any difference on a blind basis between meditation and drowsy EEGs. Raters evaluated EEG records for increased alpha amplitude, decreased alpha frequency, spread of alpha activity to frontal or temporal leads, frontal and temporal bursts, and concurrent alpha and theta activity; if slow, rolling eye movements were present, these changes were considered indicative of drowsiness, and if not, the changes were rated as meditation-related. On the basis of these criteria, judges failed to discriminate meditation-related EEG (Fenwick *et al.*, 1977).

Not all investigators have been in agreement on this point, however. Travis, Kondo, and Knott (1976) found EEG signs of sleep in 13 of 16 controls but in only 1 of 16 transcendental meditators. In a spectral analysis of the EEG during TM, Banquet (1973) recorded theta activity but found it to be dissimilar to the pattern observed during sleep. The theta pattern associated with TM, he argued, does not occur against a background of mixed frequencies, as is typical of drowsiness, and tends to consist of continuous runs of theta at a relatively constant frequency.

Perhaps part of the resolution of this mass of conflicting evidence has to do with variability in the experience of meditators. No one denies that sleep may occur during meditation; the subjects studied by Pagano *et al.* (1976) *reported* having slept during meditation. Another source of disagreement may have to do with the EEG criteria for sleep. Thus, for instance, diffuse theta has been considered the hallmark of drowsiness or sleep onset (Liberson & Liberson, 1966), but as Elson, Mauri, and Cunis (1977) have pointed out, the alpha–theta pattern of meditation is distinct from Stage I sleep onset in the fact that it is nondescending—stage II does not necessarily follow. This conclusion, based on findings in Ananda Marga Yoga meditation, like TM a mantra technique, is, however, at variance with the report of Pagano *et al.* (1976), who found substantial amounts of Stages II, III, and IV sleep in TM.

The transition from the waking state to the sleep state is marked by a diminished awareness of external reality, disorganization of normal waking consciousness into a free-associative mode, and the occurrence of spontaneous visual, auditory, and kinesthetic images that may have a hallucinatory or dreamlike quality. The psychophysiological correlates of this hypnagogic period include, first, the fragmentation of the alpha-dominant waking pattern, with intermittent alpha blocking occurring, together with the appearance of low-amplitude theta and low-voltage fast activity; changes in respiratory pattern; and low frontalis EMG (Schacter, 1976). The electroencephalographic response to sensory stimulation during this latter phase, in contrast to the alpha-blocking response during waking, is the appearance of alpha waves (the "alpha arousal reaction").

Kasamatsu and Hirai (1969) argued in their study of Zen meditators that the theta pattern of meditation could be distinguished from that occurring in the transition to sleep by two criteria. First, they reported that responses to sensory input during meditation theta consisted of desynchronization to a low-voltage fast pattern, resembling the alpha-blocking response of waking and not the alpha arousal reaction of drowsiness. Banquet (1973) described an apparently similar response during theta activity of TM. This observation suggests a possible method for empirically resolving the relationship between the meditation theta pattern and the hypnagogic theta pattern, and it should be replicated.

A second factor to be considered in comparing meditation with the hypnagogic state is the subjective experience of the subjects. Kasamatsu and Hirai (1969) and Banquet (1973) have commented on the subjective inequivalence of Zen meditation and TM, respectively, and drowsiness or sleep. One difficulty in sorting out these ideas is that it is not clear whether the occurrence of theta during meditation corresponds to fluctuations in psychological state along the sleep–wakefulness continuum or along some other psychological dimension. An empirical study of the mental experiences correlated with the occurrence of theta during meditation could be compared with similar data on subjective correlates of theta under other conditions (drowsiness, biofeedback, etc.) and might help to clarify the functional significance of its occurrence.

Some information is available relevant to this question. Hebert and Lehmann (1977) investigated the subjective experiences coincident with topographically diffuse theta bursts in four transcendental meditators selected for abundance of large-amplitude theta bursts; inasmuch as interruption of meditation was considered bad practice, however, this investigation was conducted during a period in which subjects were instructed *not* to meditate. Subjective state reports elicited during theta bursts included probable references to "peaceful, comfortable, and pleasant" experiences and "drifting or sliding" as well as "shifts of attention and reality-connected thoughts going on by themselves." Subjects reported being awake, with intact self-awareness and reality orientation, although they were not necessarily attending to the experimental situation. There were no consistent alterations in heart rate or phasic skin or muscle activity associated with the theta bursts, although bursts of eye movements sometimes occurred. In another report, episodes of theta in an adept meditator (Pelletier & Peper, 1976) corresponded to periods of reverie with rich imagery. And in yet another, albeit anecdotal, report, investigators at the Menninger Clinic quoted an Indian swami tested by them to the effect that theta is a "noisy" mental state produced by "stilling the conscious mind and bringing forward the unconscious" (Green, 1972). All of these findings appear to fit with descriptions of typical hypnagogic phenomena.

Subjects queried about their subjective experiences during meditation periods in which theta activity was prominent generally deny having been asleep (e.g., Kasamatsu & Hirai, 1969). The validity of subjective report in this regard is problematical, however. In sleep experiments, subjects showing definite EEG signs of drowsiness (occipital alpha blocking and central theta activity) will frequently deny drowsiness (Liberson & Liberson, 1966). Similarly, as Elson et al. (1977) have noted, sleep onset as assessed by unconsciousness to environmental stimuli generally occurs during the high alpha phase of Stage I sleep, and yet subjects will typically report being awake rather than asleep during this period. Clearly, there is a great deal of variability in the correspondence between the psychological phenomena of sleep onset and EEG correlates.

The most effective assessment of sleep onset is achieved with the combined measurement of EEG and eye movement (EOG) activity.

Foulkes and Vogel (1965) defined four distinct stages between waking and sleep in this way: a stage of alpha with rapid eye movements (REMs); a stage of alpha with slow rolling eye movements (SEMs); "descending Stage I," consisting of low-voltage, fast, random EEG with SEMs; and "descending Stage II," occasionally with SEMs. Hypnagogic phenomena occurred in all EEG–EOG stages of sleep onset. The associated psychological or mental activity has been characterized further by Vogel, Foulkes, and Trosman (1966) and by Liberson and Liberson (1966) in terms of the degree of reality content and of regressive (primary-process) content of each phase. Both of these ego functions were found to be usually intact in the presence of EEG alpha and absent in the later stages of drowsiness, although there is not a perfect correspondence. The duration of drowsiness, for example, accounts for some of the variance in subjective report.

It is obviously both appropriate and necessary to consider as many variables as possible in attempting to compare meditation and sleep, not merely EEG. A consideration of eye movement data as well as the relative amplitudes of abdominal and thoracic respiration (Goldie & Green, 1961) and phenomenological data would be helpful in clarifying the relationship between these states. While there is no quantitative study adequate to answer the question fully, some data are available in this regard. For instance, Hebert and Lehmann (1977) argued against a hypnagogic interpretation of meditation, citing the absence of SEMs as well as the lack of unresponsiveness to environmental stimuli, drowsiness, or other psychological phenomena of sleep onset during TM. Conflicting evidence was cited by Fenwick et al. (1977), however, who observed SEMs during TM as well as gross myoclonic jerks, which they interpreted as pathognomic of drowsiness. Tebecis (1976) also reported SEMs in a proportion of subjects experienced in TM, which were, however, not consistent between sessions. He interpreted the eye movements as similar to those seen during passive hypnosis.

Given the available evidence, there are several possible interpretations of the relationship between meditation (specifically TM) and the process of sleep onset. The first possibility, supported by Elson et al. (1977) and by Fenwich et al. (1977), is that meditation consists in practice in "freezing" the hypnagogic process, first in the predominantly alpha stage, later in the theta stage. That is, meditation may be a method of holding the level of consciousness at stage "onset" sleep. A second interpretation, a slight variation of the first, interprets the occurrence of theta during meditation in different terms (Hebert & Lehmann, 1977). According to this second hypothesis, the high-alpha phase of sleep onset is cultivated and prolonged by the practice of the TM technique, with theta bursts corresponding to transient fluctuations in level of arousal:

> Apparently the prolonged maintenance of the low arousal state which is compatible with meditation is not always successful, particularly when subjects are tired: subjects' reports as well as EEG studies have shown that sleep may occur during meditation. The theta bursts may represent a mechanism which adjusts the cerebral functional state compatible with meditation by widespread, brief neural activation. (p. 403)

This theory suggests, then, a functional interpretation of theta in terms of arousal homeostasis. This interpretation may have some bearing, also, on the occurrence of frontal theta of brief duration in normal (non-meditating) subjects (Lutzenberger, Birbaumer, & Steinmetz, 1976; Yamaguchi, 1977).

One possible interpretation of all of these data, similar to others that have been offered but somewhat different in emphasis, is that the occurrence of theta during meditation may represent a subjective point during meditation where the sleep process begins to intrude into meditation, experienced subjectively as the mind's drifting pleasantly or as a moment of reverie. In a recent review, Schacter (1976) emphasized that the hypnagogic state is defined by a particular pattern of psychophysiological changes occurring *in the context of the drowsy interval between sleep and waking* [italics added]. Perhaps in the context of a different cognitive set, meditation, the same events do not necessarily culminate in sleep and are subjectively interpreted as distinct from falling asleep. Some support for this conjecture may be found in the fact that EEG findings alone are insufficient criteria for defining the occurrence of sleep. According to Evans (1973, pp. 43–83), "there are no specific EEG criteria that define Stage I sleep; it is recognized as such only if subsequent records reveal Stages II or III sleep." Thus, EEG findings alone take on meaning only in a particular context that includes behavior.

From a psychological point of view, the hypnagogic state involves a loosening of cognitive controls, which allows the free-associative, primary-process, reverie sort of mentation to emerge. Drowsiness is only one way that such a destructuring of thought can come about. A variety of deliberate induction techniques are known that can facilitate these "altered-state" phenomena, including sensory deprivation, hypnosis, and autogenic training. A combination of features in meditation, including the passive–volitional set, the deep relaxation, and perhaps mild sensory deprivation aspects, may likewise facilitate the occurrence of hypnagogic phenomena.

Even if true, however, it does not follow that the occurrence in meditation of either hypnagogic phenomena, the theta EEG that presumably is their correlate, or for that matter outright sleep is necessarily the goal of meditation. Rather, the "goals" of meditation, as has been suggested above, have to do with the quality of awareness that is brought to whatever cognitive process goes on during meditation. Indeed, in many Eastern schools, disciples are warned not to get too drawn into hallucinatory phenomena; in Zen meditation, when the roshi perceives that the student has fallen asleep or into a trancelike state, the student is brought back to present-centered awareness with a sharp blow (or a light tap) across the back and shoulders.

7. Meditation and Attention

As suggested in the discussion earlier, meditation differs from other relaxation practices along the dimension of attention. Beyond the variety among different meditation practices, all meditations involve the selective deployment of attention. In fact, Davidson and Goleman (1977) *define* meditation as the self-regulation of attention.

As mentioned in an earlier section, two basic types of meditation that have been identified in the literature are *mindfulness* and *concentration*. Goleman (1977) summarized the differences between these methods as follows:

> In meditation, method is the seed of the goal: The contours of the state the meditator reaches depend on how he arrived. The concentrative path leads the meditator to merge with his meditation subject . . . and then to transcend it. As he reaches deeper levels, the bliss becomes more compelling, yet more subtle. In the way of mindfulness, the meditator's mind witnesses its own workings, and he comes to perceive increasingly finer segments of his stream of thought. As his perception sharpens, he becomes increasingly detached from what he witnesses, finally turning away from all awareness in the nirvanic state. In this state, there is no experience whatever. (p. 114)

Mindfulness and concentration meditations may also be distinguished in terms of the passive and active attentional strategies that typify them (Davidson & Goleman, 1977). As previously noted, mindfulness entails a passive witnessing of experience, whereas concentration involves a more active focusing of attention. These two meditational strategies have been related to alpha–theta and fast-wave EEG patterns, respectively (B. B. Brown, 1977; Brown, Fischer, Wagman, Horrom, & Marks, in press; Davidson & Goleman, 1977, Peper & Ancoli, 1977). Thus, Brown *et al.* suggested that the beta pattern in meditation connotes an active state in which there is considerable directed thought and attention, whereas slower frequencies are related to passive states of internal attention.

Case studies of individuals adept in various techniques of meditation and voluntary control of autonomic function provide some additional support for this interpretation of the EEG data. Pelletier and Peper (1976) reported on several such individuals in a recent paper. One subject, R. C. T., demonstrated his ability in the laboratory to push a sharpened bicycle spoke through one cheek and out the other in the presence of an occipital alpha density of 100%–time and an increase in alpha amplitude of 73% relative to eyes-closed baseline. Comparable psychophysiological findings occurred in J.S., while he pushed an unsterilized, sharpened knitting needle through his left bicep. Both of these individuals reported detaching their awareness from the insertion point. In contrast, J.S.L. accomplished a similar feat using a meditative process in which he intensified his focus on the sensation, and in this case, the investigators found an occipital EEG consisting mainly of beta activity with some low-amplitude alpha and some slowing in frontal leads.

As indicated in the quote from Goleman (1977) above, mindfulness and concentration practices are regarded as resulting in different experiences of altered states. In addition to differences in ongoing EEG, alleged objective correlates of this difference in state have also been identified in terms of the alpha-blocking response. Depending on the type of meditation, it has been reported either that alpha blocking fails to occur (TM: Banquet, 1973; Yoga: Anand et al., 1961) or that it occurs to a repeated series of stimuli without the expected habituation (Zen: Kasamatsu & Hirai, 1969; TM: Wallace, 1970). These data have been widely interpreted as reflecting decreased reactivity to the external environment during concentration, on the one hand, and the maintenance of an unusual degree of alertness during mindfulness practices, on the other.

There are, however, substantial difficulties with this interpretation. In the first place, as J. M. Davidson (1976) has pointed out in his excellent review, the characterization of these phenomena has been based on a very few subjects and has been very sketchily reported. By and large, these have been incidental rather than systematic observations: stimulus parameters and procedures have not been reported, criteria for alpha blocking have not been described, and the number of subjects has been quite small (three in the Kasamatsu & Hirai study and four in the Anand et al. study). Moreover, the results even as described are quite variable: the two reports on TM are inconsistent, for example.

Important methodological considerations appear to have been overlooked in these studies.[1] One important factor is the ongoing EEG (and

---

[1]A number of substantive comments were contributed to this discussion by David Becker.

experiential state) at the time of stimulus onset. For example, in Banquet's (1973) study of TM, a stimulus during alpha resulted in no alpha blocking; a stimulus during theta produced a brief desynchronization; and a stimulus during beta produced no change. Another point concerns the evaluation of the alpha-blocking response when the eyes are open, as in Zen meditation. For example, the figures in Hirai's monograph on Zen (1974) show what appear to be prominent eye-movement artifacts in response to clicks, and it may be that these are related to the persistence of the alpha-blocking response during this eyes-open practice; control subjects were tested with eyes closed. (Anand *et al.*, 1961, found blinking responses to external stimuli in the absence of any blocking of the alpha-blocking rhythm, however, although these subjects kept their eyes closed.)

Even assuming the basic effects to be replicable, it does not follow that changes in the alpha-blocking response are necessarily due to the meditative ASC achieved through mindfulness and concentration practices. Differences in cognitive set during meditation might account for differences in alpha blocking apart from the induction of an ASC. Mulholland and Runnals (1962) have shown, for instance, that different attentional sets may determine whether alpha blocking or alpha facilitation occurs even in the normal waking state. Transitory alerting to an external stimulus tends to produce alpha suppression, whereas a set for continuous or sustained attention to a stimulus tends to be associated with an absence of alpha blocking or alpha facilitation. Voluntary attention to a stimulus, and whether it has signal value, may also mean the difference between the habituation and the nonhabituation of an orienting response (e.g., Luria & Homskaya, 1970, pp. 301–330). Thus, alpha blocking and habituation might conceivably vary as a function of attentional variables quite apart from the effects of the meditation process, the meditative ASC, or even the attentional skills acquired through meditation. A number of different control procedures would be needed in order to distinguish among these possibilities.

Davidson and Goleman, in a recent review (1977), have summarized the evidence relating to psychophysiological differences between mindfulness and concentration practices. They concluded that both meditation strategies are associated with autonomic quiescence but that concentration enhances cortical specificity to a greater degree than passive meditations. In a study by Schwartz, Davidson, and Margolin (cited in Davidson and Goleman's 1977 review), EEG changes were related to two different forms of meditation, TM (a passive meditation) and a Gurdjieffian meditation, in which attention is actively focused on a series of somatic and proprioceptive stimuli. It was predicted that the skills acquired in the Gurdjieffian practice would show up in terms of a relatively greater activation in the appropriate cortical areas when the subjects were asked to attend to visual and kinesthetic stimuli. Cortical activity was assessed as the ratio of activation in occipital and sensorimotor-region EEG. As predicted, differential activation was greater in the Gurdjieffian group. These results show that different meditation practices cultivate different attentional skills. As predicted, it was also found that active attention (the Gurdjieffian exercises) produced greater EEG activation at both sites than did passive attention (TM). The success of this paradigm in discriminating *trait* effects of meditation suggests possible applications in the study of meditation itself. For example, a single meditator might be asked to meditate on some target actively and passively in turn, so that the contribution of the attentional strategy can be evaluated.

Thus, the available evidence supports the notion of *specificity* in cortical activation and suggests that EEG correlates in meditation may, in fact, be explicable in terms of specific cognitive behaviors, that is, in terms of the *content* rather than the *context* of meditation. Specific predictions follow from the nature of the behaviors involved in different meditation practices. For example, mantra meditation involves a repeating verbal loop that presumably should differentially involve the left hemisphere. Zen koan meditation, as opposed to Zazen, involves an active thinking process and should therefore result in an EEG more similar to the waking state. And so on. There may, however, be limitations inherent in this approach. As Adey (1969, pp. 194–229) commented in another context, the evaluation of EEG even by simple automated techniques may be inadequate for elucidating correlates of processes such as focused attention, in that mental processes are so rapid and changing that our windows on these processes must be equivalently refined and effective with epochs of only a second or so in duration.

It is surprising to find no experimental work on the effects of meditation on evoked potentials or contingent negative variation (save a brief note by Legrand, Toubol, Barrabino, Darcourt, and Fadeuilhe, 1977 remarking changes in amplitude, particularly late components.) Changes in reactivity to stimulation would seem to hold promise as a potential means of characterizing the meditative ASC, above and beyond changes in baseline psychophysiology. The evoked-potential method would be useful, for instance, as a direct test of the notion that concentration meditation results in an attenuation of afferent input below the cortical level (cf. Davidson & Goleman, 1977). Amplitudes of evoked potentials are known to vary with degree of attention (Tecce, 1970), so this parameter seems likely to be sensitive to meditation. Another general prediction is that there should be less associative "noise" in response to input during meditation. That is to say, if the mind is calm, it is theoretically less reactive to stimulation, and this effect might be characterized by changes in amplitude, latencies, or especially distribution of the evoked response in different cortical areas.

There have been surprisingly few direct or systematic studies of the attentional phenomena of meditation. One exception is the study of Van Nuys (1971), who reported a very simple technique applicable to the assessment of attention in meditation; the subject simply presses a telegraph key or other manipulandum every time he notices that his attention has wandered from its intended focus ("intrusions"). Kubose (1976) applied this method to an experimental investigation of Zen breath-counting meditation. Meditators showed decreased thought intrusions over 15 experimental 15-minute sessions, indicating a learning or practice effect of the meditation. There were also more intrusions within a session as the session progressed.

One of the problems in characterizing the nature of attention in meditation is that attention is not a unitary phenomenon. Pribram and McGuinness (1975) delineated three neurally distinct systems that are involved in attention: a system for visceroautonomic *arousal*, a system for somatomotor *activation*, and a system that organizes the relationship between the two. This latter mechanism, termed *effort*, is conceived of as an attentional mechanism that organizes information processing and thereby operates on the constraints that ordinarily maintain a "tight join" between arousal and activation. It is viewed as the substrate of changes in central representations of the sort called *state, set,* or *attitude.* Meditation may be associated with changes in arousal and activation, as has already been discussed, but it is a change in "effort" that seems more important to an understanding of the meditative ASC. In Pribram's words, here is a mechanism whose function it is to "*operate on the context in which . . . informational content is processed*" (italics added).

Another aspect of this theory that is relevant to meditation concerns the role of the frontal cortex, where, it will be recalled, the most prominent EEG changes are seen in meditation. Pribram and McGuinness theorized that the frontal system acts to increase internal redundancy in input channels, so that the information being processed becomes chunked into one unit (the opposite of discrimination); phenomenological descriptions suggest that just such a process takes place during meditation (Deikman, 1966, pp. 317–326). A role of the frontal system in the regulation of arousal is also described, underlying sustained attention to goal-directed behaviors (Luria & Homskaya, 1970); the activity of this system might presumably be inhibited by attention "here and now."

In summary, attention appears to be a major psychological process involved in meditation. Attentional skills are enhanced through the practice of meditation and are associated with enhanced specificity in cortical activity (cf. Davidson & Goleman, 1977). In order to further elucidate the attentional phenomena of meditation, however, there are a number of component processes that must be taken into account, including what Pribram and McGuinness (1975) termed *arousal, activation,* and *effort*.

Self-regulation of attention in meditation takes place in a particular context of psychophysiological arousal and cognitive set. In order to determine whether the specific features of this process are unique to meditation, it would be important to contrast attention in meditation with attention–vigilance in other contexts. One-pointed attention may itself engender changes in cognitive functions usually ascribed to the meditative ASC. Indeed, vigilance is one of the conditions frequently associated with the spontaneous occurrence of ASCs—for example, a pilot flying his plane or a drummer playing his drums (Ludwig, 1966).

8. Meditation and Trance

States of highly focused attention in meditation bear enough resemblance to trance states to warrant some discussion of the similarities and differences between meditation and trance. Indeed, several contributors to the scientific literature on these topics have taken the position that meditation and trance are in some respects similar or even identical phenomena (Das, 1963; Aaronson, 1973).

Trance has been defined as any state in which there is a functional nonawareness of the "structured frame of reference in the background of attention which supports, interprets, and gives meaning to experience" (Shor, 1959). (Hypnotic trance is a special type of trance state in which, through interaction with a hypnotist, there is formed a special, temporary orientation to a small range of preoccupations). Various states of mystical consciousness achieved through complete absorption in meditation seem clearly to qualify as trance states, at least according to this definition. Thus, the devotee becomes totally lost in his inner experience—motionless, eyes transfixed, apparently out of touch with external reality. This is described as a state of mind in which thinking stops and consciousness both of the world and of the body disappears:

> When the state of one-pointed, quiet and yet attenuated awareness of "I-ness" becomes so deep, or the absorption of "I-ness" in the meaning of an idea, in a God-concept, in a syllable (like the sacred syllable Aum), in some body zone (like the middle of the eyebrow), in a color, form, sound (and) or experience in the internal representation thereof becomes so drastically complete that irrelevant and fluctuant specificities of perception or thinking disappear, only the identified "I-ness" with the object of thought remains, and

stimuli from the somatic system or external world do not reach the consciousness of the meditator for a long or a short time. (Bagchi & Wenger,
1957, p. 134)

In the final stage, the mystical consciousness itself presumably disappears as well. It is said that in such states of high samadhi, bodily
functions including breathing, heartbeat, and metabolism cease, or
nearly so, and that one cannot survive longer than seven days in this
state. Interestingly, the philosopher Stace commented on the occurrence
of "abnormal bodily states" of "rapture or trance" in mystics but considered these "accidental accompaniments" of mystical consciousness
(Floor, 1976).

Trancelike states are produced by various religious practices that
involve rhythmic or repetitive elements such as chanting, drumming,
and dance (e.g., Bourgignon, 1972, pp. 331–334). For instance, a trancelike ASC produced among the dervishes by whirling is described by
Burke (1973), who experienced a state of heightened perception and loss
of all sense of time. Indeed, the rhythmic element in these practices suggests the possibility that they may in some way entrain the activity of
the CNS in a manner analogous to that of photic driving (cf. Rogers,
1976).

Attention appears to be a conceptual bridge between trance
phenomena and meditation. According to Goleman (1972, 1977), the
capacity for one-pointed attention is the gateway of access to mystical
states of consciousness. Similarly—according to some writers, at
least—a key feature in trance appears to be a narrowing of the scope of
attention, though not necessarily one-pointed (Krippner, 1974).

If hypnosis and meditation involve in any sense similar psychological processes, one might expect to find similar psychophysiological correlates. To the contrary, however, no empirical criteria for determining
when (or if) a trance exists have ever been established. In the case of
hypnosis, the most widely studied example of trance, there does not
appear to be any unique set of psychophysiological correlates that comprise a "scientific basis" for trance (as claimed for meditation). Rather,
the psychophysiology has been found to vary with the content of the
experience evoked during trance. The lack of EEG findings in hypnosis
comparable to those in meditation therefore suggests that the two states
are not entirely equivalent.

A further difference between hypnotic trance and meditation is
suggested by the following comparison. In hypnosis, there is often a
dissociation between experience and physiology; for example, a subject
may fail to experience a painful stimulus as painful and yet may react
physiologically in a manner appropriate to pain (increased heart rate,
etc.) (Hilgard, 1976). That is, information is processed but is unavailable

to consciousness. In concentrative meditation, on the other hand, the evidence tends to suggest an inhibition of information processing itself, for example, the absence of alpha blocking or autonomic response to pain (Pelletier & Peper, 1976). Davidson and Goleman (1977) have elaborated a signal detection model of this difference, regarding meditation as affecting stimulus set (d') and hypnosis as affecting the criterion for reporting pain (β).

Another important link between hypnosis and meditation (at least, TM) is the low-arousal state produced. Thus, as Paul (1969) pointed out, a typical hypnotic induction procedure is similar to relaxation training and tends to be associated with physiological measures of reduced arousal, such as decreased heart rate, muscle tension, and skin conductance in response to suggestions of being sleepy, drowsy, and relaxed; Edelman (1970), in fact, has hypothesized that neutral hypnosis and relaxation are the same phenomenon.

Hypnosis and TM have, additionally, been compared with regard to long-term effects of practice (termed "altered *traits* of consciousness" by Schwartz, 1974). Tebecis (1975) reported that in comparison with a group of nonmeditators, TM subjects exhibited significantly more theta EEG during *both* TM *and* nonmeditation control periods. A similar effect was found in a group of subjects who practiced self-hypnosis (Tebecis *et al.*, 1975). The authors interpreted these data to mean that frequent experience with self-hypnosis or TM facilitates entry into a zone of consciousness (a low-arousal state) in which hypnagogic phenomena emerge. They regarded this trait effect as evidence of a shift in equilibrium toward lower arousal produced by these practices, which accords well with the popular literature on TM (Campbell, 1974).

Tebecis *et al.* (1975) further believe that the similarity in long-term EEG effects of hypnosis and TM practitioners justifies the conclusion that both TM and self-hypnosis should be regarded as trance states. In support, they remark on the subjective reports of experienced meditators hypnotized in their laboratory to the effect that passive hypnosis and TM are similar; self-hypnosis subjects beginning to meditate reported the same thing. Along the same lines, Greenfield (1977) reported a significant correlation between hypnotizability and intensity of meditation experience. These data concur with the theoretical formulation that ASCs are a family of trance states that occur under conditions in which attention is shifted away from the *external* to an *internal* frame of reference, regardless of what specific technique is involved (Aaronson, 1973).

For the majority of meditators, it seems probable that the "altered state" experienced in meditation is a trancelike state accounted for in terms of low arousal and a shift to an internal frame of reference. In a recent study by Hunt and Chefurka (1976), it was shown that simple instructions to attend to one's subjective state coupled with "sensory deprivation" as mild as 10 minutes of isolation in a darkened room resulted in reports of altered-states phenomena such as cognitive disorganization, perceptual anomalies, and feelings of strangeness and unreality. The trancelike state produced during meditation, then, constitutes one set of conditions under which ASC phenomena might be expected to occur.

9. MEDITATION AND BRAIN-WAVE BIOFEEDBACK

Following the documentation of brain wave changes during meditation, the question naturally arose whether the meditative ASC could be induced through the expedient of brain wave control. It had been shown by Kamiya (1969, pp. 507–518) that subjects could learn to discriminate whether they were in brain wave "state" A or B (alpha or beta), and with the advent of brain-wave biofeedback techniques, it became possible for subjects to learn to produce alpha brain waves at will. The subjective reports of these subjects suggested that the so-called alpha state was indeed an ASC akin to that achieved through meditation, and brain wave biofeedback was soon hailed as nothing less than a revolutionary advance, the "Yoga of the West." Maslow (1969), for example, stated:

> What is seminal and exciting about this research is that Kamiya discovered quite fortuitously that bringing the alpha waves to a particular level could produce in the subject a state of serenity, meditativeness, and even happiness. Some follow-up studies with people who have learned the Eastern techniques of contemplation and meditation show that they spontaneously emit EEGs that are like the "serene" ones to which Kamiya was able to educate his subjects. That is to say, that it is already possible to teach people how to feel happy and serene. The revolutionary consequences not only for human betterment, but also for biological and psychological theory, are multitudinous and obvious. There are enough research projects here to keep squadrons of scientists busy for the next century. The mind–body problem, until now considered insoluble, does appear to be workable after all. (p. 725)

The general scope of these conclusions was affirmed in many popular articles and experimental studies (e.g., B. B. Brown, 1970, 1971; Nowlis & Kamiya, 1970) and became widely accepted, with, however, little critical consideration of the data on which the conclusions were based. Many of the relevant issues in regard to the alpha state have been raised in other articles in recent years (e.g., Lynch & Paskewitz, 1971; Plotkin, 1976; Plotkin & Cohen, 1976; Plotkin, Mazer, & Loewy, 1976; Travis et al., 1975; Walsh, 1974), and the details are beyond the scope of the present paper. To recapitulate briefly, the conclusions to be drawn from these various studies is that the alpha experience is not linearly related to alpha strength in the EEG but is determined by the interaction of several factors including (a) the subject's expectations; (b) the instructions given; and (c) the demand characteristics of the situation. Controlled investigations have not only failed to confirm the relationship between the alpha experience and brain wave activity but have also cast doubt on whether authentic conditioning occurs in the brain-wave biofeedback paradigm. Indeed, it has not been reliably established that brain wave feedback is associated with an increase in alpha activity.

Among the variables that can influence or potentiate biofeedback effects and that pertain especially to the ASCs under consideration here, sensory deprivation deserves particular mention. As previously mentioned, a study by Hunt and Chefurka (1976) recently demonstrated that mild sensory deprivation coupled with instructions that sensitize subjects to their subjective state produce ASC phenomena. This sort of sensitization is clearly present in the biofeedback situation and relates back to the formulation presented above that altered states occur under conditions that involve a shift from the external to the internal frame of reference (Aaronson, 1973).

One implication concerning the relationship between the "alpha state" and the meditative ASC is that biofeedback as a practice may not be essentially different from meditation. Like meditation, biofeedback involves a focusing of attention on internal (subjective) events. One might also argue that in the biofeedback paradigm, the biofeedback signal is tantamount to a meditation object—the ideal meditation object, in the sense that it provides built-in information as to the success of the meditation. Like meditation, the practice of biofeedback involves concentration and the sustained monitoring of attention. Thus, the similarity between the alpha state and the meditative ASC may derive from the behavioral similarities between biofeedback and meditation rather than the common denominator of enhanced alpha waves.

There are several possible functions served by the feedback signal vis-à-vis the biofeedback paradigm as meditation. First, as Stoyva and Kamiya (1968) pointed out, the feedback provides an explicit cue that the "correct" internal process has been found; if a measurable physiological event is associated with a discriminable mental event, they argued, then the mental event will be reinforced in the presence of the physiological event; and as a result, the subject will be able both to discriminate better whether the physiological event and the associated mental event are present and perhaps to control the occurrence of these events. Second, feedback assists in generating the low-arousal state that is prerequisite to the psychological phenomena of meditation. Yet a third function, according to Shapiro's (1977) analysis, relates to the point that "the ability to generate a given psychophysiological state and to maintain it over a course of time appears to facilitate the process of identifying and labelling certain aspects of conscious experience" and to "fix" that state of consciousness in experience, in this case the meditative ASC. It would be interesting to see an experimental investigation of the interactions between biofeedback and meditation, with regard, for instance, to whether biofeedback facilitates or impedes training in meditation and the relative effectiveness of the combined procedures.

10. THE PSYCHOPHYSIOLOGICAL PRINCIPLE

It seems clear from the foregoing that the presence of alpha in the EEG is not a sufficient condition for the occurrence of either the alpha experience (alpha "state") or the meditative ASC. This fact raises anew the question of what defines an ASC in the first place. The ASCs associated with meditation and biofeedback have, in a sense, been legitimized in terms of the brain states presumed to underlie them; measurable physiological correlates have imparted a degree of reality and scientific status to these states that hypnosis, for example, has yet to earn, despite the fact that it is subjectively just as real.

Closer examination of this model suggests that there are two assumptions involved here: (a) that an ASC is (or is associated with) a discrete brain state and (b) that a discrete brain state is identifiable in the EEG. Brain wave feedback, for example, stems directly from this model. It is based on the proposition that a particular set of experiences (the meditative ASC) implies a particular brain state, and its converse, that reproducing the brain state suffices to reproduce the experience. From this proposition comes the hope that biofeedback technology "will eventually become an effective, reliable, and objective method for monitoring and eventually altering private events . . . through the alteration of their objective correlates (Wickramasekara, 1976).

The above propositions reduce to what Elmer Green has termed "the psychophysiological principle," which states that "every change in the physiological state is accompanied by an appropriate change in the mental–emotional state, conscious or unconscious, and conversely, every change in the mental–emotional state, conscious or unconscious, is accompanied by an appropriate change in the physiological state" (Green, Green, & Walters, 1970). Implicit in this statement, and its application in biofeedback, is the belief that brain states *cause* mental experiences; the assumption appears to be that physiological correlates are the *real* or underlying basis of psychological phenomena and consequently that to produce the physiology is to cause the mental event. Even if there were a close correspondence between changes in heart action, for example, and reports of fear or anger, we would no doubt be quite reluctant to conclude that heart changes produce anger, or that anger was located in the heart. Only our *a priori* belief that brain states cause mental states allows us to give special weight to neurophysiological correlates (Grossberg, 1972).

Thus, while it may be true that a particular experience is associated with certain EEG correlates, correlation does not imply causation, and it does not necessarily follow that duplicating the same EEG pattern will always be associated with the same experience. (See Rechtschaffen 1975, pp. 135–191) for an excellent discussion of the correlation–causation issue.) While in principle there may be isomorphism between brain state and experience, it is limited by the degree to which our techniques of measurement adequately assess and describe the state of the brain. Further, events in the brain are not in theory separable from events in other physiological systems, so that ultimately all bodily activities are relevant to a description of a state of consciousness. One might also extend this argument beyond the physiology of the individual to include events in the environment and, ultimately, all events (Deikman, 1973). As Grossberg (1972) pointed out, a complete accounting of experience requires full consideration of situational and historical components rather than a narrow focus on biological events.

The underlying issue here is none other than the old mind–body problem, recurring now in the biofeedback context. For as Green (1972) has pointed out, "in actuality there is no such thing as training in brain-wave control; there is training only in the elicitation of certain subjective states that are accompanied by oscillating voltages in the cerebral cortex." Since brain waves have no known sensory representation by means of which they could possibly be detected, no direct control of brain waves is even theoretically possible. What *are* detected are attentional processes, thoughts, and feelings; physiological self-regulation is merely a by-product of the regulation of psychological events.

The use of a biofeedback strategy as a test of the psychophysiological model thus entails a rather interesting circularity; for if there *is* an isomorphism between subjective state and physiological state as the psychophysiological model supposes, and if what we are really doing in biofeedback is conditioning the occurrence of a subjective state, then by definition the only subjective state that will suffice to produce the desired physiological state is the meditative state! In other words, only the meditative state will suffice to produce the meditative state!

11. Meditation and the Psychophysiological Model

We return then to the issue of the significance of the psychophysiological correlates of ASCs.

On the one hand, the literature abounds with the suggestion that psychophysiological states underlie altered states of consciousness and are their objective correlates. The clear implication here is that psychophysiological events are not merely correlated with altered states but are in some way necessary to their occurrence; that is, that psychophysiological events (increased alpha, altered respiratory pattern, decreased skin conductance, etc.) are integrally rather than incidentally (or even artifactually) related to these states of consciousness. The strongest statement of this psychophysiological model of ASCs would be the hypothesis that certain psychophysiological events (or a pattern of such events) are *both necessary and sufficient* for the occurrence of a particular ASC. The empirical evidence reviewed above thus needs to be reconsidered in terms of the "necessary" and "sufficient" criteria.

Although there is some consistency in the reports of psychophysiological changes during meditation, the data are clearly not sufficiently robust to warrant the conclusion that any particular pattern of psychophysiology is invariably associated with the meditative ASC. Thus, there is considerable psychophysiological variation between individuals practicing the same meditation technique and within the same individual at different times. Very likely, much of this variation reflects variabilities in experience. Lacking an adequately defined phenomenology of meditation experience, we are obviously in a poor position to spell out either experiential or psychophysiological criteria for the occurrence of the "meditative ASC."

Meditation is most often associated with one or more signs of reduced autonomic, somatic, and/or cortical arousal. The evidence suggests that this low-arousal state is not substantially different from that produced by other practices (progressive relaxation, etc.). This relaxation state has trancelike features, and in all probability, this state is the main component of the experience of many meditators.

While the evidence suggests that a low-arousal state is conducive to the experience of passive awareness, the meditative ASC does not *invariably* emerge, given a background of low arousal and relaxation. Very likely, there may be important determinants of the meditation experience that are cognitive rather than specifically physiological (J. M. Davidson, 1976), including the intention and set brought to meditation. Thus, it would appear that psychophysiological variables are one class of variables associated with the meditative ASC but are not sufficient for its occurrence.

Psychophysiological processes appear to be involved in facilitating the emergence of certain psychological phenomena and/or making them accessible to being identified and labeled within awareness (Shapiro, 1977). This process may perhaps be illustrated by analogy with drug-induced ASCs. As is well-known, the marijuana experience has a learning component to it in the sense that the user must learn to discriminate the drug's effects and to label and identify the various elements of the psychoactive experience (e.g., Becker, 1967). Analogously, meditation involves a process of learning to experience in a new way, and this learning is facilitated when the body is relaxed and the mind is quiet. The possibility is left open, however, that with practice, the meditative ASC may also be experienced against a background of other psychophysiological states. There are few data that bear upon this essentially empirical question. One strategy that might be employed, for instance, would be to investigate whether the meditative ASC, *once trained* with TM or other practice, could be maintained in other psychophysiological states. On the whole, the evidence does not strongly support the conclusion that a state of low arousal is necessary for the occurrence of the meditative ASC, since it can occur during active meditations and religious practices (or spontaneously). Rather than *identifying* consciousness with the psychophysiological process, an alternative formulation might be in terms of what psychophysiological states are *compatible* with what modes of experience.

Among the specific correlates of meditation that have been discussed, one group—alpha–theta EEG and reduced autonomic/somatic arousal—appears to be related to a nonspecific relaxation response. Other findings, specifically the high-amplitude fast-wave EEG and occurrence of marked EEG coherence, appear to have some relationship to specific phenomenological features of meditation. These EEG findings are more typical of advanced meditators and concentrative meditation practices, and both have been interpreted as correlates of "samadhi" or transcendental consciousness (Das & Gastaut, 1955; Banquet, 1973; Orme-Johnson, 1977). As emphasized by Pribram and McGuinness (1975), focus of attention ("effort") acts to organize neural processes into coherently interacting patterns, which may explain the high energy in the beta band; it is not entirely clear that this phenomenon should occur only in meditation, however. Enhanced coherence, if replicable, may be a key finding. According to Orme-Johnson (1977), it represents a "low-noise" state in the brain; that is to say, it reflects that the mind–brain system has become quiet, which in turn allows the meditative ASC to emerge. Following Deikman's discussion (1973), consciousness (awareness) is "known" or appreciated through systems of organization, such as thought, which permit "knowledge of awareness"; when the mind–

brain system becomes quiet, consciousness is not bound by thought, and cosmic consciousness can occur.

States of consciousness have been viewed as stable patterns of activity among various functional subsystems that underlie perception, cognition, and behavior (Tart, 1975). In this theoretical framework, meditation can be viewed as a methodology for destabilizing the structures of normal waking consciousness, thus allowing altered patterns of activity to emerge. According to this "systems approach" to consciousness, "states" can be fully described in terms of specific patterns of cognitive activity, physiological activity, and associated dispositions to process input and to respond in particular ways ("content"); the "state" (context) is simply the total configuration of activity among subsystems at a particular time. Thus, it may be that "context" is most closely equivalent to the configuration of the mind–brain system as a whole and is ultimately specifiable only by specifying the activity of every element.

On the other hand, it is conceivable that there may be specific neural correlates of the meditative ASC. To speculate on a couple of possibilities, there might be a feedback network within the attention mechanism which resonates or "rings" in a distinct manner when the system is tracking perfectly in present time. Alternatively, there might be a neurochemical change with meditation that supplies a particular feeling-tone to experience above and beyond any altered pattern of cognition.

A thorough description of meditation on the psychophysiological level will, in all probability, ultimately depend on careful phenomenological analysis of the meditation experience—specifying the variations of physiological indices most likely to occur at different levels of practice (D. P. Brown, 1977). In the meantime, we are led, full circle, back to the conclusion of Johnson (1970) that "EEG and autonomic data cannot be used to define states of consciousness; the state of consciousness of the subject must first be known before the physiological significance and possible behavioral meaning [of these measures] can be inferred."

Acknowledgments

Thanks to the editors and to David Shapiro, John Reeves, and Mark Fleischer for valuable editorial comments and suggestions.

REFERENCES

AARONSON, B. S. ASCID trance, hypnotic trance, just trance. *American Journal of Clinical Hypnosis*, 1973, *16*(2), 110–117.

ADEY, W. R. Spectral analysis of EEG data from animals and man during alerting, orienting, and discriminative responses. In C. R. Evans & T. B. Mulholland (Eds.), *Attention in neurophysiology*. New York: Appleton-Century-Crofts, 1969.

ANAND, B. K., CHHINA, G. S., & SINGH, B. Some aspects of electroencephalographic studies in yogis. *Electroencephalography and Clinical Neurophysiology*, 1961, *13*, 452–456.

BAGCHI, B. K., & WENGER, M. A. Electrophysiological correlates of some yogi exercises. *Electroencephalography and Clinical Neurophysiology*, 1957, *7*, 132–149.

BANQUET, J. P. Spectral analysis of the EEG in meditation. *Electroencephalography and Clinical Neurophysiology*, 1973, *35*, 143–151.

BEATTY, J., GREENBERG, A., DIEBLER, W., & O'HANLON, J. Operant control of occipital theta rhythm affects performance in a radar monitoring task. *Science*, 1974, *183*, 871–873.

BEATTY, J., & KORNFELD, C. Relative independence of conditioned EEG changes from cardiac and respiratory activity. *Physiology and Behavior*, 1972, *9*, 733–736.

BECKER, H. S. History, culture, and subjective experience: An exploration of the social bases of drug-induced experiences. *Journal of Health and Social Behavior*, 1967, *8*(3), 163–176.

BENSON, H., BEARY, J. F., & CAROL, M. P. The relaxation response. *Psychiatry*, 1974, *37*(1), 37–46.

BOURGIGNON, E. Trance dance. In J. White (Ed.), *The highest state of consciousness*. New York: Doubleday/Anchor, 1972.

BROWN, B. B. Recognition of aspects of consciousness through association with EEG alpha activity represented by a light-signal. *Psychophysiology*, 1970, *6*, 442–452.

BROWN, B. B. Awareness of EEG—subjective activity relationships detected within a closed feedback system. *Psychophysiology*, 1971, *7*, 451–464.

BROWN, B. B. *Stress and the art of biofeedback*. New York: Bantam, 1977.

BROWN, C. C., FISCHER, R., WAGMAN, A. M. I., HORROM, N., & MARKS, P. The EEG in meditation and therapeutic touch healing. *Journal of Altered States of Consciousness*, in press.

BROWN, D. P. Levels of concentrative meditation. *International Journal of Clinical and Experimental Hypnosis*, 1977, *25*(4), 236–273.

BUDZYNSKI, T. H., STOYVA, J. M., & ADLER, C. S. Feedback-induced muscle relaxation: Application to tension headache. *Behavior Therapy and Experimental Psychiatry*, 1970, *1*, 205–211.

BUDZYNSKI, T. H. Some applications of biofeedback induced twilight states. *Fields within Fields within Fields*, 1972, *5*, 105–114.

BURKE, O. M. *Among the dervishes*. London: Octagon Press, 1973.

CAMPBELL, A. *Seven states of consciousness*. New York: Perennial Library, Harper & Row, 1974.

CURTIS, W. D., & WESSBERG, H. W. A comparison of heart rate, respiration, and galvanic skin response among meditators, relaxers, and controls. *Journal of Altered States of Consciousness*, 1976, *2*(4), 319–324.

DAS, J. P. Yoga and hypnosis. *International Journal of Clinical and Experimental Hypnosis*, 1963, *11*(1), 31–37.

DAS, N. N., & GASTAUT, H. Variations de l'activité électrique du cerveau, du coeur, et des muscles squelettiques au cours de la méditation et de l'extase yogique. *Electroencephalography and Clinical Neurophysiology*, 1955, Suppl. 6, 211–219.

DAVIDSON, J. M. The physiology of meditation and mystical states of consciousness. *Perspectives in Biology and Medicine*, 1976, *19*, 345–379.

DAVIDSON, R. J. Specificity and patterning in biobehavioral systems: Implications for behavior change. *American Psychologist*, 1978, *35*, 430–435.

DAVIDSON, R. J., & GOLEMAN, D. J. The role of attention in meditation and hypnosis: A psychobiological perspective on transformations of consciousness. *International Journal of Clinical and Experimental Hypnosis,* 1977, *25*(4), 291–308.

DAVIDSON, R. J., & SCHWARTZ, G. E. The psychobiology of relaxation and related states: A multi-process theory. In D. Mostofsky (Ed.), *Behavior control and modification of physiological activity.* Englewood Cliffs, N.J.: Prentice-Hall, 1976.

DAVIS, H., DAVIS, P. A., LOOMIS, A. L., HARVEY, E. N., & HOBART, G. Human brain potentials during the onset of sleep. *Journal of Neurophysiology,* 1937, *1*, 24–37.

DAVIS, K. L., HOLLISTER, L. E., OVERALL, J., JOHNSON, A. and TRAIN, K. Physostigmine: Effects on cognition and affect in normal subjects. *Psychopharmacology,* 1976, *51*, 23–27.

DEGOOD, D. E., & CHISHOLM, R. C. Multiple response comparison of parietal EEG and frontalis EMG biofeedback. *Psychophysiology,* 1977, *14*(3), 258–265.

DEIKMAN, A. Deautomatization and the mystical experience. *Psychiatry,* 1966, *29*, 324–338.

DEIKMAN, A. The meaning of everything. In R. Ornstein (Ed.), *The nature of human consciousness.* San Francisco: Freeman, 1973.

DEWAN, E. M. Occipital alpha rhythm, eye position, and lens accommodation. *Nature,* 1967, *241*, 975–977.

EDELMAN, R. I. Effects of progressive relaxation on autonomic processes. *Journal of Clinical Psychology,* 1970, *26*, 421–425.

ELSON, B. D., HAURI, P., & CUNIS, D. Physiological changes in yoga meditation. *Psychophysiology,* 1977, *14*(1), 52–57.

EVANS, F. J. Hypnosis and sleep: Techniques for exploring cognitive activity during sleep. In E. Fromm & R. E. Shor (Eds.), *Hypnosis: Research developments and perspectives.* London: Paul Elek (Scientific Books), 1973.

FENWICK, P. B. C., DONALDSON, S., GILLIS, L., BUSHMAN, J., FENTON, G. W., PERRY, I., TILSLEY, C., & SERAFINOWICZ, H. Metabolic and EEG changes during transcendental meditation: An explanation. *Biological Psychology,* 1977, *5*(2), 101–118.

FISCHER, R. A cartography of the ecstatic and meditative states. *Science,* 1971, *174*, 897–904.

FLOOR, E. R. The brain in samadhi: An hypothesis. Unpublished manuscript, Harvard University, 1976.

FOULKES, D., & VOGEL, G. Mental activity at sleep onset. *Journal of Abnormal Psychology,* 1965, *70*, 231–243.

GELLHORN, E., & KIELY, W. F. Mystical states of consciousness: Neurophysiological and clinical aspects. *Journal of Nervous and Mental Disease,* 1972, *154*, 299–405.

GELLHORN, E., & LOOFBOURROW, G. N. *Emotions and emotional disorders.* New York: Harper & Row, 1964.

GOLDIE, L. & GREEN, J. M. Changes in mode of respiration as an indication of level of awareness. *Nature,* 1961, *189*, 581–582.

GOLEMAN, D. The Buddha on meditation and states of consciousness. Part 1: The teachings. *Journal of Transpersonal Psychology,* 1972, *4*(1), 1–44.

GOLEMAN, D. *The varieties of the meditation experience.* New York: Dutton, 1977.

GOYECHE, J. R. M., CHIHARA, T., & SHIMIZU, H. Two concentration methods: A preliminary comparison. *Psychologia,* 1972, *15*, 110–111.

GREEN, E. Biofeedback for mind-body self-regulation: Healing and creativity. In D. Shapiro, T. X. Barker, L. V. DiCara, J. Kamiya, & J. Stoyva (Eds.), *Biofeedback and self-control.* Chicago: Aldine, 1972.

GREEN, E., GREEN, A., & WALTERS, E. D. Voluntary control of internal states: Psychological and physiological. *Journal of Transpersonal Psychology,* 1970, *1*, 1–26.

GREENFIELD, T. K. Individual differences and mystical experience in response to three forms of meditation. Unpublished doctoral dissertation, University of Michigan, Ann Arbor, 1977.

GROSSBERG, J. M. Brain wave feedback experiments and the concept of mental mechanisms. *Journal of Behavior Therapy and Experimental Psychiatry*, 1972, *3*, 245–251.

HARDT, J. V., & KAMIYA, J. Some comments on Plotkin's self-regulation of EEG alpha. *Journal of Experimental Psychology: General*, 1976, *105*, 100–108.

HASSETT, J., & SCHWARTZ, G. E. Relationships between heart rate and occipital alpha: A biofeedback approach. *Psychophysiology*, 1975, *12*, 228.

HEBERT, R., & LEHMANN, D. Theta bursts: An EEG pattern in normal subjects practicing the transcendental meditation technique. *Electroencephalography and Clinical Neurophysiology*, 1977, *42*, 397–405.

HILGARD, E. Neodissociation theory of multiple cognitive control systems. In G. E. Schwartz & D. Shapiro (Eds.), *Consciousness and self-regulation*, Vol. 1. New York: Plenum, 1976.

HIRAI, T. *Psychophysiology of Zen*. Tokyo: Igaku Shoin, 1974.

HUNT, H. F., & CHEFURKA, C. M. A test of the psychedelic model of altered states of consciousness. *Archives of General Psychiatry*, 1976, *33*, 867–876.

JEVENING, R., WILSON, A. F., SMITH, W. R., & MORTON, M. Redistribution of blood flow in transcendental meditation. Paper presented at the Society for Psychophysiological Research, Toronto, 1975.

JOHNSON, L. C. A psychophysiology for all states. *Psychophysiology*, 1970, *6*, 501–516.

KAMIYA, J. Operant control of the EEG alpha and some of its reported effects on consciousness. In C. Tart (Ed.), *Altered states of consciousness*. New York: Wiley, 1969.

KAMIYA, J. Autoregulation of the EEG alpha rhythm: A program for the study of consciousness. In T. X. Barber, L. V. DiCara, J. Kamiya, N. E. Miller, D. Shapiro, & J. Stoyva (Eds.), *Biofeedback and self-control*. Chicago: Aldine, 1975–1976.

KASAMATSU, A., & HIRAI, T. An electroencephalographic study on the zen meditation. In C. Tart (Ed.), *Altered states of consciousness*. New York: Wiley, 1969.

KING, C. *The states of human consciousness*. New Hyde Park, N.Y.: University Books, 1963.

KRIPPNER, S. Hypnosis and attention: A review. *American Journal of Clinical Hypnosis*, 1974, *16*(3), 166–177.

KUBOSE, S. K. An experimental investigation of psychological aspects of meditation. *Psychologia*, 1976, *19*(1), 1–10.

LEGRAND, P., TOUBOL, M., BARRABINO, J., DARCOURT, G., & FADEUILHE, A. Contingent negative variation in meditation. *Electroencephalography and Clinical Neurophysiology*, 1977, *43*(4), 532 (abstract).

LEHMANN, D. Multichannel topography of human alpha EEG fields. *Electroencephalography of Clinical Neurophysiology*, 1971, *31*, 439–449.

LIBERSON, W. T., & LIBERSON, C. W. EEG records, reaction times, eye movements, respiration, and mental content during drowsiness. *Recent Advances in Biological Psychiatry*, 1966, *8*, 295–302.

LINDSLEY, D. Psychological phenomena and the electroencephalogram. *Electroencephalography and Clinical Neurophysiology*, 1952, *4*, 443–456.

LUDWIG, A. Altered states of consciousness. *Archives of General Psychiatry*, 1966, *15*, 228–234.

LURIA, A. R., & HOMSKAYA, E. D. Frontal lobes and the regulation of arousal processes. In D. I. Mostofsky (Ed.), *Attention: Contemporary theory and analysis*. New York: Appleton-Century-Crofts, 1970.

LUTHE, W. (Ed.). *Autogenic training*. New York: Grune & Stratton, 1969.

LUTZENBERGER, W., BIRBAUMER, N., & STEINMETZ, P. Simultaneous biofeedback of heart rate and frontal EMG as a pretraining for the control of EEG theta activity. *Biofeedback and Self-Regulation*, 1976, *1*(4), 395–410.

LYNCH, J. J., & PASKEWITZ, D. A. On the mechanisms of the feedback control of human brain wave activity. *Journal of Nervous and Mental Disease*, 1971, *153*, 205.

MASLOW, A. H. Towards a humanistic biology. *American Psychologist*, 1969, *24*, 724–735.

MICHAELS, R. R., HUBER, M. J., & MCCANN, D. S. Evaluation of transcendental meditation as a method of reducing stress. *Science*, 1976, *192*, 1242–1244.

MILLS, G. K., & CAMPBELL, K. A critique of Gellhorn and Kiely's mystical states of consciousness. *Journal of Nervous and Mental Disease*, 1974, *159*(3), 191–195.

MULHOLLAND, T. B. The concept of attention and the electroencephalographic alpha rhythm. In C. R. Evans & T. M. Mulholland (Eds.), *Attention in neurophysiology*. New York: Appleton-Century-Croft, 1969.

MULHOLLAND, T., & PEPER, E. Occipital alpha and accommodative vergence, pursuit tracking, and fast eye movements. *Psychophysiology*, 1971, *8*(5), 556–575.

MULHOLLAND, T., & RUNNALS, S. Increased occurrence of EEG alpha during increased attention. *Journal of Psychology*, 1962, *54*, 317–330.

NARANJO, C. The domain of meditation. In J. White (Ed.), *What is meditation?* New York: Doubleday/Anchor, 1974.

NOWLIS, D. P., & KAMIYA, . The control of electroencephalographic alpha rhythms through auditory feedback and the associated mental activity. *Psychophysiology*, 1970, *6*, 476–484.

ORME-JOHNSON, D. W. Autonomic stability and transcendental meditation. *Psychosomatic Medicine*, 1973, *35*, 341–349.

ORME-JOHNSON, D. W. EEG coherence during transcendental consciousness. *Electroencephalography and Clinical Neurophysiology*, 1977, *43*(4), 581 (abstract).

PAGANO, R. R., ROSE, R. M., STIVERS, R. M., & WARRENBURG, S. Sleep during transcendental meditation. *Science*, 1976, *191*(4224), 308–309.

PASKEWITZ, D., LYNCH, J. J., ORNE, M., & COSTELLO, J. The feedback control of alpha activity: Conditioning or disinhibition. *Psychophysiology*, 1970, *6*, 637–638.

PAUL, G. Physiological effects of relaxation training and hypnotic suggestion. *Journal of Abnormal Psychology*, 1969, *74*, 425–437.

PELLETIER, K. R. Neurophysiological parameters of alpha, theta, and cardiovascular control. Paper presented at Western Psychological Association, San Francisco, April 24–27, 1974.

PELLETIER, K. R., & PEPER, E. The chutzpah factor in altered states of consciousness. *Journal of Humanistic Psychology*, 1976, *17*(1), 63–74.

PEPER, E., & ANCOLI, S. The two endpoints of an EEG continuum of meditation—Alpha/theta and fast beta. *Biofeedback and Self-Regulation*, 1977, *2*(3), 289–290 (abstract).

PLOTKIN, W. B. On the self-regulation of the occipital alpha rhythm control strategies, states of consciousness, and the role of physiological feedback. *Journal of Experimental Psychology*, 1976, *105*, 66–99.

PLOTKIN, W. B., & COHEN, R. Occipital alpha and the attributes of the "alpha experience." *Psychophysiology*, 1976, *13*(1), 16–21.

PLOTKIN, W. B., MAZER, C., & LOEWY, D. Alpha enhancement and the likelihood of an alpha experience. *Psychophysiology*, 1976, *13*(5), 466–471.

PORGES, S. W. Peripheral and neurochemical parallels of psychopathology: A psychophysiological model relating autonomic imbalance to hyperactivity, psychopathy, and autism. *Advances in Child Development and Behavior*, 1976, *11*, 35–65.

PRIBRAM, K. H., & McGUINNESS, D. Arousal, activation, and effort in the control of attention. *Psychological Review*, 1975, *82*(2), 116–149.

RAJNEESH, B. S. *Meditation: The art of ecstasy*. New York: Harper & Row, 1976.

RECHTSCHAFFEN, A. Scientific method in the study of altered states of consciousness with illustrations from sleep and dream research. In *Altered States of Consciousness: Current Views and Research Problems*. Washington, D.C.; Drug Abuse Council, 1975.

ROGERS, L. J. Human EEG response to certain rhythmic patterned auditory stimuli, with possible relations to EEG lateral asymmetry measures and EEG correlates of chanting. Unpublished doctoral dissertation, Department of Physiology, University of California, Los Angeles, 1976.

SCHACTER, D. L. The hypnagogic state: A critical review of the literature. *Psychological Bulletin*, 1976, *83*(3), 452–481.

SCHWARTZ, G. E. Meditation as an altered trait of consciousness: Current findings on stress reactivity, attentional flexibility, and creativity. Paper read at the 82nd Annual Convention of the American Psychological Association, New Orleans, September 1974.

SCHWARTZ, G. E., SHAW, G., & SHAPIRO, D. Specificity of alpha and heart rate control through feedback. *Psychophysiology*, 1972, *9*, 269 (abstract).

SHAPIRO, D. A biofeedback strategy in the study of consciousness. In N. E. Zinberg (Ed.), *Alternate states of consciousness*. New York: Free Press, 1977.

SHOR, R. E. Hypnosis and the concept of the generalized reality-orientation. *American Journal of Psychotherapy*, 1959, *13*, 582–602.

SITTENFELD, P., BUDZYNSKI, T., & STOYVA, J. Differential shaping of EEG theta rhythms. *Biofeedback and Self-Regulation*, 1976, *1*, 31–46.

STOYVA, J. Biofeedback techniques and the conditions for hallucinatory activity. In F. J. McGuigan & R. A. Schoonover (Eds.), *The psychophysiology of thinking*. New York: Academic, 1973.

STOYVA, J. M., & BUDZYNSKI, T. H. Cultivated low arousal—An antistress response? In L. V. DiCara (Ed.), *Recent advances in limbic and autonomic nervous systems research*. New York: Plenum, 1974.

STOYVA, J. M., & KAMIYA, J. Electrophysiological studies of dreaming as the prototype of a new strategy in the study of consciousness. *Psychological Review*, 1968, *75*, 192–205.

SUTER, S., JOHNSON, T., FRANCONI, L., & SMITH, D. Independent biofeedback control of EEG alpha and skin conductance. *Biofeedback and Self-Regulation*, 1977, *2*(3), 295 (abstract).

TART, C. *States of consciousness*. New York: Dutton, 1975.

TEBECIS, A. K. A controlled study of the EEG during transcendental meditation: Comparison with hypnosis. *Folia Psychiatrica et Neurologica Japonica*, 1975, *29*(4), 305–313.

TEBECIS, A. K. Eye movements during transcendental meditation. *Folia Psychiatrica et Neurologica Japonica*, 1976, *30*, 487–493.

TEBECIS, A. K., PROVINS, K. A., FARNBACH, R. W., & PENTONY, P. Hypnosis and the EEG. *Journal of Nervous and Mental Disease*, 1975, *161*(1), 1–17.

TECCE, J. J. Attention and evoked potentials in man. In D. I. Mostofsky (Ed.), *Attention: Contemporary theory and analysis*. New York: Appleton-Century-Crofts, 1970.

TIMMONS, B., SALAMY, J., KAMIYA, J., & GIRTON, D. Abdominal–thoracic respiratory movements and levels of arousal. *Psychonomic Science*, 1972, *27*, 173–175.

TRAVIS, T., KONDO, C., & KNOTT, J. Alpha enhancement research: A review. *Biological Psychiatry*, 1975, *10*(1), 69–90.

TRAVIS, T. A., KONDO, C. Y., & KNOTT, J. R. Heart rate, muscle tension, and alpha production of transcendental meditators and relaxation controls. *Biofeedback and Self-Regulation*, 1976, *1*(4), 387–395.

VAN NUYS, D. A novel technique for studying attention during meditation. *Journal of Transpersonal Psychology*, 1971, *2*, 125–134.

VOGEL, G., FOULKES, D., & TROSMAN, H. Ego functions and dreaming during sleep onset. *Archives of General Psychiatry*, 1966, *14*, 238–248.

WALLACE, R. K. Physiological effects of transcendental meditation. *Science*, 1970, *167*, 1751–1754.

WALLACE, R. K., BENSON, H., & WILSON, A. F. A wakeful hypometabolic physiologic state. *American Journal of Physiology*, 1971, *221*, 795.

WALRATH, L. C., & HAMILTON, D. W. Autonomic correlates of meditation and hypnosis. *American Journal of Clinical Hypnosis*, 1975, *17*(3), 190–197.

WALSH, D. Interactive effects of alpha feedback and instructional set on subjective state. *Psychophysiology*, 1974, *11*(4), 428–435.

WARRENBURG, S., PAGANO, R., WOODS, M., & HLASTALA, M. Oxygen consumption, H.R., EMG, and EEG during progressive muscle relaxation (PMR) and transcendental meditation (TM). *Biofeedback and Self-Regulation*, 1977, *2*(3), 321. (abstract)

WENGER, M. A., & BAGCHI, B. K. Studies of autonomic functions in practitioners of yoga in India. *Behavioral Science*, 1961, *6*, 312–323.

WICKRAMASEKARA, I. *Biofeedback behavior therapy and hypnosis: Potentiating the verbal control of behavior for clinicians*. Chicago: Nelson-Hall, 1976.

WOOLFOLK, R. L. Psychophysiological correlates of meditation. *Archives of General Psychiatry*, 1975, *32*, 1326–1333.

YAMAGUCHI, Y. Frontal theta burst and personality factors. *Electroencephalography and Clinical Neurophysiology*, 1977, *43*(4), 528 (abstract).

YOUNGER, J., ADRIANCE, W., & BERGER, R. Sleep during transcendental meditation. In M. H. Chase, W. C. Stern, & P. L. Walter (Eds.), *Sleep Research*, Vol. 2. Los Angeles: Brain Information Service/Brain Research Institute, University of California, Los Angeles, 1973 (abstract).

14
Toward a Psychobiology of Transcendence: God in the Brain

Arnold J. Mandell

1. An Argument for Implicit Knowledge in the Brain Sciences

Since the time of atomists like Democritus, forerunner of Plato and Aristotle, two modes of scientific explanation have been used to fill the conceptual space between mind and brain, a dualism more grudgingly resistant to resolution than that of energy and matter. One method assumes a world of hidden realities, impenetrable, to be understood by conjecture and test, observations evaluated for their consistency with hypothetical constructs. The other requires an intuitive grasp of the essence, insightful awareness of the thing itself. The first approach defines a unification of mind and brain out of the possible; the second assumes it. Feelings about these orientations still run strong. In a recent book, the philosopher of science Sir Karl Popper expressed irritation with Plato for intermixing these two thought styles without acknowledging the intermixture, concluding that only the conjectural-test approach is valid; the other kind of knowing Popper dismissed as a "will-o-the-wisp" (Popper & Eccles, 1977).

When it comes to the movements of planets and other "out-there" things, not knowing seems more likely than when we speak of the properties of the human brain, a world hidden from others but one in which we spend our days. Plato's use of myth as verisimilitude represents a tradition of model building developed most elegantly by Newton in *Principia Mathematica*, in which logical consistency and fit with observable data are mixed with a disclaimer about knowing; "Not that I affirm gravity to be essential to bodies" (Popper, 1963).

ARNOLD J. MANDELL • Department of Psychiatry, University of California, San Diego, La Jolla, California 92093. The research reported here was supported by USPHS Grant DA-00265-07. Some of this theoretical material developed as part of a symposium on emergent brain properties at the 11th Annual Winter Conference on Brain Research, Keystone, Colorado, January 1978.

An assumed ignorance of the ultimate mysteries, leading to distant and derived systems of mathematical logic and model building for work in physics and chemistry, may have created more problems than solutions in brain research. The behavioral neurobiologist's mistrust of the brain's observations of its own workings has led us to ignore (at least in our formal work) this most valuable source of insights. Descartes (Haldane & Ross, 1931) formalized our dualistic dilemma even while acknowledging that a clear and distinct subjective impression, "a gift from God," must be true. In spite of this tribute to the value of intuitive awareness, he constructed an un-unifiable cosmology in which mind (or soul) was nonmaterial, body was material, and all things interacted in the world by mechanical *push*. The metaphor eliminated mind–brain unity and made even imagining an interaction difficult. Into this breach was thrown God. Cartesians like Leibnitz said that it was He who harmonized physical and mental events as they operated in parallel (Watkins, 1965). The Occasionalists (Popper, 1959) also made such interactions miraculous, but tailored for each occasion.

We who are interested in the brain mechanisms of mind are still stuck. The physicists, scientists of the past century, taught us of empiricism, logical positivism, operational definitions, and mathematical model-building, and then in a revolutionary sequence of insights and experiments, they fused their erstwhile dualism of energy and matter and gave us a world of predictable physical events in everything from chemical reactions to red-shift tracking of our place in the cosmos after the big bang (Bohr, 1958; Weinberg, 1977). Around the turn of the century, following their example, we stopped looking for what we sensed, built models of nervous system function from externally observable events like reflexes and behavior after reinforcement, and chased the thought style and mathematical elegance of the physical scientists like a minority group trying to be white. Freud, descended via Burke from Helmholtz, revolting from Mueller's biological vitalism (Armacher, 1965), used his subjective world as noetic source but codified his observations with thermodynamics as a theoretical premise and employed a ruminative style of conceptual development that made things sound as if they had passed the test of experimental disconfirmability. He created the impression of externally derived converging evidence, using material from his patients.

John Dewey rather than William James represented Western academic psychology's move into this century, as Pavlov's cosmology (also derived from the Helmholtz school, via Sechenov) dominated experimental psychology, just as Freud's did psychiatry. Neurobiologists looking for parallel biological phenomena in brain, using indices of electrical and chemical change, focused on behavioral events reflecting

Pavlovian–Freudian concepts such as drive, conditioning, learning, reinforcement, conflict, and anxiety. Models of behavior emerging from more subjective phenomenologists—such as Hebb's (1949) organization of behavior, Hayek's (1952) sensory order, and Polanyi's (1958) personal knowledge—never found their way as orienting ideas into the laboratories of brain biologists. Wolfgang Köhler's (1970) Gestalt psychology, Piaget's (1973) developmental models, and Lévi-Strauss's (1972) structuralism are examples of other rich systems of brain-relevant concepts that are difficult to examine using Skinner-box, nigrostriatal behavioral paradigms with which to interpret the output of our scintillation counters.

As matter escapes reductionistic accounting in the new subatomic physics (five quarks by the latest count), Phillip Anderson, a recent Nobelist in physics, assured me that things down there have become quite indeterminate, and as "emergent properties" (Anderson, 1972) and "system theory" (Miller, 1978) are invoked to replenish our impoverished repertoire of researchable behavior, perhaps we should take new courage and start all over again, go back to the turn of the century, examine what we threw out as philosophy, unrigorous and subjective, and see if there is a vocabulary of human behavior that can be useful in creating new ways of looking at brain biology in relation to mind.

William James's *The Varieties of Religious Experience* (1929) serves as our inspiration. Using powerful prose and insights from his complex personal life, James examined the phenomena of religious conversion in all aspects, as it occurred in the lives of saints; in the experiences of his friend, a dentist, breathing nitrous oxide; from its developmental character to its long-lasting impact on personality. In somewhat the same way that thousands of years of personal observation about the management of pain by acupuncture of various strange and unlikely parts of the body can today be rationalized by the use of a testable system of nerve-stimulated release of endogenous opiates, we suggest that James was not in error in his confidence in his own felt truths, which led him to develop the proposition that transcendental experience was similar wherever he examined it and that its most commonly invoked source, God, was in the brain. Thought style transforming consciousness, the assumption of thousands of years of Eastern metaphysics, so different from the Pavlovian–Freudian involuntary brain-stem striate cortex of fighting and eating, bespoke a new way of looking at brain and mind for the West, which was too bothered by Darwinian and Marxian social problems to listen. The possibility that there is a biogenic amine–temporal-lobe limbic neurology for transformed consciousness, that the ethic of the experimental method can be used in meaningful dialogue with subjective behaviorism, that Western man turning inward for metaphysical solution has biological mechanisms with which to rationalize the journey, is entertained here. Following descriptions of the approach to research in biological psychiatry called the *pharmacological bridge* and the mechanisms under study in our laboratory and others that serve to control systems of forebrain limbic excitation, we examine the phenomena of transcendence in both neurobiological and behavioral contexts.

It could be argued that exploring the mind–brain interface in a locus where the descriptive boundaries of either are indefinable—the transformed consciousness of religious conversion was called "ineffable" by James—augurs failure from the beginning. For example, what we mean by *transcendence*, demanding description, will have to accrue definition as we develop the model for its neurobiological mechanisms. We have chosen a limiting case. If there appears to be the possibility of the unity of mind with brain here, perhaps other examples will seem more approachable. It is the advent of psychotropic drugs and some understanding of their chemical representations in the brain, called *neurotransmitters*, that has brought us to the capacity of linking neurochemical mechanisms with systems neurophysiology. As alterations in one amino acid in a sequence ramify through tertiary protein structure to metabolic disease, small regulatory changes in brain-biogenic amine synthesis appear through known neurophysiological mechanisms to be capable of altering world view. One might suggest that with such connections established, the reverse may be possible. Sensitive listening to the background feelings of self may make possible new hypotheses about brain-biogenic amine regulation. With such an interactional language established, it may one day be possible to demonstrate that the brain knows about itself.

2. THE PHARMACOLOGICAL BRIDGE AND THE MODULATION OF AROUSAL AND FEAR

One approach to the explanation of brain chemical mechanisms underlying human states of consciousness can be called the *pharmacological bridge* (Schildkraut, 1969). Human brain chemistry, difficult to sample *in situ*, is studied via an intermediary, a drug that, acting as definable chemical information, becomes a link between chemical events induced in the brains of experimental animals and clinical phenomena. Dose–response curves, use of congeners, and converging evidence from studies of other psychobiological systems (electroencephalography, neuroendocrinology, peripheral studies of urinary and spinal fluid metabolites) supply opportunities to test derived hypotheses (Mandell, 1969).

The ability of reserpine to decrease levels of biogenic amines (dopamine, norepinephrine, and serotonin) in the brains of experimental animals and to produce lethargy in some people and agitated or retarded depression in others under treatment for hypertension (Harris, 1957), when combined with the observation that monoamine oxidase inhibitors both increase brain levels of these amines in rats and produce elevations in mood and energy, even to the production of full-blown mania in man, led to theories of mood and mood disorder of a relatively simplified sort. Up in amines was up in mood; down in amines was down in mood; and which brain amine was prepotent constituted grounds for debate (Brodie, Spector, & Shore, 1959; Kety, 1961; Carlsson, Lindqvist, & Magnusson, 1957; Coppen & Shaw, 1963). Tricyclic antidepressant drugs, the most predictably efficacious drug family, constituted a bit of a mystery for a while because they did *not* change the brain levels of amines. Glowinski and Axelrod (1964) studied drug effects on the disposition of radioactive norepinephrine administered intraventricularly in rats and found that the tricyclics blocked the uptake of norepinephrine into the nerve cells, potentiating its activity at synapses. When this finding was considered with the discovery that the kinetic regulation of the rate-limiting enzyme in catecholamine biosynthesis, tyrosine hydroxylase, was by product inhibition (Nagatsu, Levitt, & Udenfriend, 1964)—that is product competing with tetrahydrobiopterin for the cofactor site (Kaufman, 1958)—the tricyclics could be seen as potentiating synaptic transmission both by blocking reuptake inactivation of the amine and by temporarily depleting cytoplasmic norepinphrine, releasing the enzyme to synthesize more norepinephrine and increasing its supply to the synapse.

Two aspects of this application of the pharmacological bridge using tricyclic antidepressants presented some difficulties. One was the latency to clinical effects of several weeks in man in the face of achievement of therapeutic blood levels within days (Hammer & Sjöqvist, 1967). The other was that even in patients treated chronically, there was a poor relationship between blood level of drug and affective morbidity (Coppen *et al.*, 1978). It was in this context that we undertook to study other measures of central nervous system norepinephrine function in response to tricyclics and found that chronic tricyclic administration *decreased* tyrosine hydroxylase activity in the major brain-stem norepinephrine nucleus, the locus ceruleus, as well as in the hippocampus. We speculated that this finding resulted from inhibitory feedback from postsynaptic sites, reducing the spontaneous rates of discharge of these cells, and a subsequent reduction in the level of enzyme activity (Segal, Kuczenski, & Mandell, 1974). Blood levels of drug—clinical effect transduced through this neurobiological system and the enzymatic machinery genetically determined in rats and probably subject to individual differences in humans (Segal, Kuczenski, & Mandell, 1972)—would therefore not be expected to fit well with either latency to effect or degree of clinical response.

Since that time, Nyback, Walters, Aghajanian, & Roth (1975) have reported that the tricyclic drugs decrease the discharge rate of locus ceruleus cells; Roth's group (Roth & Salzman, 1977) has conducted a series of experiments showing the dependence of brain-stem noradrenergic tyrosine hydroxylase activity on locus ceruleus electrical activity—the relationship is a direct one; and Braestrup (1974) has shown that chronic treatment with tricyclic drugs *reduces* brain catecholamine metabolites. Recent studies of the effects of electrical stimulation and ablation of the locus ceruleus in the stump-tailed monkey (Huang, Redmond, Snyder, & Maas, 1975; Redmond, Huang, Snyder, & Maas, 1976) have suggested that this system regulates arousal and fear, perhaps via its connections to the hippocampus, which is known to be involved in alerting (Passouant, Cadilhac, & Passouant-Fontaine, 1955). The monkeys with locus ceruleus ablation put on weight, dominate, and are fearless around man. Segal and Bloom's (1974a,b, 1976) elegant work showing locus-ceruleus–derived, norepinephrine-mediated inhibition of spontaneous firing rate in hippocampal pyramidal cells associated with increases in evoked activity, generating and saving "second messenger" for use by specific sensory stimuli, is a classic illustration of an arousal effect tuning a system to increase the signal-to-noise ratio. A similar action of norepinephrine has been reported for other afferent systems, also suggesting an information-processing role (Foote, Freedman, & Oliver, 1975; Freedman, Hoffer, Puro, & Woodward, 1976; Nakai & Takaori, 1974). As will be seen, the raphe serotonin pathway to the hippocampus (M. Segal, 1975) is more diffuse and appears to reduce both resting and evoked activity for another purpose, perhaps the psychomotor and endocrine expression of background feelings.

We began with a clinical effect of a drug in man: tricyclics in several weeks produce remission in a high percentage of patients with depression. We crossed the model bridge to animal brains to learn that there is a potentiation of amine transmission, but with more careful clinical studies of latency to effect and the poor relationship between blood levels and affective morbidity, we went back to the laboratory and elucidated a longer latency mechanism relating to the norepinephrine system, which appears to be a *turning down* of its electrical and biosynthetic activity presynaptically. The postsynaptic effect appears consistent; it has been shown that chronic tricyclic treatment reduces the sensitivity of the limbic–forebrain noradrenergic cyclic adenosine monophosphate (AMP)-generating system (Vetulani, Sawartz, & Sulser, 1976). It is tempting to relate this change to the immediate sedative effect of the tricyclics. The possibility of long-term effects on the parameter of sensory arousal to fear and its relation if any to the antidepressant effect lead us to some long-standing psychoanalytic observations. Fear of loss of supplies, for example, and preoccupation with poverty and starvation were reported as consistent features of the depressive syndromes by the pioneering psychoanalysts (Freud, 1925; Abraham, 1927) as well as the modern practitioners of clinical characterization by rating scales (Overall, Hollister, Johnson, & Pennington, 1966).

Without technical jargon, the clinical transformation of fear to depression could be expressed as follows. A person upon whom you feel dependent is standing on your foot. You would like to tell him to get off, but fear of loss of his approval and whatever else he can give you prevents you. So you suffer in silence, get angry, and, as with the rebound effect of amphetamine-induced anger, there is depression. Tricyclics, by reducing the subjective accompaniment of fear generated by fantasies (plans to correct the situation), lead to assertiveness ("get off my foot"), which eliminates the need to be angry, which relieves the depression. It was this kind of thinking about fear and depression that led Donald Klein to try tricyclic antidepressants on patients with phobias, and in well-conducted studies, it appears to have worked well (Klein, Zitrin, & Woerner, 1978).

In this way, the pharmacological bridge facilitates the dialogue between mind and brain. Converging data are then sought: tricyclics are shown to prevent behavioral pathology in monkeys separated from their mothers (Hrdina & von Kulmiz, 1978); tricyclic drugs are shown to *decrease* both indolamine and catecholamine metabolites in the cerebrospinal fluid of depressed patients (Bertilsson, Asberg, Mellstrom, Tybring, & Sjoquist, 1978); patients with temporal lobe tumors when infused in the internal carotid on the left, but not on the right, experience transient episodes of depressive fear (Terzian, 1958), the locus ceruleus pathway to the hippocampus perhaps modulating what Penfield has called the relevance aspects of temporal lobe learning and memory function (Penfield, 1959; Penfield & Mathieson, 1974). Threat of imagined outcome of action, a fear that was wound into the above psychodynamic sequence leading to depression, is altered by a tricyclic-induced change in amine input to the hippocampus via the norepinephrine tract outlined by Segal and Bloom (1974a,b).

Much of our work over the past 15 years has focused on secondary responses to drug action, comparable to the decrease in presynaptic tyrosine hydroxylase activity and postsynaptic norepinephrine sensitivity in receptors after chronic treatment with tricyclic drugs (Mandell, 1978a). We have come to believe that the mechanisms underlying such secondary responses are multiple neurobiological systems in biogenic amine neurons that function to maintain and/or return the biosynthetic activity of these cells to their preperturbed state after administration of psychopharmacological agents. In studies of drugs with transient effects, such as the lower doses of stimulants and sedatives, we see these metabolic mechanisms only temporarily unbalanced, with compensations occurring and some or most of the drug effect disappearing in what has been called tolerance (Mandell, 1975). With most drugs used in psychiatry, such as the tricyclics and lithium, which have long latencies and enduring action, we see the major neurobiological mechanisms underlying behavioral change to be those that cannot be undone by tolerance mechanisms either by the drug's preempting control over the normal regulatory system, as in the case of lithium's stimulating the tryptophan membrane uptake mechanism so it no longer is led by raphe unit firing rate (Glowinski, Hamon, & Héry, 1973; Mandell & Knapp, 1977), or as in the case with tricyclics and the norepinephrine system, where the treatment may be the induction of tolerance (Mandell, 1975). Another example of "treatment by tolerance induction" may be the increase in dopamine synthesis following neuroleptic administration (blockade of autoreceptors releasing firing rate and synthesis) with an accompanying increase in the inhibition of downstream striatal and limbic forebrain systems (Carlsson & Lindqvist, 1963; Siggins, 1978).

High-dose amphetamines, cocaine, and the hallucinogenic drugs, which constitute our pharmacological bridge to transcendence, are characterized by their capacity to induce acutely a temporarily uncompensated decrease in synthesis and/or release of serotonin, a loss in its inhibitory effect, and a transient "runaway" excitation of brain systems, specifically mesolimbic temporal lobe structures. Although the resulting behavioral states have been described with psychopathological terms, like William James we shall relate the chemistry and behavior of these transcendent states without value-laden diagnoses. It will then be shown that pretreatment with lithium, a drug that increases serotonin synthesis and buffers it against change by enzyme stabilization and the induction of autoreceptor subsensitivity, has the capacity, both neurobiologically and behaviorally, to prevent transcendence induced by high doses of amphetamine, cocaine, or the hallucinogens. A further relationship, recently established, between the neuronal uptake of tryptophan, affecting the rate of serotonin synthesis via its substrate curve, and the degree of lateral asymmetry of serotonin and its metabolites as influenced by lithium, when combined with the neurological evidence for affectual specialization of the two temporal lobes, may explain lithium's effects on spontaneously occurring affectual extremes such as hypomania (one name for transcendent consciousness) as well as those that are drug-induced (Mandell & Knapp, 1978).

3. The Pharmacological Bridge and the Modulation of Rage

Neurobiological transcendence, going beyond the normal limits of the mechanisms of adaptation, is exemplified by neurochemical changes induced in dopaminergic neural systems by high doses of amphetamine. Regulatory mechanisms maintaining steady-state function fail, leading to the deregulation of dopamine synthesis (Bullard, Guthrie, Russo, & Mandell, 1978; Bullard, Yellin, Russo, & Mandell, 1978). With the weight of evidence suggesting that dopamine operates downstream as an inhibitory transmitter (Siggins, 1978), failure in an adaptational increase in synthesis at a time of drug-induced high rates of release may lead to depletion of the functional dopamine pool and to runaway excitation in some brain functions. Using the pharmacological bridge of high doses of amphetamine, we will relate a drug-induced decrease in the tetrahydrobiopterin cofactor of tyrosine hydroxylase and an increase in inhibition of dopamine tyrosine hydroxylase at a time of drug-induced augmented release (Mandell & Bullard, 1978a) to a loss of dopamine inhibition to the nuclei of the amygdala (Ben-Ari & Kelly, 1974). The latter was shown to be kindled into hypersynchronous spindling by high or chronic doses of amphetamine (Ellinwood, 1974) with a resulting increase rather than a decrease in sensitivity to amphetamine with chronic drug administration (Segal & Mandell, 1974) and the induction of states of rage and paranoia (Connell, 1958).

Naturally occurring states of rage in animals and man are associated with temporal lobe pathology (Terzian & Ore, 1955), particularly the amygdala-involved "individual survival" part of the temporal lobe limbic system (MacLean, 1959). As is the case with the tricyclic antidepressants, it is speculated that drug-induced changes in biogenic amine synthesis alter the modulation of excitability of temporal lobe structures. With tricyclic drugs, the synaptic potentiation of the inhibition of uptake is counterbalanced by a decrease in biosynthetic enzyme activity and an insensitivity of receptor mechanisms, stabilizing the system. With high doses of amphetamine, however, a failure of regulation occurs, and more dopamine is needed but less is made, which we speculate leads to deregulation of amygdala function. Electrical activation of the amygdala in man has been shown to be associated with paranoid rage reactions

(Chapman, Schroeder, Geyer, Brazier, Fager, Poppen, Solomon, & Yakovlev, 1954).

A paradoxical finding that has involved us since 1968 is a *decrease* in striatal synaptosomal conversion of tyrosine to dopamine following the administration of amphetamine in doses of 1–2 mg/kg and above (Mandell & Bullard, 1978a,b). Increasing the release of dopamine failed to increase dopamine synthesis in striatal nerve-ending preparations; actually, it was reduced under circumstances in which a release of product-feedback inhibition of tyrosine hydroxylase and an increase in dopamine synthesis would have been predicted. In rats, doses in this range or higher produce behavioral stereotypy (circling, rocking, gnawing), and, unlike behavioral activity induced by lower doses of amphetamine, there is no tolerance with repeated administration. The effect does not disappear; rather, it becomes more exaggerated; the same amount of amphetamine administered regularly *increases* the amount of induced stereotypic hyperactivity (Segal & Mandell, 1974). In the rat, with high or repeated doses of amphetamine, neurobiological and behavioral adaptations fail. A recent finding of Bullard, Yellin, *et al.* (1979) might help explain these events. By the amphetamine-induced uncoupling of tyrosine hydroxylase from quinoid dihydropterin reductase, pterin oxidation, and spontaneous rearrangement, the cofactor tetrahydrobiopterin level is diminished and takes several hours to return to control levels by a slower-acting reductase. This decrement in brain-reduced pterin has a time course corresponding to that of the decrease induced by amphetamine in synaptosomal conversion of tyrosine to dopamine (Bullard, Guthrie, *et al.*, 1978; Bullard, Yellin, *et al.*, 1979; Mandell & Bullard, 1978a,b). Because the kinetic regulation of dopamine synthesis involves the competition of dopamine with tetrahydrobiopterin for the cofactor site of tyrosine hydroxylase (Nagatsu *et al.*, 1964), release of dopamine by a drug would normally lead to an increase in dopamine synthesis, compensating for loss in the cytoplasmic pool of dopamine. However, the amphetamines, by diminishing brain tetrahydrobiopterin, *increase* the sensitivity of tyrosine hydroxylase to inhibition by dopamine. After the drug-facilitated release, instead of a compensatory increase in dopamine synthesis, there is a decrease. This adaptational failure does not disappear with repeated amphetamine administration, just as abnormal stereotypic behavioral excitation does not diminish (Segal & Mandell, 1974), nor does tolerance develop to amphetamine-induced paranoid psychosis in man (Angrist & Gershon, 1970).

Fluorescence studies of the anatomy of the dopamine tracts suggest that the A-10 dopamine nucleus projects to the basolateral and central nuclei of the amygdala (Fallon & Moore, 1976; Ungerstedt, 1971), and a high ratio of tyrosine hydroxylase to dopamine-β-hydroxylase in the amygdala, useful as an index of dopamine nerve endings, has been confirmatory (Saavedra & Zivin, 1975), as has the capacity of pimozide to block amygdala influences on prolactin secretion (Straughan & Legge, 1965). Dopamine applied iontophoretically to cells in the central and basolateral nuclei of the amygdala has been shown to inhibit both spontaneous and glutamate-induced discharge (Ben-Ari & Kelly, 1976; Straughan & Legge, 1965). A decrease of dopamine synthesis under circumstances of high demand, as demonstrated in the mesostriatal system (Bullard, Guthrie, et al., 1978; Bullard, Yellin, et al., 1979), occurring in the mesolimbic system—not yet examined—can be speculated to result in release of the amygdala from inhibition with fast, hypersynchronous spindles (28–30/sec) that have been associated with high doses of amphetamine in animals (Ellinwood & Escalante, 1970), paranoid states as recorded over temporal lobe structures in man (Lester & Edwards, 1966), and in the amygdala-septal circuit with stereotyped rituals in a schizophrenic patient (Hanley, Rickles, Crandall, & Walter, 1972). Paranoid, delusional, and rage states have been described as concomitants of both ictal and interictal periods in psychomotor epileptics with temporal lobe pathology since the first descriptions of the syndrome (Falret, 1860; Gastaut, 1953; Karagulla & Robertson, 1955). These phenomena have been produced by high doses of amphetamine in normal volunteers (Griffith, Cavanaugh, & Oates, 1970), suggesting that their presence is a unique function not of the pathological features of temporal lobe syndromes or schizophrenia but of mind mechanisms lying latent in the brain.

Recent experience with a professional football team (Mandell, 1976) afforded an opportunity to observe the once-a-week use of high doses of amphetamine (as high as 125 mg orally), which led not to the pure paranoid rage of the amphetamine psychotic ingesting drugs regularly (Connell, 1958) but to the quality of ecstatic joyfulness, a peculiar mixture of killer rage and grandiose playfulness (Johnson, 1972). Speed freaks starting with high doses of amphetamines administered intravenously, in ever-increasing doses over four or five days called *bursts*, describe initially a transcendent euphoric rush, which requires larger and larger doses to be produced until the pleasurable aspect is finally lost, with increasing fear, dysphoria, and paranoia associated with continued use (Smith, 1969). As we shall see, such "joyful" rage may result from the separate release of dopamine-modulated rage and serotonin-regulated ecstasy, the first involving both amygdala and hippocampus, the second the hippocampus alone. In the following section, we report an acute inhibition of serotonergic synthesis by amphetamine, of the sort seen with cocaine and the hallucinogens, but by a different mechanism, which we see as colored by the dopamine effect. Of the three families of psychotropic agents producing transcendence, neurobiologically and subjectively, leaving sensorium and memory intact, only the amphetamine group regularly leads to a vicious aggressiveness. It is tempting to speculate that a release of the amygdala-lateral hypothalamic rage mechanism (deMolina & Hunsperger, 1959) from dopamine control may be responsible.

The sensitivity of the amygdala to kindling, electrical excitation leading to decreased threshold for further discharge, suggests the possibility that release from dopamine inhibition on a repeated basis may have more-or-less permanent ramifications in brain function and behavior (Goddard, McIntyre, & Leech, 1969). As will be seen, increased excitability in temporal lobe limbic structures as reflected in synchronous discharges from the region are associated with personality changes similar to those seen with religious conversion.

4. NEUROBIOLOGICAL TRANSCENDENCE: HIGH-DOSE AMPHETAMINE, COCAINE, AND THE HALLUCINOGENS

There is a mesolimbic serotonergic pathway that extends from the median raphe nucleus in the mesencephalon, coexistent with part of the mesencephalic reticular formation regulating arousal (Morgane & Stern, 1974), to the septum and the hippocampus (Fuxe & Jonsson, 1974; Geyer, Puerto, Dawsey, Knapp, Bullard, & Mandell, 1976; Lorens & Guldberg, 1974; Moore, 1975). Afferents to this system, as traced by the horseradish peroxidase method, have indicated that with the exception of the habenula most projections to the median nucleus also project to the mesencephalic reticular formation, including cells in the reticular formation itself (Aghajanian & Wang, 1977), so that driving by sensory input and its loss in such "brain-silencing" maneuvers as meditation, attributed in another era to the reticular formation alone (Magoun, 1954; Bradley, 1958), may involve the serotonin cells of the median raphe as well. Serotonergic input to cells in the amygdala, either by microiontophoresis or by stimulation of the dorsal raphe nucleus, a natural serotonergic input, is inhibitory (Wang & Aghanjanian, 1977), whereas both inhibitory and some excitatory effects are reported from iontophoretic studies in the hippocampus (M. Segal, 1975); the effects of activation of physiological input are not yet available. Recent work has explicated two kinds of postsynaptic serotonin receptor: facilitatory to motor nuclei and inhibitory to lateral geniculate and (of major interest in this theoretical development) to hippocampal CA_3 cells (McCall & Aghajanian, 1978).

Amphetamine, cocaine, and the hallucinogens reduce serotonin biosynthesis and/or release by separate mechanisms. Amphetamine in doses above 1–2 mg/kg within 15 minutes reduces synaptosomal conversion of tryptophan to serotonin *without* a change in solubilized tryptophan hydroxylase activity (Knapp, Mandell, & Geyer, 1974). That is, there is acute impairment of nerve-ending synthesis of serotonin without a change in either substrate (tryptophan) supply to the enzyme or the amount of enzyme activity. The mechanism of this change has led us to studies of regulation of tryptophan hydroxylase by ligands like calcium (Knapp & Mandell, 1979), but it appears more likely that the mechanism used to explain the amphetamine-induced decrease in dopamine synthesis in intact nerve endings is applicable: a drug-provoked decrease in tetrahydrobiopterin cofactor (Bullard *et al.*, 1978, 1979; Mandell & Bullard, 1978a,b) a necessary catalyst in the activity of tryptophan hydroxylase. As noted, this reduction in the pterin cofactor impairs kinetically mediated compensation in biosynthesis and constitutes an escape from regulation by product. Although inhibition of tryptophan hydroxylase by serotonin feedback has been difficult to demonstrate, such inhibition by the intermediate 5-hydroxytryptophan, has been suggested (Kaufman, 1974).

Cocaine inhibits the mechanism for neuronal membrane tryptophan uptake into serotonergic nerve endings, resulting in an acute decrease in serotonin synthesis, demonstrable in both synaptosomal preparations and intact brain (Knapp & Mandell, 1976a). Because it appears that substrate is limiting in serotonin biosynthesis (Yuwiler, Oldendorf, Geller, & Braun, 1977), and cocaine appears to work at the neuronal membrane (Mandell & Knapp, 1978a), the increase in soluble tryptophan hydroxylase activity seen following cocaine fails to work since tryptophan supply, which is limiting for the enzyme, has been decreased further; the decrease in serotonin biosynthesis is uncompensated. In this way, cocaine inhibits serotonin synthesis without the possibility for compensation. Cocaine, like other behaviorally activating drugs, also increases bilateral serotonin asymmetry (Mandell, Knapp, & Geyer, 1979).

The effects of hallucinogenic drugs on brain serotonergic systems present a third instance of neurobiological transcendence. The signal discovery of lysergic acid diethylamide's (LSD) mode of action, silencing raphe serotonergic cell firing following exquisitely low doses (Aghajanian, Foote, & Sheard, 1968; Anden, Corrodi, Fuxe, & Hökfelt, 1968), interpreted as the action of an autoreceptor agonist, has been associated with no consistent evidence of a biochemical change except a small increase in intracellular serotonin, such as might be expected from a sudden decrease in discharge rate and release (Freedman & Halaris, 1978). Although consciousness expansion and transcendent behavioral properties have been attributed to this sudden reduction in serotonergic inhibition of neurophysiological systems thought to underly such processes as sensory thresholds, dreams, and hallucinations (Barchas & Usdin, 1973), there have been two major caveats.

The first is that other families of hallucinogens, such as the phenylethylamines, notably mescaline, did not have as clear-cut a cell-silencing effect in the dorsal raphe nucleus. Recently, in our laboratories, using single-cell quantitative microspectrofluorometry of the *median* raphe nucleus (Geyer, Dawsey, & Mandell, 1975, 1978) we found that this group of serotonergic cell bodies with projections primarily to the limbic forebrain (Geyer et al., 1976) showed similar changes associated with cell silencing (small increases in intracellular serotonin without significant changes in extracellular amine) by *all hallucinogens tested*, including mescaline, LSD, and the methoxyamphetamines (Geyer, Petersen, Rose, Horwitt, Light, Adams, Zook, Hawkins, & Mandell, 1978b). Aghajanian's (1972a,b) single-unit studies have focused on the *dorsal* raphe nucleus, where the effect is apparently more heterogeneous. The median raphe nucleus, its cells more diffuse, is more difficult to hit with a microelectrode and has not been examined as systematically in electrophysiological studies.

The other inconsistency that has reduced the currency of LSD's serotonergic cell-silencing effect to explain its induction of transcendent states is that such agents as tryptophan, chlorimipramine, and monoamine oxidase inhibitors silence dorsal raphe cells without inducing comparable alterations in consciousness. It is here that adaptational failure, or neurobiological transcendence, seems to play a role. With psychoactive agents other than hallucinogens, silencing of serotonergic cells is associated with compensatory changes in biosynthetic function, increases in serotonin turnover, and tryptophan hydroxylase activity (Gallager & Aghajanian, 1975, 1976b; Mandell & Knapp, 1978a; Mandell, et al., 1979). With LSD, for example, a reduction of the base rate of raphe cell firing occurs *without* the compensatory increase in serotonin biosynthesis observed in nerve-ending preparations or intact brain (Freedman & Halaris, 1978; Mandell et al., 1979). This dissociation of firing rate and biosynthetic compensation has been unique to hallucinogenic drugs in our studies of over 40 drugs that perturb the rat brain serotonin system. Thus, the hallucinogens join the amphetamines and cocaine in their ability to decrease mesolimbic serotonin synthesis and/or release acutely, without immediate compensation.

It is suggested that all three of these drug families have the capacity to reduce acutely serotonin biosynthesis and/or release, disinhibiting the temporal lobes and leading to synchronous electrical discharges in temporal lobe limbic structures (Eidelberg, Lesse, & Gault, 1963; Ellinwood, 1971; Monroe & Heath, 1961; Radalovackey & Adey, 1965). These synchronous discharges in the temporal lobes are shown, in later sections of this chapter, to last beyond the acute drug effect and are related to increased discharge and resulting cell death in the hippocampus, associated with the appearance of a neurological state of transcendent consciousness. In some patients with temporal lobe tumors, further damage leads to another temporal lobe syndrome, a disinhibition of instinctual acting out, the Klüver-Bucy syndrome (Terzian, 1958), which can be reversed to a state of transcendent consciousness with tumor removal or antiepileptic medication. These phenomena become part of the evidence used to develop our thesis of the existence and modulation of transcendent states represented by biogenic amine–temporal lobe limbic interactions. Specifically, these drugs induce an acute loss of serotonergic regulation of temporal lobe limbic structures, releasing the affectual and cognitive processes characteristic of religious ecstasy and the permanent personality changes associated with religious conversion.

5. Neurobiological Antagonism of Amphetamine, Cocaine, the Hallucinogens, and Naturally Occurring Transient Hypomanic States by Lithium's Effect on Serotonin Biosynthesis

Since Cade's (1949) discovery of the antimanic effect of lithium, a number of mechanisms for its action have been proposed. Our work has shown that lithium has the capacity to stimulate tryptophan uptake into neurons (Knapp & Mandell, 1973, 1975), resulting in an increase in serotonin synthesis in those serotonergic cells that contain tryptophan hydroxylase (Mandell & Knapp, 1977); the enzyme appears to exist *in vivo* in an unsaturated state. This increase in serotonin synthesis can be seen in the mesostriatal system (Mandell *et al.*, 1979) as well as in the mesolimbic system; that is, both septal and hippocampal serotonin levels are augmented significantly (Mandell *et al.*, 1979). Pretreatment with lithium dampens significantly the reduction of serotonin synthesis induced by amphetamine in septal and striatal synaptosomes (Mandell & Knapp, 1976). Pretreatment with lithium appears to antagonize directly cocaine's inhibition of tryptophan uptake into synaptosomes, preventing the expected sequence of changes in the serotonergic biosynthetic system (Knapp & Mandell, 1976a). Lithium stimulates tryptophan uptake into neurons, more nearly saturating tryptophan hydroxylase and increasing the synthesis of serotonin, and these processes occur independent of cell discharge. Therefore, it is not surprising that the pattern of cell arrest (increased intracellular with no change in extracellular fluorescence) is converted to the pattern seen with cell arrestors like chlorimipramine in association with compensatory changes, that is, increases in both extracellular and intracellular amine measures (Mandell, Geyer, & Knapp, in preparation). Animal behavioral data and clinical reports have suggested that lithium antagonizes the behavioral effects of both amphetamine (Segal, Callaghan, & Mandell, 1975; Furukawa, 1975; van Kammen & Murphy, 1975) and cocaine (Cronson & Flemenbaum, 1978; Flemenbaum, 1974), and this antagonism is consistent with known serotonergic inhibition of stimulant-induced behavior (Hollister, Breese, Kuhn, Cooper, & Schanberg, 1976; Warbritton, Stewart, & Baldessarini, 1978). Consonant with this formulation is the finding that parachlorophenylalanine (PCPA) an inhibitor of tryptophan hydroxylase (Scheel-Krüger, Braestrup, Nielson, Golembiowska, & Mocilnicka, 1977), and lesions of the mesolimbic median raphe nuclei (but not the mesostriatal dorsal raphe nuclei) potentiate many of the behavioral effects of amphetamine and cocaine (Segal, 1977).

A number of manic-depressive patients on lithium in my practice have reported an almost complete loss of effect of self-administered cocaine and LSD. Challenge with these drugs on lithium effects in normal subjects has not been reported. Bunney and his co-workers have reported that in rapidly cycling manic-depressives, the day of the "switch" from depression to mania is often one of clarity, insight, empathy, and kindness, and in many ways, the patients are "much better than they are" (Bunney, Murphy, Goodwin, & Borge, 1970; Bunney, personal communication, 1978). This spontaneously occurring state, comparable to the states of transcendent consciousness induced by the hallucinogens, cocaine, and amphetamine (which differ in quality but all have the hypomanic component, to be discussed in more detail below), is also obtunded by lithium pretreatment (Goodwin, Murphy, & Bunney, 1969).

The apparent lateral specialization of affectual-cognitive function in man—the left temporal lobe with obsessional, paranoid, dysphoric, and negativistic traits, the right temporal lobe with hysterical, impulsive, and manic character—led us very recently to explore the possibility that serotonin distribution is asymmetrical, which would make one "mood" dominant, and that lithium treatment might restore relative symmetry. That such biogenic amine asymmetries occur in animals and can be altered by drugs has been reported by Glick, Jerussi, & Zimmerberg (1977) for striatal dopamine. A similar dopamine asymmetry in response to sensory stimulation has been reported by Nieoullon, Cheramy, and Glowinski (1977). Although the work is in an early stage, we have shown that there is 15% bilateral asymmetry in tryptophan concentration and about 25% asymmetry in serotonin and 5-hydroxyindolacetic acid when each hippocampus and striatum is compared with the one on the other side (Mandell *et al.*, 1979). This asymmetry is *halved* by lithium treatment. That is, a lithium-induced increase in serotonin synthesis, via an increase in tryptophan uptake, increases the symmetry of distribution of tryptophan, serotonin, and 5-hydroxyindolacetic acid in both mesostriatal and mesolimbic systems.

The mechanism seems built into the regulatory properties of the coupled tryptophan uptake and tryptophan hydroxylase biosynthetic system which has been shown to have a biphasic response to increasing substrate—activated at lower concentrations, inhibited at higher concentrations—so that increased tryptophan uptake tends differentially to reduce systems with higher synthesizing rates and to increase those with low rates (Mandell & Knapp, 1977; Mandell *et al.*, 1979; Neckers, Biggio, Moja, & Meek, 1977). Cocaine, blocking tryptophan uptake, doubles the asymmetry. Thus, the serotonin synthesis rate, controlled by the neuronal membrane uptake process for tryptophan, appears differentially to alter serotonin inhibition of the laterally specialized temporal-lobe limbic structures. This may be lithium's mechanism of action on mood, since it serves well as an antidepressant *and* an antimanic agent for *bipolar* affectual disorders (Goodwin, Murphy, Dunner, & Bunney, 1972; Noyes, Dempsey, Blum, & Cavanaugh, 1974), as does tryptophan (Coppen, Whybrow, Noguera, Maggs, & Prange, 1972; Murphy, Baker, Goodwin, Miller, Kotin, & Bunney, 1974). A periodic oscillating tryptophan uptake function has been reported by Glowinski's group (Glowinski *et al.*, 1973). Perhaps also relevant to the lithium-induced increase in serotonin symmetry is the case report of a rapidly cycling manic-depressive whose greatly asymmetric lateral distribution of EEG alpha waves in both affectual extremes was made symmetric by lithium as his moods shifted toward normal (Harding, Lölas-Stepke, & Jenner, 1976).

The coupled rate of neuronal membrane tryptophan uptake and serotonin synthesis (Glowinski *et al.*, 1973; Hamon, Bourgoin, Héry, & Glowinski, 1977; Mandell, 1975, 1978a; Mandell & Knapp, 1977; Mandell *et al.*, 1979), their close relationship to brain tryptophan content, the level of extraneuronal-serotonin–regulating rates of tryptophan uptake as studied in brain slices (Tagliamonte, Tagliamonte, Forn, Perez-Cruet, Krishna, & Gessa, 1971) and synaptosomes (Karobath, 1972), when taken in combination with substrate activation (Neckers *et al.*, 1977) and inhibition of enzyme activity (Friedman, Kappelman, & Kaufmann, 1972), explains the sinusoidal changes of serotonin synthesis over time. Since high rates would tend to be reduced and low rates increased by increases in tryptophan uptake with lithium—and a substrate-sensitive lateral asymmetry of serotonin system function has been demonstrated—it appears that an *up and down* oscillation of tryptophan uptake and serotonin synthesis is translated into a lateral, *back and forth*, distribution of serotonin inhibition of the temporal lobes. This oscillating function may be responsible for the left (verbal)-right (visual) oscillation of the REM cycle in sleep, the fantasy-thought cycle while awake, and the diurnal and seasonal cycles of mood to be explored more fully in later sections. The so-called switch in manic-depressive illness (Bunney & Gulley, 1978), a dramatic change in the clinical picture from depression to mania, or the reverse, may occur when an oscillating wave of changing serotonin inhibition shifts hemispheres. LSD and other hallucinogens, which arrest cell firing and uptake of tryptophan, may freeze the oscillating function and, via bilateral disinhibition, account for the intensification of the existent affectual state, positive or negative.

So, the lithium-induced effect on serotonin synthesis rate and symmetry in the temporal lobe limbic system antagonizing the influence of amphetamine, cocaine, and the hallucinogens—three drugs differing in mechanism but all acutely reducing mesolimbic serotonin biosynthesis and/or release—both neurobiologically and behaviorally, as well as its effect on naturally occurring hypomanic states, becomes another link in the pharmacological bridge to a neurobiological understanding of the behavioral state of transcendence. Changes induced by amphetamine, cocaine, and the hallucinogens, their effects escaping normal adaptive controls, are reversed by the increase in serotonin synthesis and symmetry effected by lithium. Connections will be made between these pharmacological effects on serotonin synthesis and the specific behavioral neurology of the structures under serotonergic control.

6. Kindling of Temporal Lobe Limbic Structures: Raphe and Hippocampal Pyramidal Cells as Double Gates to Transcendence

Kindling refers to a long-lasting or permanently reduced threshold for induced neural excitability as a result of previous excitation. The possibility that interruption of ascending inhibitory influences on temporal lobe limbic structures, of the sort described above for serotonin pathways, could produce lasting increases in excitability of the hippocampus has been noted immediately after electrolytic lesions in the mesencephalon and diencephalon, as have markedly prolonged limbic seizures produced by hippocampal stimulation (Andy, Chinn, Allen, & Shawver, 1958; Andy & Mukawa, 1960). With repeated electrical stimulation, the threshold for the induction of hippocampal afterdischarge

decreased, the length of the episodes increased, and excitation spread
beyond the hippocampus to the amygdala and the rest of the limbic
system (Andy, Chinn, Bonn, & Allen, 1958; Chatrian & Chapman, 1960;
Delgado & Selvillano, 1961; Goddard et al., 1969; Racine, Tuff, & Zaide,
1975). Cat behavior during repeated electrical-stimulation–induced
evolution of longer hippocampal afterdischarge goes through two de-
marcatable phases: when the synchronous high-voltage discharge is restricted to the hippocampus (and the septum), the behavioral ramifications include arrest, staring, and respiratory and pupillary signs; and
when the spread (propagated and induced) advances to include the
amygdala, there ensue facial twitching, tonic extension of the contralateral forepaw, and clonic convulsions (Delgado & Selvillano, 1961; Goddard et al., 1969; Sato, 1975). No behavioral automatisms or seizures
occur when the hypersynchrony is restricted to the hippocampus (Andy
& Akert, 1955). These two distinct behavioral syndromes in the cat differentiating hippocampal and amygdala involvement are clinically important because it has been shown that unconsciousness and amnesia in
man, components of clinical seizures, can be produced by amygdala but
not hippocampal stimulation (Feindel, Penfield, & Jasper, 1952; Delgado
& Hamlin, 1960).

That there are two syndromes of augmented limbic-system excitability fits the original descriptions of the full clinical picture of
psychomotor epilepsy by Gibbs (1951), who described depressed,
paranoid, and hysterical traits as interictal and *inversely* correlated with
seizure incidence in temporal lobe epileptics. Delgado (Delgado & Selvillano, 1961) reported that a refractory period for hippocampal induction
of limbic seizures lasting 15–20 minutes did not occur unless the abnormal electrical activity had spread to the amygdala. Electrical stimulation
of the amygdala in temporal lobe epileptics has been shown to duplicate
all the somatomotor, sensorial, autonomic, and behavioral phenomena
of their seizures (Chatrian & Chapman, 1960), whereas purely affectual
and personality manifestations involved the hippocampus and the septum (Heath, 1954). The confusion between ictal and interictal features in
the temporal lobe epileptic is particularly relevant to affectual
phenomena, for example, Dostoevski's episodes of religious ecstasy as
described in *The Possessed*:

> There are moments lasting five or six seconds when you suddenly feel the
> presence of external harmony . . . it is clear, indisputable, absolute feeling . . .
> you suddenly perceive the entirety of creation . . . it is a joy so great that, even
> if it were to last more than five seconds, the soul would not endure it and it
> would fade away.

Again, in his novel *The Idiot*, in the midst of sadness, oppression,
and spiritual darkness, there was a flash of light in his brain, "the very

second which was not long enough for the water to be spilt out of
Mahomet's pitcher, though the prophet had time to gaze at all the habi-
tations of Allah." These events in all probability were interictal in light of
the absolute absence of such episodes as auras to seizures in Gastaut's
(1978) large series of psychomotor epileptics. Hill (1952) also focused on
interictal impulsiveness, emotional lability, and other so-called personality problems as distinct from ictal manifestations in these temporal lobe
syndromes.

Patients with demonstrated septal and hippocampal synchronous
discharges, whose personalities included emotional intensity, acting
out, disturbed interpersonal relationships, aggression, mood lability,
and episodes of strange experiences, have tended to be *misdiagnosed* as
schizophrenic. *Missing* in them are the characteristic flattening, interpersonal isolation, or Bleulerian thought disorder. Heath's group at
Tulane did not usually make the diagnosis of affect disorder and were
strongly influenced by the Columbia psychoanalytic group as represented by the work of Hoch and Polatin to call these unusual people
"borderline" (Hoch & Polatin, 1949; Heath, 1954; Ervin, Epstein, &
King, 1955). The probability that Heath's patients were not schizophrenic was noted by Monroe (1959). The Mayo group, however, described the affectual symptoms and "queer or unusual behavior" in their
series of a hundred patients with temporal lobe spikes without resort to
the diagnosis of schizophrenia (Mulder & Daly, 1952) and also noted
that such behavior was quite distinct from the epileptic symptoms.
Temporal lobe spiking is related to the personality features of patients
with temporal lobe syndromes, including hyposexuality, religiosity, and
emotional lability and intensity, because (except for "viscosity" and obsessiveness) changes in personality constellation are demonstrable following the removal of the spike focus during temporal lobe surgery or
successful treatment with anticonvulsants (Falconer, Serafetinides, &
Corsellis, 1964; Geschwind, 1973; Falconer, 1973).

Thus, it appears that hippocampal-septal hyperexcitability induced
by loss of electrophysiological inhibition from below or direct electrical
stimulation leads to increases in excitability lasting months or years
(Andy, Chinn, Allen, & Shawver, 1958; Andy, Chinn, Bonn, & Allen,
1958; Andy & Mukawa, 1960; Chatrian & Chapman, 1960; Delgado &
Selvillano, 1961; Goddard *et al.*, 1969; Racine *et al.*, 1975; Sato, 1975),
associated with the following features: a behavioral syndrome dissociat-
able from pure motor seizure phenomena in man and animals (Andy &
Akert, 1955; Delgado & Hamlin, 1960; Delgado & Selvillano, 1961; Feindel *et al.*, 1952), with interictal personality and behavioral features that
are characterized by affectual and paranoid components (to use
psychiatric parlance) (Ervin *et al.*, 1955; Gastaut, 1978; Gibbs, 1951;

Heath, 1954; Hill, 1952; Mulder & Daly, 1952) and that can be modified by changes in the synchronous electrical discharges (Blumer & Walker, 1967; Falconer, 1973; Falconer *et al.*, 1964; Geschwind, 1973; Peters, 1971). The hippocampus now becomes a focal point for further analysis, particularly in relation to permanent changes produced there that may be invoked by drugs reducing inhibitory serotonin regulation of temporal lobe limbic function and producing transcendent consciousness.

Kindling can be induced in the limbic system by drugs belonging for the most part to the three classes of agents discussed above: local anesthetics like cocaine, stimulants like amphetamine, and the hallucinogens. In rat, cat, monkey, and man these drugs, if given chronically or in some cases acutely, lead to a lower threshold for subsequent drug-induced phenomena, continued electrophysiological signs of excitability in limbic structures, and/or progression of the drug-induced syndrome from hyperactivity to stereotypy and seizures. Post (1977) has published a comprehensive review of drug-induced kindling. The hallucinogens produce high-voltage synchronous activity in hippocampus and septum, but not in amygdala, of cat and man that may last days or weeks after one administration (Adey, Bell, & Dennis, 1962; Killam & Killam, 1958; Monroe & Heath, 1961; Winters, 1969). Septal and hippocampal synchronous activity in man has been seen on depth recordings in many pleasure states, including the euphoria induced by marijuana smoking (Heath, 1972). Cocaine and the amphetamines, when given chronically, induce hypersynchrony initially in the septal-hippocampal system, with eventual spread to the amygdala and extralimbic structures like the globus pallidus (Ellinwood, Kilbey, Castellani, & Khoury, 1977; Post, 1977; Post, Kopanda, & Black, 1976).

Fractionation of the syndrome of kindling into two behavioral patterns in animals involving separate parts of the limbic system (hippocampus–septum versus amygdala and other areas), expressed differentially as interictal versus ictal clinical phenomena as described above, may be accomplished neurochemically by the differential prominence of two inhibitory biogenic amine transmitter systems. Segal has shown that stimulant-induced hyperactivity could be potentiated by pretreatment with the inhibitor of serotonin synthesis PCPA, as well as by electrolytic destruction of the mesolimbic serotonergic cell bodies of the median raphe nucleus, whereas stimulant-induced stereotypy could not (Segal & Mandell, 1974; Segal, 1977). The necessary involvement of the spread of excitability to the amygdala for manifestation of motor phenomena, particularly stereotypy and seizures, was described above. Social isolation differentially potentiates stereotypy, but not hyperactivity, induced by stimulants, a finding similarly consistent with the independence of these two phenomena and of their underlying neural systems (Sahakian, Robbins, Morgan, & Iversen, 1975). The finding that amphetamine-induced stereotypy involves forebrain dopamine mechanisms (Costall, Naylor, & Neumayer, 1975; Randrup & Munkvad, 1967) when combined with the stimulant drug effects on dopamine synthesis as reviewed in Section 3 suggests that dopamine regulation may be more relevant to such amygdala-stereotypy-seizure phenomena as the ictal phenomena of psychomotor epilepsy, whereas serotonin inhibitory influence may regulate primarily the hippocampal-septal arrest reactions in cats, hyperactivity in rats, and limbic seizures without motor manifestations in man called pleasure or ecstasy and may be reflected in the personality syndromes of the temporal lobe epileptic and a subgroup of a psychiatrically labeled population with bipolar affect disorder.

Biogenic amine regulation of the excitability of hippocampal pyramidal cells appears central to an understanding of both the pharmacological phenomena of kindling and its clinical ramifications in the interictal personality manifestations of patients with temporal lobe limbic pathology. It is the thesis of this essay that loss of serotonin inhibitory regulation of hippocampal CA_3 cells leads immediately to their hyperexcitability and to loss of CA_3 cell system "gating" of emotionally laden associative matching of internal (temporal lobe limbic) with external events (Lennox, 1951; Penfield, 1975; Vinogradova, 1975), thence to hippocampal-septal synchronous discharges and the emotional flooding called ecstasy (depending on its subjective interpretation) (Monroe & Heath, 1961). Subsequent death of these pyramidal cells, which have a relatively unusual property of feed-forward facilitation and the tendency to become progressively excited and die (Nadler, Perry, & Cotman, 1978), may account for the permanent changes in personality following an episode of religious transcendence. These are the cells that have died in the characteristic gliosis of h1 and h3 to h5 hippocampal pyramidal cells in the brains of psychomotor epileptics with interictal features of multiple religious conversions, hyposexuality, transcendent consciousness, good nature, and emotional deepening (Bear, 1977; Blumer, 1975; Blumer & Walker, 1967; Dewhurst & Beard, 1970; Gastaut, 1953; Sano & Malamud, 1953). So loss of serotonin inhibitory tone can result from the drugs' interfering with serotonin synthesis or release, from physiological driving through activity or stress leading to serotonin release and autoreceptor-mediated median raphe cell arrest, or from reduction of sensory driving of serotonergic cells from input via sensory isolation or meditation.

Repeated or overwhelming episodes of loss of serotonin inhibition may lead to accruing excitability and then death of CA_3 cells as part of the kindling phenomena, which, we speculate, may play a key role in the "transcendence training" of such activities as prolonged and regular unning, meditation, or regular use of hallucinogens. The inadvertent gradual near-drowning of the hyperactive type of dogs in Pavlov's laboratory led to permanent changes in their personalities, so dramatic as to be called the "ultraparadoxical response" (Pavlov, 1933). The following reviews the evidence for the sequence of neurobiological mechanisms in the hippocampus. Both the serotonergic mechanisms invoked and their clinical manifestations are discussed in following sections.

The serotonin pathway to the hippocampus (Geyer et al., 1976) and specifically to CA_3 cells (Palkovits, Saavedra, Jacobowitz, Kizer, & Brownstein, 1977) has been demonstrated, and serotonin, on ionophoretic application, is depressant to spontaneous firing rate (de-Montigny & Aghajanian, 1978). It has been known that hippocampal cells of the h1 (Sommer sector) and the endfolium (h3–h5) are uniquely sensitive to excitation-induced damage in rat, cat, baboon, and man whether the agent be an excitatory glutamate analogue, a blocker of γ-aminobutyric acid inhibition, anoxia, or status epilepticus (Blackwood & Corsellis, 1976; Meldrum & Brierley, 1972; Nadler, Perry, & Cotman, 1978; Purpura & Gonzalez-Monteagudo, 1960; Schwarcz, Scholz, & Coyle, 1978; Sommer, 1880). These cells die, usually creating unilateral gliosis in the hippocampus, the most consistent neuropathological feature in patients with the temporal lobe syndrome of altered personality and transcendent consciousness (Spielmeyer, 1927; Sano & Malamud, 1953; Malamud, 1966, 1975).

The unique influence on the quality of man's consciousness and personality of the temporal lobes was reported by Jackson (Jackson, 1866; Jackson & Coleman, 1898). Penfield, reviewing more than 1,100 patients, concluded that only from stimulation of temporal lobe structures in man had he ever evoked what could be divided into experiential and interpretive responses: the first, the perception of an ongoing scene in "split" consciousness; the second, a change in the meaning of what was being experienced (Penfield, 1975). At first he called it a "memory cortex" (Penfield, 1952), but later, he acknowledged that the memories were stored elsewhere, with the temporal lobe anterior to the anastomotic vein of Labbé containing the amygdala and pes hippocampis involved as referential mechanisms (Penfield, 1958). He felt that this group of structures, along with their limbic connections, served to present interpretations of present experience to consciousness, doing for nonverbal concepts what the speech–memory mechanisms, farther back on the temporal lobe, do for words (Penfield, 1968). Affectual coloring; moods of fear, anger, boredom, and ecstasy; and nonverbal interpretive sets influence our perceptual-interpretative processes and are influenced by them. Bombarded by information from both the environment and experiences and feelings from the emotive memory banks of anterior thalamus and limbic system cortex, the temporal lobe mechanisms seem critical to the adjudicative process of comparison and decision between emotionally laden possibilities.

Functions relevant to learning—response to novelty, orienting, and habituation—have been the conventional foci in studies of the behavioral physiology of the hippocampal pyramidal cells' gating and integrating afferent paths; the strong, widespread, and prolonged inhibitory processes of these cells in the regulation of hippocampal input and output signals have been demonstrated (Anderson, 1975; Anderson & Lømo, 1970). Hyperpolarization associated with inhibition of cell discharge that follows excitation from all afferent connections is seen in these cells even without previous excitation and is probably due to collaterals of the efferent paths (Spencer & Kandel, 1961). Frequency potentiation within a narrow range, with depression of activity beyond it and long-lasting post-tetanic potentiation, has been easy to analogize to the behavioral functions of learning and memory (Anderson, 1975; Bliss & Lømo, 1973), to a high level of unit reactivity to multimodal sensory inputs and long-lasting inhibition after excitation to a gating function, and to the disappearance of cell discharges with repeated sensory stimulation to the psychological function of habituation. These studies conducted in rats, cats, and monkeys made use of objectifiable behaviors and paradigms from experimental psychology.

It will be seen from temporal lobe behavioral and electrophysiological research, as well as from psychopharmacological studies, that changes in responses to novelty and habituation are only part of larger syndromes of personality and affect when studied in man. For example, a defect in making differentiations between *allo* and *homo* significance, what Geschwind called "deepening," is a consistent feature in patients with missing hippocampal CA_3 cells with the temporal lobe syndrome of transcendent consciousness (Geschwind, 1965; Bear, 1977), and it seems consistent with findings that primates after hippocampal ablation cannot adjust their response rates down when reinforcement ratios are reduced (Clark & Isaacson, 1965); that bipolar affective disorder patients, who, as will be seen, may have bilaterally disinhibited temporal lobes, are sensory evoked-response augmenters (Buchsbaum, Goodwin, Murphy, & Borge, 1971); and that an unbridled flurry of associations (bringing from the internal memory banks material *felt* to be relevant to outside stimuli) to almost any topic is characteristic of hypomanic patients. Hypergraphia and preaching are manifestations of the increased associations and a feeling of their significance in the temporal lobe syndrome with missing hippocampal CA_3 cells (Waxman & Geschwind, 1974).

The hippocampal CA_3 cells receive reticuloseptal afferents via the medial septal nucleus (Grantyn, Grantyn, & Hang, 1971), which is important because these hippocampal cells project inhibitory axons to the mesencephalic reticular formation and median raphe serotonin cell clusters. Reticular median raphe, septal, and hippocampal CA_3 cells are sensory-driven in most modalities and undergo habituation of responses with repetition of stimuli (Bell, Sierra, Buendia, & Segunda, 1964; Bradley & Mollica, 1958; Mays & Best, 1975; Nauta, 1958; Vinogradova, 1975). The other major source of informational input to hippocampal pyramidal cells is from the entorhinal cortex, which receives from the intralaminar nuclei of the thalamus and temporal cortex and projects via the so-called perforant path through the dentate fasciculus, bringing information directly to the hippocampal CA_3 cells (cf. Pribram's concept of learning as the cortical entrenchment of the news of nonnovelty). The high concentration of norepinephrine distributed to the dentate hilus may regulate the segmental activity of the granular cells and their "transformation" during learning and habituation (Pickel, Segal, & Bloom, 1974; Vinogradova, 1975). Efferents from these cells go to the lateral septal nucleus and via the fornix and median forebrain bundle to the hypothalamus (the importance of this pathway to the peculiar pattern of glucocorticoid regulation in patients with mood disorder is discussed below) and the area of the mesencephalon where the tegmental reticular formation and the tail of the median raphe nucleus are located (Nauta, 1958; Raisman, 1969; Morgane & Stern, 1974). Thus, CA_3 cells are modulated by ascending reticular septal and median raphe projections and in turn modulate them.

An intriguing and useful proposal for the role of hippocampal CA_3 cells has been made by Vinogradova (1969, 1973, 1975), and it is not inconsistent with the suggestios of others (Adey et al., 1962; Crowne & Radcliffe, 1975; Douglas & Pribram, 1969; Grastyan, Lissak, Madarasz, & Donhoffer, 1959). She sees the hippocampus as the meeting place of two limbic circuits: (1) the circuit made by hippocampal CA_1 cells–mammillary bodies–anterior thalamic nuclei–cingulate cortex, receiving inputs from the highest levels of the convex neocortex and involved with complex information-processing, memory storage, and retrieval, which analyzes its vast source of information reflecting this analysis along the flow, beginning with gradual loss of evoked responses (habituation) and gradually being substituted by increases in evoked responses, a series of serial integrators; (2) the second circuit, the hippocampal-septal-reticular circuit with inputs from sensory collaterals in the brain stem and visceromotor, affect-related structures like amygdala and hypothalamus, bringing the quality of emotional charge as a regulatory influence on the informational activity of the first circuit. What has been called *intention* in animals, which stripped of its cognitive component in man reveals affectual tone (the "plan" riding on the feelings), has been coded in frequency patterns of the hippocampal electrical response in relation to various anticipatory behaviors (Elazar & Adey, 1967; Gray, 1970; Vanderwolf, Bland, & Whislaw, 1973). The hippocampal-septal slow waves of approach behavior can be seen as the positive expectations of the pleasure state (Heath & Gallant, 1964), incrementing as drive with frustrative nonreward (Amsel, 1958), perhaps the neurobiological substrate of the "high" of asceticism (Clark, 1965). The CA_3 cells are seen as the mediator between the two circuits, between incoming sensory information registering in the reticular-septal-hippocampal circuit and the evoked and spontaneous, emotionally colored memories of the informational circuit, with this comparison function limited by the narrow frequency range for physiological function of the CA_3 cells (Anderson & Lømo, 1970). The evaluation of new information from a data base of old memories and feelings, current affect state, and symbolic significance appears to change dramatically when the CA_3 cells are disinhibited by removal of serotonin inhibition by the amphetamines, cocaine, or hallucinogens (Adey *et al.*, 1962; Radulovacki & Adey, 1965) or when the cholinergic medial septal nuclei–hippocampal CA_3 pathway (Lewis & Shute, 1967) is blocked with anticholinergic glycolate esters like phencyclidine or ketamine (Winters, 1969; Winters, Ferrar-Allado, Guzman-Flores, & Alcarez, 1972). The endogenous opiates appear to invoke a direct effect on hippocampus, bypassing the biogenic amines (Henricksen, Bloom, Ling, & Guillemin, 1977).

It appears that a loss of hippocampal CA_3 modulation by medial septal cholinergic pathways (Fonnum, 1970), by ascending reticular (Andy, Chinn, Allen, & Shawver, 1958; Andy, Chinn, Bonn, Allen, 1958; Andy & Mukawa, 1960) or median raphe serotonergic influence (see above), or by temporary functional ablation and/or subsequent cell death (Nadler *et al.*, 1978) removes the CA_3 to CA_1 regulatory input (Blackstad, 1956) derived from sensory collaterals via the reticular formation to the medial septal nucleus (Raisman, 1966), leaving the inside world (Vinogradova, 1975) to dominate. The sudden failure of comparator function and the associated loss of the feeling of "I" will be seen to be the moment of contact with God as described by James, "unity" in most of the literature on religious conversion, luminescence in the writings of Eastern metaphysics, transcendent consciousness as used in this essay, or loss of ego boundaries and psychotic consolidation in the literature of psychopathology, that is, the sensation of "ego function" requiring the self versus nonself activities of mind. The loss of hippocampal inhibitory influence on the reticular arousal system brings the feelings of high energy (low-voltage fast waves from the scalp, high-voltage slow waves in the limbic system) along with the loss of comparator function.

Dualistic debates, conflicts, and ruminations between alternatives suddenly disappear with a feeling and perception of unity, as the internal organization, evoked symbolically by external events but demodulated as to external specificity, becomes the dominant subjective world. Henry Maudsley, the famous English neurologist, tried to explain to the demonologist Aleister Crowley the unity of subject and object as "the extreme activity of one part of the brain and lassitude in the other"—declining to indicate specifically the involved parts (Sargant, 1969). A drive–arrest sequence in the median raphe cells, due to the serotonin cell's sensitivity to autoreceptor agonist inhibitory action (Aghajanian & Haigler, 1975; deMontigny & Aghajanian, 1977), may account for the production of this state by long-distance running, hunger, thirst, sleep loss, and other stressors shown to evoke serotonin-system function (Barchas & Usdin, 1973). Meditation is speculated to silence the serotonin cells (perhaps the reticular-septal circuit as well) by removing sensory driving. John Lilly (1972) has reported that sensory isolation potentiates the pharmacological effects of two kinds of hippocampal CA_3 cell-demodulating drugs, for example, LSD and ketamine. The electrical activity associated with this CA_3 cell demodulation is high-voltage hypersynchronous activity in the limbic system (in both cats and man) (Monroe & Heath, 1961; Adey, 1964) and occlusive hypersynchrony in the reticular formation (Winters, 1975). This central nervous system state in animals tends to persist (Adey et al., 1962; Andy, Peeler, Mitchell, Joshee, & Koshino, 1968; Radulovacki & Adey, 1965), and when induced in man spontaneously or with drug, it is associated with the ecstasy of "peaking" (Pahnke, 1966).

The association of "insight" with "ecstasy," the core of the experience of religious conversion (James, 1929), appears to involve the loss of normal hippocampal comparator function. The feeling of "truth" (no more conflict between alternatives) and the feeling of ecstasy come together as personality and attitudes are changed for a long time or permanently. Whereas there has been some debate about the affectual tone accompanying septal-hippocampal hypersynchrony in animals, from pleasure to rage (Anand & Dua, 1955; MacLean, 1957), apart from considerations similar to those relevant to the psychedelic drug experience (vulnerability of interpretation to set and setting), manifold sources of pleasure such as marijuana, sexual excitement, the hallucinogens, and pleasurable fantasies have been shown to be associated with septal-hippocampal high-voltage slow waves in man (Heath, 1964, 1972; Lesse, Heath, Mickle, Monroe, & Miller, 1955; Monroe & Heath, 1961).

The extreme sensitivity of the hippocampal CA_3 cells to excited discharge from anoxia suggests the possibility that psychedelic and trancendent experiences during dying may be the result of the kind of demodulation that results from uncompensated perturbation of the serotonergic and cholinergic system input to these cells by drugs, from naturally occurring loss of these regulatory influences via various stressors, or from electrically induced septal-hippocampal hypersynchrony and are variously interpretable as frightening or ecstatic (Evans-Wentz, 1960; Otis & Haraldsson, 1977). There is also striking similarity between transcendent experiences at death involving "out of the body" perceptions, voices, an unrolling of memories, and the phenomena reported by Penfield as induced by electrical stimulation of the temporal lobes (Penfield, 1955).

7. BIPOLAR AFFECT DISORDER, THE TEMPORAL LOBES, AND TRANSCENDENT CONSCIOUSNESS

The psychiatric diagnostic description that most resembles "spontaneous" episodes of transcendent consciousness and religious conversion is that describing hypomanic episodes in patients with the so-called bipolar affective disorders, particularly Bipolar II (Dunner, Gershon, & Goodwin, 1976; Leonhard, Korff, & Schulz, 1962; Perris, 1966). James (1929) described the bipolarity of the lives of the saints in the following terms: *deepening significance... melancholy... feelings coming from deeper regions... despair... world remote... psychical neuralgia... persons move like shadows...* alternating with *wordless joy... truths known without discursive intellect... revelations... illuminations... enlargement of perceptions... insight... ecstasy... need to write and speak of spiritual life... cosmic consciousness.* Gershon, Targum, Kessler, Mazure, and Bunney (1977) summarized the criteria for bipolar affective disorder as follows: *poor appetite... sleep difficulty... malaise... agitation or retardation... self-reproach... loss of interest... slowed-up thoughts...* alternating with *hyperactivity... pressure of speech... racing thoughts... grandiosity... decreased need for sleep... easy distractability.* Dunner et al. (1976) have described a more benign form of bipolar disorder, the so-called Bipolar II. These people may be hospitalized for suicidal depression, but their manic phases tend to be under control, a hypomania that approximates the syndrome described by James. William Bunney (personal communication) has noted that on "switch" days (Bunney, Goodwin, & Murphy, 1972), emerging from depression and not yet manic, the hypomanic has clarity of thought and insight, imperturbability, empathy, kindness and awareness, and interpersonal charisma that is infectious, all of which disappear as he goes on to mania of psychotic proportions.

A characteristic peripheral hormonal manifestation of the two affectual extremes in bipolar patients may reflect underlying temporal lobe limbic mechanisms. Rapid cyclers manifest high glucocorticoids in plasma and urine during depression and low values during mania (Bunney, Mason, & Roatch, 1965; Rubin & Mandell, 1966). Stimulation of hippocampus and amygdala in man has shown that when electrically activated, the former structure produces a decrease and the latter an increase in circulating glucocorticoids (Mandell, Chapman, Rand, & Walter, 1963; Rubin, Mandell, & Crandall, 1966). Limbic regulation of these steroids becomes another evidential link between affective change and the temporal lobes, expressed through hypothalamic mechanisms (Mason, Nauta, Brady, Robinson, & Sachar, 1961). Recent work demonstrating specific corticosterone binding by pyramidal cells of the hippocampus (CA_1, CA_2, and CA_3) but not in the hypothalamus (McEwen, Wallach, & Magnus, 1974), glucocorticoid-induced changes in hippocampal pyramidal-cell firing rate (Pfaff, Silva, & Weiss, 1971), and the suggestion that glucocorticoids act on the hippocampus to shut off ACTH secretion during stress, (McEwen, Zigmond, & Gerlach, 1972) when combined with the association of hypomania (transcendent consciousness) with decreased glucocorticoid secretion, forms a psychoendocrine linkage suggesting that transcendent consciousness may be an escape from stressors such as pain, hunger, sleep loss, and depression, all elevators of adrenal corticoid secretion (Mason, 1958). Angst (1973) and others have shown that bipolar patients when stressed often go through a short period of hypomania before a clinical episode of depression, and both Freud (1925) and Abraham (1927) described the hypomanic state as a "defense" against psychological pain.

Studies of avoidance conditioning and extinction also link ACTH regulation to the hippocampus; hippocampal ablations, which retard both processes, are mimicked in effect by ACTH or polypeptide analogues (De Wied, 1969; Isaacson & Wickelgren, 1962). Decapeptides without peripheral hormonal effect also alter these behavioral functions, depending on hippocampal integrity (De Wied, Witter, & Lande, 1970; McEwen, Gerlach, & Micco, 1975). It may be that the sudden and dramatic reversal of mania by naloxone (Judd, Janowsky, Segal, & Huey, 1978), which antagonizes the effects of endogenous polypeptide opiates, involves interference with endogenous polypeptide opiate binding in the hippocampus, the key structure in the septal-hippocampal limbic hypersynchrony, which, as we have seen, is involved in pharmacologically induced transcendent states and in the neurohormonal correlates of hypomania. A recent study showed high-voltage slow waves from temporal lobe limbic sites in rats following the administration of polypeptide opiates (Henriksen et al., 1977), drugs reported to induce pleasurable states in man (Kline, Li, Lehmann, Lajtha, Laski, & Cooper, 1977).

The cortical spindles in rats following enkephalin administration (Urca, Frenk, Liebeskind, & Taylor, 1977), which resemble the electrical activity in animals that received such pleasurable stimulation as food or water (when they had been deprived) or vaginal probing or electrical stimulation (Frenk, Urca, & Liebeskind, 1978), may be the concomitant of the limbic electrophysiological events seen in hippocampal-septal sites in man from diverse sources of pleasure (Heath, 1964). The Bhagavad Gita speaks interchangeably of *transcendent* consciousness and *bliss* consciousness, pure brain pleasure without an instinctual source as a reference (Stanford, 1970). It is interesting that the extrapyramidal nuclear system containing the highest levels of intense enkephalin immunofluorescence, the globus pallidus, which also supports self-stimulation (Simantov, Kuhar, Uhl, & Snyder, 1977; Stein & Belluzzi, 1978), is the part most closely related to the hippocampal-limbic circuit (Parent & Olivier, 1970); among the thalamic nuclei, mostly devoid of enkephalin, the highest concentration is found in the nucleus paratenialis (Parent & Olivier, 1970), which too supports self-stimulation (Stein and Belluzzi, 1978) and is an important projection to the hippocampus (Valenstein & Nauta, 1959; Knook, 1966). Brain endorphins fulfill the criterion of facilitating memory consolidation to qualify as a "reinforcer" (Stein & Belluzzi, 1978), and a discriminating gate to memory is indicated by many studies as one of the hippocampus's most significant roles (Adey, 1966). The picture emerging is consistent with the formulations of both Papez (1937) and MacLean (1949): the hippocampal formation combines internal and external information ("taking orders") and regulates attention and memory and *the subjective concomitants of these activities*—that is, affective feelings—that find further elaboration and expression through other limbic structures. Bliss consciousness or transcendent consciousness, which we see as the subjective correlate of hippocampal-septal high-voltage, slow wave activity, when induced by meditation has been shown to be associated with reductions in metabolic rate (Wallace & Benson, 1972), breathing rate (Allison, 1970), cardiac output (Wallace, 1970), and skin resistance (Wallace, Benson, & Wilson, 1971), all consistent with the descending inhibitory actions of the hippocampus on cardiovascular reflexes (Hockman, Talesmik, & Livingston, 1969), visceral responsiveness (MacLean, 1957), extensor reflexes (muscle tone) (Vanegas & Flynn, 1968), and, as noted above in the context of hypomanic (transcendent) states, ACTH secretion (Endröczi & Lissak, 1959).

Thus we have seen that hippocampal-septal slow waves can be induced by drugs altering serotonergic raphe cell modulation from the brain stem such as cocaine, amphetamine, and the hallucinogens; anticholinergic drugs such as phencyclidine and ketamine, which alter septal-hippocampal relations; and polypeptide transmitters that appear to regulate neurohormonal and affective activity via their direct action on hippocampal pyramidal cells. Eastern metaphysicians have said that there is only one pleasure. It may be that the state of transcendent consciousness, Buddha's "awake," a state facilitating orienting and memory and associated with the affective feelings of pleasure and beyond (bliss consciousness), a state shown to be diversely elicitable by sexual excitement without orgasm, pleasurable fantasies, meditation, or "spiritual" exercises, constitutes what James has described as part of the primary religious experience.

Another series of studies that suggest temporal lobe involvement in what has been called *bipolar affective disorder* examined the interesting spectrum of psychiatric disorders with higher than expected incidence in relatives of bipolar probands. Many of the same behavioral patterns have been found in patients with temporal lobe disorders. These include a higher incidence of alcoholism and sociopathy (Cadoret, 1976), what Monroe (1970) called "acting out," hysteria (Shields, 1975), cycloid psychosis and atypical psychosis (Perris, 1974), minor depressive episodes and cyclothymic personality (Gershon, Mark, Cohen, Belizon, Baron, & Knobe, 1975), emotionally unstable character disorder with a favorable response to lithium (Rifkin, Quitkin, Carrillo, Blumberg, & Klein, 1972), and suicide (with higher incidence in the more psychiatrically benign Bipolar II form) (Dunner *et al.*, 1976). Affective and socially disruptive symptoms without significant cognitive disorder have been the common element in the interictal psychopathology of patients with temporal lobe electrical abnormalities, including a higher incidence of alcoholism (Blumer, 1975; Ervin *et al.*, 1955; Gastaut, Morin, & Lesevre, 1955; Gibbs, 1950; Monroe, 1970; Scott & Masland, 1953). The temporal lobe syndromes are discussed in greater detail in relation to the clinical neurology of transcendent consciousness in Section 10. Carbamazepine, a "tricyclic" drug useful in the treatment of temporal lobe seizures, has been shown to improve these patients' affective and personality problems, even without change in the seizures (Dalby, 1971; Lehmann & Ban, 1968; Tunks & Dermer, 1977). This drug, its mechanism of action not yet thoroughly explored, has been shown to suppress kindled seizures in temporal limbic structures (Babington & Horowitz, 1973) and to be an effective treatment for a significant percentage of manic patients and a small percentage of depressed patients; it has significant prophylactic action in both (Okuma, Kishimoto, Inoue, Matsumoto, Ogura, Matsushita, Nakao, & Ogura, 1973). In a recent study of double-blind, placebo-controlled, longitudinal design, 7 of 10 manic-depressive patients improved on carbamazepine; 4 of the 7 relapsed when given placebo (Ballenger & Post, 1978).

The hypothetical relationship between septal-hippocampal high-voltage, slow wave activity and hypomania (transcendent consciousness) has not been explored in suitable EEG studies. Brazier (1968) has shown in man that whereas diffuse, amygdala-led, temporal limbic abnormalities would be seen on the scalp, electrical abnormalities in the hippocampal-septal circuit alone might be missed. Phenothiazine-activated sleep EEGs with sphenoidal leads might reveal anterior temporal lobe hypersynchrony or spikes in what we call the *syndromes of temporal lobe disinhibition,* including bipolar affective disorders.

As we have seen, whereas there appears to be evidence from drug–neurotransmitter studies, temporal lobe behavioral neurology, neuroendocrinology, and psychophysiology of a septal-hippocampal mechanism for transcendent consciousness, hypomania, and high pleasure states (terms used interchangeably), evidence of a systematic neurophysiological and chemical locus for depression is less clear-cut. In view of the kind of neurohormonal linkages suggested above for the hypomanic state, it is interesting that bipolar-affective-disordered patients in the depressed state manifest increases in circulating metabolites of the glucocorticoids (Sachar, 1967), but, as has been pointed out, this phenomenon may reflect nonspecific aspects of crisis because such elevations are seen also during acute "breaks" in schizophrenic patients, crises in psychotherapeutic treatment, and postpsychotic dysphoric states, that is, times of disruption of psychological homeostasis (Sachar, MacKenzie, & Binstock, 1967; Sachar, 1969). However, analogous to the temporal lobe limbic inhibitory regulation of ACTH secretion by the hippocampus noted above, amygdala secretion in man does produce elevations in plasma glucocorticoids with latency of several minutes (Mandell *et al.,* 1963; Rubin *et al.,* 1966). The connections of the amygdala with lateral hypothalamus (pathways associated with the expression of hypothalamic rage and the Klüver–Bucy syndrome [Klüver & Bucy, 1937; Terzian & Ore, 1955]) as well as stimulant and local anesthetic drug-kindled amygdala limbic spiking (hypersynchrony spread beyond the septal-hippocampal circuit as described in Section 6) associated with stereotypy and seizures (models for paranoid psychotic states [Ellinwood, 1974; Post, 1977]) bring affects with negative valence (like fear, paranoia, and rage) under temporal lobe limbic influence, but the relationship between these states and depression is not clear-cut. As has been noted in Section 2, using antidepressant drug treatment as a model, it is likely that fear plays an important role in the genesis of what is called depression by psychiatric clinicians. The role of rage in the genesis and phenomenology of depression has always been an important aspect in psychodynamic analysis of these states (Freud, 1925), and it is interesting that a "detachment" process was seen by Freud, as well as in the Bhagavad Gita, as a treatment and/or a preventative for sorrow (Stanford, 1970). A neurology of depression apart from fear and rage is difficult to construct.

It seems likely, to remain consistent with our level of analysis, that the possibilities for depression are three: (1) Depression may emerge from the dualism, introduced in Section 6, between hypersynchrony restricted to the hippocampal-septal circuit representing pleasure/ ecstasy, which when spread to evoke amygdala spindles emerges as fear, rage, and depression, represented by typical auras in psychomotor epilepsy (Gastaut & Broughton, 1972). The temporal lobe limbic-hypothalamic pituitary representation of these states—steroids reduced with hippocampal activation and increased with amygdala stimulation—is consistent with this formulation. (2) Depression could be the subjective concomitant of malfunction, stress, overload, and disorganization, leading to the loss of slow waves in the hippocampal-septal limbic system, so whereas there is a specific neurology of pleasure and transcendent states, depression may be multifaceted—like "headache"—dysphoria as a nonspecific sign of multiple potential sources of malfunction or need, a central representation of psychic pain without specific peripheral anatomic location, and a loss of the feeling of inner harmony associated nonspecifically with elevated steroids (Sachar et al., 1967). The genitals are innervated by the protopathic pain system (Von Frey, 1895), and depression is characterized by incapacity for pleasure, anhedonia, and loss of libido. (3) Depression may be born of influences on affective specialization in the lateralization of the brain, with "negative" emotions like fear and paranoia and dysphoric feelings like sorrow and depression lying as subjective concomitants of verbal memories and analytic capacity on the left side of the brain, the left temporal lobe, and with the mute, geometrically cognitive, musical right temporal lobe specialized for joy. The evidence for this third possibility will be reviewed.

Biogenic amine lateral asymmetry in rats, functionally manifested by a turning tendency that is exaggerated by amphetamine (Glick et al., 1977; Glick & Cox, 1978), and reflected in levels of dopamine and its metabolites, suggests that lateral specialization, studied heretofore more extensively in humans and apes in the context of high cerebral symbolic activity (Milner, 1971; Rumbaugh & Gill, 1976), may have more fundamental representation in brain stem systems in all mammalian species. Recent studies have demonstrated asymmetrical norepinephrine concentrations in the human thalamus (Oke, Keller, Mefford, & Adams, 1978) and, even more relevant to our topic, that reduction of lateral asymmetry of alpha rhythm indices in a rapidly cycling manic-depressive patient after normalization with lithium (Harding et al.,

1976). We are proposing (Mandell *et al.*, 1979) an oscillating role for tryptophan uptake and serotonin synthesis that is transduced to changing lateralization of serotonin inhibition of the temporal lobes. Material relevant to affectual specialization by lateralization and what appear to be the multiple behavioral syndromes of disinhibited temporal lobes, from psychomotor epilepsy through affect disorder to syndromes of personality and character, is discussed in Section 8.

8. SYNDROMES OF TEMPORAL LOBE DISINHIBITION

The nervous system, regulated by multiple layers of inhibition, reveals its underlying organization with the loss of inhibition. The antigravity prominence of the spinal-cord motor system is seen in the spasticity that follows damage to the descending inhibitory pathways from the brain stem and the cerebrum (Jackson, 1898). In the same way, the interictal personality traits of the temporal lobe epileptic, whose lobes are disinhibited enough to evidence periodic hyperexcitability in the form of seizures, serve to teach of the underlying contributions of these structures to personality, behavior, and human experience. For this purpose, the "pure" temporal lobe syndrome is instructive, with interictal anterior temporal lobe spikes and neuropathology restricted to medial temporal sclerosis (Gibbs, 1951; Mulder & Daly, 1952; Ervin *et al.*, 1955) and a specific loss of pyramidal cells from the hippocampus (Malamud, 1967, 1975).

The seizures themselves—transient attacks of autonomic, sensory, and affectual auras; motor automatisms; confusion; and sequential behavior like "a person acting out a bad dream," with amnesia for the event (Gibbs, Gibbs, & Fuster, 1948)—are not as revealing as the progressive changes in behavior typically taking 14 years to reach exaggerated, clinically troublesome proportions (Slater & Moran, 1969) or the character of the interictal episodes, which are more expressive of the underlying content and contribution of the temporal lobes to the qualities of consciousness (Geschwind, 1975a,b). As a matter of fact, Gibbs and others have suggested that there is a reciprocal relationship between manifestations of character pathology and incidence of seizures (Gibbs, 1951), noting a worsening (intensification) of alterations in personality when seizures are treated successfully with anticonvulsants (Hill, Pond, Mitchel, & Falconer, 1957), and suggesting that temporal lobe limbic seizures may be therapeutic, via the induction of long lasting hippocampal-septal "pleasure"—slow wave afterdischarge. Interictal epochs of behavioral abnormality are associated frequently with a normalization of the EEG (Landolt, 1955), and in light of Penfield's (1975) statement that in stimulation experiments during his long study of some 1,100 patients, it was only in the temporal lobes that he produced alterations in either the interpretation of ongoing experience or the induction of unreal experience, it is not surprising that a great deal of what has constituted the purview of the psychiatrist shows up in the interictal clinical phenomena of the temporal lobe epileptic patient.

In analyzing these cases, it is important that we not be restricted to psychiatric categories of diagnosis derived from a history and politics not easily relatable to known brain function (Geschwind, 1973). For example, many reports of interictal behavioral disturbances in temporal lobe epileptics have used the rubric *schizophrenia* to label the marked deviations from reality-oriented adaptive functioning more properly called *psychotic*. The almost omnipresent affectual intensity, called by Geschwind *deepening* (Geschwind, 1975a,b; Pond, 1957) the absence of characteristic thought disorder (Bleuler, 1950), and the close although often difficult interpersonal relationships maintained (Slater & Beard, 1963) are inconsistent with a diagnosis of schizophrenia (American Psychiatric Association, 1968). Although there are unambiguous cases of paranoid "schizophrenia" (Flor-Henry, 1969a) among this group, the poor phenomenological and genetic relationship between that syndrome and the other schizophrenias is known (Winokur, 1977). *Organic* versus *functional* categories for behavioral syndromes lose their currency when the most thorough neuropsychological tests available, the Halsted–Reitan battery, fail to discriminate affective disorder from temporal lobe epilepsy or "brain damage" from schizophrenia (Donnelly, Dent, & Murphy, 1972).

When objective psychological instruments standardized on patients grouped phenomenologically or on the basis of psychodynamic personality constellations have been used to examine temporal lobe epileptic patients, there has been poor correspondence with established psychiatric diagnostic groups (Glaser, 1964; Mignone, Donnelly, & Sadowsky, 1970; Small & Small, 1967; Tizard, 1962). Yet, as we shall see, when the intrinsic cognitive and sensory–affective characteristics of each temporal lobe are examined from a review of patients with known unilateral temporal lobe lesions, it becomes possible to infer a relationship between the spectrum of personality and behavioral characteristics of patients with disinhibited temporal lobes and a spectrum of "functional" psychopathological syndromes that include affect disorder, character pathology including aggressiveness, paranoia, obsessiveness, hysteria, and alcohol and drug addiction—perhaps representing a gradient of lost serotonergic inhibition of temporal lobe subjective phenomena as well as dopaminergic nigral–amygdaloid compulsive and aggressive behaviors (Cadoret, 1976; Gershon *et al.*, 1975; Guze, Woodruff, & Clayton, 1972;

Shields, 1975; Van Valkenburg, Lowry, Winokur, & Cadoret, 1977; Winokur & Clayton, 1966). Recent studies have shown that amphetamine-induced motor behavior can be antagonized by tryptophan (Hollister *et al.*, 1976) or intraventricular administration of serotonin (Warbritton *et al.*, 1978). A recent conference reviewing the successful use of lithium in many of these apparently diverse psychiatric syndromes (Kline, Gershon, & Schou, 1978) and the elucidation of lithium's capacity to increase serotonergic inhibition of temporal lobe function with changing lateral asymmetry (Mandell, *et al.*, 1979) may be consistent with this formulation. Goodwin's group (Brown, Goodwin, Ballenger, Goyer, & Major, 1978) recently reported a strong negative correlation between the serotonin metabolite 5-hydroxyindolacetic acid in spinal fluid and life histories of outwardly or inwardly directed aggressive behavior in a population of individuals with character disorders and/or alcoholism. Van Praag, Korf, and Schut (1973) had earlier reported low CSF levels of the same metabolite in a subgroup of patients with affect disorder. The polygenic pattern of inheritance of the affective spectrum disturbances (Gershon, Targum, Kessler, Mazure, & Bunney, 1977) may represent the genetics of a continuum of differentially lateralized serotonergic inhibition.

Here we will examine the behavioral patterns revealed by those experiments of nature, humans with disinhibited temporal lobe function and histologically demonstrable neuropathological changes, and try to relate them to clusters of similar behavior patterns as studied in clinical psychopharmacology. In Section 9, we will look at the psychopharmacological induction of disinhibition and inhibition of temporal lobe function and see that there are commonalities between the syndromes revealed by neurological material and psychotropic drug-induced phenomena.

The lateral specialization of brain function for a number of activities has been established (Harnad, Doty, Goldstein, Jaynes, & Krauthamer, 1977), and a behavioral analysis of temporal lobe function serves here as a heuristic tool. The human temporal lobes are anatomically asymmetrical (Geschwind, 1968; Lemay & Culebras, 1972) and appear specialized as to style of cognitive functioning, with the left being verbal/analytic and the right spatially integrative (Milner, 1974; Sperry, 1974). Penfield's (1959) early observations that nonverbal memories serve in the right temporal lobe as verbal (speech) memories do in the left are consistent with these later formulations. A lateral specialization of affect has been suggested from the picture of high mood and denial versus low mood and exaggeration of problems when left- and right-sided stroke patients were compared (Weinstein & Kahn, 1955); from studies in which left and right intracarotid injections of amytal resulted in left lobe disinhibition being reflected in fear and right lobe disinhibition in joy (Rossi & Rosa-dini, 1967; Terzian, 1964); from the dependence of euphoria and psychedelic effect on the right temporal lobe in temporal lobe epileptics given LSD (Serafetinides, 1965); from the negative valence in behavior of temporal lobe patients with electrical abnormalities on the left (Glaser, 1964); from more optimism and denial of symptoms with cerebral lesions on the right than on the left (Gainotti, 1972); from more influence purely on mood with right-sided electroconvulsive treatment (Galin, 1972); and from leftward gaze in response to emotional questions implicating the right cerebrum (Schwartz, Davidson, & Maer, 1975).

Whereas Flor-Henry has developed a position that what he calls schizophrenia involves left temporal lobe damage and manic-depressive syndromes involve the right (Flor-Henry, 1969a,b, 1972, 1976; Flor-Henry & Yeudall, 1973), his work seems to suffer from less attention to the texture of the clinical phenomena and more reliance on conventional psychiatric diagnostic categories of the major mental illnesses, categories that undergo formal revision regularly and that were derived to deal with what amount to psychosocial syndromes of interpersonal adapta-tion to the presence of a psychiatric diagnostician. For example, the verbal-analytic mode of the left temporal lobe is the tool we use to explain our behavior and feelings to ourselves and others. It was called left temporal lobe "consciousness" by early workers like Dandy (1931), who removed various parts of the human brain as part of his neurosur-gical practice, and recently by Popper and Eccles (1977) in their theoreti-cal effort to locate the "self." What is more likely is the importance of verbal skills in maintaining the complex psychosocial work of coping, the *appearance of consciousness* to others. A sequence of Minnesota Mul-tiphasic Personality Inventory (MMPI) studies of patients with brain damage incorporating the Halstead–Reitan indices of lateralization suggests that reactive problems secondary to the loss or distortion of verbal capacity are prepotent in configuring personality reactions from left-side damage (Dikman & Reitan, 1974, 1977). In the same way, the obsessional-paranoid mode of dealing with others—described in psychological as well as in psychoanalytic studies of character pathology (Fenichel, 1945; Weintraub, 1974) and characterized by general negativism, exaggeration of difficulties through continued preoccupa-tion, projection of rage, ruminative self-concern, mistrust, emotional isolation, and other features of *dysphoric thinking style* (in contrast to the manic denial of the hysteric)—would, in extreme, appear "psychotic" and seems to be what Flor-Henry calls schizophrenia of the left lobe.

Likewise, tendencies toward bland denial (*la belle indifference*) in high moods, "emotionality," and impulsivity (due to the absence of delay function inherent in the prolonged verbal analyses of the obsessional lobe) the personality researchers would call a hysterical (Chadoff & Lyons, 1958; Lazare, 1971) or cyclothymic personality pattern (Tupin, 1974). The extreme expression of this temporal lobe personality constellation is what Flor-Henry labels *manic-depressive*. Character traits like the hyposexuality of hysterics are seen to have a biological substrate in the context of temporal lobe neurology (Blumer & Walker, 1967; Gastaut & Collomb, 1954). Mood alterations—the hysteric's apparently intense feelings, which are more subtle in expression than the paranoid fixations and passive-aggressive argumentativeness of the obsessional—become prominent when not obscured by the syndromes of temporal lobe disinhibition on the left side. Temporal lobe phenomenology, like character pathology (Walton, Foulds, Littman, & Presly, 1970; Kernberg, 1971), is most often the exaggerated and mixed expression of both ends of the obsessional/paranoid and manic/hysteric personality continuum (Beard & Slater, 1962; Chafetz & Schwab, 1959; Emerson, 1915; Ervin *et al.*, 1955; Falconer, 1954; Gibbs, 1951; Malamud, 1967; Mulder & Daly, 1952; Walker, 1973). It is probably a similar group of personality and mood disorders that have been called the *affective spectrum diseases* (Cadoret, 1976; Gershon *et al.*, 1975; Winokur & Clayton, 1966). We suggest that the access to action of both the left and the right temporal lobe styles of thinking and fantasizing, the so-called psychopathic component in these syndromes (Ervin *et al.*, 1955; Flor-Henry, 1976; Flor-Henry & Yeudall, 1973; Gibbs, 1951; Mulder & Daly, 1952) may derive from similar losses of serotonergic inhibition and an additional involvement of the behavior-emitting, dopamine-gated amygdala circuit as described in Section 3 above. Pribram and others have noted that whereas the limbic amygdala circuit drives sensorimotor activity, the hippocampal–septal pathways facilitate its inhibition (Black, 1975; Pribram, 1967).

The elegant and objective work of Bear (Bear, 1977; Bear & Fedio, 1977) clarifies the relationship between the occurrence of discrete unilateral temporal pathology and the personality syndromes of diminished temporal lobe inhibition. By using a population that for the most part had not entered the health system through psychiatric portals, by not using conventional categories of psychiatric diagnosis, by using the technique of objective ratings by self and others and multivariate analyses, he has been able to describe personality patterns and their relations to manifest electrical abnormalities in the dominant and non-dominant temporal lobes. Questions were constructed about 18 behavioral traits taken from the literature of temporal lobe epilepsy to constitute a 90-item questionnaire, to which a 10-item validity scale from the MMPI was added. The 100-item instrument was given to both the subject and someone in his environment who had known him for a long time. Bear compared patients with unilateral right or left anterior spiking foci. Both groups scored higher in all 18 categories of personality description—that is, exhibited intensification of personality trains—than control groups of normals or patients with neuromuscular disease. It was clear that the left locus facilitates the emergence of such attributes as anger, humorlessness, sadness, obsessiveness, and aggressiveness; the right locus, such attributes as emotionality and elation.

Far more revealing, however, was the difference in the personality profiles of the left versus the right temporal lobe subjects when their own ratings were compared with ratings of them by others. Here can be seen the interpersonal cognitive ("defense") style directly. Whereas the subjects with left foci saw themselves as worse than others rated them in almost all 18 categories ("tarnishing"), the right foci facilitated the reverse, an overestimation of positive attributes like elation and an underestimation of such characteristics as circumstantiality, obsessiveness, dependence, sadness, and humorlessness ("polishing"). By using a hierarchical cluster analysis, Bear was able to separate a grouping of dysphoric, socially unacceptable traits such as depression, suicidal feelings, explosive temper, peevish irritation to small disturbances, and inappropriate defensiveness from a positive cluster including feelings of self-worth, ability to see meaning behind suffering, personal etiquette, conscientiousness in personal dealings, and minimal sexual needs. Patients with left foci saw themselves in the negative cluster and were seen much less so by others; the reverse was the case for the patients with right temporal lobe foci.

In the context of Bear's work, we see that disinhibition of the temporal lobes, with a lateralization bias, leads to intensification of the spectrum of personality features that have as feeling components of cognitive style (an association observable in all patients and studied extensively by psychoanalysts working with character pathology [Fenichel, 1945]) two aspects of mood: pessimism with obsessiveness and optimism with hysteria; in the extreme, depression and elation. Thus, it appears that mood disorder as a function of the degree of asymmetric disinhibition of the temporal lobes accompanies the degree of disinhibited expression of the cognitive style of the lobe involved. In this context, observations like Glaser's (1964), "more psychopathology in left temporal lobe patients," translate to more negative impressions of the self and the environment, more paranoid ruminations about being abused, and the natural association of such thoughts with anger and counteraggression, which, when added to motor dyscontrol, can be antisocial. When examined closely, Flor-Henry's observation that there is more "schizophrenia" in patients with left lobe foci (Flor-Henry, 1969a, 1972, 1976; Flor-Henry & Yeudall, 1973) results from an association with paranoid states, which from the work of Bear we see as a component of the cognitive style of that lobe. Even the major Schneiderian sign of schizophrenia, a voice of outside influence, resembles what Penfield elicited in some cases by stimulation of the left temporal lobe (Penfield, 1955, 1959, 1975). Hypomanic states, elation, the state that determines the label *bipolar* or *manic-depressive* attributed to right lobe pathology by Flor-Henry (Flor-Henry, 1969a, 1972, 1976; Flor-Henry and Yeudall, 1973) can now be seen as an intensification of the personality trait tendencies of the right lobe.

   This pathological intensification of personality traits can be seen as the common element, speculated as due to disinhibition of temporal lobe function, in the so-called affective spectrum disorders (Winokur & Clayton, 1966; Gershon *et al.*, 1975; Cadoret, 1976). For example, a group of patients with anterior temporal lobe spikes, but *without histories of seizure,* showed episodic affectual swings, intensification of hysteric and obsessional personality traits, and "acting out" (Ervin *et al.*, 1955). Transient episodes of exaggerated temporal lobe expression, temporary disinhibition of temporal lobe function, may be the mechanism underlying stress-induced transient neurotic reactions, from the obsessive/compulsive to the hysteric. We shall suggest shortly that a drive–arrest sequence perhaps in all three biogenic amine cell systems (norepinephrine, dopamine, and serotonin), dictated by exquisite inhibitory autoreceptor sensitivity to their own transmitters, could "release" the temporal lobe temporarily from biogenic amine inhibition. Permanent disinhibition of these structures may be reflected in what have been called the *neurotic character disorders* (Fenichel, 1945). The varying course of the mood disorders, inverse to seizure incidence in the temporal lobe epileptic, *also clearly periodic* (Gibbs, 1951; Landolt, 1955; Pond, 1957; Strauss, 1959), could result from what may be harmonic lateral oscillation of serotonin inhibition with different periods (100 minutes, a day, a season). The reciprocal relations between hippocampus and amygdala in limbic circuitry (MacLean, 1958) and the relation of amygdala activation to seizures as described previously may be the biological bases for the inverse effects of treatment on seizures and personality–mood manifestations (Ervin *et al.*, 1955; Flor-Henry, 1969b; Gibbs, 1951; Gibbs, Gibbs, & Fuster, 1958; Glaus, 1931; Mulder & Daly, 1952; Strauss, 1959). The phasic nature of seizures and mood disorders led to the early diagnostic rubric of *larval epilepsy* for what is now called *bipolar affective disease* (Morel, 1873).

   As suggestive as is the range of personality trait intensification in the interictal clinical picture of the temporal lobe epileptic for the possible mechanism of neurotic character pathology and mood disorders, the quality of the patient's significant relationships is even more so. This interpersonal style—called *viscosity,* a tendency to be dependently needful of positive feedback from people in the psychomotor epileptic's life, an interpersonal stickiness, a need for reassurance and evidence of care (Geschwind, 1973; Blumer, 1975; Geschwind, personal communication, 1978)—is the neurologist's way of describing what the psychoanalyst sees as the hallmark of the severe neurotic character or borderline patient (Kernberg, 1975; Knight, 1953), the tendency to make intense and distorted transferences. These patients are easily provoked into recall of painful emotional memories under "similar" circumstances that configure ongoing experience with significant others, what Geschwind has called "intensification," as high drive levels lead to inappropriately broad stimulus generalization. The transference object out of sight, things left ambiguous, such patients are attacked by voices and images of undesirable possibilities: not being loved; being held in contempt; not being understood; being humiliated. They need to call their doctor or remain beyond the session to discuss, continuing to try to "straighten out" with him or another important person what the "facts" of the relationship are, hoping for relief from those imagined possibilities. Their emotional memories easily evoked from their disinhibited temporal lobes, relevance felt to ongoing events, they seek outside reassurance that their dysphoric reminiscences are not true. This "dependence" was elicited from both the patients and their observers by Bear's questionnaire (Bear, 1977; Bear & Fedio, 1977) and was more prominent in people with left anterior temporal EEG abnormalities.

The psychopharmacology of both the temporal lobe and the neurotic character and mood disorders can be seen as consistent with "viscosity" and "neurotic transference" arising from disinhibited temporal lobes. Klein et al. (1978) have demonstrated that the characteristic "separation anxiety" and other aspects of neurotic dependence—another way of trying to convey the neurologist's "viscosity" or the psychoanalyst's "neurotic transference distortion"—is responsive to the tricyclic antidepressant drugs and, in some cases, to the monoamine oxidase inhibitors (Blumer, 1975; Klein et al., 1978). As noted, there are a number of reports that the "best" drug for psychomotor epilepsy is carbamazepine, which improves the mood and personality problems even when it does not change the incidence of psychomotor seizures (Dalby, 1975; Lehmann & Ban, 1968). Tricyclics given acutely or chronically reduce raphe cell firing rate (Bramwell, 1974) and lead to postsynaptic supersensitivity (deMontigny & Aghajanian, 1978). Tryptophan hydroxylase activity, in another compensatory move, increases (Mandell & Knapp, 1978a). However, the presynaptic autoreceptors appear to be affected differently. Tricyclic pretreatment reduces significantly the actions of LSD (Davis, Gallager, & Aghajanian, 1977), the model autoreceptor inhibitory agonist. Might it be that tricyclic drug-induced autoreceptor *subsensitivity* protects patients from the result of stresses that might otherwise drive serotonin neurons and lead to their arrest via inhibition by their own transmitter and subsequent release of temporal lobe CA_3 cells and the temporal lobe limbic system from serotonergic inhibition? Tricyclics, early in their administration, perhaps during the phase of cell arrest before subsensitivity can take place, can lead to release of the temporal lobe limbic system and to psychotic reactions (Coppen, Ghose, & Jørgensen, 1978; Prien, Caffey, & Klett, 1973). The basic pharmacology of carbamazepine in the serotonin system remains to be explored. Our model leads to the speculation that it will work the same way the other tricyclics do, by the induction of autoreceptor subsensitivity to serotonergic inhibition while partially releasing postsynaptic CA_3 cells from inhibition, allowing the emergence of septal-hippocampal slow (pleasure) waves. The successful treatment of severe obsessional illness with tricyclics, a recent development (Group for the Advancement of Psychiatry, 1975; Klein *et al.*, 1978), is also consistent with the psychopathophysiological speculation of a disinhibited temporal lobe syndrome. Blumer (1971) has pointed out that the "viscosity" of the temporal lobe epileptic occurs only after puberty, which is suggestive of the relevance of sexuality (in the broad sense) and object significance as evocateurs.

Besides the increased intensity of personality traits and mood that lie latent in the temporal lobes, the temporal lobe epileptic experiences two other kinds of transient affectual phenomena: one, the characteristic aura of temporal lobe seizures, consisting of fear, panic, and terror (Gastaut & Broughton, 1972; Gowers, 1901; Jackson, 1880–1881; Macrae, 1954); the other, interictal episodes *not associated with seizures* that are characteristically more positive in tone, even ecstatic, and frequently interpreted as belonging in a religious context (Howden, 1872–1873; Mabille, 1899; Boven, 1919; Sedman & Hopkinson, 1966; Dewhurst & Beard, 1970). The mutual exclusiveness of the aura of fear preceding seizures and the experience of ecstasy as an interictal event has been emphasized recently by Gastaut in a reanalysis of Dostoevski's ecstatic "auras," in which Gastaut pointed out that not in 35 years and many hundreds of epileptic patients, had he seen ecstasy as an aura preceding seizure (Gastaut, 1978). Lennox's (1960) analyses of over a thousand cases revealed only nine preseizure auras that were pleasant and none that were ecstatic. Whereas Gastaut concluded that Dostoevski's religious ecstasies were invented by his literary imagination because he reported them as auras, others have pointed out that the experiences occur interictally, independent of motor or seizure phenomena (Dewhurst & Beard, 1970; Geschwind, personal communication, 1978; Waxman & Geschwind, 1974). Walker (1973) observed that "dysphoric moods characterized by increasing irritability and hypersensitivity (paranoid thinking) lasting hours or days may herald an outburst of anger or a seizure," whereas a typical interictal ecstasy occurs without warning; the patient would be "overcome with a feeling of bliss... mood was elated... mind was clear," not associated with even minor manifestations of the events of temporal lobe epileptic seizures, lip smacking, or olfactory hallucinations, and followed by long-lasting positive affect and clinical improvement (Dewhurst & Beard, 1970).

As reviewed in Section 6, the progressive stages of kindling of the temporal lobe limbic system induced by electrical stimulation are characterized first by hypersynchrony confined to the hippocampal-septal circuit (associated with behavioral arrest and staring), followed by facial movements, stereotypy and seizures when the hypersynchrony spreads to the amygdala (Delgado & Selvillano, 1961; Sato, 1975). Two forms of limbic seizure are also seen with psychopharmacological kindling. Repeated treatment with amphetamine, cocaine, or lidocaine leads to stereotypy and seizures with hypersynchrony throughout the limbic system, including amygdala spindling (Ellinwood *et al.*, 1977; Post, 1977; Segal & Mandell, 1974). The hallucinogens in animals (Killam & Killam, 1958; Adey *et al.*, 1962) and in man (Chapman, Walters, & Mandell, unpublished observations, 1962–1963) induce hypersynchrony lasting weeks after a single injection (Radulovacki & Adey, 1965), which remains restricted to the hippocampal-septal circuit of the temporal lobe limbic system, and the related behavioral signs in animals are signaled by altered orienting behavior (Radulovacki & Adey, 1965) but never by forced motor activity.

As has been reviewed in Section 4, whereas cocaine, amphetamine, and the hallucinogens reduce serotonin availability to receptors acutely by differing mechanisms, amphetamine also influences dopamine pathways, known to be important substrates of stereotypic (Cools & Van Rossum, 1970; Costall & Naylor, 1973; Creese & Iversen, 1972; Scheel-Krüger, 1972), aggressive, and paranoid behavior (Snyder, 1972) of the sort that has characterized the *ictal* behavior of temporal lobe epilepsy (Taylor, 1969; Falconer, 1973). The evidence of the involvement of the hallucinogens in altering dopamine function, especially in the low doses associated with autoreceptor agonist action, is not as compelling (Persson, 1977; Pycock & Anzelark, 1975). Whereas there is a significant dopamine input to the amygdala, the dopamine content of the hippocampus is so low as to suggest that it is there only as the norepinephrine precursor (Moore & Bloom, 1978). Unlike dopamine and norepinephrine, the serotonin supply is much higher to the hippocampus than it is to the cortex (Moore & Heller, 1967; Moore, 1975). It thus appears that the two kinds of limbic hypersynchrony—hippocampal-

septal versus amygdala-involved high-voltage activity—may be regulated prominently by serotonin and dopamine, respectively, may be
elicitable by the hallucinogens versus drugs like amphetamine, and may
involve transcendent consciousness with pleasurable benignity in contrast to fear and rage, the former being the substrate of the interictal
"attacks" of ecstasy; the latter, of irritability, anger, rage, and seizures in
the temporal lobe epileptic.

This theme can be carried into the clinical psychopharmacology of
the two families of drugs. Whereas the "high" of amphetamine is short-
lasting and usually followed by a short period of poststimulant drug
lethargy and depression (Segal & Janowsky, 1978), the hallucinogenic
drug effects are characterized by continued high mood for days or weeks
(Naranjo, 1975; Unger, 1964). Recent brain stimulation studies in man
have shown that the hippocampus has a lower threshold for and much
longer duration of hypersynchronous afterdischarge than the amygdala,
in which it was difficult or impossible to produce (Cherlow, Dymond,
Crandall, Walter, & Serafetinides, 1977). Only when a hippocampal-
septal seizure reaches the amygdala is there a refractory period of about
20 minutes (Delgado & Selvillano, 1961) before another can be induced
electrically, an interesting correspondence to the refractory period following sexual orgasm (Masters & Johnson, 1966). The long-lasting feelings of well-being after interictal episodes of ecstasy in temporal lobe
epileptics have been noted (Dewhurst & Beard, 1970; Mulder & Daly,
1952), but fear and rage last only as long as the seizure episodes (Macrae,
1954; Lennox, 1960). The relationship between the amygdala and the
lateral hypothalamus in the phenomenon of sham rage (Flynn, 1967;
Haymaker, Anderson & Nauta, 1969) and the almost consistent presence of hippocampal-septal hypersynchrony in man during the experience of a variety of pleasures—from pleasant fantasies to marijuana
smoking (Heath, 1964, 1972; Heath & Mickle, 1960; Monroe & Heath,
1961), which contrasts to the association of high-voltage waves in amygdala with negative thoughts (Lesse et al., 1955)—are consistent with two
kinds of temporal limbic hypersynchrony.

Hippocampal slow waves are seen as representing an "optimal"
level of brain activity for energy, orienting, learning, memory, and attention (Block, 1970; Vinogradova, 1975), a positive background state
optimizing brain function. It is possible that some hypomanic states are
associated with hypersynchrony restricted to the hippocampal-septal
circuit, but, as shown in simultaneous recording from depth and scalp
electrodes in man, it is amygdala not hippocampal dysrhythmia that
reaches the superficial leads (Chatrian & Chapman, 1960). There are no
studies in the literature of manic-depressive patients during either
mania or depression using nasal or sphenoidal leads and pharmacologi-

cal activation. Alpha chloralose activation studies, shown to be useful in bringing to the surface latent temporal lobe limbic electrical abnormalities (Brazier, 1954; Monroe, Heath, Miller, & Fontana, 1956), do activate differentially the EEGs of the types of mood and character disorder patients that we have here called the syndromes of disinhibited temporal lobes or the affective spectrum disturbances (Monroe & Mickle, 1967), with the exception of alcoholics, who may represent a group with some pharmacological tolerance.

As we have seen, there is a strong possibility that psychopharmacological agents that alter serotonergic function alter the amine's influence in the two brain hemispheres differentially. Although comparative studies of biogenic amine function using two sides of the brain are in their infancy, it has already been shown that the turning tendency in rats is related to a 15% bilateral differential in concentrations of dopamine and its metabolites, and that amphetamine, which exaggerates the directional proclivity of the turning, is associated with an increase in the bilateral asymmetry of concentrations of dopamine and its metabolites to 30% (Glick, Jerussi, Waters, & Green, 1974; Jerussi & Glick, 1976). We have observed about the same proportional shifts in the bilateral distribution of serotonin, its precursor tryptophan, and its metabolite 5-hydroxyindolacetic acid with cocaine; that is, the drug approximately doubles the bilateral differential, whereas with lithium, the asymmetry is halved (Mandell et al., 1979).

When these findings are considered in light of those showing that alterations in brain serotonergic function induced by specific serotonergic neurotoxins or median raphe lesions increase turning but not stereotypy in response to amphetamines (Costall & Naylor, 1975; Jacobs & Cohen, 1976; Milson & Pycock, 1976), and that amphetamine, which diminishes serotonin synthesis by decreasing the level of reduced pterin cofactor necessary for tryptophan hydroxylation (Mandell et al., 1979), is potentiated in its effect on turning by LSD in a dose that inhibits serotonergic autoreceptors (about 20 μg/kg), the idea emerges of separate but converging mechanisms (Fleischer & Glick, 1978) consonant with an LSD-induced reduction in serotonin postsynaptic inhibition.

We continue to explore our hypothesis about oscillating serotonergic asymmetry between the brain hemispheres, particularly with reference to the dramatic reduction in that asymmetry observed with lithium treatment. It appears that the lateralization in the clinical phenomena of temporal lobe epilepsy is reflective of two psychobiological syndromes: (1) A neuro-biological substrate for obsessional, paranoid, fearful, and rageful mental states, more prominent with left (dominant) temporal lobe foci or spikes and influenced by a dominant hemispheric, dopamine-regulated hypersynchrony involving the amygdala. In normal people these events may be associated with fear and rage, may be activated by drugs like amphetamine, and may have only short periods of activation followed by lethargy and depression—a dysphoric state. (2) A neurobiological substrate for transcendent consciousness, more characteristically hysterical, denying of negative possibilities, visually symbolic, intuitive, impulsive, with a more dominant right temporal lobe focus or spikes and influenced by a nondominant hemispheric, serotonin-regulated hypersynchrony involving the hippocampal-septal circuit but not the amygdala. In normal people these events may be associated with pleasure ranging from relaxed harmony to ecstasy, may be activated specifically by the hallucinogens, and may have long periods of afterdischarge associated with a positive background state of feeling—a euphoric state.

It was MacLean's (1958) suggestion that the hippocampal-limbic and amygdala-limbic systems, substrates respectively of feelings of pleasure and fear/rage, are reciprocally innervated, as are the gravity and antigravity reflexes of the spinal cord. In light of the reciprocal relationship between the presence of anterior temporal lobe abnormalities, psychomotor seizures, and the degree of psychopathology in temporal lobe patients, reviewed above, the selective activation of the hippocampal-septal system by natural means or by drugs may be a new basis for psychiatric treatment. The dramatically reconstructive effects of spontaneous or mescaline-induced transcendent or mystical states in borderline patients has been reported in the psychoanalytic literature (Horton, 1974); indeed, such healing has long been known.

9. The Activated Sleep Syndrome, the Drive–Arrest–Release Sequence in Biogenic Amine Neurons, and the Psychopharmacology of the Bipolar Affect Disorders

We have thus far developed a model for transcendent consciousness that involves the loss of serotonin inhibition to hippocampal CA_3 cells, with resulting increase in their activity, manifested in hippocampal-septal slow waves ranging from simple slowing in the harmonious pleasure of the relaxed state (perhaps reflected in the regular rate of approximately 1/sec of the "pacemaker" cells in the hippocampus, the septum, and the serotonergic raphe nuclei [Artemenko, 1972; Morales, Roig, Monte, Macador, & Budelli 1971; Mosko & Jacobs, 1974]) to the driven hypersynchrony of hippocampal-septal seizures (without spread to the amygdala), which we see as the neurobiological correlate of ecstasy—spontaneous, induced by drug or meditation, or as observed in transient interictal experiences of religious ecstasy undergone by the temporal lobe epileptic patient. The afterdischarge of this event may last days or weeks (Radulovacki & Adey, 1965) and is associated with positive feelings as a background state for optimal brain function and other aspects of the state of transcendent consciousness. In the last section of this essay, Section 10, we examine this event as reported in spontaneous occurrences of religious conversion.

Similar changes in hippocampal-septal activity are induced by such anticholinergic psychotropic drugs as phencyclidine (Adey & Dunlop, 1960) and ketamine (Winters et al., 1972), which we speculate may act in the cholinergic septal-hippocampal circuit via the pathway of Lewis and Shute (1967), and the opiates, which appear to act directly in the hippocampus, producing hippocampal-septal slow waves (Henriksen et al., 1977). The opiate effect is blocked by naloxone but not by lithium, which, as described in Section 5, obtunds the effects of cocaine, amphetamine, and the hallucinogens via its action on the serotonin system arising from the raphe nuclei. Consistent with this conceptualization is the finding that lithium fails to block the opiate "high" (Jasinski, Nutt, Haertzen, Griffith, & Bunney, 1977), while naloxone blocks spontaneous hypomania in some patients, suddenly and dramatically (Judd et al., 1978). Serotonin cells are gated locally by γ-aminobutyric acid (GABA) (Gallager & Aghajanian, 1976b), so the other drug family producing transcendent consciousness consists of GABA agonists such as muscimol (Angrist, personal communication, 1978; Tamminga, Chase, & Crayton, 1978). Thus, ignoring the important and less diffuse norepinephrine pathway to the hippocampus (Segal & Bloom, 1976), to which we have given a sensory information-processing function, and acknowledging the nigral dopamine pathway to the amygdala, to which we have ascribed a role in aggressive behavior, stereotypy, and seizures, there appears to be a psychopharmacological model for the disinhibition of hippocampal-septal slow waves associated with pleasure that involves serotonin regulation from the median raphe nucleus, cholinergic regulation from the septum, opiate regulation locally, and GABA regulation via local inhibition of serotonin cells. When these potential sites of psychopharmacological action are considered with the sedative neocortical "release" phenomena shown to activate latent temporal lobe feelings of "joy" (Terzian, 1958), only the "inibriantia" class of drugs like alcohol are missing from among the original classifications by Louis Lewin (1964) of drugs giving pleasure: euphorica (opiates), phantastica (hallucinogens), excitantia (amphetamine and cocaine), and hypnotica (sedatives).

Central to this model is the role of the serotonin inhibitory system on temporal lobe function. The clinical manifestation of the speculated asymmetric loss of this inhibition in personality and mood disorders (both kinds of patients frequently showing low 5-hydroxyindolacetic acid in their cerebrospinal fluid as noted above) have been described as seen by the neurologist, the psychoanalyst, and the psychiatrically oriented personality researcher. This chronic state of disinhibition produces a spectrum of conditions that we have seen are relatable to chronic character pathology, episodic neurotic and mood disturbances under stress, and transient episodes of religious ecstasy. James (1929) noted the long-standing "sick" personality and mood manifestations as almost constant features before the luminescent moment in the lives of saints.

Another syndrome that may be associated with a transient, diffuse loss of serotonin modulation of neural activity, analogous to that postulated for transcendent consciousness, is the state of activated or REM sleep (Aserinsky & Kleitman, 1953; Dement, 1958), shown to be driven or led by the activity of the giant cells of the pontine tegmentum (Hobson, McCarley, Pivik, & Freedman, 1974; Siegel, McGinty, & Breedlove, 1977), which, however, are not necessarily selective for activated sleep. Two biogenic amine systems serve an inhibitory role, discharging inversely with the giant cells: the locus ceruleus norepinephrine system (Jouvet & Delorme, 1965; Hobson, McCarley, Wyzinski, & Pivik, 1973) and the raphe serotonergic system (McGinty & Harper, 1972). Pontogeniculo occipital (PGO) spikes, the central signature of activated sleep, have been reported inhibited by serotonin (Brooks & Gershon, 1971; Ruch-Monachon, Jalfre, & Haefely, 1976). Although occurring in the sleep state and not emergent into behavior, the pattern of neurobiological events, if they resemble those speculated to be under serotonin regulation and released during episodes of transcendent consciousness, should show some consonance with the pattern of physiological events during activated sleep. There is evidence that this may be the case.

Activated sleep, associated with visual imagery and detailed narrative sequencing of events when examined in the sleep subject immediately after his dream, unlike the condensed and distorted versions heard by the psychoanalyst (Dement, 1960; Dement & Wolpert, 1958; Roffwarg, Dement, Muzio, & Fisher, 1962), shows precisely the sort of "memory" unfolding that Penfield and others have reported from temporal lobe stimulation (Penfield & Perot, 1963; Penfield & Mathieson, 1974). It is interesting that sleep subjects awakened during REM sleep recall visual imagery of the sort ascribed to the right temporal lobe; those awakened in slow-wave sleep characteristically are engaged in verbal discussion (or without recall), suggesting more left temporal lobe disinhibition. Lateralization has not been a prominent dimension in sleep research, but it may be that the sleep cycle represents a sequence of left–right oscillations driven by an oscillation in tryptophan uptake and serotonin synthesis, as described above (Mandell *et al.*, 1979). A daytime rhythm alternating between reality and fantasy has a similar time constant (Friedman & Fischer, 1967; Kripke & Sonnenschein, 1973). It appears that serotonin disinhibition of giant cells driving oculomotor muscles associated with the rapid eye movements of activated sleep (Keller, 1977) is associated with the imagery that we have speculated occurs with disinhibition of hippocampal CA_3 cells when the functional serotonin supply is interrupted (Roffwarg *et al.*, 1962).

A second dramatic aspect of activated sleep is the loss of muscle tone in face and neck, seen easily from periorbital and neck leads in the conventional sleep laboratory (Dement, Ferguson, Cohen, & Barchas, 1969). Expression of motor activation is prevented in activated sleep by postsynaptic inhibition (loss of facilitation) of some motor neurons (Pompeiano, 1970). This phenomenon appears to be inconsistent with serotonin's characteristic inhibitory influence: a loss of serotonin inhibition should produce high muscle tone and movement in the face and neck. However, McCall and Aghajanian (1978) have recently demonstrated the presence of serotonin receptors on cells of the facial nerve motor nucleus that *facilitate* motor cell discharge and, unlike the inhibitory serotonergic postsynaptic receptors, are blocked by agents that block serotonin's effect on smooth muscle, for example, methysergide. Thus, a loss of serotonin input to the facial muscles would *decrease* muscle tone, and both the almost parkinsonian inexpressiveness of the psychotically depressed and their short REM latency (Kupfer, 1976) may be from loss of a postsynaptic serotonin effect, expressed by the loss of facilitation of face muscles and the disinhibition of (left) temporal lobe dysphoric mentation. Maas, Redmond, and Gaven (1973) have reported that chronic administration of PCPA produced "masked facies" in their *Macaca* monkeys. However, not all brain-stem–derived muscle systems lose their facilitation. The middle ear muscles contract during activated sleep (Dewson, Dement, & Simmons, 1965), reducing the transfer of energy from the air to the cochlear fluid and unit activity in the cochlear nucleus (Jouvet, 1962). The diffuse spinal motor neuron inhibition that occurs during activated sleep (Pompeiano, 1970), duplicated by loads of 5-hydroxytryptophan (Lundberg, 1966), may not be a direct inhibitory effect as has long been thought. Rather, because tryptophan and 5-hydroxytryptophan loads *reduce* raphe firing rate (Aghajanian, 1972a; Gallager & Aghajanian, 1976b), probably secondary to autoreceptor agonist inhibition, it may be the effect of loss of serotonergic facilitation of the sort reported recently for direct serotonin nerve endings on motor neurons of the seventh nerve nucleus (McCall & Aghajanian, 1978).

A third manifestation of the activated sleep state is penile and clitoral erection (Fisher, Gross, & Zuch, 1965). Bulbospinal serotonin pathways ending in the lumbosacral area, *not as prominent in the cervical area*, are known (Dahlstrom & Fuxe, 1965; Fuxe & Jonsson, 1974), and recent work has shown them to be inhibitory (Sangdee & Franz, 1978); perhaps the inhibitor is related to the descending bulbospinal reticular tract of Magoun and Rhines (1946). Thus, serotonergic disinhibition in the lumbosacral cord may be consonant with an increase in tone in genital reflexes or a more integrated mechanism in the hypothalamus. There is recent evidence that hypothalamic serotonergic receptors modulate sexual lordosis in the female rat (Foreman & Moss, 1978). Benson found that some good meditators experience spontaneous erections and ejaculations (Geschwind, personal communication, 1978). Meditation may decrease serotonergic tone by reducing its background rate of sensory driving—an immediate response of the unit to sensory input in a 1–3/sec cell is a routine way for neurophysiologists to check their location in raphe cells (Jacobs, personal communication, 1978). We have seen that serotonin agonists in high doses produce paralysis in the hind limbs of rats.

A fourth manifestation of activated sleep is hippocampal-septal slow waves without amygdala spindling (Jouvet, Michel, & Mounier, 1960), a pattern very similar to that induced by hallucinogens or by various forms of pleasure. Amygdala units reduce their firing in slow-wave sleep (Jacobs, 1973). We observed that intravenous administration of 5-hydroxytroptophan produces earlier and longer-lasting activated sleep in human subjects (Mandell & Mandell, 1965; Mandell, Spooner, & Brunet, 1969), a finding that we could now interpret as the result of autoreceptor agonist inhibition of serotonin cells, consistent with the discovery by Muzio, Roffwarg, and Kaufman (1966) that 12–25 μg of LSD before sleep also markedly enhanced the length of the first dream as well as the percentage of activated sleep during the early part of the night. Thus, using Aghajanian's elegant and systematic work demonstrating three kinds of receptors for serotonin—autoreceptor-inhibitory, *with the most sensitivity* (Aghajanian *et al.*, 1968); post-synaptic-inhibitory, as in the lateral geniculate or hippocampal CA_3 cells (Haigler & Aghajanian, 1974; deMontigny & Aghajanian, 1978); and post-synaptic-facilitative, as in the facial nerve nucleus (McCall & Aghajanian, 1978)—we can speculate that the syndrome of activated sleep may be one of generalized loss of serotonin effect and may bear many of the same features, or perhaps represent the same neurological syndrome, when it occurs in the waking state, transcendent consciousness.

The periodicity of serotonin cell discharge, maintained even in brain slices (McGinty & Harper, 1976; Mosko & Jacobs, 1974), contrasts to the lack of periodicity in the discharge of the giant cells of the pontine tegmentum (McCarley & Hobson, 1974) and suggests that the ultradian rhythm of the sleep-stage cycle may be regulated by the raphe cells or perhaps by the in-step activity of septal and hippocampal neurons (Artemenko, 1972; Morales et al., 1971). The coupling of raphe unit discharge rate to tryptophan uptake (Hamon et al., 1977) may be the mechanism by which serotonin cell activity is locked to biosynthesis rate and thereby to the rate of lateral shuttling of the wave of serotonin inhibition to alternate temporal lobes. The dramatic alterations in time sense that occur with hypomania, meditation, and hallucinogenic drug effects may be tied to an arrest of these pacemaker cells and their shuttling mechanism.

There is an interesting correspondence among the length of the REM cycle (Hobson, 1975), the refractory period for electrical induction of REM episodes (Jouvet, 1962), postcoital afterreactions associated with hypothalamic-pituitary insensitivity to ovulation evoked by vaginal stimulation in rabbits (Sawyer & Kawakami, 1959; Khazan & Sawyer, 1964), limbic seizures that spread to the amygdala (Delgado & Selvillano, 1961), and the refractory period after sexual orgasm in man (Masters & Johnson, 1966). Aghajanian (personal communication, 1978) has noted that there is a slow return to normal discharge rate after serotonergic autoreceptor agonist inhibition by LSD as compared with the immediate return to normal after the administration of a GABA agonist.

The pharmacology of activated sleep has been reviewed recently by Gillin, Mendelson, Sitaram, and Wyatt (1978). The studies in this field are extremely difficult to interpret. For one example, many have treated the brain's multiple pathways as if they were all one unregulated gland, and the asymmetry dimension has never been addressed. For another, tryptophan loads do not duplicate postsynaptic serotonin because they also arrest serotonin cell firing via autoreceptor inhibition (Gallager & Aghajanian, 1976) and first activate (Neckers et al., 1977) and then inhibit (Friedman et al., 1972) the critical serotonin enzyme, tryptophan hydroxylase. When a manipulation like reserpine is used to "deplete" brain serotonin, what is not acknowledged is that reserpine increases reduced pterins in brain (Bullard, Guthrie, et al., 1978; Bullard, Yellin, et al., 1979; Mandell & Bullard, 1978a,b) and increases serotonin synthesis (Knapp et al., 1974) while reducing its stores. Thus, the increment in amount or tendency for the phasic events of sleep (e.g., PGO spikes) induced by reserpine (before it destroys sleep) (Dement et al., 1969) can be seen to operate similarly to tryptophan loads (Gallager & Aghajanian, 1976b) or to LSD; that is, autoreceptors mediate inhibition with loss of postsynaptic serotonin effect and a "release" of PGO spikes.

Multiple interacting adaptive mechanisms and presynaptic changes in biosynthetic rate (changing pre- and postsynaptic impingement as well as alterations in receptor supersensitivity [Mandell, 1978a]) account for the field of sleep psychopharmacology's having resisted integration. For example, PCPA, which inhibits serotonin formation via three separate mechanisms (Knapp & Mandell, 1972), initially *increases* activated sleep, and later, even when REM sleep is gone, the phasic elements continue (Dement, Henriksen, & Ferguson, 1973). Serotonin postsynaptic receptor supersensitivity, after tricyclic administration (deMontigny & Aghajanian, 1978), adds another factor. So, although PCPA markedly reduces brain serotonin, the physiological status of the serotonergic system is difficult to describe precisely. During chronic treatment with PCPA, REM "quanta" go through three phases: up, down, then up. The postamphetamine, REM-dominated recovery period (Rechtschaffen & Maron, 1964) we could view as secondary to amphetamine's capacity to diminish reduced pterins in brain, which are necessary to the function of tryptophan hydroxylase and tyrosine hydroxylase (Bullard, Guthrie, *et al.*, 1978), and the very slow return of the reduced pterin pool to control levels (Bullard, Yellin, *et al.*, 1978), and we could speculate about a synaptic serotonin deficiency's releasing tegmental-giant-cell–regulated REM sleep from serotonergic inhibition though total brain levels might be affected very little.

Consistent with the concept of a sleep cycle regulated by an oscillating rate of serotonin synthesis with an ever-changing bilateral distribution of postsynaptic inhibition are recent findings that slow-wave sleep is associated with an increase in cerebrospinal fluid 5-hydroxyindolacetic acid collected from the cisterna magna (Buckingham & Radulovacki, 1975) and that sudden and complete arrest of dorsal raphe serotonin cells occurs with the onset of activated sleep (McGinty & Harper, 1976). Using Aghajanian's complement of serotonin receptors, one could speculate that postsynaptic serotonin inhibition is consistent with depression of the neural system associated with slow-wave sleep (Dement, Holman, & Guilleminault, 1978), bearing some relation to lateralization. Serotonergic effects on autoreceptors would mean inhibition of cell firing and release from postsynaptic inhibition. Motor neurons with direct input may be facilitated by serotonin and, as Aghajanian has observed (McCall & Aghajanian, 1978), may be responsible for the hyperactivity syndrome occurring after large tryptophan loads given with monoamine oxidase inhibitors (Grahame-Smith, 1971). Thus, with graded serotonin influence, one could imagine an initial release of structures from serotonin inhibition by unit arrest, followed by serotonin inhibition of neural activity, followed by hyperactivity with, at the same time, a postsynaptic change in bilateral asymmetry of the serotonin inhibition of limbic forebrain activity. This triphasic pattern is most characteristic of behavior following graded increments of brain serotonin via tryptophan loads (Mandell *et al.*, 1969).

We have noted that, in the way the hippocampal CA_3 cells are seen as the gate to the temporal lobe limbic behavioral phenomena of mentation and feeling released from serotonergic inhibition by such drugs as LSD acting on serotonergic cells, such drugs as phencyclidine and ketamine influencing the cholinergic system may produce many of the same phenomena via cholinergic pathways. In the literature on sleep research, it has long been known that cholinergic compounds also can induce aspects of the activated sleep syndrome (Jouvet & Michel, 1960; Sitaram, Mendelson, Wyatt, & Gillin, 1977). We have developed the position that dysphoric thinking and feeling as well as hypomanic impulsive denial are qualities of the temporal lobes; that is, disinhibition of their latent function can be manifested by either kind of human experience, and which one predominates may be a function of genetically based anatomical asymmetry (Rubens, 1977). Against this supposition, we can examine what appears to be a relationship between potentiation of serotonergic influences and cholinergic influences. Subjects "stoned" on marijuana (viewed here as a raphe-cell-arresting hallucinogen) were precipitated into a syndrome undifferentiable from severe psychotic depression by physostigmine within a few minutes; this depression was readily reversed by atropine (El-Yousef, Janowsky, Davis, & Rosenblatt, 1973). Physostigmine facilitates the emergence of REM sleep only at times when the serotonin cells from below are silent physiologically because of the time in the cycle (McGinty & Harper, 1976; Sitaram *et al.*, 1977); this reaction may be an example of temporal lobe limbic "release" by septal-hippocampal cholinergic and raphe cell serotonergic mechanisms invoked simultaneously during sleep. The short latency and dominance of REM sleep in psychotic depression, comparable to narcolepsy in this regard, may be some similar combination of loss of serotonergic gating and cholinergic action (Gillin *et al.*, 1978). There is some suggestion that cholinergic function may be more influential in left than in right temporal lobe function because choline substrate loads increase memory function for *low-imagery* words (Sitaram, Weingartner, Caine, & Gillim, 1978). The psychopharmacological response of the activated sleep syndrome, aspects of the clinical response of mood disorder patients, and drug responses in patients with temporal lobe epilepsy have many similarities. Perhaps all involve laterally biased disinhibited temporal lobe function.

A vague and intuitively derived concept of "gathering instinctual pressure" is used in many apparently disparate theoretical discussions: psychoanalytic theories of drive (Freud, 1954), storing of REM or phasic event pressure with selective REM deprivation (Dement, 1960; Dement *et al.*, 1966, 1969), psychological stress leading to an ecstatic climax (Sargant, 1957), stress gathering to a "psychotic" break (Cohen, Baker, & Cohen, 1954; Paykel, Myers, Dienelt, Klerman, Lindenthal, & Pepper, 1969), sexual tension mounting to orgasm even in patients with complete spinal cord transections (Zeitlin, Cottrell, & Lloyd, 1957; Money, 1960), depressive pain gathering to the moment of the sudden "switch" to mania in manic–depressive patients (Bunney *et al.*, 1972), dysphoria preceding the transcendent effects of hallucinogens (Giarman & Freedman, 1965; Bowers & Freedman, 1975), fear and depression preceding religious conversion (James, 1929; Rattenbury, 1938), irritation and rage building to psychomotor seizures in the temporal lobe epileptic (Blumer, 1975; Sherwin, 1977), and uncomfortable dysphoria in the early period of tricyclic antidepressant treatment in some responders (Mandell, Segal, & Kuczenski, 1975). What James called the "period of unease before all ecstasy" could also describe what precedes the onset of severe dysphoria called *depression*.

It is tempting to speculate that all such sequences represent the same general neurochemical mechanism: a rhythmic or stress-driven increase in biogenic amine cell discharge and release of transmitter, which impinges on both auto- and heteroreceptors until a critical level is reached at the autoreceptor, leading to the system's sudden arrest, with resulting release of downstream systems from inhibition. Under strong stimulation producing biogenic amine cell electrophysiological synchrony—all the cell group responding at once, as when a pure autoreceptor agonist like LSD in low doses makes all the cells involved act in concert—there is sudden loss of inhibition and resulting activation of the temporal lobe limbic system where either ecstasy or agony waits to emerge, depending on the degree of excitation and/or lateralization. It is well known that LSD disinhibition can produce a dysphoric or a euphoric experience, although it has no effect on serotonin synthesis rate (Mandell *et al.*, 1979). Perhaps LSD arrests the lateral serotonin shuttle wherever it happens to be, intensifying the present emotional experience.

A drive–arrest sequence could be common to all three biogenic amine systems. Autoreceptors, with high affinity for their own agonist, mediate arrest of dopamine cells; this effect has been demonstrated by the arrest of firing with microgram quantities of apomorphine (Aghajanian & Bunney, 1973), by the arrest of locus ceruleus cells with equally small amounts of the alpha agonist clonidine (Greenberg, V'Prichard, & Snyder, 1976), and by Aghajanian's seminal finding in the serotonin cells of the dorsal raphe nucleus, with LSD, norepinephrine, and serotonin operating physiologically in a recurrent inhibition by axon collaterals (Aghajanian *et al.*, 1968, 1977; Wang & Aghajanian, 1977a).

Although postsynaptic feedback pathways for the serotonin system seem less clear than those for dopamine, the habenula at least is of major importance (Aghajanian & Wang, 1977), and it is possible that autoreceptor arrest and postsynaptic release from inhibition are associated with feedback to the GABA interneurons regulating serotonin cells (Gallager & Aghajanian, 1976), increasing or prolonging the arrest phase in what may be a cyclic process including the loss and gain of sensitivity by autoreceptors. As noted, the outcome of raphe cell arrest could depend on which temporal lobe limbic system is more prominently released, which would explain the unpredictable clinical outcome of LSD—dysphoric pain or transcendent ecstasy. If this sequence turns out to be the common mechanism underlying "gathering instinctual pressure" to a climactic but discontinuous event, it might explain (along with the presynaptic and receptor adaptive changes described above) why amino acid precursor load studies have produced such variable results in sleep experiments (Gillin *et al.*, 1978) and why there appear to be so many paradoxes in the theories of drug action related to neurotransmitters in the clinical syndromes called the *affect disorders*.

A prophylaxis against the occurrence of the drive–arrest–release of the downstream activity sequence would be the induction of autoreceptor subsensitivity. Aghajanian has recently demonstrated heteroreceptor supersensitivity of hippocampal pyramidal cells to the inhibiting effect of serotonin after chronic treatment with tricyclics (deMontigny & Aghajanian, 1978); his group has also reported that tricyclic pretreatment leads to a marked reduction in the behavioral effects of LSD (Davis *et al.*, 1977). We deduce that these results are due to facilitated serotonin transmission at the autoreceptors. Perhaps the tricyclic-LSD experiments offer a model for tricyclic prophylaxis in affect disorder: reduction by autoreceptor subsensitivity of the potential for a drive–arrest–release sequence. Some bipolar patients are precipitated into mania by tricyclics early in the course of their treatment (Bunney *et al.*, 1970; Coppen, Montgomery, Gupta, & Bailey, 1976), in the presence of postsynaptic supersensitivity but perhaps before autoreceptor subsensitivity is achieved. Aghajanian (personal communication, 1978) has found in pilot experiments that lithium, as effective as the tricyclics in the treatment of depression in bipolar patients (Goodwin *et al.*, 1972; Mendels, 1976) but never leading to manic episodes, does *not* lead to postsynaptic supersensitivity in hippocampal pyramidal cells as the tricyclics do, a finding consistent with a lithium-induced increase in postsynaptic serotonin inhibition as reported recently in a neurophysiological study (Sangdee & Franz, 1979). It may be that tricyclics and lithium, both effective prophylactically in bipolar affect disorder (Prien *et al.*, 1973), share the capacity to induce raphe neuron autoreceptor subsensitivity in addition to increasing the symmetry of temporal lobe limbic inhibition. In my clinical experience, both tricyclics and lithium obtund the euphorogenic and psychedelic actions of hallucinogens.

Against this background, it becomes possible to explain why tryptophan can be both antidepressant and antimanic (Farkas, Dunner, & Fieve, 1976; Murphy et al., 1974; Prange, Wilson, Lynn, Alltop, & Stikeleather, 1974), producing postsynaptic inhibition and autoreceptor subsensitivity in the raphe system that functions as an inhibitory gateway to the temporal lobes—the left one expressing depressive, and the right expressing manic—phenomena—as well as how tryptophan can be as effective an antidepressant as the tricyclics and in fact potentiate their effect (Coppen, Shaw, Herzberg, & Maggs, 1967; Coppen, Whybrow, et al., 1972) and how its mechanism of action may be the same as that of lithium (see Section 5). It may also be possible to understand why fenfluramine, a functional serotonin agonist (Knapp & Mandell, 1976b), reduces the clinical signs of mania (Cookson & Silverstone, 1976; Pearce, 1973) and depression in bipolar patients (Murphy, personal communication, 1978).

If episodes of affect disorder represent a loss of serotonergic inhibition of temporal lobe limbic phenomena, their valence depending upon which side predominates, and if the phasic events of activated sleep represent the same neurobiological syndrome, one would predict that drugs that reduce the incidence of affectual diathesis would also reduce the amount of activated sleep. Too few data are available to allow us to say anything about lithium in this regard, but the tricyclics, while decreasing latency to sleep and spontaneous arousals, do reduce the amount of activated sleep, and this finding has been consistent in several studies (Hartmann, 1978). The monoamine oxidase inhibitors act similarly (Hartmann, 1978). Unfortunately, most studies of the effects of tryptophan loads on sleep have used very large amounts (5–15 g), risking, as noted above, the mixed effects of activation and inhibition of tryptophan hydroxylase, so the data are difficult to interpret (Hartmann, 1978). The study best controlled for dose, starting with 1 g and going to 15 g, produced results consistent with our model: a decrease in activated sleep, although sleep in general was facilitated (Hartmann, Cravens, & List, 1974).

So far we have developed the case that affect disturbances in bipolar individuals; the interictal ecstasies in temporal lobe epileptics; the transcendent consciousness induced by the serotonergic, cholinergic, and GABAergic hallucinogens and meditation; some aspects of the clinical effects of the amphetamines and cocaine; and activated sleep epochs— all represent the same or very similar neurobiological constellations: a sequence beginning with a laterally biased loss of serotonergic inhibition of temporal lobe limbic function via the hippocampal pyramidal CA_3 cells, resulting in an increased CA_3 cell discharge, reflected in hippocampal slow waves proceeding to hypersynchronous high-voltage discharge ranging from pleasure to ecstasy, depending on lateralization and the presence or absence of amygdala involvement. The spontaneous occurrence of this phenomenon with "stress" or perhaps with calculated loading from activities like running is speculated to result from the drive–arrest–release sequence of function built into the physiology of biogenic amine neurons and their connections with the temporal lobe limbic system. It may also account for the building up of instinctual pressure to the breaking point implied in studies of REM deprivation, the pathogenesis of psychosis, or stress-induced transcendence. The concluding section of this essay addresses an additional locus for this cluster of events: religious ecstasy and conversion.

10. Religious Ecstasy and Conversion

The neurochemical, neuropharmacological, and neurophysiological model constructed here suggests that within the continuum of slow waves to hypersynchronous seizures restricted to the hippocampal-septal-reticular-raphe circuit (without amygdala involvement) lies the essential neurobiological constellation underlying positive to ecstatic feelings, and that they can be induced by the use of techniques directed toward disinhibition of that circuit. The Russians studying theta waves from scalp leads and limbic phenomena in animals have designated this state optimal for learning and memory (Belenkov, 1970). Objective studies of autonomic correlates of this end point of meditation suggest it to be ideal for cardiovascular health (Benson, Beary, & Carol, 1975). We have also speculated that hypersynchronous seizures are associated with ecstasy, a transient and "ineffable" climactic event, the primary religious experience, which leads to the several weeks or months (perhaps lifelong duration) of what James called "saintly," kind, insightful, loving, emphatic living. We have suggested that this prolonged positive background state is a concomitant of the characteristic prolonged afterdischarge of the hippocampal-septal circuit, in contrast to the amygdala (Cherlow *et al.*, 1977). In man, living for days or weeks in a new background state of optimal brain function reconfigures perceptions of life, creating more positive and harmonious interpretations of the environment. These new concepts (in concert with the positive feelings) lead to the characteristic long-lasting changes in personality and living that follow religious conversions, which objective studies have shown include the abandonment of addictions like alcoholism, devotion of energy to more creative and constructive activity, and repair of life careers and family and interpersonal relationships (Allison, 1967; Christensen, 1963; Underwood, 1925).

The major source of evidence supporting this formulation comes from clinical studies of temporal lobe epileptics who can be seen as suffering from the "local" disinhibition observed most commonly after the excitement-induced loss of hippocampal CA_3 cells resulting in medial temporal sclerosis (Sommer, 1880; Malamud, 1966). In passing, it should be noted that evidence is accruing, as reviewed in Section 6, that these cells have a tendency toward feed-forward facilitation and death, thus suggesting another possible explanation, in addition to relearning in a positive background state, for the long-standing personality changes that follow ecstatic conversional experiences. Primary religious experiences (apart from seizures), exaggerated piety as an interictal personality change, "hallucinations of God," and multiple religious conversions were reported early in the literature of epilepsy (Boven, 1919; Glaser, 1964; Mabille, 1899). It is likely that prolonged hippocampal–septal hypersynchronous discharge follows grand mal seizures (Green & Shimamoto, 1953), which perhaps accounts for the subsequent elevations in mood. Prolonged limbic afterdischarge may account for the good dispositions of temporal lobe patients with "pure" unilateral medial sclerosis (Geschwind, 1975a,b). The increased insight and empathy associated with interictal experiences of this sort (Mullan & Penfield, 1959) make them more than the sensory hallucinatory experiences of music or God's voice that may accompany the ecstatic moment (Karagulla & Robertson, 1955). In a careful statistical study of 69 psychomotor epileptics, 26 of them reported what the investigators describe as interictal "mystical delusional" experiences (Beard, 1963; Slater & Beard, 1963).

The "delusional" quality of these episodes should be addressed. The experience of a sudden attack of all-encompassing ecstasy followed by empathic beatitude with no external explanation—such as having taken a drug, having engaged in meditation, or having had a near brush with death—leads understandably to a projection of its source to God. A projective mechanism for interpreting an event felt but difficult to locate in space may be a fundamental feature of human brain function. Békésy (1963) has shown that the source of sensory stimuli applied to the ends of two adjacent fingers with a latency between them of under 2 msec is experienced as coming from some distance away, between the two in space.

The most careful documentation of the interictal ecstatic religious experience in temporal lobe epileptics was published by Dewhurst and Beard (1970); the associated personality, attitudinal, and behavioral sequelae, by Geschwind's group (Geschwind, 1964; Waxman & Geschwind, 1974, 1975), and Blumer (1975). The syndrome accompanying interictal temporal lobe spiking includes the occurrence of spontaneous ecstatic episodes, religious preoccupations, and compulsive, usually metaphysical, writing and preaching with a general feeling state of good-natured kindness. Other aspects of the personality syndrome have been described in Section 8. A marked reduction of interest in sexuality (*not* impotence), first reported in temporal lobe epileptics by Gastaut (1956), is a prominent feature accompanying the religious preoccupations. Walker (1973) reported the amazement of these patients at their friends' interest in dirty jokes and pornographic displays and "obsessions" with the libidinal aspects of sex (Blumer & Walker, 1967). If their spike foci arose before adolescence, they did not notice their own lack of sexuality; this unawareness was in contrast to their awareness of it if their foci emerged later. The most interesting aspect of what is probably maintained limbic afterdischarge—the state noted in Section 9 to be associated with refractoriness of the hypothalamic-pituitary system to the ovulation that results from vaginal stimulation in the rabbit (Sawyer & Kawakami, 1959) and part of the positive background state of transcendent consciousness—is that when the spike focus is treated successfully with anticonvulsants or by removal of the temporal lobe, eliminating the hypersynchrony, there are a worsening of the personality problems, an increase in irritability and dysphoria, a loss of religious and metaphysical preoccupations, a worsening of interpersonal problems, and *a return of sexual interest* (Blumer & Walker, 1967, 1975; Falconer, 1973; Walker & Blumer, 1977; Waxman & Geschwind, 1974, 1975). It is tempting to speculate that hippocampal-septal slow waves associated with transcendent consciousness—while improving personality features, disposition, and insightful empathy—reduce bonding with others as the source of instinctual pleasure (Swieczkowski & Walker, 1978; Westermeyer, Bush, & Wintrob, 1978). The Bhagavad Gita suggests that transcendent consciousness is associated with "detachment" from objects of desire (Mahesh Yogi, 1969), occurring automatically on the attainment of higher states of consciousness. The surgical removal of the amygdala, which releases hippocampal slow waves (MacLean, 1957), is associated with disaggregation of the social structure of primate groups living in the wild (Dicks, Meyers, & Kling, 1969); monkeys wander off alone (Mirsky, 1966; Rosvold, Mirsky, & Pribram, 1954). Recent studies of heavy marijuana users (as noted previously, the drug induces hippocampal slow waves that persist) indicate that they have experienced a reduction in their sexual interest (Maugh, 1974). Perhaps there is a neurological substrate for the Eastern metaphysical statement about the inconsistency of rage and desire, which generate attachment, with transcendent consciousness (Smith, 1958). The rage of the amygdala-dominated limbic hypothalamic system (Gloor, 1955; de-Molina & Hunsperger, 1959) may be inconsistent with the behavioral and subjective concomitants as well as the high-voltage slow waves restricted to the hippocampus and the septum (MacLean & Ploog, 1962). Blumer (1970) suggested that the Klüver–Bucy syndrome of insensitivity (psychic blindness), unbridled oral-sexual activity, and tendency toward rage is reciprocal in temporal lobe epileptics with the syndrome of religious ecstasies, kindness, sensitivity, and hyposexuality when changed with antiepileptic drugs or neurosurgical removal of the focus. The female cat's orgasm ends in a hissing rage, frightening away the male in a stereotyped "defense" reaction driven by the amygdala (Hilton & Zbrozyna, 1963), whereas sexual excitement without orgasm may not spread to the amygdala (MacLean & Ploog, 1962). Rats that undergo kindling into prolonged limbic afterdischarge manifest delayed puberty (Hilton & Zbrozyna, 1963). Sexual behavior has not been studied systematically in meditators, but an established researcher in the movement (Farrow, personal communication, 1978) indicates that sexual preoccupation is reduced among long-term meditators.

Amphetamine, a drug that mimics the energetic "high" of rage, is associated with postdrug lethargy and depression (Connell, 1958). This effect is in contradistinction to the energetic euphoria induced acutely by the hallucinogens, which we have noted is characteristically associated with a prolonged period of positive mood (Pahnke, 1966). The course of the development of the elation also differs. Amphetamine effect, like irritation and rage, accrues monotonically and then is discharged, although there have been reports that amphetamine in some normal subjects produces sleepiness (Tecce & Cole, 1974), whereas the hallucinogens induce a transitional state of tentativeness, dysphoria, discomfort, and sleepiness before euphoria is attained (Grof, 1975). Accounts of spontaneous religious ecstasy and conversion characteristically include a preceding period of depression, melancholia, pain, suffering, and duress (Leuba, 1896; Starbuck, 1897). The most characteristic pattern (1) begins with increasing discomfort and anxiety, including attempts at sleep or social withdrawal, which (2) climax in an ecstatic luminescence of insight and ecstasy and (3) are followed by long periods of "saintliness." Mimicked well by the effects of hallucinogens, this struggle to luminescence and its glowing aftermath have been called many things, depending on the context: William James called it a "mystical experience." Saint Paul called it "the peace that passeth understanding"; Thomas Merton, the "transcendental unconscious"; Maslow, "peak experience"; Gurdjieff, "objective consciousness"; the Quakers, "inner light"; Jung, "individuation"; Emerson, "Oversoul"; Lao Tse, "the absolute Tao"; Zen Buddhism, "satori"; yogis, "samadhi"; Saint John of the Cross, "living flame"; *The Tibetan Book of the Dead*, "luminosity"; Saint Teresa, "ecstasy"; Blake, "divine intuition"; Buddha, "awake"; Brother Lawrence, "unclouded vision"; Jacob Boehme, "light, which is the heart of God"; Philo Judaeus, "joyful with exceeding gravity"; Plotinus, "divine spirit"; Colin Wilson, "intensity experience"; Eliade, "shamanic ecstasy"; Arthur Clarke, "overmind"; Arthur Deikman, "deautomatization"; a Harvard undergraduate on LSD, "moment of truth"; Julian Silverman (about an aspect of the acute schizophrenic reaction), "the oceanic fusion of higher and lower referential processes"; Walter Pahnke, "unity"; Wasson (about mushrooms), "the dawning of a new world"; Myerhoff (about peyote), "mystic vision"; Tennyson, "the loss of personality seeking not extinction but the only true life"; Hinduism, "that"; and Ramon the Huichol, "Our life." Are they all the same? The Eastern comparative religionist Alan Watts, after his second LSD experience, answered "embarrassingly" so. Like sexual orgasm, however, full of many of the same ineffable qualities and similarly associated with long-lasting metaphysical feelings like "being in love," manifestations of the same nervous system reflex are often variously embellished by personality and culture (Mandell, 1978b).

The personality change in Pavlov's nearly drowned "hyperactive–stable" dogs, with complete loss of their conditioned responses (Sargant, 1969); the shift from fear and hate to idolatrous love for their captors in some victims of hijacking, called the Stockholm effect (Hacker, 1978); brainwashing to an entirely new philosophical and emotional state (Sargant, 1957); the meditative ecstasy of the "climbing Kundalini" of Gopi Krishna (1971); the ecstatic ascendency of long-distance running (Sheehan, 1978); the mystical experience in poetry, a struggle for comprehension based on old premises, discomfort, sudden insight, and delight with the perception of a new meaning as described by Colin Wilson (1969); the ecstatically creative moment after hours and days of intellectual struggle in a scientific endeavor—all may be manifestations of the drive–arrest–release sequence in biogenic amine inhibitory systems, releasing temporal lobe limbic, hippocampal-septal hypersynchrony that lasts for long periods of afterdischarge. They all may reflect the neurobiological mechanisms underlying transcendence, God in the brain.

REFERENCES

ABRAHAM, K. Notes on the psychoanalytical investigation and treatment of manic-depressive insanity and allied conditions. *Selected papers on psychoanalysis.* London: Hogarth, 1927.

ADEY, W. R. Computer analysis of hippocampal EEG activity and impedance in approach learning. Effects of psychotomimetic and hallucinogenic drugs. In *Pharmacology of conditioning, learning and retention*. New York: Academic Press, 1964.

ADEY, W. R. Neurophysiological correlates of information transaction and storage of brain tissue. In E. Steller & J. M. Sprague (Eds.), *Progress in physiological psychology*, Vol. 1. New York: Academic, 1966.

ADEY, W. R., & DUNLOP, C. W. The action of certain cyclohexamines in hippocampal system during approach performance in the cat. *Journal of Pharmacology and Experimental Therapeutics*, 1960, *130*, 418–426.

ADEY, W. R., BELL, F. R., & DENNIS, B. J. Effects of LSD, psilocybin and psilocin on temporal lobe EEG patterns and learned behavior in the cat. *Neurology*, 1962, *12*, 591–602.

ADEY, W. R., WALTER, D. O., & LINDSLEY, D. F. Effects of subthalamic lesions on learned behavior and correlated hippocampal and subcortical slow wave activity. *Archives of Neurology*, 1962, *6*, 194–207.

AGHAJANIAN, G. K. Influence of drugs on the firing of serotonin-containing neurons in brain. *Federation Proceedings*, 1972, *31*, 91–96. (a)

AGHAJANIAN, G. K. LSD and CNS transmission. *Annual Review of Pharmacology*, 1972, *12*, 157–168. (b)

AGHAJANIAN, G. K. Feedback regulation of central monoaminergic neurons: Evidence from single cell recording studies. In M. B. H. Youdim & W. Lovenberg (Eds.), *Essays in neurochemistry and neuropharmacology*. London: Wiley, 1977.

AGHAJANIAN, G. K., & BUNNEY, B. W. Central dopaminergic neurons: Neurophysiological identification and response to drugs. In E. Usdin & S. H. Snyder (Eds.), *Frontiers in catecholamine research*. Oxford: Pergamon, 1973.

AGHAJANIAN, G. K.. & HAIGLER, H. J. Hallucinogenic indoleamines: Preferential action upon presynaptic serotonin receptors. *Psychopharmacology Communications*, 1976, *1*, 619–629.

AGHAJANIAN, G. K., & WANG, R. Y. Habenular and other midbrain raphe afferents demonstrated by a modified retrograde tracing technique. *Brain Research*, 1977, *122*, 229–242.

AGHAJANIAN, G. K., & WANG, R. Y. Physiology and pharmacology of central serotonergic neurons. In M. A. Lipton, A. DiMascio, & K. F. Killam (Eds.), *Psychopharmacology: A generation of progress*. New York: Raven, 1978.

AGHAJANIAN, G. K., FOOTE, S. E., & SHEARD, M. H. Lysergic acid diethylamide: Sensitive neuronal units in the midbrain raphe. *Science*, 1968, *161*, 706–708.

AGHAJANIAN, G. K., CEDARBAUM, J. M., & WANG, R. Y. Evidence for norepinephrine-mediated collateral inhibition of locus coeruleus neurons. *Brain Research*, 1977, *136*, 570–577.

ALLISON, G. E. Psychiatric implications of religious conversion. *Canadian Psychiatric Association Journal*, 1967, *12*, 55–61.

ALLISON, J. Respiratory changes during the practice of the technique of transcendental meditation. *Lancet*, 1970, I, 833–834.

AMERICAN PSYCHIATRIC ASSOCIATION, Task Force on Nomenclature and Statistics. *Diagnostic and statistical manual of mental disease II*. Washington: American Psychiatric Association, 1968.

AMSEL, A. The role of frustrative nonreward in noncontinuous reward situations. *Psychological Bulletin*, 1958, *55*, 102–119.

ANAND, B. K., & DUA, S. Stimulation of limbic system of brain in waking animals. *Science*, 1955, *122*, 1139–1140.

ANDEN, N-E., CORRODI, H., FUXE, K., & HÖKFELT, T. Evidence for a central

5-hydroxytryptamine receptor stimulation by lysergic acid diethylamide. *British Journal of Pharmacology*, 1968, *34*, 1–7.

ANDERSON, P. Organization of hippocampal neurons and their interconnections. In R. Isaacson & K. Pribram (Eds.), *The hippocampus*, Vol. 1. New York: Plenum, 1975.

ANDERSON, P., & LØMO, T. Mode of control of hippocampal pyramidal cell discharges. In R. Whelan (Ed.), *The neural control of behavior*. New York: Academic, 1970.

ANDERSON, P. W. More is different. *Science*, 1972, *177*, 393–396.

ANDY, O. J., & AKERT, K. Seizure patterns induced by electrical stimulation of hippocampal formation in the cat. *Journal of Neuropathology and Experimental Neurology*, 1955, *14*, 198–213.

ANDY, O. J., & MUKAWA, J. Amygdaloid propagation to the brain stem (electrophysiological study). *Electroencephalography and Clinical Neurophysiology*, 1960, *12*, 333–343.

ANDY, O. J., CHINN, R., ALLEN, M. B., & SHAWVER, E. F. Influence of mesencephalic and diencephalic stimulation on limbic system seizures. A behavioral and electroencephalographic study in the cat. *Neurology*, 1958, *8*, 939–952.

ANDY, O. J., CHINN, R., BONN, P., & ALLEN, M. Effect of frontal cortical and hippocampal system after-discharges upon learned behavior. *Electroencephalography and Clinical Neurophysiology*, 1958, *10*, 206.

ANDY, O. J., PEELER, D. F., MITCHELL, J., FOSHEE, D. P., & KOSHINO, K. The hippocampal contribution to "learning and memory." *Conditioned Reflexes*, 1968, *3*, 217–228.

ANGRIST, B. M., & GERSHON, S. The phenomenology of experimentally induced amphetamine psychosis. Preliminary observations. *Biological Psychiatry*, 1970, *2*, 95–107.

ANGST, J. (Ed.). *Classification and prediction of outcome of depression*, Symposium Medicum Hoescht 8. Stuttgart: F. K. Schattauer Verlag, 1973.

ARMACHER, P. Freud's neurological education and its influence on psychoanalytic theory. *Psychological Issues*, Monograph 16, Vol. 4. New York: International Universities Press, 1965.

ARTEMENKO, D. O. Role of hippocampal neurons in theta-wave generation. *Nierofiziologiya*, 1972, *4*, 531–539.

ASERINSKY, E., & KLEITMAN, N. Regularly occurring periods of eye motility, and concomitant phenomena during sleep. *Science*, 1953, *118*, 273–274.

BABINGTON, R. G., & HOROVITZ, Z. P. Neuropharmacology of SQ 10, 996, a compound with several therapeutic indications. *Archives Internationales de Pharmacodynamie et de Therapie*, 1973, *202*, 106–118.

BALLENGER, J. C., & POST, R. M. Therapeutic effects of carbamazepine in affective illness: A preliminary report. *Communications in Psychopharmacology*, 1978, *2*, 159–175.

BARCHAS, J., & USDIN, E. (Eds.). *Serotonin and behavior*. New York: Academic, 1973.

BEAR, D. The significance of behavioral change in temporal lobe epilepsy. *McLean Hospital Journal*, June 1977, 9–21.

BEAR, D. M., & FEDIO, P. Quantitative analysis of interictal behavior in temporal lobe epilepsy. *Archives of Neurology*, 1977, *34*, 454–467.

BEARD, A. W. The schizophrenia-like psychoses of epilepsy. II. Physical aspects. *British Journal of Psychiatry*, 1963, *109*, 113–129.

BEARD, A. W., & SLATER, E. The schizophrenic-like psychoses of epilepsy. *Proceedings of the Royal Society of Medicine* (London), 1962, *55*, 311–316.

BÉKÉSY, G. VON. Interaction of paired sensory stimuli and conduction in peripheral nerves. *Journal of Applied Physiology*, 1963, *18*, 1276–1284.

BELENKOV, N. J. The conditioned reflex and the reticular formation. In *Structural and functional bases of the conditioned reflex*. Leningrad, 1970, *18*.

BELL, C., SIERRA, G., BUENDIA, N., & SEGUNDO, J. P. Sensory properties of neurons in the mesencephalic reticular formation. *Journal of Neurophysiology*, 1964, *27*, 961–987.

BEN-ARI, Y., & KELLY, J. S. Iontophoretic and intravenous effects of the neuroleptic, α-flupenthixol, on dopamine evoked inhibition. *Journal of Physiology* (London), 1974, *242*, 66P–67P.

BEN-ARI, Y., & KELLY, J. S. Dopamine evoked inhibition of single cells of the feline putamen and basolateral amygdala. *Journal of Physiology* (London), 1976, *256*, 1–21.

BENSON, H., BEARY, J. F., & CAROL, M. P. Meditation and the relaxation response. In S. R. Dean (Ed.), *Psychiatry and mysticism*. New York: Nelson-Hall, 1975.

BERTILSSON, L., ASBERG, M., MELLSTROM, B., TYBRING, G., & SJOQUIST, F. Factors determining drug effects in depressed patients—Studies of nortriptyline and chlorimipramine. In *Depressive disorders*, Symposium Medicum Hoechst 13. Stuttgart: F. K. Shattauer Verlag, 1978.

BLACK, A. H. Hippocampal electrical activity and behavior. In R. L. Isaacson & K. H. Pribram (Eds.), *The hippocampus*, Vol. 2. New York: Plenum, 1975.

BLACKSTAD, T. W. Commissural connections of the hippocampal region in the rat, with special reference to their mode of termination. *Journal of Comparative Neurology*, 1956, *105*, 417–537.

BLACKWOOD, W., & CORSELLIS, J. A. N. (Eds.). *Greenfield's neuropathology* (3d ed.). London: Arnold, 1976.

BLEULER, E. *Dementia praecox or the group of schizophrenias*. New York: International Universities Press, 1950.

BLISS, T. V. P., & LØMO, T. Long-lasting potentiation of synaptic transmission in the dentate area of the anesthetized rabbit following stimulation of the perforant path. *Journal of Physiology* (London), 1973, *232*, 331–356.

BLOCK, V. Facts and hypotheses concerning memory consolidation processes. *Brain Research*, 1970, *24*, 561–672.

BLUMER, D. Changes of sexual behavior related to temporal lobe disorders in man. *Journal of Sex Research*, 1970, *6*, 173–178.

BLUMER, D. Neuropsychiatric aspects of psychomotor and other forms of epilepsy. In S. Livingston (Ed.), *Comprehensive management of epilepsy in infancy, childhood and adolescence*. Springfield, Ill.: Thomas, 1971.

BLUMER, D. Temporal lobe epilepsy and its psychiatric significance. In D. F. Benson & D. Blumer (Eds.), *Psychiatric aspects of neurologic disease*. New York: Grune & Stratton, 1975.

BLUMER, D., & WALKER, A. E. Sexual behavior in temporal lobe epilepsy. *Archives of Neurology*, 1967, *16*, 37–43.

BLUMER, D., & WALKER, A. E. The neural basis of sexual behavior. In D. F. Benson & D. Blumer (Eds.), *Psychiatric aspects of neurologic disease*. New York: Grune & Stratton, 1975.

BOHR, N. *Atomic physics and human knowledge*. New York: Wiley, 1958.

BOVEN, W. Religiosité et épilepsie. *Schweizer Archiv fur Neurologie, Neurochirurgie und Psychiatrie* (Zurich), 1919, *4*, 153–169.

BOWERS, M. B., & FREEDMAN, D. X. Psychedelic experiences in acute psychoses. In S. R. Dean (Ed.), *Psychiatry and mysticism*. Chicago: Nelson-Hall, 1975.

BRADLEY, P. B. The central action of certain drugs in relation to the reticular formation of the brain. In H. H. Jasper (Ed.), *Reticular formation of brain*. Boston: Little, Brown, 1958.

BRADLEY, P. B., & MOLLICA, A. The effect of adrenaline and acetylcholine on single unit activity in the reticular formation of the decerebrate cat. *Archives Italiennes de Biologie* (Pisa), 1958, *96*, 168–186.

BRAESTRUP, C. Effects of phenoxybenzamine aceprone and clonidine on the level of 3-methoxy-4-hydroxyphenylblycol (MOPEG) in rat brain. *Journal of Pharmacy and Pharmacology*, 1974, *26*, 139–141.

BRAMWELL, G. J. The effects of antidepressants on unit activity in the midbrain raphe of rats. *Archives Internationales de Pharmacodynamie et de Therapie*, 1974, *211*, 24-33.

BRAZIER, M. A. B. The actions of anesthetics on the nervous system. In E. D. Adrian, F. Bremer, & H. H. Jasper (Eds.), *Brain mechanisms and consciousness*. Oxford, England: Blackwell, 1954.

BRAZIER, M. A. B. Studies of the EEG activity of limbic structures in man. *Electroencephalography and Clinical Neurophysiology*, 1968, *25*, 309-318.

BRODIE, B. B., SPECTOR, S., & SHORE, P. A. Interaction of monoamine oxidase inhibitors with physiological and biochemical mechanisms in brain. *Annals of the New York Academy of Sciences*, 1959, *80*, 609-614.

BROOKS, D. C., & GERSHON, M. D. Eye movement petentials in the oculomotor and visual systems of the cat: A comparison of reserpine induced waves with those present during wakefulness and rapid eye movement sleep. *Brain Research*, 1971, *27*, 223-239.

BROWN, G. L., GOODWIN, F. K., BALLENGER, J. C., GOYER, P. F., & MAJOR, L. F. CSF amine metabolites in human aggression. *American Psychiatric Association*, May 10, 1978, Session 11, Paper 180 (abstract).

BUCHSBAUM, M., GOODWIN, F. K., MURPHY, D. L., & BORGE, G. AER in affective disorders. *American Journal of Psychiatry*, 1971, *128*, 19-25.

BUCKINGHAM, R., & RADULOVACKI, M. 5-Hydroxyindoleacetic acid in cerebrospinal fluid: An indicator of slow wave sleep. *Brain Research*, 1975, *99*, 440-443.

BULLARD, W. P., GUTHRIE, P. B., RUSSO, P. V., & MANDELL, A. J. Regional and subcellular distribution and some factors in the regulation of reduced pterins in rat brain. *Journal of Pharmacology and Experimental Therapeutics*, 1978, *206*, 4-20.

BULLARD, W. P., YELLIN, J. B., RUSSO, P. V., & MANDELL, A. J. The pharmacology of striatal pterins and the regulation of dopamine function. In E. Usdin (Ed.), Catecholamines: Basic and clinical frontiers. New York: Pergamon, 1979.

BUNNEY, W. E., & GULLEY, B. L. The current status of research in the catecholamine theories of affective disorders. In E. Usdin & A. J. Mandell (Eds.), *Biochemistry of mental disorders*. New York: Dekker, 1978.

BUNNEY, W. E., MASON, J. W., & ROATCH, J. F. A psychoendocrine study of severe psychotic depressive crisis. *American Journal of Psychiatry*, 1965, *122*, 72-80.

BUNNEY, W. E., MURPHY, D. L., GOODWIN, F. K., & BORGE, G. F. The switch process from depression to mania: Relationship to drugs which alter brain amines. *Lancet*, 1970, *1*, 1022-1027.

BUNNEY, W. E., GOODWIN, F. K., & MURPHY, D. L. The "switch process" in manic-depressive illness. *Archives of General Psychiatry*, 1972, *27*, 312-317.

CADE, J. F. Lithium salts in the treatment of psychotic excitement. *Medical Journal of Australia*, 1949, *2*, 349-352.

CADORET, F. Genetics of affective disorders. In R. G. Grenell & S. Gabay (Eds.), *Biological foundations of psychiatry*. New York: Raven, 1976.

CARLSSON, A., & LINDQVIST, M. Effects of chlorpromazine or haloperidol on formation of 3-methoxytyramine and normetanephrine in mouse brain. *Acta Pharmacologia et Toxicologica*, 1963, *20*, 140-144.

CARLSSON, A., LINDQVIST, M., & MAGNUSSON, T. 3,4-Dihydroxyphenylalanine and 5-hydroxytryptophan as reserpine antagonists. *Nature*, 1957, *180*, 1200.

CHADOFF, P., & LYONS, H. Hysteria—The hysterical personality in hysterical conversion. *American Journal of Psychiatry*, 1958, *114*, 734-740.

CHAFETZ, M. E., & SCHWAB, R. S. Psychological factors involved in bizarre seizures. *Psychosomatic Medicine*, 1959, *21*, 96-105.

CHAPMAN, W. P., SCHROEDER, H. R., GEYER, G., BRAZIER, M. A. B., FAGER, C., POPPEN, J. L., SOLOMON, H. C., & YAKOVLEV, P. I. Physiological evidence concerning the importance of amygdaloid nuclear region in the integration of circulatory function and emotion in man. *Science*, 1954, *120*, 949–950.

CHATRIAN, G. E., & CHAPMAN, W. P. Electrographic study of the amygdaloid region with implanted electrodes in patients with temporal lobe epilepsy. In E. R. Ramey & D. S. O'Doherty (Eds.), *Electrical studies of the unanesthetized brain*. New York: Hoeber, 1960.

CHERLOW, D. G., DYMOND, A. M., CRANDALL, P. H., WALTER, R. D., & SERAFETINIDES, E. A. Evoked response and after-discharge thresholds to electrical stimulation in temporal lobe epileptics. *Archives of Neurology*, 1977, *34*, 527–531.

CHRISTENSEN, C. W. Religious conversion. *Archives of General Psychiatry*, 1963, *9*, 207–216.

CLARK, C. V. H., & ISAACSON, R. L. Effect of bilateral hippocampal ablation on DRL performance. *Journal of Comparative and Physiological Psychology*, 1965, *59*, 137–140.

CLARK, W. H. *Psychology of religion*. New York: Macmillan, 1965.

COHEN, M. B., BAKER, G., & COHEN, R. A. An intensive study of 12 cases of manic-depressive psychosis. *Psychiatry*, 1954, *17*, 103–137.

CONNELL, P. H. *Amphetamine psychosis*, Maudsley Monograph No. 5. London: Oxford University Press, 1958.

COOKSON, J., & SILVERSTONE, T. 5-Hydroxytryptamine and dopamine pathways in mania: A pilot study of fenfluramine and pimozide. *British Journal of Clinical Pharmacology*, 1976, *3*, 942–943.

COOLS, A. R., & VAN ROSSUM, J. M. Caudate dopamine and stereotyped behavior of cats. *Archives Internationales de Pharmacodynamie et de Therapie*, 1970, *197*, 163–173.

COPPEN, A., & SHAW, D. M. Potentiation of the antidepressive effect of a monoamine-oxidase inhibitor by tryptophan. *Lancet*, 1963, *I*, 79–81.

COPPEN, A., SHAW, D. M., HERZBERG, B., & MAGGS, R. Tryptophan in the treatment of depression. *Lancet*, 1967, *2*, 1178–1180.

COPPEN, A., WHYBROW, P., NOGUERA, R., MAGGS, R., & PRANGE, A. The comparative antidepressant value of L-tryptophan and imipramine with and without attempted potentiation by liothyronine. *Archives of General Psychiatry*, 1972, *26*, 234–241.

COPPEN, A., PRANGE, A. J., WHYBROW, P. C., & NOGUERA, R. Abnormalities of indoleamines in affective disorders. *Archives of General Psychiatry*, 1972, *26*, 474–478.

COPPEN, A., GUPTA, R., MONTGOMERY, S., & BAILEY, J. A double-blind comparison of lithium carbonate and Ludiomil in the prophylaxis of unipolar affective illness. *Pharmakopsychiatrie, Neuro-Psychopharmakologie*, 1976, *9*, 94–99.

COPPEN, A., MONTGOMERY, S. A., GUPTA, R. K., & BAILEY, J. E. A double-blind comparison of lithium carbonate and maprotiline in the prophylaxis of the affective disorders. *British Journal of Psychiatry*, 1976, *128* 479–485.

COPPEN, A., GHOSE, K., & JØRGENSEN, A. Prolonged treatment of depression by amitryptyline. In *Depressive disorders*, Symposium Medicum Hoescht 13. Stuttgart: F. K. Schattauer Verlag, 1978.

COSTALL, B., & NAYLOR, R. J. The role of telencephalic dopaminergic systems in the mediation of apomorphine-stereotyped behavior. *European Journal of Pharmacology*, 1973, *24*, 8–24.

COSTALL, B., & NAYLOR, R. J. Stereotyped and circling behavior induced by dopaminergic agonists after lesions of the midbrain raphe nuclei. *European Journal of Pharmacology*, 1974, *23*, 206–222.

COSTALL, B., NAYLOR, R. J., & NEUMAYER, J. L. Dissociation by the apomorphine derivatives of the stereotypic and hyperactivity responses resulting from injections into the nucleus accumbens septi. *Journal of Pharmacy and Pharmacology*, 1975, *27*, 875–877.

CREESE, I., & IVERSEN, S. D. Amphetamine response after dopamine neurone destruction. *Nature New Biology*, 1972, *238*, 247–248.

CRONSON, A. J., & FLEMENBAUM, A. antagonism of cocaine high by lithium. *American Journal of Psychiatry*, 1978, *135*, 856–857.

CROWNE, D. P., & RADCLIFFE, D. D. Some characteristics and functional relations of the electrical activity of the primate hippocampus and a hypothesis of hippocampal function. In R. Isaacson & K. Pribram (Eds.), *The hippocampus,* Vol. 2. New York: Plenum, 1975.

DAHLSTROM, A., & FUXE, K. Evidence for the existence of monoamine neurons in the central nervous system. II: Experimentally induced changes in the intraneuronal amine levels of bulbospinal neuron systems. *Acta Physiologica Scandinavica Supplement* 247, 1965, *64,* 1–36.

DALBY, M. A. Antiepileptic and psychotropic effect of carbamazepine (Tegretol ®) in the treatment of psychomotor epilepsy. *Epilepsia,* 1971, *12,* 325–334.

DALBY, M. A. Behavioral effects of carbamazepine. In J. K. Penry & D. D. Daly (Eds.), *Complex partial seizures and their treatment.* Vol. 11: *Advances in neurology.* New York: Raven, 1975.

DANDY, W. E. The brain. In D. Lewis (Ed.), *Practice of surgery.* Hagerstown, Md.: Prior, 1931.

DAVIS, M., GALLAGER, D. W., & AGHAJANIAN, G. K. Tricyclic antidepressant drugs: Attenuation of excitatory effects of d-lysergic acid diethylamide (LSD) on the acoustic startle reflex. *Life Sciences,* 1977, *20,* 1249–1258.

DELGADO, J. M. R., & HAMLIN, H. Spontaneous and evoked electrical seizures in animals and in humans. In E. R. Ramey & D. S. O'Doherty (Eds.), *Electrical studies on the unanesthetized brain.* New York: Hoeber, 1960.

DELGADO, J. M. R., & SELVILLANO, M. Evolution of repeated hippocampal seizures in the cat. *Electroencephalography and Clinical Neurophysiology,* 1961, *13,* 722–733.

DEMENT, W. The occurrences of low voltage, fast electroencephalogram patterns during behavioral sleep in the cat. *Electroencephalography and Clinical Neurophysiology,* 1958, *10,* 291–296.

DEMENT, W. The effect of dream deprivation. *Science,* 1960, *131,* 1705–1707.

DEMENT, W., and WOLPERT, E. The relation of eye movements, body motility, and external stimuli to dream content. *Journal of Experimental Psychology,* 1958, *55,* 543–553.

DEMENT, W., GREENBERG, S., & KLEIN, R. The effect of partial REM sleep deprivation and delayed recovery. *Journal of Psychiatric Research,* 1966, *4,* 141–152.

DEMENT, W., FERGUSON, J., COHEN, H., & BARCHAS, J. Nonchemical methods and data using a biochemical model: The REM quanta. In A. J. Mandell & M. P. Mandell (Eds.), *Psychochemical research in man.* New York: Academic, 1969.

DEMENT, W., HENRIKSEN, S., & FERGUSON, J. The effect of the chronic administration of parachlorophenylalanine on sleep parameters in the cat. In J. Barchas & E. Usdin (Eds.), *Serotonin and behavior.* New York: Academic, 1973.

DEMENT, W., HOLMAN, R. B., & GUILLEMINAULT, C. Neurochemical and neuropharmacological foundations of the sleep disorders. In E. Usdin & A. J. Mandell (Eds.), *Biochemistry of mental disorders.* New York: Dekker, 1978.

deMOLINA, A. F., & HUNSPERGER, R. W. Central representation of affective reactions in forebrain and brain stem: Electrical stimulation of amygdala, stria terminalis, and adjacent structures. *Journal of Physiology,* 1959, *145,* 251–265.

deMONTIGNY, C., & AGHAJANIAN, G. K. Preferential action of 5-methoxytryptamine and 5-methoxydimethyltryptamine on presynaptic serotonin receptors: A comparative iontophoretic study with LSD and serotonin. *Neuropharmacology,* 1977, *16,* 811–818.

deMONTIGNY, C., & AGHAJANIAN, G. K. Tricyclic antidepressants: Chronic treatment increases responsivity of rat forebrain neurons to serotonin. *Science,* 1978, *202,* 1303–1306.

DEWHURST, K., & BEARD, A. W. Sudden religious conversion in temporal lobe epilepsy. *British Journal of Psychiatry,* 1970, *117,* 497–507.

DeWied, D. Effects of peptide hormones on behavior. In W. F. Ganong & L. Martini (Eds.), *Frontiers in neuroendocrinology*. New York: Oxford University Press, 1969.

DeWied, D., Witter, A., & Lande, S. Anterior pituitary peptides and avoidance acquisition of hypophysectomized rats. *Progress in Brain Research*, 1970, *32*, 213–220.

Dewson, J., Dement, W., & Simmons, F. Observations on middle ear muscle activity during sleep in the cat. *Journal of Experimental Neurology*, 1965, *12*, 1–8.

Dicks, D., Myers, R. E., & Kling, A. Uncus and amygdala lesions: Effects on social behavior in the free-ranging Rhesus monkey. *Science*, 1969, *165*, 69–71.

Dikman, S., & Reitan, R. M. MMPI correlates of dysphasic language disturbances. *Journal of Abnormal Psychology*, 1974, *83*, 675–679.

Dikman, S., & Reitan, R. M. MMPI correlates of adaptive ability deficits in patients with brain lesions. *Journal of Nervous and Mental Disease*, 1977, *165*, 247–254.

Donnelly, E. F., Dent, J. K., & Murphy, D. L. Comparison of temporal lobe epileptics and affective disorders on the Halsted-Reitan test battery. *Journal of Clinical Psychology*, 1972, *28*, 61–62.

Douglas, R. J., & Pribram, K. H. Distraction and habituation in monkeys with limbic lesions. *Journal of Comparative and Physiological Psychology*, 1969, *69*, 473–480.

Dunner, D. L., Gershon, E. S., & Goodwin, F. K. Heritable factors in the severity of affective illness. *Biological Psychiatry*, 1976, *11*, 31–42.

Eidelberg, E., Lesse, H., & Gault, F. P. An experimental model of temporal lobe epilepsy: Studies on the convulsant properties of cocaine. In H. Gilbert & G. H. Glaser (Eds.), *EEG and behavior*. New York: Basic Books, 1963.

Elazar, Z., & Adey, W. R. Spectral analysis of low frequency components in the electrical activity of the hippocampus during learning. *Electroencephalography and Clinical Neurophysiology*, 1967, *23*, 225–240.

Ellinwood, E. H. Effect of chronic methamphetamine intoxication in rhesus monkeys. *Biological Psychiatry*, 1971, *3*, 25–32.

Ellinwood, E. H. Behavioral and EEG changes in the amphetamine model of psychosis. In E. Usdin (Ed.), *Neuropsychopharmacology of monoamines and their regulatory enzymes*. New York: Raven, 1974.

Ellinwood, E. H., & Escalante, D. O. Chronic amphetamine effect on the olefactory forebrain. *Biological Psychiatry*, 1970, *2*, 189–203.

Ellinwood, E. H., Kilbey, M. M., Castellani, S., & Khoury, C. Amygdala hyperspindling and seizures induced by cocaine. In E. H. Ellinwood & M. M. Kilbey (Eds.), *Cocaine and other stimulants*. New York: Plenum, 1977.

El-Yousef, M. K., Janowsky, D. S., Davis, J. M., & Rosenblatt, J. E. Induction of severe depression by physostigmine in marijuana intoxicated individuals. *British Journal of Addiction*, 1973, *68*, 321–325.

Emerson, L. E. The psychoanalytic treatment of hystero-epilepsy. *Journal of Abnormal Psychology*, 1915, *11*, 315–328.

Endröczi, E., & Lissak, K. The role of the mesencephalon and archicortex in the activation and inhibition of the pituitary-adrenocortical system. *Acta Physiologica Academiae Scientiarum Hungaricae*, 1959, *15*, 25–37.

Ervin, F., Epstein, A. W., & King, H. E. Behavior of epileptic and nonepileptic patients with temporal spikes. *Archives of Neurology and Psychiatry*, 1955, *74*, 488–496.

Evans-Wentz, W. Y. *The Tibetan book of the dead*. New York: Oxford University Press, 1960.

Falconer, M. A. Clinical manifestations of temporal lobe epilepsy and their recognition in relation to surgical treatment. *British Medical Journal*, 1954, *2*, 939–944.

Falconer, M. A. Reversibility by temporal-lobe resection of the behavioral abnormalities of temporal-lobe epilepsy. *New England Journal of Medicine*, 1973, *289*, 451–455.

FALCONER, M. A., SERAFETINIDES, E. A., & CORSELLIS, J. A. Etiology and pathogenesis of temporal lobe epilepsy. *Archives of Neurology*, 1964, *10*, 233–248.

FALLON, J. H., & MOORE, R. Y. Dopamine innervation of some basal forebrain areas in the rat. *Abstracts, The Society for Neuroscience*, 1976, *2*, 486.

FALRET, J. De l'état mental des épileptiques. *Archives Générales de Médecine.* 1860, Series 5, Vol. 16, 666–679.

FARKAS, T., DUNNER, D. L., & FIEVE, R. R. L-Tryptophan in depressions. *Biological Psychiatry*, 1976, *11*, 295–302.

FEINDEL, W., PENFIELD, W., & JASPER, H. Localization of epileptic discharge in temporal lobe automatism. *Transactions of the American Neurological Association*, 1952, *14*, 17.

FENICHEL, O. *The psychoanalytic theory of neurosis.* New York: Norton, 1945.

FISHER, C., GROSS, J., & ZUCH, J. Cycle of penile erections synchronous with dreaming (REM) sleep. *Archives of General Psychiatry*, 1965, *12*, 29–45.

FLEISCHER, L. N., & GLICK, S. D. Hallucinogen-induced rotational behavior in rats. *Psychopharmacology*, 1979, *62*, 193–200.

FLEMENBAUM, A. Does lithium block the effects of amphetamine? A report of three cases. *American Journal of Psychiatry*, 1974, *131*, 820–821.

FLOR-HENRY, P. Psychosis and temporal lobe epilepsy. A controlled investigation. *Epilepsia*, 1969, *10*, 363–395. (a)

FLOR-HENRY, P. Schizophrenic-like reactions and affective psychoses associated with temporal lobe epilepsy: Etiological factors. *American Journal of Psychiatry*, 1969, *126*, 400–404. (b)

FLOR-HENRY, P. Ictal and interictal psychiatric manifestations in epilepsy. Specific or nonspecific? *Epilepsia*, 1972, *13*, 773–783.

FLOR-HENRY, P. Lateralized temporal–limbic dysfunction and psychopathology. *Annals of the New York Academy of Science*, 1976, *280*, 777–795.

FLOR-HENRY, P., & YEUDALL, L. T. Lateralized cerebral dysfunction in depressive and in aggressive criminal psychopathy. Further observations. *Journal of International Research Communications*, July 1973, *1*(5), 31.

FLYNN, J. P. The neural basis of aggression in cats. In D. C. Glass (Ed.), *Neurophysiology and emotion.* New York: Rockefeller University Press, 1967.

FONNUM, F. Topographical and subcellular localization of choline acetyltransferase in the rat hippocampal region. *Journal of Neurochemistry*, 1970, *17*, 1029–1037.

FOOTE, S. L., FREEDMAN, R., & OLIVER, A. P. Effects of putative neurotransmitters on neuronal activity in monkey auditory cortex. *Brain Research*, 1975, *86*, 229–242.

FOOTE, W. E., SHEARD, M. H., & AGHAJANIAN, G. K. Comparison of effects of LSD and amphetamine on midbrain raphe units. *Nature*, 1969, *222*, 567–569.

FOREMAN, M. M., & MOSS, R. L. Role of hypothalamic serotonergic receptors in the control of lordosis behavior in the female rat. *Hormones and Behavior*, 1978, *10*, 97–110.

FREEDMAN, D. X., & HALARIS, A. E. Monoamines and the biochemical mode of action of LSD at synapses. In M. A. Lipton, A. DiMascio, & K. F. Killam (Eds.), *Psychopharmacology: A generation of progress.* New York: Raven, 1978.

FREEDMAN, R., HOFFER, B. J., PURO, D., & WOODWARD, D. J. Noradrenaline modulation of the responses of the cerebellar Purkinje cell to afferent synaptic activity. *British Journal of Pharmacology*, 1976, *57*, 603–605.

FRENK, H., URCA, G., & LIEBESKIND, J. C. Epileptic properties of leucine- and methionine–enkephalin: Comparison with morphine and reversibility by naloxone. *Brain Research*, 1978, *147*, 327–337.

FREUD, S. Mourning and melancholia. In *Collected Papers.* London: Hogarth, 1925, *4*, 152–170.

FREUD, S. The origins of psycho-analysis. *Letters to Wilhelm Fliess*, drafts and notes, 1887–1902. New York: Basic Books, 1954.

Friedman, P. A., Kappelman, A. H., & Kaufman, S. Partial purification and characterization of tryptophan hydroxylase from rabbit hindbrain. *Journal of Biological Chemistry,* 1972, *247,* 4165–4173.

Friedman, S., & Fischer, C. On the presence of a rhythmic, diurnal, oral instinctual drive cycle in man: A preliminary report. *Journal of the American Psychoanalytic Association,* 1967, *15,* 317–331.

Furukawa, T. Modification by lithium of behavioral responses to methamphetamine and tetrabenazine. *Psychopharmacologia,* 1975, *42,* 243–248.

Fuxe, K., & Jonsson, G. Further mapping of central 5-hydroxytryptamine neurons: Studies with the neurotoxic dihydroxytryptamines. *Advances in Biochemical Psychopharmacology,* 1974, *10,* 1–12.

Gainotti, G. Emotional behavior and hemispheric side of the lesion. *Cortex,* 1972, *8,* 41–55.

Galin, D. Implications for psychiatry of left and right cerebral specialization. *Archives of General Psychiatry,* 1972, *31,* 572–583.

Gallager, D. W., & Aghajanian, G. K. Effects of chlorimipramine and lysergic acid diethylamide on efflux of precursor-formed ^{3}H-serotonin: Correlations with serotonergic impulse flow. *Journal of Pharmacology and Experimental Therapeutics,* 1975, *193,* 785–795.

Gallager, D. W., & Aghajanian, G. K. Effect of antipsychotic drugs on the firing of dorsal raphe cells II. Reversal by picrotoxin. *European Journal of Pharmacology,* 1976, *39,* 357–364. (a)

Gallager, D. W., & Aghajanian, G. K. Inhibition of firing of raphe neurons by tryptophan and 5-hydroxytryptophan: Blocked by inhibiting serotonin synthesis with RO4-4602. *Neuropharmacology,* 1976, *15,* 149–156. (b)

Gastaut, H. So-called "psychomotor" and "temporal" epilepsy. *Epilepsia,* 1953, *2,* 59–99.

Gastaut, H. La maladie de Vincent Van Gogh envisagée à la lumière des conceptions nouvelles sur l'épilepsie psychomotrice. *Annales Médico-Psychologiques* (Paris), 1956, *114,* 196–238.

Gastaut, H. Fyodor Mikhailovitch Dostoevsky's involuntary contribution to the symptomatology and prognosis of epilepsy. *Epilepsia,* 1978, *19,* 186–201.

Gastaut, H., & Broughton, R. *Epileptic seizures: Clinical and electrographical features, diagnosis and treatment.* Springfield, Ill.: Thomas, 1972.

Gastaut, H., & Collomb, H. Étude du comportement sexuel chez les épileptiques psychomoteurs. *Annales Médico-Psychologiques* (Paris), 1954, *112,* 657–696.

Gastaut, H., Morin, G., & Lesevre, N. Étude du comportement des épileptiques psychomoteurs dans l'intervalle de leurs crises. Les troubles de l'activité globale et de la sociabilité. *Annales Médico-Psychologiques* (Paris), 1955, 113, 1–27.

Gershon, E., Mark, A., Cohen, N., Belizon, N., Baron, M., & Knobe, K. E. Transmitted factors in the morbid risk of affective disorders. A controlled study. *Journal of Psychiatric Research,* 1975, *12,* 283–299.

Gershon, E. S., Targum, S. D., Kessler, L. R., Mazure, C. M., & Bunney, W. E. Genetic studies and biological strategies in the affective disorders. *Progress in Medical Genetics,* 1977, *2,* 101–164.

Geschwind, N. Disconnexion syndromes in animals and man, Part 1. *Brain,* 1965, *88,* 237–294.

Geschwind, N. Effects of temporal-lobe surgery on behavior. *New England Journal of Medicine,* 1973, *289,* 480–481.

Geschwind, N. The borderland of neurology and psychiatry: Some common misconceptions. In D. F. Benson & D. Blumer (Eds.), *Psychiatric aspects of neurological disease.* New York: Grune & Stratton, 1975. (a)

Geschwind, N. The clinical setting of aggression in temporal lobe epilepsy. In W. Fields & W. Sweet (Eds.), *The neurobiology of violence*. Springfield, Ill.: Thomas, 1975. (b)

Geschwind, N., & Levitsky, W. Human brain: Left–right asymmetries in temporal speech area. *Science*, 1968, *161*, 186–187.

Geyer, M. A., Dawsey, W. J., & Mandell, A. J. Differential effects of caffeine, d-amphetamine, and methylphenidate on individual raphe cell fluorescence: A microspectrofluorimetric demonstration. *Brain Research*, 1975, *85*, 135–139.

Geyer, M. A., Puerto, A., Dawsey, W. J., Knapp, S., Bullard, W. P., & Mandell, A. J. Histologic and enzymatic studies of the mesolimbic and mesostriatal serotonergic pathways. *Brain Research*, 1976, *106*, 241–256.

Geyer, M. A., Dawsey, W. J., & Mandell, A. J. Fading: A new cytofluorimetric measure quantifying serotonin in the presence of catecholamines at the cellular level in brain. *Journal of Pharmacology and Experimental Therapeutics*, 1978, *207*, 650–667. (a)

Geyer, M. A., Petersen, L. R., Rose, G. J., Horwitt, D. D., Light, R. K., Adams, L. M., Zook, J. A., Hawkins, R. L., & Mandell, A. J. The effects of lysergic acid diethylamide and mescaline-derived hallucinogens on sensory-integrative function: Tactile startle. *Journal of Pharmacology and Experimental Therapeutics*, 1978, *207*, 837–847. (b)

Giarman, N. J., & Freedman, D. X. Biochemical aspects of the actions of psychotomimetic drugs. *Pharmacological Reviews*, 1965, *17*, 1–25.

Gibbs, E. L., Gibbs, F. A., & Fuster, B. Psychomotor epilepsy. *Archives of Neurology and Psychiatry*, 1948, *60*, 331–339.

Gibbs, F. A. Psychiatric disorder in temporal lobe epilepsy. In *The biology of mental health and disease* (Milbank Memorial Fund). New York: Hoeber, 1950.

Gibbs, F. A. Ictal and non-ictal psychiatric disorders in temporal lobe epilepsy. *Journal of Nervous and Mental Disease*, 1951, *113*, 522–528.

Gillin, J. C., Mendelson, W. B., Sitaram, N., & Wyatt, R. J. The neuropharmacology of sleep and wakefulness. *Annual Review of Pharmacology and Toxicology*, 1978, *18*, 563–579.

Glaser, G. H. The problem of psychosis in psychomotor temporal lobe epileptics. *Epilepsia*, 1964, *5*, 271–278.

Glaus, A. Über Kombinationen von Schizophreine und Epilepsie. *Zeitschrift Gesamte für Neurologie und Psychiatrie*, 1931, *135*, 450–500.

Glick, S. D., & Cox, R. D. Nocturnal rotation in normal rats: Correlation with amphetamine-induced rotation and effects of nigrostriatal lesions. *Brain Research*, 1978, *152*, 1–13.

Glick, S. D., Jerussi, T. P., Waters, D. H., & Green, J. P. Amphetamine-induced changes in striatal dopamine and acetylcholine levels and relationship to rotation (circling behavior) in rats. *Biochemical Pharmacology*, 1974, *23*, 3223–3225.

Glick, S. D., Jerussi, T. P., & Zimmerberg, B. Behavioral and neuropharmacological correlates of nigrostriatal asymmetry in rats. In S. Harnad, R. W. Doty, L. Goldstein, J. Jaynes, & G. Krauthamer (Eds.), *Lateralization in the nervous system*. New York: Academic, 1977.

Gloor, P. Electrophysiological studies on the connections of the amygdaloid nucleus in the cat. Part II: The electrophysiological properties of the amygdaloid projection system. *Electroencephalography and Clinical Neurophysiology*, 1955, *7*, 243–264.

Glowinski, J., & Axelrod, J. Inhibition of uptake of tritiated noradrenaline in the intact rat brain by imipramine and structurally related compounds. *Nature*, 1964, *204*, 1318–1319.

Glowinski, J., Hamon, M., & Héry, F. Regulation of 5-HT synthesis in central serotonergic neurons. In A. J. Mandell (Ed.), *New concepts in neurotransmitter regulation*. New York: Plenum, 1973.

Goddard, G. V., McIntyre, D. C., & Leech, C. K. A permanent change in brain function resulting from daily electrical stimulation. *Experimental Neurology*, 1969, 25, 295–330.

Goodwin, F. K., Murphy, D. L., & Bunney, W. E. Lithium carbonate treatment in depression and mania. *Archives of General Psychiatry*, 1969, 21, 486–496.

Goodwin, F. K., Murphy, D. L. Dunner, D. L., & Bunney, W. E. Lithium response in unipolar versus bipolar depression. *American Journal of Psychiatry*, 1972, 129, 44–47.

Gowers, W. R. *Epilepsy and other chronic convulsive diseases.* London: Churchill, 1901.

Grahame-Smith, D. G. Studies *in vivo* on the relationship between brain tryptophan, brain 5-HT synthesis and hyperactivity in rats treated with a monoamine oxidase inhibitor and L-tryptophan. *Journal of Neurochemistry*, 1971, 18, 1053–1065.

Grantyn, A., Grantyn, R., & Hang, T. L. Hippocampole Einzelzellant auf mesenzephale Reizungen nach Septumlasion. *Acta Biologica et Medica Germanica*, 1971, 26, 985–996.

Grastyan, E., Lissak, K., Madarasz, I., & Donhoffer, H. Hippocampal electrical activity during the development of conditioned reflexes. *Electroencephalography and Clinical Neurophysiology*, 1959, 11, 409–430.

Gray, J. A. Sodium amobarbital, the hippocampal theta rhythm, and the partial reinforcement extinction effect. *Psychological Review*, 1970, 77, 465–480.

Green, J. D., & Shimamoto, T. Hippocampal seizures and their propagation. *Archives of Neurology and Psychiatry*, 1953, 70, 687–702.

Greenberg, D. A., V'Prichard, D. C., & Snyder, S. H. Alpha-noradrenergic receptor binding in mammalian brain: Differential labeling of agonist and antagonist states. *Life Sciences*, 1976, 19, 69–76.

Griffith, J. J., Cavanaugh, J., & Oates, J. Psychosis induced by the administration of d-amphetamine to human volunteers. In D. H. Efron (Ed.), *Psychotomimetic drugs.* New York: Raven, 1970.

Grof, S. Varieties of transpersonal experiences: Observations from LSD psychotherapy. In S. R. Dean (Ed.), *Psychiatry and mysticism.* Chicago: Nelson-Hall, 1975.

Group for the Advancement of Psychiatry. *Psychotherapy and pharmacotherapy.* Report No. 93, 1975.

Guze, S. B., Woodruff, R. A., & Clayton, P. J. Sex, age, and the diagnosis of hysteria. *American Journal of Psychiatry*, 1972, 129, 747–748.

Hacker, F. J. *Crusaders, criminals, and crazies.* New York: Bantam, 1978.

Haigler, H. J., & Aghajanian, G. K. Lysergic acid diethylamide and serotonin: A comparison of effects on serotonergic neurons and neurons receiving a serotonergic input. *Journal of Pharmacology and Experimental Therapeutics*, 1974, 188, 688–699.

Haldane, E. S., & Ross, G. R. T. (Eds.). *The philosophical works of Descartes.* London: Cambridge University Press, 1931.

Hammer, W., & Sjöqvist, S. Plasma levels of monomethylated tricyclic antidepressants during treatment with imipramine-like compounds. *Life Sciences*, 1967, 6, 1895–1903.

Hamon, M., Bourgoin, S., Héry, F., & Glowinski, J. regulation of tryptophan hydroxylase. In E. Usdin, N. Weiner, & M. B. H. Youdim (Eds.), *Structure and function of monoamine enzymes.* New York: Dekker, 1977.

Hanley, J., Rickles, W. R., Crandall, P. H., & Walter, R. D. Automatic recognition of EEG correlates of behavior in a chronic schizophrenic patient. *American Journal of Psychiatry*, 1972, 128, 1524–1528.

Harding, G. F. A., Lölas-Stepke, F., & Jenner, F. A. Alpha rhythm laterality, lithium, and mood. *Lancet*, 1976, 2, 237.

Harnad, S., Doty, R. W., Goldstein, L., Jaynes, J., & Krauthamer, G. (Eds.). *Lateralization in the nervous system.* New York: Academic, 1977.

Harris, T. H. Depression induced by the Rauwolfia compounds. *American Journal of Psychiatry*, 1957, 113, 950–951.

Hartmann, E. Effects of psychotropic drugs on sleep: The catecholamines and sleep. In

M. A. Lipton, A. DiMascio, & K. F. Killam (Eds.), *Psychopharmacology: A generation of progress.* New York: Raven, 1978.

HARTMANN, E., CRAVENS, J., & LIST, S. Hypnotic effects of L-tryptophan. *Archives of General Psychiatry,* 1974, *31,* 394–397.

HAYEK, F. A. *The sensory order.* Chicago: University of Chicago Press, 1952.

HAYMAKER, W., ANDERSON, E., & NAUTA, W. J. H. (Eds.). *The hypothalamus.* Springfield, Ill.: Thomas, 1969.

HEATH, R. G. *Studies in schizophrenia.* Cambridge, Mass.: Harvard University Press, 1954.

HEATH, R. G. Pleasure response of human subjects to direct stimulation of the brain: Physiologic and psychodynamic considerations. In R. G. Heath (Ed.), *The role of pleasure in behavior.* New York: Hoeber,1964.

HEATH, R. G. Marihuana. Effects on deep and surface electroencephalograms of man. *Archives of General Psychiatry,* 1972, *26,* 577–584.

HEATH, R. G., & GALLANT, D. Activity of the human brain during emotional thought. In R. G. Heath (Ed.), *The role of pleasure in behavior.* New York: Hoeber, 1964.

HEATH, R. G., & MICKLE, W. A. Evaluation of seven years experience with depth electrode studies in human patients. In E. R. Ramey & D. S. O'Doherty (Eds.), *Electrical studies on the unanesthetized brain.* New York: Hoeber, 1960.

HEBB, D. O. *The organization of behavior, A neurophysiological theory.* New York: Wiley, 1949.

HENRIKSEN, S. J., BLOOM, F. E., LING, N., & GUILLEMIN, R. Induction of limbic seizures by endorphins and opiate alkaloids: Electrophysiological and behavioral correlates. *Abstracts, The Society for Neuroscience,* 1977, *3,* 293.

HILL, D. EEG in episodic psychotic and psychopathic behavior: A classification of data. *Electroencephalography and Clinical Neurophysiology,* 1952, *4,* 419–442.

HILL, D., POND, D. A., MITCHEL, W., & FALCONER, M. A. Personality changes following temporal lobectomy for epilepsy. *Journal of Mental Science,* 1957, *103,* 18.

HILTON, S. M., & ZBROZYNA, A. W. Amygdaloid region for defence reactions and its efferent pathway to the brain stem. *Journal of Physiology,* 1963, *165,* 160–173.

HOBSON, J. A. The sleep–dream cycle: A neurobiological rhythm. In H. L. Ioachim (Ed.), *Pathobiological annals.* New York: Appleton-Century-Crofts, 1975.

HOBSON, J. A., McCARLEY, R. W., WYZINSKI, P. W., & PIVIK, R. T. Reciprocal tonic firing by FTG and LC neurons during the sleep-waking cycle. *Sleep Research,* 1973, *2,* 29–37.

HOBSON, J. A., McCARLEY, R. W., PIVIK, R. T., & FREEDMAN, R. Selective firing by cat pontine brain stem neurons in desynchronized sleep. *Journal of Neurophysiology,* 1974, *37,* 497–511.

HOCH, P. H., & POLATIN, P. Pseudoneurotic forms of schizophrenia. *Psychiatric Quarterly,* 1949, *23,* 248–276.

HOCKMAN, C. H., TALESMIK, J., & LIVINGSTON, K. E. Central nervous system modulation of baroceptor reflexes. *American Journal of Physiology,* 1969, *217,* 1681–1689.

HOLLISTER, A. S., BREESE, G. R., KUHN, C. M., COOPER, B. R., & SCHANBERG, S. M. An inhibitory role for brain serotonin-containing systems in the locomotor effects of d-amphetamine. *Journal of Pharmacology and Experimental Therapeutics,* 1976, *198,* 12–21.

HORTON, P. C. The mystical experience: Substance of an illusion. *Journal of the American Psychoanalytic Association,* 1974, *22,* 364–380.

HOWDEN, J. C. The religious sentiments in epileptics. *Journal of Mental Science,* 1872–1873, *18,* 491–497.

HRDINA, P. D., & VON KULMIZ, P. Separation-induced behavioural disorder in infra-human primates: An animal model of depression. In *Depressive Disorders,* Symposium Medicum Hoescht 13. Stuttgart: F. K. Schattauer Verlag, 1978.

HUANG, Y. H., REDMOND, D. E., SNYDER, D. R., & MAAS, J. W. *In vivo* location and destruction of the locus coeruleus in the stumptail macaque. *Brain Research,* 1975, *100,* 157–162.

Isaacson, R. L., & Wickelgren, W. O. Hippocampal alblation and passive avoidance. *Science*, 1962, *138*, 1104–1106.

Jackson, J. H. Clinical remarks on the occasional occurrence of subjective sensations of smell in patients who are liable to epileptiform seizures or who have symptoms of mental derangement, and in others. *Lancet*, 1866, *1*, 659–660.

Jackson, J. H. On right or left-sided spasm at the onset of epileptic paroxysms, and on crude sensation warnings, and elaborate mental states. *Brain*, 1880–1881, *3*, 192–205.

Jackson, J. H. Remarks on the relations of different divisions of the central nervous system to one another and to parts of the body. *British Medical Journal*, 1898, *1*, 65–84.

Jackson, J. H., & Colman, W. S. Case of epilepsy with tasting movements and "dreamy state"; very small patch of softening in the left uncinate gyrus. *Brain*, 1898, *21*, 580–584.

Jacobs, B. L. Amygdala unit activity as a reflection of functional changes in brain serotonergic neurons. In J. Barchas & E. Usdin (Eds.), *Serotonin and behavior*. New York: Academic, 1973.

Jacobs, B. L., & Cohen, A. Differential behavioral effects of lesions of the median or dorsal raphe nuclei in rats: Open field and pain-elicited aggression. *Journal of Comparative and Physiological Psychology*, 1976, *90*, 102–108.

James, W. *The varieties of religious experience*. New York: Modern Library, 1929.

Jasinski, D. R., Nutt, J. G., Haertzen, C. A., Griffith, J. D., & Bunney, W. E. Lithium: Effects on subjective functioning and morphine-induced euphoria. *Science*, 1977, *195*, 582–584.

Jerussi, T. P., & Glick, S. D. Drug-induced rotation in rats without lesions: Behavioral and neurochemical indices of a normal asymmetry in nigrostriatal function. *Psychopharmacology*, 1976, *47*, 249–260.

Johnson, L. A. Amphetamine use in professional football. Doctoral dissertation, United States International University, San Diego, 1972.

Jouvet, M. Recherches sur les structures nerveuses et les mécanismes responsables des différentes phases du sommeil physiologique. *Archives Italiennes de Biologie*, 1962, *100*, 125–206.

Jouvet, M., & Delorme, F. Locus coeruleus et sommeil paradoxal. *Societé de Biologie, Paris, Comptes Rendus*, 1965, *159*, 895–899.

Jouvet, M., & Michel, F. Nouvelles recherches sur les structures responsables de la "phase paradoxale" du sommeil. *Journal de Physiologie*, 1960, *52*, 130–131.

Jouvet, M., Michel, F., & Mounier, D. Analyse électroencephalographique comparée du sommeil physiologique chez le chat et chez l'homme. *Revue Neurologique*, 1960, *103*, 180–205.

Judd, L. L., Janowsky, D. S., Segal, D. S., & Huey, L. Y. Comparison of the effects of intravenous naloxone in bipolar depressives and normal controls. *New Research Abstracts, American Psychiatric Association* Annual Meeting, Atlanta, May 8, 1978.

Karagulla, S., & Robertson, E. E. Physical phenomena in temporal lobe epilepsy and the psychoses. *British Medical Journal*, 1955, *1*, 748–752.

Karobath, M. Serotonin synthesis with rat brain synaptosomes. Effects of serotonin and monoamine oxidase inhibitors. *Biochemical Pharmacology*, 1972, *21*, 1253–1263.

Kaufman, S. A new cofactor required for the enzymatic conversion of phenylalanine to tyrosine. *Journal of Biological Chemistry*, 1958, *230*, 931–939.

Kaufman, S. Properties of pterin-dependent aromatic amino acid hydroxylases. In *Aromatic amino acids in the brain*, Ciba Foundation Symposium, 1974, *22*, 85–107.

Keller, E. L. Control of saccadic eye movements by midline brain stem neurons. In R. Baker & A. Berthoz (Eds.), *Control of gaze by brain stem neurons*, Developments in Neuroscience. New York: Elsevier, 1977.

Kernberg, O. F. A psychoanalytic classification of character pathology. *Journal of the American Psychoanalytic Association*, 1971, *18*, 800–822.

KERNBERG, O. F. Countertransference. In *Borderline conditions and pathological narcissism.* New York: Aronson, 1975.

KETY, S. S. Possible relation of central amines to behavior in schizophrenic patients. *Federation Proceedings,* 1961, *20,* 894–896.

KHAZAN, N., & SAWYER, C. H. Mechanisms of paradoxical sleep as revealed by neurophysiologic and pharmacologic approaches in the rabbit. *Psychopharmacologia,* 1964, *5,* 457–466.

KILLAM, K. F., & KILLAM, E. K. Drug action on pathways involving the reticular formation. In H. H. Jasper (Ed.), *Reticular formation of the brain.* Boston: Little, Brown, 1958.

KLEIN, D. F., ZITRIN, C. M., & WOERNER, M. Antidepressants, anxiety, panic and phobia. In M. A. Lipton, A. DiMascio, & K. F. Killam (Eds.), *Psychopharmacology: A generation of progress.* New York: Raven, 1978.

KLINE, N. S., LI, C. H., LEHMANN, H. E., LAJTHA, A., LASKI, E., & COOPER, T. B. Beta-endorphin–induced changes in schizophrenic and depressed patients. *Archives of General Psychiatry,* 1977, *34,* 1111–1113.

KLINE, N. S., GERSHON, S., & SCHOU, M. (Eds.). *Proceedings, International Lithium Conference—Controversies and Unresolved Issues.* New York: Excerpta Medica, 1979.

KLÜVER, H., & BUCY, P. C. Psychic blindness and other symptoms following bilateral temporal lobectomy in Rhesus monkeys. *American Journal of Physiology,* 1937, *119,* 352–353.

KNAPP, S., & MANDELL, A. J. Parachlorophenylalanine—Its three phase sequence of interactions with the two forms of brain tryptophan hydroxylase. *Life Sciences,* 1972, *11,* 761–771.

KNAPP, S., & MANDELL, A. J. Short- and long-term lithium administration: Effects on the brain's serotonergic biosynthetic systems. *Science,* 1973, *180,* 645–647.

KNAPP, S., & MANDELL, A. J. Effects of lithium chloride on parameters of biosynthetic capacity for 5-hydroxytryptamine in rat brain. *Journal of Pharmacology and Experimental Therapeutics,* 1975, *193,* 812–823.

KNAPP, S., & MANDELL, A. J. Cocaine and lithium: Neurobiological antagonism in the serotonin biosynthetic system in rat brain. *Life Sciences,* 1976, *18,* 679–684. (a)

KNAPP, S., & MANDELL, A. J. Coincidence of blockade of synaptosomal 5-hydroxytryptamine uptake and decrease in tryptophan hydroxylase activity: Effects of fenfluramine. *Journal of Pharmacology and Experimental Therapeutics,* 1976, *198,* 123–132. (b)

KNAPP, S., & MANDELL, A. J. Conformational influences on brain tryptophan hydroxylase by submicromolar calcium: Opposite effects of equimolar lithium. *Journal of Neural Transmission,* 1979, *15,* 1–15.

KNAPP, S., MANDELL, A. J., & GEYER, M. A. Effects of amphetamines on regional tryptophan hydroxylase activity and synaptosomal conversion of tryptophan to 5-hydroxytryptamine in rat brain. *Journal of Pharmacology and Experimental Therapeutics,* 1974, *189,* 676–689.

KNIGHT, R. P. Borderline states. In R. Knight & R. Friedman (Eds.), *Psychoanalytic psychiatry and psychology.* New York: International Universities Press, 1953.

KNOOK, H. L. *The fibre-connections of the forebrain.* Philadelphia: Davis, 1966.

KOHLER, W. *Gestalt psychology* (new ed.). New York: Liveright, 1970.

KRIPKE, D. F., & SONNENSCHEIN, D. A 90-minute daydream cycle. *Sleep Research,* 1973, *2,* 187.

KRISHNA, G. *Kundalini: The evolutionary energy in man.* Berkeley, Calif.: Shambhala, 1971.

KUPFER, D. J. REM latency: A psychobiological marker for primary depressive disease. *Biological Psychiatry,* 1976, *11,* 159–174.

LANDOLT, H. Über Verstimmungen, Dämmerzustande und Schizophrene Zustandsbilder bei Epilepsie. *Schweizer Archiv für Neurologie, Neurochirurgie und Psychiatrie,* 1955, *76,* 313–327.

LAZARE, A. The hysterical character in psychoanalytic theory—Evolution and confusion. *Archives of General Psychiatry*, 1971, *25*, 131–137.

LEHMANN, H. E., & BAN, T. A. Studies with new drugs in the treatment of convulsive disorders. *Internationale Zeitschrift fur Klinische Pharmakologie, Therapie und Toxikologie* (Munchen), 1968, *1*, 230–234.

LEMAY, M., & CULEBRAS, A. Human brain-morphologic differences in the hemispheres by carotid arteriography. *New England Journal of Medicine*, 1972, *287*, 168–170.

LENNOX, W. G. Phenomena and correlates of psychomotor triad. *Neurology*, 1951, *1*, 357–371.

LENNOX, W. *Epilepsy and related disorders*, Vol. 1. London: Churchill, 1960.

LEONHARD, K., KORFF, I., & SCHULZ, H. Die Temperaments in den Familien der monopolaren and bipolaren phasischen Psychosen. *Psychiatria et Neurologia*, 1962, *143*, 416–434.

LESSE, H., HEATH, R. G., MICKLE, W. A., MONROE, R. R., & MILLER, W. H. Rhinencephalic activity during thought. *Journal of Nervous and Mental Disease*, 1955, *122*, 433–446.

LESTER, B. K., & EDWARDS, R. J. EEG fast activity in schizophrenic and control subjects. *International Journal of Neuropsychiatry*, 1966, *2*, 143–156.

LEUBA, J. H. A study in the psychology of religious phenomena. *American Journal of Psychology*, 1896, *7*, 309–385.

LÉVI-STRAUSS, C. *Structural anthropology*. London: Harmondsworth, 1972.

LEWIN, L. *Phantastica—Narcotic and stimulating drugs*. New York: Dutton, 1964.

LEWIS, P. R., & SHUTE, C. C. D. The cholinergic limbic system: Projections to hippocampal formation, medial cortex, nuclei of ascending cholinergic reticular system, and the subfornical organ and the supra-optic crest. *Brain*, 1967, *90*, 521–540.

LILLY, J. *The center of the cyclone*. New York: Julian, 1972.

LORENS, S. A., & GULDBERG, H. C. Regional 5-hydroxytryptamine following selective midbrain raphe lesions in the rat. *Brain Research*, 1974, *78*, 45–56.

LUNDBERG, A. Integration in the reflex pathway. In R. Granit (Ed.), *Nobel symposium. I: Muscular afferents and motor control*. Stockholm: Almquist and Wiksell, 1966.

MAAS, J. W., REDMOND, D. E., & GAVEN, R. Effects of serotonin depletion on behavior in monkeys. In J. Barchas & E. Usdin (Eds.), *Serotonin and behavior*. New York: Academic, 1973.

MABILLE, H. Hallucinations religieuses et délire religieux transitore dans l'épilepsie. *Annales Médico-Psychologiques*, 1889, *57*, 76–81.

MACLEAN, P. D. Psychosomatic disease and the "visceral brain." Recent developments bearing on the Papez theory of emotion. *Psychosomatic Medicine*, 1949, *11*, 338–353.

MACLEAN, P. D. Chemical and electrical stimulation of hippocampus in unrestrained animals. *Archives of Neurology and Psychiatry*, 1957, *78*, 113–127. (a)

MACLEAN, P. D. Chemical and electrical stimulation of hippocampus in unrestrained animals. II: Behavioral findings. *Archives of Neurology and Psychiatry*, 1957, *78*, 128–142. (b)

MACLEAN, P. D. The limbic system with respect to self-preservation and the preservation of the species. *Journal of Nervous and Mental Disease*, 1958, *127*, 1–11.

MACLEAN, P. D. The limbic system with respect to two basic life principles. *Second Conference on the Central Nervous System and Behavior*. New York: Josiah Macy Foundation, 1959.

MACLEAN, P. D., & PLOOG, D. W. Cerebral representation of penile erections. *Journal of Neurophysiology*, 1962, *25*, 29–55.

MACRAE, D. On the nature of fear, with reference to its occurrence in epilepsy. *Journal of Nervous and Mental Disease*, 1954, *120*, 385–393.

MAGOUN, H. The ascending reticular formation. In E. Adrian, F. Bremer, & H. H. Jasper (Eds.), *Brain mechanisms and consciousness*. Oxford, England: Blackwell, 1954.

MAGOUN, H., & RHINES, R. An inhibitory mechanism in the bulbar reticular formation. *Journal of Neurophysiology*, 1946, 9, 165–171.

MAHESH YOGI, M. *On the Bhagavad-Gita—A new translation and commentary.* New York: Penguin, 1969.

MALAMUD, N. The epileptogenic focus in temporal lobe epilepsy from a pathological standpoint. *Archives of Neurology*, 1966, 14, 190–195.

MALAMUD, N. Psychiatric disorder with intracranial tumors of limbic system. *Archives of Neurology*, 1967, 17, 113–123.

MALAMUD, N. Organic brain disease mistaken for psychiatric disorder: A clinicopathologic study. In D. F. Benson & D. Blumer (Eds.), *Psychiatric aspects of neurologic disease.* New York: Grune & Stratton, 1975.

MANDELL, A. J. Hormonal and metabolic correlates of behavioral states in man. In A. J. Mandell & M. P. Mandell (Eds.), *Psychochemical research in man.* New York: Academic, 1969.

MANDELL, A. J. Neurobiological mechanisms of presynaptic metabolic adaptation and their organization: Implications for a pathophysiology of the affective disorders. In A. J. Mandell (Ed.), *Neurobiological mechanisms of adaptation and behavior.* New York: Raven, 1975.

MANDELL, A. J. *The nightmare season.* New York: Random House, 1976.

MANDELL, A. J. Redundant mechanisms regulating brain tyrosine and tryptophan hydroxylases. *Annual Review of Pharmacology and Toxicology*, 1978, 18, 461–493. (a)

MANDELL, A. J. The neurochemistry of religious insight and ecstasy. In K. Berrin (Ed.), *Art of the Huichol Indians.* New York: Abrams, 1978. (b)

MANDELL, A. J., & BULLARD, W. P. Striate tetrahydrobiopterin concentration: A pharmacologically regulatory factor in the biosynthesis of dopamine. In *Depressive disorders*, Symposium Medicum Hoescht 13. Stuttgart: F. K. Schattauer Verlag, 1978. (a)

MANDELL, A. J., & BULLARD, W. P. Regional and subcellular distribution and factors in the regulation of reduced pterins in rat brain. *Psychopharmacology Bulletin*, 1978, 14, 46–49. (b)

MANDELL, A. J., & KNAPP, S. Cocaine, amphetamine, and lithium interactions: Neurobiological correlates. *Annals of the New York Academy of Sciences*, 1976, 281, 441–455.

MANDELL, A. J., & KNAPP, S. Regulation of serotonin biosynthesis in brain: Role of the high affinity uptake of tryptophan into serotonergic neurons. *Federation Proceedings*, 1977, 36, 2142–2148.

MANDELL, A. J., & KNAPP, S. Adaptive regulation in central biogenic amine neurons. In M. A. Lipton, A. DiMascio, & K. F. Killam (Eds.), *Psychopharmacology: A generation of progress.* New York: Raven, 1978.

MANDELL, A. J., KNAPP, S., & GEYER, M. A. Lithium decreases and cocaine increases the bilateral asymmetry of serotonin in mesostriatal and mesolimbic systems associated with changes in the kinetic properties of tryptophan hydroxylase. In E. Usdin (Ed.), *Catecholamines: Basic and clinical frontiers.* New York: Pergamon, 1979.

MANDELL, A. J., & MANDELL, M. P. Biochemical aspects of rapid eye movement sleep. *American Journal of Psychiatry*, 1965, 122, 391–401.

MANDELL, A. J., CHAPMAN, L. F., RAND, R. W., & WALTER, R. D. Plasma corticosteroids: Changes in concentration after stimulation of hippocampus and amygdala. *Science*, 1963, 139, 1212.

MANDELL, A. J., SPOONER, C. E., & BRUNET, D. Whither the sleep transmitter? *Biological Psychiatry*, 1969, 1, 13–30.

MANDELL, A. J., SEGAL, D. S., & KUCZENSKI, R. T. Metabolic adaptation to antidepressant drugs—Implications for pathophysiology and treatment in psychiatry. In A. J. Friedhoff (Ed.), *Catecholamines and behavior*, Vol. 2. New York: Plenum, 1975.

Mandell, M. P., Mandell, A. J., & Jacobson, A. Biochemical and neurophysiological studies of paradoxical sleep. In J. Wortis (Ed.), *Recent advances in biological psychiatry.* New York: Plenum, 1964.

Mason, J. W. The central nervous system regulation of ACTH secretion. In H. H. Jasper (Ed.), *Reticular formation of the brain.* Boston: Little, Brown, 1958.

Mason, J. W., Nauta, W. J. H., Brady, J. V., Robinson, J. A., & Sachar, E. J. The role of limbic system structures in the regulation of ACTH release. *Acta Neurovegitativa,* 1961, *23,* 4–14.

Masters, W. H., & Johnson, V. E. *Human sexual response.* Boston: Little, Brown, 1966.

Maugh, T. H. Marihuana: The grass may no longer be greener. *Science,* 1974, *185,* 683–685.

Mays, L. E., & Best, P. J. Hippocampal unit responses to tonal stimuli during arousal from sleep and in awake rats. *Experimental Neurology,* 1971, *47,* 268–279.

McCall, R. B., & Aghajanian, G. K. Serotonergic facilitation of facial motoneuron excitation: A modulatory effect. *Abstracts, Society for Neuroscience,* 1978, No. 1422, 447.

McCarley, R. W., & Hobson, J. A. Clustered discharges of FTG neurons during desynchronized sleep. *Sleep Research,* 1974, *3,* 24–32.

McCarley, R. W., & Hobson, J. A. Discharge patterns of cat pontine brain stem neurons during desynchronized sleep. *Journal of Neurophysiology,* 1975, *38,* 751–766.

McEwen, B. S., Zigmond, R. E., & Gerlach, J. L. Sites of steroid binding and action in the brain. In G. H. Bourne (Ed.), *Structure and function of nervous tissue,* Vol. 5. New York: Academic, 1972.

McEwen, B. S., Wallach, G., & Magnus, C. Corticosterone binding to hippocampus: Immediate and delayed influences of the absence of adrenal secretion. *Brain Research,* 1974, *70,* 321–334.

McEwen, B. S., Gerlach, J. L., & Micco, D. J. Putative glucocorticoid receptors in hippocampus and other regions of the rat brain. In R. L. Isaacson & K. H. Pribram (Eds.), *The hippocampus,* Vol. 1. New York: Plenum, 1975.

McGinty, D. J., & Harper, R. M. 5-HT-containing neurons: Unit activity during sleep. *Sleep Research,* 1972, *1,* 27–41.

McGinty, D. J., & Harper, R. M. Dorsal raphe neurons: Depression of firing during sleep in cats. *Brain Research,* 1976, *101,* 569–575.

Meldrum, B. S., & Brierley, J. B. Neural loss and gliosis in the hippocampus following repetitive epileptic seizures induced in adolescent baboons by allylglycine. *Brain Research,* 1972, *48.* 361–365.

Mendels, J. Lithium in the treatment of depression. *American Journal of Psychiatry,* 1976, *133,* 373–378.

Mignone, R. J., Donnelly, E. F., & Sadowsky, D. Psychological and neurological comparisons of psychomotor and nonpsychomotor epileptic patients. *Epilepsia,* 1970, *11,* 345–359.

Miller, J. G. *Living systems.* New York: McGraw-Hill, 1978.

Milner, B. Interhermispheric differences in the localization of psychological processes in man. *British Medical Bulletin,* 1971, *27,* 272–277.

Milner, B. Hemispheric specialization: Scope and limits. In F. O. Schmitt & F. G. Worden (Eds.), *The neurosciences—Third study program.* Cambridge: MIT Press, 1974.

Milson, J. A., & Pycock, C. J. Effects of drugs acting on cerebral 5-hydroxytryptamine mechanisms in dopamine-dependent turning behavior in mice. *British Journal of Pharmacology,* 1976, *56,* 77–85.

Mirsky, A. F. Studies of the effects of brain lesions on social behavior in *Macaca mulatta:* Methodological and theoretical considerations. *Annals of the New York Academy of Sciences,* 1966, *85,* 785–794.

Money, J. Phantom orgasm in the dreams of paraplegic men and women. *Archives of General Psychiatry,* 1960, *3,* 373–382.

MONROE, R. R. Episodic behavioral disorders: Schizophrenia or epilepsy? *Archives of General Psychiatry*, 1959, *1*, 205–214.

MONROE, R. R. *Episodic behavioral disorders*. Cambridge, Mass.: Harvard University Press, 1970.

MONROE, R. R., & HEATH, R. G. Effects of lysergic acid and various derivatives on depth and cortical electrograms. *Journal of Neuropsychiatry*, 1961, *3*, 75–82.

MONROE, R. R., & MICKLE, W. A. Alpha chloralose-activated electroencephalograms in psychiatric patients. *Journal of Nervous and Mental Disease*, 1967, *144*, 59–68.

MONROE, R. R., HEATH, R. G., MILLER, W., & FONTANA, C. EEG activation with chloralosane. *Electroencephalography and Clinical Neurophysiology*, 1956, *8*, 279–287.

MOORE, R. Y. Monoamine neurons innervating the hippocampal formation and septum: Organization and response to injury. In R. L. Isaacson & K. H. Pribram (Eds.), *The hippocampus*, Vol. 1. New York: Plenum, 1975.

MOORE, R. Y., & BLOOM, F. E. Central cetecholamine neuron systems: Anatomy and physiology of the dopamine systems. *Annual Review of Neuroscience*, 1978, *1*, 129–169.

MOORE, R. Y., & HELLER, A. Monoamine levels and neuronal degeneration in the rat brain following lateral hypothalamic lesions. *Journal of Pharmacology and Experimental Therapeutics*, 1967, *156*, 12–22.

MORALES, F. R., ROIG, J. A., MONTE, J. M., MACADOR, O., & BUDELLI, J. Septal unit activity and hippocampal EEG during the sleep-wakefulness cycle of the rat. *Physiology and Behavior*, 1971, *6*, 563–567.

MOREL, B. A. Discussion sur l'épilepsie larvée. *Annales Medico-Psychologiques*, 1873, *31*, 155–163.

MORGANE, P. J., & STERN, W. C. Chemical anatomy of brain circuits in relation to sleep and wakefulness. *Advances in Sleep Research*, 1974. *1*, 1–131.

MOSKO, S. S., & JACOBS, B. L. Midbrain raphe neurons: Spontaneous activity and response to light. *Physiology and Behavior*, 1974, *13*, 589–593.

MULDER, D. W., & DALY, D. Psychiatric symptoms associated with lesions of temporal lobe. *Journal of the American Medical Association*, 1952, *150*, 173–176.

MULLAN, S., & PENFIELD, W. Illusions of comparative interpretations and emotions. *Archives of Neurology and Psychiatry*, 1959, *81*, 269–284.

MURPHY, D. L., BAKER, M., GOODWIN, F. K., MILLER, H., KOTIN, J., & BUNNEY, W. E. L-Tryptophan in affective disorders: Indolamine changes and differential clinical effects. *Psychopharmacologia*, 1974, *34*, 11–20.

MUZIO, J. N., ROFFWARG, H. P., & KAUFMAN, E. Alterations in the nocturnal sleep cycle resulting from LSD. *Electroencephalography and Clinical Neurophysiology*, 1966, *21*, 313–324.

NADLER, J. V., PERRY, B. W., & COTMAN, C. W. Intraventricular kainic acid preferentially destroys hippocampal pyramidal cells. *Nature*, 1978, *271*, 676–677.

NAGATSU, T., LEVITT, M., & UDENFRIEND, S. Tyrosine hydroxylase—The initial step in norepinephrine biosynthesis. *Journal of Biological Chemistry*, 1964, *239*, 2910–2917.

NAKAI, Y., & TAKAORI, S. Influence of norepinephrine-containing neurons derived from the locus coeruleus on lateral geniculate neuronal activities of cats. *Brain Research*, 1974, *71*, 47–60.

NARANJO, C. *The healing journey*. New York: Ballantine, 1975.

NAUTA, W. J. H. Hippocampal projections and related neural pathways to the mid-brain in the cat. *Brain*, 1958, *81*, 319–340.

NECKERS, L. M., BIGGIO, G., MOJA, G., & MEEK, J. L. Modulation of brain tryptophan hydroxylase by brain tryptophan content. *Journal of Pharmacology and Experimental Therapeutics*, 1977, *201*, 110–116.

NIEOULLON, A., CHERAMY, A., & GLOWINSKI, J. Nigral and striatal dopamine release under sensory stimuli. *Nature*, 1977, *269*, 340–342.

NOYES, R., DEMPSEY, G., BLUM, A., & CAVANAUGH, G. Lithium treatment in depression. *Comprehensive Psychiatry*, 1974, *15*, 187–193.

NYBACK, H. V., WALTERS, J. R., AGHAJANIAN, G. K., & ROTH, R. H. Tricyclic antidepressants: Effects on the firing rate of brain noradrenergic neurons. *European Journal of Pharmacology*, 1975, *32*, 302–312.

OKE, A. KELLER, R., MEFFORD, I., & ADAMS, R. N. Lateralization of norepinephrine in human thalamus. *Science*, 1978, *200*, 1411–1413.

OKUMA, T., KISHIMOTO, A., INOUE, K., MATSUMOTO, H., OGURA, A., MATSUSHITA, T., NAKAO, T., & OGURA, C. Anti-manic and prophylactic effects of carbamazepine (Tegretol®) on manic-depressive psychosis. *Folie Psychiatrica et Neurologica Japonica*, 1973, *27*, 283–297.

OSIS, K., & HARALDSSON, E. *At the hour of death.* New York: Avon, 1977.

OVERALL, J. E., HOLLISTER, L. E., JOHNSON, M., & PENNINGTON, V. Nosology of depression and differential response to drugs. *Journal of The American Medical Association*, 1966, *195*, 946–948.

PAHNKE, W. N. Drugs and mysticism. *International Journal of Parapsychology*, 1966, *8*, 257–294.

PALKOVITS, M., SAAVEDRA, J. M., JACOBOWITZ, D. M., KIZER, J. S., & BROWNSTEIN, M. J. Serotonergic innervation of the forebrain: Effect of lesions on serotonin and tryptophan hydroxylase levels. *Brain Research*, 1977, *130*, 121–134.

PAPEZ, J. W. A proposed mechanism of emotion. *Archives of Neurology and Psychiatry*, 1937, *38*, 725–743.

PARENT, A., & OLIVIER, A. Comparative histochemical study of the corpus striatum. *Journal fur Hirnforschung*, 1970, *12*, 75–81.

PASSOUANT, P., CADILHAC, M., & PASSOUANT-FONTAINE, T. Influence en cours de sommeil spontané de la stimulation électrique réticulaire et des stimuli sensoriels sur les rhythmes hippocampiques du chat. *Journal de Physiologie*, 1955, *47*, 715–718.

PAVLOV, I. P. Les sentiments d'emprise and the ultraparadoxical phase. *Journal de Physiologie*, 1933, *30*, 9–10.

PAYKEL, E. S., MYERS, J. K., DIENELT, M. N., KLERMAN, G. L., LINDENTHAL, J. J., & PEPPER, M. P. Life events and depression: A controlled study. *Archives of General Psychiatry*, 1969, *21*, 753–760.

PEARCE, J. B. Fenfluramine in mania. *Lancet*, 1973, *1*, 427.

PENFIELD, W. Memory mechanisms. *Archives of Neurology and Psychiatry*, 1952, *67*, 178–191.

PENFIELD, W. The role of the temporal cortex in certain psychical phenomena. Twenty-ninth Maudsley Lecture. *Journal of Mental Science*, 1955, *101*, 451–465.

PENFIELD, W. *The excitable cortex in conscious man*, Fifth Sherrington Lecture. Springfield, Ill.: Thomas, 1958.

PENFIELD, W. The interpretive cortex. *Science*, 1959, *129*, 1719–1725.

PENFIELD, W. Engrams in the human brain. *Proceedings of the Royal Society of Medicine*, 1968, *61*, 831–840.

PENFIELD, W. *The mystery of the mind.* Princeton, N.J.: Princeton University Press, 1975.

PENFIELD, W., & MATHIESON, G. Memory. Autopsy findings and comments on role of the hippocampus in experiential recall. *Archives of Neurology*, 1974, *31*, 145–154.

PENFIELD, W., & PEROT, P. The brain's record of auditory and visual experience. A final summary and discussion. *Brain*, 1963, *86*, 595–696.

PERRIS, C. A study of bipolar (manic–depressive) and unipolar recurrent depressive psychosis. *Acta Psychiatrica Scandinavica*, 1966, *42*, Supplement 194.

PERRIS, C. A study of cycloid psychoses. *Acta Psychiatrica Scandinavica*, 1974, Supplement 253.

PERSSON, S. A. The effect of LSD and 2-bromo-LSD on the striatal DOPA accumulation after decarboxylase inhibition in rats. *European Journal of Pharmacology*, 1977, 43, 73–83.

PETERS, V. H. Sexualstoerungen bei psychomotorischer Epilepsie. *Journal of Neurovisceral Relations Supplement*, 1971, 10, 491–497.

PFAFF, D. W., SILVA, M., T. A., & WEISS, J. M. Telemetered recording of hormone effects on hippocampal neurons. *Science*, 1971, 172, 394–395.

PIAGET, J. *Main trends in interdisciplinary research.* New York: Harper & Row, 1973.

PICKEL, V., SEGAL, M., & BLOOM, F. E. A radioautographic study of efferent pathways of the nucleus locus coeruleus. *Journal of Comparative Neurology*, 1974, 155, 15–42.

POLANYI, M. *Personal knowledge.* Chicago: University of Chicago Press, 1958.

POMPEIANO, O. Mechanisms of sensorimotor integration during sleep. *Progress in Physiological Psychology*, 1970, 3, 1–179.

POND, D. A. Psychiatric aspects of epilepsy. *Journal of the Indian Medical Profession*, 1957, 3, 1441.

POPPER, K. R. *The logic of scientific discovery.* London: Hutchinson, 1959.

POPPER, K. R. *Conjectures and refutations.* London: Routledge and Paul, 1963.

POPPER, K. R., & ECCLES, J. C. *The self and its brain.* New York: Springer International, 1978.

POST, R. M. Progressive changes in behavior and seizures following chronic cocaine administration: Relationship to kindling and psychosis. In E. H. Ellinwood & M. M. Kilbey (Eds.), *Cocaine and other stimulants.* New York: Plenum, 1977.

POST, R. M., KOPANDA, R. T., & BLACK, K. E. Progressive effects of cocaine on behavior and central amine metabolism in rhesus monkeys: Relationship to kindling and psychosis. *Biological Psychiatry*, 1976, 11, 403–419.

PRANGE, A. J., WILSON, I. C., LYNN, C. W., ALLTOP, L. B., & STIKELEATHER, R. A. L-Tryptophan in mania: Contribution to a permissive hypothesis of affective disorders. *Archives of General Psychiatry*, 1974, 30, 56–62.

PRIBRAM, K. H. The limbic systems, efferent control of neural inhibition and behavior. In W. Adey & T. Tokizane (Eds.), *Progress in brain research.* New York: Elsevier, 1967.

PRIEN, R. F., CAFFEY, E. M., & KLETT, C. J. Lithium carbonate and imipramine in prevention of affective episodes. *Archives of General Psychiatry*, 1973, 29, 420–425.

PURPURA, D. P., & GONZALEZ-MONTEAGUDO, O. Acute effects of methoxypyridoxine on hippocampal end-blade neurons; an experimental study of "special pathoclisis" in the cerebral cortex. *Journal of Neuropathology and Experimental Neurology*, 1960, 19, 421–432.

PYCOCK, C., & ANZELARK, G. LSD and dopamine receptors. *Nature*, 1975, 257, 69–70.

RACINE, R., TUFF, L., & ZAIDE, J. Kindling, unit discharge patterns and neural plasticity. *Canadian Journal of Neurological Sciences*, November 1975, 395–403.

RADULOVACKI, M., & ADEY, W. R. The hippocampus and the orienting reflex. *Experimental Neurology*, 1965, 12, 68–83.

RAISMAN, G. The connections of the septum. *Brain*, 1966, 89, 317–348.

RAISMAN, G. A comparison of the mode of termination of the hippocampal and hypothalamic afferents to the septal nuclei as revealed by electron microscopy of degeneration. *Experimental Brain Research*, 1969, 7, 317–343.

RANDRUP, A., & MUNKVAD, I. Stereotyped activities produced by amphetamine in several animal species and man. *Psychopharmacologia*, 1967, 11, 300–310.

RATTENBURY, J. E. *The conversion of the Wesleys.* London: Epworth, 1938.

RECHTSCHAFFEN, A., & MARON, L. The effect of amphetamine on the sleep cycle. *Electroencephalography and Clinical Neurophysiology*, 1964, 16, 438–445.

REDMOND, D. E., HUANG, Y. H., SNYDER, D. R., & MAAS, J. W. Behavioral effects of stimulation of the nucleus locus coeruleus in the stump-tailed monkey *Macaca orctoides. Brain Research*, 1976, 116, 502–510.

RIFKIN, A., QUITKIN, F., CARRILLO, C., BLUMBERG, A., & KLEIN, D. Lithium carbonate in emotionally unstable character disorder. *Archives of General Psychiatry*, 1972, 27, 519–523.

ROFFWARG, H., DEMENT, W., MUZIO, J., & FISHER, C. Dream imagery: Relationship to rapid eye movements of sleep. *Archives of General Psychiatry*, 1962, 7, 235–258.

ROSSI, G. F., & ROSADINI, G. Experimental analysis of cerebral dominance in man. In C. H. Milikan & F. L. Darley (Eds.), *Brain mechanisms underlying speech and language*. New York: Grune & Stratton, 1967.

ROSVOLD, H. E., MIRSKY, A. F., & PRIBRAM, K. H. Influence of amygdalectomy on social behavior in monkeys. *Journal of Comparative and Physiological Psychology*, 1954, 47, 173–178.

ROTH, R. H., & SALZMAN, P. M. Role of calcium in the depolarization-induced activation of tyrosine hydroxylase. In E. Usdin, N. Weiner, & M. B. H. Youdim (Eds.), *Structure and function of monoamine enzymes*. New York: Dekker, 1977.

RUBENS, A. B. Anatomical asymmetries of human cerebral cortex. In S. Harnad, R. W. Doty, L. Goldstein, J. Jaynes, & G. Krauthamer (Eds.), *Lateralization in the nervous system*. New York: Academic, 1977.

RUBIN, R. T., & MANDELL, A. J. Adrenal cortical activity in pathological states: A review. *American Journal of Psychiatry*, 1966, 123, 387–400.

RUBIN, R. T., MANDELL, A. J., & CRANDALL, P. H. Corticosteroid responses to limbic stimulation in man: Localization of stimulus sites. *Science*, 1966, 153, 767–768.

RUCH-MONACHON, M. A., JALFRE, M., & HAEFELY, W. Drugs and PGO waves in the lateral geniculate body of the curarized cat. II: PGO wave activity and brain 5-hydroxytryptamine. *Archives Internationales de Pharmacodynamie et de Therapie*, 1976, 219, 269–286.

RUMBAUGH, D. M., & GILL, T. V. The mastery of language-type skills by the chimpanzee. *Proceedings of the New York Academy of Sciences*, 1976, 280, 562–578.

SAAVEDRA, J. M., & ZIVIN, J. Tyrosine hydroxylase and dopamine-β-hydroxylase: distribution in discrete areas of the rat limbic system. *Brain Research*, 1975, 105, 517–524.

SACHAR, E. Corticosteroids in depressive illness. A longitudinal psychoendocrine study. *Archives of General Psychiatry*, 1967, 17, 544–567.

SACHAR, E. J. Psychological homeostasis and endocrine function. In A. J. Mandell & M. P. Mandell (Eds.), *Psychochemical research in man*. New York: Academic, 1969.

SACHAR, E. J., MACKENZIE, J. M., & BINSTOCK, W. A. Corticosteroid responses to psychotherapy of depressions. *Archives of General Psychiatry*, 1967, 16, 461–470.

SAHAKIAN, B. J., ROBBINS, T. W., MORGAN, M. D., & IVERSEN, S. D. The effects of psychomotor stimulants on stereotypy and locomotor activity in socially deprived and control rats. *Brain Research*, 1975, 84, 195–205.

SANGDEE, C., & FRANZ, D. N. Lithium-induced enhancement of 5-HT transmission at a central synapse. *Communications in Psychopharmacology*, in press.

SANO, K., & MALAMUD, N. Clinical significance of sclerosis of the cornu ammonis. *Archives of Neurology and Psychiatry*, 1953, 79, 40–49.

SARGANT, W. *Battle for the mind. A physiology of conversion and brain-washing*. London: Heineman, 1957.

SARGANT, W. The physiology of faith. *British Journal of Psychiatry*, 1969, 115, 505–518.

SATO, M. Hippocampal seizure and secondary epileptogenesis in the "kindled" cat preparations. *Folia Psychiatrica et Neurologica Japonica*, 1975, 29, 239–250.

SAWYER, C. H., & KAWAKAMI, M. Characteristics of behavioral and electroencephalographic after-reactions to copulation and vaginal stimulation in the female rabbit. *Endocrinology*, 1959, 65, 622–630.

SCHEEL-KRÜGER, J. Behavioral and biochemical comparison of amphetamine derivatives, cocaine, benztropine and tricyclic antidepressants. *European Journal of Pharmacology*, 1972, 18, 63–73.

SCHEEL-KRÜGER, J., BRAESTRUP, C., NIELSON, M., GOLEMBIOWSKA, K., & MOCILNICKA, E. Cocaine—Discussion on the role of dopamine in the biochemical mechanism of action. In E. H. Ellinwood & M. M. Kilbey (Eds.), *Cocaine and other stimulants*. New York: Plenum, 1977.

SCHILDKRAUT, J. J. Rationale of some approaches used in biochemical studies of the affective disorders: The pharmacological bridge. In A. J. Mandell & M. P. Mandell (Eds.), *Psychochemical research in man*. New York: Academic, 1969.

SCHWARCZ, R., SCHOLZ, D., & COYLE, D. T. Structure-activity relations for the neurotoxicity of kainic acid derivatives and glutamate analogues. *Neuropharmacology*, 1978, *17*, 145–151.

SCHWARTZ, G. E., DAVIDSON, R. J., & MAER, R. Right hemisphere lateralization for emotion in the human brain: Interactions with cognition. *Science*, 1975, *190*, 286–288.

SCOTT, J. S., & MASLAND, R. L. Occurrence of continuous symptoms in epileptic patients. *Neurology*, 1953, *3*, 297–301.

SEDMAN, D., & HOPKINSON, G. The psychopathology of mystical and religious conversion in psychiatric patients. *Confinia Neurologica*, 1966, *9*, 1–19, 65–77.

SEGAL, D. S. Differential effects of serotonin depletion on amphetamine-induced locomotion and stereotypy. In E. H. Ellinwood & M. M. Kilbey (Eds.), *Cocaine and other stimulants*. New York: Plenum, 1977.

SEGAL, D. S., & JANOWSKY, D. S. Psychostimulant-induced behavioral effects: Possible models of schizophrenia. In M. A. Lipton, A. DiMascio, & K. F. Killam (Eds.), *Psychopharmacology: A generation of progress*. New York: Raven, 1978.

SEGAL, D. S., & MANDELL, A. J. Long-term administration of amphetamine: Progressive augmentation of motor activity and stereotypy. *Pharmacology, Biochemistry, and Behavior*, 1974, *2*, 249–255.

SEGAL, D. S., KUCZENSKI, R. T., & MANDELL, A. J. Strain differences in behavior and brain tyrosine hydroxylase activity. *Behavioral Biology*, 1972, *7*, 75–81.

SEGAL, D. S., KUCZENSKI, R. T., & MANDELL, A. J. Theoretical implications of drug-induced adaptive regulation for a biogenic amine hypothesis of affective disorder. *Biological Psychiatry*, 1974, *9*, 147–159.

SEGAL, D. S., CALLAGHAN, M., & MANDELL, A. J. Alterations in behavior and catecholamine biosynthesis induced by lithium. *Nature*, 1975, *254*, 58–59.

SEGAL, M. Physiological and pharmacological evidence for a serotonergic projection to the hippocampus. *Brain Research*, 1975, *94*, 115–131.

SEGAL, M., & BLOOM, F. E. The action of norepinephrine in the rat hippocampus I. Iontophoretic studies. *Brain Research*, 1974, *72*, 79–97. (a)

SEGAL, M., & BLOOM, F. E. The action of norepinephrine in the rat hippocampus II. Activation of the input pathway. *Brain Research*, 1974, *72*, 99–114. (b)

SEGAL, M., & BLOOM, F. E. The action of norepinephrine in the rat hippocampus. III: Hippocampal cellular responses to locus coeruleus stimulation in the awake rat. *Brain Research*, 1976, *107*, 499–511.

SERAFETINIDES, E. A. The significance of the temporal lobes and of hemispheric dominance in the production of the LSD-25 symptomatology in man. *Neuropsychologia*, 1965, *3*, 69–79.

SHEEHAN, G. A. *Advice and philosophy for runners*. New York: Simon & Schuster, 1978.

SHERWIN, J. Clinical and EEG aspects of temporal lobe epilepsy with behavior disorder, the role of cerebral dominance. *McLean Hospital Journal*, June 1977, 40–50.

SHIELDS, J. Some recent developments in psychiatric genetics. *Archiv fur Psychiatrie and Nervenkranheiten* (Berlin), 1975, *220*, 347–360.

SIEGEL, J. M., McGINTY, D. J., & BREEDLOVE, S. M. Sleep and waking activity of pontine giganto cellular field neurons. *Experimental Neurology*, 1977, *56*, 553–573.

SIGGINS, G. R. Electrophysiological role of dopamine in striatum: Excitatory of inhibitory.

In M. A. Lipton, A. DiMascio, & K. F. Killam (Eds.), *Psychopharmacology: A generation of progress.* New York: Raven, 1978.

SIMANTOV, R., KUHAR, M. D., UHL, G. R., & SNYDER, S. H. Opioid peptide enkephalin: Immunohistochemical mapping in rat central nervous system. *Proceedings of the National Academy of Science,* 1977, *74,* 2167–2171.

SITARAM, N., MENDELSON, W. B., WYATT, R. J., & GILLIN, J. C. The time-dependent induction of REM sleep and arousal by physostigmine infusion during normal human sleep. *Brain Research,* 1977, *122,* 562–567.

SITARAM, N., WEINGARTNER, H., CAINE, E. D., & GILLIN, J. C. Choline selective entrancement of serial learning and encoding of low imagery words in man. *Life Sciences,* 1978, *22,* 1555–1566.

SLATER, E., & BEARD, A. W. The schizophrenia-like psychoses of epilepsy. I: Psychiatric aspects. *British Journal of Psychiatry,* 1963, *109,* 95–112.

SLATER, E., & MORAN, P. The schizophrenia-like psychoses of epilepsy: Relation between ages of onset. *British Journal of Psychiatry,* 1969, *115,* 599–600.

SMALL, J. G., & SMALL, D. F. A controlled study of mental disorders associated with epilepsy. *Biological Psychiatry,* 1967, *9,* 171–181.

SMITH, D. E. (Ed.). Amphetamine abuse. *Journal of Psychedelic Drugs,* 1969, *2,* Issue 2.

SMITH, H. *The religions of man.* New York: Harper & Row, 1958.

SNYDER, S. H. Catecholamines in the brain as mediators of amphetamine psychosis. *Archives of General Psychiatry,* 1972, *27,* 169–179.

SOMMER, W. Erkrankung des Ammonshorns als aetiologisches Moment der Epilepsie. *Archiv für Psychiatrie and Nervenkrankheiten* (Berlin), 1880, *10,* 631–675.

SPENCER, W. A., & KANDEL, E. R. Hippocampal neuron responses to selective activation of recurrent collaterals of hippocampofugal axons. *Experimental Neurology,* 1961, *4,* 149–161.

SPERRY, R. W. Lateral specialization in the surgically separated hemispheres. In F. O. Schmitt & F. G. Worden (Eds.), *The neurosciences–Third study program.* Cambridge, Mass.: The M.I.T. Press, 1974.

SPIELMEYER, W. Die Pathogenese des epileptisches Krampfes. *Zeitschrift für die Gesamte Neurologie und Psychiatrie,* 1927, *109,* 501–536.

STANFORD, A. *The Bhagavad Gita—A new verse translation.* New York: Seabury, 1970.

STARBUCK, E. D. A study of conversion. *American Journal of Psychology,* 1897, *8,* 268–308.

STEIN, L., & BELLUZZI, J. D. Brain endorphins: Possible mediators of pleasureable states. In E. Usdin, W. E. Bunney, Jr. & N. S. Kline (Eds.), *Endorphins in mental health research.* London: Macmillan, 1979.

STRAUGHAN, D. W., & LEGGE, K. F. The pharmacology of amygdaloid neurones. *Journal of Pharmacy and Pharmacology,* 1965, *17,* 675–677.

STRAUSS, H. Epileptic disorders. In *American handbook of psychiatry,* Vol. 2. New York: Basic Books, 1959.

SWIECZKOWSKI, J. B., & WALKER, C. E. Sexual behavior correlates of female orgasm and marital happiness. *Journal of Nervous and Mental Disease,* 1978, *166,* 335–342.

TAGLIAMONTE, A., TAGLIAMONTE, P., FORN, J., PEREZ-CRUET, J., KRISHNA, G., & GESSA, G. L. Stimulation of brain serotonin synthesis by dibutyryl-cyclic AMP in rats. *Journal of Neurochemistry,* 1971, *18,* 1191–1196.

TAMMINGA, C. A., CHASE, T. N., & CRAYTON, M. GABA agonist effect in schizophrenia and tardive dyskinesia. *Thirty-Third Annual Meeting, Abstracts, The Society of Biological Psychiatry,* Atlanta, May 3–7, 1978.

TAYLOR, D. E. Aggression and epilepsy. *Journal of Psychosomatic Research,* 1969, *13,* 229–236.

TECCE, J. J., & COLE, J. O. Amphetamine effect in man: Paradoxical drowsiness and lowered electrical brain activity. *Science,* 1974, *185,* 451–453.

TERZIAN, H. Observations on the clinical symptomatology of bilateral partial or total removal of the temporal lobes in man. In B. Maitland & P. Bailey (Eds.), *Temporal lobe epilepsy*. Springfield, Ill.: Thomas, 1958.

TERZIAN, H. Behavioral and EEG effects of intracarotid sodium amytal injections. *Acta Neurochirurgica*, 1964, *12*, 230–240.

TERZIAN, H., & ORE, G. D. Syndrome of Klüver and Bucy—Reproduced in man by bilateral removal of the temporal lobes. *Neurology*, 1955, *5*, 373–380.

TIZARD, B. The personality of epileptics: A discussion of the evidence. *Psychological Bulletin*, 1962, *59*, 196–210.

TUNKS, E. R., & DERMER, S. W. Carbamazepine in the dyscontrol syndrome associated with limbic system dysfunction. *Journal of Nervous and Mental Disease*, 1977, *164*, 56–63.

TUPIN, J. P. Hysterical and cyclothymic personalities. In *Personality disorders—Diagnosis and management*. Baltimore: Williams & Wilkins, 1974.

UNDERWOOD, A. C. *Conversion: Christian and non-Christian. A comparative and psychological study*. London: Allen and Unwin, 1925.

UNGER, S. M. Mescaline, LSD, psilocybin and personality change. In D. Solomon (Ed.), *LSD—The consciousness-expanding drug*. New York: Putnam, 1964.

UNGERSTEDT, U. Stereotaxic mapping of the monoamine pathways in the rat brain. *Acta Physiologica Scandinavica*, 1971, Supplement No. 367, 1–48.

URCA, G., FRENK, H., LIEBESKIND, J. C., & TAYLOR, A. N. Morphine and enkephalin: Analgesic and epileptic properties. *Science*, 1977, *197*, 83–86.

VALENSTEIN, E. S., & NAUTA, W. J. H. A comparison of the distribution of the fornix system in the rat, guinea pig, and monkey. *Journal of Comparative Neurology*, 1959, *113*, 337–364.

VANDERWOLF, C. H., BLAND, B. H., & WHISLAW, I. Q. Diencephalic, hippocampal, and neocortical mechanisms in voluntary behavior. In J. Master (Ed.), *Efferent organization and the integration of behavior*. New York: Academic, 1973.

VANEGAS, H., & FLYNN, J. P. Inhibition of cortically elicited movement by electrical stimulation of the hippocampus. *Brain Research*, 1968, *11*, 489–506.

VAN KAMMEN, D. P., & MURPHY, D. L. Attenuation of the euphoriant and activating effects of d- and l-amphetamine by lithium carbonate treatment. *Psychopharmacology*, 1975, *44*, 215–224.

VANPRAAG, H., KORF, J., & SCHUT, D. Cerebral monoamines and depression. *Archives of General Psychiatry*, 1973, *28*, 827–831.

VAN VALKENBURG, C., LOWRY, M., WINOKUR, G., & CADORET, R. Depression spectrum disease versus pure depressive disease. *Journal of Nervous and Mental Disease*, 1977, *165*, 341–347.

VETULANI, J., STAWARZ, R. J., & SULSER, F. Adaptive mechanisms of the noradrenergic cyclic AMP generating system in the limbic forebrain of the rat: Adaptation to persistent changes in the availability of norepinephrine (NE). *Journal of Neurochemistry*, 1976, *27*, 661–666.

VINOGRADOVA, O. S. Specific and nonspecific response systems in the formation of conditioned responses in man. In M. Cole & I. Maltzman (Eds.), *A handbook of contemporary soviet psychology*. New York: Basic Books, 1969.

VINOGRADOVA, O. S. Some suggestions on neuronal mechanisms of memory and on the role of the limbic system in registration of information. *Zhurnal Vysshei Nervnoi Deyatel'nosti*, 1973, *48*, 305–372.

VINOGRADOVA, O. S. Functional organization of the limbic system in the process of registration of information: Facts and hypothesis. In R. L. Isaacson & K. H. Pribram (Eds.), *The hippocampus*. New York: Plenum, 1975.

VON FREY, M. Beiträege zur Sinnesphysiologie der Haut. *Leipzig Akademie der Wissenschaften. Mathematisch-Physische Klasse. Berichte*, 1895, *47*, 166–184.

WALKER, A. E. Man and his temporal lobes. *Surgical Neurology,* 1973, *1,* 69–79.

WALKER, A. E., & BLUMER, D. Long term behavioral effects of temporal lobectomy for temporal lobe epilepsy. *McLean Hospital Journal,* June 1977.

WALLACE, R. K. *The physiological effects of transcendental meditation: A proposed fourth major state of consciousness.* Ph.D. thesis, Department of Physiology, University of California at Los Angeles, 1970.

WALLACE, R. K., & BENSON, H. The physiology of meditation. *Scientific American,* 1972, *226*(2), 84–90.

WALLACE, R. K., BENSON, H., & WILSON, A. F. A wakeful hypometabolic physiologic state. *American Journal of Physiology,* 1971, *221,* 795–799.

WALTON, H. J., FOULDS, G. A., LITTMAN, S. K., & PRESLY, A. S. Abnormal personality. *British Journal of Psychiatry,* 1970, *116,* 497–510.

WANG, R. Y., & AGHAJANIAN, G. K. Andromically identified serotonergic neurons in the rat midbrain raphe: Evidence for collateral inhibition. *Brain Research,* 1977, *132,* 186–193. (a)

WANG, R. Y., & AGHAJANIAN, G. K. Inhibition of neurons in the amygdala by dorsal raphe stimulation: Mediation through a direct serotonergic pathway *Brain Research,* 1977, *120,* 85–102. (b)

WARBRITTON, J. D., STEWART, R. M., & BALDESSARINI, R. J. Decreased locomotor activity and attenuation of amphetamine hyperactivity with intraventricular infusion of serotonin in the rat. *Brain Research,* 1978, *143,* 373–382.

WATKINS, N. W. N. *Hobbes's system of ideas.* London: Hutchinson, 1965.

WAXMAN, S. G., & GESCHWIND, N. Hypergraphia in temporal lobe epilepsy. *Neurology,* 1974, *24,* 629–636.

WAXMAN, S. G., & GESCHWIND, N. The interictal behavior syndrome of temporal lobe epilepsy. *Archives of General Psychiatry,* 1975, *32,* 1580–1586.

WEINBERG, S. *The first three minutes.* New York: Basic Books, 1977.

WEINSTEIN, E. A., & KAHN, R. C. *Denial of illness: Symbolic and physiologic aspects.* Springfield, Ill.: Thomas, 1955.

WEINTRAUB, W. Obsessive–compulsive and paranoid personalities. In *Personality disorders—Diagnosis and management.* Baltimore: Williams & Wilkins, 1974.

WESTERMEYER, J., BUSH, J., & WINTROB, R. A review of the relationship between dysphoria, pleasure, and human bonding. *Journal of Clinical Psychiatry,* 1978, *39,* 415–424.

WILSON, C. *Poetry and mysticism.* San Francisco: City Lights Books, 1969.

WINOKUR, G. Delusional disorder (paranoia). *Comprehensive Psychiatry,* 1977, *18,* 511, 521.

WINOKUR, G., & CLAYTON, P. Family history studies: Sex differences and alcoholism in primary affective illness. *British Journal of Psychiatry,* 1966, *113,* 973–979.

WINTERS, W. D. A neuropharmacological theory of psychosis. In A. J. Mandell & M. P. Mandell (Eds.), *Psychochemical research in man.* New York: Academic, 1969.

WINTERS, W. D. The continuum of CNS excitatory states and hallucinosis. In R. K. Siegel & L. J. West (Eds.), *Hallucinations; Behavior, experience, and theory.* New York: Wiley, 1975.

WINTERS, W. D., FERRAR-ALLADO, T., GUZMAN-FLORES, C., & ALCAREZ, M. The cataleptic state induced by ketamine: A review of the neuropharmacology of anesthesia. *Neuropharmacology,* 1972, *11,* 303–316.

YUWILER, A., OLDENDORF, W. H., GELLER, E., & BRAUN, L. Effect of albumin binding and amino acid competition on tryptophan uptake into brain. *Journal of Neurochemistry,* 1977, *28,* 1015–1023.

ZEITLIN, A. B., COTTRELL, T. L., & LLOYD, F. A. Sexology of the paraplegic male. *Fertility and Sterility,* 1957, *8,* 337–348.

15

Prospects for the Scientific Observer of Perceptual Consciousness

GORDON GLOBUS AND STEPHEN FRANKLIN

We are perceivers. We are an awareness; we are not objects; we have no
solidity. We are boundless. The world of objects and solidity is a way of
making our passage on earth convenient. It is only a description that was
created to help us. We, or rather our *reason*, forget that the description is only
a description and thus we entrap the totality of ourselves in a vicious circle
from which we rarely emerge in our lifetime.

—Carlos Castaneda (1974)

1. INTRODUCTION

It would seem that the prospects for the "scientific observer" of brain
and behavior are excellent, given the extraordinary advance of
twentieth-century science. Until the level of investigation descends to
the quantum domain, where peculiar difficulties in observation arise
(Bohm, 1951), there do not appear to be clear-cut conceptual barriers
that limit the scientific observation of brain and behavior and the concomitant advance of empirical knowledge about them.

However, when we turn to the prospects for the "scientific observer" of consciousness, we are immediately faced with a host of
perplexing issues, entangling confusions, definitional obscurities, and
even a formidable "ghost" or two, which Western science and philosophy have not satisfactorily laid to rest. In attempting to cope with this
situation, the present chapter utilizes insights gained from "meditation"
adepts in the non-Western tradition, where specialization in the exploration of consciousness has been especially emphasized (Naranjo & Ornstein, 1971). Our focus is on what is entailed in scientific observation;
therefore, we discriminate two kinds of knowledge, only one of which is
related to scientific observation, and consider the relations between

GORDON GLOBUS • Department of Psychiatry, University of California at Irvine, Medical
Center, Orange, California 92668. STEPHEN FRANKLIN • Department of Mathematics,
School of Physical Sciences, University of California at Irvine, Irvine, California 92664.

these kinds of knowledge. Finally, we derive the "structural identity" solution to the mind–brain problem (Globus, 1976).

We conclude that, strictly speaking, there is no scientific observation of perceptual consciousness, yet paradoxically, scientific observation can yield the *structure* of perceptual consciousness. Perhaps more importantly, in coming to this conclusion, we shall have occasion to explore the nature of the scientific enterprise as it interfaces with conscious experience and thereby move toward a conceptual foundation for the kinds of consciousness-related research reported in the present volume.

2. THE SCIENTIFIC OBSERVER AND THE PROBLEM OF MIND AND MATTER: A PHENOMENOLOGICAL ARGUMENT[1]

The presentation of a truly *phenomenological* argument requires that the reader "co-reflect" with the writer, and accordingly, I extend to you an "invitation" to co-reflect with me.[2] Of course, since you and I are not vis-à-vis, this is not a true "co"-reflection but a regressive form that cannot sustain immediate reciprocity. Be this as it may, I shall invite you to reflect on your conscious perceptual[3] experience in the manner that I reflect upon mine, in order that you may first appreciate my phenomenological argument—an argument that is primarily based not on logical conceptions but on a direct appeal to your immediate conscious experience—and then may go on to assess it critically.

Since this is a phenomenological argument, my style of presentation and locutions are accordingly also phenomenological. Rather than addressing some rather formal version of myself to some general audience "at large," I shall speak directly to you in particular from some relatively concrete description of myself, and if you, accepting my invitation, respond in the same manner, then we may get as close as we are likely to get to "true" co-reflection in a volume such as the present one. (It may prove easier to co-reflect with me if you think of it as a form of "play"!)

Suppose you were to join me at the place where I write this, and as

---

[1] Since this section was the responsibility of the first author, the first-person singular is used.

[2] See Zaner's (1970) lucid methodological discussion of what he nicely calls the "invitation" to "co-meditate."

[3] I restrict my reflection to *perceptual* experience—primarily visual and auditory—to ease the burden of exposition and to avoid being sidetracked into issues not germane to our central purpose. Despite this restriction, the argument, whatever its defects, is considered a general argument not limited to perceptual awareness.

"scientific observers," we were to perceive the "reading" on some scientific instrument, which reading we could see or touch or hear. I might enjoin you, for example, to *look at* the pointer on a speedometerlike instrument, and we could more-or-less agree as to its value with respect to the associated metric.

When we do so, as scientific observers, we participate in the process of *making distinctions*. Out of the enormous amount of stimulation presented to our eyes—from plants, a Tibetan tanka painting, an ancient bronze warrior–Buddha, and so on—we distinguish the pointer (i.e., we select a particular invariant from the input structure [Gibson, 1966]). For us, the pointer is a "physical thing," set off as a figure from its ground. The entity distinguished, which I shall call an *intentional particular* (or equivalently, an *intentional object*), is so distinguished in the visual mode, and the action of distinguishing a particular invariant in the input may be called *intentional particularization*. If the state of the scientific instrument were signaled to us by a tone of a certain frequency, the entity distinguished—a tone of a certain pitch at a certain location— would be in the auditory mode. Note that we do not confuse these two modes, which are incorrigibly different; even in a synesthesia[4] we in no way confuse the "intentional functions" (or "intentional acts") of seeing and hearing.

Returning to the speedometer, the reading we are observing is "public"—accessible in the same mode across observers—but this is not to say that the intentional particular is perceived in the same way by each of us. Suppose the distinction we are both making—the pointer reading—confirms your most cherished scientific theory and disconfirms mine. The pointer just looks different depending on our desire with regard to it—just as the pizza at the next table looks and smells different depending on whether or not we ourselves have already dined on one![5] Such desirings are examples of "intentional operators," since they transform intentional functions in this way and that, however these functions happen to be intentionally particularized.

There are many other ways in which intentional particulars come to appear different to us, for example, depending on our ideas about them. You may be rather mechanically inclined, whereas my own predilection is for aesthetic form. The pointer reading may be perceived as "machinelike" for you, whereas for me, the pointer and its circular

---

[4] A synesthesia entails a kind of "crosstalk" between two perceptual systems. For example, if one is lying relaxedly with eyes shut, an auditory stimulus perceived as a sharp sound may simultaneously be experienced as a flash of light.

[5] I do not mean here that the pointer looks the same to each of us but that we "interpret" it differently in our thought. The pointer *actually* looks different. (This is easier to appreciate in the case of the pizza.)

frame have something of a "mandala" quality. So "intentional operators" have a number of different modes: "conative" in the case of
strivings, "cognitive" in the case of ideas. Further, intentional functions,
however particularized, are transformed by our emotions, that is, intentional operators in the affective mode. When miserable, for example, I
see the world of intentional particulars "through a glass darkly." Or
again, the experience of an intentional particular may be transformed by
virtue of the use we are going to make of it; this is the action mode. My
curious hat, for example, looks different to me when I put it on to shield
me while hiking in the desert sun than when I put it on as part of my
local native "image," while drinking gin and tonic on the shaded terrace
of the Laguna Hotel!

It must be apparent by now that for you and me as scientific observers to have "the same experience" of the reading—at least, the same
within limits imposed by (presumably minimal) *genetic* differences in
our respective nervous systems—we must adopt "the same" intentional
operations, and to do so, we would have to truly *co*-reflect with each
other over extended time periods. In effect, we would establish a social
consensus with respect to permissible intentional operations. (This process is equivalent to what Castaneda [1973] calls an ordinary "description of the world.") I submit that if we persisted in open-minded good
will, we could perceive the intentional particular that is a pointer reading
in more-or-less the same way.[6] But for you to perceive my beloved in
accordance with my intentionality, or for me to experience your beloved
as do you, is far more difficult to achieve and probably impossible in
practice, given the intensely idiosyncratic nature of the intentionality
entailed in loving! (As we are wont to exclaim with regard to somebody
else's infatuation, "What in the world does he see in her?")

So when we are in the world of intentional particulars by virtue of
our making distinctions—when we make those distinctions with impeccable objectivity, methodically, in a disciplined manner, and so on,
so that we are observing *as scientists*—our conscious experience of the
distinguished intentional particulars depends on (a) invariants present

---

[6] A number of points are involved here. The claim is *not* that the pointer points to, say,
"100" only by virtue of social concensus. This "pointer reading" is an invariant that *may*
be extracted from the input structure but *need not* be extracted. A "sorcerer" (in Don
Juan's sense) would be likely to extract different invariants than a scientist, since he
operates within a different description of the world. A "sorcerer" may choose to extract
the same invariants as a "scientist," and presumably, with training, a "scientist" could
learn *willing* and extract the same invariants as the sorcerer. (See the writings of Castaneda [1973, 1974] in this regard.) These are simply different ways of cleaving that
indivisible whole (which is nature) implied by quantum interconnectedness (Bohm,
1951).

in signals from the environment (Gibson, 1966); (b) the intentional functions particularized by those signals; and (c) the intentional operators that transform these functions so particularized. The "things" of our ordinary experience that have physical properties—Stebbing's (1938) "furniture" of the world—are given in this way.

Now, suppose you and I decide to relinquish this scientific observation and meditate together. We first turn to the bronze warrior–Buddha and remind ourselves of this perspective, in order to refresh our impeccable intent and trim our spirits; we then precisely resume our former position vis-à-vis the "reading." We assume a quiet, stable posture, breathe quietly and rhythmically, turn off the trivial internal dialogue going on incessantly in our heads, and are interested in no particular thing[7] (not even interested in meditating!). (According to the Yaqui "sorcerer" "Don Juan" [Castaneda, 1973], we do not really "do" anything; it is "not-doing" that we require.)

We then achieve an experience radically different in character from before, even though stimulation from our environment has remained more-or-less constant: first, there is no longer a subject who is observing an intentional particular, and second, there are no distinctions within conscious experience. Both "we" and the "reading" have disappeared!

I want to emphasize that these two characteristics of the meditative state can be reduced to one by assuming that the ineffable way it feels to be making those distinctions is precisely that experience we denote by the terms *I, subject, ego,* and so on, and about which we can say nothing other than that it "is." The "reason" we can say nothing—that is, make no distinctions—about the subject other than that it "is" is that the very process of making distinctions *is* the subject; and the process of making distinctions (about making distinctions) *is* the subject; and so on. So the subject—I—is given as fact to our direct acquaintance, but we can say nothing about it, since it *is* the very making of distinctions entailed in saying anything. Note that the present point is *not* that the subject makes distinctions, as if this were an activity of the separate subject comparable to my driving a car. Instead, *the making of distinctions is what constitutes the subject.*

So the subject–object distinction disappears as we meditate, and with it disappears intentional particulars, such as the pointer reading.

---

[7] This can be called the "empty form" of interest. The empty form can be thought of as a function containing not a particular value but a free variable; the empty form is that set of rules to be imposed on potential stimulus inputs. (The particular value within that range is a function of the actual input and the intentional particularization.)

What remains is "consciousness *per se*"—an unbroken whole in which nothing is distinguished, because no distinctions can be made. Nor is this undivided whole distinguished from anything else; it is the totality—everything that is the case—for this consciousness. Since it contains no distinctions, we may justifiably call it a *continuum*, and since it is everything that is the case, we may say that this continuum is *unbounded*, for this consciousness can find no boundary to the *totality* unless it unjustifiably exempts itself from that totality and then distinguishes the boundary from its privileged vantage point. Further, consciousness *per se* transcends time; time presumes the making of distinctions between what is and what was or will be.

Note that to say consciousness *per se* (or "being") is an undivided whole is not to say that it is homogeneous. This whole has a particular configuration in accordance with the input to it; consciousness then carries this or that structure. Since the structure of consciousness is the case, we may call it a *fact* (or a *fact structure*). This fact is no longer transformed by intentional operators, however, since there is no subject. Further, the set of intentional functions blend into an unbroken whole as well, in which, say, seeing and hearing are not *distinguished* as different but are just experienced as simultaneously coexisting.[8]

So when we are in the nonintentional world of meditation, our experience can be an indivisible fact-structure that is the totality. Since it is without distinction, it is a continuum, rather than composed of distinct pieces providing "grainy" matter, and since it is the totality, it cannot be located "somewhere" (since the totality cannot be part of itself) and is therefore unextended. This experience, then, lacks properties of extendedness and graininess, which lack characterizes "the mental" in contrast to "the physical" (Globus, 1973, 1976), which has properties of extension and grain. *The mental qua fact structure is given through nonintentionality.*

Let us step back and see what we have tried to accomplish in Section 2. In effect, we have spelled out what we mean by *mental* (more specifically, *perceptual mind*) and what we mean by *matter,* and the difference between mind and matter is the difference in these meanings, according to our co-reflection. (Others may mean something else by

---

[8] It may well be that there are deeper stages of meditation that might be achieved if we co-reflected with a true adept. Various writings (Goleman, 1976; Longchenpa [Guenther, 1976]; Patanjali [Taimni, 1961]) suggest that in the most quiet of states, even the fact is transcended and there is at the essence an unconfigured "pure" consciousness or being. Speculatively, the engagement of receptor states with more central states, so that information can be acquired centrally from the periphery and "the fact obtains," requires some minimal intentionality; without the facilitation of intentionality, these receptor and central systems are functionally disengaged.

mind and *matter;* indeed, the mind–matter "problem" pivots on just what we mean by these terms.) Here the reader must forego co-reflection and now "critically assess" what has been discussed heretofore.

Our basic claim is that certain fundamental distinctions between matter and mind are a function of the intentionality, or lack of it, taken with regard to conscious experience. That matter is grainy and with extension, and that mind is continuous and without extension, is due to variations in our own intentional activity in shifting from "doing" to "not-doing," rather than to any fundamental differences between the properties of physical and mental "stuffs." When we make distinctions within perceptual experience, we are, perforce, in the physical domain; there is no mental object that we can point to in contradistinction to its physical correspondent. Scientific observation is the intentional activity of making distinctions *par excellence;* the nonintentional world is simply not available to it. *There is no scientific observation of perceptual awareness,* whether we are scientifically (i.e., rigorously) observing our own consciousness or asking subjects to scientifically observe their own consciousness in our behalf. In either case, "perceptual awareness" (in our sense) presupposes the foregoing of that intentional activity of making distinctions that is at the heart of scientific observation. Perceptual awareness is a timeless, unbounded, unbroken whole that has a fact structure and cannot be observed "scientifically." This unobservability would appear to be a limitation on the prospects for the scientific observer of perceptual consciousness, yet we shall see that it is nevertheless possible to observe the *structure* of perceptual consciousness, albeit in different form.

There is a particular instance of the mind–matter problem that we shall go on to consider in Section 3. In the above, we were indiscriminate in our choice of matter, which we contrasted to mind; we chose a reading on a scientific instrument, but we might have chosen any piece of "furniture" in the world. Now, there is one particular piece of furniture that has very special status when contrasted with mind; here we refer, of course, to the *brain.* We have every reason on empirical grounds to believe that our conscious experience as we are acquainted with it has something to do with our brain; this is nothing but the well-known principle of psychoneural correspondence. So we shall want to consider this very special case of the "mind–matter problem," which is the "mind–brain problem." Because mind and brain appear to be coupled in some peculiar manner, we may learn more about the *relations* between mind and matter by study of this case. In what follows, we can present our thesis more clearly if we shift over from a phenomenological to an abstract argument.

3. THE SCIENTIFIC OBSERVER AND THE PROBLEM OF MIND AND BRAIN: AN ABSTRACT ARGUMENT

3.1. Introduction

If we may proceed by reflecting on a dictionary definition of *observer*, then we can move more swiftly toward the themes we wish to consider. According to Webster (1961), the observer is:

> **a:** A representative sent to observe and listen, but not to participate officially in a gathering. **b:** *Aeronautics.* One who accompanies the pilot of an airplane in order to make observations during flight.

This definition seems to preserve the independence of the observer and that which he observes. The observer does not "participate officially" in the events under his observation. The observer does not fly the plane but passively records the flight. Indeed, the root meaning of *observe* has to do with "preserving," "saving," and "keeping." A "scientific" observer, as we have seen, is just a very good observer, and the scientific observer's report of his observations is somehow equivalent to, or can be transformed to, "knowledge."

This relation of the observer to the observed presumes a typically Western paradigm, which characterizes both empirical science and phenomenology as science. The empirical scientist, while recognizing the relativity of his frame of reference (Einstein, 1961), his disturbance of the observed by virtue of having made an observation (Heisenberg, 1958), and the arbitrariness of having cleaved that indivisible whole that is nature into observing and observed parts (Bohm, 1951), will come to know whatever it is his lot to know by virtue of the observations he can and does make. Likewise, for Husserl's (1960) phenomenological scientist, it is the self that drops the "natural standpoint" in which the world is both real and independent of the observer and adopts instead the "standpoint of consciousness." It is this observing self that comes to know (noetically and noematically) whatever it is phenomenologists are supposed to know (apodictically!) about the mind.

This typically Western coupling of the observer and knowledge is easily confused with the claim that *all* knowledge comes via the observer, that is, the notion that the observer is *requisite* for knowledge. But this view is sharply criticized by philosophers who assume certain non-Western paradigms. Indeed, according to some versions of non-Western phenomenology, ultimate knowledge entails a foregoing of the observer completely. As discussed above, it is the loss of the subject–object distinction that is the hallmark of those meditative states in which the "mystical" kind of understanding is gained. It is only in those states of "not-doing," in which all intentionality ceases, that "the world collapses"—that one "stops the world"—where *world* implies a socially inculcated consensus as to legal descriptions according to which experience can be constrained (Castaneda, 1973).

It is our thesis—which is shared by at least some in Western and non-Western traditions (Blackburn, 1971)—that these two kinds of knowledge, "scientific" (or intentional) and "meditative" (or nonintentional) are "complementary," which in our view means that the kinds of knowledge are in some sense incompatible and cannot be simultaneously gathered (or perhaps can be simultaneously gathered only at the risk of paradox), and yet at the same time there is a structure conserved across them. As we shall see, although the possibilities for the scientific observation of perceptual consciousness are nil, there is no conceptual impediment to scientific observation of objects that display structural congruency with perceptual consciousness.

3.2. Intentionality and the Abstract Observer

Our strategy is now to reconsider the issues of Section 2 in an abstract domain. Rather than choosing to observe a "real" object—a pointer reading—an abstract object, Z, is observed as intentional particular. Further, an abstract subject, S, is posited to observe this abstract object, and this observation occurs in an abstract perceptual mode (abstract intentional function). Having established this abstract domain, we vary the intentionality allowed the abstract subject in observing the abstract object.

There are several advantages in using abstract objects. Since we have complete control over their construction, we can talk about them with great precision. Furthermore, our epistemological situation is greatly simplified, because abstract objects are entirely independent of "reality"; that is, they are neither representative of nor dependent on "real" objects in the world but are self-subsistent, by virtue of our manner of creating them. Meaning, for a completely formalized abstract object, is completely intrinsic to the object; no reference to anything external is required.

As abstract object, then, we take a completely formalized arithmetic, designated Z. As an arithmetic, Z is a *particular* abstract machine—with a certain vocabulary, axioms, rules of inference, etc.—and thus is configured in a certain way.

Since we are in the domain of the abstract, we must consider the formal perceptual mode according to which S, the abstract subject, observes Z. S cannot see or hear Z. Instead, the formal mode of S's apprehending Z—S's "intentional function"—must be abstract; that is, S "perceives" not in a visual, auditory, etc., domain but in an abstractly meaningful domain. Let us consider more closely what is meant by an *abstract intentional function*, for this is central to our argument.

We may distinguish the intentional function as "ground" or "quale" from the particularization of that ground. For example, the visual ground has properties of color, brightness, extension, and so on; this ground is particularized in accordance with the input, the invariants selected, and so on.

Our abstract ground has the properties of arithmetic meaningfulness. As we shall see, depending on the rules we allow S, particular arithmetic distinctions (e.g., a number, a formula, a relationship between numbers or formulas) are made in the abstract ground, but the ground *per se* is given as arithmetically meaningful. Without the abstract ground, S is abstractly "blind," so to speak; that is, S has no modality by means of which Z can be observed. Thus, S, as abstract subject, is given an abstract perceptual mode that is inherently a mathematical manner of perceiving an abstract world. We designate the abstract intentional function by A.

It is up to us to decide how extensive an intentional repertoire we are going to give the abstract subject perceiving Z in the perceptual mode A. In an entirely informal approach, we might be willing to give S our entire personal repertoire (which, of course, includes A) so that S is a kind of "alter ego," so to speak, who can be interested in Z, or get mad at it, or have vague intuitions about it, and so on, in addition to making mathematical observations. Here, the abstract subject is none other than we ourselves, or our image of ourselves. Or we may limit the intentionality of S so that only certain kinds of rather formal mathematical observations on Z can be made; no personal feelings are allowed! S, then, systematically makes observations *about* Z, its parts and their patterns of relations. Given this degree of limitation in S's intentionality, S would be equivalent to what would be called the *metamathematical observer*.

But S's intentionality vis-à-vis Z can be reduced even further, so that S becomes an "arithmetic" observer. Suppose S could distinguish only the discrete symbols and their interrelationships that comprised the words and sentences and sequences of Z. Further, S's very observational capabilities are formalized in Z, so that S's observations are in effect limited to the "language" of Z itself; S is restricted in its observations to what Z actually can say and can directly observe nothing *about* Z. In the metamathematical case, the method of making observations that is S's intentionality is a richer kind of observational capability than that formalized in Z. As "arithmetic" observer, S cannot get outside of Z and "look it over" from the metaperspective.

For S so restricted, Z is composed of symbols arranged in a certain way. Further, S knows Z to be an "entity," that is, an "object." For S, Z is composed of distinguishable subentities; following Husserl's insight, S can at least discriminate the discreteness of Z as intentional object from the intentional acts of perceiving Z.[9] The intentional function, A, is distinguished from its object, Z.

It is crucial to note here that since Z as a completely formalized system has been drained of all *external* meanings, it is not required that S as arithmetic observer intend any meanings with regard to Z. All "meanings" required are already internal to Z by virtue of the formalization. S as arithmetic observer, then, has been reduced to only that minimal intentionality that is necessary to find the entity Z comprised of symbols (units) structured in a certain way. In effect, S can discern symbols and formulas as invariant structures within the whole stimulus, Z.

Now, consider the case of meditation, in which even this minimal intentionality is relinquished and no distinctions obtain. As we saw in Section 2, consciousness is then an undivided whole and takes on the character of a continuum; but this continuum is not homogeneous, for it carries a structure.[10]

Let us contrast the arithmetic and meditative perspectives on that object that, according to the former, is an entity comprising an arrangement of individual elements. On the meditative perspective, this entity becomes a whole unbroken configuration without distinctions.

It is crucial to our argument to appreciate that on the meditative perspective, this holistic structure *qua* structure is the same as that structure composed of interrelated parts on the arithmetic perspective. For example, we may perceive the facial structure of someone as comprising nose, eyes, mouth, etc., arranged in a certain way, or we may just perceive the whole arrangement of the face. We shall call the former *analytic structure* and the latter *synthetic structure*. (Synthetic structure is sometimes called *emergent*.) Analytic and synthetic structures are congruent structures.[11] Analytic structures, however, are composed of interrelated parts, whereas synthetic structures are an unbroken whole. The distinction between analytic and synthetic structure is not in the

---

[9] Husserl's subject distinguishes intentional object from intentional act—distinguishes between noematic and noetic poles—so that the object is an entity. (See Jones, 1969.)

[10] The strategy of our argument inclines one to think of the subject as gradually disappearing over the stages of informal, metamathematical, arithmetic, and meditative "observation."

[11] It might be thought that this claim is incompatible with the dictum that the whole is more than the sum of its parts. But the present point is that the whole is the same as the parts in their interrelatedness, not the parts as a mere aggregation.

structure *per se,* but in the intentionality adopted vis-à-vis that structure.

Before returning to our abstract observer, *S*, there is one other feature of the meditative perspective to recall. Z is no longer an "entity" on the meditative perspective, for an entity presumes distinction, and there are no distinctions (no intentionality) on this perspective. Z is instead an unbounded totality—everything that is the case.

We now need to appreciate the peculiar properties of Z as a piece of "furniture" that is also a formalized system; this conception of Z markedly reduces the difference between arithmetic and meditation perspectives (in contrast to ordinary pieces of "furniture"). Since Z has been drained of all external meaning by virtue of the formalization, there is no loss of meaning in shifting from the arithmetic to the meditative perspectives. The only difference is that on the arithmetic perspective, Z is an entity (that is, discrete) composed of interrelated pieces, whereas on the meditative perspective, Z is an indivisible configuration that is the totality; *the structure of Z is the same in either case* but is analytic on the one hand and synthetic on the other. So when *S* shifts back and forth between the arithmetic and meditative perspectives on the formalized system Z, the same structure is rendered differently in each case, depending on the perspective taken. Since there must always be *some* perspective taken, we cannot explicitly capture this structure *per se,* but only analytic or synthetic structure. The crucial difference between arithmetic and meditative perspectives has to do with the "stuff" that carries the structure. On the arithmetic perspective, there is an entity composed of interrelated "pieces," whereas on the meditative perspective, there is a configured, unbroken continuum that is an unbounded totality.

So we have two "complementary" perspectives on Z that provide the "same" structure for Z but different "stuffs" that carry the structure. We might pursue the possibility that one of these perspectives is privileged with respect to the other, but it is difficult to find any compelling justification, since these are just different stances with regard to structures, and the same structure is preserved in either case. Our Western custom of emphasizing the scientific observer and the intentionality entailed in the making of distinctions would seem to be just a paradigmatic bias and nothing more. *Pari passu,* Eastern thought emphasizes meditation and the relinquishing of intentionality and tends to deplore the making of distinctions entailed in thought. But since both perspectives find congruent structures for "what is the case," it would seem arbitrary to favor one over the other.

So the scientific observer of perceptual consciousness, whose intentionality is reduced in our abstract case to the bare minimum in which the object is a discrete "grainy" entity comprising a structure of interrelated parts, ascertains the fact of the object's structure but has a limited view of the "stuff" that carries that structure. In the complementary view, achieved in meditation where there is no intentionality, the fact of structure is quite the same, but the limited view of the "stuff" that carries that structure finds it to be continuous rather than "grainy." For an unbiased knowledge of this "stuff," complementary perspectives are required, yet the stuff has incompatible properties according to these complementary perspectives.

3.3. The Mind–Brain Problem

The discussion has been carried to the point at which we can derive the "structural identity solution" (Globus, 1976) to the mind–brain problem without much difficulty. The core properties of perceptual awareness appear to be that (a) it is not composed of material pieces but is a continuum; (b) it is not extended in space but is without location; and (c) it provides privileged (private) access to one observer who is directly acquainted with that mind, whereas all other observers can know it only indirectly by inference from behavior, physiological readings, and so on. Brain, on the other hand, is (a) composed of grainy material; (b) extended in space; and (c) equivalently accessible across observers (i.e., is "public").

We replace the abstract object, Z, by a brain, B, whose input consists of homogeneous red light, and we replace the abstract subject, S, by the ordinary observing subject, O. O now observes B as intentional particular with a reduced intentionality, so that for O, B is a discrete entity (a brain) composed of interrelated parts (neurons, electrochemical events, or whatever). But B corresponds to an awareness (on the principle of psychoneural correspondence) that has a subject, S, observing a homogeneous red field as intentional particular. For S, this field is a discrete entity but is not composed of interrelated parts (given "homogeneous" input). This is as it should be, since the brain of S, designated B_s, has a different input than the brain of O, designated B_o.

Now suppose S enters meditation and the subject–object distinction is transcended. The homogeneous red field is no longer an entity but the totality. In this case, there is a continuum that is the totality. Since the continuum is everything that is the case, it cannot be extended—that is, is not localized—since extension presumes a distinction between located "here" and not located "there," and there are no distinctions on this perspective. Where previously S had observed an intentional particular—an entity—now there is only perceptual awareness, whereas for O, there is brain.

Of course, S and O are acquainted with different structures because the input structure is different—a "homogeneous red field" in the former and a "brain" in the latter. Suppose we were to set up a *gedanken* "autocerebroscope"[12] so that S observes his own brain, B_S, on the autocerebroscope screen just as O observes B_S on the same screen; that is, the same inputs impinge on B_S and B_O. If S and O assume minimum intentionality, they each find "the same" entity composed of grainy stuff. But if S adopts the meditative perspective *sans* all intentionality, there is acquaintance with an indivisible configured continuum that is the totality. Yet the (synthetic) structure of the continuum is "the same" as the (analytic) structure according to O. This is to say that the structure *qua* structure is identical across complementary perspectives but the "stuff" that carries the structure is "mental"—continuous and unextended—on the one hand, and "physical"—grainy and extended—on the other.

Thus, in the unique case where the same input is arranged for S and O, the structure of mind with which S is acquainted is "the same" as the structure of brain with which O is acquainted, even though the stuffs that carry the structure have incompatible properties according to these complementary perspectives.[13] In effect, the "scientific observer" of consciousness is constrained to an acquaintance with fact structures as grainy, extended entities, whereas in meditation, there is acquaintance with fact structures as continuous, unextended totalities. A complete view requires complementary perspectives that if simultaneously assumed, provide *incompatible* properties (hence the possibilities for paradox) with regard to the ground stuff that embodies "the same" fact structure.

Before leaving this discussion, we need to sharpen the solution to the mind–brain enigma a bit more, and we have not yet joined the private-public issue. Strictly speaking, the fact structure of O's acquaintance is not "the same" as that of S's acquaintance, since even though O has minimized his intentionality, there are processing mechanisms that transform the input structure (e.g., lateral inhibition in the retina as a contrast mechanism). So the fact structure is different for O and S, because of genetically given forms of "intentionality" (if you will). However, knowing the constraints of these genetic givens, O can recover the structure of B_S with which S is directly acquainted; but here O is not

---

[12] Feigl (1967) has discussed the "autocerebroscope," an imaginary but technically feasible device that allows one to observe one's own brain in the manner of any other observer.

[13] There is a subtle point to be made here. We are idealizing so that B_S completely fills the visual world of S and O. But when B_S is a figure against ground and S forgoes intentionality, B_S is assimilated to a larger whole; that is, its structure is integral to a larger structure. In this more complicated case, we must say that the structure of brain with which O is acquainted is "the same" as a structure integral to the mind with which S is acquainted.

directly acquainted with the structure of B_S. (O can be directly acquainted only with the structure of B_O.) Instead, O is indirectly acquainted with the structure of B_S by inference from his acquaintance and ancillary knowledge. Following Russell (1948), we may say that O knows B_S "by description" rather than "by acquaintance." In sum, *the structure of B_S known by acquaintance during meditation is* (a) *strictly congruent with the structure of B_S known to the scientific observer by description* and (b) *a transformation of the structure of B_S known to the scientific observer by acquaintance.* [14]

The issue of privileged versus public access is explicated as follows. We say that brain is "public"—both S and O observe B_S on the autocerebroscope screen with roughly equivalent intentionalities. Equal access is in effect being able to line up one's receptors (more or less) in the same way to (more or less) the same input and by social consensus adopting (more or less) the same intentionalities with regard to that input. *Privileged access* (privacy) means *either* that S and O have different inputs—as when S has "red light" and O has a "brain" as input—*or* that input is the same (as in the autocerebroscope case), but S and O adopt differing intentionalities, as when S enters meditation and forgoes all intentionality and O retains some intentionality.

Understood in this way, the distinction between privileged and public access is vitiated. When it is mechanically difficult to arrange for each observer to have more-or-less the same input—that is, the pattern of proprioceptive input from one observer's muscles—the one observer is said to have privileged access. When it is communicationally difficult to arrange for each observer to have more-or-less the same intentionality (e.g., one observer's intention toward his beloved is notoriously difficult for a neutral observer to adopt) the one observer is said to have privileged access. But none of this denies that given enough technical virtuosity on the input side and enough adjustment on the intentionality side, so-called privileged experiences could become more-or-less "public."

On the other hand, there does not appear to be any procedure for establishing with certainty that different observers have "the same" intentionality. No matter how "public" the object—even with the pointer reading discussed in the first section—we cannot be sure that the so-called public object is perceived equivalently across observers, *even though the same invariant is abstracted from the input structure,* since intentional operations may differ.

---

[14] We assume here that O has adopted an appropriate level of observation so that the analytic structure formed by the interrelated pieces in fact shows a congruent structure with the synthetic structure of S's acquaintance. Sperry (1976) has pointed to the appropriate level as being at the very apex of the brain's organizational hierarchy.

So the distinction between public and privileged access is under-mined on both sides; the former cannot really be established, and the latter is a matter relative to technical and communicative issues. With respect to the invariants present in the input, social consensus deter-mines which we choose as meaningful figure against meaningless ground. In any case, our view of the roles of input and intentionality accounts for the apparent public access to brain and privileged access to mind.

Let us review the basic themes of the preceding discussion. We have argued for a monistic ontology whose fundamental is neither men-tal nor physical but is "structure"; *mental* and *physical* have to do with different ways of knowing this common structure. The "ground stuff"—the embodiment that carries structure—has incompatible prop-erties depending on whether there is a "scientific observer" who main-tains a subject–object distinction or a meditative state in which there is no scientific observer and accordingly no subject–object distinction. Thus, we have an irreducible epistemological dualism vis-à-vis the one ground stuff; its properties vary as a function of our manner of acquain-tance with it. However, there is no irreducible epistemological dualism with regard to structure, for the two versions of structure share a com-mon structure.

4. Conclusion

We may review the peculiar prospects for the scientific observer of perceptual consciousness. There is no scientific observation of per-ceptual consciousness *per se*, since such observation (either by the scientist with regard to his own consciousness or by a subject in the scientist's behalf) assumes the making of distinctions that provides a "physical world" rather than "perceptual consciousness." The scientific observer is limited to a grainy perceptual world in which pieces are interrelated to form an "analytic structure." Perceptual consciousness is provided by meditative observation, which is limited to a configured continuum that forms a "synthetic structure." Nevertheless, since ana-lytic and synthetic structures share a common structure (which cannot be known *per se*), the scientific observer of brain can be said to have a knowledge of the structure of perceptual consciousness, even though he cannot observe it. If the scientific observer has chosen the proper level and units of analysis, then he can know that structure "by description" and a transformation of that structure "by acquaintance." Since it is precisely the structure of consciousness that we are interested in as scientists, the prospects for the scientific observer vis-à-vis perceptual consciousness are quite good, in that there are no conceptual constraints to the gaining of such structural knowledge. (As *epistemologists*, we may be interested in the properties of the carrier of that structure; here paradox occurs.)

We can only conclude that scientists ought to continue doing what they have been doing all along; this conclusion is hardly a newsworthy item! Yet, for those of us who are concerned with such issues, and the building of bridges between mind and brain, phenomenology and behaviorism, mysticism and science, and East and West, the suggestive possibilities for a more comprehensive world view in which these bifurcations can be transcended is encouraging.

REFERENCES

BLACKBURN, T. R. Sensuous–intellectual complementary in science. *Science,* 1971, *172,* 1003–1007.

BOHM, D. *Quantum theory.* New York: Prentice-Hall, 1951.

CASTANEDA, C. *Journey to Ixtlan.* New York: Simon & Schuster, 1973.

CASTANEDA, C. *Tales of power.* New York: Simon & Schuster, 1974.

EINSTEIN, A. *Relativity, The special and general theory,* R. W. Lawson (trans.). New York: Crown, 1961.

FEIGL, H. *The mental and the physical.* Minneapolis: University of Minnesota Press, 1967.

GIBSON, J. J. *The senses considered as perceptual systems.* Boston: Houghton Mifflin, 1966.

GLOBUS, G. Unexpected symmetries in the "World Knot." *Science,* 1973, *180,* 1129–1136.

GLOBUS, G. Mind, structure and contradiction. In G. Globus, G. Maxwell, & I. Savodnik (Eds.), *Consciousness and the brain: A scientific and philosophical inquiry.* New York: Plenum, 1976.

GOLEMAN, D. The Buddha on meditation and states of consciousness. In T. X. Barber (Ed.), *Advances in altered states of consciousness and human potentialities,* Vol. 1. New York: Psychological Dimensions, 1976.

GUENTHER, H. *Kindly bent to ease us,* Part 2. Emeryville, Calif.: Dharma, 1976.

HEISENBERG, W. *Physics and philosophy; The revolution in modern science.* New York: Harper & Row, 1958.

HUSSERL, E. *Cartesian Meditations,* D. Cairns (trans.). The Hague: Martinus Nijhoff, 1960.

JONES, W. T. *A history of Western philosophy:* Vol. 4: *Kant to Wittgenstein and Sartre.* New York: Harcourt, Brace & World, 1969.

NARANJO, C., & ORNSTEIN, R. *On the psychology of meditation.* New York: Viking, 1971.

RUSSELL, B. *Human knowledge: Its scope and limits.* New York: Simon & Schuster, 1948.

SPERRY, R. W. Mental phenomena as causal determinants in brain function. In G. Globus, G. Maxwell, & I. Savodnik (Eds.), *Consciousness and the brain: A scientific and philosophical inquiry.* New York: Plenum, 1976.

STEBBING, T. S. *Philosophy and the physicist.* London: Methuen, 1938.

TAIMNI, I. K. *The science of Yoga.* Wheaton, Ill.: The Theosophical Publishing House, 1961.

Webster's New Collegiate Dictionary, J. P. Bethel (Ed.). Springfield, Mass.: G. & C. Merriam, 1961.

ZANER, R. *The way of phenomenology: Criticism as a philosophical discipline.* New York: Pegasus, 1970.

Index